D0611298

DYNAMICS OF DEVELOPMENT
AND THE
THERAPEUTIC PROCESS

DYNAMICS OF DEVELOPMENT
AND THE
THERAPEUTIC PROCESS

Richard Lasky, Ph.D.

JASON ARONSON INC.
Northvale, New Jersey
London

The author gratefully acknowledges permission to reprint the following material: "Dynamics and Problems in the Treatment of the 'Oedipal Winner,' " by Richard Lasky. Copyright © 1984 by *The Psychoanalytic Review,* vol. 71, pp. 351–374. Reprinted by permission of *The Psychoanalytic Review,* Guilford Publications.

Production Editor: Judith D. Cohen

This book was set in Schneidler by Lind Graphics of Upper Saddle River, New Jersey, and printed and bound by Haddon Craftsmen of Scranton, Pennsylvania.

Library of Congress Cataloging-in-Publication Data

Lasky, Richard.
    Dynamics of development and the therapeutic process / by
Richard Lasky.
        p.   cm.
    Includes bibliographical references and index.
    ISBN 0-87668-565-3
    1. Psychoanalysis. 2. Personality development.
    3. Psychoanalysis–Case studies. I. Title.
    [DNLM: 1. Child Development. 2. Psychoanalytic Theory.
    3. Psychoanalytic Therapy–in infancy & childhood. WS 350.2 L345d]
    RC506.L36 1993
    616.89' 17–dc20
    DNLM/DLC
    for Library of Congress   92-17808

Manufactured in the United States of America. Jason Aronson Inc. offers books and cassettes. For information and catalog write to Jason Aronson Inc., 230 Livingston Street, Northvale, New Jersey 07647.

Again for Judy,
who still makes it
all worthwhile

Contents

Part II The Therapeutic Process

Part III Development of the Therapeutic Process

A six-year, five-sessions-per-week, analysis of an obsessional neurotic woman with depressive features, problems in the management of aggression, marked sado-masochistic features, and other major sexual pathology. The presentation includes a detailed description of analytic hours. It demonstrates how an analysis is actually conducted, the fluctuations in the transference neurosis, the processes of insight and reconstruction in working through, and the points in the analysis at which one could identify structural changes.

A successful psychoanalysis, illustrating modifications in classical technique for the treatment of character-disordered patients.

Two unsuccessful analyses, illustrating why certain kinds of character pathology and psychoanalysis do not mesh well together (even when major modifications are undertaken).

Vernunft wird Unsinn,
Wohltat Plage.
(Reason becomes unreason,
And kindness torment).
                    —Goethe, *Faust* (Part 1, Scene 4)

When we remember that we are all mad,
the mysteries disappear and life stands explained.
                    —Mark Twain, *Notebook*

The best of artists has no thought to show
Which the rough stone in its superfluous shell
Includes:
To break the marble spell
Is all the hand that serves the brain can do.
                    —Michelangelo, *Sonnets*

Introduction

Over the course of a number of years of teaching analytic material on the undergraduate and graduate levels, and even more frequently in analytic training programs, I have repeatedly been asked by students whether there isn't a single, up-to-date book somewhere that covers the main points of traditional, mainstream (i.e., Freudian) psychoanalytic theory and technique in a competent way. Students are asking for a book they can use for the purpose of getting an overview; one that will serve them as an anchor, one might say, in what feels to them like the stormy seas of many separate and sometimes unrelated-seeming readings[1] that are assigned in their classes. It is a fact that most articles assigned in classes are not overview articles: they usually have a highly specified, primary focus on a particular, limited aspect of psychoanalytic theory or technique. This question, or request, has never seemed to me to be geared toward finding a way to avoid reading the assigned articles: students appear to be looking for something additional that can pull together for them a wide variety of diverse articles (and books) that they are not yet prepared to integrate on their own.

Because the breadth of field in psychoanalysis is so wide, and such a depth of conceptualization is necessary (given the complexity of this subject matter), very few authors, understandably, have attempted to write an overview of psychoanalysis. Such a task is so massive and daunting that even the idea seems overwhelming and inconceivable. Analytic writers are usually much more sensible; they pick a single topic (or concept) and then reduce the field even further. They zero in on some smaller, fractional aspect of their topic in order to force the focus of concentration on the subject into a sufficient degree of sharpness as to be manageable. This approach is not only sensible, it is usually quite productive and effective. However, when articles become so highly specialized, it sometimes becomes exceedingly hard for anyone who is not fully conversant with the literature (namely, analytic students) to see the forest for the trees.

The argument for trying to produce this kind of "overview" book (notwith-

---

[1]Many articles that beginning students view as unrelated to each other are often very closely related. The problem is simply that the students' education is not yet advanced enough for them to be able to recognize and appreciate the relationship that exists between them.

standing the cost in terms of lost depth, as long as the result is not too superficial) is obvious: if, by being able to present how and in what ways the numerous, complex, and often abstract concepts of psychoanalysis are always deeply interrelated, a book like this can give a quality of coherence to the other, more specific readings that are so difficult for analytic students to integrate.

In a different way, teaching analysts as well might find this book helpful. Let me start by stating a problem that we all face as teachers – the reverse, perhaps, of the one faced by our students. Faculty members often feel somewhat daunted because they have to choose only a comparatively few reading assignments from a pool of literature that is usually immense and that seems completely related and integrated. If most of the literature were inferior it wouldn't be a problem, but having to choose among many absolutely outstanding articles and books is not an easy task. For most psychoanalytic courses an attempt to do a systematic reading of everything in the literature could take years, not a single semester. It is wonderful that we have such a rich literature, but this is exactly the kind of situation that demonstrates that an embarrassment of riches is not always a good thing. The mathematics of the problem are quite straightforward: thousands (sometimes even tens of thousands) of pages may have been written on a subject; students cannot reasonably be expected to read more than about fifty or sixty pages a week (if we expect them to do so in any kind of critical fashion); and, the class only lasts 8, 12, or 15 weeks.

Analytic faculty have been known to spend days, or even weeks, over bibliographies of three or four hundred excellent references, trying to figure out which ten, twenty, or maybe even thirty articles will provide enough scope and sufficient depth for the course. It is my hope that this book could free the teaching analyst from having to select articles without sufficient depth just in order to provide students with scope. Teaching analysts can use selected sections of the book in conjunction with the more highly specialized papers that do provide adequate in-depth elaboration of the finer points of the subject matter of the course.

Now let me also say something about how this book might be of use to the working practitioner, who is no longer part of the training process. At professional workshops, as a member of peer-supervision groups, with friends, at conferences, and in other settings, I have met many working analysts and therapists who have felt that they have some small gaps in their mastery of analytic theory, or in their ability to comfortably conceptualize some of the underpinnings of their technique. Such gaps need not always pose problems for these analysts in their work: no one has ever learned all that there is a use for, and recognizing that one still has something left to learn doesn't automatically "cripple" an analyst. However, almost always (because they are serious people), they do express a wish in our conversations to find a reasonable way to catch up on the areas in which they feel they are weak. The literature is so massive, however, that these working professionals (who, we must remember, have been out of training for some time, and who also have lost the mental set of being a student) usually believe, perhaps correctly, that it is not really possible to pursue their goal in an efficient and time-effective way. Their lives are no longer able to accommodate the strenuous study routine of an analytic candidate, and so they sometimes joke: "Perhaps in my next life."

It is my hope that this book, despite its being an overview on psychoanalytic theory and technique, might offer a possible solution to the problem. Working analysts could use the book in two ways: first, it can give them a general, but still relatively thorough, understanding of the areas in which they feel deficient; and second, they can use both the book and the supplementary knowledge that they have gained from it as a platform, as it were, from which to launch themselves into the rest of the literature in a more sharply targeted fashion that would truly conserve their limited time and energy.

Let me now turn to my approach to writing the book itself; that is, my absolute and utter commitment to writing this book in the clearest fashion possible. I am convinced that most analytic books and papers are much harder to read than is necessary, and that this creates pointless difficulties in the learning process. I would like everyone who has read this book to be readily able to describe, with genuine confidence, the major differences between, say, object relations and identifications; or, to give a different example, the major changes between previous and contemporary concepts of how children acquire their basic gender identity; or, in yet another example, the basic differences between ubiquitous transference, symptomatic transference, the transference neurosis, floating transference, delusional transference, narcissistic transferences, and a transference psychosis; or, for one last example, the difference between an interpretation and a reconstruction. Many analysts cannot do this, and I believe that it is partly (although, obviously, not entirely) the fault of how a large proportion of the analytic literature is written. The concepts are often brilliant, but the writing is awful, and I believe that writing clearly and well about these very complicated things has half the battle won.

Psychoanalytic concepts are extremely complex and very difficult to grasp under even the very best of circumstances. Because every event in the mind is overdetermined, and because every mental event serves numerous functions simultaneously, when we try to conceptualize mental processes we are in the position of having to simultaneously consider many complicated variables, which are constantly in ever-changing interaction with one another. We should not be surprised if many analysts whose ability to do this has been dazzling—incredibly brilliant analysts— have not been able to communicate their ideas clearly in their published works. This is quite understandable in that they were trained as analysts, not writers. Their training, no matter how well they have been able to conceptualize theoretical and clinical events, has not been in the construction of language on the written page. One might say, rather, that an analyst's training is in the deconstruction of language (in the sense that they are trained to listen for and to decode the hidden, unconscious meanings of what patients have to say on the couch). We would expect to find, and we do, that the result of this is that, all too often, the value of a complex analytic contribution is obscured by a convoluted or otherwise difficult writing style. If the reader must struggle in the process of learning psychoanalysis, as one must always struggle with material of great complexity, my hope is that with this book the task will be made appreciably easier through the use of a clear and readily comprehensible style of writing.

An example of how much more difficult the material can be when it is not presented in a clear writing style can be seen in Edith Jacobson's *The Self and the Object World*. I have singled out Jacobson here because I believe that many of her contributions, which are extremely difficult to read, have been among the most important in contemporary psychoanalytic thinking. Because of the immense admiration and respect that I have for her work, I must admit to some trepidation in using Jacobson as an example of what I am describing, but discussions with colleagues and students over the years have made it clear to me that her work is indeed a good example. The reason Jacobson's style of writing is frequently criticized is that it often prevents her ideas from being fully accessible. Most analysts who know her work do not question the value of her contributions, and in fact she is idealized by many current analysts; but when it comes time to read Jacobson in study groups or classes, there is always an almost universal groan. This groan is not a reflection on what Jacobson has to say but on how she goes about saying it. One frequently hears comments, even from quite experienced analysts, that go something like: "I had to read each sentence five times before I understood what she was trying to say."

Some members of the analytic community who have criticized psychoanalytic authors such as Jacobson for their writing technique (and it must be said that she is only one of many to whom this criticism has been applied) offer the additional criticism that the problem is as much one of psychoanalytic jargon as it is of writing style. They object to the use of metapsychological language, as if it were the language itself (or, for some, the metapsychology) rather than the way it is used that is the problem. Although I understand the difficulties inherent in learning any new vernacular, and the natural resistance that may be felt at having to learn a whole new technical vocabulary, I do not believe that this is what is at the heart of the problem. Technical language is a shorthand, a shortcut, a metaphor, for concepts that could take paragraphs to describe in "plain talk." Every profession has its language, a new version of the mother tongue that must be learned by its practitioners. (Metapsychology is also a shortcut of a sort, a means of describing certain kinds of psychic phenomena at a specific level of abstraction that comes in particularly handy at times.)[2] One cannot get around the problem of having to the learn the language of psychoanalysis; however, once the technical language is absorbed into one's intellectual vocabulary, I fully believe (and I hope this book will demonstrate) that it can to be used with ease, comfort, and facility in both thinking and writing.

As a special means of achieving clarity of expression I have done something very unorthodox in this book: except where I am presenting a direct quote or where I am discussing someone's work specifically, I have left out the all the usual and expected reference citations. I have chosen to do this because I believe that citations break up

---

[2]Chapter 1 contains a thorough discussion of how metapsychology arose, how it is used, what its critics suggest is wrong with using it, and why I disagree.

the conceptual thread of a sentence. Because this material is always so dense and so very complicated, I felt that it was important to remain firmly attached to the goal of avoiding anything that might interfere with simplicity and intelligibility of presentation. I have, of course, done this with great hesitation, not merely because it disregards the scholarly tradition, which I hold in great respect, but also because it removes the means by which the originators of very important and profound contributions receive credit, thus depriving them of the acknowledgment which is theirs by right, and which I firmly believe is well deserved. I also hesitated to do this because citations are the means by which readers have access to source materials, and I consider it a serious deprivation not to have these references at one's disposal. I will explain below what I have done to rectify (at least, in part) the problems this presents, but let me first elaborate a bit further on my motives, because I do want to avoid giving the impression of ungratefulness or a lack of respect for tradition or for other people's work.

Ordinarily, as one presents one's ideas one carefully references them with the appropriate citations. Despite its importance, I have always found this to be extremely distracting. It does not merely break up the line of the sentence but, more importantly, it breaks up the reader's train of thought.

I can vividly illustrate what I mean by first demonstrating what a properly referenced presentation looks like and then comparing it with how it reads after the citations have been removed. The following example is from my (1990) article "Catastrophic Illness in the Analyst and the Analyst's Emotional Reactions to It" (*International Journal of Psycho-Analysis* 71:455–473); this excerpt occurs near the beginning of the article, on page 455:

> I found this topic (illness in the analyst) to have received relatively little attention in the literature, and although this was generally true across the board it was more true of the analytic literature than of the psychotherapy literature. In any event, even the combined literature could not be considered ample. The literature does cover a very wide range of topics having to do with critical events in the lives of analysts, such as pregnancy (Fenster et al. 1986, Lax 1969) and miscarriage (Hannet 1949); ageing (Eissler 1975) and criteria for retirement (Eissler 1977, Michaels and Schoenberg 1966); and relocation (Aarons 1975, Dewald, 1965, 1966, Mullholland and Sanguilano 1969, Rosenbaum 1977, Weiss 1975); and, there is even a growing literature on the repercussions of the analyst's death (Barbanel et al. 1989, Bolsom and Bolsom 1974, Givelber and Simon 1981, Kubie 1968, Rodman 1977).

Here is the same material with the citations removed:

> I found this topic (illness in the analyst) to have received relatively little attention in the literature, and although this was generally true across the board it was more true of the analytic literature than of the psychotherapy literature. In any event, even the combined literature could not be considered ample. The literature does cover a very wide range of topics having to do with critical events in the lives of analysts, such as pregnancy and miscarriage; ageing and criteria for retirement; and relocation; and, there is even a growing literature on the repercussions of the analyst's death.

Some readers may not find the difference between the samples particularly relevant, but it is my expectation that most readers will see the logic behind my choice to omit reference citations from the body of the text except in very special circumstances. What I have done to try to accommodate giving credit to those authors whose work have I relied on in writing this book is to list them all in a full and rather extensive bibliography. I recognize that it is a bit of a halfway measure, but it is the best compromise that I have come up with.

For those readers who are intrigued by anything in particular that they have come across in the book, no matter where it was found, and who are interested in reading in greater depth on that topic, I have included a thorough bibliographic essay at the back of the book. This essay describes some of the key articles and books in the different subject areas, including those I have found to be especially useful. The bibliographic essay follows the general outline of the table of contents. Subject areas are identified in boldface type, so that the reader can find his or her area of interest without having to read through the entire bibliographic essay. Obviously, the bibliography itself, which dwarfs the bibliographic essay, is also available to those readers who exhaust what the essay has to offer and who wish to study one of the topics in even greater detail than the essay can recommend.

Let us turn to how the contents of the book are organized. The book is divided into three sections: the dynamics of development, the therapeutic process, and the development of the therapeutic process. In the first section, on development, I have taken a longitudinal approach in which, at key developmental points, we look at psychic functioning in a "cross-sectional" fashion. Because identifications, object relations, psychic structuralization, and narcissistic regulatory processes (to mention only a few of the topics considered) are all intrinsically tied into one another and mutually interdependent, it seemed best not to discuss them separately (as if they were, in effect, separate theories of personality). Also, since many simultaneous mental operations undergo mutually reinforcing changes as development proceeds (along the course of all of the psychosexual stages), the most sensible strategy seemed to be to make an approach to this material in a manner that roughly approximates, or is at least analogous to, what a radiologist does with a CAT scan. In computerized axial tomography the radiologist gets a sense of what an entire organ is like rather than just acquiring a two-dimensional picture of the organ at a single plane. The computer, in concert with the x-ray machine, "moves across" the entire organ under study, taking pictures of the plane at microscopic intervals, until something equating a three-dimensional image of the organ is available. In this first section of the book I have presented a series of "pictures" of various "organs," showing how they function in relation to one another, and I progressively advance along the route of psychosexual development giving us, in this way, what I believe is a "three-dimensional image" of mental processes and their evolution.

Throughout the entire book, but most particularly in this first section (which has a lot of theoretical material, mostly at very high levels of abstraction), I have taken as many opportunities as possible to illustrate the material with concrete examples (most commonly with clinical vignettes). In addition to the difficulty of working with such highly abstracted material, most of analytic theory is highly metaphorical, extremely subtle, and contains more concurrent variables than we can usually juggle at one time with comfort; thus the constant use of concrete examples is indispensable in helping to keep the material grounded for the reader.

In this section on the dynamics of development as well as in the second section of the book on the therapeutic process, I provide many definitions of terms, concepts, and processes, and I have stated that in this I am representing the views of mainstream, Freudian psychoanalysis. I feel absolutely certain that for every single definition I provide, without exception, some Freudian analyst-readers will disagree. There is an old joke that traditionally has used many different groups as its target, and when it is told about analysts it goes: *When you put two analysts in a room together, you can always count on getting at least three different opinions.*

There is, in fact, no single stance on anything in the Freudian camp; Freudians occupy a spectrum of opinions on theory and technique. Freudians frequently look very different when you compare them with one another (Brenner and Loewald, for example), but they appear considerably more homogeneous, perhaps even monolithic, when compared with analysts of other schools of thought (for example, when Freudians are compared with self psychologists, interpersonal-humanists, Jungians, and so forth). Because there is no "party line" in the Freudian model (it only looks that way when compared with other, different analytic models) I have had to make something of a compromise in what I represent as being Freudian definitions. In formulating my criteria for a definition I said, *"Suppose we had ten analysts in a room, all of whom defined their orientation as Freudian, and each of whom was recognized by the others as being a Freudian analyst,*[3] *– what do I believe a significant majority of them would be able to agree on?"*

One of the special uses I have made of footnoting in this book has been to indicate where there are alternate definitions that I believe would have been preferred by a significant minority of my hypothetical group of Freudian analysts. In a similar fashion (except where I expressly wanted to contrast the views of alternate schools of psychoanalysis with the Freudian view) I have frequently used footnotes when I have thought that the reader might find some non-Freudian conceptualizations of interest. I have also used footnotes when some intriguing aside occurred to me that I did not want to include in the body of the text because I thought that it would be either diverting or distracting. Footnotes may be interesting, but they never include material that I consider absolutely essential to the book, and so readers who find

---

[3]It was important to me to require that my hypothetical group of Freudians not only define themselves in that way, but also that they be willing to define each other in that way. This was because many therapists who describe themselves as analysts are not accepted by fully trained analysts as really being analysts (the designation is, in fact, used very loosely by some professionals and by the public), and because it is equally true that not every analyst who chooses to define himself or herself as a Freudian is actually accepted by such by the majority of Freudian analysts.

footnotes distracting can choose to disregard them without fear of having missed anything of central importance.

In writing the second section of the book (on the therapeutic process), I made an intentional decision to avoid recommending therapeutic tactics. I did not want this section to have a cookbook quality about it ("If A happens, do X, and if B happens, do Y"; "A pinch of interpretation here, a dash of abstinence there"); my interest was in examining the nature of the process itself (Why is something therapeutic? How does it work? What is the nature of the analytic situation? How do we understand a clinical problem?) Although I have included a few "general rule" descriptions (for example, the order in which resistance is usually analyzed), I believe that particular analytic interventions are always guided by and subject to the specific issues and situations that are in effect for the individual patient at hand, and that any attempt to create a formula for technique will only lead to rigidity and dogmatism in the analyst and in the analysis.

In the third section of the book (on the development of the therapeutic process) I present four psychoanalytic cases in some detail. My specific reasons for picking each case are outlined in the introduction to each treatment, so there is no need to review that here. However, my wish to present actual analytic cases in detail should be explained. First, the analytic undertaking is a "protected" endeavor, protected for a number of reasons (for example: confidentiality for the patient, narcissistic vulnerability of the analyst, fear of countertransference exposure, and so forth). Because this is the case, there are very few instances in the literature where one can see exactly how an analysis is conducted. This seemed a favorable opportunity to do so. Second, it seemed important to provide a situation where the reader could tie together the first two sections of the book so that they could be formed into an integrated whole; it seems to me that the best venue for doing this is always in the conduct of an analysis itself.

I would like to conclude this introduction by expressing my appreciation to all the people who helped me in the writing of this book. Need I even say that I owe an inestimable debt to my patients, who were, and still are, after all, my best teachers? And after them come all of my "official" teachers who helped me to learn psycho-analysis and to treasure it. Very many friends and colleagues, during innumerable discussions, have taught me about psychoanalysis and have steadfastly prompted me to sharpen both my technique and my thinking–too many, in fact, to be able to name individually. However, there are two friends (who are also colleagues, but that comes second) I must single out for special thanks: Dr. Andrew Druck and Dr. Marvin Hurvich.

Gaon was the title given, in the Babylonian Jewish community (in the post-Talmudic period, approximately between the sixth and eleventh centuries), to spiritual and intellectual leaders who were also legal authorities. More recently, Gaon has become an honorific title for any leading Talmudic scholar of great authority and distinction. In Dr. Druck I have found a psychoanalytic Gaon who continually, by his example, stimulates me to greater aspirations. My contact with him, as a friend and colleague, makes me a better person and a better analyst; and his contact with this book has made it a better product than I could have produced alone without his profound insights and help. Dr. Druck went over the manuscript, line by line, catching my many errors (and my tendency to under-represent analytic positions with which I disagree). He didn't just keep me honest, however; he made significant contributions to this book in the many enlightening suggestions he so generously offered to me.

In addition to his careful criticism of this book, which I found to be of immense help, I am indebted to Dr. Hurvich for many stimulating discussions in which I directly benefited as an analyst. I, along with many others, have been the beneficiary of his extraordinary insights into both borderline phenomena and annihilatory anxiety.

I must thank Dr. Jason Aronson, who has been all any author could have hoped for in a publisher. The writing of this book went through a number of fits and starts, and through more delays (entirely my fault) than either of us would have anticipated. Throughout, he was always supportive, enthusiastic, filled with many good ideas for the book and, not least, patient. There were times when it definitely looked like this book might never get finished, and I am certain that without Dr. Aronson's constant advocacy and encouragement, it would not have been completed. I would also like to thank Judy Cohen, my editor at Jason Aronson Inc., who was the good shepherd who guided the book through production. She was always helpful, and every author appreciates having an editor like her. I would like to thank Sanford Robinson, my copy editor, not only for his thoroughness, but for his thoughtfulness in the suggestions that he made throughout.

Like a child with an Oreo cookie, I have saved the best for last. No one is owed a greater debt by me than my wife, Dr. Judith Lasky, who has been my helpmate in life as well as with this book. I could not even begin to list all that I owe her for the life we have had together; let me try to do her justice in a smaller, more manageable way by describing my bottomless, immeasurable gratitude for the help she has given me with this book. She too, like Drs. Druck and Hurvich, read this book and criticized it in manuscript form; however, Drs. Druck and Hurvich only had to read it once, and not dozens upon dozens of times. Her conceptual and clinical contributions were more than just helpful: the fact of the matter is that every time I got into trouble with anything in this book (not an unusual event in the least), she was there to bail me out. There is no way that this book could have been written without her.

Finally, let me furnish the formal assurance that all nonfiction authors are compelled by conscience to give: despite all the wonderful help I have received in writing this book, the final decision for the contents has always been mine, and I am solely responsible for any and all errors, misrepresentations, and mistakes.

I

THE DYNAMICS OF DEVELOPMENT

1

What the Infant Brings to the Environment

The Baby at Birth

Babies are subject from the moment of their birth to the influences of a number of physiological needs and requirements such as hunger, thirst, metabolic activities, evacuation of wastes, homeostatic temperature regulation, and so forth. These biological considerations, and additional physiological tensions that arise when states of need remain unmet or requirements are unfulfilled,[1] are the prime movers in the generation and continuous development of mental functioning. We can think of the earliest psychological event as an excitation, or perhaps we may wish to compare it to the notion of a pressure that constantly mounts as new needs arise, as some needs are not met, and as they continue to press individually and in combination for satisfaction or discharge. The basic and most primitive model of anxiety, which sets the stage for signal anxiety, separation anxiety, castration anxiety, and other anxieties in later psychosexual development is, then, the earliest experience of mounting uncontrollable tension or excitation.[2]

We are always, even in earliest infancy, subjected simultaneously and sequentially to a multitude of related and unrelated needs. It is not possible for one to ever be in a situation where all one's needs are being met. Thus the mind is always in a state of psychic tension. Biological conditions and events initiate mental functioning, and they continue to exert an undiminished influence on mental functioning even after environment and experiences exert their own powerful influences later in

---

[1] I am setting the stage here for a basic paradigm of conflict that is invariably related to needs and to blocks in their satisfaction.

[2] I am suggesting that anxiety has properties, in addition to the signal function developed later in life when the ego is more mature (to be discussed in detail later on), which are directly related to conflicts surrounding the satisfaction of needs. However, I am also suggesting that anxiety is a property of need itself: that anxiety in earliest infancy is reflecting the subjective experience of a need that feels overwhelming. Thus need, when it becomes too intensified or too long delayed, leads to anxiety for economic reasons, even before anxiety becomes related to conflict for dynamic reasons.

mental development. Some conflicts faced in life can be resolved according to the "fight or flight" principle; however, the mental conflicts that reflect physiological demands and requirements cannot. One cannot ultimately defeat the need for food for example, or flee from it, though one can certainly control aspects of subjective hunger. The mental pressures that emerge are inescapable because they arise in a context that is biologically, and not psychologically or environmentally, determined. We can view the emergence of mental representations of these pressures and a mental response to these pressures as the very first work of the psyche.[3] If we say that anatomical and physiological separation from the mother constitutes the physical birth of the infant, we can add that the emergence of mental representations of anatomical considerations (such as gender, functional characteristics of perceptual capacities, muscular and skeletal development, etc.), and the emergence of mental responses to ordinary and ever present physiological factors, constitutes the psychological birth of the infant.

The Drives

These most basic excitations, which form the original mental representations and which are in large part determined by genetic predisposition, are what we mean when we refer to the drives or to instincts (the terms are generally used interchangeably). In psychological terms the concept of an instinct is different from the meaning it conveys in biology. *Drive* is sometimes, but not always, the favored term because of the biological and ethological comparisons the word *instinct* calls forth. A psychological instinct is not meant to suggest the equivalent of nest building in birds, pack behavior in dogs, or antipathy between male Siamese fighting fish, although it is only natural for us to think of these unlearned but highly complicated behaviors when the concept of instinct is introduced. Psychological instincts are also not the same as simple reflexive behavior, such as "instinctively" flinching or blinking one's eyes when an object is thrown at the face, or "instinctively" grabbing for a support if one should trip and fall.

In normal development a number of drives will coalesce around qualities of experience (i.e., gratification, satisfaction, pleasure, pain, excitement, unpleasure, tension, and anger) and around complicated functions (such as sexual behavior or eating). The psychological components of eating, for example, would always

---

[3] This is a conflict theory (leading to a structural theory) model of the beginning of mental functioning. Some analysts (like, for example, Margaret Mahler), in adding the point of view of object relations theory, suggest that the psychological birth of the infant is related to conflicts related to separation/differentiation/individuation issues. I am not sure that these models really clash if one looks at Mahler's concept of psychological birth as concerning a more organized and coherent basis for mental functioning, and the conflict/structure concept I have presented here as concerning only the origins of initial, and extremely preliminary, mental operations (and not the dynamic relations that mental events will eventually have to one another).

include drive activity that is related to the tensions and unpleasure experiences associated with being hungry, as well as the satisfactions and pleasurable states associated with the gratifications of being fed. Additionally, in eating one would also find instinctual components that are intrinsic in the mental corollaries of looking, touching, tasting, smelling, and so on. The subjective experience of eating (and all it may subsequently mean) will always have within it basic and distinct instincts that are closely related to physiological and anatomical factors, and complex or "compounded" instincts that form in response to experience (a more abstract notion that involves the integration of a number of separate and initially unrelated instincts). This suggests a quantum leap in complexity within the structuring of drives, and yet in relative terms we are reviewing a development that is still quite primitive and that remains intimately related to bodily processes. A "structured" drive is often so transformed that it is no longer recognizable or functions like the simple sum of its component parts. This notion of a structured instinct (or drive) is more readily understandable as a specifically *psychological* concept than is the concept of the more primitive unstructured drive. In general, the greater its distance from a purely biological event the easier it is to conceive of a drive as being a psychological event; for example, the concept of a "quality of excitation" is much harder to understand, and to relate to in human terms, than is the concept of "being hungry." In the psychoanalytic literature one may usually assume that references to instincts and drives refer to these complex and compounded, highly organized and structured entities. In a final word on the most primitive variety of drive, one should be aware that simple drives can keep their character intact while nevertheless being used in the formation and development of compound instincts. The character of a compounded higher-order instinct, however, can be quite different from the primitive drives that make up its component parts.

Evaluating Drive Theory

Appreciating the genuinely psychological nature of the most primitive drives is quite difficult, and this has led some theorists either to ignore or to dispute drive theory as an essential and underlying fundamental principle of psychoanalysis. Those who wish to abandon drive theory in its entirety suggest that mental functioning is initiated by events in the environment alone. They see mental operations as having their origins in reactions to externally, not internally, introduced stimuli. They take the position, for example, that aggression is a response to frustration; that depression is a response to disappointment, or, as one theorist puts it, that depression is love gone hungry; that pleasure is a response to satisfaction or gratification; that love is a response to having one's needs met and that sexual excitement (in adults) naturally follows; that interest develops in response to what is available; or that mastery is developed in response to what is required by one's situation. Without question, these interrelationships can be of the utmost importance; one possible response to frustration might very well be aggression, and one possible response to disappointment or deprivation might very well be depression. However, one must ask whether these are the only responses possible, whether these responses are inevitable in the presence of those conditions, and, more importantly, whether these are the only ways such mental events can be formed. Are these indeed the only responses possible? Or is it possible for depression *and* aggression to evolve as a consequence of frustration, and is it possible that both love *and* interest might evolve from having needs met? One must ask whether particular responses are inevitable in the presence of specific conditions. Is it possible to have a response other than aggression when frustrated, or depression when deprived, or must every other possible reaction *always* be accompanied by aggression when one is frustrated, and depression when one is deprived? Are these the only ways mental events – depression and pleasure, for example – can be formed? Is there any way it would be possible for both depression and pleasure to emerge within the exact same environmental condition?

Perhaps the following example can illustrate a drawback in the purely environmental approach by demonstrating how the same environmental conditions can foster love and pleasure in one individual and frustration and disappointment in another. If we postulate (as we may do with confidence) that under normal conditions reasonably prompt and nourishing feedings administered by warm and loving parents will promote feelings of well-being and a sense of basic trust in an infant, we can hypothesize that an infant who gets these things will be satisfied, will experience pleasure, and will have relatively few barriers in the formation of love. Suppose, however, that we have a second child, one who is ill and in great pain, in exactly the same environment. We are likely to find that equally "good enough mothering" might be satisfactory in establishing a feeling of well-being in the healthy child while remaining unsatisfactory in developing that feeling in the sick child. In early infancy the tension of being hungry is not differentiated from other tensions, and although not all unpleasure experiences are experienced in the same way, an infant does not have the fine sensory and intellectual capacities to make realistic judgments about what it is feeling and why. Thus a hungry infant can be soothed by feeding even though it had no clear understanding that hunger was the specific cause of its discomfort. A wet infant can be initially soothed, in a limited way, by feeding rather than only by changing, just as a hungry infant can be initially soothed, in a limited way, by changing or by holding rather than only by feeding. Mothering acts of nurturance are experienced globally, and without clear distinction, as are the infant's subjective experiences of pleasure and unpleasure. For a sick infant in pain, being fed promptly by an affectionate adult will have only limited effects on the subjective experience of unalleviated discomfort. The infant, unable to sort out the cause of his discomfort and unable to appreciate his parent's legitimate efforts on his behalf, finds being fed highly unsatisfactory, hence disappointing and frustrating, as the major portion of his discomfort and tension remains unaffected. Here we can see that if the infant's illness and pain are considerable, more than the ordinary amount of good mothering will be necessary for the establishment of a sense of well-being and basic trust. The same environment that contributed to these positive and pleasurable experiences in a healthy, pain-free infant can be a main feature in disappointment, frustration, aggression, depression, and a major sense of deprivation in a sick and hurting infant. One chooses to make special efforts for a sick child precisely because of the interrelationship between bodily factors and how they change the meaning and experience of the environment. As bodily considerations become paramount, environment becomes less important and even, in some cases, almost irrelevant. If a sick infant's pain is too intense it is conceivable, particularly in a prolonged illness, that no amount of good mothering, even with heroic attempts, would be enough to forestall frustration and disappointment.

When we compare a healthy and a sick child we are examining the differences between the innate drive endowments of these infants. In this example the nature of the comparison involves differences in innate drive endowment that are temporary. An example of innate drive endowment that changes but is not temporary is the alteration in mental functioning brought about by the onset of puberty. An example of a permanent and unchanging innate drive endowment, which also illustrates the problems inherent in a strictly environmental theory of mental functioning, is seen in the differing thresholds of subcutaneous skin responsivity present in people from the moment of birth. Studies have described major psychological differences in infants who differ on this variable even though their environments, including specific types and qualities of mothering, were essentially the same.[4] One draws the conclusion again that the same environmental circumstances are not experienced and processed in the same way by all individuals. Even before the powerful effects of prior experience become influential in determining inner mental events, it will be useful to be aware that where kinesthetic and tactile pleasure is concerned, an infant whose stimulus barrier is high on this variable will require a greater frequency and intensity of handling, caressing, and fondling than will an infant whose barrier is low. If this alone is not sufficient to illustrate the way nature and nurture are inextricably bound together in the development of psychological functioning, one can also consider the role of a factor such as this in additional aspects of mental organization. For example, one tends to rely on some perceptual capacities more than others in one's experience of the world. Some people have an exquisite sense of smell, which they use quite actively in learning about and relating to their environment. Looking, touching, hearing, and so on either follow, or are used in, subsidiary capacities. For such people memory, too, can be clearest, best, most vivid, most complex, and most accessible when smell is involved. A factor like the threshold of subcutaneous skin responsivity can be directly involved in whether touch will be a perceptual avenue of choice, and that perceptual pathway will be critical in how one

---

[4]Studies of validity and reliability were conducted with infants between and within experimental groups to be certain that the variable of subcutaneous skin responsivity was responsible for the findings, rather than other differences that may have existed between individuals.

experiences and relates to the environment. Because it is involved not only in how the environment is experienced but also in how the individual responds, this factor is directly involved in setting up an interactive chain of events in mental development like the ever-widening ripples in a pond.

Some perceptual preferences can be quite dramatic, either by choice or by necessity, as in the exquisitely sensitive hearing of the blind. When one considers the sheer number of directly biologically influenced, and genetically predisposed, variables that operate side by side in every individual, it becomes apparent that the environment itself is considerably less important than how it is processed. This view cannot be carried to the extreme of arguing that the environment has no objectively important features, but it is designed to show the error in suggesting that the influence of the environment on mental development can be considered outside the context of the psychobiological matrix.[5] To do so is not only an oversimplification but also a reduction of psychological functioning to the level of the most elementary stimulus-response learning theory.

The Issue of Metapsychology

Different but equally important problems arise in any approach that ignores rather than disputes the critical position of drive theory in psychoanalysis. Some knowledge of the basic metapsychological assumptions of psychoanalysis is necessary in order to constructively evaluate an alternative approach (even if the alternative approach disputes the existence of those assumptions). Metapsychology describes the most elemental assumptions about mental functioning one can make.[6] It describes mental functions that must exist in every aspect of psychological life, no matter how small, fleeting, or inconsequential. Finally, it forms the unifying principles that are always necessary, but by no means sufficient, for a specifically psychoanalytic understanding of mental functioning. Metapsychology is also a way of organizing our thinking about the nature of psychological events that do not lend themselves readily to empirical study; for example, the specific source of instincts that are actively or passively experienced in terms of mental drives (or pressures), or the relationship between mental energies and conscious feelings (and thoughts). Freud's earliest use of the term was as a means of indicating that his theories addressed mental phenomena outside the realm of consciousness, but his final definition of metapsychology as the basic set of assumptions upon which

---

[5]The point I am making here is not that the infant can be detached from the environment for study (a child is born into an environment as Winnicott so aptly points out), but that the environment cannot be appraised without considering the influences brought to bear by the individual born into it. We all have our own subjective environments which are distinct from the objective environment assumed to exist for us by others, precisely because it is experienced by us with our own unique patterns of needs and endowments.

[6]It is also true that these are often also the most abstract, distant from experience, and least "provable" of assumptions.

psychoanalysis rests is the one that is in most common use today. It is usually divided into six theoretical points of view: economic, dynamic, topographical, structural, genetic, and adaptive. The economic and dynamic theories are of most interest for this discussion, and so the other theories will only be summarized now, with a fuller discussion of them to follow later when other subject matter will more readily facilitate their integration. Briefly, then, the topographical theory postulates that mental functioning occurs both consciously and unconsciously, leading inevitably to the conclusion that consciousness is not a prerequisite for mental functioning. Topographical theory was partially supplanted by structural theory, which postulates that despite some degree of overlap in both functions and contents, the id, the ego, and the superego organize mental functioning in characteristically unique ways. Adaptive theory, which is still controversial and thus not uniformly accepted as a metapsychological principle, postulates an adjustive and an adaptive inclination in one's relation to the environment, which is expedited by primarily autonomous ego functions present at birth, and which is continuously reinforced through the ongoing development of secondary ego autonomy (terms which will be defined below). The genetic theory postulates that current psychological functioning is influenced by a combination of current life events and the ways resolved and unresolved past conflicts were experienced, with a particular emphasis on how such conflicts and resolutions were expressed, abandoned, and retained in the psyche.

The Economic and Dynamic Theories

In distinction to the foregoing capsule summaries, we can begin a more complex investigation of the economic and dynamic theories by making the general statement that they were both developed by Freud, who sometimes discussed them together and at other times considered them separately, in order to make purely psychological statements without having to refer back in each case to the anatomical and physiological matrix out of which a psychological event has its origin. His interest was in being able to discuss mental events in mental terms. The notion that a mental event has its origin in the biological substrate does not necessarily mean that a biologically organized discussion of its operations is the best way to understand it. Furthermore, there is the basic difficulty (even if one did want a biologically organized discussion) of specifying the exact somatic origin of a drive at any given time. One can observe the qualities and results of drives by examining their aims and objects, their transformations, and their derivatives, but the source of a drive falls within the domain of physiology. Current research into the body–mind relationship (e.g., on the biochemical origins of mental illness, on genetic predisposition in autism, on the operation of mind-altering drugs, on mapping of the brain) may ultimately develop real precision in determining the source of drives. On the question of whether one is entitled, then, to postulate the existence of drives if their specific sources in the biological substrate are unspecifiable, we are in the position of the person who cannot know precisely what electricity is but who can nonetheless perceive its effects, understand and predict its action, control it, channel it, transform it, make it work, stop its operation, and so forth. By looking at the transformations and derivatives of instincts we can learn something specific about their aims, objects, and pressures even if we can only discuss their sources in general terms.

The use of such concepts as *aim, object,* and *pressure* are central to economic and dynamic theory. Economic theory postulates a psychic energy derived from the drives that has been previously conceptualized as the mental representation of biological substrates. This energy is the fuel for mental activity, and psychoanalytic discussion of mental functioning uses economic theory when it includes descriptions of the way mental energy is expended. An example of this in everyday terms is expressed by the harried individual who, on being asked to undertake an emotionally draining or time-consuming additional task, replies: "I'm sorry, but I just don't have the energy to get involved with that now." It is as a part of economic theory that we consider the concepts of displacement and transformation and the concept of the pleasure principle. We see these economic principles in operation in mobilization of cathexis and other mobile aspects of cathexis (e.g., hypercathexis, hypocathexis, anticathexis, and so forth, which will be described below), in the discharge capacities of affects, in sublimation and neutralization, and in the interweaving and fluctuations between primary- and secondary-process functioning.

Dynamic theory, in contrast, postulates the operation of psychic forces, not energy, in mental functioning. In dynamic terms we can think of these forces as being capable of, and subject to, variations of intensity (changes in magnitude) and as having the characteristics of direction (toward or away from something or someone).[7] If we consider the economic concept of *energy* to involve *aim,* in the sense that aim is thought of as the achievement of discharge (i.e., the pleasure principle), then we can consider the dynamic concept of *force* to involve *objects* and *pressure.*

Force involves objects in the sense that most ways of achieving the goal of discharge require the direction of mental forces toward an object. When the term object is used to mean a person, mental forces can be directed toward someone (in the external environment) who can facilitate the process of aim-satisfaction, or they can be directed at the self (the internal environment) as an object. An example of the self as object in this process would be found in acts of autoeroticism; however, it is safe to say, as a rule, that mental forces directed at the self will be expressed in a wide variety of ways (not just masturbatory), which are determined for the most part by the prevailing state of intrapsychic organization. Mental forces involve differences in pressure in the sense that the need for gratification increases when unfulfilled (a buildup of tension). This creates mental (and other) actions in the striving for the achievement of an instinctual aim. Mental forces may decrease in pressure (a reduction or absence of tension) when instinctual aims are achieved or are dormant. Another way forces may be considered to have pressure is when they are combined,

---

[7]The act of a mental force being directed at something (a wish, the self, or an object) is what is meant by *cathexis.* It is an *investment* of psychic energy. This concept is discussed in detail on p. 13.

which can occur in a variety of ways. The addition of forces can result in a propor-tional *increase* of pressure (an infant is more highly motivated to extend cathexis to its mother when the need to be held, to feed, to suck, and to make eye contact with her are operating in concert) and, in a different outcome, the addition of forces can result in a proportional *decrease* of pressure (an infant can, in the face of disappointment and frustration, decrease its inclination to make a retaliatory attack by adding to the aggressive cathexis of its mother a libidinal cathexis as a balance, or one might say, as a countermeasure). Variations, fluctuations, and alternative channeling of the pressures in mental forces are also involved in, affected by, and effected by the process of drive fusion and defusion. In the same way that a quantity of mental energy (libido) is first directed at the mother herself, and then sublimated in the service of retaining memory-traces of her in her absence, energy is also invested in the development of psychic structure. One major difference in these two cases is the extent to which sublimation and neutralization are necessary for successful achievement of the goal. Memory-traces (of the mother) require the maintenance of unsublimated libido (to serve as both the motivator and the reinforcer of memory) in addition to sublimated libido (to be used in the actual remembering itself). *Specific memory,* then, uses drive energy that is sublimated and neutralized as well as considerable drive energy that has remained instinctualized; whereas the *process of remembering* uses essentially "free" (or "autonomous") energy, and considerably less instinctualized energy.[8] We call free energy the product of drive fusion because of the freedom from instinctualization achieved in this form of combining drives, in contrast to the more highly instinc-tualized proportional increases and decreases in pressure just described. Thus we can say that although representatives of drive fusion can be found in both the contents and the functions of the psychic structures, the most valuable and impressive con-tribution of drive fusion is prominently displayed in the development of the psychic structures themselves.

The breakdown of psychic structure involves drive defusion, which causes further serious disruption in the capacity to first develop, and then maintain, sublimation and neutralization. It is a characteristic of drive fusion that it binds and transforms large quantities of aggression so that a considerable amount of libido is set free for both direct and sublimated uses. Defusion works in the opposite direction. It binds libido and frees aggression with one major difference; that is, the aggression freed by defusion is not particularly amenable to neutralization. This is in distinction to the susceptibility to ready sublimation of freed libido that occurs in drive fusion. This is not surprising when we consider that highly developed structures permit enhanced capacities for developing adaptive functioning, whereas damage to structure inevitably carries with it disruption and impediments in the area of function. Neutralization and sublimation, and the process of drive fusion, have an interactive relationship. Initially neutralization and sublimation, when accom-plished, pave the way for the development of drive fusion; drive fusion builds

---

[8]Further remarks on autonomous energy, primary autonomy, and secondary autonomy can be found in the section on ego functioning.

structuralization; greater structuralization promotes and makes possible further sublimation, neutralization, and drive fusion, which aids adaptation and progressive maturational development.

Let us return now to the "psychoanalytic" theory that ignores rather than disputes the critical position of drive theory in mental functioning. This position suggests that one can retain dynamic theory because it explains the interactions in mental functioning while remaining silent on the economic theory until the sources of instincts are definitively established. The problem with this line of thought, however, is twofold: (1) the source of a drive is of considerably less importance in a psychological theory than is the fact of its existence and the presence of its manifold effects, and (2) determining the source of a drive would have little or no effect on economic theory, which is concerned only with the mental aspects and representations of drives. A more important problem in any approach that attempts to ignore drive theory, however, is that one cannot work with dynamics without implicit acceptance and use of economic theory, as one may have already concluded from the preceding discussion. One usually discusses mental dynamics without explicitly differentiating dynamic and economic viewpoints because of their essential interrelatedness; however, there are times – such as when one wants to describe the relationship of anxiety to differences in innate drive endowment – that one might wish to consider aspects of them separately. To consider aspects of them separately, as in this example, in no way suggests that as metapsychological and practical viewpoints they can ultimately be kept so artificially apart. In consequence, the claim that one is suspending judgment on economic theory until the source of drives is determined is at best inaccurate and at worst a self-deception, as long as one uses any aspect of the dynamic theory.

The situation is somewhat analogous to the topographical theory, in which there is postulated an unconscious, a preconscious, and a conscious mode of functioning. Each mode seems to function as if it were a separate entity; however, this is only superficially true because the preconscious is part of the conscious system and it is truly subordinate to consciousness's guiding principles and not to those of the unconscious system. In the same way, economic and dynamic viewpoints are inextricably intertwined even if they sometimes give the deceptive appearance of being readily separable. One either rejects drive theory in favor of an exclusively environmental (hence behavioral) approach, or one includes both drives and environment in one's view of mental functioning; those who imagine they have withheld a "decision" on drive theory participate in economic thinking without being aware of it, in the same way that a person would be discussing the *conscious system* even if he insisted he was only addressing preconsciousness alone. This can be illustrated by a concrete example of how economic and dynamic viewpoints are actually used in conceptualizing the dynamics of mental functioning, as we also introduce the metaphor of a closed hydraulic system, so often used in describing the psychoanalytic position.

When we work with the concept of mental energy, and we have in mind an economic and dynamic model that we describe as operating on a principle closely related to a closed hydraulic system, what we mean to say is that there is a specific amount of mental energy which can increase or decrease only as a by-product of anatomy and physiology, and which only can be split and channeled (although in an infinite variety of ways) as a psychological phenomenon. For example, we may be reading and listening to music at the same time. If we become more absorbed in reading, it is likely that we will attend less to the music. If we are deeply involved in our book, the music may fade to a barely perceived background noise; and if our attention is absolutely riveted to our book, it is even possible for the music to fade out of our awareness entirely and to be perceived only subliminally. The word *cathexis* refers to our investment of psychic energy; in the act of reading we cathect the book, the meaning of the words, the story, the act of looking and what we see as a result, as we do the music to which we are listening. Each and every function, whether in consciousness or unconsciousness, uses a part of the total resource of mental energy, and there are hundreds (or even thousands) of these allotments of mental energy in effect all the time. This idea of the ever-changing infinite and multiple allotments of a finite amount of psychic energy is included within the economic point of view. When we refer to the whys and wherefores of the specific allotments, we are reflecting the dynamic point of view. The dynamic approach explains why cathexis increases and decreases, and describes the net results of an economic shift. Going back to the example of reading and listening to music, the *economic* statement would be: At time A, reading uses x amount of energy and listening uses y amount of energy; at time B, reading uses $x + 1/2\, y$ amount of energy and listening uses $1/2\, y$ amount of energy; at time C, reading uses $x + 9/10\, y$ amount of psychic energy and listening to music uses $1/10\, y$ amount of psychic energy; and so on. The *dynamic* statement would be: As the act of reading becomes more absorbing, energy is shifted away from listening to music to provide the resources with which to fuel, and thereby increase, our involvement in reading; as we are less absorbed in listening, we need, or can tolerate, less psychic energy for that activity, and so we can use some of that energy for other tasks (such as reading) that are making a greater claim on our psychic energy resources. Obviously the potential for a conflict of interests is enormous, and incompatible and mutually exclusive and competing interests always keep the psychic apparatus in a state of considerable tension.[9]

---

[9]Although my preference clearly is to give all the metapsychological theories full equivalence, it should be noted before we proceed any further that many analysts (usually non-Freudians but including also quite a few Freudians) tend to view dynamic theory as critical while downplaying the economic point of view, both theoretically and clinically. My point of view, with which they would disagree, is that in accepting dynamic theory one implicitly accepts the equivalent centrality of economic variables. Because one does not usually have the same clinical need to define the exact influences of economic issues that one always does with dynamic considerations, economic considerations seem only abstract and reduced in importance to the point where it seems that they do not even need to be acknowledged. The necessity to clinically define economic factors becomes clearer in situations in which their role is

Transformations of Libido and Aggression

Let us now turn our attention to the specifically dual-drive theory of instincts, *libido* and *aggression,* that characterizes psychoanalysis. Libido and aggression are two descriptions of internal drive constellations that are mutually dependent. They have

---

unmistakable – for example, in the power puberty exerts over latent oedipal object relations. But where economic influences are particularly subtle, such as the relationship between early preferred pathways of perception and later preferred pathways of defense, they may not become clinically highlighted, and it is precisely in an example like this that the need for an economic point of view generates a great deal of controversy and disagreement.

Some analysts reject the economic point of view entirely and others reject only certain parts of it – for example, a reworking of economic theory so that the concept of "instinct" is rejected, but not the concept of "psychic drive." Other analysts have linked their rejection of economic theory to a rejection of the whole concept of metapsychology itself (in which economic theory is only a single component). Much of my discussion here, and in what follows, supports ideas that make some classical analysts uncomfortable, and which they try, whenever possible, not to emphasize. Let me indicate at this point the nature of some of their objections, to both economic theory and to metapsychological description, so that the reader may measure their criticisms against the ideas that I will put forward throughout the rest of this chapter.

There are analysts who feel that metapsychological modes of description are too abstract and removed from experience, as I have already noted in Footnote 6, being unwilling to accept (especially for the concept of drives, and other energy metaphors) the kind of hidden, inaccessible, and often unknowable quality that they readily can accept for the concept of the unconscious and its processes. Others prefer exclusively clinical descriptions to metapsychological ones, feeling that what may be lost (in the economy of thinking that metapsychology affords) is more than gained back by descriptions that are subjectively and observably recognizable (Schafer's call for an "action language" is a good case in point). They believe that anything that needs to be said about a patient's functioning can be said in clinically descriptive terms, thus making metapsychological description superfluous. Still others prefer clinical and "action" descriptions because they feel that metapsychological descriptions are too mechanistic and, as such, reductionistic, inevitably leaving out important and subtle variables of experience.

Some analysts have rejected metapsychology as too mechanistic on rather different grounds; they feel that the mechanism it reflects is connected to outdated concepts of physiological functioning that were popular in Freud's day but which are no longer valid. Also, some critics go even further and consider the development of metapsychology, and particularly the economic point of view, as being almost dishonest – as much a political statement on Freud's part as it was a scientific statement. In other words, that metapsychology, and particularly the economic point of view, was merely Freud's attempt to legitimize psychological concepts by describing them in the prevailing "scientific" terms of the day (the idea being that Freud was willing to subordinate the specifically psychological underpinnings of psychoanalysis to the demands of the "scientific," that is, "medical," community – or as others suggest, to meet his personal need for psychoanalysis to be seen as a science – by recasting many of his ideas into a form, namely the physiological model that was politically correct for the time and place in which he found himself).

Some analysts have difficulty with the "hydraulic" concept of Freud's energy theories, finding it difficult to accept the "closed" nature of his model. Others fault all the metapsychological assumptions because of their closeness (in how they are organized, conceptually) to conflict and to structure and their relative distance from the influence of object relations; and this is particularly the case, they feel, once again, with the economic point of view. For example, some analysts, particularly those whose model of personality is based on an object relations theory, suggest that the long period of interpenetrability between the psyches of a mother and her young infant make the notion of the infant's constitutional drive endowments essentially irrelevant.

evolved from the same source, the psychobiological matrix, and they, as "the instincts," are what we have been discussing as being the motive force behind the organization of complex mental activity. Libido is usually thought of as a sexual drive, a loving drive, a sexualized drive, a life-preserving drive, a pleasure-seeking drive, and so forth. Aggression has been conceived of as an assertion drive, a negation drive, a drive to remain in the status quo, a drive to regress, the sadistic and masochistic drives, among others (in addition to being thought of as a death instinct, a philosophical interest of Freud's that became most well known despite his considerable emphasis on the myriad other aspects of aggression).

Some further clarification of the definitions of sublimation and neutralization may be warranted at this point. When libido is desexualized (deinstinctualized) we say that it is sublimated. Sublimation gives us energy to use in pursuits outside the arena of immediate instinctual gratifications; for example, we first attach ourselves to, and then begin to learn about, our mothers because they are instinctually gratifying, but we use essentially sublimated libidinal energy to learn spelling and arithmetic (which play almost no role in immediate instinctual gratification). The deinstinctualization of aggression is known as neutralization. The methods by which the ego achieves these transformations will be detailed below.[10] Because libido is not ultimately destructive to either self or object, it has more pathways of discharge, and more flexibility within these pathways. This tends to make its derivations readily observable; however, there is much less clarity in describing and elaborating the derivatives of aggression. There is an unfortunate tendency to equate aggression with sadism, hostility, and destructiveness, and to be unaware of and unclear about the more disguised derivatives of aggression, even though they are crucial in understanding mental functioning. Neutralized derivatives of aggression, and aspects of the aggressive drive which have undergone drive fusion, are so highly transformed (in the service of protecting self and object) that they are often unrecognizable as having had destructive origins. For example, because there is only affirmation in libido, it is aggression that we use in developing the concept of negation. One goes beyond wholesale, global negation and to a much more sophisticated use of aggression when one becomes involved in developing fine shades of negation, which inevitably becomes an absolute necessity in the development of rational judgment. To consider a more primitive context, transformed aggression, with its capacity for negation, is the major vehicle for the discriminations between inner and outer, self and object, and even the specific qualities of

---

[10]Drive fusion describes a synthesis between libido and aggression (as described earlier in this chapter) that not only creates sublimated and neutralized energy (as they balance each other out), but that also results in a third kind of energy (available to the ego) that is more greatly removed from the drives and which, most importantly, is not the simple sum of the libidinal and aggressive energies that were fused. The greater distance from drives makes this energy more impervious to reinstinctualization than is simple sublimated and neutralized energy, and the greater "maturity" of this energy strengthens it even further; it is primarily a person's capacity to engage in successful drive fusion that dictates his or her capacity for secondary autonomy in the ego.

objects (the specific role of the instincts alone, not experience and frustration, in differentiating the self from objects, will be considered in detail below). In the area of defense, neutralized aggressive energy is employed extensively (most notably in countercathexis, which is a process of distraction, to enable suppression, inhibition, prohibition, and repression to be effected). In the anal stage, control over the instincts, as well as control over the body itself, depends on the constructive use of aggressive energy. These, and many more activities that have no overtly observable sadistic overtones, are derivatives of primarily aggressive energic states. Just as we differentiate between libidinal energy and feeling sexually aroused, we must differentiate between aggressive drives and feelings of anger.

An interesting aspect of the relationship between libido and aggression is that aggressive tensions frequently develop within the demand for libidinal satisfaction. We see this, for example, when aggression is mobilized to communicate an infant's hunger to its mother, or in the way aggression is elicited to be transformed into the concrete acts of feeding. Another interesting thing about the relationship between libido and aggression is that aggressive tensions are frequently satisfied, sometimes in their entirety, when one is successful in satisfying libidinal demands. One should keep in mind, however, that libido and aggression are fully separate instinctual motivators of mental functioning even though they are often channeled together or successfully merged, and thus we prefer not to view them as drives that must *always* act in concert with one another. This reminder is also necessary, in part, because of the relatively invisible character of aggression as compared with libido when one examines their derivatives in normal functioning. As described previously, in complex mental functioning it is usually difficult, if not sometimes impossible, to specify exactly which components (and derivations) originate from libido and which originate from aggression. In addition one would also wish to avoid a fairly common fallacy about the relationship of libido and aggression to the pleasure and unpleasure principles. It is unconditionally and absolutely *not* true that all pleasure is synonymous with libido and all unpleasure (mounting tension, deprivation, frustration, delay, and so on) is synonymous with, or is the equivalent of, aggression. Frustration of either libidinal or aggressive needs, as well as the mounting libidinal and aggressive tensions (which precedes gratification or frustration) that alert the individual to the presence of a need, are equally experienced in terms of unpleasure. Gratification and other methods of achieving discharge are experienced by the individual as pleasurable; and this too is equally true about both the libidinal and aggressive drives.

We can see examples from the clinical setting that illustrate how the gratification of aggression can be experienced with pleasure. One patient, who was describing a humiliating incident with his employer, was further shamed by having had to not reply or defend himself in order to keep his job. In his analytic session he began to describe all the things he wished he could have said, becoming progressively more and more angry. Eventually he worked himself into quite a rage, describing in vivid detail how he imagined beating up his boss, sabotaging the business, and recounting other imagined acts of retaliatory destructiveness. Each act of fantasied vengeance was accompanied by much affective delight, and one could observe both increasing rage and increasing delight occurring side by side as he described his escalating reprisals and retribution. In addition to the pleasure that attended each fantasy, the lengthy and intense experience was quite cathartic for him, and he felt both relieved and vindicated by the passage of this affect-storm accompanied by its imagined triumphs. If one looked hard enough one could find some hidden libidinal derivatives in this, because no mental action can be entirely composed of one of the drives to the full exclusion of the other; however, it seems clear that the predominating drive was aggression. The accompanying pleasure was tied to its satisfaction through the act of talking, through other muscular and mobile actions (fist clenching, teeth gnashing, arm waving, and other isotonic and isometric activity on the couch), and through the generation of wish-fulfilling fantasies.

In order to consider examples of aggressive gratifications that lead to pleasure where varying quantities of libido are present, we can jump forward for a moment into the clinical realm, where it is possible to look at some of the ways silence can be used by patients in analysis. Conspicuous silence, as one sees in extended periods of silence within an analytic hour, or for the entire hour, or for a number of hours, may represent, in very disturbed individuals, an identification with an absent or dead person. It may be a graphic representation of an inner feeling of emptiness. It may be a highly personified identification with the analyst, who often remains silent for extended periods. It may be a form of "hoarding" in which thoughts and feelings are treated as if they are concrete things to be tangibly given or withheld, or a form of hoarding where thoughts and feelings are treated as if they were actual parts of the individual (almost as though thoughts and feelings were like arms or legs that could be amputated), who remains intact only so long as they are "preserved" internally. It may be an anal-erotic activity in which both the reservation and yielding of the stream of free associations is the mental equivalent of infantile masturbatory involvements in containing, transporting, and releasing the fecal column or the stream of urine. Silence may also harbor a reflection of the struggle over yielding to forbidden wishes, and in this connection it could express some central conflicts about submission in the oedipal conflict (to both love-objects and competitors). It can help to bind anxiety as well as being a means of instituting and maintaining repression, suppression, inhibition, and other denial-based defenses. It can be a response to shame, guilt, or embarrassment, and it can be used to avoid future humiliation. It can be a way of sadistically punishing the analyst or an attempt to immobilize and restrain the analyst, or it can be an invitation to punitive or retaliatory action from the analyst. In this brief list one can see aggression serving the pleasure principle by preventing unpleasure as well as by causing active pleasure. In some of these examples aggression seems subordinated by libido, in some aggression seems principally neutralized, and in others untransformed aspects of primitive aggression are patently clear; but in every case frustration or gratification of aggression operates according to the pleasure principle.

The Dual-Drive Theory

The discussion thus far has presented current views on aggression. However, it would be of value now to discuss the evolution of drive theory, specifically of the dual-drive theory, and most particularly of aggression, because they have undergone considerable change and revision by Freud and by others over the years. As a result of his earliest clinical work, mainly treating young women suffering from conversion and anxiety hysterias, Freud's first theory postulated the presence of a sexual drive, which he called *libido*. It was this sexual drive, libido, repressed and suppressed but nonetheless pressing hard for expression, that Freud initially assumed was responsible for both the central conflict and the symptoms of neurosis. Although a well-organized and sophisticated theory of psychic structure (id, ego and superego) would not be presented by Freud until almost 30 years later, he did even then have some rudimentary ideas about the nature of the ego and the id. In those early years libido, unconsciousness, primary process functioning, and the id were lumped together and discussed as if they were synonymous. To the ego Freud ascribed another, separate, instinct: self-preservation. Freud found himself having to struggle with such major exceptions to his theory of both libido and a self-preservative instinct, such as suicide and celibacy; it was from these and other significant exceptions that he developed his ideas about the vicissitudes instincts undergo, and it was on just such exceptions that he based his descriptions of how widely various and radical can be the transformations of aim and object in the course of normal development. The two most critical renovations of drive theory, the development of Freud's notion of a death instinct and the location of the instincts in the id alone (and not in both the id and the ego as he had previously postulated), were also direct outgrowths of Freud's clinical experiences. In order to understand how Freud was influenced against seeing the ego as the reservoir of drives, and to know why he ultimately chose to lodge them entirely in the id, we must first look at what caused him to augment his topographical metapsychological theory with the development of a structural metapsychological point of view. We will return somewhat later to how and why Freud developed the notion of a death instinct, but first we must detour back to our discussion of the nature, meaning, and contents of metapsychological theories so that we can understand these two, which were deferred until now. To pick up the thread of our thinking where we left off, let us remember the analogy of reading while listening to music.

Topographical and Structural Theories

When we spoke of music that registered only subliminally, we introduced that point of view known as the topographical theory. The topographical point of view diagrams the idea of consciousness, preconsciousness, and unconsciousness. Unconsciousness refers to all mental functioning that is both unknown and inaccessible to us; however, things that are unknown to us but are potentially or readily accessible to us are thought to reside in preconsciousness (about which more will be said below). The contents of the unconscious, which may include ideas, wishes, and feelings, can exist in different forms. Drive derivatives that began in the unconscious and that go through a process of evolution may freely pass into consciousness at a later time (some instincts are so primitive that they never enter consciousness). Thoughts, wishes, and feelings that are anxiety-provoking, and thus disorganizing, are retained in the unconscious and are actively prevented from emerging into consciousness (because of the "dangers" they carry with them). Thoughts and feelings that were at one time conscious but were too anxiety-provoking, disorganizing, or unacceptable to remain so, can be caused to be moved into unconsciousness as a defense. When something in the unconscious is prevented from emerging into consciousness, as in the former case, we describe that operation as *repression*. The operation of pushing something from consciousness back into the unconscious, as in the latter case, is called *suppression*. The concept of preconsciousness is a subcategory of consciousness. It refers to things that are right at the threshold of consciousness, things in the process of emergence into consciousness, and things that are readily available to consciousness. Although professionals view preconsciousness as a form of consciousness, the layman's concept of the *subconscious* blends together preconsciousness with the unconscious. Topographical theory is responsible for the popular "iceberg" imagery, in which the tip (consciousness) shows above the water and looks to us to be of itself immense, but whose main portion (unconsciousness) is actually hidden under water, giving little obvious indication of its presence, let alone its true size. Consciousness looms in the vision of the observer, giving the impression that one has seen all, or just about all, of what there is to be seen. Because in reality the major portion of mental functioning is unconscious, we should be aware of the crucially important fact that nowhere in any part of psychoanalytic theory is consciousness a prerequisite for mental functioning.

Some limitations in the capacity of the topographical theory to adequately describe and explain mental functioning become apparent when an attempt is made to examine the operating principles of *repression* and *suppression*. In both operations (which belong to the generic classification defenses) we have implied that a censor exists, which examines psychological events (in consciousness and in the unconscious) for acceptability, for anxiety-provoking capacities, and for mentally disorganizing potentials. If such problematic mental activity or functioning is identified as imminent, or already occurring, the censor must either refuse it admission into consciousness or push it out of consciousness, depending on the topographical level in which the unacceptable influence originated, or is in operation at the time of the discovery. The problem with this purely topographical approach is that if we postulate that the censor is in the unconscious, how then can it operate in consciousness as the agent of suppression? We are inevitably led to the conclusion that if the capacity for censorship is located in the unconscious, suppression (which takes place in conscious regions) would be impossible. On the other hand, if we describe censorship as functioning in the realm of consciousness, how then can it operate in the unconscious to prevent unacceptable material from emerging into consciousness? Here we are led to conclude that if material needs to be conscious to come into contact with the censorship "device," we would only be capable of suppression and the concept of repression would be unworkable. When this theoretical difficulty became apparent to Freud, he was forced to introduce an additional point of view to explain phenomena that can occur in both consciousness and the unconscious; it was to meet this requirement that he formulated the structural metapsychological theory. The structural point of view separates mental functioning into three areas of organization: the id, the ego, and the superego; and it was with this development that the id came to be thought of as the reservoir of the drives. The ego was conceived of as being responsible for adaptation to the environment (both internal and external). To solve the topographical dilemma Freud postulated that it was the ego, operating in both consciousness and in the unconscious, that was responsible for all of the censoring activities in every topographical layer. With the addition of structural theory the question of where the censor was actually located no longer posed any problem; the ego, in this view, recognizes and attempts to avoid danger at *all* levels from total unconsciousness to complete consciousness. Thus we see again some important additional verification of the idea that consciousness is no prerequisite for mental functioning.

Our example thus far was one of an internal danger: we postulated a need for censorship to control a *psychological* event that threatened psychic equilibrium. The ego also provides the mode of operation and is the organ or the structure used to cope with external danger. Its prime functions cause it to be more properly viewed as a drive regulator and not as a *source* of drive pressures. The ego develops and administers our defenses. It can, as we have seen, cause us to forget (suppress) something that threatens our capacity to function, and on a more drastic scale it has been known to bring about massive somatic reactions (on the order of hysterical blindness) when there is something we do not wish to "see" (and in such an instance the censored material can have its origins in either internal or external events, or both). The capacity of the ego is not limited only to refusing to acknowledge or understand something that will cause us emotional suffering or disorganization. The ego is also responsible for the organization of our intelligence and for the constant applications of our knowledge (as in our ability to know that we must step out of the way of a moving vehicle, our remembering not to draw breath under water, and our caution around a growling dog). The ego is also the mental entity by which we relate to reality, and through which our attempts at adaptation are governed. We use the ego to process reality and to remember things, to alert us to that which (based on past experience or rational evaluation) we can expect to happen, to help us understand that which *is* happening, to integrate and organize our experiences, to synthesize (from a multitude of things) that which is necessary for our welfare, and to exercise all of the "executive" and "sovereign" roles in organizing mental functioning. This list of operational definitions by no means exhausts the potentials and responsibilities of the ego, which will be discussed in considerably greater detail in Chapter 7.

Primary Process and the Reality Principle

All mental operations that function in accordance with the restraints of reality, logic, rational thinking, and adaptation come under the organizing functions of the ego. Mental functioning that is governed by the need for pleasure, that is, in the service of "discharge," and which is immune to the constraints of reality (which includes causality, logic, and the concepts of time and space) can be said to be organized by (or are functions of) the id. The special role of the regulatory principles of mental functioning, which includes the pleasure principle and the reality principle, will be discussed below. We can summarize this by saying that with articulation of the structural theory Freud now saw *all* the mental entities developed by the pressures of physiological activities (which he conceived of as drives) as residing within, and constituting the total contents of, the id; and it was his view that they always press for immediate and total gratification. The mental processes that are used to achieve those goals or to deflect them if they create danger he conceived of as functions of the ego, which he viewed as operating in accordance with the demands of reality and the goals of adaptation (and with the pleasure principle in the service of defense).

As a preliminary to our fuller discussion of the regulatory principles of mental functioning, which we will return to at the end of this chapter, we can begin to outline some of the characteristics of primary-process and secondary-process functioning that have special relevance to the distinctions that apply to the structural differentiations between the ego and the id. We call the mental operations associated with the id "primary-process" functioning, and the mental processes associated with the ego "secondary-process" functioning. The hallmarks of primary process are condensation and displacement. *Condensation* is the expression of two or more drives, wishes, feelings, or thoughts through only one channel. For example, the act of downhill skiing may condense a wish to be free; a need for danger and the wish for mastery; a need to stay fit; a fantasy satisfaction associated with the idea of looking reckless, brave, or just plain good; concerns about body damage; a way of relieving tension; a means of achieving a physical or psychological elation; a mode of manipulating fear, and so on. All these mental issues can be expressed (all together, one at a time, or in combination) in a single act or in a single mental representation. As one might anticipate, the process of condensation may be a mode of primary-process functioning, but the specifics of what is being condensed need not necessarily be so. The substance of condensation may be all primary process (as in the schizophrenic's "I am you and you are me. There is only one person here."), or it may consist of secondary-process material ("We often think and feel alike, we react so much in the same way, it's almost as if we are one and the same person. When I relate to you it is almost as if I am relating to me."). *Displacement* is the expression of a single drive, wish, feeling, or thought, through a channel other than the original one or through two or more channels (which may or may not also include the original one). For example, people who give up smoking often feel very hungry. Their hunger exists, in part, because nicotine raises the blood sugar level (and so the blood sugar level is lowered in the absence of nicotine when they give up smoking); thus some of their hunger reflects an essentially physiological event despite its psychological concomitants, but they may also be hungry as a direct psychological substitute for wanting a cigarette. Displacement exists, in this case, when the longing for food represents the longing for smoking, and things can be further complicated because this can be occurring even if one feels a longing for a cigarette at the same time as one is experiencing the longing to eat in displacement. We also are using displacement if eating decreases some or all of the longing for a cigarette. In this particular example, physiology conspires with psychological principles so that one can never be entirely sure exactly how much hunger for food really represents a hunger for a cigarette; but then, true examples of displacement and condensation never do appear in pristine forms. In order to examine a more exclusively psycho-logical example we may imagine a man who has been humiliated at work and who, as a result, comes home quite short-tempered, and who then snaps at his family all evening; here we see displacement of his anger from the work setting where he could not (or should not) express it, to the home setting where its expression was safer (or more possible). This will still properly be described as displacement whether or not he is aware of having been angry (or at having been humiliated) at work, and whether or not he is aware of that connection when he takes the anger out on his family.

We should, before leaving the metapsychological assumptions of the structural theory, comment briefly on the superego and also describe some of the distinctions between a psychic structure and its contents and functions. The superego is the mental structure that acts as a reservoir of our identifications. It contains, in addition, our aspirations (which are mostly a part of the subsystem known as the ego-ideal), and the superego is what we often think of as being our "conscience." The superego is often described as the "heir to the oedipal complex" because, although many of its contents and functions are present at earlier developmental periods, the superego is not *structuralized* until the time of the oedipal complex (this will be adequately clarified later in our discussion of the phallic stage in Chapter 4). The concept of structuralization is an abstraction meant to suggest a mental entity that is organized in a specific and distinctive way. We can think of a psychic structure as an organizer of mental activity, and each of the mental structures (id, ego, superego) as making use of contents (and often, even functions) that may or may not be represented in the other psychic structures. The following example may shed some light on the difference between a structure and its functions and contents. Bricks and mortar, copper pipes, glass, wood, and steel, are used in the construction of a house and in the construction of a store; we can view these items as *contents*. Both a house and a store offer protection from the elements, safety, storage of property, a setting for interaction, considerable equity, and so on; these we may view as *functions*. Despite their similarities in contents and functions, homes are used for living in and stores are used for commerce, and this tends to influence our conceptions so radically that we tend to think of them as *completely* different from one another. In many ways this is an entirely accurate conception because we dress differently at home and in the office, we use different criteria for admitting people to our home or our office, there are a number of activities (such as sleep, sex, listening to music or watching television, selling, having a party, cleaning) that are appropriate for home or for office but not usually for both. Thus we can see that the psychic structures (id, ego, and superego) cannot be defined or understood only by identifying their contents and functions (even though they are important and enlightening), but must also be considered on the basis of the unique way they organize mental life. This is also true of the distinction between primary process and secondary process, which are so profoundly dissimilar even though they may have some very similar characteristics *out of context*.

Intrapsychic and Interpsychic Conflict

The question of conflict between and within the psychic structures, and its resolution, necessitates some further description of the differences between the structures, with special attention given to the ego, which mediates all conflicts that may develop between and within the psychic structures (including itself). For example, the need to eat emerges from dynamics organized within the id and this need is experienced by the individual as a powerful hunger. The solution in terms of the id is, without any other considerations, simply to eat. If weight gain is an important consideration or if, in a different case, eating (through both condensation and displacement) is part of an unconscious and forbidden masturbatory activity, the superego might oppose eating and might call upon the ego to generate considerable guilt, agitation, or depression. As a "mediator" the ego might also try to reduce the pressure for immediate gratification by noting (or emphasizing) the small amount of time left to wait until the next meal; or it might attempt to interfere with the processing of our perceptions and our sensations in such a way so that we are no longer aware of being hungry. It might interfere with aspects of our reality-testing capacities and aspects of our memory so that we will not know what is bothering us, and will then seek some other more acceptable channel for discharging tension (like, for example, masturbation to a conscious thought that is not forbidden); or it might surrender some of its sovereignty and permit, or be unable to stop, an uncontrolled regression so that one hallucinates being fed. These possible activities of the ego are all in the service of meeting, and thus reducing, the demands of the id. A decrease in the demands of the id, for these or for other reasons, will lead to an easing of the tensions between the id and the superego, and between the ego and the superego.

If the pressures stemming from demands of the id cannot be reduced in the manner just described or in a similar manner, the ego might also use similar attempts at compromise formations in trying to mediate the demands of the superego. The ego might alert the individual to the presence of low-calorie foodstuffs to reduce potential weight gain; or, for another example, it might distort its reality-testing functions (by imposing primary-process functioning on secondary-process reasoning) so that we believe that weight loss can only be achieved by immediately eating lots of high-calorie food. In a more adaptive approach, it might determine that the demands of the superego are inappropriate because weight loss is not a problem or because the eating being contemplated will not contribute to a weight gain. It might also use its relation to logic and reality to differentiate for the individual between eating and masturbating so that the inhibitions attached to one need not automatically be associated with the other.

One can see from this that the activities of the psychic structures occur both in relation to factors *within* the structure, and in relation to factors *between* the structures. Conflicts that exist in a structure will be related to all the other factors within a structure, but the degree of interrelationships within a structure may vary; this is also true for the conflicts (and relationships) that occur between the psychic structures, so that variables in each structure have connections to variables in the other structures. In addition, one does not see correspondence between only two structures, even though a particular interaction between two structures may be more visible or seem to be of greater importance at a given time. All psychic structures play a significant role in every mental event, no matter how variable, subtle, covert, or minor their relative participation seems. Among the above examples were a number of instances in which a single structure seemed to predominate, in which a single structure seemed to capitulate, where some functions (or contents) were strengthened, and where others seemed weakened; but whether this was determined by nonpathological processes, or fragmented and weakened by trauma or pathology, or by a combination of both, one sees a highly concentrated field in which mental events can be described as the simultaneously occurring multiple interactions of multiple variables. Another aspect of the difficult mediating responsibility of the ego is that it must engage in a dual function within which it must judge itself objectively while meeting its own unique goals in the process. Even as the ego is in direct conflict with the id or the superego, it must also press for its own interests while evolving a compromise solution satisfactory to diminish the conflict exclusively between the other structures as well as the struggle between itself and the other structures. The heroic task of the ego is to be constructive in a situation where the solutions for each structure, and between structures, inevitably have some unresolvable and competing interests.

In a final note about conflict and these structures, we must guard against what could turn into an animistic flaw in our conceptions. There really isn't, after all, such a thing as an id, or an ego, or a superego. These are not anatomical or physiological entities. They exist as intellectual constructs to help us think about mental events and they organize for us some mental events that have things in common with other mental events and some mental events which can also be systematically differentiated from others. No surgeon or endocrinologist can find the id in the human body. Mental activity is different from physical activity despite the fact that it produces things that can be demonstrably measured, such as the interaction between fear and adrenalin. Many concepts in psychoanalytic psychology are concretized in this manner, but only as heuristic devices to help organize our thinking.

The Regulatory Principles of Mental Functioning

In the theoretical step that led Freud to locate the drives exclusively in the id, the ego was considered to have (as one of its many attributes) the *function* of self-preservation and was no longer considered to have a self-preservative instinct of its own. Having taken that step, we can now return to the question of how aggression joined libido, and how that conceptualization was responsible for a specifically dual-drive theory, in Freud's thinking. Although he initially wrote of many instincts and often focused on the juxtaposition of libido (which he originally viewed as representing sexual drives) and self-preservation (which he originally viewed as representing a life instinct), Freud's dual-drive theory refers only to libido and aggression. This is an important point because the term *dual drive* is not intended to suggest just a specifically numerical quality (as in the statement that there is in human beings *two* drives, or as in the statement that of all human instincts only *two* are important as psychological factors), but means to highlight instead the hostility to one another of libido and aggression, the mutual exclusivity of libido and aggression although their derivatives are capable of being merged or fused, and to focus our thinking on the fact that libido and aggression by their very nature exist in a state of competitive tension. The limits of their cooperation was expressed by Freud in his notion that before each person dies he has genetically predetermined tasks to accomplish, the foremost and most notable of which is the conjugation of germ-plasm to serve the goal of preservation of the species. In this notion libido now has the life instincts, which were previously assumed to be part of the ego, added to its sexual instincts, as it delays the death instinct long enough for conjugation of germ-plasm to occur. The new idea, that libido did not preserve life so much as it served to postpone death,[11]

---

[11] In describing the role of man's needs for self-preservation, self-assertion, and mastery, Freud called them "component instincts whose function it is to assure that the organism shall follow its own path to death, and to ward off any possible ways of returning to inorganic existence other than those which are immanent in the organism itself. We have no longer to reckon with the organism's puzzling determination (so hard to fit into any context) to maintain its own existence in the face of every obstacle. What we are left with is the fact that the organism wishes to die only in its own fashion. Thus these guardians of life, too, were originally the myrmidons of death. Hence arises the paradoxical situation that the living organism struggles most energetically against events (dangers, in fact) which might help it to attain its life's aim rapidly—by a kind of short-circuit. Such behavior is, however, precisely what characterizes purely instinctual as contrasted with intelligent efforts." S. Freud (1920). Beyond the pleasure principle. *Standard Edition* 18:39.

redefining libido not as a coequal drive with the death instinct but as a respondent that modifies it, had sweeping ramifications for psychoanalytic theory. This description of the relationship between the instincts led to a major renovation in how Freud viewed the regulatory principles of mental functioning. Until then, Freud thought that the pleasure and unpleasure principles were the earliest and most compelling regulatory principles of mental functioning, but with this new dual-drive theory he came to see the Nirvana (which in Sanskrit means "annihilation," although in current cultural idiom the term is thought to reflect a concept something akin to "paradise") and the constancy principles as having precedence. This led, too, to pleasure being dispossessed by the repetition compulsion as the earliest, most basic and primary, derivative of the regulatory principles of mental functioning.

The pleasure principle, and pleasure–unpleasure experiences, were identified but not sufficiently described in the previous discussion of the economic concept of *aim* and the dynamic concept of *pressure*. In the next chapter, when we discuss the development of object relations and the early development of love, we will again see the pleasure/unpleasure principles acting as the hidden architects in the process of identification. Before this theoretical shift Freud thought that first and foremost the unpleasure principle, joined almost immediately afterward by the pleasure principle, guided the dynamics of the mental representations of, and responses to, the drives. In the dynamic and economic state of an infant at birth, all cathexis of libido (and of aggression, too) is directed at the self. Attention to the environment, and to the object world in particular, requires detachment of some of the self-directed libido (a lowering of narcissistic libido) and a reinvestment of that cathexis into someone or something else (extending object libido). This phenomenon, although somewhat less intense, also occurs even in so rudimentary an activity as perceiving the environment, wherein narcissistic libido that was invested centripetally (inward with great pressure, as in the opposite of centrifugal) is shifted to the surface of the body, that is, to the perceptual "rind." In either case, the shifting of cathexis away from the central or visceral self is experienced as a loss or a depletion, and so a mode of functioning is developed to prevent this activity, called *negative hallucination*. Contrary to its implication, negative hallucination is not a way of hallucinating a satisfaction, gratification, or pleasure; it is not a hallucination in which the initial narcissistic libido is fully restored, nor is it a hallucination in which the loss of narcissistic libido becomes inconsequential, nor is it a hallucination in which narcissistic libido was never extended. Negative hallucination is the erection of a stimulus barrier. It is an attempt to prevent the necessity of transforming narcissistic libido into object libido. One aspect of the well-known fable of the ostrich with its head in the sand is that he believes that when he cannot see himself no one else can see him, and if no one can see him (to hurt him) he has therefore escaped from danger; in terms of the stimulus barrier erected in negative hallucination, which is the real point of the fable, the danger itself does not exist as long as his head is in the sand and he does not see it. A common misconception about the unpleasure principle is that its object is to diminish unpleasure. Diminishing unpleasure and acquiring pleasure are two sides of the pleasure principle, not the unpleasure principle.

The work of the unpleasure principle, with negative hallucination as its agent, is to prevent the development of unpleasure; once unpleasure occurs and is in the process of being reduced, we are seeing an aspect of the pleasure principle in operation. In our discussion of object love in the next chapter, we will see how the relationship of the infant to its mother goes first through stages of indifference and hatred before love is achieved, as the infant's mental processes move from the influence of the unpleasure principle to the attempted domination of the pleasure principle. We will also see in this process, as the nascent ego exercises its function, the introduction of the reality principle and its eventual striving for sovereignty (at least in consciousness and in conjunction with secondary-process functioning).

Without diminishing their attributes as just described, these regulatory principles and their derivatives became overshadowed by the death instinct, the Nirvana and constancy principles, and the repetition compulsion when Freud attempted to clarify some puzzling clinical phenomena. Freud noticed that people, in general and in treatment, tend to repeat in the present significant relationships, events, attitudes, beliefs, feelings, expectations, and action tendencies from the past (which he called *transference*); and that frequently these repetitions do not lead to, or enhance, pleasure; that in fact, some repetitive functioning leads quite actively to unpleasure and pain. Freud noted a similar phenomenon in the dreams that emerge in a traumatic neurosis. It was his theory that dreams were a way of fulfilling wishes that in waking life were entirely frustrated or unable to be fully gratified. In the dreams associated with traumatic neuroses, however, the trauma was replayed again and again in ways that did not lead to pleasure. It had been previously assumed that wish fulfillment in dreams was regulated by primary process and the pleasure principle, and yet the wish fulfillment in these dreams did not follow that model. In another of Freud's numerous changes in theory, when the existing theory no longer adequately explained what he observed in situ, he hypothesized that in the dreams associated with a traumatic neurosis, the wishes being fulfilled have little to do with pleasure and are mainly an attempt at mastery of the traumatic situation; for example, in a repetitive anxiety-laden nightmare (of the traumatic event), the dreamer has included a subjective anxiety that may have been absent or insufficient in the traumatic event and that might have served a protective function had it been present before or during that event; in a repetitive nightmare (of the traumatic event) the dreamer moves from passive to active by being the creator of the event itself through its creation in the dream, and from passive vulnerability to a more active role within the dream as he makes the traumatic event occur repeatedly. Based on these factors (the transference neurosis and, to a lesser extent, transference in general, and the dreams in traumatic neuroses) and some others (such as the meaning of repetitive play in childhood), Freud came to the conclusion that the compulsion to repeat is more powerful in mental functioning than is the search for pleasure. Were this not so, we would not see such painful repetitions in the transference neurosis or in dreams, nor would we ever see the common escalations in these phenomena that lead directly away from pleasure toward increased pain, frustration, disappointment, deprivation, fear, and so on. Although it is true that we often see mergers between libido and aggression in the repetitions of the transference neurosis (e.g., as in most forms of sadism and masochism), there is a sufficient number of instances where repetition takes precedence over pleasure, in both treatment and general mental functioning, for this modification in psychoanalytic theory to obtain.

Repetition and growth (not to be confused with *practice* and growth), repetition and progress, repetition and novelty, and repetition and continuously evolving development, are incompatible when repetition occurs as a *compulsion* to repeat. The repetition compulsion prefers to repeat what is, rather than move to something new; and it prefers to repeat what was, rather than engage in anything that may be occurring in the present.

In some ways Freud's description of the repetition compulsion in mental functioning, with its complex resistances to alterations in its condition, is reminiscent of the laws of both inertia and momentum in physics (just as his dynamic theory is reminiscent of the laws of fluid dynamics). Mental functioning resists change except insofar as it continuously presses for a return to what has just been its prior condition; this is the regulating principle of the repetition compulsion. If we then trace this backward, as Freud did, we see that eventually we come to the point where the only prior condition left is the inanimate state just prior to life. If we are at that point, we find ourselves in the position of demanding death with more power (if the repetition compulsion has precedence over pleasure) and with more intensity than we give to our aspirations for life. Based on this inevitable conclusion, Freud developed his specific theory of the death instinct and its power relative to libido, and so it was in response to this hierarchical ordering of the instincts that he came to the view that the life instincts (libido) served the purpose of postponing the paradoxical coming to fruition of the death instinct. Freud saw the pleasure principle as a reflection of libido's demands for gratification, and the Nirvana principle as a confederate of Thanatos (the death instinct). The constancy principle, intended to resist all change and to keep inactive the tensions arising from within and without, is another regulatory principle aligned with the death instinct and whose goals the repetition compulsion also serves. As we know, libido may be transformed from narcissistic libido into object libido, and in a similar way the death instinct can, and in this case must, be deflected outward and invested in others. It is in this context that the death instinct is transformed into the aggressive drive; the capacity to engage in external aggressive cathexes is of course, along with maturation and some environmental considerations, responsible in large part for delaying immediate gratification of the death instinct. It is, in addition, responsible for protecting the individual from a damaging overabundance of self-directed lethal and nonlethal aggressive cathexes, for helping to bleed off enough aggression for the process of neutralization to proceed, and for freeing both libido and (at a later stage) the ego to participate in strengthening the primacy of aggression over the death instinct.

We have already discussed the next level of transformation of the death instinct, that is, the transformations of aggression, at various places in this chapter, and thus there seems to be no need to pursue them any further now. Without returning to concrete illustrations, we see that in the service of maintaining life, the death instinct is reduced (or perhaps we should say that its tension or pressure is reduced) by a partial deflection outward, and it undergoes further internal vicissitudes by which it is transformed into aggression. This description is compatible with, and does not alter, the polarizing and congregating of drives in the psychobiological matrix discussed at the beginning of this chapter. The earlier description covers the nature of drives as mental initiators and points up the necessity of including the interaction between nature and nurture in our thinking about mental functioning, whereas the current description highlights the meaning and consequences of antagonistic (and ambivalent, and dichotomous) factions within the id, and for mental functioning in general. As a benefit of having been able to deflect the death instinct outward, and with the help of maturation and numerous possible factors of the environment, much residual aggression will be able to be neutralized, merged and fused with libido, offset and balanced by libido, and ultimately will be subject to greater leverage from the ego as it strives toward sovereignty. The most critical derivative of the death instinct, the repetition compulsion – mainly untouched by these attempts to defeat (however temporarily) the demand of the death instinct – serves as a constant reminder to us, however, that in its very core psychoanalytic theory posits a highly conflictual dual-drive conceptualization as the basis of its understanding of both normal and pathological mental functioning.

In addition to the essential notion that libido can not postpone death unless some portion of the death instinct is externally directed, the need to deflect the death instinct is also important in the very earliest steps in the development of object relations; deflection away from the self serves as a precursor to the infant's capacity to develop distinctions between himself and others, and to appreciate the boundaries of where he ends and the rest of the world, including others, begins. We are most used to thinking of these developmental achievements as occurring in the context of the infant's early development with his mother and, as we shall see in the next chapter, we often place enormous importance (quite correctly) on the extent to which the environment is libidinally gratifying or frustrating. However, it is important nonetheless to recognize the preparatory field for the development of object relations and of other capacities for understanding the differences between the inner and outer worlds that is laid down by the infant's necessity to deflect the death instinct away from the self. It should also be noted that this model is different from Melanie Klein's theories, because for Klein the deflection is taken up in its entirety by *projection* (following closely on the heels of primitive, defensively motivated, *splitting*). In the more traditional view, an aggressive cathexis invested externally is a smaller and more circumscribed unit of mental functioning than is the more highly organized action of projection. Also, the use of a defense (rather than a reaction or a vicissitude) is a somewhat premature expectation; if possible, it could only occur at the most primitive levels in early infancy because of the nascent and undeveloped nature of the ego at that stage. Hating someone, or wishing to harm someone, employs an aggressive hypercathexis but need not necessarily involve the use of projection or splitting. Externalization is not splitting or projection, nor is the attachment of an aggressive cathexis. We would not wish to view externalization or aggressive investments as a form of splitting or projection simply because they involve interactions with the object world. The attachment of an aggressive cathexis, although serving a defensive purpose, is a far cry from the more complex nature of a defense that we are usually accustomed to; and whereas the transformation of aggression is the underlying foundation for the development of defenses, it would be nonetheless confusing and inaccurate from a developmental perspective to consider the concept of cathexis to be the rough equivalent of a defense. Aggressive cathexes, like those of libido, are not limited only to people but are also directed at inanimate objects, animals, situations, and events. Despite our model's differences from Klein's metapsychology, it is interesting to see how the early relation to the object world emerges first from the nature of instinct-life rather than from the environment, as we might assume if we looked only at the finished form.

Returning once again to the questions of metapsychology and regulatory principles, it will be clear that the internal organization of the adaptive and genetic theories has been insufficiently discussed, and that the regulatory principle of "internalization" has been discussed not at all. Examination of these issues will be facilitated by deferring their discussion until we have reached a context in which their operation is most notable. For example, internalization can be most productively described in the context of studying the processes of identification; the adaptive theory can be examined most fruitfully in our study of the ego and its attributes; and genetic theory can be made clearest in our discussions of dreams, neurosis, and reconstruction. Before ending this chapter, however, let us consider the question of where within metapsychology the regulatory principles of mental functioning lie. These principles seem to be so meaningful and omnipresent in psychic life that one wonders why, as a group, they are not considered the equivalent in importance to the adaptive, dynamic, economic, genetic, structural, and topographical theories. If we have defined metapsychology as those most basic principles without which psychoanalytic theory cannot exist; as those principles that always apply (without exception) in every psychological event (even where considerable emphasis is placed on other factors); as those principles for which consciousness is not a prerequisite; and as those principles that do not readily lend themselves to empirical investigation, we see that the regulatory principles as a class fit the definition most closely. We say that metapsychological theories are absolutely necessary, even though they are not in and of themselves sufficient for a psychoanalytic explanation of mental functioning; just as we could not imagine discussing psychic life without including the attributes of the unconscious, the ego, and mental dynamics, so does it seem impossible to conceive realistically of a psychology unaffected by the regulatory principles of mental functioning. Particularly now, with the contributions of ego psychology, and increased attention to developmental and maturational processes in infancy and in preoedipal childhood, the value of familiarity with the regulatory principles of mental functioning is underscored. Much in the same way that the ego has autonomy from the drives on one hand and the environment on the other, the regulatory principles bridge both drives and environment in keeping mental functioning stable. Just as we view the analyst's behavior in treatment as being a form of benign, hovering attention, out of which specific interactions with the analysand emerge, we may view the regulatory principles as an ever-present context in which specific mental events occur. Let us now shift our attention to the influences on psychic life that occur in response to our interactions with the environment, looking closely at the developmental events that emerge from the collaboration between nature and nurture. We have thus far indicated what it is that the child brings to the environment; we can now begin to study what happens psychologically within the environment.

2

The Infant's Interactions with the Environment

Why Define It as an Oral Stage?

The first psychosexual stage of development is known as the *oral* stage. The infant is capable of experiencing the world through many senses. Some senses function fully at birth; others will be available, or fully functional, shortly after birth. The infant can relieve tension through a variety of outlets and activities, such as eating, crying, yawning, vocalizing, moving, looking, and listening. All activity, physical or mental, from the most arduous physical actions to the simplest and most insignificant-seeming attention cathexis, uses energy. All action functions as a safety valve to bleed off psychological pressure. Many needs are capable of being satisfied by the infant himself: he needs no one else to yawn, cry, perspire, spit up, urinate, defecate, sleep, waken, or stir about. Other needs, however, such as the need for fuel for the body must be met by someone else. As this is unique in his experience (and repeatedly traumatic), a special involvement arises around feeding that will be considerably greater in importance, psychologically, than will most other activities in the earliest stages of infancy. Feeding is special because it masters and dissipates unpleasant experiences of mounting, uncomfortable psychological tension. Feeding is the pathway of the most actively pleasurable experiences available to the infant (one must remember that the experience of being fed also includes being held, cuddled, caressed, and so on). Feeding meets, and on the other hand sustains, the very need for self-preservation. Each time hallucinatory wish fulfillment fails and the baby is successfully fed, the hypercathexis of the feeding activity and of oral sensation is increased, and hypercathexis of the feeder (presumably the mother) is intensified. The oral activity, oral sensations, and all other actions related to feeding will be expanded upon and greatly generalized later in life, so that these earliest feeding experiences serve as the precursors of what will eventually become adult sexual sensations and pleasures. The image of the initial supplier of libidinal gratification will evolve in a parallel fashion, so that ultimately she will come to serve as the original, and still influential, model for the adult's eventual nonincestuous love object (male or female). Finally, one may also add that there is a biological determinant present that conspires to form an initially oral relation to the world for the infant: feeding becomes so very special because of the exquisite sensitivity of the mouth in comparison with the rest of the infant's body. The hypercathexis of orality reflects, at this stage in the infant's development, the most efficient pathway for the discharge of tension and the most efficient pathway for the acquisition of pleasure.

The concept of an oral stage does not deny the presence or importance of other activities and capabilities in early infancy, but it suggests the existence of a major organizing factor in early mental life that causes the infant's comprehension of himself and the world to operate on a model of oral incorporation. Babies tend to explore the world with their mouths. From a rattle or a blanket to the family cat, if a baby wants to investigate it he will put it in his mouth. Certain character disorders such as the narcissistic character disorder, the infantile personality, the passive-dependent personality; certain psychoses such as schizophrenia; and other very primitive mental states can be traced to fixations in the oral stage. Particular affects such as those primitive aspects of rage that are characterized by mental images of chewing, biting, and other destructively intended sadistic wishes, or a "hungry" sort of envy that never is relieved or satisfied, can be traced to fixations in the oral stage. Many of the more archaic and vestigial elements in dissociative disorders are linked to the oral stage, particularly to the portion that predates the infant's capacity to integrate and comprehend causality, and particularly to the portion of the oral stage in which the infant's relation to reality and to the object world is based entirely on impulsive determinants and their gratification. Virtually every psychological event described thus far has its origin in the oral stage. The oral stage may be characterized by development in a variety of psychological areas; however, it is given its name from only its libidinally gratifying determinants.

The Early Mother–Child Relationship

To describe other people, such as an infant's mother, the word *object* rather than *person* was decided upon by Freud because of the earliest ways an infant relates to the significant others in his environment. Readiness to make an emotional bond is inherent, not in biology, but in the very nature of the relationship between mother and child, even though some mothers and their children do not take advantage of it. This first relationship may well be the strongest and most significant attachment in one's personal history, and it will undoubtedly be the prototype for all future love relationships. Contrary to what the layman might expect, this readiness may exist more in the mother than in her child at the time of birth and shortly thereafter. The child's relationship to his mother is in some ways both simple and complex, and much time will have to pass before the child is capable of loving his mother in the ordinary romantic or altruistic sense in which we customarily use the word. At first the child is attuned to his mother physiologically as a result of their long biological union. He then may come to be psychologically attuned to his mother as an outgrowth of their earlier physiological association (heartbeat, smell, the common hormonal balance reflected in the physiology of the feeding experience, temperature, and so on), which he may recognize in his postpartum relationship with his mother and remember in a primitive way. His recognition and remembrance of his mother will at first occur through sensational more than through cognitive channels, and his sensations and their associated memory traces will have their effects specifically in the form of mental events despite the fact that they will be extremely primitive. The child's relation to his mother has frequently been described as symbiotic at the time of birth; however, this biological term is being used rather loosely, for there is a parasitic quality to the relationship that frequently is underemphasized. For the newborn infant there is no concept of "mother" who loves, or "mother" who is loved. The newborn exists in a state of primary narcissism (where no capacity to differentiate between the self and that which is not the self yet exists), and in a state of primary identification (where the infant is not yet capable of differentiating that which originates from within and that which originates from without), with virtually all cathexis directed primarily at the self. When the mother attends the child, as in feeding, some cathexis is drawn away and given over to the process of feeding, and some is invested in the immediate presence of the mother, who at that moment is acting as a libidinally gratifying *object* (not as a person, but as a thing that has met a pressing need, the way a glass of water meets the need of a thirsty man). Before the pressure to be fed has reached a point that drives the child to action, cathexis is not extended to the "object" that is biologically his mother, and after feeding (when the drive has been reduced) cathexis is withdrawn from the act of feeding and from "objects" (in this case his mother), and it is once again reinvested in the self. Whether the child exists in primary narcissism (and identification) as a primitive developmental level, or when as a defense (later in infancy or early childhood) he is attempting to recreate it in order to redirect cathexis to the self, two things are clear: (1) cathexis that is directed outward is experienced as a depletion (and this is one primary source of unpleasure, along with mounting excitation), and cathexis that is directed centripetally is experienced as a narcissistic enhancement (and is one primary source of pleasure along with the reduction of tension); (2) the child is indifferent to everything in the object world that is not instinctually gratifying; he tries to keep externally directed cathexes as minimal as possible (even in the act of being instinctually gratified), and he withdraws cathexes as quickly and as totally as possible, once an instinctual gratification has been achieved. From this description one sees the development of object attention but not object love. The mother is used as an object designed to meet whatever instinctual needs the infant has at a given moment; there is an economic pressure on the child to experience her as, quite literally, nonexistent otherwise. Mothers can never actually fulfill the economic ideal (in line with the demands of the constancy principle) of being nonexistent, which in this sense means that they give without taking, because babies have a lot of different needs practically all the time, which forces them to always be economically involved even if it is at first only on the level of object attention. The word *object,* then, derives from the child's initial use of his mother, and it is intended to clarify the newborn's true relation to his mother so that we do not maintain for ourselves the unrealistic but more romantic (and certainly more palatable) idea that we would prefer to have, of an infant having always been capable of an innate *love* for his mother. One can liken this to the way one uses a light bulb: we don't think about a light bulb before we want light in a room or after we don't need light anymore; we only think about it when we want to turn it on, or when we think we forgot to turn it off, or when it's blown out and won't give us what we want. To the newborn infant, his mother is used like a light bulb instead of a person; hence she is spoken of as an object. Because all mental events are related to the dynamic modes that precede them, we extend this aspect of our language beyond the duration of these primitive relationships so that the metaphor remains intact, and we consequently continue to speak of the "object world" even later when a child or adult is capable of, and is engaged in, object love.

As Freud has pointed out, the first stage in loving and the earliest motivated activity after achieving secondary narcissism is indifference. This is followed swiftly by hatred. Indifference, because the child erects a stimulus barrier designed to prevent anything from drawing cathexis away from the self (an example of a stimulus barrier in an adult would be when someone is concentrating so hard that he doesn't hear when his name is called); hating, because cathexis that has been drawn away from the self is experienced as a depletion, and subjectively it feels like damage or harm to oneself.

Infants do not have the capacity for rational thinking (particularly where cause and effect is concerned). They go through the satisfactions (and libidinal gratifications) of being fed as if that experience of pleasure were unrelated to the competing unpleasure of lost cathexis (that occurs when the giving over of object attention takes place in feeding). This primitive splitting is a measure of the child's inability to integrate related aspects of things, people and events. This primitive incapacity, along with the *defense* of splitting (where one intentionally, even if unconsciously, separates and keeps apart aspects of things, people, and events that were already integrated), and the child's growth beyond it, is central in understanding the early psychological climate and thus will now be presented in fuller detail.

In an environment that is basically normal, adaptation requires that the child not be indifferent or, most importantly, not feel hatred toward his mother. Mother and child must be in an affectionate and libidinally gratifying bond in order for an environment (physical or psychological) to exist in which the infant has optimal opportunity for development. In the economy of mental functioning the child must find a means of first being able to tolerate object attention, and then of going beyond object attention to develop object love. This must be achieved without experiencing narcissistic injury as a consequence. The child achieves this through the evolution, after innumerable feedings, of a double-cathexis process in which there is no difference between narcissistic libido (self-directed libidinal cathexis) and object libido (object-directed libidinal cathexis). This process is the most primitive identification technique in secondary identification[1] (from here on, "identification" will be used to denote secondary identification unless otherwise noted), and it is called *incorporative identification* or just *incorporation*. In incorporation the child takes into itself the characteristics and libidinally gratifying aspects of the mother during feeding. At this stage the child is unable, developmentally, to recognize or distinguish (or even to marginally separate) mother, milk, feeling good, self, other actions associated with feeding, the boundaries of self and of objects, or the multiple characteristics of self and object, from one another.

For the infant, being fed is not just the ingestion of mother's milk or formula, it is ingestion of the mother herself. An adult eating an apple does not experience himself as "a person with an apple inside of him," he thinks of himself as only "himself" before, during, and after feeding. His identity is not changed unless there are special circumstances involved. For example, someone on a rigorous diet may view himself as "himself" *with* the conscious representation, or imagery, of an apple in him. He uses the mental images of both eating and the apple itself to control his appetite. He may also use the mental image of how he imagines himself to be with an apple inside his stomach (the image of the apple inside him may be of a chewed-up apple and/or, paradoxically, a whole apple as it looked before it was eaten) as a way of trying to control his hunger. Most likely, he will use all three. This process, with considerably less sophistication and reality testing, can be likened to the infant's use of incorporative identification. For baby, his mother is both inside him and outside of him. His experience of himself is merged with a maternal representation that now will cross the boundaries of where he begins and ends. Thus, libido that is directed toward mother is no longer traumatic because this intentional psychological maneuver makes it possible for the distinctions between self and object to be blurred. Actually it is not the mother so much as it is the mothering functions (that is, the subjective experiences associated with being mothered) that are cathected, and that are merged with self-representations. At this stage the child's mother is not integrated into a whole object representation but exists, instead, as a relatively loose aggregation of part object representations which are sometimes connected to one another and sometimes not. These primitive representations are not primarily based on a reality that includes such factors as the objective characteristics of his mother that make her unique. Clearly, these considerations are less important, and less accessible to the baby, than his mother's ability to be instinctually gratifying. If mother and baby are "one," then object libido and narcissistic libido are the same; "loving" the mother is the same as "loving" one's

---

[1]In secondary narcissism one is aware, no matter how primitively, that things exist that are not part of the self: an archaic precursor to the more psychologically advanced "I-Thou" relationship, if you will. In secondary identification one attempts to merge with the self that which originates from without: a merger of that which is separate, and a denial of that separation should its "separateness" call forth anxiety.

self, and the first step is taken in the process of evolution from the infant's grudgingly limited capacity for object attention to the welcome extension of object love.

Another important benefit is made available to the infant when this dual-cathexis process is developed. He can, almost paradoxically, use his identification with his mother (whom he experiences as absolutely omnipotent because of her capacity to meet, and because of her potential of continuing to meet, at least in his mind, all his instinctual needs) as a means of restitution, when his own grandiose self-representations and the omnipotence of his own narcissism, based on his identifications with her, are injured and diminished by failures in reality. The child begins with the even more primitive and magical notion that he is all-powerful. If he is hungry, he hallucinates being fed; if he is cold, he hallucinates being warm; if he is tired, he sleeps, and awakens miraculously revived; for him, nothing is impossible. When this primitive magic is not successful, the child's self-esteem is lowered, and as the duration of his "failure" lengthens, he becomes progressively more trauma-tized. If one can conceive of "wit" in a nearly newborn infant, one can say that by the time the baby is faced with the unalterable reality that he is not omnipotent (for example, unless someone comes to feed him soon, he will die) he is at his "wit's" end. He is faced with two alternatives, and depending on how nurturing his environment is, he will remain fixated in the first or he will be able to proceed to the second.

Under the impact of trauma people tend to regress, and they try to cope by using methods that they are familiar with. They lean heavily toward old methods that have either worked or seemed to work, whether or not the context was similar; this has been observed in both clinical and nonclinical settings. In addition, whether or not the defense *remained* successful over time is usually not an important consideration. In the face of a reality failure the child's first reaction is to call into effect negative hallucination, and when that fails, to call hallucinatory wish-fulfillment to the rescue, attempting to regulate his inner experience via the unpleasure and pleasure principles in the absence of a working, functioning reality principle. The immature ego cannot yet make use of the fact that the functional capacity of these two defensive operations is both limited and short-lived. In an environment that is generally adequate, rescue from hunger, for example, will come from his mother and not from within. After repeated successful feedings the child's second reaction is to hold on to the images of having been happily fed, as traces of memory, and then with these memory traces (or engrams) he will be able to begin to differentiate himself from the object-world (whose sole occupant, at this time, is his mother). In this operation his failure to meet his own needs forces his attention to the object world, insofar as his mother was successful where he was not, and he then begins to invest his mother with the primitive omnipotence he formerly attributed to himself. By incorporatively identifying with his mother he reconstitutes his lost omnipotence and repairs the injury to his narcissism, as her powers have become a part of him once again. These restitutions, primitive and magically unrealistic as they are, give the child (or in his view, restore to him) the ability to face the next step in acknowledging the object world and in confronting failure, frustration and disappointment.

Frustration then, plays a large role in the child's relation to the object world. Frustration in an environment that is deprivational, and at its base disappointing, leads the infant away from the object world (since there is nothing in it for him). His reactive fixation on hallucinatory wish fulfillment and other primary-process "solutions" may lead to death, morbid psychotic depressions, autism, childhood schizophrenia, dissociative psychoses, and so forth. Frustration in an environment that is generally, but not totally, disappointing and only moderately, but significantly, deprivational leads the child away from the development of object love, and is commonly thought to be a central consideration in the development of the narcissistic character disorder. In the narcissistic character disorder, not to be confused with an intense narcissistic injury, people are treated as if they were inanimate objects that exist only to gratify whichever instinctual longings happen to be paramount at any given moment. Once used, people are to be discarded in much the same way that any used-up thing is to be thrown away. Frustration in an environment that is for the most part good and libidinally gratifying causes the child to turn to, and eventually welcome, the object world. It gives the child an opportunity to learn his limitations in a context that is supportive, and therefore his experience of being limited is not harmfully injurious to his basic, developing self-esteem. His subjective, but transitory, injury in being faced with his limitations is thus kept within constructive bounds, and it turns the child not away from his mother, but in the direction of the development of genuine object love. It is in this circumstance, because there has been sufficient gratification, that others will eventually be cherished because they are to be valued, even though the first steps in the development of object love often hinges on self-interest alone. Too little frustration in an environment that is overly gratifying causes the child to hold on to his illusions of omnipotence. Unless some needs are left unmet, and unless others are met only after his inability to make them happen himself is undeniable, the child will not be under sufficient pressure to acknowledge the necessity and the impact of the object world. This can lead to the maintenance of inappropriately infantile grandiosity; an enduring lack of frustration tolerance; a lack of establishment of, or the loss of, impulse control; the development in later life of a generally infantile and/or passive dependent personality; psychotic functioning which might include delusions or hallucinations, fantasies of merger, or a lack of reality testing; and so on.

As time passes, the child's anatomical and psychological maturing gives him greater and more accurate exposure to his surroundings. Memory engrams and traces are formed and become increasingly sophisticated, encompassing the child's experiences with the world and lending it both consistency and constancy. As we have seen, children are motivated to attend to, and to remember, those events and people that are involved in the gratification of instincts. These modes of attention and learning are also directly influenced by the health, body state, and genetic makeup of the individual. For example, as has been earlier demonstrated, a child who sees poorly may gear his relation to the world primarily through smell or taste or through touch; we can safely assume that in numerous ways a male child will experience things differently from a female child (particularly in later childhood, and certainly this is even more true in adolescence, with sexual maturity, and in adulthood); or, a child in pain, as stated previously, will experience equivalent "mothering" differently from a child who is not in pain. Most, in fact almost all, learning and development are focused around and stimulated by the gratification and frustration of drives, and, even more importantly, around the resolution of conflicts. The things we learn first are those that are involved in reducing the psychological tensions that mount continuously in states of unfulfilled drive demands. The way we learn about the world, and especially the people in it who will be significant to us, is based on how they are with us, and this is inextricably and intimately related to our anatomy and physiology and to the mental demands they make upon us. In service to the pleasure, reality, constancy, internalization, and unpleasure principles, we attend most significantly to gratification and to frustration, and we attempt to be selectively inattentive to that which lies between, or outside, those specifically drive-related circumstances and people.

In considering the role of conflict resolution it must be emphasized that it is not actually conflicts themselves that make us grow, but their successful resolutions. If we didn't have libidinal and aggressive drives that press for discharge, and if we were entirely self-sufficient at birth, conflict itself would be considerably less in evidence, if in fact it was present at all. Finding a way to successfully master conflicts removes the psychologically disorganizing consequences that result from the presence of conflicts. Conflict resolution directly strengthens the ego so that it will be better able to cope with repetitions of that conflict (as in the repetition compulsion) or with similar or related conflicts, and it readies the ego to subsequently meet future conflicts, and conflicts of greater magnitude.

Conflict-Free Spheres of the Ego

In the earliest days of psychoanalysis it was assumed that all growth and all progression in the ego was directly due to the mastery of psychological conflict. This position suggests that the ego's functions and its contents are never entirely free of conflict, even though the ego's organizational tasks include the reduction and resolution of conflict. In the evolution of psychoanalysis, attention was initially focused on the nature of drives, their psychological expression, and the conflicts they produced; with the development of the structural theory the ego and its mechanisms came under closer scrutiny, and a major area of ego functioning was discovered that appeared to be conflict-free and therefore has become known as "autonomous." Examples of primary ego autonomy include our capacity to perceive, our capacity to initiate motion, our capacity to remember, and, at the heart of many of the regulatory principles of mental functioning, our threshold apparatuses. What we perceive, how we perceive, what we do with our perceptions, the reliance we develop on favored modes of perception will be closely related to, and influenced by, conflict; the *capacity to perceive,* however, is not induced by conflict, and it exists in each individual in ways that are genetically predetermined. Anatomically and physiologically determined poor vision is a physical event, not a psychological one, even though poor eyesight can also develop in response to conflicts about seeing and knowing. Why we move, when we move, where we move, how we move, and similar possibilities concerning choices not to move are usually related to conflict; however, our *capacity to move,* that is, our capacity to use motility as a vehicle for the expression and resolution of conflict, is not. Similar factors also are true for memory. The point is not that primarily autonomous ego functioning is impervious to conflict, but that it *originates* (whether or not it continues to exist) independent of conflict. Ego functioning that was formerly fully or relatively autonomous but which has become "instinctualized" can be, with sufficient resolution of conflict, returned to its previous autonomous state. The concept of *primary* autonomy indicates that the origins of some ego functions are not dependent for their development on the presence of conflict; thus one need not view them (unlike all other ego functions) as being necessarily involved with conflict; the concept of *secondary* autonomy refers to a previous conflictually bound ego attribute that has become deinstinctualized and which now has an imperviousness (or at least a relatively successful resistance) to reinstinctualization. For example, the use of "word salad" in hebephrenic schizophrenia illustrates secondary (or "relative") autonomy in the use of language for expression and for communication, although the thought disorder, and the subsequent idiosyncratic grammar and vocabulary, make the use to which language is put incomprehensible to everyone but the psychotic. Properly or improperly used, language is retained as an intrinsic capacity of the hebephrenic's mental and interpersonal functioning. In contrast, a catatonic schizophrenic may be absolutely and totally mute and may remain so for years. In this case the use of language (or perhaps only speech), and not just thoughts, vocabulary, syntax and grammar, has become instinctualized.

Thus far we have been considering aspects of the ego's autonomy from the id. We can also speak of another aspect of ego autonomy, that is, the ego's autonomy from the environment. In conceptualizing the ego's autonomy (primary and secondary, but with most of our emphasis on secondary autonomy) we describe the ego as using its relation to reality, to secondary process, to the reality and constancy principles; and as using its capacity for both compromise and defense, to abandon, delay, and transform drive demands originating in the id. Where the ego's autonomy from the environment is concerned we can no longer cite the hereditary inbuilt apparatuses (perception, memory, motility, and threshold mechanisms) that support the ego's obligatory relation to reality. Autonomy from the environment is made possible through the pressures engendered from the drives themselves. Drives, always exerting their influences on mental functioning, make it impossible for the ego to enter into a Pavlovian relationship with the environment and its demands. Just as the ego's unbreakable connection to reality and to the external environment compromises a direct fulfillment (or full and immediate gratification) of the drives, so the demands of the drives always impinge on the relationship the ego has with the environment, protecting us from stimulus-response slavery. Put most succinctly by Rapaport (1958): "Thus, while the *ultimate* (primary) *guarantees of the ego's autonomy from the id* are man's constitutionally given apparatuses of reality relatedness, the *ultimate guarantees of the ego's autonomy from the environment* are man's constitutionally given drives" (p. 19). It should be clear that when one speaks of autonomy, whether from the id or from the environment, one has in mind a relative rather than a total or absolute measure, and also that with the exception of primary autonomy we think in terms of constantly fluctuating (hence the term "relative") autonomy in both areas. This view of relative autonomy has critical implications not only for conceptualizing mental functioning but also for the process of treatment.

The question of treatment is covered in the second section of this book, but as a brief aside we can consider for a moment an interesting ramification for treatment in the development of the concept of ego autonomy. If we are able to evaluate ego autonomy and its vicissitudes, we know something about the strengths of an individual's defenses, particularly under stress; and many other important factors in the structure of personality and character are made accessible when we know about the ego's capacity to resist regression and reinstinctualization. Should regression and reinstinctualization occur, a knowledge of a person's capacity to effectively use secondarily autonomous ego functions will permit us to estimate the speed, and degree, of "rebound" at their disposal. The questions of "rebound" and maintenance of ego autonomy are critical in formulating a treatment of choice: the psychoanalytic treatment modality makes use of a regressive condition in which infantile conflict is intended to emerge for scrutiny and extended examination; psychoanalytic psychotherapy relies on this to a lesser extent; some treatment modalities actively discourage any and all regressions; and other treatment modalities are rather indifferent to the question of regression. In any case, it should be noted that the degree of (re-) instinctualization will often be in direct proportion to the depth of a regression, that all ego functions are not affected equally (which is the saving grace for those individuals with solidly developed levels of secondary autonomy), and that there is a mutually reinforcing relationship between reinstinctualization and regression that continually gathers momentum.

To return to the oral stage, we can state that identifications are an important tool in the development of secondarily autonomous ego functions, and in the management of regression. A baby traumatized by hunger uses incorporative identifications with his mother, in addition to his memories of having been fed and hallucinatory wish fulfillment, to help him tolerate the wait for the bottle without a major disorganizing regression. Babies who have not achieved this level of functioning, or who have been made to wait too long for hallucination, memory, and identification to remain effective, can become so disorganized that they may be unable to feed when the breast (or bottle) is finally offered to them; they may have reached a point where biting, spitting, vomiting, crying, or throwing themselves around is so intense that it is impossible to eat. The older child also uses identification as one of his tools for resisting regression and disorganization. For example, an older child might enhance his ability to tolerate the frustration of waiting on a long, slow-moving line by watching how his parents are able to wait. He might tap his feet (superficially as a means of showing impatience, but dynamically as a way of draining off aggression in response to frustration) if he sees that this is one of the things his parents are doing. If his parents complain to the manager about the long wait, the child might subsequently play a game, in order to stabilize the regulatory capacities of the identification, where there is a long wait and in which he complains to the manager (both as a safety valve for aggression and as a way of constructively reducing the waiting time). These identifications are called imitative identifications; incorporation and imitation are the primary forms of preoedipal identifications in early childhood.

Some Preliminary Remarks on Infantile Sexuality

One may see, after our discussion of the organizing potentials of libido in the previous chapter and our discussion in this chapter of the child's instinctually determined relations to the world and to significant others, that it is the intense childhood love-relations that will be transformed into adult love (with the addition of sexuality) after puberty. We use the term *infantile sexuality* to mean both: (1) the childhood nonerotic precursors to adult sexual life, and (2) the immature expression of genital excitement. The initial feelings of mounting tension produced by drive states in children is the original model for sexual excitement in adults; the constellation of feelings of relief and elation that accompanies the gratification of drive demands in childhood is the original model for climacteric pleasure in the orgasm of adults. The intensity of childhood excitement is very real even though it is expressed in infantile forms. Unlike the specifically focused genital sexuality of the adult, infantile sexuality is more like the feeling of scratching an intense itch, like the feeling of urinating after having had to hold in an uncomfortably full bladder for a very long time, like the first food after one has been starving or the first water when one has been parched. Children express the continuum of sexual and loving feelings in whichever way is appropriate for the developmental stage they are in, but the underlying dynamic (that is, the aim and object of erotic libido) transcends stage-specific modes of expression and will be found to be very much in evidence in the basic fabric of every developmental stage, without exception. We now can begin our discussion of the anal stage, in which striking transformations of infantile sexuality may be observed.

3

The Anal Stage

Anality, Narcissistic Trauma, and Other Dynamic Ramifications of Toilet Training

Psychoanalytic developmental theory separates psychological growth into six psychosexual stages: *the oral stage*, which occurs in early infancy; *the anal stage*, which spans late infancy and early childhood; *the phallic stage*, in which the Oedipus complex occurs, and which is associated with the middle phase of childhood; *latency*, which covers late childhood; *the genital stage*, which emerges in adolescence and is triggered by puberty; and finally (if all goes well), *adulthood*. So much happens in the course of mental development, particularly in the early years, that one may ask why the primary consideration in characterizing psychological maturation has been specifically *psychosexual*. For example: remembering, and learning to use intellect are among the primary tasks of childhood; why, then, do we not have a *cognitive* or *educational* phase? Learning to walk, and to master the mechanics of the body in other respects, are momentous activities of childhood; why then do we not have a *locomotor, mastery,* or *mobilization* stage? Because the nervous system and other aspects of anatomy are not fully developed at birth, why do we not have specific stages that are organized around, or which commemorate, these important events as they progress? Major steps in development are undertaken when children move from parallel to cooperative play, and in their shift from total involvement in the nuclear family to new allegiances with peer groups, so why has psychoanalysis chosen not to postulate a specifically *social* phase? There are so many significant events from birth to death that one could, if one wished to make random choices, point to hundreds of developmental phases and stages. Indeed, some (such as Fairbairn, Sullivan, and Erikson) have proposed alternative views to the traditional and established psychosexual model of development.[1]

---

[1]One might also wish to posit an object relations set of stages from a Freudian perspective, and if one were to do so one would look at the work of Margaret Mahler, for example, who suggests the following sequence (not as a substitute for psychosexual stages, but as a kind of elaboration): a normal autistic phase and next a normal symbiotic phase, which are forerunners of the separation-individuation process, followed by the first separation-individuation subphase, known as *hatching* (in which initial differentiation and development of the body image take place); then the second subphase, known as *practicing* (in

The psychosexual model was not chosen by default; that is to say, because of the motive force of the dual-drive configuration we do not consider the psychosexual model to be one of a number of equally important paradigms. It has been chosen neither for the sake of comfort or convenience (as in not being able to make a selection from a varied and interesting menu), nor because it exemplifies a tight set of well-organized theoretical constructs, but because psychosexual considerations dictate and color every mental event, with relatively few exceptions, in a way that is not duplicated by any other (that is, noninstinctual) psychological component. In fact, excepting the few autonomous ego functions present at birth, we can state the psychosexual considerations are capable of dictating and coloring every mental event, whatsoever, in every instance. We are able to make this assertion because we know that under the pressure of psychosexual influences it is possible for aspects of ego functions that originated outside the realm of conflict to subsequently become highly instinctualized.[2] If we accept that psychosexual influence is so pervasive that an entire model of development can be oriented toward always taking it into account, we are still left with the question of why primarily libidinal, rather than some other, influences came to play such a central role in mental development. We must remember that, in part, the very nature of instinct-life itself and its psychological vicissitudes automatically organize psychological experience around the predetermined poles of libido and aggression. Libido does not operate under the same necessity for transformation as does aggression, and thus it determines and ensures that there will always be a psychosexual context to mental functioning, even in those circumstances having no discernible sexual attributes prior to their inclusion in the psychological matrix. In addition, the overriding and compelling sovereignty of the unpleasure–pleasure principles in early mental life reduces even the most complex of events to the oversimplified levels of frustration versus gratification, anticathexis and hypercathexis, indifference and hatred juxtaposed with object love, and tension versus satisfaction. This obscures many other important factors that cannot be conveniently stated in those terms although they might be of considerably greater objective significance than that which has become so disproportionately exaggerated. Finally, if we keep in mind the distinctions raised at the end of the last chapter, between mature sexuality and infantile sexuality, we can see that the definition of sexuality in no way pits psychosexual considerations against other

---

which initial separations are attempted); then the third subphase, known as *rapprochement* (in which optimal distance from the object is tried out); and then the fourth and final subphase (in which the child consolidates its individuality and begins to develop emotional object constancy).

[2]In an assertion like this, one always takes for granted that there is a rich and complex interrelationship between drives and environment. However, one must also take for granted (which is to say, not to either ignore or to underrate) the impact that both object relationships and the subsequently internalized object relations have on the organization of mental functioning in each of the psychosexual stages. Very early in his writings, Freud pointed out the almost immediate connection between narcissistic libido/aggression, object libido/aggression, and the development of both psychic structure and object relations, which proceed hand-in-hand through all the stages of psychosexual development.

mental considerations in an either-or configuration. We can also include many other considerations without finding ourselves forced into the position of being required to challenge the primacy of the psychosexual model.

Let us now move to the transformations of the anal stage and consider why the shift becomes necessary and how it becomes possible. We have previously described how the exquisite sensitivity of the oral cavity, and its relationship to the most gratifying experiences of infancy, being fed and mothered, has organized the earliest stage of mental functioning into a period of conspicuous psychosexual orality. The oral stage was dictated essentially by anatomical and physiological factors, whereas the anal stage is initiated by traumatic pressures originating in the external, not the internal, world. The oral stage translated the environment into instinctual terms for processing, whereas the environment channels drive derivatives into its terms for processing in the anal stage.

The anal stage is brought about because of the parent's attempts to toilet train the child. In general, sufficient control over the anal sphincter is achieved, in anatomical and physiological maturity, by about the eighteenth month, and this is the optimal time for the child to begin to be toilet trained. Control over the anal sphincter can be achieved significantly earlier because of precocious anatomical development or in response to traumatic repetitive demands made by the parents; infants who are toilet trained by the age of 8 or 9 months are not unique.

Some children who are anatomically ready to be toilet trained when they are 18 months of age do not accomplish it until their third or fourth year. This might be due to a variety of physical and psychological factors, for example: slower anatomical development; parents who do not know how to toilet train a child because of unresolved conflicts about their own toilet training; parents who give the child double messages during toilet training (overtly they insist that toilet training occur, but tacitly they communicate to the child that he is to act out for them all their own hidden rebellion against rules and regulations); or parents who have directed at the child unconscious aggression, which takes the form of not properly helping him to achieve skills necessary for a happy adjustment. Prolonged toilet training might also be due to a child's intense preoccupation with winning what he sees as a power struggle between him and his parents, to an attempt to preserve narcissistic intactness if he has not been able (for related or unrelated reasons) to distinguish between himself and his "productions," or because toilet training and/or other toilet activity has become eroticized and thus prolonged in the service of pleasure.

Prior to their decision to toilet train their child his parents have loosened some of the hold that reaction formation has had on their own interest and pleasure in anal activity and anal products. Reaction formation is a defense developed by the ego during the anal stage that causes one to reverse one's feelings, thoughts, ideas, wishes, and so on. If it feels good to have a warm, wet bowel movement in one's pants, reaction formation changes that feeling to disgust and discomfort. If the smell of vomit, sweat, urine, anal gas, and feces is both interesting and pleasurable to an infant (one sees such interest and pleasure evinced throughout the animal kingdom), reaction formation changes that to nauseating revulsion. If the sight of vomit or stool is fascinating, reaction formation makes the sight repulsive and motivates us to avoid it wherever possible. If it is fun to play with mucus, vomit, or bowel products, reaction formation will make those activities so abhorrent to us that we will develop an avoidance bordering on phobia regarding them. The reaction formations of parents do not become loosened as if by magic at the moment a baby is born. Much of the joking around in the months immediately preceding delivery about changing diapers and wearing clothes that they are willing to have soiled, is a preparatory activity expressly designed to reduce the power of many of their reaction formations in this area. This is necessary for them to be able to tolerate a re-immersion in excretory activities that they have guarded against unrelentingly since their own toilet training. After the birth of their child, they are constantly exposed to vomit, urine, mucus, and feces, which paradoxically help to make the experience more tolerable. Cleaning their baby will be a pleasure, an *active* pleasure as an act of love, so that removing his wastes is not actively aversive even though handling his excretory products themselves will never become an active pleasure. In addition, parents, because of the way archaic things are retained in the psyche and in identification with their child, experience a revival of their own unconscious equation between one's self and one's products. This primitive view is activated in the unconscious, and remains unconscious, so that their love for the baby includes an ability to successfully counter a rejection of him that, once in operation, would lead to being revolted by the baby himself in addition to his waste products. At the very same time parents retain the main bulk of their conscious and intellectual awareness of the difference between one's self and one's products, which permits them to continue in this way to love and adore their baby even if they are unconsciously and on occasion consciously appalled and disgusted by his vomit, urine, mucus, and bowel contents. The passage of time, repeated exposure, and the reduction (or loosening) of reaction formations enables parents to love their baby with a minimum of disgust and without wishing to avoid him.

A child is not born with anal reaction formations already in place. He begins life with a total inability to differentiate between himself and his products. His initial ventures into the object world find him unequipped to measure and comprehend subtle shades of unconscious feeling in his parents. If his parents are in active conflict about soiling he will try to deny, or to selectively inattend to, any conflictual or negative cues that he has recognized in his parents' unconscious feelings (the child now has a conflict about how to deal with his parent's conflicts). His parents are striving consciously and unconsciously to love him both totally and unambiva-lently, and this also aids the infant to feel, before the pressures of toilet training, at least neutral and at other times quite positively toward his productions. Regarding his waste products, the infant frequently sees no reason for disgust or for feelings of alienation prior to toilet training.

As the time approaches when the child's parents are contemplating toilet train-ing, their reaction formations begin to redevelop and return to their old configurations. Because they know their child will soon be able to exercise control over himself, they are free to gradually reinstitute their almost lifelong prohibitions and disgusts. By the time toilet training is begun, the parents are in a kind of middle stage of reaction formation where they are able to clean their child when necessary but find it actively unpleasant. This change in attitude is extremely traumatic for the child. Up until then he was loved totally and without reservation, and suddenly he causes revulsion and disgust in his mother.

When his mother reacts with disgust to the child's soiling himself, the child (who imagines that his mother functions exactly as he does), being unable to distinguish between himself and his feces, and being unable to distinguish between himself and his actions, takes her disgust and rejection to be aimed at him (not just his soiling) and is dealt a powerful narcissistic injury. He cannot appreciate the true intrapsychic nature of her reactions and takes them to mean only a change in her feelings about him. Never before has she as unambivalently taken a position of such determined rejection. His mother's angers and frustrations in the past were reactive (for example, because she was overtired, or had some specific pressure she was under) and were passing phenomena. If, like every mother, she has been rejecting at one time or another, never before has she taken such an uncompromising position with her child. It must be emphasized that his mother's stance with him is not defined by the demand in reality that she is making on him: "You must learn to use the potty, and then the toilet." Her relationship to him is changing and is defined by her feelings of anger, revulsion, frustration, impatience, and hostility each time she has to change a "filthy" diaper. One also wishes to emphasize that whereas this new posture exists to some extent in his mother's conscious functioning, it gains its power for the child in that it exists in her unconscious as reaction formations that reassert themselves, even in those cases where his mother is most patient and laudably enlightened (in consciousness) about toilet training.

From baby's point of view, enlightened mothers are bad and unenlightened mothers are worse, because in both cases they threaten him with loss of love and more. Loss of love stands for loss of life. He assumes that if mother no longer loves him, she will no longer provide for him. Just as he is unable, and intentionally unwilling, to deflect libidinal resources toward an object he does not love, and just as he actively withdraws libidinal cathexis when he is angry, he assumes the same dynamic configurations in his mother. He doesn't think it out and measure it against reality, he just fears and dreads it. Many children express these concerns quite openly, and this has been demonstrated to occur just as much with children who have not verbalized these fears. One of the major variables in the child's compliance with toilet training is primitive self-preservation. Learning to comply causes to occur in the present (and for the future) the sought-after past experiences of being loved. The infant is made safe and is provided for by a mother who will once again be unreserved in her long-term general feelings toward her child; thus we can see that although being successfully toilet trained is a developmental move forward, part of the motivation of the child (demonstrating an adaptive as well as a regressive aspect of the repetition and Nirvana principles) involves the wish to regress to the happy past as the means of implementing the forward step into the future. It is apparent then that where development is concerned, clear and unequivocal distinctions between forward and backward are impossible.

We must also recall that, economically, to love is a narcissistic depletion, and that being loved is narcissistically expanding. The feelings and thoughts of a child are affected by this economic circumstance more greatly than would be the case for an adult, who has ways of coping that the child will not have for years to come. Under the traumatic impact of the primary process experience of toilet training (which goes on forever, or so it seems to the child, in that once toilet training has begun it will continue until it is successful, and the infant's sense of time is entirely unrealistic), some of his hard-won ego functions threaten to crumble as he is required to comply with behavioral demands that are frustrating and alien, and with which he has had no experience whatsoever (and as he is "punished" and "threatened" each time he fails, as fail he must). His initial experiences in toilet training are failures, and not only is such failure increasingly unacceptable to his mother and father as time goes by, it also disorganizes the child's feelings of narcissistic integrity, which potentially diminishes his coping mechanisms in other areas (which can lead in turn to additional narcissistic injuries).

Some of the child's omnipotence and grandiosity was diminished when he realized that he needed his mother to do things for him that he couldn't do for himself, but much of it has been able to remain intact in those situations where it was not explicitly challenged. An important mechanism used by children to recapture their lost sense of omnipotence, and to ensure the continuity of their inner experience of grandiosity and power, is to identify with their mother and to thereby make her strengths their own. Most people are resistant to, and have understandable difficulties in, experiencing themselves as weak, helpless, exposed, vulnerable, and defenseless; this is most especially so for an infant when he is without a caretaker, for he is not simply having an experience but is, in reality, in genuine peril. When his mother withholds love (not a hateful mother who doesn't care for her child, and not even a loving mother who is frustrated; just the mother who normally continues to press for compliance in toilet training), she also cuts the child off from her "supply" of power so that subjectively his sense of self is diminished, and he feels himself to be defenseless. Every child feels that his parents are the most powerful people in the world, and the withdrawal of their protection (even if their *absolute* withdrawal is primarily a fantasy, and the parents are in most important ways still completely available) is terribly frightening for the child.

A child is able to use his mother's love for him and his awareness of his importance for her in the maintenance of omnipotence and grandiosity. When a mother truly expresses love for her child, he is aggrandized and nurtured. He then uses her loving and positive regard to ward off drops in self-esteem, and other narcissistic injuries, as the reality disconfirmations of his omnipotence inevitably accrue in proportion to his successes and failures in reality. By augmenting his damaged narcissism with his mother's omnipotence, he can make appropriate use of failures to form a more realistic picture of himself, the world, and his relationship to it. His ability to be constructive in the face of failure, and not just traumatized, relies heavily on the "loan" of his mother's omnipotent representation, which he merges with self-representations through incorporative and imitative identifications. This ability also relies heavily on the "loan" of his mother's mature and autonomous ego attributes as she actively teaches him things, does things for him, sets limits for him, and so on.

To return to what the child's mother feels: her reservations about his behavior extend, in part, to him as well, because it is not possible to completely separate him from his actions. For the child, however, her reservations about his behavior are the same as her having those reservations entirely about *him;* thus he experiences her demands on him, and her affective repugnance (fueled once again by the institution of reaction formation), as more than just a difficult learning experience. Toilet training is an extraordinary trauma of monumental proportions, and as we can see, more hangs in the balance for the child than just a behavioral compliance. His crisis is experienced as being of life-threatening proportions, even where he has in reality the kindest, most loving, and most supportive of mothers. His fantasy, which is not distinguished from reality, is that all his mother's power, love, support and comforting is withdrawn when she reacts to his being soiled. It has been said that bowel movements are the first medium of exchange, and here we can see that this is an apt phrase.

Both mother and child engage in a trading relationship, and it is from this model that much having to do with withholding, generosity, and power relationships in adulthood has its origins. Before commenting further on the adult representations of anal-stage developmental factors, we will need to view another element of this stage that makes it traumatic, and consequently, very highly cathected. Until the parents' attempts at toilet training, the child has never been required to inhibit or delay gratification of an impulse. Certain actions have been inhibited (baby can't poke mother in the eye, he can't run in the street, he can't put his hand in fire or hot coffee, he can't play with sharp knives), but they do not use the ego strengths of the child as much as they rely on the ego strengths and the intelligence of the mother for their initiation and maintenance. Within the process of toilet training one finds that for the very first time, the child is required to develop an internal capacity for self-regulation, and despite the pleasure associated with success when achieved, this is difficult and unpleasant for him. Thus far, his experiences have been centered around affirmation and the gratification of his wishes, and he has indiscriminately attempted to satisfy every impulse without considering the consequences, without exception and without reservation. Learning to say no to oneself would not or could not be accomplished if that which is at stake – that is, if the cost of noncompliance – were minimal or unimportant. It is precisely because of the traumatic "threats" and "deprivations" described above that the child is motivated to learn how to negate or postpone the gratification of his impulses. Biological dictates and the wish to gratify impulses act in concert on the child. We should remember that holding in his excreta and waste products makes no sense to the child. These products are meant to be discharged and expelled, and toilet training goes against biological common sense. Unexpelled wastes build up in the body and act as pollutants and contaminants, and ultimately they are destructive to life. Outside of the very special circumstances of toilet training, a child who consciously and intentionally permitted and fostered the retention of body poisons would be described as directing unneutralized aggressive energy at himself. Transformation, through neutralization and drive fusion, and the augmenting of libidinal drive elements, changes this potentially dangerous and destructive activity into an adaptive and constructive adjustment. This is a major accomplishment, even though the transition is by no means smooth, and even though it occurs amidst considerable conflict and tension.

Here, once more, we see conflict and its resolution playing a major role in mental development. Throughout this chapter and within succeeding chapters conflict will be addressed again and again. One of the things that most characterizes psychoanalytic thinking is its attention to conflict. For psychoanalytic psychology the relationships between (1) conflict and regression, (2) conflict and fixation, and (3) conflict resolution and growth are inseparable. In toilet training the psychological pressure (danger) initiated by the child's mother is ultimately more threatening, more immediate, more consistent, and more constant than the initial drive stages aroused by physiological determinants; thus, given this lack of balance, the child is motivated to learn "clean" habits.

Let us now consider how the child's growth is aided and provided for by the satisfaction and pleasure he experiences innately and when mastery is achieved. Mastery over his bowels is pleasurably extended to include mastery over a wide range of other functions, over the functions of others, and over others themselves. This rise in libido helps to transform, balance, and cancel some intense aspects of aggression that are generated in the search for mastery, and it also initiates an "erotic" feature in bowel control and in related toilet activities. Neutralized aggression, in combination with libidinal cathexes, focuses the child's attention on the operation of his bowels and on associated factors in his toilet functioning, so that excretion will never again be an automatic and unremarkable event. By imbuing successful toilet training with pleasurable characteristics, the child can both maintain and increase passive rewards (such as an uninterrupted, generally libidinal relationship with his mother) and active rewards (such as an erotically pleasurable experience when he complies). There is, in addition, a general feeling of well-being and pleasure connected to the strengthening of the ego achieved during mastery. A wide variety of secondary gains are made available in many other areas as well, because each act of mastery increases the general sovereignty of ego and its capacities across broad ranges of mental functioning.

Power, as distinguished from mastery, is an issue of paramount importance in the anal stage. Power signifies more than just mastery, more than a general strengthening of the ego, and more than a simple decrease in dependency; power signifies a victory over the narcissistic injuries of the oral stage (when the child could not meet his needs), and a victory over the narcissistic injuries of the anal stage (when he could not prevent withdrawal of the libidinal cathexes of his mother).

The feelings of power that accompany mastery experiences in toilet training are narcissistically enhancing. They bring about a decrease in the child's sense of vulnerability and provide (or reinstate) the impression that control over the supply of instinctual gratifications is completely within his capacity. Power, then, is valued for what it can do in reality, but it becomes truly beloved for what it can do in fantasy. These dynamics underlie the behavior of the "terrible twos" who glory in saying no, and who peremptorily order around every animate (and inanimate) object in sight (or mind). Through play in which they are omnipotent and masterful, and with much repetition, they gain sovereignty over their own impulses as they test out the impact of "no" on the world around them. Through renewed reparatory fantasies of omnipotence and a continual measuring of this against reality, they are able to tolerate some of the more disorganizing aspects possible in experiencing frustration and disappointment. It is within this context that the child can learn to delay gratification of his impulses and, beyond that, to derive gratification and pleasure from the ability to delay. This subtle combination of aggression (saying no to oneself) and libido (pleasure in being able to do so) helps to ensure that life does not turn into nothing more than a simple Pavlovian game of waiting. The acquisition of this psychological skill frees the child from a total dependency on his instincts and makes possible the complex mental patterns of adult functioning which, in most ways, are not tied to simple reward and punishment or stimulus–response operations. This marks the first intersystemic psychic struggle (id vs. ego) and sets the model for future structural reorganization. In addition, it marks the first collaboration of the id with the ego in frustrating one of its own demands. We see in this a new level of complexity in the nature of the psychic structures (as they simultaneously work against, for, and with one another).

Most of our adult capacities to delay our impulses, or to deprive ourselves of things we want which we feel we should not have (for whatever reasons), originate in the anal stage. Because toilet training is a form of habit development, much of our physical and psychological regularity has its roots in the anal stage. Our attitudes toward general cleanliness and orderliness emerge from our toilet training and its emphasis on personal cleanliness. If parents have an outstanding conflict in this area that they pass on to their child (even unconsciously and inadvertently), he, as an adult, is likely to have an exaggerated interest in (or disregard for) cleanliness and neatness. It is unusual, except in the most seriously disturbed adults, to come across people who wallow in or play with their own body wastes; it is not unusual, however, to find relatively healthy adults who pick their nose, who pick at scabs, who visually examine their bowel movements and urine carefully before flushing the toilet, who derive great pleasure from belching or breaking wind, who enjoy squeezing pimples or enjoy spitting, who *never* show up late or who *always* show up late, who use foul language, who take every situation and turn it into a power struggle, who make long and elaborate lists of questionable reality value (or who use other strikingly compulsive or obsessive mechanisms), and so on. These are a few of the ordinary sequelae of the anal stage in the generally healthy personality that are frequently, but not necessarily, a cause for shame, conflict, or ambivalence.

Overdetermination and the Genetic Viewpoint

Even when we focus our attention on the anal stage for heuristic purposes, we will want to remember that we are viewing phenomena that are subject in every case, without exception, to the influence of oral-stage and anal-stage processing. It is not possible for any mental event to be a production of only the oral stage or only the anal stage. Frequently it might seem as if only oral stage-specific or anal stage-specific features are present, but it is usually just a matter of the extent to which one or the other predominates, or it may be only a matter of greater visibility. As the result of a conflict, a fixation may occur that carries with it such strong signs of the origin of the conflict, the stage in which the conflict was most intense, or the stage in which it was most unsolvable, that we may be led to the incorrect assumption that this stage was the only one involved. In formulating the *genetic* metapsychological theory we have postulated a historical component in our thinking that views psychological maturation as following a pattern where everything that has ever happened to an individual is used (to a greater or lesser extent, depending on the circumstances) in the development of all current mental events and in the evolution of all future psychological activity. The second half of genetic theory describes the intrusion of infantile conflict into the mental functioning of an adult, with the emphasis on *conflict* from the past. We use the word *overdetermination* to express the idea that every single mental event has within it more than one genetic or historical antecedent.

A clinical example may help to make this somewhat more clear:

A striking and repetitive characteristic of one woman who was in treatment was that she would come to sessions regularly and on time, but once there, she often refused to speak. Not only could an entire session go by without her saying a word, but sometimes a number of sessions in a row would go by without a sound from her. When she was asked what she was thinking, she felt nagged. When asked if there was anything her therapist could do to help her say what was going on, she felt harassed (an instructive, amusing and poetic pun [har "assed"], as we shall soon see). When her silence was interpreted, to show her how it was a symbolic repetition of a highly conflictual set of circumstances and events carried forward from her childhood, she felt persecuted rather than enlightened. Prior to her eventually successful analysis of this, her general feeling was that her analyst's interpretations did more harm than good.

This 32-year-old woman was born without a proper anus, without proper sphincter musculature, and with other severe rectal deformities. Her rural southern family relocated to the urban Northeast because the extensive surgery and physical therapy procedures that were needed to keep her alive were not available where they lived. Bowel movements were mostly painful ordeals, always unpleasant and in her early years quite uncontrollable. From birth to midlatency she suffered severe bouts of constipation in which her feces became so impacted that her parents were frequently required to remove them by digging them out with their fingers. Laxatives, enemas, and other purgatives alternated with explosive diarrhea, and with an ever-leaking rectum that caused her intense suffering, shame, and humiliation. As she experienced it in her childhood, and as she remembered it as an adult, everything connected to bowel control and evacuation was perceived as a destructive assault. This involved numerous penetrations of her body with varying implements in addition to her parents' fingers, unremitting pain, damage to her insides (real and fantasied) and, in her child's mind, a wholesale robbery and victimization of her that was perpetrated by the very people who were supposed to protect her from such things – her mother and father. Inevitably, anything related to toilet training became a battleground.

Being only a child, she could not appreciate the effort expended by her parents in keeping her alive. They did an unusually good job of coping with a demoralizing and perpetually demanding situation in which they were also exposed to great hardship and suffering (exemplified by, but not limited to, their pulling up roots and moving to a location where she could get desirable and necessary, in fact life-preserving, treatment). It is by no means a certainty that all parents, if confronted with even just the daily tasks required by such a circumstance, could have done the job at all, let alone do it as well as hers did. She was entirely unable to appreciate this as a child. Even as an adult, the context of her lifelong situation was too traumatic for her to be able to attend to all the objective realities and the inevitable ramifications of her congenital defect.

An important aspect of her development was her need to gain a sense of active control over her bowel functioning because it was unbearable for her to be entirely helpless and passive. Given the natural limitations of the infantile ego, she felt victimized by her body and victimized by her parents. As a defense, she developed the belief that when she had diarrhea, it occurred because she *wanted* to have diarrhea. In the service of this defensive belief, she fought the medical binding of her bowel contents and resisted her parents' attempts to teach her how to acquire (limited) control of her anal sphincter. In a parallel maneuver she came to believe, in the service of feeling more actively in control, that when she was constipated she *wanted* to be constipated. She resisted passing urges to defecate, and she would lie to her parents claiming that she had moved her bowels when she hadn't. This intentional blurring of cause and effect doesn't solve anything in reality, but it was the best compromise formation (in the defense of her narcissistic injury) available to her as a little girl.

Knowing all this, it comes as no surprise that she remained silent in precisely the type of treatment where the prime rule is to say *everything* that comes to mind, without censorship or other reservations, and where withholding, while not uncommon, is nonetheless considered to be taboo. It is also clear, if not blatantly obvious, how she came to experience her analyst's interventions as persecutory and hostile. Another factor, drawn now from a developmental consideration of her oral stage rather than from her circumstances in toilet training, will help us to more fully appreciate her conviction that her therapist's interpretations would do more harm than good. Interpretations and what they were designed to achieve were experienced by this woman as being so much like, and reminiscent of, those childhood attempts to evacuate, which were so painful and so humiliating for her and which made her feel so vulnerable and victimized, that she was too traumatized to experience or to then appreciate the feelings of health and relief they were supposed to effect. As a child she was simply too young to be able to connect cause and effect in that way, and as an adult the situation was one of such long-standing trauma that the pleasure and relief were bought at too high a cost in pain, shame, and humiliation.

Additional factors from the oral stage make her stubborn conviction even more comprehensible. When we eat, we set into motion the rippling action of the digestive tract known as peristalsis. Much of the physiology of the digestive tract occurs outside of conscious awareness, but peristalsis, its sequelae, and a few other gastrointestinal actions can make themselves sensationally known consciously. They frequently may begin to function, and thus make their presence felt, as soon as one starts eating. Each time when as a baby this woman was fed, peristalsis and other digestive tract activity stimulated intense pain and discomfort. Eating, which is usually the prime vehicle for libidinal gratification in the oral stage, was paradoxical, because her damaged digestive tract caused subjective experiences that were colored by sensations (and affective states) more closely related to death and destruction. This left her in a state of conflict and disorganization and, unlike normal children who use libidinal gratification to balance and reduce the possible predominance of aggression in their lives, she was subject to levels of aggression that could never be outweighed by the minimal libidinal gratifications available in her uniquely complex feeding situation. Eating kept her alive and of course provided some secondary satisfactions, but this woman's experience of being fed was that it did her more harm than good. She was in no position, as an infant, to appreciate anything beyond the fact that hunger was dreadful but being fed, too, led to pain, frustration, disappointment, and rage. The offered interpretation was for this woman the symbolic equivalent, via condensation and displacement in primary process, of being fed symbolically by her therapist. Given her special and peculiar history, interpretations that should have reduced anxiety and made her feel better were something to be feared and avoided. Her conviction, that interpretations and other interventions would harm her, was perfectly understandable considering the net result of the contamination by pain and discomfort of the feeding process in her infancy.

Another aspect of her fear and expectation that therapeutic interventions could cause her harm rather than benefit is that her mother, who should have been the agent of protection and libidinal gratification for her, was through no fault of her own the agent of anxiety and pain. In numerous repetitive situations (feeding; changing surgical dressings; cleaning sensitive scar tissue when changing diapers; holding and cuddling in situations where movement carries with it some discomfort during healing; removing impacted feces; administering unpleasant or bad-tasting medicines that sometimes, as in the case of purgatives, created further pain and discomfort) her mother "caused" her much pain, discomfort, anguish, and despair. From our perspective as adults and from our position of greater objectivity, not having been caught up in this ourselves, we can see that it was not her mother's fault nor was it her mother's intention that her child should be subjected to these awful experiences. Excluding her parents' genetic material, it cannot be said to be their fault that she felt miserable at the very time she should have been mostly feeling pleasurably gratified and generally feeling loved and safely protected. However, it is also clear that an infant has neither the distance nor the mental capacity to appreciate the subtleties of this dilemma. We see from this unfortunate set of circumstances that not just the food but the feeder as well, *subjectively* did more harm than good. By extension, under primary-process influence, the interpretation and the interpreter became a source of danger. Although she often had sufficient ego strength to know otherwise, it was frequently this woman's worst fear that the whole process of psychoanalysis had either the potential or the intention to be more harmful than helpful. It was the ego strengths she had at her disposal as an adult that permitted her to enter treatment initially, and it was the increased sovereignty of ego functioning achieved in the treatment itself that enabled her to remain in, and to derive continued benefit from, the treatment; within the process of psychoanalysis it became clear that this overdetermined confluence of oral-stage and anal-stage dynamics and conflicts had contributed greatly to, and helped to shape, her fears, her silences, and her initial resistances to interpretation.

It is obvious that this description does not include influences from subsequent psycho-sexual stages; for example, there was in the full analysis much rich material about castration anxiety (beginning in the anal stage, coalescing in the phallic stage, and recrudescing in both latency and adolescence) that also contributed greatly to this woman's fears, and to certain aspects of a "stubbornness" she frequently engaged in with her therapist.

It was for heuristic purposes that the concept of overdetermination and the workings of the genetic metapsychological principle were undertaken at this junc-ture. Ordinarily, we would want to examine this woman's mental functioning only after we take into consideration the full range of psychosexual developmental stages (which, in this case, has not yet been sufficiently presented). These confluent events are so numerous and complex that the addition of dynamics from following stages should wait until the basic concepts of overdetermination and the genetic theory are fully appreciated and understood. The task in this case was to see how aspects of the past (particularly conflicts) are simultaneously in operation, or are exerting an influence, in the present. We have not attempted an identification of all the origins of this woman's silences, but that presents us with no particular problem as long as we know, and keep constantly in mind, that we have not yet exhausted the field. As we bring this subject to a close, we find ourselves ready to move ahead into the highly complex phallic stage.

4

The Phallic Stage

Why Define It as a Phallic Stage?

In the process of mastering the developmental tasks of the anal stage, the child's attention (and the focus of instinctual tensions) is peripherally directed to the genitals. When toilet training has been accomplished, the child's involvement with his genitals increases. By directing his attention to the genitals the child escapes what would be a trauma to newly won ego functioning if he maintained, increased, or renewed anal eroticism.[1] The specific ego function of reaction formation, the primary defense developed in the anal stage, inhibits further involvement in anal eroticism causing libidinal interests to require, create, and thus take advantage of, new aims and pathways of gratification. The residue of anal eroticism that does remain can be, and usually is, camouflaged by sharing the means of an associated body part in discharging tension and in achieving pleasure. The physiology of the urogenital system is remarkable for its high degree of innervation, and the external genital is uniquely accessible; as a consequence, the genitals are a particularly satisfactory site for the discharge of tension. Manipulation of the genitals (and the future sexual activities associated with them) are predetermined by biology to be intensely pleasurable. The child resists a regression to oral modes of gaining gratification, that is, a retreat to the immediately preceding stage, because movements in non-stage-specific directions are regressive and the primitive ego recognizes that psychological movement in a regressive direction is destructive.[2]

Not every oral wish (and dynamic) is abandoned when the child enters the anal stage, nor is every anal wish (and dynamic) abandoned with the child's entrance into the phallic stage. We should conceptualize the flow of impulses (instincts, drives, wishes) through the psychosexual stages as a process where basic psychic phenomena (instincts, their vicissitudes, and defenses) undergo transformations of

---

[1]Increased ego capacities are narcissistically rewarding, and a continued interest in anality would bring about a trauma not only to the ego, in its capacity to progressively develop, but to the sense of narcissistic integrity that accompanies the ego's maturational achievements as well.

[2]These insights and choices are in response to (and in the service of) both the adaptive and the reality principles.

purpose and expression. These transformations are dependent on, and are governed by, stage-specific characteristics that are themselves a response to a combination of environmental circumstances and biologically predetermined factors. The underlying wishes, tensions, and conflicts may remain the same throughout all the psychosexual stages, but even where they do not they are rarely as changed as their derivatives. They continuously exert unceasing pressures for discharge and gratification, and it is this which moves us through the psychosexual developmental stages. As a consequence, our method of mental functioning progressively matures and becomes more adaptive over time.

The stage we are considering in this chapter is called the phallic stage rather than the genital stage for two reasons: (1) the genital, and its associated sexual physiology, is not yet fully developed, and thus the concept of a genital stage is more appropriate to adolescence when puberty prepares the individual for fully adult sexual functioning; and (2) children have a ubiquitous fantasy that the significant difference between boys and girls is merely the presence or absence of a penis. Children have only a vague and rather amorphous understanding of anatomy. This is true with regard to identification, location, and knowledge about their bodily parts – even their arms and legs – and this is most especially true with their internal organs. Thus it is not surprising that both empirical and clinical research have verified that when children become aware of the anatomical differences between the sexes their reactions include ways of trying to understand why boys have a penis and girls do not.[3]

The Power of Fantasy over Reality and Its Impact on Perception, Sensation, and Memory

The deflection of drives (and not only intellect, as one might expect) from anal interests to the genitals can serve to prevent the development of a clear comprehension regarding the nature of the genitalia. The intrusion of primitive or poorly transformed drive elements may readily prevent optimal use of the ego and its potential for intellectual and practical understanding. Interference with cognition may often be a consequence of unregulated drive intrusions in the functioning of the ego. Further interference with comprehension can be created when reaction formation (against anal-erotic pleasure) is directed to the phallus or, in the case of girls, to

---

[3]In the figure drawings of adults (which are often used for diagnostic purposes) one repeatedly encounters mistaken impressions about how the body is formed. In direct questioning many "healthy" and well-educated adults are unable to accurately describe the working principles of human physiology, anatomical placement, and the appearance of many internal organs. These "healthy" adults frequently are unable to describe the proper configuration of much of the external aspects of the human body of both their own, and the opposite, gender. Given the hazy and mistaken notions held by adults, we can more fully appreciate why 3- and 4-year-olds are unable to properly understand the differences between internal and external genitalia, and how they can mistake a vagina for an absence of a penis.

the entire genital area. When reaction formation is relatively global, it is easy to understand its impact on other ego functions. Sometimes reaction formation is applied to only a single part of a complicated situation where a multitude of variables superficially look very much alike and therefore seem to be indistinguishable; for example, as it applies to displaced anal libido which is superficially indistinguishable from phallic libido (as a result first of displacement and then of condensation). In this case, too, reaction formation will inevitably spill over into areas that are both indiscriminate and otherwise inappropriate. The ego's interest in, and capacity to comprehend, the true anatomy of the genitalia can be either relatively accurate or an intellectual "casualty" (depending, in part, on the extent of spillover of reaction formation into the cognitive area of mental functioning, and its effects on the individual's capacity to remain organized by secondary-process operations and the reality principle). Deficits of this type can often bring about inhibitions affecting ego functioning and in addition have an effect on selected drive configurations. Residual anal libido commonly causes cognitive interference in varying degrees to remain perpetually in effect because anal reaction formation is never completely successful. This is often the underlying problem in adult misconceptions of anatomy, physiology, and body-image inaccuracies. Numerous aspects of ego functioning may be, and often are, initially and then continuously affected. In the dynamics of primary-process functioning, if the primary objective or impulse cannot be effected, a secondary (frequently, not always related) objective or impulse may be substituted (although it may make no objectifiable sense, which is after all not a feature of primary-process but of secondary-process activity). An interference in becoming clearly informed about sexual anatomy can occur as a form of, or a substitute for, forbidden excitement and can, under the influence of reaction formation and other primary-process operations, begin in early childhood and continue throughout life. In addition, because primary-process operations are not based on reality, one can be informed, uninformed, and misinformed all at the very same time.

We have described the fulcrum of the phallic stage as being whether one does or does not have a penis. The preceding material explains much of why and how children focus so concretely and exclusively on the penis, and why and how children, and adults, may harbor the fantasy that girls are merely castrated/emasculated boys; they describe, and give a fair sense of, the quality and the mechanisms involved in such inaccurate and unreasonable assumptions and conclusions. These ideas, even though far-fetched, are part of the normal developmental sequence. We do not consider these ideas to be a sign of pathology in a child for a number of reasons, the two most important of which are their ubiquity, and the fact that we do not expect a 3- or 4-year-old child to have the ego strength (which includes the maturity of intellect necessary) to correctly and objectively evaluate such ideas. When we see these, or related, fantasies and ideas intact – or especially, predominating – in the mental functioning of an adult, it is of course a signal of psychopathology.

One of the most customary and relatively benign (although still pathological) mechanisms of this in adulthood is the conviction of essential superiority that some men feel, so that even in the best of their relationships a woman is implicitly and irrevocably inferior; and on the other side, an acceptance by some women of their innate "inferiority" to men. Some even less adaptive mechanisms include primitive feelings of contempt, humiliation, rage, arrogance, envy, and hatred held in concert with this idea, or the use of the concrete image of the penis itself, and its presence or absence, as a way of reflecting positive and negative, and favored and unfavored, aspects of being male or female. The self-satisfaction of men who are contemptuous of women, and who are convinced of the basic and intrinsic inferiority of women, is the male counterpart of penis envy in women.

Penis Envy

Thus far we have spoken about how, in the absence of accurate anatomical knowledge, the penis becomes such an important symbol that it characterizes a whole developmental era, but we have not yet addressed why it is the vehicle for values. That is to say, if we have adequately described how and why the penis is so emphasized, we must now discuss how it is that children conclude that having a penis is good and not having one is bad. One reason has already been hinted at in our discussion of toilet training. Loss of feces (which is the equivalent of losing irreplaceable body parts, and which is how the very young child views it) is an injury to one's narcissism that lowers self-esteem and traumatically disrupts related areas of the psyche: to have suffered the loss is bad and to have avoided the loss is good; to be damaged is bad and to be intact is good; to have a mother who did not protect one from this "destruction" of one's body is bad, and to have a successfully protective mother is good; more is better and less is worse. These infantile and archaic approaches reflect both oral and anal explanations (and preoccupations) and are only marginally influenced by reality testing, secondary-process functioning, and other sovereign ego attributes. This is in part because this is a traumatic and hurtful discovery (that one has been, or can be, castrated and emasculated). In times of stress a regression to this belief is frequently present (usually in children, and on occasion in primitive adults). Where children are concerned, this is compounded by the developmental limitations of the ego at that stage of life. However, there are also higher-order factors that contribute to this misconception. These are factors that reflect the superior status of men in our society, and these factors are also condensed into the "have/have not" configuration. In many ways children are exposed to situations where men are figures of authority and women are represented variously as passive, dependent, and simple-minded (for example, in a now defunct television show called *Father Knows Best;* in a commercial where successful housecleaning is accomplished not by the housecleaner, who is always a woman, but by "Mr. Clean"; in another commercial where the husband works, earns money, and has an impact on his environment while his wife is wholly concerned with "ring around the collar," since she is so superficial and incompetent that she couldn't even launder a shirt properly the first time around; policemen are seen as powerful models for emulation, whereas women police officers or women in the military are seen as misfits, or at the very least are thought of as strange; physicians, who give orders, are stereotypically male, and nurses, who take orders, are stereotypically female; and so on). There are other ways, too, in which males are privileged and women, conspicuously, are not (all-male clubs and bars, looser restrictions on impulses such as fighting and sexual behavior; deference to husbands and fathers as head of the house; more pay for the same job; less double-talk and exploitation from service personnel such as auto mechanics, waiters, and clerical staff; a greater number of administrative or managerial positions in government, where most senators, congresspersons, and cabinet members are male, too; whether one is required to act stupid, incompetent, helpless, or masochistic to be attractive to the opposite sex). From the time a child learns that there is a world that goes beyond the mother–child relationship, he finds an implicit depreciation of women in the background, and an explicit depreciation of women occupying the foreground. Initially the impact of this knowledge is superficial and at the beginning of this stage still mostly irrelevant because the child is almost entirely preoccupied with himself and his mother, and also because his mother's ability to meet virtually all his needs serves as a barrier to a wholesale depreciation of her. Over time the child's depreciation of women adds up, and it will eventually be used quite actively by children of both genders in their attempts to abandon, first in the anal and now in the phallic stage, their hypercathected oral links to their mother as an instinctually gratifying object. Another consideration involves the parents' unconscious and irrational attitudes about the penis, which are transmitted to the child and which then become unconsciously incorporated into the child's self-representations so that these very same views evolve into being his own. The residue of his parents' infantile attitudes, no matter how unconscious or how drastically their conscious attitudes differ, are in this way not just understood but incorporated into the personality of the child. There is often a close parallel between the primary process that dominates an infant's mental functioning and the primary process used in the generally unconscious and most archaic modes of mental functioning of an adult. Not uncommonly, it can be his parents' unrealistic prejudices and aggrandizements that are most accepted and are most tenaciously retained by the child. Additional factors in the idealization of males (and the penis) and in the denigration of females (as persons without a penis) will be further discussed in the context of the oedipal complex, the relationship of feminine masochism to female sexuality, and the fate of bisexual identifications in latency, which follows.

Differentiation, Separation, and Individuation in Relation to the Oedipal Conflict

The oedipal conflict pits a child against the same-gender parent, in competition for "possession" of the opposite-gender parent; boys compete with their fathers for their mothers, and girls compete with their mothers for their fathers. The term *possession* is used even though the conflict is phallic because the model for love is based on infantile, rather than mature, sexuality. Boys and girls employ many similar dynamics and go through substages of the conflict that bear a strong resemblance, but it is not true that boys and girls go through the oedipal complex in the same way, and in the same order, with only the genders reversed. After some brief comments on differentiation, separation, and individuation, which appear to be similar in both genders, first the oedipal conflict in boys will be presented and then the oedipal conflict in girls. The development of the superego (which is the third element of the structural metapsychological theory and which we have put off until now) will be discussed in this context, and in special detail in Chapter 5, because the structuralization process (as opposed to contents and functions that have been in existence all along but which have been uncoordinated with one another) occurs as a consequence of, and as a mode of resolving, the oedipal complex.

By the time toilet training is complete, the infant has fully made the transition to "toddlerhood," and his capacity for attending to the presence and the meaning of the world around him is greatly enhanced. As he gains in motility and he is able to get around more freely, he is also beginning the process of differentiating himself psychologically from his mother; the task of separation will be enhanced by successful differentiation and individuation. As the child is increasingly able to turn his interests and his activities, beyond the mother–child dyad, both he and his mother begin a gradual process of individuation, which is simultaneously satisfying and anxiety-provoking. It is satisfying for many obvious reasons: excitement and interest in new and changing things; greater mastery over his body and his impulses; enlarged opportunity for stimuli and, through them, for self-gratifications; increased self-esteem and a greater sense of security in response to developing self-reliance, and so forth. These advances may be minuscule when compared with the functioning of an adult but they are, in fact, radical changes when compared with the child's prior psychological state. Each step the child takes in the separation process, and each degree of relinquishment achieved by the mother, is a mixed event because it carries with it anxieties about abandonment. Ambivalence about separation from his mother is also high because individuation reduces primitive, narcissistically gratifying feelings of omnipotence. The child's maternal grandiose self-representations are decreased by his concrete and literal separation from his mother in this continuously progressing process. Furthermore, and playing directly into oedipal considerations, exploration of the world around him alerts the child to aspects of the family triad that were previously unacknowledged or unappreciated. As his mother gradually reindividuates from her child (the initial individuating having occurred in her own differentiation as a child) and reduces her narcissistic investment in him, much of the psychological energy in her attachment to her child (which was most intense in response to the total helplessness and dependency of her baby) can be redirected back to her husband (from whom, in part, it was originally deflected). As the child perceives this realignment in his mother's involvements, and as he becomes aware of the strengthening in his mother's affectional and dependency ties to his father, his cognizance of the family triad is increased and his feelings toward his father begin to shift; his father is no longer experienced as a loving and protective "auxiliary mother" but takes on the appearance instead of a depriving interloper. Thus far the sequence has not differed much for boys and girls, and for both genders a return to earlier forms of involvement with their mother is resisted (not altogether success-fully) because of the destructive elements that inevitably must accompany a whole-sale regression. Thus we see another reason for the development of a phallic, precociously sexual stage; the phallic stage permits the child an arena of interaction with his mother that is instinctually very intense without, except for temporary and mild regressions, necessitating a return to either the oral or the anal stage. Children are also aware of erotic components in the parental relationship, and even if the child is unable to know (or even imagine) the specifics, this also plays a part in the shaping of the specific arena in which wishes and conflicts will be expressed. We see once again the complexities of overdetermination in the emergence of a psychosexual stage in which conflict is centered on genital metaphors, allusions, illusions, and concerns.

The Oedipal Conflict in Boys

When the little boy experiences his father as a competitor, he feels a sense of indignant outrage. His mother has, for the most part, been entirely available to him, and he resents both the interference of his father and his mother's withdrawal from him. One withdrawal occurs in his imagination when he becomes aware of his mother's divided loyalties, and the other withdrawal actually occurs in reality in his mother's redirection of cathectic investment to her adult lover, in most cases the little boy's father. As is the case with most children when they are in situations that are frustrating and depriving, the boy's rage is total and uncompromising; if it were within his power, he would dispose of his father without the slightest qualm.[4] He responds to his father's "intrusion" with oral annihilatory rage compounded by anal sadistic rage. These rages are unbound by immediate stress and by the anticipation of future disappointments. Oral and anal rages are then joined to stage-specific (phallic) aggression, which is liberated by oedipal-complex anxiety and by his continuously enlarging feelings of competitiveness with his father. In this state of mind he assumes that his father is aware of all the destructive and murderous wishes in him that are surfacing. That his father is aware of all this seems not unreasonable to him because it is impossible to hide all these intentions and "hopes," and because

---

[4]This readiness to kill stems from a combination of rage, limited impulse control, and an unrealistic understanding of the nature and permanence of death. Similar considerations also apply, in varying degree, to the wish to injure and do harm. The father's reactions to this are discussed in detail in Chapter 5.

the "omniscient" parent (as all parents are in the eyes of young children) will be aware of even that which is not explicitly visible.[5] Children also assume that the world is made in their image, and knowing how unmanageable and punitively destructive his own aggression is at this time, the little boy expects that his father will automatically respond in kind.

Castration Anxiety

Because the phallus is hypercathected in this stage, the boy's primary-process operation links up murder and castration, and his fears take the form of castration anxiety; life and death are mere abstractions for a child in this stage. (Additional comments on the relationship between castration anxiety and the regulatory principles of mental functioning are presented in Chapter 5.) The child's secondary-process functioning, limited as it is but growing daily, makes it perfectly clear that a very young child, no matter how enraged, is no match for an enraged adult male. The boy takes for reality what he imagines his father is about to do, and this is terrifying (even if he kills his father ten thousand times over in a day in his fantasies). In fact, the boy's fantasies of waging a successful war against his father are double-edged. Each fantasy victory is exhilarating, which is why the little boy has them, but each fantasy also calls into play an additional fantasy of a devastating defeat at the hands of his father; the more you are successful in fantasy, the more frequently and ruthlessly you are destroyed.

Having (as he sees it) his back to the wall, the little boy tries to extricate himself from the inevitable – (1) loss of his mother, and (2) castration – through two operations. He attempts to reduce the level of his intense desire for his mother, and he tries to transform and thereby undo his father's retaliatory anger. His interest in his mother was based on his view of her as having everything good as either an integral part of herself, or as having everything good entirely at her disposal. Small narcissistic injuries have been mastered up until now, in part, by his feeling of being united with someone who was perfect. He reduces his attachments to her by changing his view of her, and he focuses on her lack of a penis as a sufficient cause for depreciation. If he finds her wanting (for lack of a penis, which has become a powerful symbol by this time), he is able, in the service of protecting himself (his penis) from his father, to reduce his wanting. If she is somewhat less desirable his interests are not so all-encompassing. By reducing the intensity of his wishes he can diminish his father's reactive impulses. A second approach is employed when he also attempts to transform what he understands to be his father's hostile intentions by offering himself up to the father as a love object. He presents himself as an alternate to his mother so that his father will direct loving feelings and erotic libido toward him instead of aggression. Normally, one does not destroy or damage love

---

[5]Children are often convinced that their parents can read their minds. In addition, they often cannot distinguish between what they imagine and wish, and what has happened or will happen.

objects. The motives for this go beyond the wish to transform danger, however, and are related, as well, to the wish to rob and murder his father. Children's imagery of sexual intercourse usually includes the conflicting ideas that it is highly pleasurable, that the father is attacking the mother, and that the interchange between his parents is the equivalent of the exchange of oral supplies (typical of the mother–child feeding situation). When he was an infant the little boy literally did incorporate his mother; what was physically part of her became a physical part of him; he assumes in the phallic stage that he can take his father's penis, and keep it internally as a part of himself, in precisely the same way as he did with mother in the oral stage. Both father and the penis are, in the little boy's fantasies, symbols of power (transferred from the anal stage). By stealing his father's penis he disarms his father and invalidates his threat; he increases his own destructive powers in fantasy, which he believes will aid him in disposing of his father; using the "more is better" principle he acquires a bigger and better organ (in primary-process terms, this symbolically stands for all pleasure); possessing his father's penis, he becomes less dependent on others (but not independent), including his depreciated mother, for the acquisition of gratification; and in addition, he now has what his mother found so attractive in his father.

The little boy depreciates his mother to make her less desirable and tempting, but it is important to remember that his depreciation of her is relative not to reality but to his original exaggerated and aggrandized view of her and her desirability (which is related but not the same thing). That the little boy finds means of giving up his mother does not mean that he no longer needs and wants her; she was, and will remain, his primary love object. What it means is that he tries to find ways to reduce the demand that she be totally available to him in all ways. On the other hand, it is also true that modifications in his insistence that he replace his father do not mean that he has abandoned hope entirely. It means that active oedipal demands give way, and the energy that was used in the struggle is freed to act on behalf of the ego in other, noninstinctualized, pursuits. Giving up his mother means the ruthless suppression of active oedipal wishes, but this does not imply abandonment of those wishes and abandonment of her as a primary love-object, nor does it diminish her role as the model for all his lovers in the future. In order to aid in the process of offering himself to his father as a love object, the little boy generates a libidinal interest in his father which enables him to value his father and what his father has; and which transforms somewhat the absolute wish to make it his own through stealing and murder. This serves to further delibidinize his "damaged" mother as it cuts into and lowers the level of aggression directed toward his father. When love juxtaposes, and then to a large extent cancels, hate and the wish to destroy, the threat of "retaliation" is markedly reduced. This is known as the passive-negative phase of the oedipal complex.[6] The continued maintenance of a passive-negative

---

[6]*Passive* means to take in, *active* means to enter or to penetrate, *positive* means heterosexual, and *negative* means homosexual in this use of the language of psychoanalysis.

oedipal stance is ultimately unacceptable to the little boy because (1) it involves a greater rejection of libidinal interaction with his mother than he is capable of at this time, and (2) this stance puts him in the role, vis-à-vis his father, of a girl. His father's love object is female, which will lead the boy to a change in gender identity in order to be his father's love object, which means the loss of his penis – which is, paradoxically, what he was trying to avoid in the first place. Being identified primarily with his mother, in primary-process terms, provides some interesting secondary gains; for example, it means that he will be able to have all her resources, internally, as part of himself. The outcome of his secondary-process reasoning, as an overlay to more powerful and influential primary-process functioning (which is, in addition, strongly stage-specific), insists, however, that more is lost than gained in a renunciation of the penis.

To summarize the above, and to lead us to the next step in the process, we can say that at the onset of the oedipal conflict the little boy was in a positive oedipal stance, which had both active and passive elements; when active aims began to predominate in response to his long-standing hypercathexis of his mother and his more recent hypercathexis of his penis, he found himself in conflict with his father; his solution was to move to a passive-negative oedipal position. This shift not fulfilling its promise, the little boy then becomes aware that he must seek other means of resolution in order to maintain narcissistic integrity (which in this stage is represented by intactness of the genital). In order to do this he must repress, suppress, inhibit, and transform his libidinal attachments even further. The major element in helping the little boy to manage his instinctual wishes is castration anxiety. Were it not for this, there would be no impetus for the regulation and transformation of his incestuous wishes. One may have the reaction (to the concept of castration anxiety) that it is a terrible thing for a child, or for an adult for that matter, to have to go through; and although it is true that the experiences of castration anxiety and for girls, penis envy, are most unpleasant, this is a good example of the point expressed earlier in this chapter, that without conflict there is no growth. Without castration anxiety to combat incestuous object choices, and without the mechanisms developed to cope with it, the situation might very well be that if little boys couldn't grow up to marry their mothers they wouldn't want to get married at all! In effect the little boy plays a waiting game; he uses a tactic learned in the anal stage as he resigns himself to coping with a delay in the gratification of his wishes. In order to do this he lowers the intensity of his incestuous wishes through balancing opposing drives, through the progressive transformation of drives, and through repression and other dissociative defenses. To have oedipal interests remain at their original level of demand would make the waiting, and the things one needs to learn while waiting, impossible. Some lowering of the intensity is also achieved through a strengthening of his pride in his penis and in his masculinity, and by overemphasizing this he is able to develop further rationales for depreciating his mother. Thus a support system develops that permits him to develop a greater level of dichotomy and ambivalence in his relationship with her.[7]

In normal circumstances the little boy now begins to identify with his father. This is an intense identification process, where the boy identifies with specific characteristics of his father as an individual, and with his father's masculinity in general. This process is actually in the service of oedipal goals while providing an opportunity to simultaneously push oedipal wishes out of sight. He attempts to weaken the demand for immediate oedipal gratification by substituting his father as a love object for his mother. He attempts in the relationship with his mother to introduce abstractions and mental images, in the form of limited identifications, in place of the demand for instinctualized gratifications that would occur in an incestuous oedipal liaison. He repeats earlier and more primitive attempts to acquire that which draws his mother to his father (the penis, in its symbolic representation of power and masculinity), except this time in a more psychologically and developmentally mature fashion, so that instead of an oral robbery (and an anal hoarding of the "spoils") he uses identification. If women are attracted by men, then he will grow up to be a man; and if his mother is attracted by both masculine and other more specific characteristics of his father, then he will grow up to be the kind of man his father is, *except more so*. In this effort his oedipal wishes will become dormant and will be a latently motivating force, as the little boy practices learning how to be a man and waits for the time when he can successfully challenge his father for his mother. And finally, by identifying with the aggressor (his father) he learns to fight fire with fire. If his father will emasculate him in the contest, he will wait until he has grown strong enough physically to use his father's very weapons and powers to castrate (or kill) him instead. By becoming even more like his father than his father is himself, the boy will be that much more attractive to his mother and that much more powerful than his father.[8]

The boy is not in a position to compete sexually for his mother, and so he abandons clearly oedipal aims for the present. However, it is not really possible for a child to abandon the major portion of his attachments to his mother, partly because he is still entirely (or almost entirely) dependent on her and partly because she has been the primary source of instinctual gratification throughout his whole life.

Even if he directs libidinal cathexis toward his father and toward playmates and

---

[7]Although not the only explanation, this is often at the root of sexism in adult males who treat women with hatred and contempt. They are unable to develop loving and sexual relationships with women because they have never been able to separate the woman they are with (and of course, all women who they may potentially be with) from the mental image of their mothers, who are the archetypes of all women.

[8]Such fantasies are repressed and suppressed as the child grows older, demonstrating one important purpose in the development of infantile amnesia. Young children in the midst of this process, however, frequently express such wishes and intentions quite openly.

other significant others, his mother still remains his primary love object. He manages to keep his attachments intact throughout this period by desexualizing them. He transforms the love that led to the wish to instinctually possess his mother into a love that has the essential quality of nonsexualized enduring affection. The transformation of instinctual aims into conscious feelings of affection and love permits the maintenance of a noneroticized libidinal relationship at a sufficient distance so that reality and fantasy interactions with her will not degenerate into the deadly competition he just avoided.

From this point on virtually all identifications with his mother will be much more complex than previously. Some early identifications may have to be abandoned or renounced, and others that might have occurred may have instead to be avoided, because of the "dangers" inherent in wholesale identifications with a woman (which in the little boy's mind leads to castration). The whole process of identification itself also must become more dependent on abstract, rather than concrete, qualities so as to avoid internal (as well as external) conditions that would be too instinctually stimulating. Both the motives and the basis for identifying begin to take on a new character. Previously, identification was based on instinctual gratification (it was an attempt to merge with, and thus have possession and control of, an instinctually gratifying object or experience), and the maintenance of an identification was directly dependent on the continuance of gratification. Now a new class of identifications is developed, called *introjects,* that are specifically designed to separate the prior connections between aim (oedipal) and object (mother) while maintaining the merged mental representations intact. Introjects are more stable than the preoedipal forms of identifications since as they are not developed in the direct matrix of instinctual gratifications they are not abandoned when instinctual gratifications cease (which is the opposite of the case with incorporative and imitative identifications). Many archaic identifications with mother are transformed into introjects, and future introjective identification is freely possible as long as they are not feminized. In this way the boy does not have to entirely give up his mother. Instead of killing his father and marrying his mother, he can have his mother for the rest of his life by carrying her inside him, and as part of himself, through introjection. Although the mechanisms of incorporation and introjection are designed to achieve the same goals (merger, control, possession, and so on), their development, operation, and qualities of endurance are intimately related to their attachment to, or separation from, directly instinctual aims.

These principles are also in operation concerning the boy's relationship with his father, except in the case of his father the operation lies in an even more delicate balance. The boy must separate his instinctual wishes from his relationship with his father in order to have the wish to identify replace the wish to kill and rob. As mentioned earlier, the boy substitutes his father as a love object for his mother in order to reduce some of his instinctual ties to her, but if the substitution is too directly linked to libido (and therefore his relation to his father is frankly erotic) he is once again in the position of a woman, and therefore vulnerable to castration. If his identification with his father remains too closely tied to the wish to rob and murder him, it will not be possible to relate to him as a love object. If it remains too concretely the case that the only point of identifying is to kill the competition, then each successful operation of identifying would raise traumatic revitalizations of the oedipal wish. Introjection is a mechanism that solves the circularity of this process by rendering free the instinctualized component so that admiration can replace hatred, and so that the process of identification does not carry within it the seeds of trauma. The section on the superego, which is the "heir" to the oedipal complex, will elaborate different aspects of the superego more fully.

The Oedipal Conflict in Girls

It is now time to focus on girls and follow their passage through the oedipal complex. The little girl suffers the same narcissistic insult as does the little boy when she is confronted with the reality of the family triad and its implications. However, she has in addition the extra narcissistic injury of being a girl; a narcissistic injury in the sense that being a girl is the equivalent, in the mental functioning of young children, of having been castrated. Turning her interests toward her father serves a variety of purposes for a little girl. One aspect of this is that it enables her to have an alternate love object that will help her at some levels to break, and at other levels to modify, many of her infantile ties to her mother. Most maternal ties are still enormously seductive, and the little girl's "abandonment" of her original love object occurs only in the most relative terms. The maternal instinctual connection is more difficult for a girl to break than for a boy because (1) a girl can identify both openly and concretely with her mother; and, (2) she is not motivated, by the same degree of castration anxiety, to degrade her mother (in order to resist the very identificatory merger with her mother that would, because of castration anxiety, be intolerable for an ordinary boy). Girls are not actively subject to castration anxiety (which does not mean they have no conflicts or other anxieties), so that identifying with women is not potentially, or inevitably, self-destructive. In identifying with her mother the little girl has a problem in that incorporation and imitation, which are oral stage--specific mechanisms, are the primary, if not exclusive, models of identification. This becomes a problem because without more mature mechanisms available to her the little girl is subject to a tendency to regress when she identifies with her mother. She must develop some complicated mechanisms to balance the need to identify and the tendency to regress.

One measure involves the use of her fantasy that she is a castrated boy, and therefore inferior. When she develops the conviction that her mother also suffers from this "handicap" she finds herself able to modify some of her prior assumptions about her mother (as being the reservoir of everything good and thus the agent of all gratification). This serves the little girl's wish to experience her mother as a bit less attractive and therefore less compelling. The little girl uses penis envy for a healthy and progressive purpose; she uses this as a form of leverage that can enable her to continue to identify with her mother while controlling the speed and depth of a regressive momentum. One can find many examples of infantile mental functioning that are highly pathological and grossly inappropriate when seen in an adult; and conversely, others like this, which are inaccurate and indeed barely related to reality, but nonetheless beneficial and ofttimes necessary in the mental functioning of children. The little girl's attachments and idealizations of her mother are tempered with devaluations and ambivalence resting squarely on infantile beliefs about women really being castrated men, and this acts in concert with a heightened appraisal of her father who, by virtue of his penis, has all that is ultimately good (and presently unobtainable for the little girl). Despite the narcissistic injury inherent in penis envy for girls, they cleave to it dearly in this special stage of their development as the main tool to combat the seductiveness of regressive inclinations when they identify with their mothers. Some retaliatory impulses are generated by her mother in response to the little girl's devaluation of her and the child's partial withdrawal; some competitive and aggressive inclinations arise in her mother in response to the little girl's oedipal dynamics. These reactions create a complex problem in identification. Putting aside for the moment the question of regression (which will be considered directly), the little girl cannot engage in a fully encompassing identification with her mother without also including her mother's aggression toward her. The young girl's growing ego will use anything, including this conflict, that helps her to discriminate between, and moderate, the complicated nature of her identifications with her mother. The girl's conflicts and reservations about the contents and nature of her identifications serves the goal of reducing or eliminating self-destructive components, and this feature of the process will also help to make actively positive and beneficial identifications with her mother more conflict free.

Some of the little girl's interest in her father is designed to diminish some of the regressive potential in maternal identifications, but it also has additional goals beyond the direct regulation of both regressive potential and the specific contents of maternal identifications. In part, the little girl's interest in her father is reminiscent of the little boy's interest in him. She too wants to acquire from her father the key features and attributes that make him attractive to her mother. If she believes that she has what she imagines her father has, she will be able to compete successfully; she will be able to reverse the traumatic recognition of the triadic family relationship and to restore a dyad that excludes all but herself from the investments of her mother. Moving away, for the moment, from the expression of aggressive aims to examine more carefully the gratification of libidinal wishes, there is also a positive goal in the little girl's interest in her father. The child imagines adult sexual love to be, as has been mentioned previously, an activity that most closely approximates the exchange of oral-libidinal supplies that occurs in the feeding process between mother and infant. She nurtures the belief that her father's penis is somehow shared, or co-owned, by her mother as a result of sexual intercourse, and in a primitive fellatio-fantasy she imagines that she can undo the "feminine insult" to her narcissism by swallowing (through mouth), incorporating (through vagina), and by withholding (in the archaic imago of the fecal column) her father's penis. Possession of a penis will elevate her to a privileged status. Beyond repairing the initial rent in the fabric of her narcissism, "possessing" a penis will make her eligible for numerous fantasied gratifications and for the continued expansion of her narcissism (based, in primary-process terms, on uninterrupted fantasy about total "masculine" satisfaction). The very inability of the girl, who is after all only a little child, to accurately assess the value of a penis and her infantile desire for (and emotional attachment to) the penis per se, contributes to progressively greater aggrandizements and thus the establishment of even more intense hypercathexes of the penis itself as if, once having one, all her problems will be solved.

An additional reason for the little girl's interest in her father's penis is genetic predispositions that everyone of all ages has, which ultimately – that is, in appropriate stage-specific ways – includes a predetermined readiness to engage in procreative functioning. In her oedipal relationship with both her parents the little girl has major advantages over the little boy in that (1) she is not competing with the more dangerous parent; and (2) she is biologically and culturally adapted to offer herself as a love object to the more dangerous parent. The girl's oedipal competition with her mother is greatly qualified by the fact that throughout the girl's entire life her mother has been, and still currently is, a consistent source of pleasure and gratification. For both genders, mother is a figure of greater ambivalence than is father, and therefore she is a much less dangerous enemy. The girl has everything to gain and little to lose in her relationship with her father, who is an enemy in an abstracted and far-removed way after having been "neutralized" by his daughter's seduction. What is seriously less to her advantage as compared with boys, and which is a direct result of having neutralized the dangerous (castrating/mutilating) potential of her father, is the less structuralized (not synonymous with inferior) nature of her superego development (more will be said in Chapter 5 about the different, but not less adequate, superego of females).

Female Sexuality and Feminine Masochism

An immediate difficulty encountered by the little girl when her sexual interest in her father heightens is the need for a shift in sexual orientation; her task is to move away from an *active* to a decidedly *passive* sexual posture. These are terms that have special meanings in the technical language of psychoanalysis. The shift from an active to a passive sexual orientation is often at the root of some significant differences in female sexual functioning that are often incomprehensible to males. A question is also raised as to whether it is possible for each of two anatomically and physiologically distinct groups to fully and properly comprehend one another. These issues are compounded by the critical fact that boys actively resist building empathy with girls, because empathy is based on identification. This consideration means that men are specifically motivated not to understand much of the sexual, and other, experiences of women.

Up until the time the little girl shifts her sexual interests to her father, her masturbation has been predominantly clitoral rather than vaginal. There is no absolute distinction between clitoris and vagina, and so one would not wish to advance the argument that clitoral masturbation precludes, and is totally separate from, vaginal sensation. This does not change the fact, however, that the primary sexual and psychological orientation of the preoedipal girl was markedly clitoral. Children, even female children who are most affected by it, have little or no understanding of the internal anatomy of the female sexual organs. For all practical purposes the little girl is limited to conceptualizations that are dependent on the examination of that which is externally visible and subject to superficial manipulation. Little girls frequently try to make up for not having a penis by treating the clitoris as if it were a penis; this is reflected in commonly expressed fantasies that describe the clitoris as a little penis, a vestigial penis, and a budding penis. The clitoris also carries a strong hypercathexis for physiological reasons as well. It is richly supplied with nerves (as is the penis) and serves as an exquisite pathway for both discharge and gratification.

It is particularly difficult, given the intense satisfactions of the clitoris, for the girl to shift major cathexis away from the clitoris and to reinvest cathexis in the vagina. Many alternating shifts will occur in the mastery of that goal.[9] The little girl has had, relative to her clitoris, comparatively little concrete and positive experience with her vagina precisely because it has been a less readily accessible and understood organ. If the vagina was as entirely accessible as the clitoris and it served the girl equally well in discharging tension, acquiring pleasure, and undoing severe narcissistic injuries, it would be no great feat for her to reduce (not abandon) her clitoral investment in favor of a greater (not exclusive) vaginal investment. This shift is an impressive feat for a little girl, and the "vaginal reinvestment" is remarkable not only because it trades on her primitive capacity to delay the gratification of powerful wishes and impulses (which will shortly be discussed), but also because it reflects an acknowledgment that she is in fact a girl. This indicates a genuine (if not total) renunciation of the fantasy that she has a hidden or an unacknowledged penis. To achieve the shift in investment from the clitoris to the vagina the girl relies, in large part, on her understanding of the differences between the assumption of a gratification which will be, quite concretely, advantageous in the long run, and on the other hand the *renunciation forever* of her wish. The successful shift to the realm of passive (accepting penetration) vaginal investments is what ultimately makes it possible for

---

[9]The alternating shifts between the clitoris and the vagina are akin to the alternating shifting and rubbing of both masturbation and intercourse. In addition, the investment of cathexis *in* the vagina has its parallels too in the envelopment of the penis in the vagina (and in the potential for the restoration of damaged narcissism they both can achieve). These primary-process gratifications aid in the achievement of this goal even though they operate on a purely unconscious level.

women to experience penile penetration (in fantasy for the little girl, and in reality for the woman) as a positive and pleasurable event. If women maintained their attachments to an active (penetrating) stance in which they remained deeply involved in the external, self-accessible, and self-stimulating clitoris, they would not be able to accept pleasure from penetration nor would they be as directed toward the use of a partner in the acquisition of pleasure; in that case, they would experience penetration as a "castration" (for little girls at the initiation of their fathers) much in the way a little boy does when he is in a passive-negative oedipal phase.

The little girl does not have the ability to identify with her father as freely as does the little boy because she cannot fall back upon the anatomical similarities the boy shares with his father. She must face the evidence of her genital if she is to pursue a course toward its restitution, for only with a vagina will she be able to incorporate her father's penis and make it her own. The pathway of oral incorporation poses too great a threat of regression so the little girl must rely on a form of "self-castration" to engage in the only progressive incorporation at her disposal. The only progressive incorporation is the current stage-specific one, which is in this case the biologically predetermined genital incorporation. In effect the little girl places her trust in the hope that what she will get will be worth more than what she is giving up; a skill developed just previously in the anal stage during toilet training. If we consider that the only reality basis for her expectation that she will be gratified is the primary-process recollection of merger during feeding, if we recall that her father has never been the primary model of libidinal gratification, and if we attend to the irrational psychological enormity of what she is giving up, it is clear what a difficult task she faces. Certainly we can argue that genetic and biological factors make the reorganization of aims and their pathways inevitable, and that this *inevitability* facilitates the process by virtue of there being a clear biological imperative at work. However, it is also true that the psychological factors that accompany the shift, from an almost total cathexis of the clitoris to a feminine stance in which the vagina also becomes highly cathected, are more complex than the anatomical dictates of gender.

The girl's willingness to *renounce* in the phallic stage, as an outgrowth of her psychological readiness to delay and renounce (as learned in the anal stage) pleasure, status, privilege, and narcissistic intactness (in order to be accessible to her father's penis), has been central in the psychoanalytic formulation that there is a powerful strain of masochism in the makeup of the feminine personality. It must be emphasized, however, that "feminine masochism" is not the equivalent of sexual masochism. Feminine masochism should not be confused with the pathological masochism to be found in persons who thrive on "hurt me, it feels so good." It is an adaptive posture that permits girls to make constructive approaches to the inaccuracies of childhood fantasy-life, and therefore should not be viewed simply as something negative. Despite the fact that it does have some negative features, feminine masochism is not pathological and should not be considered to be a form of self-hatred. The layman uses the term *masochism* in the ordinary way, which is limited essentially to pathological manifestations, and therefore the layman attaches to this concept a negative value judgment that serves normative goals. For our purposes one wishes to avoid such value judgments, which tend primarily to interfere with descriptive clarity.

Another element in the development of feminine masochism is the reevaluation which the girl must make in her understanding of the sexual act itself. She must convert her infantile impression of coitus (as an attack made by her father on her mother) to an event where the pleasure and gains experienced by a woman in intercourse are either worth the "attack" or are isolated (mentally) from the "attack." In the development of feminine masochism, and most particularly in the former case, this means that she is transforming what was once understood to be an attack into the very agent of pleasure itself. This particular aspect of female sexuality/masochism is the one that is most susceptible to degeneration into erotic masochism in adulthood; however, it is a clear demonstration (in nonpathological terms) of the resiliency and healthy adaptiveness of the little girl's developing ego in a stressful situation that has the clear potential to be continuously and repetitively traumatic.

The healthy aspect of feminine masochism aids women to transform adversity so that situations that originated in unfavorable or harmful contexts can be at least tolerated, and at best, turned to their advantage. Before the advent of the women's movement, men were expected to hold doors open for women, and women were expected to wait until doors were held for them before they went through. The practice of holding doors for women started as a way of making women passive (in English this time, not "psychoanalese"), helpless, and dependent on men. The original intention to hierarchically demean women was, for many years, obscured by history and by the transformation of this into a mark of respect rather than disdain. Experiencing having a door held open for one as something positive is a way of making the experience less damaging to one's self-esteem even though the original intention, albeit unconscious, was to demonstrate the inferior status of the female gender. As the relatively recent women's movement has addressed itself to the true purpose behind this and other similarly disguised hostile practices, as it has stressed the ingrained attachment of both men and women to a broad range of gender-related inequities, and as it has heightened growing dissatisfaction with numerous tacit and implicit derogations of women, one can point to a reduction of this specific activity (doorholding) and one can see in a portion of the population other such attitudes and activities occurring with decreasing frequency (particularly among relatively well-educated young people in liberal urban settings who have grown up in the midst of this social revolution). But for generations in Western culture, women were offended if a door was *not* held open for them, and this was not a way of asking to be treated badly; quite the opposite of its original meaning, it has been transformed into a way of asking to be treated well. Having a door held for women was (and, in the majority of the population, still is) a way for men to say "I see you as feminine and I acknowledge this through my ritual behavior." To *not* hold a door came to be an offense and an insult. It is only recently, and by no means universally true even now, that not holding a door for a woman has come to signify a statement by men of their acceptance of women's equality.

The capacity to come to terms with a situation that one cannot change is a healthy development in personality. To give up and to resign oneself to a situation that one actually *has* a hope of changing is certainly pathological. To transform, where possible, the passive acceptance of a bad situation into a form of genuinely active participation that diminishes both covert and overt undesirable characteristics in the situation is a sign of growth and adaptation. Prior to the impact of the women's movement, when political, social, and economic factors conspired unrelentingly against women, their ability to take pride and pleasure in the "deference" of men demonstrated a healthy derivative of feminine masochism.

Healthy derivatives of feminine masochism are sometimes in conflict with the economic/political/social goals of the feminist movement; the point at which healthy derivatives of feminine masochism degenerate into moral masochism (pathological masochism of a nonsexual nature) is extremely complex. Over time, feminine masochism may fluctuate between pathological and nonpathological manifestations, and between adaptive and maladaptive functioning, but the question of where psychology leaves off and politics begins is not always clear. For example, is a seemingly happy housewife really a hidden, deluded masochist? Is an unending struggle against genuinely unfair situations a compulsion, a masochistic search for frustration, or a sign of health? Is adaptation (even through acquiescence) to an inequitable situation always a pathologically masochistic solution? Is depression, which is so much more prevalent in women than in men, a characterological inevitability for women as a class because of (generically) feminine masochism, or would the statistics change if women as a class were less "oppressed" in economic/political/social areas? Are male psychoanalysts harming female patients if they discover in them signs of feminine masochism (as distinguished from non-gender-related masochism); and, having found what they take to be evidence of feminine masochism, do they foist on their women patients an injustice if they point out to them how feminine masochism has worked *for* them, as well as against them? Can male therapists (because they are part of the "system") ever help female patients resolve pathological characteristics of feminine masochism, or must they inevitably worsen their women patients' problems? Is the opposite true for female therapists? Will purely economic/political/social change bring about changes in conscious and unconscious attitudes, and changes in the contents of unconscious fantasy? These and other questions too numerous to list here are often matters of debate between psychologists and sociologists, and between feminists and psychoanalysts; this is debated hotly within some differing orientations in psychoanalysis as well (Freudians vs. interpersonalists, existentialists, Frommians, Horneyans, and so on). In a similar fashion some feminists, some sociologists, and some psychoanalysts of differing orientations take issue with another phenomenon discussed by Freudians which is closely related to feminine masochism: that is, penis envy. Their views are often that Freudians wish to inculcate penis envy in their female patients; the Freudian view differs in that they see penis envy as an ubiquitous infantile fantasy in women which needs resolution through analysis when it interferes or predominates in the functioning of an adult. One must wonder whether these divers and sundry views can ever be reconciled, and if so, how?

The impact of the women's movement has already changed some of the vehicles for the expression of both feminine masochism and penis envy. Remembering that the development of feminine masochism and penis envy occurs at an extremely early time in life when reality is profoundly influenced by fantasy, one may express some serious and considerable doubt about the extent to which even radical changes in the general economic/political/social status of women will be able to diminish the primary-process factors that lead to feminine masochism and to penis envy, and which are so intrinsic to oedipal development in little girls. Spectacular and revolutionary changes in feminine psychology due to the impact of a political shift seems somewhat unlikely if one keeps in mind the stage of life in which feminine masochism and penis envy are fixed in place, and the multiple roles that feminine masochism and penis envy play in the general development of feminine mental functioning. This assertion is based on a concept of mental functioning that is analogous to the way that primitive mental representations of one's parents are often as influential as, and frequently even more influential than, their adult counterparts. This does not suggest that men and women will be unaffected by the influence of social change, nor does it suggest that social change is worthless or that it should not be taken seriously. Its value will probably be most apparent, however, in the arena of mental functioning that is allotted to the ego and to secondary-process functioning. Despite its very real limitations it is, after all, this realm of mental functioning that frees us somewhat from the total tyranny of archaic, primitive, and infantile mental operations. This realm of mental functioning, in contact with the intended purposes of social change, strengthens our ability to lead our lives more in conformity with what we consciously believe to be right, even if we need to continue to struggle against the influence of what we believe unconsciously.

The macho concept of fighting to the bitter end, despite overwhelming odds and often a guaranteed negative outcome, is understandable (as a primary-process resistance to castration, in unconscious fantasy) but destructive in the male psyche because it interferes with the ability to engage in realistic processes of adjustment. These considerations, for both men and women, illustrate the value of abandoning the negative value judgments that are usually associated with the concept of masochism, and they reinforce further the usefulness of separating the generic concept of feminine masochism from the more specifically pathological concepts of sexual and moral masochism.

Another consequence of the shift in cathexis away from the external clitoris (which can be examined, evaluated, and stored in memory) to the vagina (which is internal, not available for as thorough an examination, and which is hazy and poorly defined as a mental image) is an increased quality of generalization regarding sexual feelings and sensations. The girl cathects her insides nonspecifically because she has no accurate understanding of where her vagina begins and ends. Although the clitoris has retained a powerful cathexis, and even though much cathexis remains in the genital area, a considerable cathexis is extended across a wide internal area. This internal/external genital cathexis is bounded only by the child's mental image of her internal anatomy. The nonspecific and relatively undifferentiated genital imagery of the little girl extends cathexis further than to just her insides, and she also cathects the skin surface of her body since, via the vagina, the outside of the body is intimately related to the inside. Thus girls develop an ability to have a wider range of body sensation in sexuality as adults than do boys. If the clitoris remained invested with the major portion of erotic cathexis, girls would have sexual sensations in a manner similar to boys, for whom other parts of the body have very mild erotic potential and the vast majority of erotic sensation is localized specifically in the genital itself.

Because of the boy's need to separate erotic objects and love objects (which will be elaborated on in the discussion of superego development in the next chapter), and because sexual sensation itself is isolated in the penis and away from the rest of the body (not totally, but very considerably), the boy can too easily split off parts of a woman which he then uses to represent for him the complete woman (as in being a "leg man"). In becoming a man, the boy will have to learn to do that which comes more readily to women, who can integrate their feelings, sensations, and ideas. Women and girls can comfortably develop and maintain an integrated mental image of their erotic love objects. This development in little girls is of extreme importance in the difference between male and female attitudes to romantic attraction. Whereas boys are usually first attracted to a girl for sexual reasons, girls are usually first attracted to boys for emotional reasons. Men may, of course, be initially attracted to women emotionally, but it is generally true that their level of emotional involvement makes its greatest increases in the context of an intense genital sexuality. Women may be initially attracted to men sexually, but it is generally true that their level of sexual intensification makes its greatest increases in the context of an emotional investment.

In the next chapter, on the dissolution of the Oedipus complex and the development of the structuralized superego, the capacity for integration of sexual and loving feelings will be discussed. This essentially feminine capacity in the latency period is also critical in the girl's oedipal attraction to her father, since the lines between what is good (love) and what is bad (sex) can be, and usually are, blurred. If there is no essential difference between love and sex there is no question but that the girl's oedipal wishes are legitimized, for who would suggest that a daughter should not love her father? And in this, we see again the complex multipurposed properties of mental dynamics; the integration is a natural form of sexual evolution which permits the little girl to maintain a conscious love for her father that includes a powerful sexual component hidden in unconsciousness while at the same time freeing her from superego attacks that would occur if her interest in her father were solely or primarily erotic. It also removes the explicit sexuality from her relationship to her father that could, if it was too apparent, draw competitive and punitive retaliatory actions from her mother.

5

The Dissolution
of the Oedipus Complex

The Superego in Boys

For boys, the dissolution of the Oedipus complex is achieved because of the pressures of castration anxiety. However, the vicissitudes of a boy's relationship with his father are not composed only of variations on the theme of aggression and fears. They include, as well, much reciprocal love and affection, which will ultimately become stabilized in the *structuralized* superego. This fact notwithstanding, the menace of emasculation does tend to be the prevailing influence on the Oedipus complex in the end-phase of the phallic stage. Despite the unsettling intensity of both his conscious and unconscious fears and the paradox this seems to create, the little boy actively seizes, nonetheless, on any available reality confirmations of his expectation of harm. If need be, he will create "proofs" in reality which are in conformity with his inner needs. Castration anxiety is not simply an unwelcome fear. It is also—and this can not be emphasized strongly enough—that castration anxiety is an inner need to which the boy is strongly attached. This is because only the looming fear of castration is strong enough to weaken the understandably immense power of a boy's incestuous ties to his mother.[1] His conviction that he is imminently in danger of genital mutilation ultimately forces him to abandon the phallic stage and drives him into latency, where he will learn to modify and transform his object instinctual striving.[2]

Although castration, in primary-process terms, stands for death as well as damage, the concept of death for a child of this age is abstract, poorly defined, and unrealistic. Of more importance is the loss of the penis and what that implies. Castration would deprive the boy of his ability to regulate mental functioning according to the pleasure and constancy principles. On the most obvious level,

---

[1] And this is then joined by identification with the father, used for the purpose of defense.

[2] Having discussed the concept of death as an abstraction for children at this age, I would like to be quite direct in stating that loss of the penis is *not* an abstraction: it is a concrete and highly specific fear. It is also, on another level, the way in which death (as something horrible) is experienced.

castration removes the most effective stage-specific pathway for actively acquiring or achieving instinctual pleasure. In global primary-process considerations, the pleasure principle gives way to the significantly less satisfying operation of negative hallucination, which operates in the service of the unpleasure principle. This means, subjectively, that the active search for and acquisition of pleasure would be replaced, after castration, by nothing more than the avoidance of unpleasure. In addition to its role as an organ of pleasure, the penis also serves the purpose of being the most effective stage-specific pathway (followed closely by motility) for the discharge of psychic tension.[3] This fantasy of castration seriously undermines the little boy's limited, and at this stage still fragile, defenses against the disruptions in psychic functioning that occur as a result of undesirable quantities of mounting tension. One also wishes to keep in mind that mounting uncontrollable tension is subjectively experienced as the most terrible and painful form of anxiety. This factor lends itself most readily to the child's overwhelming (albeit unrealistic) dread of castration. This fantasized narcissistic injury is compounded by the belief that once castration has occurred it can never be undone, as is demonstrated so graphically by his mother and other adult women. The little boy, after having learned to delay the immediate gratification of wishes in the anal stage, attempts to avoid castration by reducing his most intense incestuous attachments to his mother, believing that they can be more successfully reinstituted at a later time. He expects that he can also diminish his aggressive wishes toward his father at the same time and have them, too, return more successfully upon demand when he is bigger and stronger (two hidden expectations that make latency tolerable). The little boy postpones the struggle with his father indefinitely because he knows that once he is castrated, as he must be by his more powerful competitor, he has lost his genital forever. These considerations, individually and when combined, illustrate once again the major role played by the regulatory principles of mental functioning (in this case the pleasure, unpleasure, and constancy principles) in all the psychosexual developmental stages. Having added to how the little boy was forced into latency by castration anxiety, the stage is set for an examination of some further factors in the process of superego structuralization. This realm of investigation is concerned with how the superego and its structuralization, above and beyond castration anxiety, facilitates movement from the phallic stage into latency, and with how factors that obtain during latency participate in the yet further structuralization of the superego. We have, thus far, discussed factors that push the boy into preparation for structuralizing the superego, and having differentiated between the groundwork for structuralization and structuralization itself, we may now examine the process by which the actual structuralization of the superego itself takes place.

The process of introjection is the primary structuralizing event of the superego. The superego is commonly thought of by the layperson as the conscience, and it is,

---

[3]Although the discharge of psychic tension is often pleasurable, pleasure and discharge should not be thought of as synonymous.

indeed, the mental agency in which morals, ethics, and other psychological and behavioral strictures are to be found. But the superego has some other even more basic attributes (that are less well known) upon which moral judgments rest, and which are in fact considerably more central in mental functioning. All our identifications exist in the superego with the exception of a single class of identifications specifically known as *ego identifications*.[4] Moral and ethical attitudes are artifacts of object representations which reside in the superego. Those object representations, as mental phenomena, are themselves based on attributes of objects in reality, in combination with reality distortions determined by one's inner needs.

If one child does not hit another child because he knows that the other child will strike him back, he is making use of a variety of well-functioning ego strengths. Such a mode of controlling impulses would not correctly be attributed to the influence of the superego. When he wants to hit the other child but does not do so *because his mother will punish him* if he misbehaves, he is displaying what has variously been referred to as *maternal superego, external superego, sphincter-morality, nascent superego, function of the superego, preoedipal superego,* or *precursor to the superego.* What one means by these terms is that there is a particular way in which the child's internal object representation of his mother (and/or his father, but more usually his mother) is strong enough to exert an influence on his behavior even when his mother herself is not present. However, the maternal representation is effective only because there is an active threat of instinctual deprivation (no candy, no cuddling, and so on) and/or an active threat of instinctual overstimulation (spanking, restraint, being yelled at). In this case internal restraints exist in direct relation to the realistic possibilities involved in external behavioral actions by his mother that regulate, or are in an active relation to, the child's instinct-life. If the *actual presence* of the mother and *her responses* were withdrawn as a realistic consideration, her internal representation in the child would not, at this stage, be sufficient to restrain his aggression in the hypothetical situation described above. These are early superego contents and functions that are not abandoned but used and transformed in the ultimate formation of the structuralized superego (when the necessity of developing an identificatory reservoir based on the process of introjection mobilizes its unique organization). After the superego becomes structuralized one refrains from hitting others (in ordinary circumstances) because the casual use of violence is wrong, not because one will be harmed or punished. Although possible harm, deprivation, and punishment are important considerations, one chooses not to behave badly because one has internalized and made one's own the prohibition against random and impulsive

---

[4]In general, ego identifications are accurate self-descriptions (such as: I am obese because I am 5 feet tall and weigh 300 pounds; or, I am socially adept because I mix easily and most people seem to like me; or they are accurate memories that one has of the attributes of others. In this latter case one has an internal object representation of the person, which—as is always the case in memory—serves as the matrix from which the recollection is drawn. All other identifications are contained by the superego, although superego identifications, like most all of the other attributes of mental functioning, are often at the disposal of the other psychic structures as well.

violence once structuralization of the superego has been accomplished. Thus one can see a progressive sequence of development in the structuralization of superego organization that moves from the direct intervention of a parent to the use of an object representation, and from that, a further transformation into a moral principle. This can be conceptualized in the following way: one walks around with internalized aspects of one's parents within the main body of the superego, and those parental introjects (which are substitutive love objects, that is, the internalized parents whom one can now love and forever retain as love objects because the object relation is no longer incestuously determined) can cause one emotional pain (through guilt and the loss of love rather than through punishment) when one does not live up to one's (their) principles. On the other hand it is also those very same parental introjects, to anthropomorphize for a moment for heuristic purposes, who reward one (through heightened self-esteem and an unimpeded flow of love) when one is in compliance with one's (their) internalized values. Based on this imagery, Roy Schafer (in his classic 1960 paper) described this quality of self-qua-parental interaction as the "loving and beloved" superego. It is almost as if the superego is "the parent" and the ego is "the self." The superego/"parent" rewards the ego/"self" when moral principles have been upheld (and does the opposite when they have not), and it then directs the ego to create a sense of well-being, a sense of narcissistic expansion, an increase in self-esteem, and feelings of happiness and pleasure.[5]

Developmentally, the superego is a precipitate of the ego. It develops from ego functions that inform us about the world and its animate and inanimate objects. The development of the superego is based first on perception and then on internalization of external realities.[6] Because the ego plays such a critical role in the development of the superego, the superego's contents and functions may be extremely unrealistic and highly pathological in many other ways if perceptions are inaccurate, or if there is a fault in the ego's capacity to process internal and external material adaptively. A different problem can emerge if the functions of the ego are subverted and then placed at the service of the superego. Subversion of the ego is one result, but not necessarily the only one, when the ego is unable to realistically mediate the demands of the superego.

The following examples illustrate the shape this problem may take. If the superego demands a harsh retribution for a small breach of morals (suppose the

---

[5]It is a common misconception, which cannot be overemphasized, that the superego creates guilt. The superego has no capacity for creating feelings and ideas. The superego directs the ego to subjectively cause the experience of feelings and ideas. Only the ego can place affect and cognition into operation, consciously and in the unconscious. When one is not in compliance with one's moral and ethical standards, for example, the superego (like an angry and punishing parent) interacts with the ego (which is treated by the superego as if it is the totality of one's sense of oneself). It is the ego that is directed, without restraint, to create self-punitive ideas and which is directed to generate feelings of guilt and anxiety.

[6]Also on specific dynamic factors which differ from person to person; for example, the degree of rage directed at the father, which then affects both perception and instinctualization as well as the strength of the superego.

grocer gives one too much in change, which one chooses not to return; and suppose this leads, at the request of the superego, to inordinate self-hatred and to a prolonged depression), the ego must have sufficient strength to ignore the overly harsh demands of the superego and to create only the amount of punishment that fits the crime. It is the ego too, and not the superego, which must have the capacity to learn from the experience in order to prevent future dangerous oedipal repetitions. Despite its general evolution from the ego and from reality, the superego can also owe some facets of its contents and functions to that which does not exist in reality. A boy with a seductive mother and a father who is absent (or one who is so weak that it is impossible to feel threatened by him) may develop an object representation of his father that includes a powerful component unjustified by reality. This fantasy imago is as capable as is the imago of the most realistically powerful of fathers (and even realistically sadistic fathers) to deal out massive, punitive retribution and punishments. If his father cannot, in reality, stimulate enough castration-anxiety (either through weakness or absence) to reduce the overstimulating and perpetually disorganizing wishes attached to his mother, and if his mother overstimulates him and encourages his advances instead of rejecting them, the child's resources will remain instinctually bound. As a result he runs the risk of not having sufficient conflict-free energy at his disposal for progress through school, for learning social skills, for acquiring masculine identifications, and so forth. One could, if one wished, insist that it is primarily a form of superego pathology when the little boy tries to develop an object representation so far from the truth, but it is, on balance, a healthier alternative than having most of his ego functions disrupted. It certainly is better than the other obvious alternative of his going through life with significant lacunae (gaps to match the absence of a stable paternal object representation) in the superego.[7]

---

[7]Psychological events that are simultaneously healthy and pathological, progressive and regressive, are commonplace in mental functioning. From a conceptual point of view one is reminded of Rapaport's dissatisfaction with Kris's concept that in creative functioning one sees a "regression in the service of the ego." Although fantasy is a regressive phenomenon because it operates according to primary process dynamics, Rapaport was uncomfortable with describing its use in artistic and other creative activities as essentially, or even primarily, regressive. For example: Is it regressive to fantasize how something might happen in order to try out, and practice for, a variety of eventualities? Is it regressive to suspend one's critical faculties in order to engage in free association during psychoanalysis? Is it regressive to speculate on the outcome of something, or to anticipate? Was it regressive for Einstein to dream the theory of relativity? Rapaport argued that in these and other contexts, just as when an artist successfully transposes material in his unconscious into a form that deeply touches the unconscious of his audience, the regressive element is less consequential than the fact that the phenomenon serves a healthy and developmentally progressive function. Such transformation, according to Rapaport, was to be thought of as an adaptive stage-specific event despite the fact that some element of it employed a process that could be defined, technically, as regressive. He asserted that emphasizing the primary-process characteristics in healthy adult creativity as if they were the single most important element in the creative process (which is exactly what he thinks the use of the term *regression* connotes in this context) significantly distorts the main thrust of Kris's idea, which is to emphasize that this mental operation is being used specifically to place portions of the artist's inner life *at the service of the ego* rather than the id. Rapaport thought that one would be more accurate, by avoiding the inevitable negative connotations connected with the idea of regression, if one

Alternatively, one can develop a pliant and compromising superego even if (or more to the point, precisely because) one's parents may be inordinately harsh and aggressive (in response to even the slightest lapse in what they consider proper). If this is an intolerable burden for the child he may, at the earliest opportunity, rebound with values and ethical standards that have a wider latitude than ordinarily exists. Here again we see what some might choose to call a pathology of the superego in its narrowest definition. This solution too, however, if it doesn't go too far, is a better compromise than living one's entire life inappropriately obsessed with an irrational morality and consumed by hateful self-directed aggression.[8]

Many attributes of the superego develop in ways that are closely tied to reality as a precipitate of, or a form of distillation of, the ego. The superego also has many unrealistic attributes that superficially make it appear as if the superego is more related to the id than to the ego. For example, the superego signals the ego to demand punishment, but it does not itself regulate the amount of punishment or the type of punishment created. The superego is impartial in its demands for punishment. It makes claims on the ego almost equally, in normal circumstances, for "high crimes" and for "low." It is the ego alone, however, that controls the adaptiveness and appropriateness of the response. If the ego is functioning well it will mediate the superego's almost nondiscriminating demands so that a realistic outcome will be possible. One can see, then, that although the superego forms from the ego, and is dependent for the most part on reality features of significant others for its contents, it also functions in many ways that use the primary-process factors we customarily have associated with the id. With some exceptions we can say that in the portions of the superego that represent a reservoir for identifications, and in those portions that contribute to the development of our "conscience," its contents operate in a fashion we generally associate with the ego and its functions operate in a fashion we generally associate with the id.

The most noteworthy example of an exception to this, in nonpathological

---

used the term *reversibility of the functions of the ego* in place of the phrase *regression in the service of the ego*. This view of mental functioning is readily applicable to the little boy with an "inflated" paternal imago, who uses this "pathological" belief and identification to successfully negotiate the Oedipus complex. This development might have repercussions of a different nature in terms of its effects on other ego and superego contents and functions, and it would certainly be a cause for concern if it was maintained unmodified into adulthood, but in terms of its ability to help the little boy finally renounce his actively incestuous ties to his mother nothing could be more welcome. Thus one sees that context, as much as content and function, influences one's view about whether a particular piece of mental functioning is adaptive or maladaptive; and by viewing the context one also determines the role a specific psychic event plays in the general organization of mental functioning.

[8]In this example the boy develops his posture because of a distortion of reality in the contents of the superego, and not because secondary process elements of the ego are set into motion. If his freedom from harsh and unreasonable rules and demands was based on a realistic (and distanced) rejection of observably pathological aspects of his parents and their values, no one would suggest a pathological underpinning to his developmental achievement. Needless to say, boys of this age are nowhere near the stage in which such ego resources are possible.

development, is that major segment of the superego known as the *ego ideal*. As its name implies, it refers to an inventory of our aspirations. A few further words on the differences between ego identifications and superego identifications are necessary before proceeding to the considerably more complex nature of identifications and aspirations in the ego ideal. If self-descriptions are simply measures of how one is, and what one is like, they would be considered (because they are reality-based assessments) to be narcissistic ego identifications.[9] Also, on the other hand, the stored mnemonic representations of objects and their attributes (that involve specific evaluations based on, and limited to, reality considerations) are considered to be non-narcissistic ego identifications. Mergers between aspects of one's self and aspects of others, so that attributes of a significant other is contained in a self-representation, belong to the generic class known as superego identifications. The development of aspirations in the ego ideal make use of self ego identifications and representations which are combined with self superego identifications and representations.[10] The products of these mergers are then further combined with object ego identifications and representations, object superego identifications and representations, and additional self and object representations in the superego which have not developed into identifications and which were not included in the original mergers.

In a healthy ego ideal, aspirations are generally realistic and attainable. For example, a sales trainee can aspire to being as good as his firm's leading salesperson, a teacher can aspire to being as good as his own best teacher, a person can aspire to being as kind and thoughtful as is a particular person he knows, a person can aspire to being as slim and well-groomed as the models are in clothing advertisements, or a person can aspire to being as good a parent as his own or as good a spouse as his own. Pathology in the ego ideal usually involves unreasonable and unrealistic ambitions or identifications with inappropriate or pathological figures. For example: a man who strives to be as feminine and beautiful as was his mother or a movie star, and his female counterpart who may strive to undo all her feminine qualities and who aspires to be entirely masculine; the boy who wants to grow up to be as successful a criminal as Al Capone; the psychoanalyst who can never take pride in his work and pleasure in his ability to help people unless he reaches a stature in his profession equal to Freud's; the individual for whom nothing less than perfection is enough. From these differing examples, with a full range of goals, one can see how in healthy individuals the ego ideal serves as a sort of bridge function between the ego and the rest of the superego. When the little boy's superego is structuralized (in response to castration anxiety), he has initiated the process that will make taboos

---

[9]In this context the term narcissistic does not refer to a diagnostic categorization but, rather, reflects economic and dynamic concepts as in the process of self (also known as narcissistic) cathexis and object cathexis.

[10]Descriptions of, and clarification of the differences between, *identifications* and *representations* are extensively discussed at various points in Chapters 1 and 2.

against incest and patricide his own. This process of structuralization eventually permits the development of personal masculinity in the superego in general, and in the ego ideal specifically, for its own sake and not as just a response to direct threats or as a means to an incestuous end. In a final word about male oedipal competition in the phallic stage, there is a distinct possibility that the little boy's anxieties may have a partial basis in reality. Suppose the little boy's father becomes an active competitor (as he should) in his son's highly overdetermined and insistent oedipal drama. It is more than likely that this will bring to the surface actual residuals of his own unresolved oedipal conflicts, which have been dormant and have suddenly become triggered in reaction to his son's wishes to depose him and to dispose of him. In the primitive realms of the adult's mind, his son may be equated unconsciously with his own father (since in primary process all competitors are equal; that is, one competitor equals all competitors). In this context the little boy's father (unconsciously remembering being a little boy himself) finds that the wish to castrate and murder his father (who now takes the form of his son) is once again revived in himself. As a grown man the little boy's father will be able (consciously) to discount this wish for the most part, to keep it under control, to keep it essentially in the realm of the unconscious. Should it become preconscious he even may be able, in defense and adaptively, to find it somewhat comical as he observes it accidentally in himself. But on more archaic levels (that fortunately for both father and son do not predominate), these wishes are in deadly earnest, and the child picks up the trail even when the healthiest resolution possible had been achieved by his father.[11] The little boy may recognize this murderous intention in his father without being able to appreciate its realistic insignificance (it would not be insignificant if it was occurring in the boy himself, who believes that all others function exactly as he does), and this becomes proof positive for him of the "reality dangers" he dreads. If he can use this "proof in reality," which occurs in reality even if it does not qualify as proof of anything realistically, to reinforce his conviction that his worst possible fears may actually come to pass, then we can see even more comprehensively why castration anxiety plays such a critical and central role in the initial resolution of the oedipal complex. And it explains for us in addition why castration anxiety moves the boy into latency, and the role that castration anxiety plays in the structuralization of the superego. The more real something seems, the greater its capacity to stoke psychological fires.

Latency in Boys

In latency, boys usually shun girls, lest they trigger sexual feelings that might revive aspects of the oedipal conflict. This is the stage when boys are highly ambivalent about their relationship with their mothers, and they frequently alternate between keeping their distance and needing the loving contact that their mothers provide.

---

[11]Again one must note that successful resolution of a conflict does not mean its total absence, but the significant diminishment of its tendency to predominate in mental functioning.

This is the stage of "no girls allowed" clubs, of sports teams that exclude girls.[12] In latency one observes "heroic" figures that embody the most unequivocal stereotypes of masculine attributes (Superman, Batman, the Incredible Hulk, et al.) introduced into the ego ideal. It is a stage where any feminine identifications are ridiculed, and boys who have them in evidence are degraded by other boys (as in being called a sissy) and despised. Of course this is not because there is anything objectively despicable in femininity. Rather, it occurs in the service of keeping his oedipal wishes submerged. The latency-aged boy has had to denigrate femininity as a way of insuring that he is not attracted to women or to anything about them. In addition, he denigrates feminine characteristics because he is afraid that feminine identifications in his playmates will be contagious. He fears this in the sense that he is convinced that his own identifications with his mother – and there are many – will surface if he plays in an atmosphere where too much freedom of expression is possible. He avoids maternal identifications, at least the overtly feminine aspects of what could become a maternally influenced self-representation, conscientiously because of his infantile belief that women are castrated men – castration is precisely what structuralization of his superego and his move into latency are designed to prevent. To the extent that he is free from the extreme pressures of oedipal interests and dangers, which are an entrapment of the energy of his psychic resources, he can learn in school, engage in play, and develop his role of masculinity.

The high level of physical activity that characterizes latency for most boys may have two of its sources in oedipal dynamics. If libido and aggression balance one another (not necessarily equally), then the redistribution of libido (which is considerably greater than the redistribution of aggression) that occurs in solving the oedipal complex may unbind considerable quantities of aggression, which remain "free-floating" and unattached. If this is the case, we can see the use of high activity levels (increased motility) as well as the role of competition (and in competition, certain direct displays of assaultive hostility) as modes of constructively discharging aggression that would (or perhaps inevitably) reflect back onto the self and onto love objects were these outlets not available. In addition, it may also be the case that additional aggression is mobilized in the latency-age boy in response to the frustration, anxiety, deprivations, and disappointment that attends the renunciation, in their pristine forms, of many of his original instinctual ties to his mother. This would increase even further whatever natural tendency might exist toward hyperactive (compared with very young children, and with adults) modes of discharge.

Latency and the Female Superego

Oedipal development is different for girls than for boys because so much conspires to keep girls' libidinal ties active. The relative absence of castration anxiety, which,

---

[12]Although this is beginning to change, it must be remembered that the changes first began at the insistence of girls and female adults, and it was not initially an expression of the wishes of little boys or their counterparts, grown men.

as we know from our discussion of boys, is the most important motivator for inhibition and repression of starkly oedipal wishes, moves the girl through the phallic stage and into latency with a significant degree of oedipal wishes and other libidinized interests still relatively intact. Throughout the phallic stage and latency the girl continues to identify with her mother. The primary identification thus far has been with her mother as a source of power and of goodness, within which one sees hints of both the oral-stage and the anal-stage mother. She identifies, in both the phallic stage and in latency, with the phallic-stage mother to learn how to be a woman. A very specific goal for the latency-age girl is to learn how to be enough of a woman to attract a man. In the primary-process functioning of a latency-age girl, her mother equals all women and her father equals all men. Throughout the phallic stage and throughout latency the girl is considerably more libidinally related to her father than is the boy to his mother, because the girl is not so powerfully subjected to the inhibiting effects of the threat of body mutilation (castration). She uses both childish seduction and attempts to intensify archaic-grandiose maternal identifications, as she tries to do something that will reduce the injury to her narcissism brought about by her femininity.[13] This being the case, it is clear that the structuralizing factors in the organization of the female superego are markedly different from those in operation for males. The most obvious difference is in the motivating force in developing introjection, which was directly due to castration anxiety in boys.

Girls are motivated to diminish their libidinal ties with their mothers because the possibility of massive regressive temptations is too dangerous to face frequently and regularly. Both boys and girls resist regressive solutions that would have to lead them back to prior, infantile, orality and anality. Many such ties (more than with boys) may remain intact, but for girls the solution is to strive to alter the most concretely seductive ties of the phallic stage so that these also may be transformed into introjects. Primitive residuals may remain as archaic elements in her superego, but for the most part of the girl's transformation of oral and anal libidinal ties into introjects lets her retain the most rewarding aspects of her relationship to her mother in a safer, nondestructive way (just as the boy, who has had to give up even more oral and anal attachments, maintains his delibidinized connection to his mother by replacing phallic sexual love with affection). In this regard, because the girl is not so ruthlessly motivated to sever her libidinal ties to her mother (as dramatically and "totally" as the boy had to because of the unequal allotment of castration anxiety), it is generally true that introjective identificatory processes play a somewhat smaller role in the organization of the girl's superego. It also follows then that there will be both less distance from the drives in the superego of girls and a greater susceptibility to object loss, narcissistic injury, and depression (which combines with penis loss,

---

[13]We must remember that we are speaking of very little girls whose attitudes about masculinity and femininity are simultaneously similar and different, each gender in its own ways, but just as primitive and unrealistic as are the beliefs of their little boy counterparts.

narcissistic injury, and depression) when reality gratifications from loved ones are reduced or discontinued.

To reduce specifically phallic-narcissistic vulnerability further, the girl makes use of reaction formation, a skill developed much earlier, in the anal stage, to guard against and reduce the child's actual involvement in "forbidden" pleasures and to firmly establish the incest taboo in her psyche. This strengthens her identification with her mother's goodness, her mother's cleanliness, and most importantly, it strengthens her identification with her mother's distance from her own drives and drive-related pleasures. Reaction formation against anal pleasure is extended to reaction formations against both regressive and phallic libidinal pleasures in general, in the service of transforming (maternal) incorporative and imitative identifications into introjects. Thus, although the superego has been called the heir to the oedipal complex because of its structuralization in boys at the end of the phallic stage when active oedipal wishes are making way for latency, in the girl the superego begins its process of structuralization at the end of the anal stage as she begins to move into the phallic stage and as the first elements of the oedipal complex begin to make their presence known.

The girl's relationship with her father is equally dangerous in terms of its regressive pulls and forbidden wishes, and much of the girl's interest in her father sexually (which is the most primitive and infantile expectation of how one can go about the task of getting a penis) is replaced by identification. These identifications may be quite concrete. Some may be intense but attached to less dangerous instinctual longings or objects, and others may have become transformed (to protect herself from continuously disruptive tensions and demands) into introjects. The boy gives up his explicit oedipal demand entirely because of the threat of castration, and the girl gives up her explicit oedipal demands in large part, but not entirely, because of the threat of damage to her immature mental organization (particularly in regard to nonerotic narcissism). This also suggests some things that may be seen regularly by anyone in frequent contact with latency-age boys and girls. First, girls in latency are much more obviously involved in sexualized relationships with their fathers (openly as well as symbolically), to a dramatically greater extent, than are boys with their mothers; and second, girls are comfortable with bisexual identifications because, unlike boys who lose drastically if they openly identify with their mothers, girls will gain by identifications with mother and father both (oral and anal power and intactness from the mother, and phallic power and intactness from the father). Evidence of comfort in bisexual identification for girls (and this is not a statement of sexual orientation although it is not entirely unrelated) is easy to see: girls are frequently tomboys, and no one is even distressed as they might well be with a latency-age boy who is markedly effeminate; women wear dresses or slacks but men never (except for a kilt) wear skirts; women can hold hands, kiss, put their arms around one another, dance together at parties, and so on, without becoming threatened and panicky about their sexual identification. Many latency-age girls regularly say, with little or no conflict, that they would like to be boys but almost no latency-age boys would say that they want to be girls (and if they secretly do, they certainly wouldn't admit it). One result of all of this is that in most areas of mental functioning women will be able to empathize more easily with men than men will be able to empathize with women. This is true in sexual functioning as well as in many other areas.

These dynamics can sometimes be applied to siblings instead of parents, resulting either from the absence of a parent or as a way of choosing an incestuous object with a weaker taboo. In general, one more often sees aggressive cathexes directed at siblings without the intense libidinal component that is directed to an oedipally loved parent. This is an area where boys and girls have much in common, because gender is not necessarily a factor in a sibling's competition for the parents.

Recent Thinking on Feminine Psychology

Before leaving the general topic of feminine development it is necessary to say that there have been considerable changes in thinking, particularly in the past two decades, about the questions of feminine gender identity, feminine castration anxiety, and the superego organization of little girls. Many recent contributions do not directly challenge the general description of development as it has been described here, but they do alter it in some important ways. Mainly, they have placed drive considerations in a secondary place, and they emphasize instead issues of identification that are specific to the oral stage; in particular, they focus on the role played by self–object differentiation in the oral stage in the development of both male and female gender identity.

Refinement in our thinking about female psychology has a long history in psychoanalysis. In the 1920s, both Melanie Klein and, especially, Karen Horney posed alternative views of superego development, castration anxiety, and penis envy. Jones, in both the 1920s and the 1930s, associated himself with Horney's views about the defensive nature of penis envy (as opposed to Freud's notion that it was a "primary" phenomenon) and made further contributions of his own. In the late 1930s, Jones was joined by Jacobson who, in some ways, revolutionized Freudian thinking about the nature of both castration anxiety and superego organization in girls. The 1940s gave us the work of Zilboorg; the 1950s gave us Greenacre's extensive contributions; the 1960s ushered in the work of Barnett, Greenson, Stoller, and Zetzel; the 1970s introduced us to the work of Applegarth, Blum, Chasseguet-Smirgel, Fliegel, Galenson, Grossman, Kleeman, Kubie, Moore, and Parens and associates; the 1980s brought to our attention the work of Bernstein, Mayer, Roiphe, and Tyson. Needless to say, this list is very incomplete: it is intended only to show that many analysts have been thinking about these questions for many years (and, surely, it is not intended to ignore the many others who have made considerable contributions to the question of feminine psychology). Also, this list is a representative sample of analysts who have worked within the Freudian tradition; many other analysts not mentioned here have taken positions on feminine psychology that are antithetical to the traditional analytic model. In fact, some of the most severe criticism of the Freudian model is based on opposition to the "standard" Freudian view of female psychology, a dissatisfaction second only, perhaps, to an antagonism to drive theory. Among some feminists, both professionals and laypersons alike, the traditional view of feminine psychology is seen as an active attempt to perpetuate phallocentricity and male dominance.

Much current thinking suggests a very new idea: that the development of gender identity begins at birth and, in addition, that there may be a kind of "primary femininity." That is, that little girls seem, somehow, to be feminine from a very early age, and that this is based on a core gender identity[14] that is learned by the girl through her earliest contacts with her mother. The idea is that boys and girls are held differently by their mothers, that they are related to differently, and that these quite stereotypic differences give babies the immediate nucleus of a gender identity. This core or nuclear gender identity exists from the earliest interactions with the girl's mother, and great emphasis has been placed on how early it develops (even though it will also, over time, become consolidated into the girl's superego and into the formation of her ego). Stoller stresses that it grows directly out of the primal symbiotic stage, pointing out that girls develop a primary gender identity that is based essentially on the earliest, most primitive and archaic, primary identification with the mother.[15] Bernstein, who states quite forcefully that she thinks the phallic stage is *not* the source of either gender identity or of the superego,[16] puts it this way: "Every mother experiences with her boy and girl baby . . . the child's gender in relation to her own. I propose that the mother's experience of the girl as like herself, and the boy as different from herself, ties the girl to the mother in a reciprocal relationship and orients the boy to differentiate, from birth onward" (p. 194).[17] She goes on to say: "In the body of her infant daughter, a mother can see her own past self; the body is known and familiar, one with which she can have total identifica-

---

[14]Actually, this core gender identity is presumed to exist for boy babies, too.

[15]Stoller points out that, in contrast, boys develop a sense of gender identity via a disidentification with the mother (a concept also made known to us by Greenson) and that, because of this, early male gender identity is strongly defended in a way that is not necessary for girls. On the other hand, Fliegel points out that there are costs as well as advantages in the girl's gender identity being rooted in her primary identification with her mother; these costs include a greater difficulty in establishing autonomy, independence, and a clearly delineated self-representation.

[16]D. Bernstein (1983) The female superego: a different perspective. *International Journal of Psycho-Analysis* 64:187–202.

[17]Bernstein is forwarding her own version of the conviction that "anatomy is destiny" (now, however, on the basis of an oral-stage dynamic, rather than on the basis of the phallic-stage concept of penis envy). Despite being very much aware of the power and influence of fantasy in mental functioning, Bernstein takes this suggestion yet another step further when she argues in opposition to some approaches (and here she was referring to some of the works of Freud, Nagera, and Chasseguet-Smirgel) which she felt "g(a)ve too much credence to fantasy and not enough weight to the body experience" (p. 194).

tion. In contrast, a boy can only be experienced by a woman as different from herself; there cannot be the deep biological understanding of the male body experience that a woman has with her daughter. The mother's experience of her daughter as like herself, and her experience of her son as different, is overtly and subtly communicated to her children." (p. 191).[18]

In considering revised opinions about dynamic events in the phallic stage, we know of Horney's argument that "penis envy" is defensive rather than innate and primary; she suggested that it is reactive to the little girl's feminine ambitions and longings (which, of course, are conflictual because of the threat they present in relation to the little girl's incestuous yearnings toward her father). Some authors have more recently challenged the primacy of the penis envy concept in a different way. They have questioned whether meaningful conceptualization of the nature of the child's anatomy need wait until the phallic stage; they suggest that little girls have a preliminary, that is, preoedipal, awareness of their vaginas (before phallic-stage fantasy pressures reorganize their perceptions of their genitals, placing special emphasis *at that time* on their not having penises), or of, at least, a concept of "some kind of inner space."[19] Very early on (1966), Barnett suggested that little girls do have a preliminary awareness of their vagina; not a concept, or a fully formed notion, of what their genital is like, but a kind of precursor to a fuller awareness that they eventually will achieve at a later point in development. This preliminary awareness, or precursor, is based on the child's perception of her vulva and the introitus (a space behind the external opening that sets the stage for a later conceptualization of a vagina). Barnett is at pains to make the important point that the representation of the vagina is *not* necessary for the girl to have a representation of an

---

[18]Bernstein does not take up, in her account here, the issue of innate, inherent bisexuality and the effect it may have on these developmental events. Kubie (1974), as well as Fast (1979), emphasize that because of the innate bisexuality of all children, boys and girls alike wish to be possessed of everything, that is, wish to have *both* male and female genitals. Of course Bernstein is referring to a developmental period before children become aware of sexual anatomy, and both Kubie and Fast are discussing children after they have become aware of the fact that everyone is not genitally made in the same way. One wonders, nevertheless, what the effect of innate bisexuality might be on primary identification processes and defensive processes of disidentification in the earliest stages of childhood.

[19]On the other hand, early awareness of some of the attributes of the girl's genitals need not necessarily lead to a clarification of gender identity. For example, Lerner (1977) points out that inadequacies of how such information is processed, particularly when the parent teaches her child that she has a vagina but does not clarify the nature of the rest of her genital—that is, the relationship between labia, vulva, introitus, and clitoris—may readily lead to active penis envy. In this case, penis envy is not merely a wish to have a penis but—and here is the crux of Lerner's point—a wish to have "permission" for female sexual organs and (in later development) to be a sexually operative female. She makes the further point that the sometimes caricatured, so-called fuzzy thinking of women, as opposed to the clear-headed precision attributed to the thinking of men, may frequently be traced to unresolved difficulties caused by parental mislabeling of the child's genital (either by commission or, even more frequently, by omission), and this reflects and grows out of the lack of precision and clarity the little girl suffers in trying to understand the nature of her genital anatomy.

opening and a potential inside space. In this way Barnett is able to describe the possibility of a female castration anxiety that precedes the later, overlaying, and more typical phallic-stage castration fantasies; preoedipal female castration anxiety is about *being closed up,* whereas phallic stage castration anxiety is about *losing something.* Almost 20 years later, Mayer (1985) expanded on this theme in a paper about how children always assume that everybody must be just like they are, well before they begin to worry about how they might be different from other people. In Mayer's view the preoedipal mental representation of genital femaleness consists of an opening and an "inside space" which the little girl assumes everyone has. Mayer suggests that there is a female castration anxiety that precedes the later "penis-envy type." The preoedipal female castration anxiety is based on the fantasy in little girls, that males represent the "frightening possibility that such an opening *in a female* could be endangered, lost, or closed up as the opening is imagined to be in males" (p. 345).

Chasseguet-Smirgel suggests, in addition, the possibility of a preoedipal penis envy. This preoedipal penis envy occurs after the little girl recognizes the anatomical differences between herself and little boys, but before she enters into the phallic stage where the differences acquire their "classic" penis-envy characteristics. The little girl is deeply entwined with her mother at the beginning of life in an archaic relationship that will soon require modification, as the little girl needs to differentiate and individuate herself. Whether the mother hinders her child or facilitates her progress, the little girl is under an internal developmental obligation to emancipate herself from this symbiosis. Even with the mother's help, and under the best of circumstances, it is an immense struggle for the little girl. Here, awareness of the distinguishing physical attributes that make boys and girls very different from one another, and awareness of the way this differentiates the boy from his mother[20] and thus aids him in his gaining separateness from her, brings about a kind of penis envy that is very different, and which occurs very much earlier, than the kind we think of in the phallic stage.[21]

The relationship of castration anxiety to superego organization is undisputed by most writers (like Mayer and Chasseguet-Smirgel) on feminine psychology, but there is considerable difference in how many of them (for example, Applegarth, Bernstein, or Fliegel) conceive of the contents and strengths of the female superego. Still others (like Jacobson, and Greenacre, and especially Bernstein) suggest very different modes of female superego organization and formation. Although for both boys and girls alike the superego is generally considered to be the "heir to the Oedipus complex." Jacobson suggested (in 1937) that for girls the superego was

---

[20]It involves something that he automatically *is,* and not something that he has to do, or to be, that is against his very nature.

[21]She describes a very different type of penis envy as well in which, conversely, the penis is envied by the little girl because it lets the little boy have his mother.

"heir," specifically, "to the *negative* Oedipus complex." When the little girl gives up the immediacy of her preoedipal ties to her mother she retains her mother as an altered love object and as an altered primary object of identification, by installing her original phallic-maternal representation of her mother[22] as the nucleus itself of her superego. This occurs at the beginning of the phallic stage, under pressure of castration anxieties that cause the little girl to doubt the normality of her genital, leading her to conflicts about both masturbation and her attachments to her mother. Thus, for Jacobson (1937), the consolidation of the superego as a psychic structure occurs considerably earlier in the phallic stage for girls than for boys. This is then augmented, and given particular power, by the little girl's reaction-formations against anal pleasure through the "development of intense efforts to be good and to build up the ego ideal of a modest, gentle, obedient, clean little girl, perhaps in opposition to an unruly, cheeky, dirty little boy" (pp. 533–534).[23]

Fifteen years later, Greenacre (1952) described a "fund of guilt" in girls, which she viewed as related to an imbedded conviction that they were castrated as a punishment for masturbation and, thus, as related directly to their struggle against sexuality. This, then, contributes *independently* (and greatly) to guilt feelings in later situations of conflict. Greenacre called this *diffuse or aimless conscientiousness* and thought that it should be conceptualized as different from the more consolidated kind of "conscience" one finds in the male superego.[24]

Some of the more recent work on the nature of the female superego directly challenges Freud's idea that women have weaker, less inexorable, superegos than do men (based on his notion that this is so because their superego identifications are more transient and less aim-inhibited than are those of men). Bernstein, for example, has argued rather forcefully that the male superego is rigid and the female superego is flexible; she feels that male superego rigidity is often taken as a sign of superego strength, mistakenly in her opinion, and she suggests that the flexibility of the female superego should not be confused with weakness. In addition, she emphasizes that the female superego also has, in addition to its areas of flexibility, considerable strength and *inflexibility* and even, in certain areas, a quite relentless quality. As evidence of this she cites women whose sexuality is "frozen, unexpressed . . . and frightening" (1983, p. 187). She understands that expression of sexuality to be representative of early prohibitions that are easily and regularly able to defeat the impact of the social changes currently taking place in sexual attitudes and values. She argues that the flexibility of the female superego is no less desirable

---

[22]Ruth Lax (August 1990, personal communication) considers the concept of the phallic woman to be a "male fantasy," and theoretically insupportable.

[23]Jacobson (1964) also has an excellent description of this dynamic on pp. 112–115 of *The Self and the Object World*.

[24]A number of authors of this period have also suggested that the little girl has a fear that internal damage will be caused by the father's penis: this is another kind of castration anxiety entirely; that is, it is one that is organized by concerns about internal damage, a more global injury as it were, rather than by loss of the genital.

than the concept of superego firmness that is usually described as being characteristic of male superego organization.

Moreover, Bernstein argues for an earlier development of the superego as a psychic agency. She suggests that the core of the superego is based on the irrationality of preoedipal processes, which include introjection/projection operations of an extremely primitive nature. She suggests that these archaic dynamics (that are usually considered by traditional theorists only to be superego *precursors*) are central to–in fact, at the very core of–the superego. The usual assumption applied to the superego is that aim-inhibited identifications serve to coalesce the superego into an autonomous psychic structure, in the stressful context of castration anxiety and oedipal conflict; Bernstein suggests that archaic operations at the "core" of the superego, occurring much earlier in development, are more characteristic of superego organization than are the more "advanced" identifications that develop in the phallic stage and latency. In this proposition she is making no distinctions based on the gender of the child. She feels that these archaic processes, in the core of the superego, determine the quality and the nature of the later, phallic-stage, superego identifications as much as, if not more than, does castration anxiety. When she does separate female from male superego development, she sees the greater tendency toward obedience and compliance found in girls during the anal stage, and the greater ease with which they are toilet trained, as evidence of established (even if not fully developed) superego formation.

We can focus on Bernstein's considerable work on the female superego as a good example of how the classical model is continuously under pressure to change in response to advances in theory, research, and clinical practice. According to Bernstein (1983): "(Superego) *contents* refers to the specific admonitions and prohibitions–which drives are allowed expression, in which ways drives may be expressed, which are prohibited" (p. 189). Usually we are more used to thinking about the dynamics of *how* drives are prohibited or expressed, or *how* prohibited drives may finally reach expression, as being a matter of function rather than content (although, certainly, the specific content demands of the superego are included as one part of the superego's contents). And in addition, although it is true that one usually considers the judgments about which drives may or may not be expressed (actually, only their derivatives, not the drives themselves) to be part of superego *functioning*, the ways that drives become transformed into derivative wishes and then actually come to be expressed, further transformed, or inhibited are usually thought of as belonging to the functions of the ego, not the superego, in its role as a mediator of the superego's requirements. A nonspecific understanding of superego *contents* (most clearly, as it applies to the question of conscience) certainly does include what is specifically acceptable or unacceptable to the superego. But a more specific understanding of the superego's contents refers to much more than this; the nucleus of the superego, the superordinate contents of the superego, upon which everything else–including "content demands"–rests, is usually thought to be composed of a combination of (1) the child's not particularly aim-inhibited identification with parental superego *organization;* and (2) a special class of quite aim-inhibited identifications (in both the superego proper and in the ego ideal) which have been developed, and then further organized into a cohesive psychic agency, in response to the demands of resolving oedipal conflicts. Both of these kinds of identifications will carry within them highly specific contents of their own; for example, some may carry certain parental attitudes (conscious and unconscious) and others may carry certain attributes of a parental superego.[25] Also, we do not want to confuse the various (and varying) contents of an identification with the identification itself; the main point being that the identification is a *process,* just as the superego is a process.[26] The contents of parental identifications that enter into the child's superego are sometimes represented directly, sometimes indirectly, sometimes in reaction-formation, sometimes in exaggerated or in diminished form, sometimes in compensatory or otherwise defensive form, but *always* in forms that are subject to distortion and to fantasy reorganization so that they are not the exact equivalent of the object (or its attributes) on which the identification rests. Looked at from a more conventional view, these contents of the superego's resident identifications (the contents of contents, as it were, or a subset of a larger set in the superego) are the superego contents that Bernstein is referring to, which determine the superego's attitudes about right and wrong, and about what is acceptable or unacceptable, and permitted or prohibited. She has chosen to revise the concept of superego content to also include what we usually think of as function, that is, the *way* (but not how powerfully) things are enforced, and has particularly chosen to avoid the question of aim-inhibition as an organizing feature of the superego, in order to accommodate aspects of the superego that she feels have more to do with preoedipal than with oedipal contributions.

In Bernstein's (1983) view, "(Superego) *strength* refers to the efficiency with which the contents are regulated" (p. 189). She views the superego's strength as a form of efficiency in how powerfully the contents are enforced, whereas we are more used to thinking of *efficiency of enforcement* as a combined event involving participation from all three psychic agencies: the power of the impulse to be warded off (the id), the demand that it be proscribed (the superego), and ego's ability to regulate and mediate between the opposing demands of the two other psychic agencies. For example, we expect a strong ego to be able to prevent a condition of unconditional obedience in meeting the demands of even a very harsh superego (or of an exceedingly powerful wish, in the case of the id); conversely, we expect that a less adequately organized ego will result, comparatively, in a much more total kind of obedience to the superego, even if every feature of the harsh superego remained

---

[25]There is not a direct, unaltered incorporation into the child's superego of the conscious and unconscious parental attitudes and of other parental superego attributes. These are, nevertheless, a *primary* influence on the child's superego contents and functions, without necessarily having to be directly replicated there.

[26]We only treat identifications, and the superego, as if they were "things" in how we think about them because, as "thing" metaphors, that way of conceptualizing about them is easier and more convenient, even if it is not strictly accurate. It is a valuable luxury, albeit sometimes a dangerous one.

completely unchanged (or, in the case of the id, we would expect a greater capitulation to impulsive demands). In each of these cases, it is the nature of the ego, and not the nature of the superego (or the id), that plays the central role in regulating the efficiency and power of enforcement.

In more traditional thinking, the strength of the superego is measured not by how well it enforces its demands but, rather, by its maturity.[27] The superego's maturity means its degree of distance from the drives. On one hand, an immature superego, one that lacks distance from the drives owing to insufficient aim-inhibition in its contents, will be sadistic, ruthless, and inexorable (and very much like a "pure culture of the death instinct" in the sense that Freud described), or it will be too compliant with the id's libidinous demands (not being, itself, sufficiently distanced from them). On the "sadistic" side of this equation, the punitive and destructive qualities of the immature superego may frequently be viewed as extremely, and even unbearably, powerful. On the other hand, a particularly mature superego is also extremely powerful, in the sense that the aim-inhibited identifications within it, and which organize it, lend it a particular and certain stability: the strength of its "conscience" includes firmness, permanence, and steadiness, being based as it is on special kinds of enduring identifications, identifications that are immune to casual change (as compared with the more transient quality of identifications that are not aim-inhibited and that are maintained or abandoned in response to instinctual gratification and deprivations).

We also tend to think of the superego's strength in relation to the ability it has to exist and maintain itself as an autonomous psychic structure; that is, its ability to resist disorganizing regressions that would lead its functions and contents back into archaic and primitively organized operations, in effect restoring them to the state of superego precursors. This particular concept of superego strength is completely analogous to the concept of ego autonomy, in the sense that the ego's autonomy represents a measure of the ego's resistance to reinstinctualization. In this concept, too, we find at bottom the centrality of aim-inhibition in the identifications in the superego; here again, distance from the drives (derived from solving the castration-anxiety conflicts of the Oedipus complex) is the stabilizing element that provides the superego with *strength* in situations that have the potential to trigger (in a weaker superego) regression and instinctualization.

From Bernstein's (1983) perspective, "(Superego) *structure* refers to the organization or inter-relationships of the contents; the contents can have different strengths" (p. 189). She views the male superego as having mainly "fixed contents," and the female superego as having less-fixed contents; that is, female superegos have relative strengths of their contents, differing contents each with differing strengths, that "vary according to the situation." Here Bernstein is using the concept of structure not in the sense of "structuralization," or in the sense of the superego as a separate

---

[27]Use of the term *maturity* as regards the superego is roughly equivalent to how the term *autonomy* is used in reference to the ego.

"structural" agency, but in the sense that we more ordinarily reserve for our description of *function;* that is, in defining how male and female superegos differ in their functioning. She means structure in a more colloquial sense, that is, *Let us look at the different structure (i.e., ways of functioning) of the male superego as opposed to the female superego.* And, of course, in defining how the structures differ, Bernstein places considerable emphasis on early maternal identifications in the female superego that lend the female superego as much "legitimacy," and "moral strength of character," as has always been attributed to the superego of boys.

In all of the examples I have given of "traditional" conceptualizing about superego *contents, strength,* and *structure,* the issue of aim-inhibited identifications always takes a central position; Bernstein necessarily rejects this way of thinking about superego contents, strength, and structure because she unequivocally rejects castration anxiety as the nuclear motivation in the organization of the superego as a psychic agency (and in the organization of its contents and functions). She prefers, instead, to place its development much earlier in childhood, less in response to drive-related considerations, and more in response to object-related influences. Bernstein's work exemplifies how new propositions may have to balance on a tightrope between being an expansion of classical theory and a substitutive revision of it; sometimes new ideas serve as an addition to our theory, and at other times what may seem like an augmentation is really the proposal of a replacement theory in its stead. The problem she has had to face in rethinking a complicated issue like female superego development and organization, while attempting still to remain within the classical model, is most evident in how she departs from the standard meanings of these concepts, which departure she sees as essential to understanding feminine superego organization.

In the sense that it challenges some areas of accepted theory, Bernstein's work is very characteristic of much else that is currently being written on female gender identity, female sexuality, and feminine superego organization. Whether the classical theory changes sufficiently to accommodate all of Bernstein's ideas, and even more challenging and radical correctives of some other current theoreticians – as it may well do – or whether these, and other even more exclusively object-defined views, will serve as the nucleus for another school of psychoanalytic thinking about female development, remains to be seen. Obviously, the issue here is not the Freudian model for its own sake. One does not discard certain essentials of one's model lightly, and we usually expect that if the model has been particularly adequate in most ways, it will be able to accommodate important changes without the model itself having to be abandoned. Certainly the model is not holy, it should not be treated like received information, and it should be constantly subjected to careful scrutiny; but, radical revisions require that there be no way in which the current model can accommodate certain new data (and if this is true when making radical revisions, it is even more necessary when one offers an alternative that rejects central components of the model or the entire model itself). When our current way of conceptualizing is inadequate to explain what we see clinically (or in research), we revise before we discard and then, if it proves necessary, we may have no choice but to discard in favor of a new way of thinking about the material. In changing, altering, revising, and discarding, we might be well advised to use as a model in our theoretical decision making some of the same special conditions that Eissler suggested in choosing to use parameters, the subtle modifications of analytic treatment. He recommended that one does not alter the analytic frame unless the treatment has reached a point where absolutely nothing else is a possibility—that is, only where the treatment is at a total standstill or it is about to come to an inappropriate and premature termination. He also recommended that the departure from the analytic frame should always be the barest minimum possible that is necessary to keep the analysis intact. The analogy of this to how we think about our theory seems clear. Some patients need to be shifted from a psychoanalysis to a psychotherapy when it becomes clear that their character structure is such that the analytic procedure was not really the treatment of choice for them; analogously, we need to be able to revise and even reject any portion of our model that does not seem useful or adequate any longer. However, just as in the therapeutic situation, this is always a measure of last resort taken when no other possible alternatives are left to us. For psychoanalysts "theory" can be very comforting in that it gives a frame of reference in a very complex and frequently conflictual situation, and there is a danger in being so wedded to the comfort and safety that one's theory offers that one will maintain ways of thinking that seem to fly in the face of facts; there is, however, an equal danger in being too ready to reject ideas that are inconvenient, politically incorrect, or too conflictual, and in substituting well-rationalized claims that the traditionally accepted ways of thinking are inadequate to the task. A considerable amount of the current literature on this topic falls into a borderland in which it is not absolutely clear in what ways the material has been confirmed, and perhaps this must always be the case when theory is being subjected to significant revisions. If it presents some problems to us, it also presents us with some interesting and not unpleasant, challenges as we attempt to match the theoretical contributions we have just read about to what our own experience is like in the consultation room.

Further Considerations in the Latency Period

In Freud's 1926 essay, "The Question of Lay Analysis," he suggests that the onset of latency is biologically determined as well as a result of repression, reaction-formation and castration anxiety. He states (vol. 20, p. 210) that with the onset of the latency period, "sexuality normally advances no further; on the contrary, the sexual urges diminish in strength." In much of his other writing (particularly in his later writings) he supports a view of latency that focuses on the role of biology and the id, and this can be seen most clearly in his formulations concerning what he described as the diphasic onset of sexual development. He reinforced his idea of latency being ushered into existence as a physiological event, in an added footnote

(1935) to the description of the diphasic onset of sexual life that he offered in "An Autobiographical Study" (1924): "the most remarkable feature of the sexual life of man is its diphasic onset, its onset in two waves, with an interval between them. It reaches a first climax in the fourth or fifth year of a child's life. But thereafter this early efflorescence of sexuality passes off; the sexual impulses which have shown such liveliness are overcome by repression, and a period of latency follows, which lasts until puberty" (p. 37).

Clearly, from both the above quote and the greatest bulk of his writings, Freud did not mean to replace his psychological theory of latency with an exclusively biological and hereditary theory. In fact, in comparative terms he devoted considerably more attention to the role of psychological dynamics in the institution of latency than he ever did to physiological explanations. There seems to be little specific data available to us about a unique physiological decrease of sexual drive at the onset of latency; at least no data exist that are comparable to the obvious and measurable physiological changes that accompany the onset of puberty. And the question of the biological contribution to the structuralizations of the ego and the superego in bringing the phallic stage (and the Oedipus complex) to a close, and in maintaining the period of latency, is hard to sort out given the complexity and high visibility of psychological activity in these events. Other theoreticians, most notably Anna Freud, have taken the assumption of biological predisposition in latency much further than Freud ever did in his lifetime. She (1965), for example, frequently refers to a "post-oedipal lessening of drive urgency." The psychobiological matrix she forwards is clearly expressed in her assertion that ". . . extreme castration fear, death fears and wishes, together with the defenses against them, which dominate the scene at the height of the phallic-oedipal phase, and which create the well-known inhibitions, masculine overcompensations, [and] passive and regressive modes of the period disappear as if by magic as soon as the child takes the first steps into the latency period [and this occurs] as an immediate reaction to the biologically determined lessening of drive activity" (p. 163). Given the fact that a lessening of drive activity in latency is widely (but not universally) assumed, but remains nonetheless unproven, we find ourselves in the same relatively ambiguous position we were in when we considered the role of instincts in mental functioning – but with a slight twist.

By subscribing to the view that latency is biologically predetermined, one takes the position that, were drive activity not substantially lessened, the system of defenses could not (or at least, might not) have formed in such a way as to ensure movement out of the phallic-oedipal phase. That is, one argues that psychological defense and subsequent structuralization are dependent on the lessening of drive activity in latency in exactly the same way that the remodeling of object relations, and the renovations in psychic structure, during adolescence are directly dependent on the increase in drive activity of puberty. This position is not empirically based; it is based on a combination of inductive and deductive reasoning. It seems not unreasonable to assume that the marked shift in mental functioning during latency is accompanied, because the shift is so very radical, by concomitant fluctuations in biological factors. On the surface this seems to be a sensible assumption, but does it really follow that radical psychological change reflects an inevitable biological change? With more careful, or perhaps more demanding, review one can readily find numerous examples of biological changes that are not directly represented psychologically, and numerous examples of psychological changes that are not directly related to biological changes. Without in any way needing to diminish the role of drives in mental functioning, one may nonetheless question the assumption that the psychological changes of latency automatically reflect biologically determined lessening of drive activity. It is one thing to say that biological events have an impact on or representation in mental functioning, and quite another to suggest that biological events have a directly observable or readily recognizable representation in all mental functioning; to suggest that one can identify or understand the nature of biological events by what is apparent in mental functioning seems to be a leap in reasoning of unrealistic magnitude, and although in special cases such a thing may be possible, to present this as a general rule seems not justifiable. Thus, until strictly biological data can be specifically identified medically, we must exercise caution in accepting the view that drive activity is significantly reduced in latency. Withholding judgment on, or even rejecting, this assertion need not interfere with a psychoanalytic understanding of the vicissitudes of latency. After all, as one may recall from the earlier chapter on drive theory, metapsychology was "invented" in order to permit one to consider psychological functioning without constant recourse to the biological substrate out of which the psyche emerges, and in situations where one is frankly unable to be clear about the source and pressure of the drives.

One can appreciate the nature of the latency period best if one thinks of it as a time during which the child is able to develop the kinds of superego maturity and ego autonomy he will need to cope with the increase of drive endowment that is a consequence of puberty. In latency the superego more fully develops its structuralized form. The child withdraws considerable cathexis from infantile love objects and reinvests it in object relations (that is, in the inner and purely mental realm rather than in acted-out object-libidinal and narcissistic-libidinal striving) and in interpersonal relations. The ability to divert incestuous wishes into the structuralizing of the psychic apparatus, the capacity to deflect incestuous aims from forbidden love objects without subsequently experiencing freely sexual and aggressive pressures, the aptitude for shifting one's attachments from outer objects to internalized objects, and the relatively increased hardening (into autonomy) of many ego attributes (such as thinking, remembering, learning, perceiving, gaining coordination, separating, and differentiating) are primary attributes of the latency period. One may speculate that there are probably no increases in drive tensions in the latency period even if one is unwilling to postulate an actual decrease in drive during latency. Essentially, then, what one sees in latency is a growing control over mental functioning by the ego and the superego. Instinctual pressures that would have been either disruptive or disorganizing prior to the latency period are now taken more or less in stride by the child. Lest the last few statements be misunderstood, one would wish to remember that the development of resistance to regression that has just been described represents the development of a secondary ego autonomy rather than the continued reflection of primary ego autonomy. This developmental process reduces the emotional lability that characterized the prelatency stages, and lends a quality of stability to emotional life in general for the child. As the superego keeps pace with the ego in its development, the latency-age child is able to better regulate feelings of self-esteem and self-worth by realistic achievements and by interactions with peers, and he is consequently better able to decrease his dependency on his parents for the maintenance of narcissistic equilibrium. Another consequence of the combination of repression and inhibition on the one hand, and advances in ego development on the other, is seen in the child's use of language rather than his body for the expression of drive representations. Drives are increasingly expressed through language and fantasy, and in the later stages of latency through a decrease in fantasy and an increased capacity for rational and realistic thinking.

6

Adolescence

Adolescence in Boys

With the onset of puberty, latency comes to an end and adolescence is begun. Adolescence is a stormy and tumultuous time, in part because there is an upsurge of oedipal wishes and in part because the adolescent makes a binding, final, and irreversible renunciation of his drive- and pleasure-regulated incestuous and erotic ties to his mother. In the remodeling of object relations that occurs in adolescence, the transformation of the boy's relationship with his mother is more complete and final than the earlier shifts made in the phallic stage. In the earlier context the child could always carry with him an internal "mother," and he did not experience a deep sense of object loss because his activities continued to evolve in concert with his unconscious expectation that his estrangement from his mother was only temporary. The adolescent experiences a profound sense of object loss, and he must master a variety of depressive struggles as it becomes clear that the reunion he was waiting (and practicing) for will never occur. The process of reinstinctualization occurs because physiological changes in puberty alter the adolescent's basic state of drive endowment. The boy's oedipal wishes were essentially fantasy wishes that were attached to pleasurable infantile experiences, and the defenses that were erected were designed to cope with disruptive infantile mental events. When puberty occurs, the infantile oedipal wishes are augmented by a major physiological component, and defenses that were initially adequate to deal with exclusively mental events are no longer capable of dealing with the intensification that arises as a result of the physiological increase and reinforcement of drive.

As is usually the case with trauma, an initial reaction is to regress to an earlier mode of functioning. When the boy is incestuously aroused (which in consciousness may only include nonincestuous sexual arousal) and he is anatomically and physiologically prepared for adult genital sexuality, he first reverts to a homosexual stance as a method of deflecting erotic interests away from his mother. This time his homosexual interests are not shaped by the phallic stage and do not take the form of sexual submission to his father. His fantasy partners and his reality partners are his peers. We think of this as a phase of pseudohomosexuality because it is a comparatively brief and passing phenomenon rather than an intrinsic character variable or a stable sexual orientation. The pubescent boy cannot control his physiology, nor can he control his physical and psychological need for genitally sexual expression. Turning to male playmates is regressive, but it is also the safest behavior for him until he has had sufficient practice in constructively channeling and directing his sexuality toward females. By turning to peers instead of his father, the act of submission (leading to castration if he plays the female role) and the dangers that intensify his sense of vulnerability (to his father's retaliation if the boy tries to emasculate him by taking the masculine active role) are decreased considerably. In this phase boys may engage in eroticized wrestling, fellatio, anal sodomy, mutual masturbation, masturbation in the presence of others, and so on. It is very common for grown men to initially express anxiety (about anything and everything) in the form of being concerned about their sexual orientation. A man may be extremely concerned with his marital future, for instance, but he might be entirely unaware of that; he might very well enter treatment (or be upset privately with himself) in a "homosexual panic," that is, he may be obsessively concerned about the possibility of his being a homosexual. And it may be some time (if ever) before the true source of his anxiety surfaces. Often, men will recollect adolescent pseudohomosexual experiences, which they give as proof that they may be homosexual. The memory of those experiences often acquires in retrospect a power and importance well beyond the significance of the experiences themselves at the time they occur in early adolescence. The movement of the boy into a pseudohomosexual phase also has roots in reactions to taboos against incest and patricide that have become firmly entrenched in the superego as it has matured during latency. However, pseudohomosexuality is not a phase that can be successfully used forever. Eventually he will begin to feel some of the same concerns (about his physical and sexual safety) with his peers that he had felt in the passive-negative oedipal stance with his father, and he will also suffer conflict about the superego attitudes toward homosexuality per se he has developed throughout latency.

    In order to preserve his narcissistic integrity, the adolescent boy must discard a pseudohomosexual orientation and actively begin to develop a heterosexual orientation. In normal circumstances he cannot just give up a homosexual object-choice and then *not* develop heterosexual interests. He cannot normally develop an asexual stance because sexuality normally requires some form of expression. The demand for expression occurs as a result of the boy's lifelong history with infantile sexuality combined with the physiological origin of the current pressures for erotic satisfaction. The adolescent boy is still grossly unprepared for genuine relationships with women, and the next phase he moves to from pseudohomosexuality may be thought of as pseudoheterosexual: pseudoheterosexual, because his turn toward women is primarily a defensive maneuver rather than a sign of combined emotional and libidinal maturity. He still is unable to adequately separate his mental image of his mother from the idea of Woman in general; much of his effort during this phase will go toward the dual development of sexual objects on the one hand that have minimal loving (and by this one means nonerotic affectional) potentials, and love objects on the other hand that are nonerotic. The split is designed to permit him to have sexual but not loving feelings for some girls, and loving but not sexual feelings for other girls. The aim is to permit the emergence of sexual feelings for females that do not automatically trigger oedipal disruptions.

In this stage boys may be predatory and exploitive with some girls, while idealizing and behaving protectively toward others. In Western culture the biblical analogy sums the situation up quite nicely: Mary the virgin mother, and the Mary of the stoning. The idealized girlfriend is "pure as driven snow," she is treated with holy reverence, she has no bodily functions and no sexual feelings (as if she, also, could become pregnant without the benefit of intercourse). She is the archetype of all mothers, whom one loves abstractly and on a loftier plane than the "base" affection one develops in the context of a sexually "tainted" connection. Much to the shock and dismay of the adolescent boy, if she chafes against the artificial height of the pedestal he puts her on, and if she indicates that she would like to cuddle and kiss, be thrilled and even excited, and that she would like to be both good *and bad,* she is swiftly and roughly deposed and despised. She becomes the slut whom anyone can have, an object of scorn, derision, and exploitation, a betrayer, and very, very exciting.

Girls who are "permitted" to have sexual feelings are safe only insofar as the adolescent boy is able to differentiate them from his mother (and her representatives in both object relations and object relationships). This is a stage when boys can be very cruel and destructive to girls, in part because the substitution of sadism (a retreat to an anal-erotic trend) for sexuality is both exciting and in and of itself more acceptable, and in part because they suffer from a compulsion to differentiate these exciting and confusing persons from their mothers, and this is their first primitive erotic step in that direction. If loving behavior characterizes the relationship with the paragons who are their mothers, then merely human girls are fair game for sexually unfair, hateful, and exploitive behavior.

The adolescent boy begins next to become more comfortable developing and maintaining more normalized heterosexual object attachments, and the body changes of puberty and his newly active sexuality carry less potential for disorganization of his ego and superego than had been previously the case at the high point of pseudoheterosexuality. This is achieved, in part, by the passage of time that provides him with a greater opportunity for experimentation and practice in feeling sexual and in directing such feelings toward girls who are also, simultaneously, developing as love objects for him. The more extended his familiarity, the less traumatic are these integrated aims and investments; the less traumatic these object involvements, the richer and more developed can his attachments become. Another factor that plays no small role in the integration of loving and erotic cathexes is the boy's lengthy battle to abandon incestuous object choices throughout latency and with renewed vigor in adolescence. That permits him to distinguish more clearly between his mother and all other women. This makes his involvement with other women rewarding instead of threatening and poses no moral problems for the superego. Furthermore, despite the initiation of some major depressive struggles that the boy will have to master as he renounces, finally, the last of his infantile hopes and detaches himself from the original instinctual bond to his mother, he is enriched and helped to succeed by his ability to give and take love from females who can meet his needs as an adult, appropriately and realistically.

The importance of this factor, *specificity,* cannot be overemphasized and may be illustrated by a somewhat related clinical vignette. A patient, recalling many genuine deprivations throughout his childhood, tearfully and with angry determination said: "I didn't get what I should have received as a child. Other children received love, they were held and caressed by their mothers, and their mothers were proud to have them. My mother was psychotic [she was quite psychotic in reality and this was not just an angry figure of speech], she fed me indigestible foods, she never held me in her arms even once, and I was kept in a dark room for the first months of my life instead of being taken in a carriage for walks in the sunlight and the fresh air [all of which was true]. Well, dammit, I'm not going to accept it! I didn't get it then, and I should have, so I'm going to get it now! It is owed to me and I am going to get it now, no matter what! If I can't get it elsewhere, then you are going to give it to me, whether you like it or not, because I'm not a helpless infant now and I can take it from you if you won't give it willingly!" If this patient meant what he said, he would be satisfied only if his (male) therapist held him in his lap and bottle-fed him warm milk. He would thrive if his therapist could find a carriage big enough to fit him into, and walked him up and down the street in it. This seems silly, and the reader might well think that the patient is obviously speaking in metaphors. That is, however, only partly correct. The actual condition of this patient was that he couldn't find a way of relating satisfactorily as an adult, and poisoned every relationship with bitter recriminations and demands. He didn't say to people "Get me cute baby clothes," but he did say "You never give me what I need. You are selfish." He didn't say "Take me for a walk in a stroller," but he did say "Stop interfering with my pleasure; if I want to buy a Rolls Royce and I have to sacrifice everything I own for the downpayment, that's my business! Who are you to tell me what I can or cannot afford?" Although it is obvious that we were not meant to take him literally, it is also clear that his use of the present is only a stage-specific way of trying to get what his mother couldn't, or wouldn't, give him in an earlier stage. Because his accusations and denunciations are not related to the actual behavior of his partner in relationships (male or female), his conversation and attitudes reflect his continuing attachment to the infantile dyad and its shortcomings. This is precisely the circumstances of the adolescent boy who relates to girls via a stage of pseudoheterosexuality. If this patient found a woman who made him feel good as an adult, using the tools of adult relating, so as to provide in a current stage-specific relationship that which he should have had in stage-specific terms as a baby from his mother, or if he could buy a car that he could afford and be pleased and excited with it, we would still see many of the antecedents of his choices and how they were made, but it would also be evident that he has been able to give up his infantile object-investments and get mature and appropriate satisfactions from appropriate individuals. This too is precisely the task for the pseudoheterosexual adolescent boy. When he makes the shift, through experience, continued development, and regularly increasing structuralization, that enables him to get stage-appropriate gratifications from stage-appropriate women, abandoning permanently (except in the deeper reaches of the unconscious, of primary process, and in the most archaic of object- and self-representations) the hope for a bond with his mother that excludes both his father and all other women, we can say that he has passed into genuine heterosexuality, which also marks for him the beginning of adulthood.[1]

Adolescence in Girls

Puberty marks the beginning of adolescence for girls just as it does for boys, and their new anatomical and physiological capacities are frightening for girls for equivalent reasons. Instead of a pseudohomosexual orientation as we see in boys, girls enter a phase of pseudoheterosexuality. Girls don't have a history of compulsively avoiding the opposite sex throughout the latency stage. Their more mature and well-integrated relationship to the opposite sex (which is based on a combination of coherent and consistent experience with boys and men, and which is also based on their active bisexual identification) permits them to develop a more measured response to puberty. Their response to puberty is strong but not as extreme as the boy's phobic flight from the opposite sex. By adolescence the girl's superego, although somewhat different from the boy's in structure, functions, and contents, is well consolidated. Because of the high level of superego structuralization the girl has achieved, she experiences the upsurge in oedipal striving as very disorganizing despite the immediately preceding mitigating consideration. Her solution is somewhat counterphobic in the sense that she throws herself into sexuality quite actively. She defends against sexual longings for her father by developing a sexual interest in boys her own age, and those slightly older. The pubescent girl's intense romantic preoccupation with boys is a sign of an increase of drive (as a result of puberty) and thus cannot be viewed only as an active defense. She deflects her interest from her father onto boys. The quality of her interest in boys is usually well in excess of their capacities to respond. This is just as well, and perhaps the choice of immature males is no accident, since adolescent girls in this pseudoheterosexual stage may be physically ready for an adult sexual relationship but are far from ready for it emotionally and psychologically. This is the stage of "boy-craziness," the stage where some promiscuous acting out may be experimented with, and the stage where former scholars become functional illiterates and scholastic deadbeats. It is thought of as pseudoheterosexual rather than heterosexual because the girl's interest in boys is more a flight from her father than a mature attraction to the opposite sex. Her notions about sexuality, while considerably more sophisticated than the boy's,

---

[1]Upon reading this section one of my critical readers, who is the father of three young girls, jokingly wrote in the margin: "I won't let my girls see any boys till the boys are 21 and have been 3 years into analysis."

are still immature and essentially oedipal. This is so despite the fact that she can physically function (as she sometimes does) in a manner we consider to be customary and appropriate only for adults.

The adolescent girl's rebellion reflects much the same misery one sees in boys, as she too struggles to give up her oedipal love object and her childhood attachments to her mother. As hard-earned ego strengths and superego restraints assert themselves once again with the passage of time, she will pass through and out of the pseudo-heterosexual phase into a less overstimulating and overstimulated phase thought of as a pseudohomosexual phase. In this phase adolescent girls develop close friendships with girls of their own age, and they sometimes generate idealized interests in older women who may be available to them. These relationships have sexual undertones which, on occasion, develop into passing homosexual love affairs (or at least experimentations). This is a reinvestment of libidinal cathexis in symbolic maternal substitutes even as, paradoxically, the girl begins to relinquish her infantile oedipal desires in favor of adult genitality. She turns to women as she would have to the nurturing mother if she were still a baby, to soothe away her misery as she suffers depressive reactions in having to give up her father. She maintains women at this time as dual love objects, as her relation to them reflects both oral and genital investments.

Another part of the adolescent girl's reaction to pseudoheterosexuality involves reducing, as best she can, the pressures of overt sexuality. This reduction eventually acts to move her out of the pseudoheterosexual posture. That is because she is making a compromise by which she can hold onto her father as a partially erotic (or at least an erotically tinged) object as long as she can specifically keep the major portion of her sexuality under control. Because her father is a libidinized object, and because it is not possible simply to reduce or to transform such intense wishes, reducing her overt sexuality is helpful but not a sufficiently effective way of keeping her longing for her father under control. The adolescent girl, unable to abandon sexuality (aim), must abandon her father (object) and turn toward women. Her turn toward women is an attempt to replace the loss of her father, and it expresses the need to be taken care of by her mother; however, it is also an acknowledgment, or a declaration of her intention to develop other object choices. Despite her shift away from her father, much of the closeness in her relationships with girls and women in this phase is geared toward learning how to be a sexual woman so that the adolescent girl will be attractive to, and attracted to, appropriate males outside the family. When explicitly sexual feelings or actions do surface in this pseudohomosexual phase, it is usually an attempt to deflect irrepressible sexuality away from male objects who are, at this time, uniformly viewed as incestuous. This is a compromise formation wherein one form of misdirected sexuality is used as a defense against a different, and more disorganizing, form of misdirected sexuality. Even where some homosexual erotic play has occurred in adolescence, one need not consider the adolescent girl to be truly homosexual, because her behavior is a passing phenomenon in direct response to a revitalized oedipal conflict rather than a stable sexual orientation. Given the fact that she has identified with both genders, given the fact that sexual taboos are not as rigid in girls as in boys,[2] and given the fact that women are sexually stimulated by deeply felt feelings of love (not just erotic genitality), it is not surprising that some degree of sexuality should emerge in these intense love relationships.

With the passage of time the girl will find these relationships understandably lacking because of her maturing need to be with someone whom she can love sexually as well as emotionally. Earlier relationships are not devalued or rejected, but they are experienced as being unsatisfactory because they are incomplete. Because homosexual relationships are in the class of "forbidden" relationships they also stand, in primary-process terms, for oedipal relationships. When the girl is able to give up these no longer appropriate but intensely satisfying relationships, she is, in effect, giving up her last expectations of an oedipal union with her father. When she finds properly appropriate males to love her and to be loved by her in ways that are stage-specifically correct, she moves away from infantile and archaic demands for narcissistic restitution such as one sees in primitive penis envy and its derivatives. Outside of those cases where a woman is involved with married men or with men who are very much older than she is, who are obviously oedipal substitutes, this turn to men is her entry into true heterosexuality. In the deepest and least mature recesses of the mind's symbolic matrix, where nothing ever goes away or is lost, the woman's integrity is restored in a good love affair and even more so in a good marriage, because of the quality of union in such relationships; getting a man or having a man also has the meaning of getting and having a penis. His penis is hers quite concretely in the regular and frequent insertions during lovemaking, and it is a stable "possession" in a formalized relationship like marriage because this, more so than an affair, signifies each party's intention to form a permanent union in which the penis will not be irretrievably withdrawn as had "happened" in childhood. These are unconscious and primitive operations that are not considered to be pathological unless they predominate in the quality of a woman's experience of herself and in the quality of her relationships with men (i.e., if she feels incomplete if she is not involved with a man, if her longing for a man is experienced with desperation, if she gives up her entire identity and becomes a satellite of her husband, and so on). Another reason why marriage, rather than love affairs, can reduce the pressures for oedipal expression is because marriage was the condition of her parents; in primary-process functioning she has embarked upon an oedipal love relationship where she or any woman stands for mother, where her husband or any man stands for her father, and where marriage stands for the relationship between them.

---

[2]Despite the claim that their vigilance protects their daughters from the predatory attentions of adolescent boys, this may be why so much extra attention has to be given over by parents to the prevention and policing of their adolescent daughter's sexual life, and why so many social rules exist to hinder and restrain female sexuality in general; all these rules are a form of external (or maternal) superego controls designed to provide, in terms of "sphincter morality," some of the internalized restraints absent in the feminine superego.

Another solidification, or resolution of the oedipal striving, occurs when a woman has a baby. Here she has finally made the transition from child to mother, which was the original goal of the earliest oral incorporations that began the whole process of identification. Her ability to nurture her child satisfactorily demonstrates her "ownership" of maternal goodness, maternal supplies, and loving resources. In other words, she has not simply become a mother – she has become Mother. If this did not exist in her, she wouldn't have it to give to her baby, and thus another instinctual tie is broken as a woman no longer needs exaggerated libidinal attachments to her mother. If this is part of who she is, then she doesn't have to get it from outside sources. Breaking instinctual ties to her mother increases a woman's capacity to engage in introjection, and this permits her a more enduring relationship to her mother than when the connection was so heavily based on instinctual gratification.

The most complete resolution will occur when a woman gives birth to a male child. The male child grows inside of her and for many months prior to birth is not a separate person but an actual part of the woman's body. In "growing" a male child she has "grown" a literal, not metaphoric, penis *of her own;* thus having grown her own she no longer needs her father's and she is no longer irreparably damaged.[3] She is made considerably more effective in engaging in constructive activities, and in mature adult relationships, when a major portion of the psychic energy that was previously bound up in penis envy and the oedipal complex now becomes available to her.

Beyond Adolescence

We may now consider as complete this section's review of psychoanalytic developmental and conflict theories. Much of the psychological activity of adulthood is a refinement or an elaboration of the material just presented. Most psychological phenomena of importance that will occur in adulthood are not economical to pursue at this time, but a few should be mentioned before moving to questions of psychoanalytic treatment and technique. Loss of a loved one, serious illness, moving one's home, reaching menopause, changing careers, changing economic circumstances, and making new work-related friends are all situations in which major reactive psychological responses will occur. It is generally true that these reactive reverberations trigger old conflicts (which are never entirely resolved), and one may recall that even things that are secondarily autonomous are subject to reinstinctualization if sufficient conflictual pressure is brought to bear. It is also true, however, that the adult has a greater capacity to effectively use established defenses and is

---

[3]It cannot be emphasized strongly enough that this is not normally conscious in women, and that it is not desirable that such primitive primary-process notions should predominate in the greatest part of adolescent girl's mental functioning.

more able to develop other conflict-specific and stage-specific defenses. There are situations that adults find themselves in, and which they must respond to (becoming parents, for example), that do not usually confront a child or an adolescent. Ego and superego functioning matures and becomes more autonomous with the passage of time, and the sovereignty of the ego becomes established in large part because of the adult's relative freedom from the tumultuous psychological storms of adolescence and the earlier stages of childhood. Thus adults are less subject to regression in the presence of a new situation or in response to the emergence of conflict. One might say that a persistent resistance to regression and an increasing sovereignty of the ego (which includes major advances in its integrative, synthetic, autonomous and executive functioning) are two of the more important criteria we may want to use to describe a state of healthy adulthood. A review of the literature of the developmental processes of adulthood makes the following point: "A successful transition from the early to the later stage of [adult] life involves the acceptance of one's aging and eventual death, and the surrender of one's youth, just as at an earlier stage the acceptance of the responsibility of adulthood involved the surrender of one's childhood (J. Lasky 1985, p. 329). The author presents works that make the point that some adult tasks, particularly those of middle age, include the development of mature civic and social responsibilities, the establishment and maintenance of economic stability for oneself and one's children, providing and mentally preparing for one's retirement, developing a mode of functioning with and/or caring for one's aging parents, and dealing with what has commonly come to be known as "midlife crisis." She goes on to say that a number of the issues that can be identified as salient for the individual at midlife have to do with a changing perspective on time. Just as adolescence is the time when people first become aware of the reality of death, so midlife seems to be the time when people become aware of the circumscription of their life span: time is viewed in terms of time left to live rather than time since birth. With this changed awareness there is the increased sense that old wishes and dreams that were laid aside in the struggle to become an adult need either to be finally acknowledged or else laid to rest. There is the paradoxical position of being at the prime of life, the peak of one's abilities and accomplishments, and yet alert to the signs of impending change. There is the increased sense of actual or potential physical vulnerability, due in part to seeing one's parents age and in part to seeing changes within one's own body. Depression must be mastered, and new ways of moving beyond one's immediate personal concerns to a concern with the younger and future generations must be found.[4]

---

[4]Lasky cites numerous researchers and clinicians working in the area of adult developmental activity, who are not represented (for the sake of brevity) in this selective excerpt. Other authors, such as Erikson and Fromm, have developed consistent psychoanalytically oriented theories of various subphases in adult development that are well worth one's attention, but which are outside the scope of this present volume.

II

THE THERAPEUTIC PROCESS

7

The Psychoanalytic Situation

Undertaking a psychoanalysis, even under the most ideal of circumstances, and even when it is working at its very best, is a rather strange and unorthodox experience. The participants are required to engage in what can only be called an extremely artificial relationship: one which is based neither on friendship, education, nor mentorship, and one in which many of the ordinary social conventions are intentionally abandoned. There are major differences in the nature and quality of both of the participants' involvements that frequently impose a considerable degree of discomfort (more on the patient than on the analyst, of course; however, the peculiarities of the relationship are not borne on the shoulders of the patient alone: the experience for the analyst is not any less unusual and by no means more social, nor is it especially agreeable or comfortable in the customary sense of those terms).

As a condition of the treatment, the patient must regularly say everything that enters his mind, without exception. This is, at least, what he attempts to do insofar as he has conscious control over what he does. In this way *(free association)* the patient attempts to bring into the analysis all of the aspects of his psychic functioning, particularly the most difficult aspects of his conflicts, wishes, and defenses, which are, as a part of normal adjustment, rigorously and consistently prevented from emerging into his active conscious awareness under ordinary circumstances. In daily living one devotes enormous quantities of one's mental energies to keeping both one's impulse life and the conflicts it generates hidden in the unconscious, transformed into unrecognizable derivatives (should they become conscious) or, generally, through the activities of sublimation, neutralization, and drive fusions, constructively obscured. Paradoxically, these very same things that one spends so much effort in keeping hidden from oneself and from others (at least in their original forms, or in recognizable forms) are the very things that will have to be unearthed – and, in fact, which necessarily must emerge – for the analytic process to occur.

This is at best a difficult and almost (but not entirely) impossible task, entered upon by the patient in a context that is doubly compounded by the fact that a psychoanalysis progresses only at the cost of a series of intense (and often functionally disruptive) regressions that occur throughout the procedure. As the patient regresses, the pattern of his associations changes and the nature of his relationship to the analyst changes. Associations remain free in the sense that they continue to be reports of whatever enters the patient's mind, but they also become highly structured and predetermined. The patient's thoughts and feelings (which are spoken aloud) may superficially still seem almost random, but they become more closely organized around the conflictual issues represented within the regressive context of his changed relationship to the analyst. Because conscious thoughts are only derivative (of the underlying unconscious motivations), the material may be presented in a variety of forms: but it is recapitulated, echoes itself, and reverberates endlessly as an expression of the repetition compulsion.

It is through this combination of free association and transference regression that the transference neurosis is elucidated (in which the conflicts and defenses are reflected in their more original, i.e., infantile, forms). At points of resistance, and at moments when material breaks from unconsciousness into preconsciousness, it is interpretively addressed by the analyst. Ultimately, working through of the transference neurosis accomplishes the beneficial, that is, curative, effects of the analysis.

Some critics of this traditional analytic model have suggested that the analytic undertaking is directed away from the "whole" person because of its special focus on fantasy and regressive conflictual processes in the analysand's mental functioning. This is a misconception which may be due to either an incomplete or faulty understanding of the strength and influence of unconscious processes in the general schema of mental functioning. It is also likely to reflect a lack of appreciation of the pervasiveness of the effects of transference phenomena on a consciousness that is "innocently" unaware of this force. In many instances it is not merely an influential force, and it becomes an actual matter of domination of the transference processes in mental functioning.

Within the analytic process the patient will engage in a perpetual interplay between instinctualized, reinstinctualized, and secondarily autonomous ego functioning. As the analysis progresses and the material becomes worked through, a process of higher structuralization occurs that gives the patient increasingly more adaptive potentials as he seeks solutions to what is troubling him. This broad overview is not generally accepted by analysts outside the mainstream, classical, Freudian point of view, and this deserves some attention before moving on.

Basic Assumptions about How Psychoanalysis Cures

Different Orientations in Psychoanalysis Make Very Different Assumptions

Not everyone shares the same assumptions about how psychoanalysis cures, because the psychoanalytic situation itself is understood differently by proponents of various orientations within the field. One's view as to what the psychoanalytic situation is all about is central to one's assumptions about how a cure is to be achieved, and how could that be otherwise?

In the Kleinian model, for example, the patient is assumed to be projecting onto the analyst his inner conflicts. These are current conflicts that are perpetual representatives of the earliest infantile conflicts, and these conflicts are based more on infantile fantasies than on the reality experiences of either infancy or the present. In the Freudian model the patient is assumed to be displacing onto the analyst conflicts and relationships which have been carried forward from the past and which also have undergone alterations based on conscious and unconscious fantasies. In this case, it is a matter of fantasies being overlaid onto reality experiences with, ultimately, a greater integration between them. The key difference here is in the transference being viewed by Kleinians as a *projection* versus its being viewed by Freudians as a *displacement* (that has been altered by fantasies). One's conception of how one works with transference material is substantially influenced by whether it is to be understood as a projection or as a displacement.

In the interpersonal model it is assumed that the relationship between the patient and the analyst is healthier than were the patient's past relationships and, thus, it is the very relationship itself which is a corrective emotional experience with a curative effect. In the Freudian model, by way of contrast, only the verbal interpretations of the analyst are considered to be the tool of cure: interpretations reconstruct how past relationships are altered by fantasy and are reenacted in the present, which then leads to insight and to working-through. The working through of the insight, and not the relationship itself, is what is considered curative in the Freudian model.

Another difference between the interpersonal model and the Freudian model has to do with what is considered "primary data": the interpersonal model considers the relationship between patient and analyst as primary data, whereas the Freudian model views the relationship between patient and analyst as a means of getting to primary data. In this case the primary data are not interpersonal or interactional, they are viewed as a set of purely psychological events: they are the contents of the internal world of the patient, particularly with regard to how conflictual past relationships are integrated into, and expressed by, the patient's mental life.

In the Self Psychology model, interpretations are not made as a means of imparting information specifically in order to permit a reconstruction of a troubling past event. Interpretations are considered curative when they reestablish empathic relatedness after any break in empathy has occurred between patient and analyst. The content of the interpretation is geared to that purpose even though it may contain considerable reference to the past and to past relationships. This is a different concept of cure which is also based on the idea of a corrective emotional experience, rooted in the relationship itself between the analyst and the patient. In the Freudian model, interpretations are not used for the purpose of object-related repair.

The concept of a corrective emotional experience does exist within the Freudian model, but it plays a different role and has a very different meaning—a successful analysis has the net effect of being a corrective emotional experience, but it is not considered the means by which cure is effected.

Some proponents of the object relations point of view consider cure to be directly dependent on the analyst being a better object for the patient than were the significant objects of the patient's past. In many of the object relations approaches we see yet another "reparative" concept, using the corrective emotional experience between patient and analyst (as the analyst *is* a "better" object in the present for the patient) as the means of cure. The Freudian model views cure as related to insight and working-through, which are essentially *internal* events, not really interactional ones. The curative effect of working internally with one's own psychic phenomena is not based particularly on specific properties of the analyst or on anything special that he does but, rather, on a progressive enhancement of the synthetic and other executive functions of the patient's ego.

These differences in opinion about what is curative suggest a number of ideas, some incompatible with each other, about just what constitutes the psychoanalytic situation. As we can see, they are not minor theoretical disputes, and they have an important bearing on the entire undertaking.

This book is focused on the Freudian model. In that model the relationship between the analyst and the patient is critical. However, its importance is not for the purpose of doing something better a second time but as a tool for understanding what is important, and what is still a matter of continuing conflict, for the patient. The current relationship between analyst and patient is a means of examining the nature of the patient's past relationships, and the conflicts and fantasies surrounding them, which unconsciously still affect the patient in the present.

How the Freudian Model Conceptualizes the Relationship Between Conflicts and Symptoms

It is assumed that conflicts from childhood that were not adequately resolved will continue to exert an influence in the present. They are not immediately recognizable as childhood conflicts because, under the influence of the healthy and adaptive part of the person's ego, they have undergone many defensive transformations over the years. In neurotic individuals they are expressed as symptoms which, for self-protective purposes, are not initially recognizable. The meanings of symptoms seem, in fact, unfathomable at first. They do not permeate the entire mental life of the patient but are triggered in situations that are unconsciously reminiscent of the past situations in which they originated. It is useful to remember that one of the things that makes a neurotic *only neurotic,* and not more profoundly disturbed, is the fact that general psychological development has not been arrested. In the midst of adequate and adaptive functioning the neurotic's symptoms form as a means of defending against, as well as secretly gratifying, unresolved infantile conflicts. We can say that aspects of the ego and of the superego have become fixated in those areas of conflict. The personality of the neurotic continues to develop despite this fixation of part of the ego and the superego. As we will see in a later discussion, the same is not true for patients who suffer from the character disorders and the psychoses.

The Ego's Role in Keeping Conflicts Disguised: Stage-Specific Transformations

We choose to describe these conflict areas as fixation points because in these particular areas the ego's autonomy and the superego's maturity have been somewhat compromised. A fixation suggests an area of functioning that retains the character of infantile conflict. It is not necessary that it be recognizable as such. Because this is not the equivalent of having those conflicts act as the primary organizer of mental functioning, the ego remains essentially functional. The ego is able to transform conflicts so that they can be hidden and, hence, less anxiety-provoking, in two important ways: through the use of stage-specific transformations and through the use of defensive maneuvers.

As an example of how conflicts are reorganized by succeeding stages of development, so that they become stage-specific, we can consider how it is that oral deprivation (or frustration, or overexcitation) is not limited only to oral modes of expression. An oral conflict can be expressed genitally when, for defensive purposes, sexual intercourse is merged in unconsciousness with the developmentally earlier concept of an oral exchange of libidinal supplies. We are already familiar with the common infantile fantasy that genital intercourse is the equivalent of an oral exchange. When this fantasy is carried forward to the phallic stage in either consciousness or unconsciousness, and then is maintained from that point on unconsciously in the mind, an adult who appears on the surface to be "oversexed" might, in reality, be compulsively making up (in this symbolic fashion) for deprivations in the oral period. In such a case the fixation refers to the unconsciously distorted meaning of the act, and to the continuing need for satisfaction of an infantile wish. On the other hand, one cannot discount the fact that there has been some important progressive development (signaling only a disorder of neurotic proportions). The continuation of psychological growth is evidenced by the way of expressing the conflict, that is, in the sense that it is behaviorally and psychologically advanced to a genital means of defending and of obtaining satisfaction. On the surface, prior to any analytic investigation, it would look as if this were a genital conflict only, and that is because the earlier issues are being reorganized by the genital stage, which the adult has otherwise reached in a psychologically satisfactory fashion.

In contrast, a patient with more severe pathology, perhaps someone with a character disorder, might express the same issue by having little or no interest in genital sexuality. When sexuality does become a vehicle for the conflict, the individual might be unable in sexual contacts to achieve satisfaction or orgasm except through oral sex, or by demanding some symbolically oral fetishistic activity on the part of his partner in the place of more expected kinds of sexual contacts (which normally are characterized by genital primacy). With such a patient the symptoms are more transparent, and one would not be led to assume that genital issues are involved, even where the conflicts are manifestly expressed through sexuality.

In this example the transformation of the oral conflict into a stage-specific genital mechanism is designed to protect the individual from having to be consciously aware of archaic and primitive anxieties and fantasies related to unsatisfying (or perhaps to overly satisfying) experiences in the oral stage. In order to understand the true nature of the neurotic individual's conflict, it is necessary to unravel the complicated and highly organized and structured stage-specific disguise. The neurotic's ego is motivated to disguise his real conflicts and to maintain the camouflage as a self-protective measure, even at the very moment he presents himself for analysis with the conflicting motive of wanting to address, explore, and resolve these very conflicts.

The Ego's Role in Keeping Conflicts Disguised: Defensive Operations

The second important way the ego uses to transform conflicts is not so directly linked to psychosexual developmental stage specificity. A neurotic's ego, that is, an ego that is not overwhelmed or primarily altered by conflict, is capable of a variety of defensive operations designed to reduce anxiety, to secretly gratify unacceptable wishes, and to avoid any further escalation of already existing conflicts. Maturation always adds to the ego's resources, and without having to point to any specific psychosexual stages, the ego is capable of defensive actions of considerable scope and complexity. Conflictual wishes can be kept from emerging into consciousness through repression, or pushed into unconsciousness through suppression; they can be split off, compartmentalized, isolated, or denied (with the substitution of alternative wishes or fantasies in their place); ego functions that are too closely related to conflict can be inhibited; activity (or passivity) can be transformed to passivity (or activity); a different drive derivative may be substitute for the conflictual one; and both condensation and displacement (which are hallmarks of primary process) are operations that can serve the ego in its mission to obscure. This list is virtually endless when one postulates an ego that has a wide range of defenses at its disposal. Thus it is impossible to know what anything really means when it is first presented in an analysis. And here, too, just as we saw in stage-specific symptom transformation, the defenses that achieve this are strongly guarded and protected even when the patient truly wishes to get to his conflicts in order to resolve them.

What Do We Know about the Underlying Conflicts at the Beginning of Treatment?

It is axiomatic in the Freudian model that, in the earliest stage of a psychoanalysis, neither the patient nor the analyst can have an accurate idea of what the problem is: we may surmise that some of the patient's defenses no longer work as well as they once did, or that new pressures may be more powerful than the old defenses were equipped to manage, and so increased anxiety or increased symptomatic discomfort impelled the patient to seek some relief in treatment. But one can know nothing about the contents of the underlying conflict from the specific defenses, anxieties, symptoms, ideas or feelings that the patient presents at the beginning of an analysis.

Is This View Shared by Every Orientation?

The only thing one can postulate with any certainty is that the patient is in some sort of conflict, but the nature of the conflict is not clarified by symptoms or by what the patient knows he feels or thinks. This may seem self-evident, but it is not a point of view shared by analysts of every orientation. Some orientations do have assumptions about the contents of patients' conflicts. For example, Self psychologists assume the conflict is always, at bottom, related to some difficulty in narcissistic and self organization; some of the "British" object relations people believe that the conflict is always about inadequate internalization of object representations, or internalization of "bad" object representations, due to early frustrations; interpersonalists tend to understand the contents of conflicts as being directly related to things that actually happened between the patient and his parents (excluding the possibility of non-object-related drive conflicts, and of the role of fantasy reorganization of conflicts); and Kleinians understand the contents of conflicts to be dominated by persecutory anxiety (as a derivative of the death instinct). Critics of the Freudian model sometimes suggest that the centrality of the oedipal conflict is the automatic assumption of this model, and that Freudians automatically will assume that oedipal issues will be the "inevitable" contents of patients' conflicts. Actually, the only assumptions made in that direction are those that suggest that if development has progressed adequately up until the emergence of the Oedipus complex, disruptions of the psyche in that area will most likely be in the neurotic range rather than being in the range of the more profound psychopathologies. If anything, Freudian thinking suggests that in every analysis one will find derivatives of every psychosexual stage. Some pathologies will be more related to one or another psychosexual stage as their central organizing feature, but there is no presumption that the genesis of psychopathology will be located in the Oedipus complex. If Freudian psychoanalysis can be said to have assumptions, they are its developmental psychology (that is, a psychosexual view of development); its view of mental contents being an amalgamation of drive derivatives, reality experiences, and the effects of fantasy upon them; and that it is essentially a conflict theory (regarding both healthy adaptation and psychopathology).

Insight, Working Through, Symptom Amelioration versus Structural Change, and the Ego's Integrative and Synthetic Functions

The concepts of insight and working through are inseparable in psychoanalysis because, unlike its meaning in other contexts, psychoanalytic insight is not the equivalent of intellectual recognition. There is a great deal the patient needs to learn about, but just learning about it will not suffice. But even if the issue were only just to intellectually learn about oneself, and in one sense it is (as the important first step in a more complex process), so much conspires against self-knowledge that it makes the task rather formidable. We must remember that defenses are erected to protect the individual from danger, and that some areas of self-knowledge are dangerous because they consist of wishes and impulses that are forbidden, or are potentially destructive to one's self or to a loved object, or are overstimulating, and so forth. Particularly when defenses are maladaptive there is an even greater constraint against self-knowledge. It is not invariably the case, but it often is true that the more intense and potentially disorganizing conflicts develop fixed defensive structures (including compromise formations), and that the inflexibility of these defensive organizations is due to both the heightened potential for danger and the fact that their very rigidity prevents them from maturing into more appropriate forms. Thus even the most well-intentioned seeker after self-knowledge will also have a powerful opponent in an unconscious area of his ego (representing not only itself, but also the demands of the superego). Frequently people who think that they are sufficiently motivated so that, with enough persistence, they will find out what they need to about themselves have, ironically, no idea that their conscious wishes to know about themselves are matched (usually more than matched) by unconscious wishes to remain as consciously ignorant about their conflicts as is humanly possible. What, then, does the patient know about when he presents himself for treatment? And if he feels that he does have some insight about himself, how deep does it run?

To begin with, most conflicts are either mainly or entirely unconscious: the patient may be aware of the existence of a conflict through derivative mechanisms, such as anxiety and symptoms, but the nature of the conflict itself will be unknown. What the patient has "insight" about is that he is having a difficulty, which he usually equates with his symptoms. The task of learning about one's inner conflicts, and eventually acquiring some real insight, becomes even more daunting when we consider that people do not have just one conflict, but many conflicts. In all of these conflicts the associated symptoms and expressions of anxiety undergo the usual processes of condensation and displacement. Each single symptom, for example, can reflect a wide variety of conflicts, and on the other hand, many symptoms that may appear to be unrelated on the surface may all be reflective of a single particular conflict. If one imagines the matrix of possibilities for only one conflict and then multiplies that by a number of simultaneous conflicts, the possibilities are mind-boggling. And, in fact, mind-boggling is just what it is and what it is designed to be by the ego, which is engaged in processes intended to defend against unacceptable wishes while at the very same time also being engaged in processes engineered to secretly gratify those wishes. Thus the inevitable application of primary-process operations is another cause of the original wishes becoming unknowable. As if this did not raise obstacles enough, the defenses (which are an additional means of keeping them from being known) are also hidden and obscured. Despite the fact that they operate closer to the surface than the wish or impulse, defenses are not immediately recognizable as such.

Unacceptable wishes and impulses are not defended against on only a single level but on multiple levels. That is to say that the first line of defenses is hidden behind a second line of defenses, and the second line behind a third, almost ad infinitum. There is a great deal of intelligence in forming such layers of defending and in placing them for the most part in unconsciousness. The layering of defenses protects the individual from the anxiety and disorganization that would occur if there were only a single defense, and if that single defense collapsed under some unusual pressure. And the placement of most defensive organization in unconsciousness serves the same purpose, in that a defensive breakdown would not automatically force the conflictual wish or impulse into consciousness. From the point of view of how much self-knowledge is possible at the beginning of an analysis, the most one can expect in a very reflective person is for some partial, usually preconscious, awareness of the most superficial level of the defenses. By and large, the major portion of the defensive system is just as unaccessible to consciousness and insight as are the wishes to which they are responding.

One of the most powerful of defenses is the inhibition of the specific memories connected to conflicts. The unavailability of crucial memories makes learning about oneself virtually impossible, and they need to be retrieved in order for an analysis to progress. (The question of whether the memory needs to be accurate is important, but not nearly as important as whether or not remembering is possible.) A motivated inhibition of memory works hand-in-glove with the other defenses to make sure that anxiety-provoking and disorganizing material does not surface into consciousness; part of the job of acquiring insight will, at some point in the analysis, include retrieving suppressed and inhibited memories. Much the same is true for memories as was true for defenses, in the sense that one does not retrieve memories fully intact and in a fully accurate form. Rather, in a slow process of discovery much like the unraveling of a system of layered defenses, memories emerge piecemeal and haltingly and, specifically with regard to memory, greatly influenced by fantasy.

Considerably more could be said about much else that needs to be learned in an analysis, but this discussion of how primary-process operations apply to symptoms and anxiety, of defensive layering, and of the interplay of all that with memory adequately illustrates that the analytic process has at its center a special, difficult, and even formidable kind of learning process. The point should also be clear by now that no one thing that is learned is the equivalent of having "insight" about one's problems, and as we shall see, even having insight about one's problems is not the equivalent to knowing enough about them to change anything.

The method by which we do learn anything of value (and not merely of intellectual interest) is the process called working through. The first step in gaining insight is in acquiring a knowledge of the kinds of things just described—that is, memories that were previously unavailable, the nature of one's defenses, the underlying wishes and impulses at the heart of conflicts, the nature and meaning of one's symptoms, and so on. But we all too often see that just having the information itself, although essential, is insufficient, mainly because it is not a "working knowledge" of the material. For example, a patient might say, "I know that I fear and distrust women because my mother was both sadistic and inconsistent, but even though I know this I still don't like them." Or another patient might say, "I know that I challenge every authority figure that I encounter because my father tried to perpetually dominate me, but even knowing this, I find myself getting into trouble with my supervisor every time he gives me an order." So the question still remains about what else has to happen with the information in order to actively put it to use. But this assumes that one has the information that one needs, and that the problem is in knowing how to work effectively with it. In fact, a more basic question precedes this, namely, how does one acquire that kind of information to begin with? If the things we are unaware of are the result of a highly motivated set of operations designed expressly to keep them unknowable, what actually happens in an analysis to unlock the barriers against self-knowledge, so that it is finally permitted to surface? The answer to how material becomes available also includes within it the answer to how gaining and using the information can become more than just an intellectual exercise.

The process of working through both unlocks and puts to use the information acquired in an analysis, and these two subprocesses are highly interactional. As a preliminary statement we can say that working through involves the retrieval of memories in an affectively enhanced state. It is not just a process of information gathering and retrieval in which the patient and the analyst join intellectual forces but is, rather, a process in which a connection is made between the feelings and the ideas that are involved. For example, the person who said that he knew that his mother was sadistic and inconsistent would have reached that conclusion, in an analysis, through cognitively remembering his mother's behavior while simultaneously feeling the anger, pain, frustration, and insecurity that he felt with her as a little boy. Whether it emerged directly or in the transference it would be, for him, as if it were happening all over again, now, in the present, at the moment when he arrives at it in his analysis.

Actually, there is a different way that he regularly does reexperience those feelings in the present: not as a recognizable memory but as a symptom. It happens every time he fears, distrusts, and dislikes the women he meets. When the patient comes into contact with a woman, any woman, it causes a memory to emerge. But this memory is in an unconventional form: instead of actively and consciously remembering in the normal way, all of the feelings surface consciously and the idea (the specific conscious remembrance of things that actually happened when he was a little boy with his mother) remains unconscious. The feelings are, instead, attached to the contemporary event, which in this case means the contact with the woman that he is engaged with at the moment. Consciously, what he knows is that he dislikes her. It is fully as if she were the person to whom his archaic feelings were really responding. Because he does in fact dislike her, on one level what he thinks is true. But on another level she is only a representative for his mother, so that his dislike for her is not based on what is actually likable or unlikable about this woman but, instead, is based on what happened between him and his mother. We recognize this as being a transference event, but when he is actually experiencing it he does not understand it as transferential but as a current event, with all of its properties in the here and now. He thinks that he dislikes the woman without having any awareness that he is actively having a memory (because the idea part is still unconscious). Without being able to identify it as such, it becomes in his mind, for all practical purposes, a current reality. But from our perspective we can see how blurred the edges are between the present and his past.

The transference neurosis is the tool by which symptoms such as these are reorganized so that they become directed onto the analyst and become reenacted within the analysis, and thus it too plays a critical role in the working-through process. The concepts of transference and the transference neurosis are discussed in considerable detail in the chapter on transference. To use a capsule summary, we can start by saying that the patient undergoes a regression in the analysis. As part of this regression he withdraws the feelings and conflicts he has been expressing every-where in his life, so that they are diminished in those other areas (sometimes symptoms are so reduced that a casual observer might assume that there had already been a cure). The feelings and conflicts are then re-invested in the analysis, and are made (because of the regression) especially intensified in the analysis. To put this concretely: if we were still considering the same patient, he begins to dislike, fear, and distrust the analyst whom he experiences as being both sadistic and inconsistent. And again, just the way it happened in his symptom, it feels real to the patient, as if it were justified by his actual experiences with the analyst. We know that the analyst has not acted toward him the way that his mother did, and that he is once again having a memory (in an affective, but noncognitive form); but he does not. As far as he can tell, the things that he thinks and feels about the analyst are justified and true.

One essential difference between his experience of the analyst in the transference neurosis and the things that happened in the past with his mother is that when they happened in childhood, he had only a child's ego, and when he reexperiences a childhood event in the present, he has an adult's ego to bring to bear on the problem. For one example of the difference, let us assume for the moment (even though it is a bad assumption) that his descriptions of his mother are entirely accurate and uninfluenced by fantasy. A child's ego might not be capable of understanding this as a flaw, but an adult's can. A child, unable both to understand his mother's behavior as a weakness and to get any distance on the problem because of his physical and emotional dependence on her, is in a very different position from that of an adult, who can recognize the nature of a deficiency and who is no longer in a totally passive and dependent relationship with his mother. There is a profound difference between an adult's dependency, which is entirely emotional, and the dependency of a child, which in addition to being emotional is also obliged by the power of an absolute physical necessity. The importance of having a considerably more mature ego with which to approach one's conflicts cannot be too highly emphasized.

This combination of factors gives an adult, even an adult in a regression, tools that are inconceivable for a little child. After all, if we remember the description of how neurotics differ from persons with more profound pathologies, we recollect that the entire ego is not affected by a conflict or a regression. Only the part of the ego that is in "immediate contact" with the neurotic conflict becomes compromised, and although that may be a powerful event, it is not the equivalent of the entire ego becoming crippled by the conflict. Many other areas in both the child's ego and the adult's ego are intact and functional. In the child, given his dependant circumstances and the closeness of his instinctual ties to his mother (and father, and siblings), perhaps more of the ego would be colored by the conflict than one would see in an adult, but it would still not entirely overwhelm the ego. In an adult, considerably less of the ego would become involved (quantitatively and qualitatively), and the ego itself (including, or especially, the portion that is nonconflictually available) is much more highly sophisticated in the management of conflict. Thus the patient, who is an adult no matter how much he feels like a child, no longer has only the tools of a child.

One of the bases for assigning a patient to psychoanalysis rather than some other psychotherapy, as is discussed in greater detail later, is a careful consideration (in the initial period of consultation) of the patient's ego strengths. By definition, a patient without a basically adequate ego structure is not able to withstand the stresses of an analytic regression, and conversely, a patient for whom psychoanalysis is appropriate retains, despite the regression, enough ego autonomy to bring considerable resources to bear on the problem of analyzing what he is experiencing in the analysis. A significant part of the working-through process involves fluctuations between reinstinctualized and autonomous functioning, fluctuations between regressive and progressively adaptive functioning, and fluctuations between being entirely caught up in the experience and being able to achieve some distance from it. It is not a straightforward process of unlayering, as in the popular metaphor of peeling off the layers of an onion, but is a true series of fluctuations between things that are sometimes closely related in time and function, and things that are not.

Let us return once again to our hypothetical patient with the sadistic and inconsistent mother, to illustrate the difference between how the transference experience would be handled by a neurotic patient as compared with a patient who is more profoundly disturbed. A profoundly disturbed patient might, after such a regression has been established, refuse to continue the treatment on the grounds that it is impossible to be in a treatment with such a sadistic and inconsistent analyst, thus negating any possibility of working anything through. A neurotic patient would certainly feel that the analyst was sadistic and inconsistent but would also be aware of the possibility that this is a product of his imagination. If the analyst has not been like his mother in reality, many experiences that actively disconfirm that view of the analyst will have taken place; the patient will be in conflict about what he thinks and feels and what he knows from his actual experiences with the analyst. The neurotic patient can feel more than one feeling and have more than one idea about the analyst simultaneously, mixing his ambivalence and his dichotomous feelings and ideas without entirely losing hold on his awareness of the event as being partly rooted in reality and partly rooted in his mind. In patients who are more profoundly disturbed, an intense idea or feeling can frequently flood the ego and prevent reality testing about this, as well as disrupt a number of other executive ego functions. Thus the neurotic experiences transference events at a much higher level of complexity than does the more profoundly disturbed patient, is deeply and regressively immersed in them while also being capable of obtaining some distance from them, and has regular access to the synthetic and other executive functions of the ego which make the working-through process possible.

We have touched upon a number of ego functions that are involved in, and essential to, the working-through process: defense, reality testing, controlled regression, objectivity, fantasy, and intellect. What we have not yet said anything about, except to name it, is the ego's synthetic function. In a sense, everything that has been described thus far has been something of an introduction, setting the stage for an examination of the ego's synthetic function and its unparalleled role in the process of working through. Without the influence of the synthetic function the best we could hope for in an analysis would be a highly "educated" patient whose cure is dependent on suggestion or support. It is what finally moves the material from being simply a powerful repetitive experience, or a form of information, into something that the patient can actually put to use. It makes the experience and the information usable because it is the primary tool of progressively higher structuralization. This is particularly important because a higher degree of psychic structuralization, i.e., greater ego autonomy, greater superego maturity, and even more structuring of the id, is what we define as "being cured."

The synthetic function of the ego is not a particularly controversial concept although it has variously been described in different ways: these differences are essentially a matter of emphasis. Hartmann (1964) equated the synthetic function with a "special functional control and integration" (p. 145). Nunberg (1931) described it as a process "toward binding and assimilation;" according to Rapaport (1967), the synthetic function keeps various of the ego's aspects coordinated so that it maintains a cohesive organization. [Gill, his editor, interjects in a footnote that there is some question about whether Rapaport meant *cohesive* or *coherent*.] It puts things together, helps them fall into place, so that understanding or any other equivalent higher-order process is possible, quasi-automatically, without the individual having to make deliberate efforts to do so (pp. 589–590). What they are saying, in somewhat more complex language, is that the synthetic function organizes a variety of integrative activities in a special way; it is able to put things together in a way that makes the eventual product greater than the sum of the parts that were available to begin with. It makes sense out of incomplete information, filling in the gaps correctly. It requires no conscious effort when things "fall into place," and in fact attempting to cause things to fall into place by intention is impossible. It is what we are referring to when we speak of intuition, imaginative connections, and leaps of logic. It sorts and re-sorts the cognitive and emotional experiences of an analysis, putting them together to form a new perspective. This is not only a new way of looking at things, it also involves a genuinely new way of experiencing them. The ego's *integrative* function forms the material of an analysis, constantly, as it emerges, into a cohesive aggregate which the *synthetic* function then compounds and blends, yielding something of an even higher order: the very "insight" that the layman means when he is referring to the kind of knowledge that actively gets put to constructive use. The integrative function of the ego without its synthetic counterpart would collate the many, sometimes contradictory and some-times unrelated, aspects of an analysis so that the patient could formulate a coherent picture of his inner life, his motives, and his behavior. This is the function that "educates" the patient. The synthetic function takes what has been only learned to another plane of understanding. In working through, the transference elucidates the nature of the conflicts and defenses, the interpretation brings them into a new relationship with each other, and we count on the synthetic function of the ego to do the rest.

Let us return, one last time, to our hypothetical patient with the inconsistent and sadistic mother, for an example of how this would work in practice. Let us assume that the patient has reached the stage of understanding that his symptoms, and his transference experiences with the analyst, reflect symbolic repetitions of earlier experiences with his mother. He enters a transference regression (remember that transference regression is a fluctuating experience rather than a linear one that stretches across the analysis) and the analyst points out, with an interpretation, what is really going on. At this point the regression is reversed, in large part due to the interpretive intervention of the analyst. The patient recognizes the truth in the analyst's interpretation and readily agrees, perhaps even giving other examples of this phenomenon, as they occur elsewhere, to reinforce his understanding of the current situation. This, so far, speaks to the ego's integrative function. Now, assuming that this patient began the analysis with a relatively intact ego (a wide array of constructive defenses, a relative resistance to reinstinctualization, and so on), the autonomous and virtually automatic synthetic ego function will kick into gear and take it a step further. After repeated experiences of this sort, the patient will one day enter into an analytic regression, and before the analyst can point it out or needs to do so, the patient himself abruptly reverses the regression with the comment: "Hey! I'm doing it again, aren't I?" This first flash of independent recog-nition coupled with the ability to reverse the regression because of it, is an example of how the ego's synthetic function would operate in an actual analysis. This process happens again and again, continually enlarging its scope of influence as structural changes take place, and it is at the very heart of the working-through process.

Cure is not an absolute. In this sense it is reminiscent of how we think about reality testing: it is not something that one either has or does not have. In one area the ego's reality-testing abilities may be superlative while at the very same time, in a different area, reality testing may suffer considerable interference. Cure is relative; each step up the ladder of psychic structuralization is a cure; and the deeper regressions made possible by the ego's added strength may also be signs of a cure. It is the quality of the event and not what shows on the surface, and the quality itself may have very different vehicles of expression (so that one moment it is reflected by a progressive step and at another moment it is reflected by a regression that would have been impossible, or uncontrollable, if the ego had not been strengthened). We do not view the amelioration or removal of symptoms as a measure of cure, because one can achieve that result without structural growth – for example, in response to the analyst's influence or suggestion (in which case we describe it as a "transference cure"). What we are after is the ability to remove symptoms as the sign of a conflict having been resolved, or if the conflict is not fully resolvable, because it is better and more adaptively able to be managed. The falling away of symptoms under these conditions is not the measure of cure, or the proof of it; it is the result of cure.

The Analytic Contract and the Analytic Object Relationship

Much has been said about the patient being an adult no matter how much he may feel like a child at various points in the analysis. The patient enters into an adult working contract with the analyst at the time an analysis is started, even if certain transference elements are present right from the beginning. Patient and analyst make fee and scheduling arrangements that include the ground rules applicable to missed sessions, lateness, vacations, method and time of payment, and so on. There is usually some discussion very early in the consultative stage about large issues such as what kind of treatment seems to be most advisable for the patient. One would not ordinarily provide, indiscriminately, whatever kind of treatment the patient requested just because it was what he said he wanted; if the therapist feels that it is not advisable he would want to explore the issue as well as give the patient consultation about the treatment modality that he recommends instead, or even a referral elsewhere if appropriate. Frequency of sessions is an early issue in making the analytic contract, and the agreement regarding free association and censorship usually comes up rather quickly, depending on how appropriate and sophisticated the patient is; perhaps even in the very first session. Other technical aspects of the treatment arise somewhat later (but still in a very early phase of treatment), such as sitting up or lying down on the couch. And somewhat later yet, other technical issues arise which may require some discussion, or at least some preparation, before they can be implemented in the treatment, such as not answering personal questions by the patient (e.g., How was your vacation? Have you seen that movie? Do you know that person?), not answering questions the patient may have about the contents of what he is bringing up in a session (What do *you* think my dream means?

Do *you* think she stands for my mother? What do *you* think my "slip" means?), not answering questions about technique (Should I write down my dreams? Do you think everyone reacts to interpretations this way? When do you think I'll be ready to stop?), or other technical decisions, such as whether or not the analyst will repeat something he has said if the patient requests him to do so.

These are just a few examples of the kinds of things that are included in the analytic contract, and this list is by no means exhaustive. These kinds of examples address themselves to both the business arrangements between the parties and the reality aspects of the undertaking, and they ignore the fact that the relationship is subject to transference from the outset because it is presumed that the patient is not in the kind of regressive condition in which the transference would hold him fully within its power. The patient makes these arrangements with the analyst using the healthiest and most autonomous parts of his ego even if, later on, the arrangements become reorganized in the patient's mind in accordance with the nature of his conflicts. Most of the working agreement begins by being rooted in reality; for example, unless the patient is completely naive about the analytic process, which is always a possibility, the patient already knows that there will be times when the analyst can see something that he himself cannot, and that it will be part of his end of the contract to look seriously at (but not necessarily accept carte blanche) what the analyst brings to his attention. In fact, the patient's ability to make such arrangements, to agree to certain frustrations and deprivations, is one indicator that he has sufficient ego structure to undertake an analysis.

We can pick one of these examples—let us take the case of the patient asking the analyst to repeat himself—and show how it becomes part of the analytic contract. Suppose the patient has been dealing with a conflictual issue and the analyst makes a comment that arouses intense anxiety. If in this case the patient were to say "What were you saying? I couldn't hear you, a truck was passing by," the analyst might not want to answer the patient for good technical reasons. If this were the first instance in the analysis in which the analyst wished to act that way (there might have been previous instances in which the analyst did choose to repeat himself, for other technical reasons), the patient requires an explanation. An explanation is warranted because the patient is not expected to understand the technical and operational features of a psychoanalysis and because in normal circumstances this is an unorthodox, in fact a socially unacceptable, behavior. Without an agreement about some of the technical rules, particularly those that in other circumstances would be discourteous, the behavior becomes something that the analyst imposes on the patient. The power to impose this comes from the transference, in which some of the authority originally vested in the parents is given over to the analyst (this uses the same dynamics one sees when teachers become authority figures for children). If the analyst capitalizes on that power it erodes the analytic contract, which by necessity must be based on reality and not on the power of suggestion. And it is for this reason that the analyst and the patient must explicitly come to a mutually agreed-upon understanding that permits such behavior by the analyst when it will further the goals of the treatment. Prior to the establishment of a deeply regressed transference neurosis (in which some reality issues of the working agreement are going to be pushed into unconsciousness), having an agreed-upon understanding that the analyst's behavior is in the service of the analysis permits the patient to allow behaviors on the analyst's part that might even be considered offensive in any other circumstances. From their very first meeting to the point where a major regression occurs in the transference neurosis, the patient has had adequate reality-based therapeutic experiences that would lead him to expect that the analyst would never knowingly abuse the right to behave in this way; but that does not obviate the need for a clear agreement, because when the transference regression does deepen, it will not always remain obvious to the patient that the analyst is not abusing the privilege.

On that first occasion when the analyst chooses not to repeat himself, he might say to the patient: *"This is a situation in which I would prefer not to repeat what I said. It is true that there is some traffic noise, but it is also true that what you were talking about was making you uncomfortable. I know that you actually did not hear what I said and I am not questioning that, but I can't tell whether it was because of the truck that was passing by or because what I said had the potential to make you even more uncomfortable. If it was just the street noise, and I felt that I could be reasonably sure about that, there is no question but that I should repeat what I said. But if your not having heard me was a sign that I made you more anxious than you felt you could manage, then my repeating what I said would be a way of disregarding the only way you had to tell me that I might have said too much, too fast. Throughout our work together, in situations like this one, where I can't be sure why you didn't hear me and where there is a reasonable possibility that it may have a psychological component, I think that I'd be doing you a disservice if I repeated what I said, even though you have asked me to."* This is only one of a number of possible ways that the analyst could prepare the patient for his nonresponsiveness: whatever specific approach the analyst takes to communicating his motives for not repeating himself, he will forge a working contract with the patient that makes it clear that when he does not reply to a question or he chooses not to repeat himself, it is not because he is disrespectful, exercising illegitimate power, or treating the patient in a cavalier fashion. Such explanations only need to be made once, and as long as the patient can objectively appreciate it at the time, an analytic contract is established that remains intact even when, later in the analysis, the analyst's behavior is reinterpreted by the patient along the lines of the transference and the patient's conflicts.

The patient's need for the analyst's participation in his transferentially based regression, as if the analyst were an equal player on the stage, is the polar opposite of the analytic contract. One can say that such transference demands follow the fantasy distortions of the patient's object relations. The patient demands implicitly, and in a variety of symbolic forms explicitly, that the analyst act out the transference with him; he expects that he should have his object relations come to life in the analysis with the analyst playing the roles assigned to the significant figures in his inner life (either directly, or sometimes in reversal). Despite his awareness that this is an analysis and that the analyst is the analyst, transference regressions cause him to make simultaneous demands (which he is consciously unaware of) that the analyst *not* be just an analyst and that this is something *more* than an analysis. The patient's experience of this, when subject to a transferential regression, is quite concrete, and he has no clear recognition of how it departs from the analytic contract. From his point of view it is not in opposition to the analytic contract, it is now implicitly *part* of the analytic contract. The expectations aroused in the transference, and the belief that they can be satisfied (or unconsciously gratified), attempts to replace the analytic contract, and they have the feeling of considerable legitimacy for the patient.

We know that the transference neurosis is both the tool by which we conduct the analysis and the greatest resistance against psychoanalysis. It acts as the greatest resistance because it demands satisfaction, not analysis, at the height of an analytic regression; the patient does not just come in to talk about, understand, and recognize his conflict: the neurotic component of his personality thrives on the idea that satisfying his transferential demands and expectations may actually be possible, and at these times the patient goes about insisting (against all objective wishes and disconfirmations) that it be so. We find this very helpful in the analysis because it informs us about what the issues are in a less defended, and also more original, form; it gives us a perspective from which to view both what we reconstruct to be true about the patient's past, and the role that fantasy has played in reorganizing and distorting it. If we did not have this, we would be lost in trying to understand the inner life of the patient. On the other hand, the patient's insistence that the analyst participate in the patient's inner life, as if it were the equivalent of the analyst's external reality, presents formidable problems (essentially, we see this as the motive force, as well as the underlying meaning, of most resistances).

The belief that one can change one's past, undo it, or do it over is very different from the expectation that one can change one's *relation* to the past and the effects that it has had upon one. The latter expectation is governed by reality testing and other secondary-process operations, whereas the former expectation is governed primarily by wish fulfillment and other primary-process operations. The patient's unrealistic beliefs are designed not only to undo or to change the past, they are also a mirror of the degree to which the past gets reenacted in the present within their symptomatology. Features of infantile and archaic expectations are unconsciously merged with realistic expectations in the analytic contract, and they become indistinguishable from one another. Subjectively, when the patient loses distance from what is happening because of the regression, his expectations seem to him to be perfectly natural and reasonable. Examples of this are the bread and butter of psychoanalysis, simply because any resistance or any other transferential phenomenon qualifies. This is to say that everything that arises out of the transference in an analysis is experienced by the patient as legitimate until he gets some insight about how it is related more closely to his conflicts than to the current reality. Transference wishes are experienced as perfectly reasonable, transference fears are experienced as if they have a basis in current reality, and resistances are not experienced as something that is concretely being acted out in a symbolic form. The "truth" of the patient's experience is something that he expects the analyst to share, even if he also, on another level, expects the analyst to *analyze* rather than share. And it is in this expectation that the analyst not only will recognize the validity of his experiences but also will behave in accordance with them, that we see the patient's conflictual wishes asserting themselves in opposition to the analytic contract.

A case example will make the distinctions clear. Mr. K. came for a consultation having prematurely terminated four previous therapies, each time because he felt that he could no longer afford them, and he still owed each of his previous therapists the final month's payment at the time he wished to begin (his fifth) treatment. Exploration of this naturally raised questions about why the old debts were never paid, which then led both patient and analyst to the conclusion that there must have been more going on for Mr. K. than just the issue of what he could afford at the time. If it were only a matter of finances, the debts would have been promptly paid. Mr. K. readily acknowledged that something else must have been going on, but he was at a complete loss as to what else it might have been. Further investigation revealed that a pattern of slowly growing indebtedness developed in each of the prior treatments: first Mr. K. would pay his bills a few days late, which escalated into needing at times to pay a week or more late, which escalated into needing to defer payment for a month at a time, and then for a few months at a time. Finally, the analyst would catch on to the fact that Mr. K. was not only in some genuine financial difficulty but also very much taking advantage of his financial situation in order to act out something in the transference. Usually this was brought to Mr. K.'s attention by the analyst, rather than having entered the analysis because Mr. K. recognized the repetitive pattern. Mr. K. would become angry, feel unjustly accused, become intensely humiliated, and silently vow to himself to stay in treatment only until his current debt was paid up, at which point he would say to the therapist (this was his fantasy): "I am now paid up to date. Fuck you, fuck this treatment, and stick the check up your ass! I'm out of here, and if you don't like it, fuck you where you breathe!," slam the door (still his fantasy), and be gone forever. In reality what would happen was that he would silently seethe, "go through the motions of free associating" (as he put it), refuse to discuss the matter with the analyst, manage to get to the point where he was almost fully paid up (so that the debt was hardly more than the current month's fees), and then (this is still as he depicted the situation) get into a pitched battle over some trivial issue on the last day of the current billing month, upon which he would tempestuously quit the therapy in the last moment of the last hour of the month. He would then send in a check for the very small debt that remained, *without* including payment for the final month of treatment, and refuse any and all overtures from his previous therapists to come back to talk about this (in fact, he even returned one therapist's letter unopened because he assumed it was an invitation to try to work things out).

What I have described thus far raises some serious questions about whether Mr. K. was a good candidate for psychoanalytic treatment; however, we do not have to answer that question here because this dynamic is something that would have to be addressed consultatively in some way, no matter what modality was ultimately decided upon for Mr. K. Based on the contents of the fantasies that he reported, one could have speculated, not unreasonably, that on some level Mr. K. was acting out an anal-sadistic homoerotic transference with his prior therapists. Or one might have also speculated about his behavior as an angry narcissistic transference related to separation or to fears about a parasitic symbiosis, expressed through a developmentally later anal organization with some phallic coloring. Whether or not the subsequent treatment proved any of this to be true, one is not in a position to approach any of that material in a consultation (first, because one has no supporting data for one's speculative ideas, and second, because even if one did, it would be too early in the treatment for the patient to be able to hear an interpretation about it without being overwhelmed by anxiety). What was approachable, however, was his recognition that he was acting something out repetitively, even if he could not concretely identify what it might have been in terms of content. The analytic contract is, of course, more complex than a single agreement, but one clear part of it did involve an agreement between Mr. K. and the analyst that if anything like that did begin to appear in this therapy, whoever saw it first would bring it to the other's attention – and beyond that, that it was something that could be talked about. An even more concrete aspect of the analytic contract forged between Mr. K. and the analyst was an agreement that they would not, at any time or for any reason, get into a situation where late payment would become legitimized as part of their working arrangement.

Some time later, as the treatment progressed, Mr. K. mentioned that he had had some financial reverses (which appeared to be true and not a convenient fiction) and that he would pay what he could for that month and pay the rest at the end of the next month. He was reminded of the agreement about not making any late payment arrangements, and he vacillated between being unreasonably angry and recognizing that this might be an important psychological event that deserved closer investigation before any actions should be taken. What he focused on at the time was an assumption that the analyst only had to be told about it and then he would have no other reaction (or choice) but to acquiesce. This led into some important and revealing information about his relationship with his father, who frequently immobilized him (physically and emotionally), and Mr. K. ventured the hypothesis that he was doing to his analyst what his father did to him. Initially, however, when he was reminded of the arrangement not to permit late payment, Mr. K. did not concede that either he or his analyst had any choices in the matter, but after making the connection to his father he abandoned his demand to be allowed to pay late. Before going any further with this vignette, one can already identify the emergence of some aspects of the patient's neurotic opposition to the analytic contract. It is apparent in his initial assumption that the analyst would be as limited in his options as Mr. K. was in his, and also in his assumption that the analyst would be so identified with Mr. K.'s needs that he would automatically abandon the earlier working agreement about late payments. When Mr. K. first brought up his wish (need) for deferred payment in the current treatment, he had completely "forgotten" that this had been mutually identified in the consultation as a repetitive, established, stereotypic behavior; that it had even been talked about at all in any previous meeting; that there had ever been a discussion about how to handle it if it recurred in this treatment; and even that it could have a psychological meaning. At the moment that he introduced the idea it was, as he saw it, just an objective description of his current reality and of the inevitable implications, and he was outraged that his analyst might suggest any other possibilities (other possibilities are automatically implied, even thought they might not have been stated outright, in the notion that no change in the working arrangement should be made).

As might be predicted, repetitions of this soon followed. Each time, it became harder and harder for Mr. K. to see that his financial reverses were, at least in part, engineered by him so that he could have a reason "in reality" to justify the demand for a change in payment arrangements. And each time he repeated this request ("demand"), it became more difficult for Mr. K. to focus in on this as an unconsciously motivated repetition. At one point, Mr. K. took the position that if he was not allowed to owe money, he would have to reduce the number of sessions per week. Here we see another aspect of opposition to the analytic contract that emerged in the transference regression: Mr. K. believed that it was the analyst alone who had made a rule about not permitting deferred payment, completely forgetting that it was mutually agreed upon because it seemed at the time to both of them that it was in Mr. K.'s best long-range interests. His introduction of the possibility of reducing the number of sessions per week was first a refusal to work on the psychological aspects of how he suffered financial reverses, and also an attempt to pressure the therapist into abandoning the arrangement not to permit deferred payment. Mr. K. insisted repeatedly that this time it was a purely realistic matter, and he chose to reorganize the agreement in his mind as a rigidity on the part of the analyst. Another part of his rejection of the analytic contract, perhaps a bit more obscure, existed in Mr. K.'s assumption that the analyst had such a powerful investment in keeping Mr. K. in treatment (the very same way that a parent has a tremendous stake in his or her child) that he would agree to anything rather than see Mr. K. reduce the number of sessions per week (or, by intended implication, leave entirely). Unconsciously and then consciously the commitment was seen as going both ways, and the analyst was explicitly expected to have the same degree of intensity and neediness in his connection to Mr. K. as Mr. K. had toward the analyst.

Mr. K. was astounded when, after making it clear to the analyst that these were the only choices that he would permit, the analyst still did not agree to change their arrangement and agree to deferred payment. More and more forcefully Mr. K. insisted that *the analyst* had "made the rules," and that if the analyst would not give his permission for a deferred payment, then it was the analyst, and not he, who was making him reduce the number of sessions per week. By acting this out, that is, by actually acting on the threat to reduce the number of sessions per week when the analyst held to their prior agreement, Mr. K. put the analyst in an untenable position regarding the therapeutic contract (which included neither of these options, and certainly not a unilateral decision-making process). If the analyst agreed to deferred payment, he would be perpetuating, and perhaps even legitimizing through his participation, a long-term destructive pattern that was very much against Mr. K.'s best interests. If the analyst had no choice but to meet with Mr. K. on a reduced schedule of sessions, he would be considerably neutralized in his capacity to subject this to analysis (inasmuch as the point of acting out, or at least one of the primary purposes, is to prevent analysis). By putting it into action in this way, transference demands became dominant and the analytic contract was partially set aside. Mr. K. saw his behavior as reasonable and as being based on realistic necessity, and he was entirely unable to recognize this as a personally meaningful psychological event. From his point of view it was the analyst, and not he, who had abandoned the analytic contract, by putting him into a situation where he had "no choice but to reduce the number of sessions in order not to have an outstanding debt at the end of the month which (he) could not afford to pay, given (his) financial situation, which (he) had absolutely no control over whatsoever."

This sequence also demonstrates how, even in the early stages of an analysis, transference demands and expectations seem to be rooted in what seems to be reality. With regression (as the analysis progresses) the demands become more intense, but on the other hand, the infantile nature of the conflict also becomes more expressly visible, thereby making it more difficult to so absolutely couch it in what seems to be reality. The subjective experience early in the treatment, that it is an immediate, current event, is completely understandable and expectable before the transferential (and consequently, infantile) elements are successfully subjected to analysis. We choose our analytic patients with some care, not arbitrarily assigning everyone who comes to treatment to psychoanalysis, because we are dependent on the general strength of the patient's ego when regressions occur as a natural and expected part of the treatment. We rely on a strong ego (expecting as a given that the patient will show strong resistance to reinstinctualization, will have good reality-testing abilities, considerable autonomy, and sufficient synthetic and other executive functions) to keep superimposing the analytic contract onto infantile, transferential, and other and neurotic expectations. We depend on this, and try to assess the potential for this when we evaluate analyzability, as a means of preventing the very kind of acting out that Mr. K. displayed. We aid the patient in this process by making relevant interpretations, at various levels, which are designed to alert him to underlying psychological aspects of the situation that he has not yet recognized as having an influence on his thoughts, feelings, and behaviors. Without a basic matrix of adequate ego attributes, however, the analyst might as well not be making interpretations at all, no matter how correct they may be.

Interpretation is, of course, our most important intervention, but many other interventions take place in an analysis, and we need to think out all interventions just as carefully as we do when we are considering questions about the timing and depth of our interpretations. Because interpretation is so central to analysis, it overshadows many of the other interventions in an analysis, and there is a danger in treating noninterpretive interventions too casually. Some of the noninterpretive interventions are related to the analytic arrangements (e.g., accommodating to changes when necessary after the treatment is in progress; sending bills and receiving payment; telephone interactions; and asking the patient into the consulting room and informing him when the session has come to an end). Some of the noninterpretive interventions are related specifically to the analytic processes (e.g., assessing the need for parameters, which are special departures from the traditional analytic stance, carefully circumscribed by special conditions and subsequently analyzable at a later date; asking questions; obtaining clarifications; frustrating transference demands; and intentionally gratifying transference demands, an example of a parameter, under certain conditions). Given the peculiarities of some of the interventions in a psychoanalysis, like, for example, the practice of not answering questions, the patient finds the psychoanalytic situation to be very unorthodox in its social organization, and it is probably not like any other social relationship the patient has ever had. Every little thing counts in ways that would never be possible, or reasonable, in any other kind of social relationship: even the things that seem automatic, such as whether one calls the patient by his first name or his last name, have an important influence and meaning in the analytic process.

The context in which this all happens is the analytic object relationship. Interpretation is a powerful tool, but it does not take place in an object-relational vacuum: the analytic object relationship is the context that allows unconscious and conflictual material to emerge, and it permits the leverage (added to properties of the patient's ego) that makes interpretation curative rather than merely informative.

Before proceeding any further, this would be a good time to take a moment to review the differences between identifications, object relations, and object relationships because the analytic object relationship shifts the established balance of these operations in the patient as an essential part of the analytic work. This will enable us to think not only about the analytic object relationship, but also about analytic identifications, modeling, and the transference cure. One's object relationships (and one's relation to the object world in its entirety) are one's interpersonal relations. One's interpersonal relations are continuously modifying, and being modified by, one's object relations. One's object relations are part of the internal sphere of mental representations, which exists as a psychological and not an interpersonal event. When mental representations of the object world enter into various levels of merger with self-representations (also an exclusively internal psychic phenomenon), they compose the set of one's identifications. Object representations also exist in the psyche independently from identifications, and one's love and hate attachments to these mental representations of objects are one's object relations. A classic example of the interplay between these operations is when a man (in response to an infantile aim, but also in identification with his father) neurotically makes incestuous object choices based on unresolved oedipal wishes (object relations) in his current love life (object relationships). Identifications, object relations, and object relationships (interpersonal relations) exist in a continuously interactive matrix of mutual modification, with some identifications, some object representations, some self-representations, some object relations, and some object relationships having more stability than others.

Now let us focus in on the analytic object relationship more closely, because it is a complex relationship in which special operations take place that are similar to the object relationships of the patient's childhood, but with some significant differences. One way of addressing this is to examine what it is that is unique to the analytic object relationship, rather than to interpretation, that fosters the analytic process. How, for example, does the analytic object relationship alter the balance of the patient's psychic economy? One place to begin is to look at the effect it has on superego functioning.

The superego is, in part, composed of aim-inhibited identifications based originally on parental attributes (particularly with regard to the question of morality). The precursors of these superego operations existed in the parents' prohibitions (against, for example, anal pleasures), and they were joined by later prohibitions against incestuous and parenticidal wishes. The ego, in response to current superego demands, keeps these wishes unconscious and in so doing avoids anxiety and guilt. After the Oedipus complex, beginning at the latency period, the superego has internalized its functions (through the device of developing aim-inhibited identifica-tions) so that they are not dependent on regular reinforcement from external objects. These stable superego functions serve as a constant internalized regulator which serves to keep the patient very well defended against the emergence of those infantile wishes throughout adult life. This is why the patient, entering an analysis, is strongly defended against the very material that needs to emerge. The strength of the ego, in concert with the demands of the superego, maintains defenses intact because that material is conflictual, anxiety-provoking, and productive of shame and guilt.

One aspect of the analytic object relationship that permits such material to emerge in an analysis is a regression in superego functioning that unbinds some of the superego's self-regulatory properties and makes them once again dependent on an external object. In this case the analyst is substituted for the parents. The patient regresses to the stage where prohibitions and morality are controlled by an external object, and in this process the analyst is the focus of the patient's externalized superego functioning. The psychic regression is to a level of superego precursors, before the superego was internalized as a psychic structure with its own unique organizing potentials. Originally this was a time during which the child depended on parents and parental substitutes for guidance and restraints. In the analytic process the patient regresses in this way and, instead, uses the analyst for these functions but with a powerful difference: originally the contents of the identifica-tions were with the parents' repressive trends, whereas now the contents of the identification are centered on the analyst's nonpunitive and curious attitude toward the ordinarily forbidden wishes and impulses. The economy of the superego is changed so that it is no longer representative exclusively of the parents' traditionally repressive attitudes. This regression that defines a part of the analytic object relationship permits material to surface that would ordinarily have had intractable defenses ranged against it if the patient's customary superego attitudes had prevailed. On this basis, material can be brought into consciousness and then the executive functions of the now adult ego can have the opportunity to act upon it. This is an aspect of the analytic object relationship that is not an acting out of an infantile object relation but is, rather, a regression in part of the patient's functioning which then, in identification, uses realistic attributes of the analyst and the analytic situation as a tool of achieving a new psychic organization.

The regression that permits the patient to capitalize on this reorganization of superego functioning is no different from, and is in fact a part of, the very same regression that brings the most infantile and maladaptive features of the patient's functioning to the surface in the transference neurosis. Both ways of organizing the regression are simply an example of the principle of multiple function, in which something can serve a number of different purposes simultaneously. The depth of the regression may bring about maladaptive functioning on the side of the patient's neurosis, and highly adaptive functioning on the side of the analytic object relation-ship.

Another point of interest here is that this regression is not the equivalent of turning back the clock, in the sense that both the neurotic regressive functioning that the patient brought to the analysis and the analytic regression of the transference neurosis are not the same functioning that one would actually have seen in the patient when he was a child (and actually psychologically and materially enmeshed with his parents). Psychic functioning is indelibly changed by passage into adulthood: this is true whether one is neurotic, character-disordered, or psychotic. There are some schools of thought, notably those that postulate theories of arrested development (at various levels), which suggest that when one sees infantile conflict and regressed functioning in an adult, one is dealing, more or less, with a child's mental functioning in someone who is only chronologically an adult. This notion is flawed on a number of counts, the most obvious of which is that, given such a position, one should never, ever, see any functioning whatsoever that derives from a psychosexual stage later than the one the patient was supposed to have been arrested in (for example, if one postulates a developmental arrest in the separation-individuation phase as the etiology of borderline phenomena, one should never see any active signs of oedipal conflict in the patient: the very definition of a developmental arrest requires that everything stops at the point of the arrest), and we know from clinical experience that every patient, no matter what the diagnosis, evidences derivatives of unresolved instinctual aims from every psychosexual developmental stage in the treatment. A more important flaw in this notion, for our present purposes, is in the idea that a child's mind can exist in an adult, which totally ignores every developmental achievement subsequent to an infantile conflict. An adult's mental functioning has numerous operations that have become secondarily autonomous over the years, and the adult mental apparatus has made irreversible advances over the situation of a child, even in the midst of the presence of infantile conflict. Whatever else may be lost, these advances have a degree of stability that makes them only partially incapacitated, even by deep regressions. This point, and similar ones about not regarding any mental function in a total and absolute way, have been emphasized repeatedly in a number of different contexts: it is no less true here that only portions of any psychic function, contents, or structure are affected in regressive functioning and that other areas of the function, contents, and other mature areas of the structure are still available to the individual; and that contents, functions, and structure that have achieved some degree of autonomy coexist side by side with the infantile operations. A child does not have this at his disposal and an adult does, whether or not he is able to put it to use in the momentary depth of a regression.

In the regression accompanying the deepening transference neurosis, the psyche is truly segmented: one segment of the ego and superego apparatus demands satisfactions and gratifications related to infantile wishes; another segment is capable of observing, of testing reality, of synthetic and other executive ego functions including those that oppose infantile instinctual aims; and yet a different segment is able to use the regression directly in developing the analytic object relationship, a constructive engagement in which there is a blending together of infantile and adult functioning in a new way—one that is not in the service of obtaining infantile gratifications and satisfactions but, rather, which is in the direct service of the analysis, and which is productive of continuing psychic structuralization.

Another good example of this curious blending together of regressed functioning with adult resources exists in a different aspect of the analytic object relationship. Children, with only incomplete ego and superego structuralization at their disposal, rely on their parents as an external source of psychic organization at times of stress. Slowly, over time, they internalize the help that they get from their parents and, using that help, they develop their own ego and superego functions, which enriches psychic structuralization and eventually furnishes them with the tools of adult independence and judgement. In an analytic regression one sees the reactivation and expression of those very areas of ego and superego functioning in which the patient was least successful in achieving that kind of maturity. In the analytic object relationship the patient turns to the analyst, enlisting the analyst's more autonomous ego functioning and more mature superego functioning, in very much the same way that a child turns, appropriately, to his parents for help with that which he is unable to do for himself.

Thus far, our discussion of the analytic object relationship has centered on processes that involve some action on the part of the patient (as in his turn to the analyst for help), or which have some degree of automaticity (that is, which depend not so much on what the patient or the analyst does but, rather, on the nature of their respective psychic structuralizations: in discussing the realignment of superego economy, for example, we have described a process that has had considerably less to do with actions and more to do with an unconscious collaboration between the healthiest parts of the ego and superego of the patient and the analyst). There is, however, an aspect of the analytic object relationship that does depend on the analyst's contributions, in a more active sense, and this has to do with what and how the analyst chooses to interpret. Freud wrote very little about technique, preferring to write about mental functioning. In part this was because he was interested in developing psychoanalysis as a general psychology, but it also had to do with his view that technique should not be cast in stone. Advances in theory lead us to advances in technique, and advances in technique lead us to theoretical advances (and one or the other is always struggling to catch up). Freud was aware that major technical advances were always possible as our conceptualization of mental functioning broadened, and he did not want to limit either our technique or our ability to use advances in technique to teach us more about mental functioning, and thus he decided to say very little about how a psychoanalysis should be conducted. He did choose to comment on what he called "wild analysis," however, by which he meant making interpretations that were disorganizing rather than helpful because the analyst did not take into account the possibility that the interpretation might cause more anxiety than the patient could handle. Not only the content of the interpretation itself but also the net effect of making the interpretation must be taken into account, and it is in this area that the analytic object relationship once again becomes relevant.

The analyst has at his disposal a number of measures for assessing whether to make an interpretation: Is the material purely unconscious or has it entered into preconsciousness? Is the patient's material genuinely associative or do the contents of what he has to say seem defensive? Is this an interpretation of transference or of symptoms? Is this an interpretation of resistance or a form of censure? Is there enough evidence to feel assured that the interpretation is accurate? Is there a genuine need for an interpretation at this time, inasmuch as it will have the net effect of interrupting the free-associative process? Is there a need for an interpretation, or is it an "action defense" of the analyst's? Can the patient tolerate this kind of an interpretation? (Some patients cannot tolerate against-the-grain interpretations early in the analysis, whereas others can, frequently depending on diagnostic category; some patients, also depending on diagnostic considerations, cannot tolerate any interpretations until the treatment is relatively advanced; some interpretations, particularly those that have to do with body gestures, grimaces, and so on are better not interpreted early in a treatment because, as somatized events, they have achieved too much displacement from the psychic realm for an early interpretation.) The analyst consciously considers these issues and many more in determining whether to interpret, and if so, when and how. But there is something more at work here than just intelligent decision-making in the patient's interests; there is the net effect of making good interpretations, at the right time and in the right way, on the continuing analytic process.

We can look again to the parent–child interactions of early infancy to draw a useful analogy to an important part of the analytic object relationship. An infant can experience sensation and perception in a limited way at birth and has the possibility of a rudimentary way of remembering experiences. Organizing his experiences and making some kind of sense out of them, no matter how primitive, is another matter entirely. His primarily autonomous ego functions are of help in the first set of operations but of no help in organizing his experiences, because they are not the equivalent of a structuralized ego (which, we know, does not exist at birth). Before relying on the structured ego the baby relies on his mother to make sense of his world. One of the earliest identifications, which precedes even those based on incorporative operations, is the method by which the child's ego, as it forms into a structure, is modeled on the structure of his mother's ego. This is not a statement about the contents of the ego, even though this primitive identification uses the manipulation of contents and functions; it is a statement about the child's learning to use the ego to organize and "hold" his experiences because that is what his mother does with her ego. The structure of his ego, including its contents and functions, will have as its first model the structure (but not all of the specific contents and functions) of his mother's ego. The subsequent organization of his experiences will be based on a slowly growing ego apparatus that is based on reality (and on the possibility of experiencing objective reality), and which will, over time, bring more and more into its orbit of influence. There are some striking similarities in all of this to the situation of an analytic patient, unable to sort out his mental life, seeking a means of organization from the analyst.

We can look at how the mother does this with her baby for some clues as to how the ego of the patient begins to take on some of the character of the analyst's ego. Generally babies have different cries to indicate different states of being–for example, one kind of crying for wanting to be fed and another cry, subtly different, for wanting to be held. One need not assume, however, that these differentiated communications indicate a conceptual distinction between feeling states: the greatest likelihood is that initially the baby cannot discriminate between the various feelings of unpleasure even if they have characteristically different modes of expression (although one would also not want to overstate the differences, which are really a matter of small degrees and subtle nuances). It is entirely possible that the selectivity of the communications is more closely tied to biologically prepatterned discharge pathways than to psychologically determined choices. A stranger probably could not tell the difference between the baby's cries, but an attentive mother can and does. A well-attuned mother not only hears the differences, she can also tell what they mean (because of her vastly superior ego functioning) even when the baby himself cannot. An attuned analyst carefully attends to the patient's communications and makes sense out of them for himself, even when the patient has no way of sorting them out intelligibly.

In order to help the baby make sense of his experiences, so that he can get beyond the stage of undifferentiated tension and unpleasure, the mother responds in an appropriate fashion to the need that she has discerned in her infant. She feeds her baby when he is hungry, and she picks him up when he wants to be held. She does not feed him when he only wants to be picked up, and she does not only pick him up when he wants to be fed. Slowly, over time, he begins to distinguish between the subtleties of his discomforts, based on his mother's responses to him, until he is in the position of knowing what is bothering him and what it is that he wants. He then differentiates his communications even further in order to facilitate getting his needs met. This sequence is dependent on an accurate appraisal of the baby's experience, reflecting the mother's capacity to make sense of both their worlds. If she were poorly attuned (because of inadequate ego functions of her own), we would predict a rather pathological outcome in the child's ability to process reality, again reflecting the power that the organization of the mother's ego has on the baby's organizational capabilities. The analyst sifts through the patient's experiences and, assuming (based on his ego strength) that he is property attuned, helps the patient to organize his experiences through interpretations that are on target, and through interventions that reflect the patient's experiences with a high degree of accuracy.

A mere reflection of the baby's or the patient's experiences would be inadequate, however, no matter how accurate. The response must be at a level that the baby's ego, and the patient's ego, can grasp and make use of. Suppose a mother could tell what was bothering her baby but she responded on an inappropriate level: the baby cries for food, his mother recognizes that her baby wants to be fed, not held, and says to her infant; "You have two kinds of cries that I have come to recognize; one is when you want to be held and the other is when you want to be fed. This is the one that indicates that you want to be fed." Despite her accuracy we would not expect her infant to learn to differentiate his experiences from such a response. Here her superior ego served her quite well in recognizing her baby's need. If it were a different situation it might have served her quite well in also being able to articulate it so clearly. But her ego became inaccessible to the baby for use in structuring his own ego, because her level of response to him did not take into account the fact that he had not yet learned to talk (i.e., the limitations of his ego functions). And in the same way, the analyst must not only recognize and sort out the patient's experiences accurately but also find a way of communicating their nature to the patient in a manner that can be grasped. For the baby, only being picked up and fed–rather than being talked *at*–will suffice. The analyst, also, must find a way to gear his interpretations to an appropriate level: one at which active participation in mastering the event becomes possible for the patient. In finding such a means of intervention, two things, not one, become possible. First, the interpretation itself becomes more than just accurate information, and it can be integrated into the patient's psyche and do its work. Second, the patient's ego is subtly reorganized in a new fashion based on the superior (because they are autonomous) capacities of the analyst's ego, just as we saw with the infant and his mother (except, of course, that because the patient is not an infant this all goes on at a much higher level of sophistication). These two events work in concert, collaborating on making deeper and more complete interpretations possible and providing a framework within which the interpretations have a better chance of being metabolized into further acts of psychic structuralization. All of this is despite the fact that the dynamic operating in the analytic object relationship hinges on one of the earliest and most primitive processes of identification.

One may raise the following question: are there not patients who are insightful and self-analytic even before coming to the analysis? In answer, one can only say that certainly there are people who are capable of insight and self-analytic activity prior to being analyzed, but these capabilities, impressive as they may seem in some people, are nevertheless limited because no one, prior to an analysis, is as privy to his unconscious as he will be after having been analyzed (successfully, we presume). One should not be too satisfied with the considerable amount of self-knowledge and self-analytic abilities some patients appear to have when they arrive for a consultation: they may truly have much more than some people, or even more than one expects to see in the average patient, but we do not measure such things between different patients, we measure them within the same patient over time. When one does find such a patient, who seems to have some of these strengths even before the analysis begins, it is not a sign that analysis is unnecessary (the conflicts that bring him to the consulting room demonstrate that the analysis is necessary) but, rather, it is a good prognostic indicator of his potential for being able to use the analysis constructively.

Before moving to the next section, on analytic identification (about which we have already said a great deal), modeling, and the transference cure, there are two issues that warrant some discussion. First, there are some schools of thought, particularly those that place a heavy clinical reliance on the concept of empathy (which they have raised to new heights of meaning), that suggest that the analyst's identification with the patient's experience is not only desirable but necessary. With development of the *selfobject* concept, and the idea that the patient uses the analyst as a selfobject and that the analyst also uses the patient as a selfobject, a lack of distinction has been made about the differing dynamic reasons why people experience themselves as merged with other people, and a new distinction is made which emphasizes the experience of not knowing where one's boundaries leave off and someone else's boundaries begin (and vice versa) as a means of regulating inner experiences (which are usually, in this school of thought, related to narcissistic, or "self-," organization). In the Freudian perspective, the patient's and the analyst's experiences are *not* the same, and perhaps even more significantly, their character and psychic organization are *not* the same, no matter how well attuned the analyst is to the patient. If they really were the same, all we would have (by analogy) would be two screaming babies that could not identify the sources of their discomfort. If anything, it is the *difference* in their relative psychic organizations, and specifically the way in which the analyst's experience and psyche are *not* the same as the patient's, that make it possible for the patient to grow. Even in the concept of analytic empathy one needs to be careful about assuming too direct a correspondence between the inner lives of the analyst and the patient, just as one would not want to assume a direct equivalence of experience and functioning.

Concerning the second issue: there is a "left wing" and a "right wing" in Freudian psychoanalysis, and it is around the issues of interpretation and the analytic object relationship that some of their differences become most pronounced. The most extreme statement of the left wing emphasizes that there are personal characteristics of the analyst that come into play in every analysis and every analytic object relationship, and that the personal characteristics of the analyst will influence how the analysis will unfold and what the patient will identify with in the analytic object relationship. From this point of view, different analysts foster different analyses. The most extreme statement of the right wing emphasizes that the sole tool of cure is the interpretation itself and that, given the "correct" interpretations, analysts are entirely interchangeable. These positions seem irreconcilable only when they are taken to the extreme for polemical purposes, and their commonalities are obscured by viewing them as if they were polar opposites.

One can chip away at the most extreme left-wing position by noting that the identifications the patient makes with the analyst are limited to those that are related to the analyzing functions. This is not a form of modeling or imitative identification, and the identifications do not include the analyst's personal, idiosyncratic characteristics. Reality features of the analyst do have an effect on the treatment: for example, the analyst's gender may cause the transference to one parent to surface significantly earlier than the transference to the other parent; or the analyst's ability to resonate with some of the patient's issues more readily than with others will influence the order and sometimes the manner in which the patient integrates the material. On the other hand, the left wing fully accepts the premise that the compulsion to repeat traumatic and unresolved conflicts is the primary regulator of what will emerge in the transference, rather than the reality situation of the therapy (including the specific qualities of the analyst). Following that premise, it becomes clear that the attributes of the analyst will only influence the order and the vehicles by which the patient's conflicts are addressed. If one views the transference as being dominated by the patient's conflicts, knowing how its emergence is influenced by characteristics of the analyst can be very helpful in learning about the patient's defenses and transformational processes, but whatever the order or vehicle of expression, it will nevertheless be the patient's conflicts that have center stage in the analysis. Looked at in this way, the personal attributes of the analyst have considerable significance, but only the patient's conflicts (and not the personal traits of the analyst) can determine the kind of an analysis it will be.

One can chip away at the most extreme right-wing position by noting that there is an implicit assumption that the analyst will not be so neurotic that he will not let the analysis progress. Following that assumption, which does not preclude the inevitability of countertransferences in every analysis (because they are transitory and do not dictate the general course of the work), the autonomous ego and mature superego of the analyst will be informing his general conduct of the treatment and his behaviors will be fully in accordance with what we have described as occurring in the analytic object relationship. Based on this assumption, even if the order and vehicles of expression differ from analyst to analyst, the nature of the patient's conflicts and psychic organization will dictate the issues that arise and how they eventually will become metabolized. Given this way of looking at the situation, analysts really are interchangeable so long as their personal conflicts do not hamper their analyzing functions. Even though analysts have neurotic conflicts, there is no automatic assumption that their conflicts will necessarily contaminate the treatment unduly, any more than the fact that life is full of conflicts and frustrations prevents us from conceiving of an "average expectable environment" in which a child can learn to have basic trust. The right-wing view takes the routine position that unless there is proof to the contrary (in any specific case), the analyst is free to analyze. And that being the case, it is the patient's ego's grasp on the interpretation rather than on the object relationship (which only sets the stage for interpretations) that makes the difference. Although polemical supporters of these wings can readily point to ways in which the two approaches are *not* saying exactly the same things, these positions may, in fact, be much more compatible than is immediately apparent.

Analytic Identifications, Modeling, and the Transference Cure

The kinds of identifications discussed thus far are, by and large, expected not to outlive the analysis. They are part of the analysis, beginning in an analytic regression and being abandoned when the analysis is terminated. Regressions in ego and superego functioning that enable the patient to use selective ego and superego attributes of the analyst are only temporary, and as the analysis proceeds, advances in psychic structuralization make the patient progressively less dependent on the analyst as a means of external psychic support. However, there is a kind of analytic identification that *is* expected to outlive the analysis, and it has to do with the patient's identification with the analyst's analyzing functions. This is in distinction to identifications with the personal characteristics of the analyst, and it is in distinction to using specific aspects (that is, the contents and manner of functioning) of the analyst's psychic structure. By identifying with the analyzing functions of the analyst, the patient becomes his own analyst (setting the stage and creating the conditions for an ongoing capacity for self-analysis) and in this way, the process outlives the procedure.

Particularly in the early stages of an analysis the patient places a considerable amount of reliance on using the analyst as a means of psychic support (which, as we know, is in the service of establishing the character of the analytic object relationship). In the early and middle stages of an analysis one also can observe many imitative identifications based on concrete attributes of the analyst (such as style of dress, mannerisms, attitudes and opinions that the patient may have been able to discern, physical characteristics, action tendencies, taste in furniture, art, waiting-room music, and so on). For example, patients who are therapists sometimes find that they are making interpretations to their patients that are similar in style or content to the interpretations made to them by their analyst; or they might invite their patients into the consulting room, or indicate to their patients that a session is over, the way their analyst does. Both middle-aged patients and not-so-middle-aged patients sometimes search out gray in their hair if their analyst is gray-haired, or begin to worry about baldness if their analyst is bald. Sometimes in trying to understand a problem, a patient will fantasize what his analyst might say or how his analyst might handle it. These are all imitative identifications, which can be viewed as forms of modeling. They are comparatively primitive, first because they are so highly personified, and second because they are still very tied into the immediacy of the relationship with the analyst. Even though they serve adaptive purposes, these identifications are not aim-inhibited, and their very strength and persistence depends in large part on the instinctualized relationship that the patient has to the analyst. This relative infantilism of identifications is equally true of both the reliance on the analyst's psychic functions and the more concrete forms of modeling just exemplified. Although we willingly make use of some of these kinds of identifications in the analytic object relationship, the kind of analytic identification we ultimately want to forge is an aim-inhibited, abstract identification that will not be subject to the vicissitudes of an interpersonal relationship (no matter how healthy or adaptive it may be).

The principle involved here is no different from the way the process of aim-inhibition structuralizes the superego, permits the superego identifications (including many of those in the ego ideal) to be abstractions rather than concrete, representations of the parents or of their attitudes, and then permits the superego to serve as an independently self-regulating organizer of mental functioning. The child moves from fear of punishment (and at a later level, castration), to fear of loss of the object, to fear of losing the love of the object, to guilt – at which point the process becomes one of internal self-regulation. The patient moves from regressive identifications with the analyst and imitative forms of modeling, to the condition of being constantly curious about his inner life and his motivations in a way that is no longer inhibited by unreasonable or conflictually organized superego demands – at which point the ego's executive functions are empowered and the analytic process has been internalized and is self-regulating.

When an analysis comes to a conclusion because neurotic symptoms seem no longer to be operating but appear to have been diminished or removed only because of the patient's regressive identifications and modeling techniques, we view this as a "transference cure." We understand the basis of the patient's progress as being dependent on suggestion, not because the analyst has explicitly suggested some other way of functioning (although that, too, can happen) but because the patient's way of functioning is suggested by the analyst's capacity to function (through transient, conditionally determined identifications). Reliance on the analyst's skills or characteristics involves a dependent relationship that is modeled after a child's reliance on his parents: hence the term *transference cure*.

A second, and more pernicious, form of transference cure occurs when the patient behaves (even if it looks quite healthy) in accordance with what he assumes are the analyst's expectations of him. Such transference cures usually have a quality of impermanence, the gains falling away when the infantile and instinctual gratifications of the analysis are discontinued. However, there is a way that this kind of transference cure can achieve some degree of permanence; that is, when the patient has incorporated the analyst into his object relations. As an object of identification the analyst is considerably more transitory than when he is integrated into the instinctualized matrix of the patient's object relations (which are not so dependent on external gratifications to achieve some measure of constancy). In this case, compliance with the patient's fantasy of the analyst's expectations of him are the psychic equivalent of satisfying the fantasied (and perhaps real) demands and expectations of his parents. Certainly, even a transference cure of this nature is better than nothing – but even this has to be qualified by considering the very real possibility of obscured symptom substitution in response to conflicts that have not been resolved as a result of higher structuralization but because of the transference.

The patient, no matter what else he may want on a healthier level, always presses for a transference cure, and the analyst must constantly guard against acceding to this demand. In the case of supportive and expressive psychotherapies, perhaps a transference cure is not so problematic or is even welcome, considering the limitations in structuralization a psychotherapy is capable of, and considering the diagnostic assumptions that caused the patient to be assigned to a psychotherapy instead of to a psychoanalysis. In the case of psychoanalytic patients, a transference cure is as much the enemy of psychic structuralization as were the patient's original conflicts and fixations. This, of course, brings us back to the notion that "cure" is not related to behavior (symptom removal) but to the capacity to function at higher levels of ego autonomy and higher levels of superego maturity.

The Analyst's Contribution: Neutrality, Abstinence, and the "Blank Screen"

No discussion of what makes the psychoanalytic situation *psychoanalytic* can draw to a close before one considers the nature of the analyst's stance in relation to the patient, to the patient's productions, and to the treatment context itself. The concepts of neutrality and abstinence are directly related to what the analyst actively tries to bring to the analytic situation, and the concept of the "blank screen" describes a subcondition of the neutrality and abstinence that the analyst hopes to foster. The blank-screen metaphor is sufficiently complicated and evocative that it has become subject to considerable misunderstanding, confusion, and even misrepresentation. Before trying to clarify the nature of this metaphor it would be useful to look at the concepts of neutrality and abstinence (in that they must exist before the metaphor of the blank screen can be put into practice).

Neutrality is another of those concepts that has acquired different meanings depending on one's analytic orientation. In the Freudian model it basically means that the analyst does not take sides in any of the patient's conflicts. Conflicts exist between the psychic structures (e.g., an incestuous wish and the prohibition against it is a conflict between the id and the superego; an aggressive wish and the need to modify it in order to protect both self and objects is a conflict between the id and the ego; and the demand that all sexual wishes be ruthlessly suppressed versus the need to distinguish those that have a legitimate right to exist from those that do not is a conflict between the ego and the superego); conflicts exist within each psychic structure (e.g., simultaneous sexual and aggressive investments are a conflict within the id; defensive activity that compromises the ego's autonomy is a conflict within the ego; and moral issues that are inconsistent with each other, such as the belief that one should be charitable and contempt for street beggars, is a conflict within the superego); and conflicts exist between subjective needs, which constitute the inner world of the individual, and reality, which also includes the demands made upon the individual by the environment, which may be in opposition to his inner needs (e.g., the wish to remain in a constant condition of tension-free emotional homeostasis and the necessity to respond to inescapable drive demands; the wish to remain dependently secure and the need to achieve differentiation and independence in order to better meet one's needs; and the infantile wish only to achieve instinctual gratifications and the necessity of becoming both educated and socialized, which is, of course, imposed externally). The analyst's neutrality depends on his ability not to be caught up in one side of the struggle against the other. From the analyst's perspective the legitimacy of both sides of any conflict has to become apparent, and siding with one part of a conflict introduces the influence of the analyst's personal attitudes and conflicts, which interfere with his ability to understand and appreciate the power of each side of the conflict for the patient. In addition, the analyst's taking the side of one part of the conflict will prevent the patient from resolving it in a way that is consistent with his own psychic structure and character organization. In other words, it will tempt the patient into modeling. In general, it inhibits the patient's freedom to explore the conflict and limits the possibility of his appreciating the fullest implications of what is involved in his conflicts. The loss of neutrality does not lead only to a modeling effect but also to either a deadlock in the treatment or other types of transference cure.

Perhaps the only exception to the position of neutrality (and on closer examination it may turn out not to be an exception even if it looks like one) is in the analyst's long-range commitment to autonomous ego functioning, to mature superego functioning (that is, with adequate distance from the drives), and to the patient's ability to adapt to the demands of reality. Even though this is a real investment, it is possible to suspend it as an activity in the short run – that is, at the moment that a patient is expressing a conflict in the analysis; the analyst's ability to suspend his abstract goals in the immediacy of any particular conflict becomes one of the bases for the long-range achievement of those goals. When this breaks down and the analyst loses his neutrality, the treatment is no longer a psychoanalysis (e.g., an analyst who takes the side of the superego is conducting a supportive psychotherapy designed to promote social conformity; an analyst who sides with defenses is also conducting a supportive psychotherapy, this time designed to inhibit both spontaneity and immediacy; an analyst who is on the side of the impulses is merely undermining the defensive operations and superego functioning of the patient; and an analyst who is too attached to reality is actually sabotaging an important aspect of the ego's autonomy). The requirements of neutrality place a heavy burden on the analyst, but it is unquestionably necessary if an analysis is to remain *an analysis*. No one, of course, is without reactions, opinions, attitudes, or values, and in order to achieve some neutrality in the analytic situation the analyst relies on a kind of heightened ego autonomy that is quite specific to the work and not necessarily available to him at all other times. This suspension of the analyst's personal investments is possible in the carefully circumscribed circumstances of the work and serves the goals of neutrality and abstinence. This would naturally lead us directly to a discussion of the concept of abstinence, but before doing so there is another aspect of the concept of neutrality (which actually overlaps the concept of abstinence to a great extent) that needs consideration.

The analyst's complimentary task to the patient's task of free associating (in which certain critical faculties are suspended in order to say everything that comes to mind) is to conduct the treatment in a state of free-floating, evenly hovering attention. This ability, too, is part of the concept of neutrality, in the sense that the analyst does not intentionally choose to take a special interest in some of what the patient is saying and take less interest in other things the patient may be saying: this is directly analogous to not taking sides with one part of a conflict, with any psychic structure, or with reality.

Customarily, when two people are in a room and talking takes place, it is part of a dialogue in which both share equivalent responsibility for the conversation. Ordinarily, when one listens to someone else, one tries to follow the thread of the conversation. When one person in a conversation tries to make a point, the other tries to follow the logic. If one of the people seems to become confusing, then the other attempts to clarify, either by asking questions or by trying to sort it out in his own mind, as the confusing person continues to speak. If one of the people seems to become confused, the other will try to help him resolve his confusion. If something captures the attention of one of the participants, he may very well become willing to abandon whatever else may be going on in order to follow up on what interested him.

None of those possibilities is allowable for the analyst. This is partly because it is not a conversation in the usual sense of the word, but is mainly because the moment his attention is captured too closely by anything that is going on, he is no longer free to continue to move along in pace with the patient (who may continue to move on because his attention may not have been captured by what he just said); and because it is necessary for the analyst to be as aware of what events precede and follow each other, and in what order, as it is to be aware of the contents of the things themselves. The condition of the analyst's attention does change, but it is not usually dependent on the highly variable kinds of things that ordinarily account for shifts of attention. Rather, the analyst's active attention is usually captured by events that signal a shift in the transference, the emergence of a resistance, or the eruption of material from unconsciousness into preconsciousness. The analyst's attention to these kinds of events does not suggest that he is not listening to, and attending to, everything the patient is saying. It does suggest, however, that most of what the patient is saying (and doing) is shaped by the analyst into a kind of passive background of awareness. The analyst experiences and then retains that information (passively rather than actively) to be used again when needed. The intention to function in this way is conscious, but the mechanisms are carried out unconsciously and automatically. Some of the patient's productions can have certain signal properties in the fore-ground, especially when they do not fit into the analyst's unconsciously formed expectations, but the analyst becomes most alerted when something changes the balance of the patient's mental economy or the balance of the transference neurosis.

The analyst works in a state of altered consciousness that closely resembles a dream, meditation, or reverie. He does not seek to follow what the patient is talking about, he does not try to figure out what is going on in the transference or in the patient's dynamics, he does not try to connect anything up with what he knows about the patient's history, he does not care what the patient talks about as long as the patient is saying what is on his mind, he does not go back to something that may have happened in a previous session or back to a dream that was previously presented (even if the end of the last session interrupted the examination of it), he does not care whether or not the patient is making sense (in the sense of his not feeling the necessity of immediately doing something about that); in sum, he lets the material wash over him, as it were, and he waits for the synthetic function of his own ego to organize the material rather than trying to actively remember it or actively trying to make sense out of it. The analyst *abstains* from these actions in order not to interfere with the patient's associative processes, in order to get a more accurate understanding of the patient's underlying motivations, and in order to give the patient the widest scope of expression that is possible for him.

Abstinence, in the context of how the analyst takes in the experience, basically refers to the analyst's commitment not to use activity in the treatment to defensively satisfy his own needs. His highly abstracted curiosity and his equally abstract wish to be of genuine help to the patient are not at issue here. The overlap of neutrality with the concept of abstinence has to do with the analyst being able to sacrifice personal needs in the communicative interchange; that is, his not being able to satisfy immediate curiosity, his not being able to acquire closure, and his not being able to be active rather than passive with regard to the patient's material and the patient's use of the hour. The active application of intellect, and active emotional identification, are more satisfying than passively permitting the process to occur and passively accepting the patient's control over what emerges in the hour: intellectual and emotional activity are tempting to the analyst because they hold out the promise and reassuring feeling of being able to be in control of the situation. Analysts who cannot abstain from such gratifications may gain the delusive impression of being in control of the analysis, but whatever control they gain has to do more with their own needs than with the structure of the analysis. The illusion of control is gained at the cost of the loss of neutrality, and with the loss of neutrality they genuinely sacrifice the actual long-range control of the analysis itself. Maintaining both abstinence and neutrality is considerably easier for the analyst who, as a result of experience, has learned to trust and rely on the synthetic and other executive functions of his ego to "understand" the experience; although usually the loss is not due to a lack of experience but to neurotic conflicts that impose themselves on the analyst's functioning. Unless considerable sublimation and neutralization characterize his work, it is very difficult for the analyst to comfortably achieve the level of abstinence necessary for the kind of neutrality in "listening" that allows the work to progress.

In addition to its role in fostering enough neutrality for the analyst to maintain himself during the hour in a state of free-floating evenly hovering attention, the concept of abstinence is also relevant to the analyst not acquiring personal gratifications from the patient. The analytic situation is rife with opportunity for the analyst to seize satisfaction of his neurotic needs from the patient, and in this sense the possibility of undermining the treatment works in both directions. The patient does not abstain from making transference demands; indeed it is part of the "job description" of an analysand. What the mature part of the patient abstains from is the absolute and unconditional demand for gratification. Making the demand is essential if one is to fully understand what is at issue for the patient, and the patient being able to tolerate the frustration of not having it gratified is essential if that understanding is to be brought into the patient's consciousness (and then worked with even further). The patient must, at least initially, seek many neurotic satisfactions and gratifications from the analyst, but (if one could live up to a pure theory) the analyst is not permitted, *ever,* to use the patient in that way. There are *no* exceptions. The patient treats the immediacy of his neurotic needs and expectations, and his assumption that they will be gratified by the analyst (and his displeasure when they are not), as the "real" relationship since he is initially unaware of any of his infantile motivations: the analyst recognizes those motivations as transferential and neurotic and views the analytic arrangement as the only basis of a "real" relationship.

If the patient engages in an idealizing transference, the analyst is not free to derive narcissistic and grandiose satisfaction from that fact; he is obligated to see it as transference and nothing more. If the patient disparages the analyst and vilifies him as a reflection of negative transference, the analyst is not free to derive masochistic gratification from it; he is obligated to see it as transference and nothing more. If the patient is abusive, the analyst may not obtain retaliatory gratifications; if the patient falls in love with the analyst, the analyst is obligated to see that event as only a reflection of the patient's object relations; if the patient is a pleasant and likable person, the analyst is not free to exploit the situation by forming a friendship with him; if the patient is curious about the analyst, the analyst is constrained against engaging in any exhibitionistic pleasures; if the patient is self-defeating and destructive, the analyst cannot indulge in any messianic wishes to save the patient; if the patient has admirable qualities, the analyst is not free to use him as an active object of identification in order to regulate his own self-esteem; if the patient is miserable, the analyst's wish to alleviate his misery through concrete support (since one motive for entering this field is to help people) must be frustrated; even when the patient is clearly getting better, the analyst is not free to take personal satisfaction from that fact: there are *no* exceptions, if our theory could live up to reality.

Of course some exceptions will always occur because analysts are always subject to some countertransferential reactions, but these exceptions are not intentionally planned-for experiences in the treatment: they are only inevitable, and not legitimately desirable. Fortunately for the analysis, most countertransferences are transitory phenomena, in that every act of obtaining gratification from the patient works against the analyst's capacity to maintain neutrality. This is not to suggest that there are no legitimate satisfactions and gratifications available to the analyst: the aim-inhibited pleasure in a patient's growth because of what it means for the patient and because of what it does for the patient, rather than serving as some kind of "proof" of the analyst's competence, is perfectly legitimate; the aim-inhibited pleasure that analysts get from being able to see the world through other peoples' eyes, rather than being a voyeuristic operation, is entirely legitimate; satisfying one's fascination with how the mind works, or about the nature of psychopathology, need not be treated with suspicion simply because it is something that the analyst is interested in: that which we have to be concerned about is entirely limited to those interests of the analyst that in some way exploit the patient's transference or the analytic situation in achieving gratification and satisfaction. Abstinence is the antithesis of neurotic self-indulgence, and it not only makes neutrality possible but also makes the "blank screen" metaphor a mode of working that can be put into practice.

Freud's use of the metaphor of a "blank screen" was conceptualized at a time when he was considering the interrelationships between fantasy, transference, and analytic regression, particularly in regard to what would advantageously promote them as analytic activities and in special regard to what kinds of activities on the part of the analyst might diminish their analytic usefulness. In recognizing transference phenomena as belonging to the patient's history and to the patient's object relations, Freud discovered that, no matter how much he might wish it otherwise, patients would continue to experience him through the distortions of their transference as long as the repetition compulsion (reflecting the patient's neurotic conflicts) regulated the patient's mental functioning. In an analysis we hope to find a means of making the patient's transferences recognizable as such, rather than having them maintained consciously in the mind of the patient as "reality" relationships and "reality" events. The profound regression that is generated by the transference neurosis causes transference events and relationships to progressively lose their veneer of reality and their camouflage of transformation. The transferential significance of an event becomes more explicitly articulated by the regression. The immediate object of the transference relation becomes more clearly representative of the archaic object (and the archaic nature of the object attachment becomes somewhat more conspicuous), thus shedding the disguise of being a current event as the transferential meanings are progressively decoded. It is true that initially patients cannot be prevented from experiencing their analysts transferentially, but the analysis of the patient's transference fantasies (capitalizing on the endogenous strength of the patient's ego) is the catalyst for helping the patient to eventually achieve a realistic balance between the events and relationships of the past and the present. The analyst promotes a transference regression by frustrating transference demands. If he gratifies transference demands, he causes the transference to remain unchanged and to be expressed in its current, unintelligible, form. The analyst, through frustration or gratification of transference demands, can facilitate or interfere with the patient's freedom to bring the transference to a position of scrutiny in the analysis.

Transference gratification is not the only way an analyst can make it harder for the patient to get to the underlying meanings of his transferential anticipations. The analyst can also interfere with the process by inhibiting the full range of the patient's fantasy life. For example, if in a relatively early stage of the treatment the patient accuses the analyst, as a matter of transference, of being stingy "like his father was," he is expressing a fantasy about the analyst and a memory about his relationship with his father (or a fantasy about his father, or a memory of his father that has been influenced by fantasy). The analyst can abruptly cut short the analytic process by insisting to the patient that this is not true, that it is just a fantasy, that the analyst is, in reality, a very generous person, and by reminding the patient how this has been evidenced many times in the analysis. Objectification of the relationship too early in the analysis, that is, insisting on replacing the patient's fantasy with the assumed reality, prevents the very regression that is necessary to make it analytically available. Neither acknowledgment nor disconfirmation of the fantasy would serve this patient's best interests: in addition to preventing a very necessary regression, responding to the issue in a realistic way would make it harder for the patient to keep the fantasy alive (not impossible perhaps, the repetition compulsion being what it is, but harder nevertheless, and for no good reason).

Similarly, if a patient asks the analyst a personal question about himself, a realistic reply would have the same effect. For example, suppose a patient asks the analyst whether he has any children. Why is he asking this question? Not every patient asks this question. And one must also wonder why the patient is asking about that at this particular time. Why not two sessions ago, or five sessions later? It seems entirely reasonable to assume that patients do not ask such questions out of idle curiosity. What is the patient imagining, and what does the imagined answer to his question have to do with any transference assumptions he may be making about the analyst? Suppose, for example, this was a patient who was unloved by his own parents: suppose he imagines that the analyst has no children, and that he has further developed the fantasy that the analyst made the choice not to have children because he was aware of being so neurotically disturbed as to be unable to love children properly. Would the patient be as free to elaborate this fantasy if the analyst were to say, "I have five children. My wife and I love children, and we plan to have a few more children, too"? And do we imagine that it would have the same net effect on the patient's fantasy if, instead, the analyst were to say, "No, I haven't any children"? Whatever the analyst might say, it would have an effect not only on the current fantasy but also on the organization of future fantasies associated with this issue. The analyst is not in a position to disclose anything about whether or not he has children if he wants to keep this matter alive as an analytic issue. The analyst is not supposed to be in the business of helping to organize the kind and nature of the patient's fantasies, but only to more clearly elicit them and then to subject them to the analytic process itself.

Suppose the patient has set great store in the analyst's being very much older than the patient is in order to have a father figure to look up to: what effect will it have, not only on the patient's ability to express his fantasies but also on the subsequent nature of the treatment, if the analyst says, "Actually, you are wrong. I am, in fact, a year younger than you are"? If the analyst is older than the patient, and confirms that fact, what happens to the fantasy element that made the patient assume that he was older (since it was not based on anything he knew to be the case in reality)? The patient would seem to be best served by the analyst indicating nothing about his age.

Suppose, after a year of treatment, a patient (who knew the answer to his question when the treatment began) says, "By the way, it has slipped my mind: are you a physician or a psychologist?" A realistic answer, at this point in the analysis, would defeat any examination of why the question was arising at that time, and why the information slipped the patient's mind. Suppose the word "slipped" was a pun, and was the only available signal of a breakthrough of something into preconsciousness: an answer to the question (simply because it seemed to be a question about reality) would entirely miss the point. Suppose the therapist was a social worker? Clarifying that fact would bypass entirely whatever fantasies the patient was having about who, and what, the therapist was.

If a patient imagines that the therapist is angry at him, what is to be gained by confirming this fantasy or by disconfirming this fantasy, and what is to be lost by confirming this fantasy or by disconfirming this fantasy? And what is to be gained or lost by neither confirming nor disconfirming this fantasy? These are the issues that are at stake, not the truth or falsity of the patient's fantasy. Certainly it makes a difference if an analyst is actually angry at a patient, and if the patient has been able to recognize the analyst's anger as an event in reality. But we are speaking now of patient's fantasies, not veridical perceptions.

When patients project their fantasies onto the analyst (project in the sense of catapulting, and not in the sense we mean when we describe it as a defense), the analyst must do everything in his power not to interfere with this process prematurely. One way that Freud meant the blank-screen metaphor to be understood was in the sense that the patient should be given the opportunity to project his fantasies onto the analyst the way a movie is projected onto a screen. The analyst should refrain from cluttering up the screen with realities, since inappropriately offered realities only have the effect of inhibiting the free rein of the patient's fantasy life.

To stay within the analogy of a movie: one of the most satisfying aspects of moviegoing is the ability to lose oneself, to become totally immersed in the movie, to identify with the characters, and to "live" within the movie in an engrossingly absorbed way. We know, of course, that we are not one of the movie characters and that the story is not something that is really happening to us, but the illusion of participation that goes with the temporary lowering of one's ego boundaries is extremely pleasurable. Imagine how disruptive it would be if there were periodic announcements on the loudspeaker that this was only a movie, that the story was only a fiction, and that whatever we felt in common with the characters was only illusory. Suppose we were trying to get absorbed in a movie and the words This Is Only a Movie were printed on the screen and visible throughout the movie. These examples (the clinical examples and the hypothetical examples of being at the movies) illustrate the kinds of things Freud was concerned about when he developed the metaphorical concept of the blank screen, and it was his ambition to try, in the analysis, to develop a psychological environment analogous to the blank screen as a means of protecting the originality, individuality, and authenticity of the patient's fantasy life. By not being casually and inappropriately self-disclosing the analyst permits the patient's inner life to be expressed in the analysis with a quality of vividness and immediacy, and he avoids the complications of stimulating the patient with interfering distractions.

Freud was never so naive that he imagined that the analyst could be a cipher, a totally anonymous figure, for the patient. The blank-screen image is a metaphor that was never intended to be taken literally. There are innumerable things that a patient knows, or can learn, about the analyst. No one, least of all Freud, assumed that the analyst is in control of everything that the patient can know or eventually learn, including the things that the analyst would not wish to disclose, given a choice. The patient knows whether his analyst is male or female. In some circumstances, for example with an 80-year-old analyst, the patient (assuming he is not psychotic) will have a limited scope of possibilities when it comes time to guess the analyst's age. The patient knows something about the analyst if the analyst speaks with a foreign or a regional accent. He sees how the analyst dresses, he knows where the analyst has chosen to locate his office, he has some sense of the analyst's taste in furniture (or at least as it involves his office), and he may be able to infer something about the analyst's taste in music if the analyst has music playing in his waiting room. He knows something about the analyst's interests from the waiting-room magazines, and may learn even more from the books the analyst has in the consulting room. And not least by any means, he learns a great deal about the analyst's personality from having had years of intimate experience with him, even if the relationship does have certain artificial limitations.

There is a considerable difference, however, between what the patient is able to learn on his own and any additional information that he could only get from the analyst's decision to be self-revealing. Everything that the patient can objectively learn about the analyst acts in an inhibiting fashion to a greater or lesser extent where fantasy production is concerned. We accept the inevitability that the patient will acquire some knowledge about the analyst no matter what, that this is unavoidable, and we see this as an unfortunate liability: all that we can do is to try to work around it. Life is full of such compromises, but the fact that we are subject to them does not imply that we cannot, or that we should not, try to limit those liabilities only to those that are out of our control and about which we can do nothing. Freud meant to suggest that the fact that patients can know something about the analyst is no justification for then telling the patient anything about the analyst that he could not find out on his own. Paradoxically, patients also create a version of the "blank-screen analyst" for themselves. Many of the things the patient objectively can learn about the analyst become reorganized in the patient's mind in conformity with, and under the influence of, fantasy. By overlaying his fantasies onto what he objectively knows, the patient imposes a blank-screen attribute to the analyst as much as the analyst himself does when he tries to remain relatively anonymous. Thus, through intentionality and unintentionality, both patient and analyst collaborate in using this metaphor of the blank screen to preserve the integrity of the patient's fantasies and to facilitate their being brought into the analysis.

With this discussion we come to an end of our basic investigation of the nature of the psychoanalytic situation itself. We have considered some notions about how the concept of cure is understood in the Freudian model, and have provided a general description of some of the techniques by which we attempt to achieve higher levels of psychic structuralization. With this as a background we now find ourselves in a position to look more closely, and with even greater detail, at some further elements of the basic treatment model. We will now include questions about how we do the work, in addition to considering why we do it in a particular way.

8

Transference

A psychoanalysis is usually initiated in response to symptoms or anxieties that the patient consciously wishes to have ameliorated or removed. One cannot properly state only that a psychoanalysis analyzes symptoms and anxieties, despite the fact that symptoms and anxieties motivated the patient to seek treatment and that the relief of anxiety and symptoms are the patient's most important conscious goals. A psychoanalysis does analyze symptoms and anxieties, as well as defenses and resistances, but it does so as part of the analysis of the transference neurosis. Thus the resolution of symptoms and anxieties are a by-product of the analysis of the transference neurosis. One also, for the same reason, cannot only say that a psychoanalysis analyzes transference; the analysis of the transference, too, is a by-product of the analysis of the transference neurosis.

Psychoanalysis is frequently described as a method of treatment that analyzes transference and resistance, and one often sees assertions that any method of treatment that analyzes transference and resistance is legitimately to be regarded as a psychoanalysis. It would be more correct to say that symptoms, anxieties, transferences, and resistances are examined within the context of a transference neurosis, and that one should properly regard a treatment as a psychoanalysis when analysis of the transference neurosis is the method by which they are all addressed therapeutically.

The reasons one often sees the suggestion that a psychoanalysis *analyzes the transference* are: (1) because symptoms are usually expressive of pathological transference phenomena; and (2) because symptom formation is usually examined through a careful scrutiny and investigation of the transference manifestations that are introduced into the treatment by the patient. The problem with describing analysis in this way is that the characterization *analyzing the transference* is too broad, too encompassing, and too general a statement. One does not analyze any, and every, aspect of the transference.

Transference phenomena are, after all, quite ubiquitous in mental functioning. At times transference phenomena pathologically dominate mental functioning but, that fact notwithstanding, one may still assume that for everyone, at all times, without exception, not a single mental event can take place without some transferential displacement, however small. In psychoanalysis, only a particular aspect of the transference is analyzed. And, to take this one step further, only when that relatively limited transference display emerges under special conditions, and with an unique and exceptional intensity, will it become the subject of the analysis. To be more precise, one must limit one's description of a psychoanalysis to say that *what is analyzed is the transference neurosis, and not the transference.* To clarify the difference between the generic concept of transference and the more specific concept of the transference neurosis, considering that they have obvious similarities and many parallel mechanics, it will be of value to describe what happens in each process.

The Basic Concept: Displacement Theories
versus Projection Theories

Transference, the generic concept, involves what is essentially a process of displacement. Most commonly it involves a displacement from the past into the present situation, and more often than not it involves a fantasy-altered recapitulation of the relationship with the significant objects of one's past. However, not every displacement should be thought of as simply a variety of transference: expressing anger at one's spouse by kicking the dog, for example, is a nontransferential displacement. What becomes displaced in transference can at times be highly limited and quite specific, but usually transference involves the displacement of large organizations of complex and interactive apperceptive masses, which generally will include a combination of feelings, ideas, action tendencies, beliefs, expectations, memories, opinions, attitudes, wishes, fears, attachments, and so on. Transference may often include or involve other mental processes in addition to displacement, but the inclusion or involvement of other mental processes does not change the basic nature of the transference maneuver as a displacement activity, first and foremost. To clarify this statement we can look at how a process like *projection* can exist both independently of, and then also within, transference activity. The choice of projection is particularly useful because transference is frequently misunderstood to be either a process of projection, or a process of both displacement and projection in collaboration.

If someone cannot tolerate having a particular wish or aim, for whatever reason, one of the many possible mechanisms for coping with the discomfort it generates is to deny to oneself that one has the wish and to imagine that it exists in someone else – in other words, projection (also a displacement process). We think of projection in this case as being a defense that also serves the purposes of other defenses. To be more concrete: if a child in the midst of the oedipal conflict has conflicting wishes involving, for example, attacking his father as well as wishing to protect his father from harm, a projection of his aggression would cause him to be unaware of any hostile wishes toward his father, while at the same time causing him to fear that his father might wish to attack him; the projected aggression is treated consciously as if the destructive wish were the father's (directed toward the child) rather than a reflection of his own destructive wishes toward his father. This defense mechanism, although only a single mental operation dynamically, serves multiple defensive purposes beyond alleviating the discomfort of having an unacceptable aggressive wish, and it can realign many issues of the conflict for the child; for example, it actively protects the father from harm (in the child's fantasies the father *can* be harmed by him); it protects the child from defeat in a realistically unequal struggle should he be tempted to try to act on his aggressive wishes (one cannot act on what is not there), consciousness of any aggression toward his father would interfere with the conscious development of respect, admiration, and love, and with the child's unconscious positive identification processes; using a fear of his father's "aggressive inclinations toward him" helps the child to reduce, or to otherwise gain control over, the intensity of his incestuous wishes toward his mother; the projection, in these ways, also promotes structuralization of the superego; in addition, the projection counters the child's passive-negative oedipal posture toward his father, forcing him back into an active positive posture to avoid being "damaged by his father" sexually. One could go on, inasmuch as there are many other realignments of the conflict that the single act of projection could support, but the point is obvious that the implications of this particular kind of displacement operation are quite significant.

Projection, as a defense in such a case, is a mechanism instituted against something that is occurring *at the present moment* in the individual concerned, even if it has been going on for some considerable amount of time. Projective activity in this instance does not recapitulate the past, although it is greatly influenced by the past. Rather, it displaces something unacceptable from one *present* psychological location to another (in this case, from inside the person into the inside of someone else). The fact that something, anything, has been displaced from one psychological place, elsewhere, does not lead one to characterize this particular defensive mechanism, projection, as transference. That is because – and this is the essential difference – it is a present event based primarily on an inner conflict rather than being an event in which there is a reminder of the past, or one in which we see a repetition or recapitulation of the past itself, replete with the past's conflicts.

Transference and the Repetition Compulsion

Now let us consider the man who was that conflicted child in our example, as a conflicted adult, in order to illustrate some points about transference and projection together, rather than only about projection or transference alone. Suppose this man, who used projection in the way that was described in childhood, meets someone as an adult who reminds him of his father. Even, and especially, if our man is not particularly experiencing aggressive tensions at this time, his transferential reaction to the person who reminds him of his father may very well include his childhood projections. That is, he may experience that person as being hostile to him with all the subjective reality, now, of how he experienced his father's aggression toward him (the projection of his aggression onto his father) during childhood. In this event, insofar as he is not currently projecting aggression onto the person he recently met, we are faced not with a projection but with a transference phenomenon that includes the net result of an earlier projection. The seeming projection in this example would not be a defensive response to a current inter- or intrasystemic conflict, although current conflicts (including his transference response) may be triggered by, and influenced by, unresolved past conflicts. The projection has become part of his object relations, and perhaps part of his relationship with his father in reality as well, and consequently also with anyone who reminds him, transferentially, of his father. Even if this man also developed a continuing tendency to project (aggression, or anything else), we would not classify this particular experience as an active form of projection. The key operation here is a transference displacement and not a projection of currently active aggression onto the man who reminded him of his father. This point could be made even more powerfully if we postulate (since this is only an hypothetical person in an hypothetical example) that this man no longer characteristically relied much on projective defenses in the present. And, of course, we can also take the opposite perspective, whereby it becomes much more complicated, if we postulate that he does rely quite heavily on projections in the present. If this were the case, we might be seeing current projections onto a transferentially endowed person in the present who has already been invested (because of the transference) with past projections. Such situations, in the clinical setting, are extremely complex and difficult to unravel, with the greatest difficulty being in clarifying the differences between current projections and projections that have been transferentially carried forward into the present.

Projection was singled out here for the reasons described above, but one wishes to keep in mind that it is only one of a number of mental operations that can occur within, or side by side with, transference. Sometimes environmental events, or other events that are psychological, can entirely mask the presence and extent of transference phenomena, and at other times they may only partially camouflage the representation of transference phenomena. The important point to remember, however, is that transference repeats, in a new context, something that was specific to a previous context. This is sometimes, but certainly not always, best articulated for the patient and for the analyst when the patient is expressing in his functioning a point of fixation. We can look at some typical examples of transference phenomena that exhibit this displacement process as they do become expressed in fixated functioning.

Someone caught up in a struggle with his father may find himself constantly in inappropriate struggles with all authority figures who are reminiscent of his father, yet in each individual struggle he may be able to point to, or to conjure up, seemingly legitimate reasons in reality that appear to justify each battle. Or a child might be inclined to fear a fourth-grade teacher because of the harshness of his third-grade teacher. In fact, even genuine warmth and kindness of the fourth-grade teacher may be insufficient to dispel the damage done the year before. In terms of some of the aspects of positive transferences, children pass on to their teachers the authority, omniscience, and omnipotence (particularly in the areas of externalized superego and ego functioning) that was originally in the domain of their parents. In this case they would be entirely unaware, consciously, of how their teachers became so important and powerful. To go on to some additional examples: having been bitten once, an individual might fear all dogs for the rest of his life; or one might love all elderly persons, without qualification, because of the sheltering love of a kind grandparent in a generally unloving environment.

Let us now complicate our examples a bit, since actual transferences are never really so simple. As a sign of appropriate anxiety, one's heart may race during school examinations. This may be transferentially intensified in someone whose heart raced when he was examined physically by a parent during childhood, or in someone who was examined about some wrongdoing repeatedly during childhood, or in someone whose toilet behavior was too closely monitored during childhood. The smell of disinfectant or the sound of a hospital paging system might trigger distressing feelings of grief in someone who, entirely unconsciously, is reminded of a hospital environment that was associated with the death of a loved one. The sight of flowers might always bring joy to someone, even if they are a funeral arrangement, if flowers have become associated with some happy childhood experience.

The above examples, although a bit more complex, are nevertheless directly and immediately recognizable as transference events. Transference need not be so easily identifiable, and, in fact, usually is not. Transference phenomena themselves, as well as the various modes of expressing transference, are readily capable of undergoing disfiguring and obscuring transformations. This regularly occurs because transference, whether it is conscious or unconscious or both, can and does undergo developmental vicissitudes, which are also overlaid by defensive vicissitudes. Additionally, transference is not limited only to displacements from the very distant past. It also includes displacements from the recent past, and even includes condensations between events, things, people, and psychological operations that are virtually simultaneous, and which occur in immediate proximity to one another in the present. Such a disguised, evolved, and transfigured transference manifestation took place in the following (actual, not hypothetical) example:

A patient who was deeply fixated in a passive-negative oedipal relation to his father (i.e., he wanted to be his father's love object and had many derivative fantasies of oral and anal incorporation of his father's penis) defended against the unconscious wish for this fixated homosexual love by developing intense reaction formations. Rather than having directly presented himself only passively and homosexually as a child to his father, and as an adult (even in symbolic form) to other adult males, this man developed and then rigorously maintained an exaggerated repugnance toward the idea of homosexuality, which also included an unreasoning hatred toward homosexual men and women as a class. In fact, there was a quality of hating them defiantly and without exception (he had no "some of my best friends are homosexuals" stories, and he never suggested, as so many people with such conflicts do, that although he despised them as a group there had been some, individually, whom he had liked "as people"). This was a mechanism developed by his ego and "fueled" by his superego, using copious amounts of shame, guilt, humiliation, mortification, and abstract considerations of morality, without any commensurate interposition of pity, sympathy, or empathy for the objects of his unconscious homosexual attractions: such is the nature of reaction formation. Thus, in order to reinforce the renunciation of his specifically homosexual attachment to his father, through the development of reaction formations against it, homosexuality became anathema to him. The degree of aggression inherent in this, discharged by both the ego and the superego, was so partially and incompletely neutralized that it also subjected this defense to a "concretizing" process over the passage of the years it took for him to reach adulthood. Every homosexual person he so exaggeratedly hated represented not only himself (projection) and his own wishes (converted by reaction formation) but also represented to him his father (and here we specifically see the transference), to whom in unconscious and primary-process terms he longed to surrender himself. In this transference relation his archaic loves, fears, and hatreds concerning his father were carried over into the present and continued to be stimulated, additionally, by currently unconscious homosexual wishes and his intense reaction to them. Both the seductive pull of his love for his father and his defense against it became expressed in this malicious and troubled way. That his hateful preoccupations were channeled toward substitutes for his father, and that they were feelings and reactions brought forward from the past that reflected a powerful and archaic object relation in the present, is what makes them so significantly a form of transference: this is despite the circuitous form of its representation, in which homosexuality was represented by adamant heterosexuality; where love was expressed by hatred, contempt, and disdain; and where the original object of his attachments was initially totally obscured from view.

In a very different kind of example we can observe a form of transference that seems to affect memory, and by so doing seems to be working in reverse; that is, it can seem as if events in the present can have an effect on the past. Of course this is not really a possibility: transference can shape the present and it can distort memory, but one thing that it cannot do is to change the past; nothing, of course, can change the past, not even psychoanalysis, which at best can only change one's relations to the past. However, the illusion (which in this transference array is even more complex and compounded than in the previous example) of being able to change the past can seem quite real:

A young married woman, notwithstanding her high intelligence, considerable perceptiveness, and real expertise in many interpersonal situations and relationships, was relatively unsuccessful in differentiating (unconsciously) between her father and all other men, including her husband, as objects of her love. Quite naturally, even after marriage, she had difficulties in keeping the mental representations of her husband from merging with the mental representations of her father. It will come as no surprise to hear that she chose her husband in large part because of a number of realistic similarities, concrete attributes that he shared with her father. To introduce this situation properly one may say, then, that for this woman the actual correspondence between her husband and her father was both an essential ingredient in the relationship in reality (without which she would have not been attracted to him consciously, even if she made no conscious connection between the two), and in the transference (which is what lent him his attractiveness to her in consciousness and in reality, although she was not aware of the portion of this that was an unconscious transference reenactment). The choice of her husband was enhanced by a combination of accurate perceptions, heightened selective perceptions, and selective inattentions, which were regulated by the unconscious need to experience him as if he were her father. She did make use of many unconscious psychic manipulations to minimize the reality discrepancies between her husband and her father, but in many realistic ways her husband *was* like her father, and this was a factor that was both predetermined and reinforcing.

When this woman was in treatment for about a year, her husband decided to begin an analysis of his own. The information about him was provided in bit and pieces throughout the course of her analysis, more frequently than not in retrospect. At the time he entered treatment this man was on the verge of consolidating a number of important changes in his inner life that had been evolving for quite some time. These changes had been crystallizing especially in the previous 2 years, independent of any psychotherapy (analysis is not, by any means, the only way by which one may grow) and this was, parenthetically, the very underlying disruption in their relationship that triggered his wife's need to enter treatment (the previous year). Her presenting problems were a general anxiety that was incomprehensible to her and, even more confusing to her, repetitive attacks of panic accompanied by an increasingly mounting depression. She was not at that time aware of the relationship between her symptoms and the changes that her husband was making (that caused him to be, progressively, less and less like her father, and which she was having trouble denying). Her husband's conscious intention in beginning his own treatment was to help him to facilitate changes that he felt, paradoxically, both ready to make and blocked from acting upon. He also wished help in identifying additional changes that might be necessary but that were even further from implementation. On the very margin of his awareness he suspected that his wife's problems were related to the changes he was making, and he also had the hope that being in analysis could shield him from unpleasantness with her as he continued to change (as he had a preconscious insight into the relationship between his changes and her unhappiness). He felt quite guilty when she perceived him as undergoing a change (although his recognitions were still preconscious) and feared not only having to stop changing to satisfy her, but also the emotional responses it drew from her when he refused to inhibit the changes he felt it was necessary to make: whether she might become intensely upset or directly attack him, as she sometimes did, he wanted to be in a position to say to her, *"Blame the analysis, not me!"* It was not that he did not want to stay married; he did, and very much so, but he was concerned about the possible consequences to his marriage if significant changes in him continued to occur (consciously, at least, and about a number of other issues in which this was embedded unconsciously).

To a naive observer, who might not know how ready for change he was and how much work he had put into setting the stage for changing over the past 2 years, it might have looked as if he made some very rapid and far-reaching changes through the intervention of analysis, and in a very short time. In truth the majority of these changes were inevitable, were about to become apparent in any event, and were not really as stimulated by, or as dependent upon, the process of his treatment as it seemed. His wife's reactions were numerous, and of course very complex, and one of the most interesting reactions (particularly for the purposes of this discussion) was an actual alteration in her memories of her father (a form of denial, with its typical substitutive fantasies, designed to keep these mental representations consonant with each other when reality interpositions threatened their symmetry).

In the course of her analysis this patient had reported many memories and other descriptions of her father, which were accompanied by meticulous accounts of their relationship throughout her childhood. Those productions, which occurred prior to the alterations in her memory as just described, had a strong quality of both constancy and consistency, with no indications that might lead one to question their general reliability (the question of whether memories can ever be entirely accurate is of considerable importance and will be discussed below). Her first reactions to significant changes in her husband, besides the imposition of continuous anxiety, was to ignore them, and when that was unsuccessful, to actively reject her perceptions that these changes were taking place. Increasingly, when some of the more profound changes required (and her husband demanded) acknowledgment, thereby challenging her reluctance (including her initial refusal) to see them, she began to suffer a more acute form of mounting anxiety. She was able to say, however (it must be stressed), without profound psychological recognition, that her discomfort was in some way connected to her husband becoming "a stranger" to her. Although she consciously knew that to some extent he was changing, and some of the reasons why, what she was emotionally most aware of was how "altered" he seemed to be, which was experienced as disorienting despite whatever she seemed to know. What she did not know, at least what she was in no way meaningfully aware of, was that there was a direct and highly specific link between a growing sense of abandonment, alienation, and danger, and those changes in her husband that specifically differentiated him from her father in her mind. Although she knew that his changing was important, she did not appreciate the underlying significance of the changes that particularly mattered to her (only the ones that created dissonance between the representations of her father and her husband mattered, the others were insignificant to her because they threatened nothing). It was not necessary that her husband be like her father in every way imaginable, and in fact if he were, her prohibitions would not permit her to be attracted to him. The changes that did matter caused her to despair, and here we come to the crux of this example, for when she was in conflict because her husband's changes did infringe on the shared representations, and therefore did become threatening and made her terribly unhappy, her ultimate solution was to "spontaneously recover" what she claimed were "previously unremembered" attributes of her father. These unconsciously developed fabrications were intended to remake her memories of her father so that they would not be discordant with her current and unfortunately ever-changing husband's attributes.

It was this patient's genuine belief that the new picture she was painting of her father had always been true, but simply "forgotten." This involution of her transference needs did, in fact, permit her to feel reassured and less vulnerable as the evolution of her husband's character progressed. Her anxieties were considerably relieved (in consciousness and in preconsciousness) when her husband no longer felt so alien (that is, unlike her father) to her, and this was achieved through a transformation of her memory of her father. When she transformed her memory and in that way presented herself as if she had a new, or at least a different, past she could feel closer and emotionally safer with her husband, and she experienced an enormous sense of relief. Thus we can see how, with the contrivance (subordination) of her ego, transference needs were able to influence ideas both forward and backward in her memory, clearly influencing the present and even seeming to be able to change the past. The clinical danger in such situations is for the new material to be misconstrued by the analyst and thought of as material that has broken past the barrier of repression.

Ubiquitous Transference and the Ego's Autonomous Functions

Transference may or may not play a role in psychopathological processes. The previous examples were drawn from the treatment context, which could conceivably lead one into making the mistake of characterizing transference as something that is essentially in conflict with "good mental health" and in conflict with "constructive adjustment" to the world's demands. One would be quite wrong to view transference exclusively as an unremitting opponent of the requirements of reality. Transference has some notable regressive features, of course, in much the same way that *fantasy* has regressive elements: but, like fantasy, transference can be used for progressive and adaptive goals. To further investigate this idea, the reader is referred back to the section of this book dealing with theory (Part I), to review the discussion of *reversibility of the ego* and how it contrasts with the idea of *regression in the service of the ego*. Regression in the service of the ego and reversibility of the ego are concepts usually linked to the question of creativity, and in keeping with this context let us look at how some nonpathological aspects of transference can play a role in the development of the artist. Suppose an artist's initial interest in looking and in seeing grew, in part, from having seen specific things in childhood that were both exciting and gratifying. Naturally, the circumstances in which things have been seen, and whether what was observed was permitted or forbidden, will play a significant role in how the experience will eventually be utilized.

So as not to overstate the case, one will also want to recall that looking, seeing, and their vicissitudes are not dependent solely on those particular variables, most especially in the life of a future artist. Also, this example is not limited only to future artists; looking and seeing inevitably, as a by-product of development, becomes bound by (but not necessarily crippled by) conflict.

If, in the childhood of our hypothetical artist, looking was highly instinctualized (that is, if seeing and looking and other activities that were intimately related to visual production, and to visual reproduction, were very closely tied to both the stimulation and gratification of his drive-related wishes), but there were also adequate opportunities for sublimation, neutralization, and drive fusion, the instinctualized looking and seeing could quite readily have become transformed into a better-than-average visual acuity, a better-than-average visual perceptivity, a better-than-average visual sensitivity, a talent for, and a special interest in, visual art.

The action of transference is, in this example, intricately interwoven with other dynamic processes (in addition to sublimation, neutralization, and drive fusion); for example, repression, hypercathexis, countercathexis, cognitive and other intellectual development (esthetics, criticality, and so on), and reaction formation. Certainly one would not want to ascribe the artist's proficiency in distinguishing subtle differences in shades of color and his appreciation of form and composition only to transference; that is, merely as a displacement (however transformed) of an infantile interest (infantile aims with infantile objects) into the interests of an adult. And yet the intensity of the artist's gaze, the love of his model no matter what the subject, the uniqueness of his view (which may include an extremely idiosyncratic vision of the world), may well be based to a considerable extent on underlying reminiscences of his childhood aims and objects that are displaced into the present. It may rest on such possibilities (or, more likely, combined possibilities) as having seen his mother disrobed, on an early view of the primal scene, on the visual memories of having been breast-fed, on having seen his father shaving or his mother at her toilet, or on other early scenes with an equivalent impact employing visual cues.

We also might want to think about this as possibly having roots in genetically predetermined pathways of perception, as well as being otherwise conflictually hypercathected. The example of the artist also illustrates how transference need not be equated with, or inevitably linked up with, the idea of pathology. And it demonstrates, too, how transference does not have to be limited to mental events of a cognitive nature, or to mental events that are always directly linked to specific other people. Here we can see transference in the displacement of expectations, wishes, action tendencies, and modes of relating to the world through one's perceptions.

Pathological Forms of Transference

Transference phenomena can of course become deeply involved with pathology, even though transference also has the potential to exist apart from conflict. Transference may be expressed within symptoms or alongside of them. Transference is frequently implicated in the motives for symptom formation and also often determines the forms symptoms will take. To remain with the example of looking and seeing, let us suppose one finds certain inhibitions in an artist in later life that are associated with conflictual and hence, fixated, looking and seeing (one may safely presume that pathological transference phenomena will not exist in the absence of conflict or in the absence of attempts at conflict resolution). After all, in situations that are, because of the conflicts revived by transference, reminiscent of infantile conflict-ridden situations, particularly those in which looking and seeing were specifically of particular importance, one would not be surprised to meet with an inhibition in an artist's ability to pursue his work entirely, or in a particular aspect of his work.

One relatively young man, a gifted artist, judging from his success in the art world, came to treatment suffering from a creative block. We will focus here on one extremely pathological representation of a transference phenomenon that emerged in his work; a repetition of a highly pathological eye-contact scenario with his mother in early childhood interfering in his work, and its symbolic and destructive representation in his art.

Approximately 6 months before beginning treatment, this artist began to become unable to put his artistic wishes into action. He had always been able to draw accurately, mix colors exactly, and create effects of his choosing, and yet suddenly, everything he tried to paint or draw came out other than as he had intended. He became obsessed with drawing a series of self-portraits in which one could observe pathological transference representations affecting looking and seeing. The repetition included, as usual, transferences of a wide range of apperceptive experience and memory. He would begin to draw a self-portrait and begin to notice that one of the eyes was not exactly right. He would erase and redraw, over and over, until he was in a circular frenzy of frustrating and enraging activity. Eventually, he would stab the pencil through the eye of the drawing and then rip the drawing to shreds; in the later stages of these episodes he would come to be so out of control that he would explode into a rage, and would proceed to break up much of the furniture in his house. Both he and his wife were upset and terrified by these outbursts (even though they had cause to get used to them, because he had a prior history of temper tantrums). In these episodes of rage he would scream and yell, literally frothing at the corners of his mouth in a "fit" of frustration, smashing everything in his path, until he fell into exhaustion. He would be sick from anger and humiliation, for hours afterward.

Both of this man's parents seem to have been quite disturbed, the mother more so than the father. Throughout infancy and early childhood his mother would hold him in her arms, rocking him and crooning to him as they stared wordlessly into one another's eyes. Mother and child spent hours this way, and the patient remembered those times with his mother vividly. Unfortunately this activity, while perhaps appropriate to infancy, was not limited only to his earliest years, and some of his most painful memories were of him struggling to free himself from his mother's grasp, even as late as the age of 5. "She would hold me down and lock me in. She had herself wrapped around me somehow, so that I couldn't get free. I'd wriggle and twist and try to get out of her grip, but she was like an octopus with millions of arms. I would scream at her and bite and kick and scratch, but she'd always manage to hold me down. So there we'd be, the two of us, with me lying exhausted, locked in her embrace, sobbing and gasping for air and knowing that I could never get away; and this crazy person would be rocking and humming and looking at me with her weird smile . . . she wasn't even out of breath . . . as if we were the 'lovey-dovey' mother-and-child. I was 5 years old and she still tried to relate to me as if I were 5 *months* old!"

This patient's mother looked down into her son's eyes with what she thought was love, and he stared back up at her in wordless, helpless hatred. Having this information, we can see how the eye of his self-portrait (the mirror image of the mother's merged self and object representations as embodied in her child) came to be the locus of his adult conflict and the focus of his rage. This is an extremely complex pathological transference vehicle, effect, and representation.

The Transference Neurosis as an Artifact of Psychoanalysis

Having considered various aspects and presentations of transference, as it appears both in and outside of pathology, and always as an endemic phenomenon, we may now shift our discussion to the nature of *the transference neurosis* and its role in psychoanalysis. In the most general terms, we can say that the transference neurosis is an artificial neurosis. In the ordinary course of people's lives there can be no such thing as a transference neurosis. People may be said to enter analysis to solve their neuroses, but one can never properly make the claim that someone comes to an analysis for the treatment and cure of a transference neurosis. What is special, then, about a transference neurosis that makes it different from transference as a general concept, and why do we look to it in an analysis rather than to the general circumstances of the patient's life, to his symptoms, or to his general expression of transferences?

The transference neurosis is, as a specific by-product of the analytic process, a clearer, more purified, and more extravagant version within the treatment situation of the infantile conflicts that are usually disguised by defense and by adaptive transformation. The purpose of the transference neurosis is to unmask those defenses and transformations that hide the true nature of the infantile motives at work. In addition to defenses and other transformations, reality issues are also interwoven with transferential needs so that their infantile elements are even further obscured. For example, a man entered treatment to solve a problem in his romantic relationships. Over a number of years, and with a number of women, his relation-ships ended with his partner leaving him. They all claimed that he was intolerably jealous, and although he could see that he did have that problem, he was unable to understand why, if he knew that it was a neurotic problem, he could not be less jealous. In every instance of a jealous argument he could point to things that his partner had done that could be cause for some jealousy. Not until the relationship had come to an end could he see that his interpretation of the event was not the only one possible. He knew that his jealousy was inappropriate, as an abstraction but not concretely, because even while reviewing his past relationships in analysis he would slip back and forth between seeing other interpretations of an event and then only the one that triggered his jealousy.

This man's mother was deeply disturbed, and she sadistically provoked him on a regular basis throughout his childhood. Sometimes she did this by being intention-ally withholding, and at other times she would scare him for fun. Mainly she thought that his frustration was amusing, and most of her provocations were designed to drive him into a rage, which she thought was hysterically funny. She was sufficiently disturbed as to openly admit this without even the slightest hint of recognition of how inappropriate it was. Her ability to rationalize this behavior was supported by the claim that it was "only a joke" and, if anything, she thought that he was rather weird for reacting so strongly. She insisted that he relate to her conscious classification of this as "only a joke" as if it were the entire, and only, reality. He was able to describe numerous occasions of this in his analysis without, at first, recognizing how very disturbed she was (having taken their relationship for granted before entering analysis), and without recognizing this as an important element in his jealous rages (which, at heart, were not about jealousy at all). This man also reported a repetitious series of conflicts at work in which someone would frustrate him, or prefer someone else (although this was the more infrequent case), and he would respond so furiously that he usually had to be asked to change jobs. This, too, he did not connect with either his jealous rages or with his relationship to his mother. In both his jealous romantic rages and his work-related altercations he became focused on the possible reality features that might serve as a justification for his feelings, partly as a way of remaining unconscious of his sadomasochistic connection to his mother, and partly as a way of conforming with his mother's demand that he view only a superficial aspect of the event as if it were the full reality. For these reasons, the way he began to express this in the treatment was couched in events that could hardly be separated out from reality (at least on a manifest level).

Not long after the treatment had begun he introduced into the analysis this transferential inclination in a way that was not particularly regressed (thus keeping the infantile elements unclear), and he did so in a way that seemed only to do with reality (rather than clearly being a transference event). He mentioned that he had been reading one of the waiting-room magazines while waiting for his session and that he had not had time to finish the article he was reading. He then asked if he could borrow the magazine, so that he could finish reading the article at home. One might not ordinarily give this a great deal of consideration if one did not know anything about his history; that is, one might assume that it represented something transferential, without making any particular assumptions about what it may have stood for, transferentially. But knowing what we do, it would appear that the latent meaning of the request is fairly obvious. It does not take any great leap of the imagination to hypothesize that his request had nothing to do with the reality of the magazine and the article that he was reading. If this is true, and if the event remains on this level, how will it become possible for him to see that he is (1) trying to find out whether the analyst will be as withholding as his mother was; and (2) inviting the analyst to refuse the request (which the analyst has no choice but to do, since lending magazines is not part of the undertaking, and on some level the patient recognizes this) in order to repeat with the analyst the sadomasochistic relationship he had with his mother? If it remains on this level, how will it be possible for the patient to see that (1) just this kind of request was usually involved in his altercations at work, and (2) his jealous rages usually began when a woman did not give him something that he wanted? Something has to happen that will remove it from the realm of a concrete reality issue, if it is to be understood on any deeper level. Left in this form, the patient will treat it like a reality issue–"Can I have the magazine, or not?"–and never move any deeper into what it may mean. Simply showing the patient how they are all interrelated does not have much of a point, in that the process is analytic rather than educational, and so an analytic solution must be found.

An analytic solution would be one that caused the material to be expressed differently. At this point the question of insight is irrelevant, and we must find a way to help the patient to see more accurately just *what* is going on. Only after that has taken place can we afford to explore *why* it happens in a particular way, and what that means. If we have a method of observing the patient's conflicts in a more regressed way, it gives the patient a better chance of perceiving the infantile character of the conflict. A moderate degree of regression will not globally affect all of psychic structure and will bring the material out in a clearer way, since with regression the patient gives up some of the defensive and transformational advances he has achieved regarding his conflicts. The psychoanalytic situation is inherently frustrating and we know that frustration is experienced as traumatic (traumatic in the sense that it is painful and partially disorganizing, and not in the sense that it is inescapable and overwhelming). Trauma induces regression, and one of the net results of frustrating a patient's transference demands, wishes, and expectations will be the very regression that we need in order to see the issue more clearly. One must carefully gauge a patient's ego strength before choosing psychoanalysis as the treatment of choice, paying careful attention to the limits of the patient's frustration tolerance, since too great a trauma quickly does become overwhelming and will cause an unwanted regression in other areas of functioning that, when sufficiently severe, would work against the treatment.

The idea of bringing about a trauma, even such a limited trauma, in a patient is an emotionally loaded concept. It carries with it the specter of the analyst mistreating the patient and of the analyst secretly gratifying unconscious sadistic impulses in the name of technique. Initiating a traumatic event as a controlled technical procedure, capitalizing on a traumatic event, or turning a traumatic event into a tool need not necessarily carry those implications. Every time a physician probes the abdomen to find out where it hurts, he is inflicting a trauma on the patient. He does this not because the patient's pain gives him pleasure but because it is necessary if he is to find out what he needs to know in order to help the patient. A general report, such as "My stomach hurts," or "I have a bellyache," or "Down there, on the lower left," is insufficient: nothing less than the painful probe will do, despite the fact that it is inflicting a further trauma on a patient who is already in pain. An analogous situation exists for the analyst and analysand: our form of probing takes the form of frustrating the patient's transference demands. This induces a mild traumatic regression which is necessary in order for the treatment ultimately (and even in the short run) to be of help. Certainly, this aspect of both examinations may play into any sadistic tendencies and inclinations the physician or the analyst may have, but it is not initiated by them. An analyst lives as uncomfortably with the necessity of bringing about psychic pain as does the physician who needs to test what hurts, and in neither case would we want to avoid that action which is in fact therapeutic, or to construe a malignant motive, simply because in some cases of disturbed physicians and analysts it does have the potential to meet unconscious and inappropriate wishes. By recognizing that it is the traumatic effect of transference frustration (and facing this event squarely and unapologetically), we have an explanation of why regression occurs in a psychoanalysis that is not simply attributable to the repetition compulsion alone (which would be satisfied with any repetition, never concerning itself with whether the repetition takes a stage-specific form or has regressive features).

An additional problem that sometimes comes up when one identifies trauma as a tool in the development of the transference neurosis is that we are used to considering trauma as a negative event, one that raises anxiety and prompts defense, because we associate the concept with the disorganizing consequences of "the traumatic moment" or "the traumatic situation" (in which the outcome is determined by the psychic apparatus having been overwhelmed). Trauma, in low doses, can be both disorganizing and productive, in the same way that fantasy, in low doses, can be simultaneously regressive and adaptive. The transference frustration strips away some of the defensive camouflage from the conflict by stimulating a regression, which by definition is a sign of disorganization, and if this were the only outcome it *would* be a negative event. If the analytically traumatic event is limited enough not to be entirely overwhelming (and we know that trauma and its consequences is not an all-or-nothing proposition), then other attributes of the mature ego still remain available to capitalize on this clearer, because regressed, view of the problem, which is the positive and adaptive side of the situation.

The simplest way to achieve this goal, and the easiest way to keep the trauma at the minimum level possible, is for the analyst to frustrate a transference demand that the patient is making. This must not be confused with the analyst trying to recreate, in the present treatment, a traumatic event from the past. The repetition compulsion is the mental regulator that brings past conflicts into the treatment, quite readily, and for the analyst to actually do something to try to recreate the past would be destructive to the patient and to the treatment. The patient recreates the past on the basis of his transference needs, and this is fueled with the power of unresolved conflict: it needs no introduction into the treatment by the analyst. We manipulate the transference that the patient introduces by frustrating, and thereby focusing, his transference expectations, and we differentiate this from any active attempt on the part of the analyst to reproduce (by acting it out) some part of the transference. In this case, it would only be necessary not to agree to let the patient take the magazine home. For the analyst to try to conjure up some temptation so as to then frustrate it would only be adding insult to injury. Unconscious defensive organization operates very effectively in both permitting material access into the analysis and denying access to material that would be too traumatically disorganizing, and this part of the patient's ego is very much in operation when he introduces transferential and conflictual elements into the treatment. The patient is an unconscious collaborator, and we rely not only on the analyst's judgments but also the implicit judgment expressed by the patient in how quickly and how deeply the treatment intensifies: when the analyst introduces the transference instead of the patient, he runs the risk of overwhelming the patient by recreating in the present an actual "traumatic moment," and he undermines the collaborative aspects of the working relationship. When one only frustrates an already existing transferential demand, one does not bring about a wholesale regression but, rather, a regression that takes place only in small increments, and in this fashion we try to keep the requisite trauma to the smallest amount necessary for the treatment to progress at any given time. We would expect at first to see nothing more than an intensification of the transference demand, and we would not expect to see clearly regressed material emerging after only one transference frustration. Over a period of time, however, as the intensity of the demands increases and as the demands are frustrated as systematically as possible, one does expect to see regression in the content of the demand.

This patient's initial response to not being permitted to take the magazine home was incredulity: he said, "Are you afraid that I won't bring it back? What's the big deal?" But he said this in an affectively more intense way than he had been using with the analyst until that point, and the greater lability of affect was the first hint of a regressive intensification of the conflict with the analyst. As the intensity of his demands increased, and yet more affect was invested in them, new associative material (material that was previously repressed and suppressed) began to surface. Not on this very first occasion, but increasingly so as the treatment deepened.

Not long afterward this patient had occasion to make another request of the analyst. He had noticed a piece of art in the office that interested him and he asked about its provenance. Again, this was understood by the analyst to be a repetition (in another form) of the same issues that were inherent in the earlier request about the magazine. The analyst's response was to ask the patient what it was about that piece of art that had attracted his attention, and the patient then escalated what he understood as a struggle between them over the information by insisting that he would not answer the analyst's question before the analyst answered his. This, of course, was also a replication of the very kinds of difficulties that he often got into at work. One can see the parallels more readily now because the reality issues in the "dispute" clearly are diminished as the patient becomes less reasonable and cooperative. We can perceive this, and at that stage the analyst saw it, but the patient still only experienced it as a struggle between the analyst and him over the artwork questions and had not yet connected it with anything else. It would have been premature to interpret this, because only the analyst recognized its meaning (which had not entered into the patient's preconsciousness at that time). It would also have been premature to have interpreted it at that time, because an interpretation of it would have caused the patient (if he had accepted it) to have become more realistic, and hence, less regressed. One does not wish to interfere with the regression before the infantile nature of the conflict emerges into the patient's awareness. Too early an interpretation defeats the deepening of the transference neurosis.

This remained unresolved, the patient refusing to discuss the analyst's questions because the analyst did not first answer his. The patient wondered why the analyst would not do so, and the analyst asked him what he thought might be the reason. The patient dismissed both the question about the artwork and the question about the patient's fantasy about the analyst's motives, as a "peculiarity" of the analyst's and went on to talk about something else.

Regression and the Expression of Infantile Conflict

Before going on to follow the establishment of this patient's transference neurosis we will take a brief detour to look at an example of how the patient regulated the speed and depth of his transferential regression. The importance of only frustrating the patient's transference demands and nothing else, as opposed to attempting to introduce a transferential repetition into the treatment, was clearly illustrated by an event that occurred in the analysis about 2½ years later. The patient had achieved some insight into the infantile contribution to his current interpersonal conflicts and was working on the ways that he replicated his relationship with his mother with people in his current life. He was examining his identifications with his mother and, in particular, was looking at how he was identified with some of her most troubled traits. He had recognized that some of her behavior toward him may have been due to profound psychopathology and was trying to understand what motive he might have had for identifying with such disturbed functioning. To summarize his eventual understanding of the situation (using analytic terminology, and not his): he saw the identification with his disturbed mother as helpful and as promoting structure-building in the earliest stages of his childhood because it enabled him to extract libidinal supplies from his mother, through incorporative internalization, even when she consciously and behaviorally attempted to frustrate and deprive him. As he came to this recognition he felt a very great sense of relief, because previously he had always experienced vague and unsettling feelings, approaching terror and revulsion, when preconscious aspects of his maternal identification surfaced into his current functioning. As a very young child he used the identification in a way that was diametrically opposed to his mother's pathological inclinations, and as such he experienced the identification as a "life saver." As an adult, however, he had previously experienced the identification only as a source of shame and dissatisfaction. That shame and dissatisfaction was associated with the enduring nature of that identification; that is, with the retention of the identification into adulthood. After recognizing that the identification had an extremely valuable purpose in early childhood, even if that aspect of it had become obsolete in adulthood, the depth of his shame about it and the associated feelings of shame and self-disgust became markedly diminished. Also, the power of the identification (with his mother's pathology) was somewhat reduced. A measure of the structural reorganization of this insight is reflected in an attenuation of the ominous feelings of terror and revulsion that, previously, always saturated the event no matter what else, even adaptively, was going on.

The patient suddenly, in the midst of all this, recalled to mind the interaction earlier in the analysis, when he had refused to answer the analyst's question about the artwork unless the analyst first answered his question. He remembered thinking that the analyst was "peculiar" and recalled the analyst's query as to what motives he thought the analyst might have had in order for him to have been acting in that "peculiar" way. At the time it happened, the patient said, he had simply dismissed the question about the analyst's possible motives and went on to speak of something else; but now, he said, he could see that when the analyst asked that question he had had a "sick feeling," which he quickly and rather actively pushed out of consciousness and forgot until just this minute. The "sick feeling" about the analyst was exactly the same as the "sick feeling" that he felt about himself when he recognized some of the worst parts of his mother in himself. The invasive "sick feeling" that was so unpleasant and which seemed inescapable was not only representative of the terror and revulsion he felt about this aspect of his mother, and about his identification with her on this level: it also reflected his consciously subjective experience of the potentially and actually disorganizing features of this identification. This affect, like anxiety (and perhaps, also, a form of anxiety) was a signal (from one part of the ego to other parts of the ego) about the potential and actual dangers to psychic structure of relying on this aspect of his maternal identifications after childhood had passed and it was no longer appropriate for an adult. The dangers include decompensation, or at the very least, too heavy a reliance on primitive modes of narcissistic and affect control in an adult, notwithstanding any organizing features it may actually have had years ago in infancy and in earliest childhood.

In looking back at that interchange he said that he must have felt then that he was with his "insane" mother, and that the "vile" thought that the analyst was also "crazy" was too terrifying to acknowledge (even to himself) or to retain. So, he said, he "pushed it down" and changed the subject: how could he have remained in treatment, he wondered, if the analyst really was as horrible and as crazy as his mother?

Optimal Frustration of Transference Demands

We can well imagine what effect it would have had on the treatment if the analyst had attempted to be frustrating and depriving, *in the ways that the patient's mother actually was,* as a means of "bringing the transference into the treatment." This is the pitfall of attempting to manipulate the transference instead of only choosing to frustrate it. Just frustrating the specific, limited transference demand was quite enough to activate this transferential view of the analyst, and it also gave the patient the room he needed not to regress any deeper into this terrifying and repellant experience of the analyst. The patient shifted the subject when it became clear (unconsciously, and perhaps preconsciously) that he could not continue the treatment if this regression deepened any further at that time. Surely the patient's behaviors with the analyst reflected an aspect of the patient's identification with the frustrating and depriving nature of his mother, but beyond this, and perhaps more importantly, it was the patient's recognition (despite its not being conscious) that the regression was about to become destructively disorganizing – and not a random shift in attention – that caused him to change the subject as a way of preserving his ability to continue to be in the analysis.

Returning now to the early stage of the analysis, in which the transference neurosis was just beginning to deepen significantly, the patient asked the analyst a short time later to reschedule a session so that he could attend an office party. The analyst did not, and the patient became quite angry. He began to accuse the analyst of having "some kind of problem" with giving and saw this as strictly a problem of the analyst's. Not dismissing it so rapidly this time, he went on to speak of the irritations he had to put up with at work with people who "had problems they imposed" on him. Here we see an associative event which, although not clarifying any genetic meaning, did move him to examine his work-related problems in an affectively enhanced manner. He still, even though he had previously had a "preconscious" glimpse which he then suppressed, did not make any conscious connections to his mother as someone who had "some kind of problem," but the combination of anxiety and of being at this early stage in the process makes that not unexpected. This reference, because of how he phrased it, seemed to be more concretely reflective of his conflicts with his mother than his previous, more general, and even more symbolic references to her: thus we might view this as the first genetic representative in the transference. It would be valuable to make a brief aside at this point to clarify some of the differences between the patient's history and the nature of genetic conflicts.

The genetic theory is frequently misunderstood, and the commonest error is to assume that it stands for the patient's history, in the sense that everything that happens or that is experienced in the present is processed through the sum of everything that has had an effect on the individual in the past. That is merely a statement identifying the power of history in human development – certainly not a small or unimportant notion on its own, but a limited one in the context of genetic theory. The genetic postulation may be stated as follows: in every human experience, without exception, there will reside, to a greater or lesser extent, some kernel of infantile conflict (and not merely one's general historical experiences). In most healthy adult functioning the degree of influence determined by infantile conflict is minimal; in most unhealthy adult functioning the degree to which infantile conflict exercises its influence will be excessive and may, in its worst condition, even come to be the predominating factor in the mental event. Thus genetic theory, in full complicity with the compulsion to repeat (as a regulatory principle of mental functioning), calls to our attention the fact that anything and everything, if traced long and diligently enough, will go beyond narrating history and will eventually also lead the analysand to some kind of inherent childhood conflict. The importance of this is clear in regard to the transference neurosis, in which a highly focused view of vestigial infantile conflict is made possible, and it is interesting to see how it all simultaneously converges with the techniques of free association and of neutrality, which are so essential to the development of the entire analytic process. It clarifies the analyst's consistently attentive interest, without favor or bias, to anything the analysand happens to say. It explains why the analyst, who attempts to perceive the latent conflictual content of what is being said, will listen just as carefully (although with evenly suspended attention, or perhaps it is more true to say *because of* evenly suspended attention) to material that manifestly has no obvious relation to infantile conflict as he will to material that is obviously charged with conflict. It does not matter to the analyst what the patient talks about: everything is of importance and interest – baseball, incest, movies, food, social relationships, music, clothes, aches and pains, memories, dogs and cats, work, parents, money, school, writing a book such as this one – when the analyst automatically listens with an implicit attention to genetic considerations. And when Freud suggested, as a genetic inevitability, that whatever the patient chooses to bring up, no matter how seemingly mundane, should be taken seriously as the leading edge of the patient's unconscious, he wished to make four points: (1) that there is an unconscious; (2) that the unconscious operates according to a set of rules that are systematically organized; (3) that when one is alerted to those facts it is possible to understand more about what is being said than is immediately obvious from its manifest content; and (4) that when one attends to the latent contents of the patient's productions one can begin to acquire some sense of what the patient's infantile conflicts are, how they affect the patient's current mental and behavioral functioning, and how the patient employs defenses to manage the presence of those conflicts. Ultimately, if the patient makes a total attempt to engage in fully free association, he too will arrive at the genetic contents of his thoughts and feelings. But this will only be achieved within a process of regression. In this regression he will be in conflict about overcoming newly motivated resistances to uncensored communication, and he will exhibit considerable conflict about overcoming transference resistances; and so the work goes rather slowly. If the analyst does not interpret too quickly and lets the patient present the material in slowly deepening stages, they will inevitably be led into the patient's history and, subsequently, into the areas of the patient's continuing infantile conflicts.

As transference demands are frustrated and the regression deepens, not only the intensity but also the rate of transference demands increases. A transference demand is only an occasional event early in the treatment but it becomes a more frequent event as the analysis progresses. The patient begins the analysis telling about his life and his experiences in both the past and the present, and he is not particularly focused on the nature of the relationship between the analyst and himself. The analytic relationship becomes more of a focus as the patient's insistence on transference gratifications is frustrated: the transference demand is a piece of "unfinished business" which is returned to again and again, paralleling the process of the repetition compulsion in connection with the patient's original infantile conflicts. Slowly the treatment changes its character as the previously exclusive focus on symptoms, current experiences, and descriptions of the patient's history becomes broadened by the conflicts the patient experiences with the analyst over his transference demands. Eventually the patient tends to withdraw his conflictual attachments in many of the other areas of his life and reinvests them in the analysis and on the person of the analyst. He becomes "less neurotic" in everyday living and considerably *more* neurotic in his relations with the analyst. It often looks, on the surface, as if the patient is "cured," and it is not uncommon for some patients to terminate their treatments at this point, believing that their problems have been solved because they no longer seem to be complicating their lives outside of the analysis. Patients sometimes express this by saying, *"You don't really have any idea of what I am actually like, in real life. Do you think that I am like this elsewhere, and this way with other people? Ridiculous! You are the only one I ever behave this way with,"* not realizing that the only reason their symptoms have disappeared outside of the analysis is because they have been so powerfully invested in the analysis: the patient, in this circumstance, does not recognize the fact that if symptoms were not so invested in the analysis and with the analyst, they *would* be occurring again elsewhere, just as they did before beginning the analysis.

The "Floating" Transference

The patient whom we are using in this example had not yet reached that stage. His condition would be described as somewhere between his original neurosis and exhibiting a fully developed transference neurosis. The concept of *floating transference* refers to this intermediate condition. His transference responses to the analyst are now more intense and more regressed, but they still have some distance to go before the infantile conflictual elements can become fully enacted and, consequently, more visible.

Over the course of many months this patient initiated a number of power struggles with the analyst, all ushered in with a request that the analyst give him something. One of the striking features of these requests was that they were always for something that he knew, before making the demand, that the analyst would not give him. For example, at one point he began to insist on being permitted to shake the analyst's hand at the end of sessions. One can immediately recognize the transferential nature of this demand by how he rationalized the need for hand-shaking at the end of sessions. He said that, given how often he was angry at the analyst, he was concerned that the analyst would have his own angry counterre-sponse toward the patient's behavior (from our perspective, like his mother who could not master her own impulses when faced with the impulses of her child), and that the analyst would act out his own anger by withholding interpretations and other important information from him (again, from our perspective, as his mother sadistically withheld things from him and intentionally frustrated him). Shaking hands at the end of a session would be "proof" to the patient, he said, that the analyst was not harboring any hard feelings. He acknowledged that this would be a striking change in their customary way of ending a session and that, on some level, he recognized that it was unusual to ask the analyst to make some concrete statement of "no hard feelings" at the end of a session; but, nevertheless, he felt that it was definitely necessary. The way it came up the first time was when, at the end of a session, instead of leaving the office the patient walked over to the analyst's chair behind the couch and extended his hand. Although somewhat nonplussed by the patient's behavior, and despite being taken quite by surprise, the analyst resisted the impulse to reach out and shake the patient's offered hand. The patient reddened after a few moments, shook his head, hissed "Jesus H. Christ" through clenched teeth, turned, and stormed out of the office. This came up first thing, next session, and it was then that the patient explained what he had wanted, and why. As part of his frankly infuriated response to the analyst not having shaken his hand when it was offered, the patient said that he knew, even as he approached the analyst, that the analyst would be too "uptight and tight-assed" to respond to what was clearly, from the patient's point of view, "a friendly overture", thus demonstrating his knowledge (possibly fully conscious but more probably fully in the patient's preconscious) that he was asking for something he was unlikely to get.

This patient knew that he was provocative and knew that he looked for opportunities to engage in power struggles with his analyst. The transference neurosis was significantly deepened when, some time later, he began to express the idea that his behavior was entirely legitimate and fully justified by the need to demonstrate that, behind the analyst's "hypocritical reliance on technique," he was enjoying the patient's discomfort and that he acquired pleasure from frustrating the patient. He began to wage a campaign against the analyst, firmly having come to believe that the purpose of the analysis now was to get the analyst to drop his "bullshit claim to neutrality" (this patient had some knowledge of the field) so that the patient, and the analyst, and the whole world, could see the analyst's "true colors." [Much could be said about the patient's relationship with his father, his obvious anality, and other dynamic and structural considerations, especially considering how narrowly focused this example has been on the patient's relationship to his mother, but it would distract us from our discussion of how a transference neurosis slowly comes to fruition.] At this point the transference neurosis is quite fully developed: the patient has lost touch with that portion of reality that previously kept him aware that it was only "as if" this were all true about the analyst; the patient now "believes" that it *is* entirely true about the analyst, and the analyst is experienced with all the emotional vitality that originally was lodged in the relationship the patient had with his mother. All of the other attributes of the analyst, and all other aspects of the analytic relationship that were previously satisfactory, have become lost to the patient's perception and memory, not permanently but for the moment quite completely. The patient is reexperiencing his relationship with his mother, not just remembering it, as if it were truly happening in the here and now. At this time the patient has no insight yet that it is not actually about the analyst but about his mother; that will come later, as executive functions of the ego are brought to bear on what he is going through with the analyst. When the patient is in this temporary regression, in which so many of his reality-testing functions are interfered with that he is not experiencing it as being with someone who reminds him of his mother, but experiences it instead as if he were, for all practical purposes, with his mother again (even if he is not hallucinating her presence), we describe him as being in a *delusional transference* (which is an important and necessary event if the infantile conflicts are going to come to life and be fully expressed in the analysis).

Transference Delusions, Delusional Transferences, and Transference Psychosis

It is not uncommon for some patients to suggest that the treatment should be terminated when this point has been reached, using the rationale that the analyst is too "disturbed" to be able to conduct the analysis in a professional manner. This patient had not lost all traces of objectivity nor had he lost the main portion of his reality-testing abilities. Even though some reality-testing functions suffered an impairment in this particular area, they were not totally damaged. He always knew that he was in the room with *the analyst* and that it *was* a psychoanalysis, despite the many distortions that overlaid those facts. He had too much ego strength to simply quit, or to imperiously announce his intention to leave (and here we see the value in assessing the ego strengths of persons we are considering assigning to analysis rather than to a psychotherapy of a different and less demanding variety), but he did pose the following question with a great deal of seriousness: "How is it possible for me to benefit from being in an analysis with someone who is so much like my mother?" At this point he was still in what we would consider a delusional transference, but if he had quit instead of asking the question (which kept it in the analysis), his delusional transference could be said to have further regressed into a *psychotic transference*. In a psychotic transference the seeming reality of the transferential experience completely overwhelms important ego functions and, consequently, the residual working alliance that previously existed between patient and analyst becomes too deeply eroded, or even destroyed. The patient's internal reality, now very heavily influenced by pathological fantasy formation, becomes more powerful than is his ability to manage it objectively, and no possibility exists any longer for patient and analyst to continue working on the problem as a psychological event (rather than as a catastrophe in reality).

The concepts of delusional and psychotic transferences are not usually used unless one is talking about a psychoanalysis or, to be more specific, outside the context of a transference neurosis (which, by definition, only exists within a psychoanalysis). However, unlike the concept of a transference neurosis, which has no analogues in the patient's life outside the analysis, both delusional and psychotic transferences do have analogues in everyday living. Each time the patient initiated a power struggle with a lover or a boss, leading to a highly conflicted relationship, we can view this as analogous to many of the features of a delusional transference. And each time that he pushed them, or the argument, so far that a lover left him or he left her, or a boss fired him or he felt that he had no choice but to quit, we can see how this is analogous to many of the features of a psychotic transference.

Moving back now to the question that this patient had posed, we find ourselves in a position unique in the history of his analysis. The transference neurosis is now sufficiently regressed, by virtue of its delusional qualities, for the analyst not to be concerned about interfering with its development by making a premature interpretation. Any interpretations the analyst makes at this point (assuming, of course, that they are correct and accessible to the patient) will cause the transference to lose some of its delusional qualities and will begin to reverse some of the most regressive features of the transference neurosis. Now, however, this turn of events is quite welcome (as long as it is based on there having been an efflorescence of the infantile conflicts in the transference neurosis, and not on the analyst's wish to "get out of the line of fire"). The patient has accused the analyst, berated him, and made clear all of the condemnations he felt but could never have expressed as a child to his mother, but which he has been leveling at her ever since in the symbolic form of his relationships with other people. Finally, now, it may be possible in the analysis, for the first time, for him to give these issues a closer and more objective examination.

At this point, however, the analyst does not simply begin to make genetic interpretations for the patient's edification. Nor does the patient automatically snap out of his delusional transference in order to observe it from the distanced vantage point of his more mature ego functions. The difference, as it affects technical considerations, lies not in any immediate action taken by the analyst or, for that matter, by the patient; it is found in the analyst's license to introduce genetic constructions and reconstructions when the opportunity presents itself (a choice not possible before this point if he wanted to preserve the integrity of the transference neurosis). Previously, the analyst limited his interventions to those regarding the emergence of resistances. Despite the power that we attribute to genetic interpretations we must nevertheless not give short shrift to the interpretation of resistance. Resistance interpretations helped the patient to deepen the transference neurosis by removing obstacles to the emergence of preconscious and unconscious material, and by removing obstacles to deeper levels of regression within the transference. In doing so the patient learned a great deal about his defensive organization, a higher level of structuralization was achieved, and as a result, the patient had an enhanced ability to bring into the analysis more highly conflicted material and to have permitted a deeper regression in the analysis. The patient's ability to continue to intensify the transference neurosis in this way was based only partially on the information that the analyst had given him about his resistances and his defenses (of course this information was indispensable, but only as a first step in the process); the main advance was essentially based on the structure-building consequences of analyzing resistances, which had been an ongoing process throughout the analysis. The ability to bring in archaic conflicts and to demonstrate transference on a more infantile level was not, at this point in the analysis, only a measure of the patient's pathology or of the repetition compulsion alone. It was also a measure of the patient's improved capacity for the work of analysis, an enhanced capacity that was based on his having made important gains in psychic structuralization already in the analysis. Before he began his analysis, the patient suffered from "sick" behavior in the form of symptoms that took place in many areas of his life. His initial resistance, like any neurotic's, to regressively enacting his conflicts in the early phase of the analysis was not a sign of disorder, it was a demonstration of "healthy" ego and superego functioning. At this advanced point in the analysis, however, his ability to be more regressed and to be more unreasonable, that is, to demonstrate how very "sick" he was, now within the analysis, was actually a sign of health. It reflected a strengthened ego that now had additional resources with which to withstand the increased stresses that accompanied the more directly representative expressions of his conflicts. Thus the patient's capacity to enter into a fully developed transference neurosis, including all of its quite delusional features, was not achieved solely because the analyst had frustrated transference demands and expectations but also because of the patient's improved ability, fostered in the analysis of resistances, to withstand the more intense and regressed experience without a commensurate decompensation or counterreaction away from the analysis.

As a direct result of the gains made in psychic structuralization during the systematic analysis of the patient's resistances, delusional transferences do not enter into a regressive spiral leading to diminished returns (i.e., a psychotic transference) nor do they "bleed out" into the patient's everyday life outside the analysis (in the form of intensified symptoms). In fact, one of the interesting features of a transference neurosis that distinguishes it from the patient's "clinical" neurosis is that it is self-limiting to the analysis. It is not just that the patient has withdrawn his symptoms from his outside life and re-invested them in the analysis but that the regressive intensity of the transference neurosis tends to begin and end, generally, with the beginning and ending of the analytic hour. It is not as if at the moment that the hour begins the regression instantly takes place, and at the moment that the hour is over the regression instantly disappears. Rather, as the time of the hour begins to approach, the regression begins to intensify, so that when the hour actually begins, the regression is in place. An analogy to this is in the way one likes to have a few minutes to settle in before the first note of a concert is struck, a few moments to get in the mood. And an analogous example to the end of the regression when the hour is over is the way, after one has been particularly touched by a movie or a play, one is still quite caught up in it at the moment the event has ended and only slowly, over a brief passage of time, does one get back to oneself. One begins to anticipate the hour as it draws closer during the day, and in this anticipatory experience conflicted and regressed feelings start to surface so that they are ready for expression when the hour begins. One leaves the analytic hour gripped by the experience of it, and as one gets reintegrated into the (nonanalytic) rest of the day, the power of the regressed experiences of the analytic hour fades into the background, and one's attention and emotionality are matched once again to the ordinary activities of daily living. In the intensity of the hour itself, the prepared patient first brings to mind associations to related material (that has previously emerged in the analysis) and then brings into consciousness directly connected associations of a newer sort, new associations to the old associations that deal with the material on a deeper level, breaking past suppression and repression.

This act of bringing consciously to mind memories that previously were inaccessible to consciousness, sometimes referred to as "the return of the repressed," is a significant transformation of psychic life that has important ramifications for the success of the analysis. The work of the hour now moves to a different level, capitalizing on awarenesses acquired as a result of new material having arisen because of the regression. The conscious retrieval of early, fantasy-laden, formative experiences places them, and their influence, in a new relation to the patient. It gives him a window into the hidden motives that have been exercising a disproportionately high influence on him, including even the ways they affected how he organized his experience of reality. Things that he had previously taken for granted, and about which he would never have even thought to have raised a question, now begin to be recognized, with considerable surprise, as highly motivated events. The emergence of these memories into consciousness, a direct consequence of the intensity of the transference neurosis, promotes a translation of his conflicts (which prior to this time were expressed as disconnected affects, unconscious wishes, and symbolic behaviors that took the form of symptoms) into affectively rich conscious thoughts. Once they have achieved consciousness in the analysis as emotionally enriched ideas that are organized and expressed by words, they are finally ready to be made subject to the influence of the patient's mature ego and its current executive functions. In addition to the effect this has on the patient's ability to sort through his inner experiences with mature (and thus more powerful and effective) resources, it also has ramifications for the analytic object relationship. A more comprehensive understanding of his feelings and reactions, which will now include an awareness of previously hidden motives that had been affecting his experience of the analyst, sharply affects the idea to which the patient has become so attached, namely, that the analyst is as terrible and destructive as was the patient's offending mother.

We can see how this evolves by returning to the point where we left off in the description of this patient's analysis. After wondering how he could be helped by an analyst who was "so much like" his mother, the patient began to elaborate on both the pointlessness and the impossibility of continuing the analysis with this "carbon copy" of the person who he felt was so destructive to him. And he supported this by giving numerous examples of how destructive and hateful his mother was. In giving these examples he was unaware that he was relating memories of his childhood that he had not previously brought into the analysis. He was, in fact, retrieving memories, this time consciously, that he had been unconsciously reacting to all along. Although some of these accusations were linked to old memories that had been introduced into the analysis previously, much more of this material consisted of memories that were new to the analysis, and they emerged in direct response to the stress that he was under in the transference neurosis (experiencing the analyst as "so much like" his mother). These prompted more new memories, which triggered yet more new memories.

From our perspective these memories are not really new, insofar as they have been primary unconscious motivators of the patient's functioning, but from the vantage point of the patient's experience the emergence of these memories from unconsciousness into consciousness gives them the impression of being new, and, looked at from that perspective, they are "new." There is, of course, a distinction between those memories that the patient had previously been aware of but had chosen not to discuss in the analysis, and memories that seem to be recovered by the patient for the first time in the analysis at this point. But even in the case of those memories that previously were intentionally censored, we see an important shift in dynamic organization: the act of introducing them into the analysis at this time indicates a readiness to expose them to the analytic process, and this is in distinction to having used the withholding of them earlier as a means of acting out a resistance in the analysis. Even though the context of bringing them into the analysis is initially to use them as "evidence" against the analyst, the inclusion of them into the analytic process reflects an important advance, which demonstrates how the balance of conflicts and defenses is altered in an analysis.

The patient becomes flooded with memories under these circumstances, and his memories are not limited only to experiences with his mother; he finds his thoughts weaving back and forth between past and present, distant past and recent past, and he brings into the analysis memories of old injustices, old disappointments, and old frustrations with other family members, friends, lovers, supervisors, bosses, colleagues and, of course, with the analyst. In this context, where the conflicts have "come alive," the connections between frustrations of the past and frustrations of the present, and the connections between what he felt with his mother and what he feels with other people, can finally become apparent to him. He sees how they are related because of their proximity in his mind, consciously, as he relates them in the analysis. Previously, each ordeal or episode was experienced as if it stood alone; a separate, independent event without direct connection to his other experiences. Now, however, one emotionally charged thought leads into another emotionally charged thought in such a way as to make it more possible for him to see their relation to one another. Together, he and the analyst observe the fluidity of how they follow from one another, and how they blend into one another, talking to each other about how they are all a part of a single picture. This is where the work of the analyst's interpretations blends into the interpretations that the patient is also arriving at, himself. It is in this process that they both arrive at constructions of how many of the events and memories of the past and the present have become psychologically interchangeable, at reconstructions of the early events of the patient's life that have been ruthlessly torturing him ever since, and at some understanding of the power that the patient's fantasies have played both in his experience of his mother and of others whom he has since invested with her image (including the analyst in the most regressed versions of the transference neurosis).

With this work the transference neurosis becomes less regressed and the patient has summoned the forces of his mature psychic organization to the task of analysis. Major advances in structuralization are achieved by this process, and these gains make the patient better equipped to deal more realistically and less conflictually with events in the present and with other people in his life (including the analyst). This was not the end of the analysis for this patient, however; we have followed only a single transference distortion in our example. In reality, the complexities of what needs to be addressed in an analysis are never limited to a single parent, to a single conflict, or to a single kind of conflict, and after a period of objectivity and mature psychic participation, the transference neurosis begins to build again to its next point of neurotic regression as it did numerous times for this man. But the advance in structuralization is not lost, because it is the very thing that permits the analysis to progress to the next point of regression; it is precisely this added power of the psyche that will tolerate, for this patient and for all patients who undergo this process, the transference regression being at an even deeper level than the one just achieved, and that will permit work in relation to even more profound conflicts the next time around.

9

The Ground Rules

Use of the Analytic Couch

Perhaps the most popular image of psychoanalysis is of the patient who attends sessions four or five times a week, lying down on a couch, with the analyst sitting behind him taking notes. That image in a newspaper or magazine cartoon immediately signals the reader that the joke is about psychoanalysis. The only element of the picture that is incorrect is the image of the analyst taking notes. There are some circumstances when note-taking occurs, for example, in training situations; however, it is more usually the case that the analyst writes up the sessions after they are over rather than while they are taking place. This is because the act of writing can disturb the condition of free-floating, evenly suspended attention. If the analyst is concentrating on writing, he is not free to have spontaneously formed thoughts and resonating emotional reactions to what is going on in the session at the moment. In addition, it causes the analyst to always lag behind the patient if he takes notes while the session is in progress, since he would be currently writing about something that the patient has already left. The difficulty with this is that he would be unable to be attentive to where the patient has moved in the stream of free associations. Unless there is a special reason to do so, taking notes during a session is often an action defense, related to things like looking out the window, daydreaming, and falling asleep, and designed to insulate the therapist from unresolved personal conflicts that the patient threatens to arouse in him.

The other parts of the picture, that is, the patient on the couch four or five times a week and the analyst sitting behind him, are based on sound technical principles and have not been generated by any conflict that the analyst may be feeling. It is true that the analyst is made more comfortable when the patient is not carefully scrutinizing him for his reactions, when he does not have to actively work to keep his reactions from becoming apparent to the patient, and when he can shift around in his chair or scratch an itch (also sometimes action defenses) in relative privacy. But these benefits to the analyst are all results of the arrangement and not motivating causes for using those arrangements, even though when Freud originally initiated them they were intended to make the analytic setting more comfortable for him. Over time some of Freud's working arrangements have been abandoned – for example, pressing the patient's forehead and insisting that when the analyst's hand is raised the patient will remember, or using hypnosis to defeat resistances – because continued practice clarified for Freud and for later analysts that they worked against the analysis instead of for it; other working arrangements that were devised at first to ease some situational stresses for the analyst were retained, not for that reason but because it was found that they worked particularly well for the analytic process, and it remained only incidental that they made the analyst more comfortable. The use of the couch, for example, is a kind of sensory deprivation device, intended to help the patient to achieve a greater degree of self-reflectiveness. Choosing to sit out of the line of sight of the patient is also a sensory deprivation technique. By breaking the habit of eye contact and by remaining out of sight, the analyst does not give intentional or unintentional cues to the patient. It is natural for the patient to seek such cues, and necessary for the analyst to minimize those cues as much as is possible.

We all come into this world profoundly object-hungry because of our inability to meet our own instinctual needs (please note: object hunger describes a kind of dependency, reflecting needs that cannot be met without the intervention of an object, and it should not be confused with an awareness of the object world or with the concept of object seeking, which involves a level of object relatedness and of differentiation between self and object that only comes much later in development). The frustration and gratification of our instinctual needs fosters object relatedness, and the depth and length of our dependence on mothering objects guarantees that a considerable degree of object relatedness will become an autonomous feature of the ego as we develop into adults. This object relatedness is brought to the analysis and can never be fully interrupted. We would not want to fully interrupt it even if we could, because it lays the basis for the transference neurosis and for the alliance between the healthy parts of the patient's ego with the healthy parts of the analyst's ego (conscious and unconscious). The need for an enaction of an object-related nature is the greatest resistance to analysis (because it demands gratification of the transference) and, at the very same time, one of the most powerful tools we have to work with in an analysis. We promote a deepening of object relatedness in order to develop a regressive transference neurosis and simultaneously wish to discourage other aspects of it. In particular, we wish to interfere with object-related activities of an immediate nature, such as eye contact and other nonverbal behaviors, because of their tendency to influence the patient's attention, perceptions, and intentions.

The analyst's attentiveness or inattentiveness, agreement or disagreement, comfort or discomfort, approval or disapproval, pleasure or distress can have a powerful influence on the thoughts and feelings that occur to the patient. Agreements about not censoring and about the use of free association notwithstanding, the patient may not even know that he is responding to anything in the analyst. The influence of the analyst's immediate reactions acts in opposition to the patient's need (and ability) to "remake" the image of the analyst so that it will fit the mental images of the significant objects of the patient's past. Therefore, the less reaction the patient can perceive, the more reaction the patient can imagine. By interrupting the opportunity for visual cues, we give the patient a considerably enhanced freedom of imagination as well as permitting a greater degree of sustained concentration on himself. Obviously, many other nonverbal cues still exist, particularly the aural cues reflected in the analyst's tone of voice; changes in timbre, pitch, rhythm and volume; and differences in expressivity. Other aural cues exist in when the analyst chooses to speak as opposed to when he chooses to be silent, when he sits still and when he shifts around in his chair, and so forth. We recognize the impossibility of depriving the patient of all possible signals from the analyst even while making our best efforts to keep our interferences at an absolute minimum. Thus, in sitting behind the patient, we are making the best physical arrangement that we can to keep visual cues from the patient's attention, with the expectation that it will benefit the patient's autonomy of expression.

There is another change in the normal character of object relatedness when the analyst is sitting behind a reclining patient; that is, it alters the normal pattern of dialogue in communication. Ordinarily, two people talk together, to each other; that is, they engage in a dialogue. It is most uncommon for one person to engage in an extended monologue for long periods, sometimes whole hours, and sometimes even days, with the other person as a mostly silent listener. Dialogue presents a problem for the analytic task because it keeps the material on a superficial and manifest level. In a dialogue, communication is conversational, the patient talks *to* the analyst, the material is kept on a "linear" plane (that is, it becomes almost a kind of "story telling" that always makes logical sense, where subjects usually follow in a rational order so that the line of thought, and of communication, can be readily followed in secondary-process terms), and, most importantly, it inhibits meditative and reflective thinking and spontaneous emotional reactivity. Free association is extremely difficult, even in ideal circumstances, because of the forces of resistance, which tend, quite regularly and despite the patient's best intentions, to encourage censorship and inhibition. It is virtually impossible in a dialogue because, in conversation, one tends to automatically inhibit or to intentionally ignore or censor thoughts and feelings that seem illogical, irrational, arbitrary, random, unexpected, unwelcome, unrelated to the topic, and so on, in order to maintain concentration on what one wants to be saying and in order to allow the other person to follow the normal lines of reasoning that are necessary for an intelligible discussion to take place between two people. If seemingly random, inappropriate, or irrelevant thoughts and feelings do enter into a conversation they tend to place the participants at cross-purposes in talking to one another, and any such *free associative* comments would naturally be experienced by the other person in the conversation as puzzling and incomprehensible intrusions. It is not realistic to assume that in a dialogue, even one between an analyst and an analysand, the conversants could simply make an agreement to include one of the speaker's free associations; the very nature of the back-and-forth quality of a conversation prevents free association. It might permit a single free association to emerge, but the constant interchange of responses in a dialogue would prevent any long series of free associations to occur. Once the patient goes off on a string of seemingly tangential thoughts, each apparently unrelated on the surface to the thoughts that preceded and followed it, a dialogue no longer exists. As long as dialogue is the agreed-upon form of communication, only a conversation is possible. Rather than speaking *to* the analyst, the patient should be speaking *in the presence of* the analyst. Having the analyst sitting behind a patient, especially a reclining patient, is very effective in changing any inclination the patient may have to converse with the analyst, judge the analyst's reactions, control the analyst's reactions, or draw the analyst into a dialogue for any other defensive reasons. It is obviously not a guaranteed preventative, inasmuch as a sufficiently dedicated patient could always defeat any and all arrangements the analyst may have initiated when the need to be defensive (or resistive, or transferentially gratified) is paramount. However, it is an arrangement that has the potential to be particularly useful in supporting the patient's other analytically constructive needs – for example, the very wish to be able to free associate undistracted by the immediacy of the physical or social relationship with the analyst.

Before going on to a fuller discussion of the use of the couch, and many of the other working arrangements of psychoanalysis, it is worth noting that the various orientations in psychoanalysis frequently have very different ideas about how the work should be conducted. Probably the most hotly debated issue is the frequency of sessions per week, with some schools of thought suggesting that analysis can be conducted, even optimally, on a once-per-week basis, to the Freudian model presented here, which suggests that four sessions per week are a necessary mini-mum, and which recommends five sessions per week (or even six, if one can find an analyst who works six days a week) as optimal. Similarly, one finds points of view that discourage the development or expression of fantasy material; points of view that eschew the use of the couch in favor of face-to-face, sitting-up interactions; points of view that prefer "guided fantasy" to free association; points of view that encourage some forms of limited self-revelation by the analyst; points of view that use confrontation of resistances; points of view that prefer to interpret to the deepest levels of the unconscious; and so on. At their most polemical the different orienta-tions sometimes accuse each other of having points of view that have been arbitrarily developed, or that have been developed for political reasons or that are either reactionary or rebellious, or that merely reflect the similarities in psychopa-thology of the practitioners in a particular group (as if a whole orientation could develop and flourish on the basis of shared psychopathology alone). A careful scholar of each of the points of view will find that none of their conventions is based on anything arbitrary, or on a mindless commitment to the past, or on change for its own sake but, rather, that opposing views are based on different ways of inter-preting clinical experience. Many competitive viewpoints, in fact, use the very same case material to "prove" different theoretical and technical assumptions. The very least that can be said for each of the different orientations, whether or not one agrees with them, is that they are carefully thought-out formulations combining complex theories and working techniques that have been based on different ways of understanding the meaning of clinical events and their theoretical implications. Sometimes the theoretical assumptions (which also are not arbitrary) lead the technical advances, and at other times clinical advances modify the theories, but in each of the different points of view one can find a reasoned method of explaining their preferences for their own working arrangements.

What has preceded this slight detour has been how the Freudian model conceptualizes some of the reasons it is felt to be preferable that the analyst sit behind the patient (we have not yet fully addressed the question of the patient's reclining posture, although we have begun to touch upon it in a preliminary way). It is hoped that the theoretical, clinical, and technical issues that form the rationale for all of the working arrangements, the "ground rules," of the Freudian model will become clear as this chapter progresses.

The use of the couch, as has been already stated, is a way of promoting a kind of sensory deprivation designed to reduce distractions from the environment (physical and social) that might have a tendency to interfere with self-reflection, a meditative posture, the retrieval of memories, a partial abandonment of reliance on secondary-process functioning, and especially, reverielike experiences. The considerable value of such sensory deprivation techniques is not based on a theoretical abstraction; it is a readily observable technique, employed quite regularly by virtually everyone in the course of daily living, which people seem innately to know how to make use of, although without ever intellectually recognizing that they are engaging in an active sensory deprivation technique. One can see the principle in operation, as an automatic and unconscious aspect of everyday experience, by performing the following experiment: if, in the middle of a conversation about something else, you ask people to tell you what they ate for lunch three days ago you will see, in almost every case, that they will break eye contact with you and look off into the distance (usually looking up, and off to the left or to the right) as they try to retrieve the memory. Their glance becomes actively unfocused; it is not that they are specifically looking at something over your shoulder. By behaving in this way they are trying to block out the distracting stimuli of the environment (including their talk with you) in order to better immerse themselves in their inner world of ideas, feelings, and memories. This is the very purpose that the use of the couch is intended to achieve. It changes the orientation of the patient, both to the analyst and to the distractions of the consulting room, in much the same way as does the unfocused glance of the "rememberer" to his distracting environment. Now in both the unfocused glance away and in the use of the couch, the environment (including the people in it) is not totally obliterated, but the balance of attention has nevertheless undergone a substantial shift from the "outside" to the "inside." Many patients report that they also close their eyes during some part, or all, of a session while on the couch, attempting to reduce outside distractions even further. Parenthetically, it makes an interesting analytic study when one investigates why patients who usually keep their eyes closed during sessions sometimes choose to keep them open.

Patients who are actively in some form of resistance, or who cannot tolerate the lack of structure or of contact in using the couch, can easily defeat the potential it offers. They can, for example, actively choose to focus their attention on the environment: this may be exemplified by the patient who reports that "I find myself scanning the titles of the books on the wall in front of me," or by the patient who remains hypervigilant to any sound emanating from the analyst (noticing a slight shift in the analyst's position in his chair from the rustling of the material, or a change in the pattern of the analyst's breathing) or, in more extreme cases, by sitting up on the couch, by leaving the couch for the chair, or by looking back over his shoulder at the analyst. In the former cases these may be transient defensive maneuvers in which some internal events may be being expressed externally and projectively, and they are often able to be analyzed either in the context of a resistance or some form of a transferential enactment: in the latter cases, however, their behavior raises the question as to whether these patients have the ego strengths to tolerate the lack of structure, the lack of instinctual object relatedness, and the other frustrations that attend a psychoanalysis. It is not necessarily a foregone conclusion that once a patient sits up or looks over his shoulder at the analyst he unquestionably requires a different from of psychotherapy, but it does prompt the analyst at such times to make yet an additional evaluation of the patient's appropriateness for psychoanalysis as a natural part of trying to understand what role this action may have played in the patient's mental economy. If nothing else, it does at least give the analyst a better appreciation of some of the particular circumstances in which various aspects of the patient's autonomous ego functions are susceptible to being compromised. By attending to those times when the patient seems easily able to function on the couch and contrasting them with those times when functioning on the couch seems more difficult or impossible for the patient, the analyst can learn a great deal about the nature of the patient's conflicts, the relative power of various conflicts in the patient's general psychic organization, some of the strengths and weaknesses in the patient's defensive capabilities, and the resilience of both superego and ego functioning of the patient under varying conditions of stress, disappointment, frustration, and so on. These considerations can, and should, strongly influence the subsequent conduct of the treatment whether it is changed to a different form of psychotherapy or whether it remains a psychoanalysis. Although it was never intended specifically to be a measuring device, the way the patient makes use of the couch can clarify much about the patient's internal mental organization (including conflicts, defenses, object relations, and narcissistic regulatory processes); it can reflect important issues in the nature and the expression of the transference; and it can even serve diagnostic and prognostic purposes.

It should be clear from this discussion that any patient who cannot tolerate using the couch, cannot tolerate a traditional analytic therapy. The very same reasons that militate against the use of the couch suggest that a more supportive and less stressful treatment would probably be more beneficial for the patient. The inability to use the couch suggests structural difficulties that would prevent a transference neurosis of sufficient depth for a psychoanalysis, even though it does not suggest the impossibility of deep and profound regression. Difficulty in being able to use the couch may suggest that the necessary tolerance for frustration involved in being analyzed may not be available to the patient, or it may suggest, in particular, a lack of tolerance for the necessary regression involved in being analyzed. The inability to profitably use the couch could be because a patient is simply too highly guarded and too concretely defended (a condition that may or may not change in the future, depending on the nature of the patient and the effects of any intervening therapy), or alternatively, it might reflect an appropriate fear by the patient that too deep and therefore uncontrolled a regression might occur for him to be able to manage it successfully (also a condition that may or not change in the future, depending on the nature of the patient and the effects of any intervening therapy). In this latter case, the patient is unable to use the couch because he is unconsciously aware of the fragility of his defensive capabilities, and therefore of the dangers that it, and psychoanalysis, present to him. He is appropriately protecting himself from the structural disorganization that would occur from a psychotic transference. If it is true that the inability to work on the couch is evidence that the work cannot be a psychoanalysis, it is not true that the ability to work on the couch is prima facie evidence of the treatment being a psychoanalysis. The couch is one, and only one, of many tools of a psychoanalysis, and its use may be employed in many other kinds of psychotherapies (just as they have been able to make good use for their own purposes of the concept of the unconscious, the practice of interpretation, working with transferential material, working with dreams, and so on). Whether or not the patient uses the couch can define when a treatment is *not* a psychoanalysis, but it cannot define when the treatment *is* a psychoanalysis.

One sometimes comes across the suggestion that the use of the couch promotes regression by virtue of being roughly equivalent to an infant lying in a crib with an adult standing over him, or to a child being read a bedtime story by an adult seated near his head on the bed. No doubt, for some patients, using the couch may elicit such reminiscences or fantasies, just as for other patients it may bring up, or be reminiscent of, sexual scenes or bath scenes. As reminiscent, and at times even evocative, as it may be in some ways for patients, this potential is only an artifact of the arrangement and not the reason itself for having the patient recline. Even if using the couch was not designed to be evocative of any particular fantasies or reminiscences, we always try to capitalize on the fortuitous circumstance that it does have the possibility of being suggestive to patients. Of course, what it suggests varies from patient to patient, and for some patients the things it may suggest might encourage a certain degree of accompanying regression. On balance, however, the main external inductor of regression in the patient, the working technique in the analysis that it can be most attributed to, is the frustration of transference wishes, expectations, and demands (as has been described in the preceding chapter), and not the use of the couch.

Free Association and Censorship

These physical arrangements that we have been discussing, namely, the patient reclining on a couch with the analyst sitting behind him, are designed to create an environment in which the patient has the opportunity (because of the "altered" state of consciousness it induces) to engage in free associative rumination. Because we have discussed (in a number of different places in this book) the natural and adaptive tendency in normal circumstances to order consciousness along the lines of secondary-process functioning, it would be redundant to repeat what has already been said about the mechanisms of condensation, displacement, sublimation, neutralization, compromise formation, and defense except to remind the reader about how very difficult it is to get to the underlying meanings of things, and why this difficulty necessitates the use of special procedures to get beyond what people can be aware of on only a manifest level. We rely on the use of free association to achieve for the patient that which cannot be achieved by the patient's force of will and conscious intentions. Free association stimulates the emergence of preconscious material and adds to the material that we get from slips of the tongue, parapraxes, puns, misdefinitions, malapropisms, changes in the details of a story told more than once, idiosyncratic use of words, aphorisms, and so forth. It also gives us a window, in many ways that are similar to how dreams give us a window, into the patient's unconscious processes, his means of symbolization, and his preferred modes of transformation. That is because in free associating, just like in the way a dream is remembered upon awakening, the patient is displaying a compromise between primary- and secondary-process functioning. In dreaming, the compromise is formed as part of the dream work and as a feature of secondary revision; in free associating, the compromise is made possible by the patient's commitment to describe, without conscious censorship, thoughts and feelings that are occurring to him while they are happening (and not afterward). Excepting the acting-out of resistances, which are frequently also very revealing, almost everything that is of importance that emerges in an analysis (including the patient's dynamics, history, conflicts, fantasies, object relations, narcissistic regulatory processes, transference reactions, defenses, and resistances) comes to our attention as a result of hearing the contents themselves of the patient's free associations, or as a result of attending to fluctuations in the ease, or difficulty, with which the patient free associates.

Free association is often referred to as *the basic rule* in psychoanalysis. Simply stated, one is supposed to say everything that comes to mind. In normal conversation the rules of secondary process apply and one is expected to "make sense," that is to follow the rules of logic; to suppress random or unrelated thoughts; to keep one's emotionality within reasonable limits (or at least, appropriately related to what one is talking about); to be polite, tactful, discreet, and cooperative; to give the other person an equal chance to speak or respond (or at least, to say what they want to before the conversation is over); to make an effort to be understood, to be clear, to be relevant, to be interpersonally related; to exhaust a topic to both persons' satisfaction before it is abandoned (or not to switch topics without, at least, the tacit agreement of the other person); to limit the exhibitionistic gratifications, or to not give in to the exhibitionistic inhibitions, that might interfere with a mutual participation of the conversants; and to have an interest in what the other person is saying (and what they want from one) as a counterbalance to speaking one's own mind and getting what one needs from the other person. The use of secondary process in normal conversation requires the imposition of a number of highly adaptive defenses operating with a significant degree of automaticity. Intelligent, reasonable adult communication would otherwise be impossible. This also holds true to a surprisingly large extent for how people think, consciously, to themselves (even though more than words alone occur in thinking processes). Random and inappropriate thoughts, feelings, and images (sometimes even including sensations) often occur in silent thought as well as in conversation, and in much the same way the thinker frequently shunts them aside for many of the same reasons (including also purely defensive reasons that are not involved in interpersonal, conversational relationships). In both cases the censorship that keeps conversing and thinking rational and attuned to secondary-process principles, is virtually automatic. Random and inappropriate thought processes (which are actually overdetermined by unconscious motivations and which serve, despite their seeming irrelevance, a variety of multiple functions) are quickly dismissed and as quickly – usually instantaneously – forgotten, as an event that does not even require conscious intention or intervention. This capacity to maintain secondary-process functioning even in one's private thoughts is, despite its defensive origins and purposes, a feature of highly valuable autonomous ego functioning. Free association is difficult, despite one's best intentions, because of its reinstinctualizing capacities. Reinstinctualization is opposed by the ego because it challenges the ego's autonomy, and subjectively, for the patient, the reinstinctualizing consequence of free association threatens to consciously revive painful conflicts, thoughts, affects, and memories.

A patient engaged in free association makes a conscious effort to defeat the natural, oppositional tendency to censor the things that come to mind. One of our first clues to the emergence of infantile conflict is the patient's inability to inhibit censorship. Even if we disregard the issue of censorship (some of which can never be avoided, simply because unconscious areas of the ego are involved in defensive organization), the very act itself of saying things out loud is often enough to provide the speaker with more information about himself than he usually is able to know when he only thinks things, to himself, without speaking them aloud. Patients are regularly surprised by many of the things that emerge in this way, usually having suppressed them in the ordinary, silent way that they think about things. Not only do they find out more about what they are feeling and thinking, they also now have the opportunity to investigate these things, a possibility that is not available when this material is automatically suppressed in processes that involve unverbalized thoughts.

This is the essence of free association: material emerges that is usually suppressed; these things trigger additional material; the additional material is also said out loud; this adds yet more material that would have been suppressed; and the process continues in this fashion. Metapsychologically, free association is a method of moving material from preconsciousness into consciousness in a progressively revealing sequence as the "vacuum" in preconsciousness draws up additional material from unconsciousness (this is an admittedly inexact metaphor; a more thorough description of the process can be found in Part I of this book in the sections dealing with the dynamic and descriptive unconscious; the unconscious, preconscious and conscious systems; and the role of word cathexes in the management of impulses, wishes, affects and ideas). Other important consequences of free association are worth noting. One is the greater potential, when one does not attempt to control the material, for puns, inexact definitions, alterations, slips of the tongue, and other parapraxes to emerge, and we know how important they are in giving the patient access to preconscious processes. Another is that it supports and reinforces a meditative and self-reflective posture, as opposed to the more interpersonally interactive frame that exists in conversations and dialogues. Free association, relying on the analyst's discipline in not interrupting the patient too frequently with distractions, does not encourage the expectation that what is said will be met with a complimentary response from the analyst. In this regard, free association operates in partnership with the use of the couch and with the position of the analyst sitting behind the patient. Finally, free association is not just a way of getting to hidden material, it is also a way of defining the analytic process as a method of *self-investigation,* albeit with the help of the analyst. It becomes clear from the context of the process itself that the investigation is primarily an action of the patient's, and that the analyst's participation is only supplementary (clarifying, realigning, alerting, interpreting, what the patient himself discovers in his mind). One can draw an analogy, perhaps, to a surgeon and a pathologist working with a questionable mass of tissue: the surgeon (patient) does the exploratory operation, he opens the patient, discovers what is inside, and the pathologist (analyst) helps him determine what it was, precisely, that he discovered, which then influences how the surgeon (patient) continues and concludes the operation. In this example it is *the patient* who is metaphorically represented in the role of a surgeon: one is naturally reminded of Freud's metaphorical representation of *the analyst* in the role of a surgeon, in his early technical papers. This is not contradictory or an inconsistency but merely a case of different contexts with different points to be made drawing forth different allusions.

As a technical intervention the actual instruction to the patient is fairly straightforward. In whatever words the analyst prefers, the patient is instructed to say everything that comes to mind without exception. Depending on the patient's analytic sophistication the analyst may feel the necessity to go into some detail about not censoring random, irrelevant, fleeting, embarrassing, and distracting thoughts and feelings. Or the analyst might wish to inform selected patients that it is not necessary to prepare anything prior to the analytic hour. Initially, this latter instruction can be helpful to certain patients who (because of their general personality style, or because of specific defensive purposes) tend to take a problem-solving approach to life and thus would be inclined to approach analytic hours in this way also: but where such behavior is entrenched, the instruction will quickly give way to an analysis of the preparation as a resistance. Some analysts find metaphors helpful in explaining technical instructions: in describing how the patient is to engage in free associative functioning, Freud is reputed to have told some patients that it is like sitting in a train with a person who is blind, faithfully describing everything about the scenery that is passing by the window. The use of metaphors, or allegories, operates on the "one picture is worth a thousand words" principle and is often quite effective (and a great time saver), but there is also a danger that in introducing such images from the analyst's repertoire one could end up substituting the analyst's images (and, hence, fantasies) for those of the patient, and if that does not happen, there is still the danger that one may be providing a superstructure made up of the analyst's fantasies upon which the patient then embosses his own. We take it for granted that unconscious areas of the patient's ego are in contact with unconscious areas of the analyst's ego, and therefore that some aspects of the analyst's fantasy life (including his conflicts) are accessible to the patient despite the analyst's best (conscious) intentions not to let his own personality influence the treatment. To the extent that neither the analyst nor the patient has conscious control over the patient's ability to read the analyst's unconscious, we accept this as an inevitable (even if unwelcome) influence on the treatment. Given this vulnerability, or perhaps we should say this degree of permeability, as a fact of analytic life, one might take the position that (since the patient already has a "take" on the analyst) it does not matter if the analyst expresses his fantasies to the patient. The argument does not necessarily follow, however, because there is a considerable difference between the things that patients can learn about the analyst without the analyst's cooperation and, on the other hand, the analyst freely deciding to give information about his inner life to the patient that the patient may not have been able to obtain, automatically, in an unconscious fashion. We reluctantly have no choice but to accept the compromise that there is no real possibility of presenting the patient with an absolutely blank screen, without using it as a spuriously theoretical excuse for acting out exhibitionistic impulses.

We can see that the manner in which one gives instructions can have important consequences beyond the literal information that one is conveying to the patient. It is not uncommon for some analysts to strike a bargain with their patients about censorship: after instructing patients not to give in to any tendencies to censor their verbalizations, they tell their patients that if they should find themselves censoring something, they should at least say that they are doing so. Because considerable censorship can be observed by the analyst without the patient expressly informing him about it (e.g., in silences, too logical a progression of thought, conspicuous omissions), does striking such a bargain imply not just a recognition that some degree of censorship is inevitable, but instead signal that it is acceptable to the analyst as long as he is "officially" informed that it is taking place? One would not wish such an instruction to be construed as an invitation to censor as long as certain requirements are met (namely, that the patient tells the analyst that it is happening). One finds other kinds of instructions that are also vulnerable to being a tacit bargain between the patient and the analyst. For example, an analyst may tell patients, just prior to leaving for a vacation: "Here is a telephone number where I can be reached in an emergency," or he may tell patients, in early consultative visits: "Except in case of an emergency, I am not usually available at night or on the weekends." These communications appear to set limits for the patient, but there are some patients for whom it would imply a tacit invitation: an invitation to have an emergency in order to justify (and in this way also to legitimize) a need to be in contact with the analyst outside of regularly scheduled analytic hours. This would be especially problematic (and tantalizing) for patients with such a need who would ordinarily be able to resist it but who, because the invitation has been extended by the analyst *in the latent part of his communication,* can no longer rely on their original resources to resist the temptation to act out in this way. Not every patient would find the situation irresistible, but those who do suffer an iatrogenic compromise in their ego autonomy. The fact that latent communications exist within the manifest interventions of the analyst makes it necessary to not simply take for granted the impact that even an apparently simple communication may have on a patient. Thus, to return to the example of making a contract with patients about censorship, one must have some concern that an analyst who tells a patient to at least indicate when he is censoring something (instead of just addressing censorship if and when it emerges, and being willing to tolerate missing it when it occurs but does not emerge) may be subtly indicating to the patient that he will not treat it as resistance, and therefore something that needs actively to be analyzed, as long as the patient tells him aloud that it is happening.

Before moving on to the number of sessions per week that are considered necessary, or optimal, an issue that is closely related to what has just been discussed deserves some further consideration: that is, the general reasoning behind the analyst's decisions to engage in interventions of every kind (interpretations of resistance, transference, dynamic conflict, defense, and preconscious material; clarifications; instructions; and the like). In a general sense, what informs how and when an analyst chooses to make an intervention? The more specific questions surrounding the depth and timing of interpretations will be discussed in Chapter 11 (which is entirely devoted to the topic of interpretation), but prior to such specifics we do have this more general consideration at hand. Frequently, and particularly in treatments in which more emphasis is placed on manifest factors, therapists take a position that as long as there is no obvious reason why they should not do something, it is all right for them to do it. In other words, if a therapist is not aware of any reason why he should not be interpreting something, he may do so; if there is no reason that suggests that a confrontation may be contraindicated, a confrontation is permissible, and so on. In psychoanalysis, however, the reverse principle is followed: one only takes an action when there is a specific, particular reason for doing so. Thus, for example, one does not interrupt the patient's flow of free associations (even when it has continued for a very long time without interruption) unless there is a definite reason for doing so (e.g., the emergence of a significant resistance, or the eruption of material from preconsciousness). Even when resistance and preconscious material emerges, the analyst must make a conscious, intentional choice about whether more is to be gained from following up on that particular material, or from letting the patient go on without interruption. Inexperienced analysts sometimes rely on a rule of thumb that calls for some response whenever a resistance or preconscious material emerges, but more experienced analysts treat each instance as a particular question of choice. There are times, for example, when one can have an educated expectation (based on all the previous work with a patient) that the patient would be guarded and defensive about being shown the resistive or preconscious aspect of what he may have said; so much so, that he would only begin to harden his opposition to consciously becoming aware of it if the therapist attempted to show it to him. In such a situation the analyst might prefer to let it pass unremarked upon, knowing that the repetition compulsion will cause it to reemerge at a different time, and he would wait to choose a time when he expects that the patient will be more receptive to his intervention. On the other hand, all experienced analysts are familiar with the situation of a patient saying "Do you remember that thing you told me 4 or 5 years ago? I dismissed it then, thinking to myself that you did not know what you were talking about. But it has recently been entering my mind once again and I finally realize that you were right, after all," and the patient then goes on to provide the associations, links, fantasies, or memories, that may have been suppressed but which were nevertheless connected to the analyst's observation that had been made years ago. There are certainly instances when a deep, unwelcome, or against the grain interpretation is made despite knowing that the patient's immediate reaction might be unfavorable, because one is laying the groundwork for the future examination of something (or for a later genetic interpretation of something). This, too, reflects on the question of whether it makes sense to interrupt the flow of free associations, even when it is clear that it will only cause a more profound resistance at the moment. Whether one chooses to take an action by interrupting the flow of free associations or chooses to take an action by not interrupting the flow (it is only on the most superficial behavioral level that not interrupting the flow of free association gets defined as inaction instead of as action) is determined by at least preconsciously intentional decisions in psychoanalysis and not because there was no reason not to do so.

As one becomes more experienced, one becomes better able to make such choices instantaneously, automatically, and preconsciously; but these seemingly immediate responses still remain active choices based on analytic principles even when not being thought out consciously, in real time, prior to the intervention. Analysts eventually reach a point where they do not need to consciously think ahead before each intervention, and they frequently do not consciously know why they are doing something at any given moment; however, when they review their interventions later it becomes clear (unless they are engaged in pure rationalization, and there is no reason to assume that this must be the case) that the interventions were highly considered even if not consciously done so at the time. Analysts get used to doing analysis, and their behavior becomes somewhat automatic in much the same way that an experienced driver does not have to consciously think about gear position and clutching when shifting, or how much to compensate with the steering wheel because of fluctuations in the pavement or road direction in order to remain in lane. The automaticity does not imply that his behavior is shallow or stereotypic, or that the individuality of different patients is discarded in favor of an analytic "ritual." It is a reflection of having acquired enough experience so that questions of technique can reside in the background rather than always having to remain in the foreground. And, if anything, it permits the experienced analyst to be more spontaneous and to have greater emotional resonance, as the patient's material becomes the foreground of the analyst's experience of the hour (in partial, or "trial" identification with the patient): the analyst is "with" the patient in the hour instead of having to be preoccupied with questions of technique. Despite the essentially preconscious and automatic spontaneity of the analyst's reactions and interventions, the actions he takes are always taken (except in countertransference, of course) for considered technical reasons.

Frequency of Sessions

Let us now move to the frequency issue, which is one of the most strongly held positions of the traditional Freudian approach, and which is also a particular point of disagreement in the arguments posed by some critics of the traditional model. What is it about the high frequency of sessions that is so important in the classical model? It is our dependence on the transference neurosis and the need to keep tensions that arise in the treatment from dissipating outside of the analysis that dictates the necessity of at least four, and preferably five, analytic sessions per week. As we already know, a systematic (although not necessarily all-inclusive) frustration of the patient's demands for (and expectations of) transference repetitions tends to promote regression. In the normal course of events, when transference needs are frustrated by someone, one ordinarily puts pressure on that person to give one what one is after. If that person continues to be frustrating, one eventually looks elsewhere for the gratification and satisfaction of one's transferential needs (this departs from what is ideal for the analytic situation because it interferes with the development of a progressively deepening transference neurosis). When one finds a different person who will enact the transference indulgences that one is under pressure to repeat, one frequently severs the attachment to (and abandons) the original, frustrating, person. If we exclude from our consideration those patients who undertake a treatment more for the gratification of transference needs than they do to resolve their transferentially motivated conflicts (frequently the case in psychoses and in the character disorders), and who would thus discontinue a treatment that frustrated narcissistic-instinctual wishes, we know that the average analytic patient does not have the freedom (by his own choice, that is, because of his commitment to analyze conflicts) to abandon the analyst when he finds himself frustrated and feeling (consciously or unconsciously) deprived. Now, once again, in the normal course of anyone's life, as well as in an analysis, there are times when one does not have the freedom to reject transferentially frustrating persons (either because of situational factors, contractual factors, or because some important transferential needs are being met even if others are not). In such instances – but, we hope, not in an analysis – one may take what one can get from that partially frustrating person and then try to find others in one's life who will meet the unsatisfied remaining portion of one's transferential needs. One fairly common example of this is when a married person enters into an affair, and another example is seen in how, and why, one picks one's friends (and, especially, in why a single friend is usually not enough).

In the analytic situation the frustrations that are encountered in the treatment, or triggered by it, can be partially reversed when the patient seeks to obtain his transferential needs elsewhere and with other people, between sessions. We view this as understandable and appreciate why patients are impelled to do this (the compulsion to repeat), but nevertheless recognize this to be a form of acting out that imperils the welfare of an analysis. Clearly, it is impossible to completely avoid this simply by scheduling four or five sessions per week, because even a patient in treatment 7 days a week would still have the other 23 hours in each day in which to obtain the transference needs that have been made unavailable to him in the analysis. It seems obvious, however, despite the lack of any guarantees provided by high-frequency scheduling, that the more time that exists between sessions the greater is the opportunity for the patient to acquire transferential satisfactions and gratifications elsewhere, and that the less time that exists between sessions the more diminished is the opportunity for the patient to get his needs met in other ways and with other persons.

In addition, the degree of depth and intensity of the transference neurosis is not regulated solely by gratification or frustration of the transference, it also is partially dependent on the frequency of sessions. First (and, again, let us automatically exclude character-disordered patients from this discussion, this time because of their tendency to flood the treatment with transference from the outset), the depth and intensity of the treatment increases only gradually over time, in small but progressive increments, as the patient's transference neurosis is developing. Where the depth and intensity of a transference neurosis is not governed primarily by character pathology, or by situational crises, both deepening and intensification are greatly affected by opportunity, that is, high-frequency scheduling. Even when one takes into account the natural fluctuations of resistance, an event that occurs every day has more potential for depth and intensity than an event that occurs with less frequency. This commonly known principle is not unique to psychoanalysis, and it is regularly employed in many other undertakings: for example, one sees it at work in the immersion method of learning a new language, in which the student goes to class every day for a week (or a month) instead of attending one or two classes each week for a year or so; or in the special week-long (or month-long) brainstorming sessions at times of particular crisis at think tanks, which then supplement the regular, less intensive, study of an issue; and in the popularity of weekend (and week-long) retreats used in management training with the expectation that, in this way, the group process as well as the individual participants can capitalize on the greater depth and intensity that concentrated frequency of meetings can produce. Trading on this commonly known phenomenon, analysts attempt to exploit the concentrating effects of having so many sessions each week, and they hope in this way to structure a situation in which it is more difficult for patients to act out against their own interests in the analysis (which, by definition, includes opportunities to diminish the power of the transference neurosis).

Many analysts have reported on an interesting phenomenon, often described as a crust, that forms as a result of the weekend break (by which they mean a temporary reduction of the depth, intensity, and regressive power of the transference neurosis). In psychotherapies that rely on other technical principles (e.g., support; bolstering of defenses; developing specific coping techniques for dynamic or interpersonal conflicts; symptom amelioration or substitution; reinforcing reality testing; learning how to be more "expressive"; many forms of crisis intervention; "lending" the therapist's ego and superego capacities to patients; capitalizing on the interpersonal relationship between patient and therapist), periods of time between sessions do not usually constitute such a threat to the treatment. But where a progressively deepening transference neurosis is both the central source of data and an indispensable tool by which the treatment itself is conducted, gaps of time between sessions inevitably must work against the treatment because they promote a dilution of the transference neurosis. Thus, one way in which frequency of sessions is important is in response to a quite natural tendency toward depth and intensity that normally seems to accompany high-frequency engagements.

Another way, which we began discussing earlier, involves the added consideration of regression. Regression compounds depth and intensity, even though it does not automatically follow from high-frequency scheduling. In immersion language teaching, for example, regression does not occur simply because of the depth and intensity achieved by the immersion. In fact, since both controlled and uncontrolled forms of regression would work against its goals, a concentrated method of study would all too quickly reach a point of diminishing returns if regression were as automatic a tendency as is the tendency toward depth and intensity in high-frequency situations. Uncontrolled regression would work against a psychoanalysis, too; but controlled regression (as one finds in a transference neurosis) is crucial to a psychoanalysis, and controlled regression adds a special dimension to the depth and intensity of an analysis. Controlling an analytic regression must regularly work in two directions simultaneously: (1) the analyst is promoting an increase in regression by carefully frustrating transference demands; and (2) primarily using interpretation but, when necessary, also resorting to planned and measured transference gratifications, the analyst attempts to prevent active resistances to regression that would then act to interfere with the adequate development of a transference neurosis. When a patient does resist the necessary degree of regression, as patients periodically do as the transference neurosis intensifies, one of the tools at the analyst's disposal is the interpretive exploration of the resistance. However, this implies that an effective transference neurosis is in place so that the nature, meaning, and purposes of the resistance can surface. If an insufficient number of sessions per week acts to weaken the depth and the intensity of the transference neurosis, then the tool with which the analyst can conduct an examination of the resistance is not available, and the only tool left to the analyst is an educational intervention (or a gratification of the transference demand, to counteract the regression, which further weakens the transference neurosis, making the analysis even more compromised). Approaching resistances to transference regressions analytically, making use of the transference neurosis, requires one kind of regression as a tool to analyze the fear of further regression. Thus, high-frequency scheduling, designed to keep the transference neurosis protected, acts in the service of analyzing even the most powerful resistances to the analysis; less frequently scheduled sessions compound the resistance by diminishing the very tool by which it can come to be understood and, consequently, be worked through.

Although it is true that a high frequency of scheduling will not automatically foster regressive functioning, it is also true that a regular frustration of transference demands (with the least opportunity to gratify them elsewhere) will act to promote regressive functioning. It is this that causes immersion learning to be intensified without being inherently regressive, and psychoanalysis to be both intensified and to have regressive potential. However, we need not focus only on the way transference regressions are defeated by gratifying the patient's needs outside the analysis. We can also focus on the relationship of transference regression to the progressive effect of regularity. Even patients who attend five sessions a week demonstrate a crust from session to session (as well as over the weekend). Unless there is a specific dynamic reason at work for a particular patient, we can generally say that the crust between weekday sessions is usually less problematic than the crust that develops between Friday and Monday. A regressively more intact experience occurs when the crust is less powerful at the beginning of each session. If one needs to overcome a thicker crust at the start of a session, one usually has less time in which to deepen the process in that session, and if the crust is thin at the start of a session one can usually go further in that hour (assuming that all other things, like resistances, for example, remain constant). This is almost a simple mathematical proposition: it is like having an hour in which to drive one's car, and needing to take time out to get gas and to check the oil and the tires before one can begin the trip itself. Of course, resistance is a factor in the process and frequently it has a considerably more powerful effect than frequent scheduling can overcome; but as a general principle, sessions that are scheduled on an everyday basis do afford the patient the opportunity to begin each hour in a closer position to where the preceding hour left off, and thus less time has to be devoted to making up lost ground in the transference neurosis at the beginning of each session.

The analytic standard of four or more sessions per week was arrived at through simple trial and error examination of the differences in the development of the transference neurosis at different rates of scheduling. The early analytic patients were all seen every day, and in fact, Freud worked 6 days a week and saw his patients 6 days a week. Over time, and for a number of reasons, analysts began to reduce the number of sessions per week and quickly found that the cut-off point seemed to be four sessions per week. This was never the object of an official study, but it became common knowledge among the analysts who had done such unofficial "experimenting." Since then, other analysts have looked more closely at the issue, and by consensus they have agreed that scheduling fewer than four sessions per week seems to interfere with the regressive development necessary to establish a full-blown transference neurosis (for all of the reasons thus far cited). This is no archaic requirement held over from the past like a vestigial limb, it is the currently accepted standard of the International Psychoanalytical Association, which is the parent body of psychoanalysis, worldwide. The official training requirements that they demand of their member institutes is that analysis be conducted at a minimum rate of four sessions per week, although everyone seems to informally agree that five sessions are optimal. This specification of a minimum of four sessions per week has not been arrived at in an arbitrary fashion (as some critics of the classical approach contend). It is, rather, a reflection of a great deal of common experience that seems objectively to support that view.

Some therapists who have not had the experience of being in an analysis four or five times a week, and who have not had the opportunity themselves to work with patients four or five times a week, challenge this standard. They feel justified in doing so because their own treatment at the rate of three sessions a week (and their treatment of patients on a three-times-per-week basis) has demonstrated to them the extremely powerful differences between twice-weekly therapy and a therapy conducted three times a week. They confuse this profound difference with the establishment of an analytically effective transference neurosis. This is not a position based only on intellectual assumptions: their experience of the power of adding the third session per week convinces them, incorrectly, that it is the equivalent of an analytically viable transference neurosis. The upshot is that they believe that they have drawn the conclusion, on the basis of clinical experience, that an analysis can be effectively conducted at the rate of three sessions per week. This is, in many ways, like the difference between a person who has some genuine insight about having unconscious motives, and someone who has been absolutely awed by how much more powerful his unconscious is than he ever could have imagined (or predicted) previously, after being in an actual analysis. To put it simply, one can say that the person who has not had the experience is not in a position to know what he is missing, no matter how much he thinks he can assume things correctly based on the experience that he has had.

When Freud described the training analysis (i.e., the analysis that candidates themselves undergo as part of their formal training) as being *educational,* he did not mean that the analyst instructed the candidate in theory or in technique, or that the analyst's technique would serve as a model for the candidate, or that the analyst would supervise the candidate's clinical work (candidates have separate supervisors for this). He meant that even the most thorough intellectual understanding of how the unconscious works pales in comparison to the understanding of unconscious motivation that one achieves by being analyzed oneself. The education Freud was referring to is the recognition of how much more the candidate is influenced by unconscious factors than even his education about the unconscious could have prepared him for, and Freud felt that only in this way could the candidate be in a position to pursue his patient's deepest unconscious motivations with an adequate conviction of their power and extent. An unanalyzed person, including people training to be analysts, maintains a motivated belief that his conscious processes are powerful determinants of his thoughts, feelings, and actions (partly for specific defensive reasons, and partly because recognizing how subject to one's unconscious one is can be experienced as a narcissistic insult: one likes to imagine that, at least basically, one is in relative control of oneself). Freud once made a joking reference to consciousness, suggesting that it was only about as significant as a symptom. He was commenting on how superficial consciousness is, and on how little one can learn about mental life from it alone. Undergoing an analysis is always (if it succeeds) a revelation about the hidden parts of one's mind, no matter how prepared one is to accept the power of unconscious motivation as an intellectual concept prior to the analysis. A training analysis is useful in resolving conflicts that potentially interfere with the candidate's analytic functioning and in building ego strengths to withstand the special stresses that they are exposed to in the work (when they must identify with and permit emotional resonances to their patient's most disordered and conflictual functioning), but its educational function is specifically in regard to the power and extent of the candidate's unconscious processes which cannot be fully appreciated in any other way. The educational analysis, with its goal of demonstrating the profound influences of the unconscious, is a parallel that fits the differing situations of therapists who have been in (and conducted) intensive psychotherapy (three times a week), and therapists who have been in (and conducted) analysis (four or five sessions a week). No intellectual argument has the power that having the actual experience does to convince the therapist that four sessions per week is necessary for the adequate development of a transference neurosis.

Let us finish our discussion about frequency of scheduling by considering the relationship of frequency to resistance, especially as it is related to the organization of an enduring, aim-inhibited identification with the analytic ideal in the ego ideal. Curiosity about one's unconscious motives and the inclination to be self-reflective should be possible as an everyday event, and we hope that one of the outcomes of a successful analysis will be an ability to engage in regular self-analysis after the analytic procedure itself has been brought to a conclusion. We have the expectation, and the intention, that the process will outlive the procedure, or to put it more succinctly, that analyzing will not stop when the analysis ends. In fact, this is one of the criteria we use in considering the patient's readiness for termination: that is, does the patient have the ability to continue to be analytically interested in himself even if the treatment is no longer in effect? Does he have both the curiosity and the tools to stay in touch with many of the more important trends of his inner life? Part of the structuralizing process of an analysis involves the analytic ideal becoming a stable part of the ego ideal.

A patient who freely chooses to work in analysis every day that his analyst works (that is, usually 5 days per week), and who takes the weekend off only because his analyst does not work on Saturdays and Sundays, has made a commitment to self-examination and to the analytic process that is quite different from the commitment made by a patient who is only willing to attend the minimum number of sessions per week considered essential for the process to take place. Unless there is some compelling external reality that prevents the patient from scheduling analytic hours every day, we need to seriously address, in the analysis, why the patient might not want to work on his analysis in as fully committed a way as possible. Why is the patient willing to make a compromise, to settle for the minimal, when the optimal condition is within his means? Sometimes patients will inappropriately overextend themselves, and in the name of commitment to the analytic process but really for neurotic reasons, they may schedule more sessions than they can realistically support (acting out a masochistic submission, for example, or reflecting a fantasy of magical and symbiotic rescue in which the analyst/savior is expected to go along with the overextension of the patient because he is supposed, in the patient's fantasy, to be as unaffected by reality considerations as is the patient). Except for these neurotic and therefore inappropriate commitments to five sessions per week, a full-time commitment to the analytic *procedure* suggests a full-time commitment to the analytic *process*. And anything less than a full commitment reflects, at the very least, some ambivalence (certainly on the part of the patient, and probably on the analyst's part as well). If the analyst agrees, without analytically examining the issue, to schedule fewer hours than what is considered to be optimal (and assuming of course that this arrangement is entered into not as a necessary response to reality events that are objective and out of either party's control), he plays right into the patient's ambivalence. Patients who actively make a choice to work at only the minimum number of sessions considered necessary are expressing a resistance which may be hidden, and then rationalized in the "reworking" of it, by their apparent willingness and agreement to be analyzed (which they do, however, by agreeing to the absolute minimum only). By collaborating in the arrangement to work at the minimum frequency when the optimal frequency is, in fact, a genuine possibility for the patient, the analyst unwittingly engages in a tacit conspiracy with the patient to resist the analysis. Supporting this resistance has a detrimental effect on the development of an analytic ego ideal. The message the patient gets is that it is not a full-time job, that it is acceptable not to be analytically engaged every day, that it is all right not to be analytically invested some of the time as long as one has satisfied a theoretical requirement to be analytically invested at other times. It sends the message that analysis, as a procedure or as a process, can be relegated to a partial and circumscribed area of one's life instead of being part of the very fabric of one's daily existence. When the frequency of scheduling becomes a pro forma exercise and the patient's resistance is supported by the analyst's complicity (for example, when the analyst in consultation suggests the minimal number of sessions because he believes that analysis is possible under those conditions, rather than suggesting what he considers to be optimally in the patient's best analytic interests, even if it is more than the bare minimum and even if it is not in line with the patient's original wish to only meet the minimum requirement), we can expect that it will have a different consequence on the development of an analytic ego ideal than when both patient and analyst share a commitment to analytic investigation as frequently and as intensively as their reality circumstances will permit (and who consequently determine whether four or five sessions is advisable on the basis of what is possible rather than on the basis of what minimally satisfies a theoretical requirement).

Patients often come to treatment knowing that the traditional analytic minimum standard is four sessions per week, and when informed of the optimal standard of five sessions per week, refuse to take advantage of the optimal condition because, they rationalize, it is uneconomical. There is no question but that analysis is extremely expensive in terms of money, time, effort, and discomfort; and it is also true that in most other contexts it makes sense for people to satisfy their needs in as economical a fashion as is possible. However, when a patient chooses to limit his analysis to the minimum rather than the optimal level, based on the notion of simple economy of effort and resources, it is only another example of how readily people can use reality as a means of supporting their inner needs. In determining the frequency of scheduling, we wish to be as careful as possible not to also use, in unconscious complicity with the patient, an apparent reality consideration, based on a supportable theoretical position, in such a way as to ultimately interfere with the appropriate development of the patient's analytic ego ideal.

In a sense, we can separate the ground rules of psychoanalysis into rules that we consider to be major and those that we consider to be minor. The major rules can be thought of as the rules that are absolutely essential to the establishment of a specifically psychoanalytic situation; for example, free association, use of the couch with the analyst sitting out of sight, and the high frequency of sessions each week are the basic working components that are necessary for the analytic condition. Other arrangements may be psychotherapeutic, but they will not be psychoanalytic, partly because the conditions that are necessary for a psychoanalysis are not equivalent to the conditions that apply to other forms of psychotherapy, and, more specifically because of how those particular working arrangements foster uniquely psychoanalytic conditions. A patient's inability to tolerate or accept those working arrangements is a signal that psychoanalysis may not be the treatment of choice for that person; not because he does not have the right to accept or to tolerate what he wishes, but because the intolerance may indicate a deficiency in the specific kind of ego functioning that is necessary for psychoanalytic rather than psychotherapeutic work. The minor rules (e.g., those concerning time and lateness, other issues in scheduling, billing and payment procedures, vacations and other interruptions, explanations and instructions) are rather more technical than essential, in the sense that they are applied with patients for whom psychoanalysis does seem to be the treatment of choice, and because in those situations they tend to "fine tune" the analysis rather than to establish the basic conditions of the analysis. Of course, if mishandled, they can have an unwelcome (and even a destructive) influence on the development and maintenance of an analytic frame.[1]

Explanations and Instructions

The way an analyst introduces an instruction, or explains an unexpected behavior (like, for example, not repeating oneself upon request, or not responding to a direct question from the patient) is a good case in point. Because we have already had some discussion about instructions and their implications (when we considered free association and censorship, and in our consideration of scheduling the frequency of sessions per week), let us focus on the issue of explanation. We can first use the example of how an analyst may approach the issue of not repeating himself when the patient requests it, and then examine how he may introduce not replying to a direct question. These are very common technical procedures that occur with considerable frequency in every analysis, but in every analysis there is a first time for each, and the issue of how that is handled is not uncomplicated.

A patient in her fifth session (a lengthy consultation, prior to beginning an analysis) revealed some sexual conflict in a way that did not make it immediately

---

[1] For just a single example: some analysts suggest that one *must* charge for a missed session as if this were a major rule, and as if this were the *only* way to deal with it. Of course, there are very many ways one can deal with this.

clear to the analyst that she appreciated its depth. In consultative sessions an analyst will sometimes identify a problem or make an observation of an unconscious (or mainly preconscious) event as a diagnostic tool rather than as an analytic intervention. The purpose of making a comment that would be premature in an analytic context is to evaluate the patient's insight, reflectiveness, defenses, and autonomous ego functioning in order to determine whether or not psychoanalysis is the treatment of choice for that patient. Naturally, the intervention would not be one that the analyst would consider to be potentially too disruptive, but one which would be, nevertheless, somewhat anxiety-provoking. Ordinarily, if a patient were to bring up something in a particularly derivative way, or in a highly defended way, the analyst might choose to approach it rather obliquely (in order to avoid provoking too much anxiety) or he might choose to wait for a more opportune time to address the issue. In consultative sessions, however, the analyst might choose to comment (still tactfully, of course) in a somewhat deeper fashion to make evaluative judgments about the patient's strengths and weaknesses. In this instance the analyst said: "It sounds like you have some real restrictions in your ability to enjoy sexual relations; restrictions in your pleasure that are more profound than you are aware of, and which go back very far in your life." The patient flushed a bright red and asked: "What did you say? I didn't quite get that."

At this point, whether in consultation or in an analysis, the analyst has a number of possible approaches. He can, of course, simply repeat what he said. Or he can choose to make some comment about the patient asking him to repeat himself; that is, he can begin to examine the event as a resistance. Were he to repeat what he said, he would be ignoring the fact that the patient actually did hear him and that her response was defensive in nature. One need not feel any uncertainty about whether the analyst spoke loudly enough or clearly enough, because the patient's very apparent blush suggested that she did, in fact, hear what he said. If one's purpose in the intervention were educational, it might make sense to ignore the fact that it made the patient uneasy, and to repeat the remark. But with an analytic purpose in mind, one must become curious about why she might not let herself hear it (or, more correctly, why she could not acknowledge, even to herself, that she *had* heard it). One must then decide whether the best course of action, in exploring this as a resistance, is to just remain silent, letting the tension continue to mount, or to make some observational remark about the event that would lead into an examination of its defensive purposes. Although we say that in an analysis we work with transference, resistance, the unconscious, interpretations, and so forth, this statement only presents a gross overview of the process. The basic unit of what we do when working with all of these things is: the patient's expression of a resistance; the analyst's interpretation of it; and then, the patient's reaction to the interpretation. The means of clarifying the event as an instance of resistance need not necessarily always involve an immediate interpretive response, and remaining silent has some distinct advantages in a situation such as this. First of all, any comment that the analyst makes at this point will generate further anxiety, and the analyst must make a judgment about whether the anxiety generated by a comment will be more or less beneficial (or destructive) than the anxiety generated by the analyst's remaining silent. Second, if the patient were to begin examining the event as a resistance without the analyst's intervention (which one could not know unless one kept silent in response), one would not wish to short-circuit that process by substituting the analyst's ego functions in the place of the patient's (which is what happens if the analyst speaks before it is necessary to do so). In addition, not responding to the patient's request for a repetition of the analyst's comment would be preferable to repeating the statement or to making the statement in another way because it does not confront the patient with something she seems unprepared, as yet, to face more directly. It might also be preferable because it puts the patient in a position to begin to examine the resistive aspects of her reaction, in that a response to her request would tend to treat the fact that "she had not heard it" as if she really did not hear it (and we know from her involuntary blush that she did). One has no guarantee that the patient will begin to examine this as a resistance; she might simply go on to talk about something else if the analyst does not respond. This is sometimes a signal, which should not be ignored, that the event was too anxiety-provoking to remain with, and the analyst would choose then to wait and to approach it at another time (knowing that the repetition compulsion will bring it up again repeatedly, providing no dearth of opportunities).

The very act itself of not responding to the request for a repetition of the analyst's comment serves as a signal to the patient that there is more to be looked at in this situation, and it has the further advantage of being able to do so without offering any suggestions about the nature of the defenses and the underlying conflicts that may be at work in the resistance. It alerts the patient, while simultaneously giving her room in which to maneuver, so that she can completely avoid it if that is what is necessary for her at this time, or, alternatively, to relate to some feature of it at this time if it is possible for her to do so. The ambiguity in silence, rather than direction, permits her to choose which aspect of it she will address.

Similarly, when a patient asks a direct question (rather than asking for a repetition of something the analyst said), it is also sometimes useful not to respond. For example, when a patient asks something like "Which of the things that I said do you think it would be most valuable for me to continue talking about?" the patient is clearly in a resistance and is attempting to draw the analyst into a collusion to abandon the free associative method. And when a patient asks: "How are *you* today," the reason for not giving a direct reply is even more obvious. A direct reply to such questions as: Where did you go on your vacation? Are you going to write a professional article about me? Do you like me? and so on, inhibits the emergence and verbalization of fantasy material about the analyst (and prevents the patient from ever seeing how those fantasies are mainly about significant others in her past with whom the analyst's mental representation is unconsciously merged in the transference).

10

Resistance

The Concept of Resistance

A good place to begin to look at the question of resistance would be to consider differences in how resistance is approached by psychotherapists versus psychoanalysts. Resistance is thought by both groups to be anything that blocks advancement or progress in the treatment. From that point on, however, there are significant differences between psychotherapists and psychoanalysts in the dynamic way resistances are understood (that is, *why* and *how* resistances come into being); in the importance that is attributed to the timing of a resistance (that is, what governs the specific moments when resistances make their appearances in a treatment); and finally, in how they are managed by the therapist. For example, in a behavioral approach the reason why a resistance might occur is not always of interest, in a cognitive approach the particular form that a resistance takes may not be considered important, and in a systems-theory approach the timing of resistances may not be of particular interest (or may be of differing interests, depending on the approach). The dynamic psychotherapy approaches (usually depending on how dynamic they are) often place considerable importance on these questions, and it is the dynamic therapies[1] that I want to contrast with psychoanalysis in their differing attitudes toward resistance. For the most part, dynamic psychotherapy approaches to managing resistances tend to try to overcome them or bypass them, with interventions that may be either supportive or confrontational. The main thrust is to get past the resistance, so as to get the treatment "back on

---

[1]There is, of course, a wide variety of dynamic or "insight-oriented" psychotherapies, and they tend, not surprisingly, to emphasize slightly different aspects of the therapeutic undertaking (with some focusing more on support, others on ego functions, some more on object relations, others on reparative or corrective emotional experiences with the therapist, some more on symptom amelioration, others on interpersonal relationships, and so on). Despite their many differences in emphasis, they have much in common; for example, all attempt, each in its own way, to use insight and an understanding of past influences (whether supplied by the patient or by the therapist) as fundamental tools in achieving a "cure." The more psychoanalytically oriented therapies tend to overlap somewhat more closely with psychoanalysis in their methods of understanding and working with resistances than do the less analytic (but nevertheless *dynamic*) therapy approaches.

track." Their attention seems mainly to be focused on how a resistance is designed to stalemate or defeat the treatment; it is seen as a challenge to the therapist and a contest of wills, as it were, between the persistent therapist and the resistant patient. Their responses are essentially reactive and sometimes even combative: when they find themselves in an adversarial relation to the resistance, viewing it as "the enemy" and trying to defeat it, they are excluding many of its important elements and are responding to it as if it were nothing more than simply an impediment to the treatment.

In contrast, psychoanalysts view the emergence of a resistance as an important "entry point" for deepening the treatment. They do not attempt to defeat resistances (one might even go so far as to say that they welcome the appearance of resistances) because resistance is considered as having a dual role in psychoanalysis: it is certainly understood to be unconsciously motivated to serve as an adversary to the analysis but it is also highly valued, nevertheless, as one of the four primary tools of psychoanalysis (the other three being *free association, the transference neurosis,* and *interpretation*). In psychoanalysis, resistance is an agreeable event, not a disagreeable one, because it is uniquely suited to help the analyst to understand the deeply hidden and otherwise obscured motivations of the patient. It is particularly through the examination of how the deepening of the transference neurosis is disrupted by resistances, and how the free association process is disrupted by the emergence of resistances, that the analyst can begin to understand many important things about the patient's inter- and intrasystemic conflicts, the patient's object relations and identifications, the unconscious defensive structure of the patient, and even about the interpersonal conflicts of the patient. Resistances give the analyst crucial insights that one could not gain from an examination of free associations and the transference neurosis alone. Let us turn to the kind of clinical situation common in the supervisory setting, to clarify some of these differences.

I will describe a problem that a therapist in the early stage of analytic training was faced with, while conducting a psychotherapy that had been in progress for about 4 months. The therapist's hope was that the work that had been done up until that point would be a kind of preliminary or preparatory psychotherapy, leading to an analysis. The therapist was convinced that the treatment did need to be converted into a psychoanalysis before substantial progress could take place, and identified the hold-up in the conversion as hinging on a particular kind of resistance that had been quite troublesome. It is quite common for supervisees to complain about entrenched resistances. Beginning analytic candidates are not especially immune to this reaction when they encounter strong resistance, but their complaint to the supervisor is usually accompanied by the assumption that once they are able to find a way to resolve the resistance, the patient will then be amenable to converting the treatment into a psychoanalysis: they do not ordinarily, at the beginning of their training, see that the manner in which they deal with the resistance may, in fact, be the very means of converting the treatment into a psychoanalysis. An analytic approach to resistance needs to be learned: one does not automatically know, even if one is an experienced therapist, how resistances are managed *psychoanalytically*.

The therapist reported, "I have a patient who never expresses any feelings. He will tell me in great detail about some terribly painful situation, or about a very joyous occasion in considerable detail, but never communicates anything that he feels about it. It seems very important that he be able to get in touch with his feelings about these things, and in touch with his feelings in general, but he seems to be so highly defended against them that he only reports (on even the most striking events) with completely muted affect. I need to know how to get beyond his intense defensiveness about his feelings, because it feels to me that this is the most important issue for his treatment, and because it feels like his treatment is going nowhere. I have the impression that if I cannot find a way past this resistance he will come in, regularly, for the next 10 years, faithfully reporting the events of his life, describing everything in exquisite detail except, of course, not any of his feelings, and that this treatment will never turn into an analysis and this patient will be no further along 10 years from now than he is right now."

This is a rather typical psychotherapy approach to the problem in which the predicament is posed as follows: *How do I get the patient to give up his resistance and to talk about his feelings?* In this manner, the resistance is treated like something that needs to be undone, bypassed, removed, eliminated, dislodged, dodged, overturned. From that view the resistance is seen rather unidimensionally, that is, only as a problem of defense. Certainly one would not argue that the inability to feel or to express affect is not a serious problem for the patient; however, it is by no means clear that it is only related to defense (an inhibition against having or expressing feelings, or specific defenses erected against experiencing them). It does not automatically follow that challenging or directly interpreting the defensive aspect is the best way to use the resistance.

As it turned out, this patient had a very provocative mother who, in the phallic stage and later, frequently overstimulated him. His father was, for the most part, a verbally and emotionally silent member of the family who would, on a rare occasion now and then, erupt into short-lived but very intense rages. In addition to his mother's seductiveness, she was also very controlling and intrusive: toilet training involved the regular use of enemas (given by the mother) because the process was fraught with battles in which this patient withheld feces as a means of maintaining feelings of body-ego integrity and self-definition. Subsequently, he employed this same anal-stage withholding behavior in masturbatory activity: during masturbation fantasies he found it extremely exciting to repeatedly, using active muscular control, partially squeeze out and then withdraw some stool. In this we can see how toilet training became precociously libidinized, and how masturbatory (and, presumably, other sexual) feelings became anally dominated as development progressed into later stages.

Now if we take a psychoanalytic approach to his resistance, we will not ask what can be done to get him to feel and express his feelings, but instead we will ask: *What purposes are served by his never being aware of his feelings or, if he does have any feelings that he is actually aware of in a session, never expressing them to the therapist?* In subsequent work with this patient it became clear that the expression of feelings triggered intense anxiety: this happened because, each in their own ways, his parents overwhelmed and disorganized him with *their* feelings. With her out-of-control feelings in the phallic stage, his mother sexually overstimulated him and made him unable to control his own feelings; earlier, during toilet training, she had stimulated disorganizing and intensely reactive anxieties in him about prephallic body damage and anxieties about self-cohesion. His father was terrifying in his rages, partly because they occurred so very infrequently. The patient was never able to predict when his father's rages would occur. They seemed particularly frightening because they were inconsistent with the representation he had formed (and come to expect) of his father as a placid, rather taciturn man. And he was never able to develop enough experience with these outbursts to be able to form in himself either a more complex, integrated, and enduring representation of his father, or an adequate set of defensive coping mechanisms in response to these events.

It became clear, after a period of analytically discussing his resistive behavior, that an aspect of his conduct in the treatment was indeed defensive; he viewed emotionality as dangerous, essentially as something incestuous, and he needed to avoid the threat of becoming forbiddenly overstimulated. He achieved this by flattening affect. On another, deeper level, his sexualized feelings were exciting events that he could manage to preserve and even to preconsciously experience by keeping them hidden. He could acquire these gratifications and satisfactions, however, only if they were undertaken in secret, and it was later discovered that he "played with them" much as he "played" with his fecal column during masturbation. Deeper yet, and along very different lines, keeping his feelings hidden "deeply inside" was a means of acquiring a defined and nonfragmented experience of himself during treatment hours (much as he was forced to withhold his stools in toilet training as a means of self-delineation). Here we can see the resistance not only as a defense but also in two very different ways. On one hand, his resistance was a means of acquiring and retaining instinctual pleasures: secret and hidden libidinized anal interests and exciting oedipal feelings. They could be maintained and protected so long as they were not expressed. On the other hand, it was an anally organized and very direct transference reenactment, with the therapist in the role of enema-giving and sexually exciting Mother.

Although the initial therapeutic focus, when this meaning of the resistance finally emerged, was on how his behavior in sessions transferentially represented the struggle with his mother over his bowel productions, his emotional inaccessibility later came also to be understood as a transference repetition of the quiet times he loved and longed to repeat with his father. The very same lack of emotional tone that represented a victory over his mother also stood for the happy, quietly nonemotional times he had with his father. In subsequent analytic work, that is to say, after this particular transference meaning of his resistance was understood, the patient was then able to learn how his emotional flatness also represented an idealized identification with his father: the father who did not disorganize and terrify him with too much feeling. With further analytic work it also became possible to see how his emotional flatness also served the purpose of a direct counteridentification with his mother.

None of these understandings could have been possible if the therapist had suggested to the patient that he should try to talk more about his feelings; or if, in the patient's telling of an emotionally arid story, the therapist asked the patient to describe what he had been feeling in that event. At best, all one could hope for would be a concrete response to the question, in which the patient does manage to conjure up some highly constricted "pseudofeeling" to escort the manifest experience being described; at worst, the patient is left confused by the question, unable to give an "acceptable" answer, and feels either chastised by the therapist or that he has disappointed the therapist, who keeps demanding that he do what seems to the patient to be honestly impossible or even inconceivable.

All of this comparatively rich understanding of the patient, and in particular of the peculiarity of his flat or nonexistent affect, became possible when the resistance was treated by the therapist as a highly motivated event with a psychological, rather than purely adversarial, character. It was in consequence of a supervisory discussion of this problem that, following one particularly horrendous tale, rather than suggesting that the patient *"say whatever feelings you can think of, anyhow,"* the therapist began to observe to the patient that he told many stories, very much like this one, in which one would have expected him to have had very strong emotional reactions and responses, and that, somewhat curiously, the feelings that might have been expected to be aroused in those stories, and even right then in the telling of them, never occurred. Never, not once. The therapist then wondered out loud, in a somewhat idle-seeming fashion, almost as if the question were rhetorical, how it could be possible for a person to go through such incredibly powerful events without ever, not even once, having any emotional reactions to them. In this way it began to dawn on the patient that the absence of feeling that he systematically presented was not simple matter-of-factness, as he had always assumed, but instead a rather conspicuous omission. That was the first step in a long analytic process that handles the resistance as a psychological event, rather than as an unpleasant obstacle to be defeated.

The History of the Concept

The evolution of this beginning analyst's way of understanding and working with resistance, from first seeing resistance only as something to be overcome, to eventually prizing resistance as a major tool in the treatment, has an interesting parallel to the development of Freud's ideas about resistance. Freud was originally drawn to hypnosis as a means of reducing his patients' resistances, which he did not distinguish, in those earliest days of nascent psychoanalysis, from repression. To be more exact, Freud thought that exactly the same forces were responsible for both repression and resistance. He saw resistance as the correspondent outcome of repression, working inevitably against the treatment, and keeping symptoms undecipherable; he attempted initially to overcome resistance directly through the use of suggestion and persuasion (and, in fact, there were times when he did not merely try to persuade or to suggest – he insisted!). He had first looked to hypnosis, and later, when he had given that up, he actually would press his hand upon his patients' brow, telling them that when he removed his hand, their previously hidden memories would enter consciously into their minds.

As we now know, and as Freud quickly learned, it did not work with all patients, nor did it work every time even with those patients with whom it did seem, quite often, to work. In addition, he found that suggestion was also frequently ineffective when hidden memories did surface from unconsciousness; for example, he found that interpretation of the patient's symptoms (using the information gleaned from those memories) did not eliminate either repression or the patient's symptoms. Faced with the clinical facts that (1) some patients could not be hypnotized, (2) some patients would not produce memories on demand, (3) some patients continued to show evidence of deeper repressions despite the emergence of certain appropriately relevant memories, and (4) some patients continued to have symptoms despite what appeared to be the correct interpretations of them, Freud had no other choice but to begin to differentiate between resistance and repression despite the many similarities they seemed to share.

The first way Freud eventually worked it out was with the following model: (1) Unconscious material presses constantly and without conflict for clear, undisguised, open expression and satisfaction in thought, in feeling, in behavior, or in any other discharge avenues or mechanisms available to it. (2) Conflictual events occur in which the possibility of discharge of these wishes become frustrated. (3) This creates a pathogenic nucleus. (4) Memories are associated with this pathogenic nucleus. (5) These memories occur in a kind of "layered" fashion, with some closer to the pathogenic nucleus and others further away. (6) They all have the character of being unpleasurable.[2] (7) The intensity of unpleasure associated with these memories is increased in direct relation to how close the memory is to the pathogenic nucleus. (8) *Repression,* that is, a kind of force, is exercised to protect the individual from unpleasurable experience.[3] (9) The power with which repression is executed is in direct relation to the degree of unpleasure which is, in turn, directly related to the

---

[2]In this stage of Freud's theorizing, unpleasure is subjectively experienced as *anxiety.*

[3]At this early point, Freud's thinking was dynamic, economic, and topographical, and he had not yet conceptualized a systematic view of the ego and how it functions as a structure. He had an idea of a repressive *force* without having defined its origins or its mechanics, beyond the basic idea that it exercises some inhibitory power where unpleasure is concerned.

amount of distance of the memory from the pathogenic nucleus: in other words, memories furthest from the pathogenic nucleus, being the least unpleasurable, suffer the least amount of repression. Thus, (10) each time one unearths a repressed memory one crosses a barrier which moves one closer to the pathogenic nucleus and, in consequence, closer to painful and unpleasurable experience. Therefore (11), *resistance* is another force, similar to repression, that acts almost like a knee-jerk reflex in the "unlayering" process of treatment; and (12) resistance arises in response to the unpleasure that inevitably occurs when an obstruction to a deeper layer of repression has been traversed (simply because the process of unlayering moves the patient closer to painful, conflictual, aspects of the pathogenic nucleus). And, finally, (13) whereas *repression* is ubiquitous in its relation to all mental functioning, *resistance* arises specifically in the context of analytic treatment as a means of keeping deeper levels of repression intact in an attempt to avoid any further experiences of unpleasure (anxiety). In this model we see that Freud had two ideas about resistance: first, that it is regulated by its distance from repressed material; and second, that it is a defensive operation.

As he was developing this model of repression and resistance, Freud was also beginning to get a glimmer of the concept of transference. Initially, transference did not have the prominence it eventually came to have in the psychoanalytic undertaking, mainly because in the first stage of his work Freud's focus was primarily on making unconscious conflicts conscious. As he became more aware of transference, and the special intensity it achieved in psychoanalytic treatment (what we now think of as the transference neurosis), he realized that transference was also a form of resistance. He came to understand that the patient's transference demand (or expectation) was a call upon the analyst to engage in an emotionally charged behavioral enactment, or, more properly, a symbolic reenactment, of the patient's conflicts and infantile relationships. Freud realized that this was intended, unconsciously by the patient, to serve as a direct substitution for the evocation of memories and their verbalized recollection in the treatment, which is why he came to the conclusion that transference was perhaps the greatest and most pervasive form of resistance. And, in the same way that earlier he began to make differentiations between repression and resistance, Freud rethought the relationship of resistance to transference, finally drawing the conclusion that although resistance made use of the transference, transference was considerably more complex than simply being a resistance.[4] This revolutionized the psychoanalytic method, in that analysis stopped being only an interpretive survey of the unconscious and now involved a

---

[4]The concept of transference (including the concepts of transference neurosis, symptomatic transference, ubiquitous transference, delusional transference, psychotic transference, positive transference, negative transference, and the unobjectionable transference) was discussed in Chapter 8. A consideration of transference dynamics beyond how it may function as a resistance is fully elaborated there; the main points here are, however, not to equate transference with resistance, and not to confuse transference and resistance merely because resistance makes such thoroughly good use of transference.

detailed examination of the interplay between transference, resistance, and the unconscious.

Ego Resistance

As Freud elaborated the metapsychology of psychoanalysis and added the structural theory (that is, the concepts of the id, the ego, and the superego as superordinate regulatory bodies), the concept of resistance became more focused in its role as a defense. Indeed, Anna Freud eventually took the position that analyzing resistance was essentially indistinguishable from the analysis of all of the defenses that may emerge in the context of a treatment. When Freud developed his second theory of anxiety, that is, that anxiety is a signal to the ego of an internal danger (signal anxiety), he also further elaborated his ideas about resistance by defining resistance as occurring in five characteristic types. He now gave fuller scope to his ideas about the way in which resistance capitalizes on transference (the transference resistance). He deepened his understanding of the mechanics of repression and its relation to resistance. And he elaborated a theory of secondary gain as a resistance.

In the notion of secondary gain as a resistance, Freud pointed out how certain aspects of the patient's illness will gratify unconscious needs and how this acts, therefore, in dedicated opposition to a cure. One may recall the old joke from the first section of this book (in the discussion of the concept of secondary gains) that illustrates this so nicely: *A woman was in the hospital, recovering from her eleventh surgical procedure in the span of about 6 years. A visitor commiserating with her remarked on how difficult this must be for her; to be in such bad health, to have had to go through so much pain, so much expense, so much trauma, so much discomfort, so much inconvenience. The woman says, "Yes, it's true." She remains in a reflective silence for a few moments, and then says, in a somewhat offhand way, "But then, you know, it's the only way I can get my kids to visit."*

In the clinical setting, a clear example of how secondary gain acted as a resistance became apparent in the treatment of a man with a passive and infantile character, who had developed both his characterological style as well as a constellation of symptoms as a method, early in childhood, of competing with a sibling for their parents' love and attention. This man was the youngest of two children, his older sister having been born 4 years before him. He was the baby of the family and gloried in that role, and this special position of being the baby was reinforced by his parents' delight in having had a male child. They were quite happy with their daughter when she was born, even though they had hoped for their first child to be a son. Although this frustrated wish was obviously important to them, the fact that their first child was not a boy did not become a clearly conflictual issue for his parents until after the patient's mother became pregnant with him. His parents had assumed that they would have a large family, with many children, and that they quite naturally would have an "adequate number" of both boys and girls among the children, based just on the law of averages. As a veiled mode of expressing their preconscious disappointment in not having first had a son, they are reported to have joked around with each other about having another daughter when his mother became pregnant for the second time (with him), kidding each other about how many additional chances they would still have for "making a son" if this child was not a boy. During his mother's second pregnancy (with him), his father suffered an illness that rendered him sterile. Naturally, this focused their attention on the fact that the current pregnancy was their only opportunity to have a son. If this child were a girl they would have lost their opportunity, forever, of having the son they had really wanted to have the first time, the son who, in their many mutually shared fantasies, they fondly imagined as carrying on the family name and as following in his father's footsteps (into a very successful family business). As can be readily supposed, they were absolutely thrilled by the birth of their son, whose gender became so disproportionately important because of the father's sterility, and who fulfilled, perhaps also on some neurotic levels, so many of their imagined dreams and wishes. The patient was a pampered baby, a wish come true for his parents, and he was given (under these special circumstances) an enormous amount of attention and affection: his parents absolutely doted on him.

When the patient was 2 years old, his sister contracted poliomyelitis and the emotional balance of the family was radically altered. Virtually all of his parents' attention and concern was shifted away from the patient, in favor of his sister who was critically ill. This was an abrupt and devastating blow to him, in part because they had been so attached to him and so very involved with him (in a way that made it clear to him, even at the age of 2, that he was very much the favored child), and in part because he did not have the cognitive or emotional maturity to understand that his sister's illness made this a necessity. His experience of it was that she had stolen them away from him, very much the way a young child feels when a new baby is introduced into the family, despite the fact that in his case this was his *older* sister. The patient was in the toilet training process when this happened and, as his parents later told him, his achievements and mastery abruptly deteriorated; he was not fully toilet trained until the age of 4, and suffered from enuresis until the age of 13. His sister lived through the acute phase of her illness but she was quite badly crippled by the disease, and her illness became the new focus of concentration in the family, as one might expect. The patient is reported as having severely regressed in the following year, using exclusively baby talk sounds instead of language and attempting to cling to his mother constantly. His parents, recognizing his regressive behavior as a sign of distress and disorganization, responded quite negatively to him (under the assumption that he should not be rewarded for acting like a baby, or he would never grow up), which he experienced as a further rejection. Rather than spurring further development, this tactic embedded the regression: however, because open displays of immaturity were treated uncharitably, the patient employed a slowing of development instead, and he evolved a pervasive infantile character style in his attempt to overcome feelings of separation and abandonment and as a way of obtaining extra attention (in the form of needing extra help to accomplish developmental achievements). In his third and fourth years the patient developed a number of mild-to-moderate physical problems, which may have been psychosomatic in origin (eczema, allergies, and so on). If they were attempts to compete with his sister through sickness, they were apparently unsuccessful: he reports his parents as having been slow to comfort him and slow in bringing his conditions to medical attention. As an adult, he understood why they might not have done so, given their preoccupation with the catastrophic condition of his sister who was, at that time, living in an iron lung, but as a child this was a clear message to him that displays of physical disturbance would not suffice to regain the lost idealized relationship with his parents. It is likely that if his parents had been more responsive he might have chosen psychosomatic illness as his compromise of choice. But given their response, he was left only with slow development and immaturity as a means of refocusing his parents' attentions on him.

When he undertook an analysis as an adult, he made progress at a snail's pace, with every achievement being lost repeatedly, and regained only after unusually lengthy periods of working through. His psychic "illness"–that is, his infantile character organization–and his slow analytic progress were attempts to capture and keep the engrossed attention of the analyst, which he found immensely gratifying. Rapid analytic progress and mature psychic functioning were unconsciously equated with losing his parents once again to his sister, and retarded analytic progress signaled, in primary-process terms, the treasured relationship with his parents in which he was their ideal and idealized baby. In this way the *secondary gains* of his difficulties worked, resistively, against the treatment in a very effective manner.

Secondary gains, repression, and the transference resistance were all viewed by Freud as resistances that are organized by the ego, despite the infiltration of important influences into each of them from the id and from the superego. Freud described two more resistances attributed to other psychic agencies: (1) *id resistance,* by which he meant the power of the repetition compulsion to reiterate, incessantly, unresolved conflicts as well as the demands of wishes that have remained unsatisfied (i.e., that have been inadequately sublimated and neutralized); and (2) *superego resistance,* the most striking example of which is the "negative therapeutic reaction."

Id Resistance

Id resistance is also sometimes called the resistance of the unconscious, but whatever one chooses to call it, it refers to the way that unconscious impulses and wishes (which are currently repressed) remain in a constant, unyielding struggle for expression and make a constant demand for satisfaction and gratification. We can differentiate this from symptom formation in the following way: in the formation of a symptom, unconscious infantile impulses break past the force of repression and find symbolic expressions that are still, nevertheless, subject to many other defensive processes (thus, in a symptom one sees "the return of the repressed" in the form of a substitution, a compromise formation, or a reaction formation); whereas in id (or unconscious) resistance, the demand is that repression simply be lifted, entirely. In the case of id resistances (as contrasted with the formation of symptoms), the defensive elements that would account for symbolic and partial modes of gratification are both irrelevant and nonexistent. Thus the "demand" made by the id resistance is unaltered by defensive considerations in how it strives for fulfillment.

Freud's abrupt encounters with the ease with which id resistance (and the repetition compulsion) regularly overpowered the pleasure and the reality principles came fairly early in his career, certainly well before he systematically articulated the structural theory (and the myriad roles of the ego in the organization of conflict, defense, resistance, fantasy, symptoms, and so on). He became uncomfortably aware of the resistive power that transference and repetition wielded in the treatment, and Freud formulated his ideas about *working through* in direct response to the tenacity of his patients' constant demands to repeat, rather than to remember – and then to give up – their conflicts.[5] Despite having not yet conceptualized structural theory, Freud recognized the need for something more than just his previously educative interpretation of unconscious motives if his patients were to begin to give up their resistances to the treatment. He eventually came to the position that working through was essential to the resolution of resistance: in practice this involves, in addition to making unconscious motives conscious, changing the balance between conflicts and defenses, and renovating object relations and identifications (always, of course, through a process of judicious interpretation).[6] Freud found that the process of working through – this additional work, time-consuming and repetitive and rife with halting progressions and regressions – is always required before resistance can be abandoned; in other words, that it is through the accomplishment of long-term therapeutic acts of working through, and not especially because of so-called deep interpretations,[7] that the ego will come to be able to incorporate and reorganize infantile conflicts and their derivative expressions. It is now considered axiomatic that working through is the only way that will permit a patient to finally forgo his resistances, most especially his deepest unconscious resistances, to the treatment. This change in therapeutic alignment is clearly epitomized by Freud's wish to amend his early dictum: *Where there is unconsciousness,*

---

[5]I am referring here to Freud's 1914 paper, "Remembering, Repeating, and Working-Through." Of course, this paper was a preliminary attempt to deal with a complicated concept that really did need the later structural theory (that Freud did not fully articulate until 1923, in *The Ego and the Id*) before it could be addressed more comprehensively. After structural theory was developed as an integral part of psychoanalysis, Freud published (in 1926), *Inhibitions, Symptoms, and Anxiety*, in which he gave the question of resistance and the problem of working through resistances fuller and more inclusive treatment. Despite this, almost everything he said back in 1914 is still thought to be valid, conceptually and clinically, today. Very little else in psychoanalysis has been handed down directly from Freud in so intact a form.

[6]The dynamics of working through have been described in considerable detail in Chapter 7.

[7]"Magic bullet" interpretations serve to caricature psychoanalysis rather than to define it.

consciousness shall be, with the subsequent intent that *Where there was Id, Ego shall be.* Resistance in general, but *id resistance more than any other,* pushed Freud to radically alter the psychoanalytic method (and much of later psychoanalytic thinking).

Superego Resistance

Superego resistance, the last of Freud's five categories of resistance, is fueled by specific superego demands that conflict with the goals of treatment. Although "the negative therapeutic reaction" (in which some unconscious guilt brings about an unconscious need for punishment, a punishment that is satisfied only by the failure of the treatment) is the most commonly recognized superego resistance, it is by no means the only one, and other forms of superego resistance are not particularly uncommon. For example, the taboos against incestuous wishes, against other sexual wishes, and against many of the aggressive childhood wishes – taboos that exist within the superego – regularly prevent a wide range of material that is considered to be "forbidden," including thoughts, feelings, and memories, from surfacing into consciousness and thus into the analysis.[8] It frequently takes considerable effort, expended in a number of directions simultaneously, before such material can exist anywhere outside of unconsciousness. This should not be confused with the anxiety felt by the ego as a signal of danger when such material is approached in an analysis: anxiety (which leads to repressive efforts) and superego resistance operate in concert with each other; they collaborate in their resistive exertions, seeking the same goal for rather different dynamic reasons.

As another example of a superego resistance, one might wish to consider the conflicts of persons for whom the status of being a patient diminishes self-esteem, and who consequently resist the process rather forcefully. This can occur for many reasons, but in the condition being considered here – a superego resistance – there is usually some moderate-to-severe pathology in the ego ideal and, in particular, in the way that self-esteem is regulated in the ego ideal. Here narcissistic balance is

---

[8]One would wish to make a distinction between the ego's responses to superego demands in everyday life, and superego resistance in analytic treatment. In both cases forbidden thoughts and wishes are kept from consciousness and actualization. However, where everyday life is concerned, that which is forbidden by the superego might be adequately or inadequately repressed by the ego, using a variety of defenses, such as inhibition, denial, reaction formation, and so on; or it might emerge in symptoms (where expression and gratification are partially accomplished); or it might even be "allowed," if one transforms that which is forbidden into that which is permitted through the mechanisms of sublimation and neutralization. In superego resistance, only a part of the above is to be seen; that is, the ego's inhibitory and repressive operations in the service of the superego – and it is that alone which is manifested in the analysis. Superego resistance makes use of these defensive functions of the ego in the same way that the superego (as an agency) does in everyday life; the difference, however, is that superego resistance will not permit any of the other, alternative modes of discharge that would be possible outside of analysis.

disrupted by being a patient, which is understood to be a subordinate and passive, rather than an active and superior, position in the therapeutic relationship. This is particularly true with patients who employ archaic identification mechanisms within the ego ideal, involving the merger of grandiose and omnipotent object representations (for example, the all-powerful mother of earliest infancy, or the destructively aggressive, castrating father of the oedipal conflict) with self-representations, as a primitive and rather infantile means of regulating self-esteem. In other words, when their self-esteem becomes diminished, for whatever reason—including being a patient—they imagine themselves, as children often do, to be big, great, powerful, indomitable, indefatigable, unconquerable; and certain aspects of their reality-testing skills (at least about this) also become sufficiently impaired in the process (or perhaps one should say, to advance the process), so that they actually become unable to tell the difference between themselves as they are, as they would like to be, and how they *would be* if they actually could live up to these "aspirations." In sum, an archaic identification surfaces and becomes the current self-representation, displacing the previous, now "diminished" and cast-off self-representation. Such persons may powerfully resist analytic activity, despite very much wanting to be helped, because it diminishes their self-esteem, reminding them that they are, after all, the "weak," "diminished" and "depreciated" patient. Successful resistance, a superego resistance in this instance, brings about the fantasy that the tables have been turned, that now the analyst is the weak partner with the patient having been made the powerful one, and this not infrequently results in attitudes of condescension and contempt toward the analyst and toward analysis. In persons with a fragile narcissistic balance, who are particularly susceptible to problems of lowered self-esteem, and who have evolved this immature mode of self-esteem regulation, superego resistances of this sort are frequently the rule, and they present great difficulties because analytic efforts are contraindicated, one might say, by the ego ideal.

This process was typified by one patient who initially greeted almost all of his analyst's interventions with a grandiose "analysis" of the analyst's functioning. The specific contents of the analyst's interventions were quickly deflected and replaced by the patient's "analysis" of why the analyst chose to speak at that very moment as opposed, for example, to any other time during the hour up until that point; or the patient's suppositions about why the analyst chose the particular contents of that comment, for example, rather than having focused on something else that "might have been of equal interest"; or, in other instances, the patient would provide an "analysis" of the possible latent motives that might have contributed to the analyst's behavior, "discussing" the analyst's "countertransference difficulties" with grandiloquent and seemingly omniscient interpretations of both the nature of the analyst's "unconscious fantasies" and who it may have been that he (the patient) "stood for, transferentially, in the unconscious" of the analyst; and so forth. The patient behaved as if his analyst were a stumbling beginner and he were his analyst's rather critical supervisor. After these early, rather aggressive reactions to an intervention, the patient would then have a series of fantasies in which he himself was a "world-famous analyst." In these fantasies he would be developing a new "school" of psychoanalysis, "revolutionizing the analytic scene," collecting around himself a large group of admirers, followers, and disciples. With considerable disdain, in an icy voice dripping with scorn, he would inform the analyst that it was not very likely that he (the analyst) would be allowed to become a member of this "group." With everything in the analysis having come to such a resistive impasse, it took a great deal of time and considerable effort to analyze these manifestations of injured narcissism, pathological ego-ideal formation, and this patient's disturbed method of self-esteem regulation.

Other Resistances that Overlap Freud's
Original Five Categories

Acting Out

Acting out is one of those concepts that has more than one meaning. On the one hand it refers to any action tendency, that is, any mode of expressing a psychic event through action. This would include, for example, things like stretching, yawning, pacing the floor, or shaking one's leg as a means of reducing tension, eating as a means of regulating separation anxiety, any demands for the satisfaction of transferential wishes in an analysis, and so on.[9] When discussing, specifically, *resistive acting out,* the concept has come to mean any attempt, through the use of an action, that the patient makes to avoid the emergence of memories, and their associated affects and ideas, into consciousness and into the analysis. For example, a patient who attempts to acquire, between sessions, symbolic gratification or satisfaction of the tensions and wishes that arise within analytic sessions, as a means of defeating the frustrations of the analysis (which then serves to keep conflictual memories, associated disturbing affects, and subsequent insights contained and inaccessible) would be said to be *acting out.* Similarly, all requests that the analyst look at a picture, read a book, listen to a piece of music, shake hands at the beginning or at the end of an hour, attend a play, see a movie, read a letter; any insistence that the analyst must repeat a statement simply upon request, that he speak louder (when he has been sufficiently audible), or that he further clarify an already intelligible statement; or any expectation or assumption that the analyst will unnecessarily change his fee or his schedule on demand would all be considered other examples of acting out.

Less commonly now, but in the early days of psychoanalysis when analyses were of more limited duration (lasting a few months rather than many years), patients were expected not to make any significant life changes or, if possible, even insignif-

---

[9]In this sense, even the transference neurosis itself would be considered a form of acting out.

icant life changes, for the time they were to be in treatment, and this explicit agreement was made specifically in order to avoid any acting-out potentials these activities might harbor. That expectation, even if we do not demand it at present because of how much longer a current analysis lasts, was not as immoderate as one might imagine; consider how often we encounter patients who enter into a marriage or disrupt a marriage, or who change jobs in order to change their schedules or their financial circumstances, in an attempt to avoid certain issues that have arisen in their analyses.

Some forms of acting out are blatant, such as the ones just described, whereas others may be quite subtle. For example, a patient who, after crying, continues to hold the tissue and then, without conscious thought, proceeds to shred it while talking is engaged in a form of acting out;[10] a patient who wishes to make a referral may, depending on the circumstances, be engaged in acting out; a patient who needs to interrupt a session to use the bathroom is acting out; a patient who comes late to session or who pays late is acting out; some telephone calls to the analyst between sessions, or certain other extra-analytic contacts, again depending on the circumstances, are forms of acting out; every demand for transference gratification, while also being a transference resistance, is a form of acting out, to the extent that the wish is for an *enacted* object relationship as a substitute for conscious psychological experience, remembering, and verbalization in the analysis; the choice of sending payment through the mail versus physically making payment directly to the analyst, or between handing a check to the analyst versus giving the analyst an envelope with the check inside, has acting out components as long as it is unanalyzed and performed as if it were merely a matter of course.[11]

---

[10]In fact, even the act of crying itself is a form of enactment. This was the earliest notion of acting out that occurred to Freud; that is, any discharge via action, a concept that is best exemplified by any use of motility (in the "classic" sense of a kinesthetic discharge event), motion, or anatomical-physiological discharge that is made by a patient during a session. In this most extreme of definitions, even the act of talking while free associating involves acting out. It should be obvious why the definition became narrowed to refer specifically to *attempts to enact as a substitution for remembering,* since the broadest definition quickly acquires a reductio ad absurdum quality in practice.

[11]Some of those who have discussed this subject in the literature have thought that it might be useful to make a distinction between *acting out* and *acting in;* the difference being that acting out refers to actions that the patient takes outside the specific context of the analytic hours to prevent material from emerging within the analysis itself, and *acting in* refers to the kinds of enactments that take place—for exactly the same purpose—within the analytic hour itself (an early definition of *acting in,* which no longer seems to be in much use, is that it refers to gestures or body movements made on the couch). Thus an unnecessary telephone call to the analyst between sessions would be *acting out,* and interrupting a session to use the bathroom would be *acting in.* Motivatedly changing one's work schedule so that it conflicts with the analytic schedule would be *acting out,* and arriving late for a session would be *acting in.* Smearing the analyst's reputation would be *acting out,* and overturning an ashtray, or picking one's nose, during a session would be *acting in.* The necessity of making the distinction between these two concepts is not readily evident, except perhaps to make a phenomenological point, inasmuch as their dynamic operations appear to be identical.

Resistance to Analytic Regression

Analytic regression, the controlled regression that accompanies the deepening of the transference neurosis, has, like any regression (no matter what other purposes a regression may serve, and no matter what a regression may also gratify), certain anxiety-provoking and disorganizing features. In fact, it is the intention of an analytic regression to have certain disorganizing characteristics; for example, we count on analytic regression to disorganize an established defensive structure so that the infantile nature of the patient's conflicts can be more readily and directly observable. Instead of remaining hidden within highly transformed and symbolic events, designed to give the appearance of having their central basis in current reality, we need a way to be able to look at how the patient's functioning continues to reflect infantile conflicts.

Persons who have incestuous object relations, for example, tend to experience their sexualized object choices as if they were attractive essentially because of current, and externally determined, reasons. No one who manages to be attracted only to married, or otherwise unavailable, men says to herself, *"He turns me on because, with him, I can achieve the fantasy that I am having a sexual relationship with my father."* Rather, they usually manage to rationalize their choices on what seems to be current reality (*"Younger men are too immature for me,"* or *"Married men are safe because they are not likely to make too many demands on me"*). When they do have some recognition that these attachments are pathological, they may still be in the position of having no conscious understanding about why their love affairs always evolve in that particular, repetitive way. Analytic regression helps to strip away the guise that is supported so well by partial sublimation and other defensive transformations, so that the patient can eventually see the incestuous nature of her object choices. But it is a disorganizing and difficult experience for the patient, because it can be anxiety-provoking and painful.

The example above is only one of a number of ways that the analytic regression is intended to be disorganizing to the patient. To give an example of a different way, analytic regression is also intended to disorganize certain features of reality testing. We need a diminution of some aspects of reality testing in an analysis (although certainly not of *all* reality testing[12]) so that the patient can begin to reexperience conflicted relationships with significant past objects as if they were occurring in the present with the analyst. Without a disruption of some areas of reality testing, the "as if" quality of the transference could never take hold, and deeply felt transferential relations would never flicker in and out of the patient's analytic experience as if they were a reality. In yet a different example, analytic regression is intended to destabilize identifications so that we can understand the developmental processes and choices involved in the degree to which identifications have become aim-inhibited,

---

[12]Technically, it is probably impossible for someone to lose *all* of his reality testing, inasmuch as reality testing is not an all-or-nothing phenomenon.

in how some entered the ego whereas others were taken up by the superego, in the nature and quality of the self- and object representations (at many different levels) of which identifications are formed, and so forth. (These are only a few, perhaps the few most obvious, examples of the disorganizing potentials that are achieved with deepening of the transference neurosis; optimally, the speed and depth of regression in the transference neurosis is under some degree of control.)

This is a controlled regression from the analyst's point of view, guided by a careful gradation of transference gratifications and frustrations in response to what appear to be the patient's structural strengths and weaknesses. From the point of view of the patient, however, who is the one who has to go through it, it is not usually experienced as being a controlled event. If anything, it is in many ways a subjectively unpleasant experience, and one that is treated consciously and unconsciously in a complex fashion. On the one hand, the autonomous and observant part of the ego recognizes the adaptive aspects of the regression, and even if it does not welcome the regression with open arms, so to speak, it will at least tolerate the regression as a useful tool in the analysis. On the other hand, the superego correctly recognizes the unacceptable conflicts that the regression will inevitably liberate and puts considerable pressure on the ego to block the process. In addition to the force of superego demands, which are experienced as a danger (signal anxiety), the deepening of the transference neurosis necessarily involves, as an intrinsic part of the process, an incremental regression in many areas of ego functioning (to mention only a few: reality testing, impulse control, and frustration tolerance); this too is experienced as a danger (more signal anxiety). Signal anxiety does not concern itself with making an evaluation of the analytic method and what may be gained by it in the long run. That is left to other areas of the ego (which may or may not be operative, or which may be more or less operative, at any given time). Signal anxiety operates as a mounting pressure to take action against (resist) all dangers, whether intrasystemic (i.e., within the ego itself) or intersystemic (i.e., between psychic structures; for example, between the superego and the ego). The patient has good reality reasons as well as good neurotic reasons to resist analytic regression, and some resistance against analytic regression is a constant in every analysis. There may be more or less of this resistance at different points in the analysis, but there will be no point in the analysis at which there will be no resistance to the analytic regression. Ordinarily this resistance is as interpretable and modifiable as any other. However, there are some patients, particularly fragile and more profoundly disturbed patients, who seem to be unanalyzable precisely because they are unable to permit or tolerate the various and not insignificant regressions that are necessary to the establishment of a developed transference neurosis. This may reflect some lack of structural development and resilience in such patients, but from another point of view it also reflects some very good reality-testing abilities (in their being unconsciously able to make the assessment, which they then act on, that their psychological balance is too susceptible to disorganization and would not adequately withstand such a procedure).

The Role of Character and Character Pathology in Resistance

Character

Character is molded within the matrix of the id, the ego, and most especially, the superego. It is greatly influenced by identifications and object relations; it is forged from the tensions between the wish to indiscriminately gratify infantile instinctual aims and the opposing demands of the environment; it stabilizes the balance between drives and defenses; and it consolidates a secure relationship between fantasy and reality. It is, perhaps, the psyche's most elaborate and adaptive compromise formation. Character, which has a variety of functions in everyday life, serves as a resistance in analytic treatment.

Character is generally thought to be the overall way that infantile conflicts have been incorporated, adaptively, into the personality as a whole. Reaction formation and other, later defenses (e.g., intellectualization, asceticism, denial, externalization, displacement) initially develop in response to conflict. After having served their purposes in specific conflicts, defenses may then take on pleasurable qualities of their own; that is to say, they can achieve a considerable degree of secondary autonomy as characterologic operations. In this way, now in relative independence from conflict, defenses stop operating only as defenses, per se, and become integrated into the structure of character itself. For example, a reaction formation opposing ardent anal-erotic excitement may eventually develop into a passion for cleanliness.

The development of such autonomy does not remove our need to think in terms of specific defenses that may be actively operating in response to specific unresolved conflicts; however, simultaneously, we can now also conceptualize a somewhat more neutral, that is, characterological, use of defenses. We should also note two other important points about character: first, that character is intrinsically dependent on both ego and superego identifications for its organization;[13] second, that character reflects a continuance, a continuity, and a permanence of infantile life, in the sense that the extensive range of identifications that is blended into character is an indelible record of past aims and object choices. In addition, it is also useful to suggest some of the important ways character differs from symptoms, given their mutual relation to conflict. Symptoms are compromises that are closely associated with conflicts that have remained highly active and are closely associated with defenses that are still *relatively* instinctualized. They are "solutions" that have limited adaptive value, and they are most commonly experienced as subjectively distressing (i.e., ego dystonic). In the development of character, infantile conflicts and the responding defenses are subjected to a greater degree of both sublimation and neutralization than is the case with symptoms. Thus character shapes broader and more general features

---

[13]Ego identifications determine the individual's variously derived ego attitudes, ego interests, ego pursuits, and so forth. On the side of the superego, the internalized wish to sublimate instinctual strivings usually suggests the acceptance of a moral, or higher authority, as well as *an identification with its goals.*

of psychic organization. Character becomes an amalgam of mainly ego-syntonic traits (not defenses and not symptoms); character traits and the way they are integrated into character itself generally have the capacity to serve more adaptive purposes than one sees with defenses or, certainly, than one sees with symptoms.

To suggest just a few possibilities: *conflicts in the oral stage* can lead to certain difficulties in narcissistic regulatory processes; for example, temporary regressions into grandiosity as an initial response to narcissistic frustrations (this would be a symptom)–or they can lead to a characteristic posture of dependency on others, to generalized immaturity, or to the development of exclusively "extractive" object relationships (these would be character traits). *Conflicts in the anal stage* can frequently lead to obsessive-compulsive rituals (symptoms)–as well as to a tendency toward orderliness, toward parsimony, or to a high need for achievement (character traits). *Conflicts in the phallic stage* can lead to a wide range of phobias and anxieties (including exaggerated fears of body damage), or to pathological phallic grandiosity (symptoms)–or they can lead to a general policy of self-effacement, to a moralistic and punitive world view, or to a highly active and assertive stance toward the world (character traits). *Oedipal conflicts* can lead to compulsive masturbation, or to incestuous object choices (symptoms)–as well as to a tendency to always be on the side of the underdog, or to a mainly seductive (or, instead, challenging) posture in one's interpersonal relationships (character traits). *Conflicts around identification processes* can lead to difficulties in differentiation, or to a pathological fear of being "swallowed up" in relationships (symptoms)–as well as to an easy reversibility of object attachments (a character trait). *Conflicted object relations* can lead to sexual sadism, or to sexual masochism, or to a turning away from the object world in general (symptoms)–or they can lead to a generalized quality of unrelatedness or indifference toward others, or to a particularly vibrant and lively way of relating to others (character traits).

Because they are so much more neutralized and sublimated, and especially because they are usually ego syntonic, even *pathological* features of character and character traits are less accessible to analysis than are symptoms or defenses. It is this stability, ego syntonicity, and resistance of character traits to analysis that led Wilhelm Reich to describe the formal aspects of character as "character armor." He made many distinctions between defenses, symptoms, and character: however, one important difference in Reich's views is that he did not consider character to be as neutralized a structure as we do today. His preferred way of thinking about character was to emphasize its compromising qualities–that is, how it is designed to master anxiety (which is caused by wishes that are barred from expression), and how it also, simultaneously, manages to gratify (in an ego-syntonic fashion) those very same wishes.[14] Reich introduced some of the earliest distinctions between *transference resistance* and *character resistance*. He suggested that careful attention to "character

---

[14]This comparatively limited definition of character would seem to be the equivalent of how we define a symptom, except for the question of ego syntonicity versus ego dystonicity.

analysis" (the analysis of pathological character resistance) would move psychoanalysis from a method of analyzing symptoms to one of analyzing the whole person.

In fact, Reich believed that "transference analysis" was made possible only after a preliminary "character analysis" was successfully undertaken. His position may have been developed in reaction to a couple of sources. First, he was opposed to the earliest method of analyzing, known as "content analysis," which, at the time he was developing his ideas, still retained some adherents, and in which interpretations of deeply unconscious material were presented to the patient. Reich considered much of that to be "wild analysis," as did Freud, and was attempting to redirect the endeavor away from the immediate interpretation of deep content and instead toward the analysis of deep character resistances. Second, he balked against the general practice of leaving the analysis of negative transference until late in the analysis. The delay was designed to give the patient the opportunity to establish an operative working alliance with the analyst, the assumption being that the clear emergence of negative transference too early in the analysis would be disruptive. Reich not only rejected this, he believed that a working alliance was only possible *after,* and *because of,* an analysis of the patient's negative transference. In Reich's (1949) approach, "we isolate the character trait and confront the patient with it repeatedly until he begins to look at it objectively and to experience it like a painful symptom; thus, the character trait begins to be experienced as a foreign body which the patient wants to get rid of" (p. 50). His forceful and confrontational technique, which frequently caused patients a great deal of anxiety, was met with considerable opposition because it was seen as the equivalent of a kind of "wild analysis," involving *defenses* instead of *content.* His basic position about the importance of needing to analyze pathological character traits was, and still is, not controversial, but his confrontational method was seen as being too aggressive, and as being potentially too overpowering (at best, and as being actively destructive at worst: some patients experienced his methods with great suffering and there were reports of patients having temporary breakdowns. Reich believed that such things were unavoidable and necessary if the patient was, ultimately, to achieve a cure.). Opposition by the vast majority of the analytic community to his insistent and aggressive confrontation of character defenses was based on the argument that it was not absolutely necessary, and that it blocks the process rather than facilitating it. The criticism was that aggressive confrontation of character defenses has the same net result as one finds when one makes interpretations of content that are too deep or greatly premature: disorganization, and exponentially increased defensiveness. Eventually Reich took the even more extreme position that the entire work of an analysis could, and should, be done in the examination of character resistances; that is, that once having analyzed character resistance, the work of transference analysis was unnecessary. This, too, has been met with great opposition.

Fenichel was greatly opposed to the work of Reich because of its exclusive attention to character resistance and its inattention to the analysis of transference, and he was greatly opposed to the opposite extreme as well (exemplified for him in the work of Melanie Klein, or in the work of Theodor Reik, whose approach involved – as he saw it – interpretation of the unconscious without concern for the patient's readiness to make use of the information constructively). The introduction of ego psychology and its integration into "classical" psychoanalysis has greatly modified our approach to the analysis of the unconscious, of symptoms, of conflicts, of defenses, of resistance, and of character. Today we have reached a balance in our analytic approach in which we address unconscious conflicts, defenses, resistances, neurotic and character symptoms, ego pursuits and interests, adaptive ego functions, pregenital fixations and arrests, the superego and its introjects, conflicting identifications based on archaic fantasy–influenced parental representations, object relations, character traits, and character. We consider them all to be important and consider it essential to include the analysis of all of them in our work with every patient, no matter what their diagnostic category may be. In fact, it may be fair to say that at present the distinction between psychoanalysis and character analysis, so emphasized more than a half century ago by Reich, is no longer necessary.

Character Pathology

The above discussion has described how the nonpathological aspects of character, as well as how certain mildly pathological character *traits* (as they exist in the general, nonpathological framework of character), were understood to serve resistive functions in an analysis. It also addressed some of the changes, historically, in how we have come to analyze character (and character traits) in their resistive manifestations. Thus far we have understood character to be the modern inheritor (as well as the descendant of) infantile wishes, fantasies, conflicts, defenses, identifications, and object relations, and we consider character a vehicle of past and present symbolic satisfactions; its subtlety as a resistance is because it is primarily ego syntonic and, most especially, because it operates on relatively neutralized and abstracted levels.[15] This is why, compared with many other resistances, and certainly in comparison with symptoms, we view character as presenting special analytic difficulties.[16]

Character pathology poses certain resistive difficulties that character (and character traits) ordinarily do not. Even though nonpathological character structure (even including the possibility of a number of mildly pathological character traits) is acknowledged to be harder to analyze than many other resistances, it is only that it

---

[15]Relatively pathological character traits (within a basically nonpathological character structure) are usually organized in this same manner, and therefore they are just as ego syntonic as are the essentially nonpathological character traits. And because this is so, they are just as difficult to bring into an analysis despite their having relatively pathological qualities. However, nothing that has been said thus far about them suggests that they are impossible to bring into an analysis.

[16]Parenthetically, even significant aspects of character do not usually present insurmountable problems to analysis, whereas some neurotic conflicts can be doggedly obstructive: for example, the negative therapeutic reaction frequently is considerably harder to analyze than the resistive aspects of either passive-aggressive character pathology or infantile-dependent character pathology.

is rather more subtle and a bit more complicated; on balance, it requires a more careful and painstaking examination but it usually poses no unsolvable problems in an analysis. Severe and generalized character pathology often, and very regularly, does present serious difficulties in an analysis (even if the complications and challenges it presents are not always, necessarily, insurmountable). And at worst, certain character pathologies *are* insurmountable: they are not just difficult, they are impossible to analyze.

For example, some patients who exhibit borderline phenomena have a potential for regression that cannot withstand the stresses of an analysis. There are, undoubtedly, patients with borderline phenomena who do well in an analysis, or in an analysis with some modifications of technique, but others may enter into a spiraling regression that ultimately brings them to an unresolvable psychotic transference. The ones who do not do well in an analysis usually do better with treatment conditions that serve to support defenses, rather than being seen in a treatment that plunges them regressively ever deeper, past barely stable defenses, into even more profound areas of conflict. The nature of their character pathology makes traditional psychoanalysis a poor choice of treatment for them. This is a situation where the patient and the treatment are mismatched, and in fact, in such cases character pathology makes analytic treatment contraindicated: this is not just a matter of the patient being "too resistant," it is a matter of an incompatibility between the nature of the patient's character structure and the limited methods that psychoanalysis has at its disposal.[17]

---

[17]A thorough and detailed consideration of borderline conditions is beyond the scope of this book – it would take a whole book of its own. However, a brief description of a few of the important features of borderline functioning may be in order here, because the question of what "borderline" means is a matter of interest and controversy in the literature. There is currently no universal agreement among psychoanalytic theorists and clinicians about whether, on one hand, there is a clear diagnostic category, the Borderline Personality Disorder, with centrally organizing problems of adjustment located in a particular stage of development, a coherently predictable organization of object relations (and of identifications), and a special hierarchy of defenses (as Kernberg would have it); or whether, on the other hand, there are simply certain patients – in a wide variety of diagnostic categories – who display extremely disturbed functioning that can broadly be described as "borderline phenomena" (as Abend, Porder, and Willick would prefer). There is general agreement, however, about some specific aspects of these patients' functioning that most analysts do seem comfortable in describing as "borderline," regardless of their position on the question of diagnosis.

These patients seem to show areas of profound ego weakness and ego fragility, which leads, when they are suffering conflict, to wide fluctuations in many aspects of their reality-testing abilities. One often encounters the considerable use of denial and projection. These defenses are quite pervasive and they are utilized with a great deal of rigidity. One also observes a strong reliance on identification with the aggressor and on the defensive substitution of one drive derivative for another, particularly the substitution of aggression for other drive derivatives. The nature of their regressions frequently has sadomasochistic libidinal qualities, most especially when such patients are using regression for defensive purposes. It is hardly possible to overemphasize the seriousness of the problems that they have in managing aggression in all its aspects (drive dominated, reactive, and defensive).

These patients usually show both oedipal and pregenital conflicts of great intensity, often with important hindrances in the resolution of phallic-stage conflicts and with distortions in the ultimate

A few clinical examples can serve to illustrate this problem:[18]

A patient who suffered a wide variety of borderline phenomena was particularly susceptible to psychotic regressions in response to treatment experiences in which she felt abandoned. She suffered anxiety of annihilating proportions when she felt abandoned (which for her also meant being deserted, forsaken, neglected, and rejected), and she experienced a profound dissolution of self in that process. Her response to the experience of herself "coming apart" was a psychotic regression in which a defensive refusion of self and object images was designed to undo the sense of being catastrophically alone and the associated feeling of escalating self-deterioration. As is often the case with such patients, the self- and object representations involved in the refusion experience were not whole object images, did not have true constancy, and did not have adequate consistency (although they were, at least in this case, quite consistent in their aggressive qualities); they were, by and large, extremely fragmentary, expressing the basic difficulty she had in the areas of both object relations and identification processes (this was always true for her, even when she was not reactively regressed).

One day her therapist had the flu. He had been feeling ill, but not quite ill enough

---

organization of more mature development; these hindrances and distortions seem to be due to the patient having only been able to achieve rather faulty pregenital adjustments, which were then carried forward to affect later stages of development. These patients are often extremely narcissistic, suffer exaggerated fears of loss of the object itself as well as exaggerated fears about losing the love of the object, and are highly exploitive in their object relations (usually having been raised by seriously disturbed parents with whom, also, they are often closely identified). The inability to manage aggression causes their object relations (and also their sexual lives and their interpersonal relations) to be permeated by sadomasochistic compromise formations, in which aggression is directed at objects, at the self, or both; the projected aggression of these patients leads them to fear objects and to need to control them, and in analytic treatment this leads to paranoid reactions, manipulation, demands for reality gratification, acting out, and (just as with other objects) the analyst—when experienced as the feared object—is treated with a general lack of empathy, sympathy or pity.

Poor self–object differentiation is a common problem in certain circumstances for these patients; this is often exacerbated by an excessive dependence on projective defenses, which frequently causes these patients to have faulty self-representations, faulty self-perception, and distorted object perceptions and representations.

Finally, many of these patients have elaborate conscious and unconscious sadistic and masochistic fantasies, paranoid concerns, self-destructive impulses and inclinations, body damage concerns, and severe depressive episodes as a method of compromise between the demands of their sexual and aggressive wishes and the harsh demands of their superegos (which are usually quite primitive in terms of the degree of unneutralized aggression they contain).

[18]All of the patients in these vignettes (and in fact, it is true for all the clinical examples in this book, thus far) were considerably more complicated than they appear to be here, where the goal was to isolate and especially emphasize those factors that are relevant to the specific point under consideration: the nature of resistive character pathology. Unfortunately, in illustrating an idea, real limitations usually exist in how much of a person's dynamics can be presented, in effect treating the rest of the patient's dynamics as if they were nonexistent; this is always a problem when the purpose of the example is anything other than to provide a full case presentation. In Part III of this book, in the presentation of *The Case of Dr. A.* and, to a somewhat lesser extent, in the three additional cases that follow "*Dr. A.*," an attempt is made to present cases with many more of their complications included.

to cancel sessions. The patient had a marvelous, almost radarlike ability to read his emotional states and immediately recognized his lack of full attentiveness, despite his genuine wish to be fully attentive (which she did not as readily appreciate) and despite his wish not to give indications of being preoccupied (against his will) with his physical sensations. This patient was primitive in the sense that much of her reality testing (particularly at times of stress) was imaginative, idiosyncratic, and not closely linked to secondary process; many of her conflicts were preverbal; most of her phallic and postphallic development was rigidly altered by preoedipal conflicts and, in consequence, she suffered from grossly inadequate means of symbolization. The other side of this developmental picture was that she had a remarkable sensitivity to the nonverbal states of her therapist and, in fact, of everyone in her world (very much the way a child, before it has developed the capacity for verbal symbolization, is intuitively sensitive to the emotional states of its mother).

Recognizing that something was amiss with the therapist but not knowing how to make adequate sense of it, the patient painfully experienced his self-preoccupation as if it were a willful, rejecting abandonment of her. Within seconds of sitting down she flew into a towering rage, spewing up accusations; it was as if they were poisonous internal entities that she was ridding herself of, while also being deadly things she could, in retaliation, destroy the therapist with: "You stinking mother-fucker! I know what you're thinking. You're thinking, *'What is she doing here, this cunt? What do I need her here for, this bitch? This dumb-shit, with her sappy fantasies, and her baby dependencies. I laugh at her. She's an object of ridicule to me. What a pathetic creature!'* "

She went on to say, "I know what's going on inside your head because I'm in there with you. You think like I do, and I think like you do. There's no difference between us. We're one and the same, cut from the same cloth, so don't think you can get away with this, you miserable bastard! I ought to kill you. I ought to cut your fucking balls off, pull your fucking eyes out of your head, reach up inside your ass and pull your goddamned guts out!" The patient burst out of the office at this point, but within minutes she called from a public phone booth, continuing to rage at the therapist, and continuing to include many allusions to how they shared the same psychology because they were, as she put it, "for all practical purposes, one person." On the telephone she also was able to communicate that she absolutely had no choice but to leave when she did, in order to protect the therapist, since she would not have been able to refrain from attacking him if she had remained in the office with him any longer. In this at least, her judgment seems not to have been impaired. Later on that evening, however, the patient again called, telling the therapist that she was, at the moment of their conversation, slicing her arms with a razor. She tortured them both for a few more moments and then hung up.

The therapist called back to ascertain whether she needed immediate physical help, and the patient was then able to communicate that the cuts were essentially superficial and that she was not actively suicidal. Despite this patient's capacity for immediate and crippling regression, she also had an amazing resilience and could quickly spring back from even such an intense regression if given some facilitative

psychological assistance. The patient was in despair, and tearfully wondered why this had happened, feeling that everything was hopeless and that the therapist would never want her back. As she began to develop another head of steam, her anger once again began to surface, this time directed at herself. She was "stupid, paranoid, psychotic, disgusting, and a menace," she had "no reason for getting so nuts," and all of this proved that there was no hope for her. "At least if there were a reason why I acted the way I did, there might be a chance for me, but it all came out of the blue, and there's never a way of ever understanding anything. I'm lost. I'm forever lost."

The therapist interrupted her at this point to say that she was not just *acting*, but *reacting* to something; that her reaction was not "out of the blue"; that it had to do with something that had happened between them, something which she had correctly perceived but had not known how to correctly understand. He explained that he had not been feeling well, that he had been preoccupied, and that she had correctly perceived that he was not as connected to her, or as ready to be with her as she needed him to be and, as she was used to, with him. He went on to explain that the difficulty was that she had not been able to make adequate sense out of this very real change that she had accurately perceived in him, and that the conclusion she jumped to, that he hated her and that he wanted to get rid of her, was the problem – not her perception that he was somehow changed, and not her recognition that he was not quite there for her.

Identifying the fact that she had responded to something very real, even if she misunderstood its meaning, was very helpful to her and she was then able to go to sleep without any further disturbance. When she came in the next morning for her regular session, and for a number of sessions afterwards, she still needed considerable support in sorting out what had really happened. Her relatively limited and tenuous understanding of this was as a result of solidly supportive dynamic psychotherapy and not psychoanalysis, which her character pathology clearly could not have tolerated.

Borderline patients are famous for their rages, and the above patient was obviously no exception. Although much has been written on the maladaptive borderline use of primitive oral and anal rage, one does not usually see the adaptive uses of aggression discussed in respect to borderline patients. The next examples are interesting because, while presenting resistive character pathology that is too severe for the analytic method, they also illustrate some adaptive uses of aggression in two borderline patients. In the first case, the patient continually abused the limits of the therapeutic relationship. For example, he "borrowed" a yogurt from his therapist's refrigerator (the kitchen and the office area were separated by a door that was closed but unlocked, and the kitchen was clearly identified with a Private sign); he regularly, like clockwork, attempted to pay less than what he owed at the end of each month and adamantly insisted that it was the therapist who had made the "mistake," and not he; he completely, and rather conspicuously, ignored the Thank You For Not Smoking sign in his therapist's waiting room. When the therapist did not comment on his cigarette smoking, the patient escalated – he began to smoke cigars, filling the waiting room with billowing, "fragrant" clouds; he thought nothing of calling the therapist on weekends or late at night to ask about a schedule change, or to request clarification of something the therapist might have said during a session; he attempted to engage other patients (in the waiting room) in unwelcome conversations; he repeatedly asked the doorman at the therapist's building for personal information about the therapist; he behaved provocatively in the lobby and in the elevator of the therapist's building, which led to complaints from neighbors about the patient's conduct; and, to give just one more example, he could always be counted on to tie up the bathroom in the waiting room for excessive periods of time, both before and after sessions.

When this patient was about 2½ years old his mother underwent a severe, perhaps psychotic, depression, secondary to a serious physical illness. He had a close and very gratifying early relationship with her and, abruptly, he found that his mother had become inconsistent (depending on her limited ability to mobilize herself) and, frequently, extremely disappointing. This happened to him exactly at that point in the anal stage where power issues had taken on the utmost importance.[19] He fought bitterly, but to no avail, against seeing his mother as having been made powerless and defeated by her depression. The patient's father was not living at home, and so this patient did not have a strong masculine figure to turn to, in substitution for his erratically available, often helpless mother. As can be imagined, toilet training was significantly delayed. This was not a simple result of his mother's weakened enforcement functions but also, and much more importantly, an angry refusal on his part to comply with the strong expectations she had clearly expressed before she became depressed, in the vain hope (as it turned out) that her earlier, quite vigorous investments in his toilet training would be revived. Not only was toilet training delayed, the patient began to regress into episodes of angry smearing of feces. This was expressly designed to provoke his mother into action so that she would, through exercising power over him, reinstate herself in his world. If she could not be the loving mother he had before, the consistent source of pleasurable internal and external support she had once been – if she was only there physically, but actually quite absent emotionally[20] – he would gladly accept an oppressive but powerful and dominating substitute. He cast about desperately as a child to find some way to provoke his mother "back into being his mother" to control not just his angry anal behavior but also his own mounting depression in response to having "lost her love." This is, of course, what he was doing with his therapist. He was attempting to get the therapist to exercise powerful controls over

---

[19]As you will no doubt recall (from the detailed description of the anal stage in the first part of this book), during toilet training children begin to love power, seemingly almost as if it were for its own sake, but actually as a defense against losing the love of their mother.

[20]This is a perfect example of fear of losing the love of the object rather than fear of losing the object itself.

his behavior, to inhibit his acting out, and to prohibit his "naughtiness," as a means of attaining a safe holding environment. It was unquestionably very aggressive but not meant to be essentially destructive; it was meant to be a prod to the therapist, an inspiration as it were, for a display of "counteraggression" which the patient would then translate as a show of love and support. For this patient, interpretation was ineffective, and a simple setting of limits by the analyst did not suffice to change any of his behavior. Actually, attempting to set limits usually caused the patient to escalate his attempts to be irritating. The literature is rife with examples of this kind of behavior in borderline patients, and despite our understanding of the motive dynamics behind such behavior, numerous reports indicate that interpretation, and often even limit setting, is found to be refractory. Passionate counteraggression was the only thing this patient would accept, and the only thing this patient could understand, as proof that the analyst was engaged. In this distorted way, he was trying to reinstate with the analyst the equivalent of the happy earlier time he once had with his mother, before she became depressed, and the nature of this kind of character pathology successfully resisted any attempts at analysis.[21]

The second of these patients, with marked ego fragility, and raised by a mother whose relationship to him was parasitically symbiotic, suffered extreme fears of merger. His apprehension about merging – the dread of it and the horror it held for him – was not just a reasonable reality-based response to having had an invasively exploitive mother, although on one level it certainly was that. It was also a disguised wish to be merged, masochistically, with his mother; a disguised wish *in fantasy* to be sadistically merged with his mother, partly in identification and partly as an expression of his own sadism, but mainly so as to turn her aggression away from him and back onto her in the merger; and a disguised wish to be merged *in fantasy* with an idealized version of his mother (in which he would be completely at her mercy and totally defenseless without having to worry about any of her aggressive impulses). This was further complicated by merger fantasies growing directly from his close identification with his mother's aggression and from the disposition of his defensive preferences, which principally employed projection. In addition, he had considerable difficulty with self–object differentiation, which naturally contributed greatly to the development of his merger fantasies and to his subsequent reactions against them. And to give some indication of how convoluted these all were, the merger fantasies that were based on his underlying identificatory and defensive dynamics added considerably to his not insignificant problems in self–object differentiation, fueling yet further and more extreme merger fantasies and reactions

---

[21] The idea that aggression in borderline patients is designed to be a method of trying to get the analyst to perform containment functions is not new, but the emphasis is usually placed on the maladaptive character of the aggression because for an adult it is clearly pathological, and because it is so refractory to analytic intervention. Looked at from the patient's point of view, however (his unconscious point of view, obviously), his aggression was an adaptive attempt to restore a desperately needed but broken object tie in the only way left to him, because his mother was no longer available to him as a libidinal object.

against them. In effect, this was a kind of "snowballing" phenomenon, highly interactive and self-perpetuating, involving a destructive cycle where his difficulties in self–object differentiation led to merger fantasies, and the merger fantasies led to further difficulties in self–object differentiation, which led him to even more merger fantasies, which led him to yet poorer self–object differentiation, and so on.

The net result of the unconscious fantasies of merging that underlay his conscious fears of merger – an intricate web of sadomasochistic object relations, and defensive, identificatory and regressive events – was an intense ambivalence conflict. On one hand, his ambivalence reinforced and greatly intensified his conscious and unconscious fears of either merger itself, or any mergerlike experiences; on the other hand, his ambivalence also led him, unconsciously, to repeatedly seek merger with both sadistic-parasitic and idealized objects, a hidden wish he then had to savagely defend against.

His treatment had a bit of a slow start, as can be imagined, but rapidly thereafter led to an increase in feelings of intimacy and, eventually, idealized trust toward the therapist. This was accompanied by the reported experience of being abstractly happy (that is, his pleasure was not related by him to anything specific), and feelings that he was being well protected by the therapist. He was elated, almost hypomanic, at how safe he felt in the treatment, and then wistfully expressed his longing desire: "I wish I could have had such a good mother when I was a baby." Not surprisingly, this highly libidinized attachment, and the fantasies it created about the nature of his relationship with the therapist, increased his merger wishes and fantasies. And naturally, this led to an intensely self-protective and extremely defensive withdrawal from the therapist, in which the worst of his paranoid concerns emerged. From this, there emerged a long period of rage, accusations, and threats against the therapist (including the threat that he would never leave treatment and that he would be there for the rest of both of their lives, "so as to be able to torture [his therapist] forever"). Over a very considerable time this rage would gradually dissipate and the patient could then adopt a wary and guarded attitude toward the therapist, but without overt hostility. As certain of the patient's reality-testing capacities became more intact (unconscious needs of the patient were being satisfied, and unconscious stresses relieved, by the reduction of the precipitating wish to be, and reactive fear against being, merged with the therapist), the patient's paranoia, agitation, and aggression decreased. Slowly but inexorably, unconscious wishes to become attached once again to the therapist reasserted themselves. His reattachments eventually led to a similar idealized investment in the therapist, with associated wishes for merger. This sequence was a prototype for a series of repetitive enactments, with each repetition growing more severe and more disorganizing for the patient. The patient was entirely unresponsive to any attempt at interpretation throughout all the repetitive cycles of these mutually reinforcing conflicts; he was as immune to interpretation in the idealizing phase as he was in the period of rage, persecutory accusation, and threat. Only in the brief in-between periods was there any accessibility to the patient's observing ego, and this resource then disappeared as the cycle would intensify.

The way that this patient's needs and pathological character dynamics prevented an analytic therapy undertaking was clear, despite being rather complicated. To mention only a few of the most obvious: he was, of course, attempting to ward off his terrifying wish to be merged with his therapist/mother, that much is patently evident. The experience of having a "therapist/mother" was not just a displacement-based transference fantasy, as it might have been with a neurotic patient, it was also an almost (but not quite) psychotic mergerlike experience based on his difficulties in differentiating self- and object images, multiple images of self, and in this case, the multiple images of objects. The patient was also expressing a deeply embedded, highly pathological identification with his mother, as well as satisfying an additional merger fantasy – one in which he and his mother were sadistically consolidated against the victim (*note:* the victim as a "therapist/patient unit" should itself be understood as yet another merger fantasy operating in the treatment). His wish to be symbiotically united with his mother, both in defensive form (as a protection against her aggression) and as an identification (as a mode of deflecting the aggression away from both his mother – in her role as *idealized object* – and himself), could clearly be seen in his threat to remain a persecutory part of the therapist's life forever.

This patient, having had the kind of mother that he did, had more than ample cause to fear merger (all these other wishes to be merged, notwithstanding), and one very important part of the immensely aggressive investments he was capable of was very much in the service of adaptation. Jacobson,[22] in the general context of discussing feelings of envy and rivalry in the separation-individuation phase, has written (rather eloquently) about the importance of aggression toward rivals and other important persons, in the establishment of the child's capacity for self-delineation. Her views are quite relevant here: merger fantasies caused an inescapable exacerbation of this patient's difficulties in self–object differentiation with, as a consequence, a loss of self-boundaries, self-delineation and self-experience. This man experienced losing the capacity to retain self-delineation as a loss of the self to a sadistic, parasitic object and, naturally, this was an overwhelming and terrifying experience. Thus, much of his aggression served the urgent purpose of shoring up the experience of protective self-boundaries and the intactness of his self-experience. Experience of himself as actually separate and, more importantly, as delineated from his mother became a necessity for psychic survival (the fact that he could not always do it did not make it any less necessary). Having had no external support in this developmental effort (from parents, as most children do) and, in fact, having had only active opposition to it, he had no option or resource other than the channeling of massive amounts of aggression toward this purpose. This highly adaptive organization of aggression that was developed in early childhood remained,

---

[22]In *The Self and the Object World* (1964) and also in her work on psychotic depression.

unfortunately, as a fixed part of his character, and it played the major part in why his aggressive relation to the therapist was so rigidly fixed, so intensely gratifying, and so immune to transformation.

Perhaps the most definitive and clear-cut example of character pathology, excluding psychosis, that is exceptionally resistant to analysis may be seen in patients who have severe narcissistic character disorders. These patients frequently display an inability to form a transference neurosis. Within the analysis, with the analyst, the patient does not recapitulate conflicted relationships with significant past objects; instead, the patient attempts to have the analyst directly or indirectly gratify instinctual needs (whichever instinctual longings are paramount at the time). These patients do often come to treatment seeking some kind of relief, but wanting to be made to feel better is not the same thing as having the wish (even if ambivalently held) to resolve one's conflicts. What makes them unable to develop transferential relations in an analysis is the deformed nature of their attachments to the object world, in which they display the ability for perfectly adequate object attention without any equivalent capacity for object love. In severe form, people with a narcissistic character disorder are capable of only shallow, rather empty relationships that may, at times, superficially mimic the depth and richness one ordinarily sees in interpersonal life, but without the extent of relatedness and empathic resonance that ordinarily is an intrinsic element in human relationships.

These patients are often the children of shallow, essentially cold, self-absorbed parents who do sometimes idealize their child, but usually only as an extension of some grandiose or exhibitionistic need of their own. In the treatment situation these patients are capable of idealizing the therapist in exactly the same way that their parents may have idealized them: as a mirror of what they wish to be. Most commonly these patients have been able to achieve better self–object differentiation than have borderline patients, because they have different kinds of parental deficits in their histories, with the result that they often have stronger and more well-organized egos. Thus, despite their shallow capacity for relatedness, they are often able to achieve excellent life situations which incorporate a high degree of intellectual and organizational success and satisfaction. They function best in individual and social situations that make few demands on personal warmth and investment, but in intimate relationships they cannot get beyond the exploitive, manipulating use of others. Kernberg[23] uses an evocative metaphor in his description of the typically extractive nature of the narcissistic patient's object relationships. He writes, "A narcissistic patient experiences his relationships with other people as being purely exploitative, as if he were 'squeezing a lemon and then dropping the remains.'"[24] Except as a response to frustration, they are less prone to massive

---

[23]O. F. Kernberg, "Factors in the Treatment of Narcissistic Personalities," *Journal of the American Psychoanalytic Association,* vol. 18 (1970) p. 57.

[24]One may disagree with Kernberg about whether the patient *experiences* his relationships with other people in this way, because to experience the relationship in *that* way implies that the narcissist actually

regression and to diffusion of self-experience than are borderline patients. However, when frustrated, in life or in their therapy, their expressions of oral-sadistic and anal-sadistic rage can be most extreme, often matching the most profound rages of the borderline patient. Not having had any experience in mastering the depressive struggles that attend object loss, in the sense that they tend to discard disappointing objects, they are prone either to warding off depressive affects entirely or to severe, self-destructive depressions.

Severely narcissistic patients are usually considered to be untreatable in the psychoanalytic method, given this type of character pathology. Even less profoundly disturbed narcissists frequently have difficulties in analysis, because they often have an inability to experience the *"as-if*ness" of the situation: they are unable to experience the analyst or the analysis as anything but "real." Their expectations of gratification are concrete and their ability to experience the treatment is limited to the "here and now." One such patient insisted on the "right" to use the therapist's telephone in order to cancel theater tickets for later that evening (so that, she thought, she would not be charged for them) and was entirely unable to consider the clearly transferential nature of her demand – or even that such an event could have a nature other than the one it had in "reality" for her. A different patient could not understand why the therapist would not see him at no fee, or at a suspended fee, so that the patient could make a business investment with the money that was "sure to be a killing" and a "once-in-a-lifetime opportunity." The patient's frustration was so great that he furiously terminated the treatment. Narcissistic characters are also thought by some to be untreatable in *any* type of therapy. However, most analysts seem to feel that because no therapy that currently exists seems of any particular use to them, they should be seen, as a *heroic measure,* in psychoanalysis. Their reasoning (with which one can disagree) is that if any method of treatment has the potential to be of help, it is *probably* psychoanalysis, and that these extremely narcissistically disturbed patients should at least be offered something. Others feel that they can frequently, although certainly not always, be helped by supportive techniques that improve their frustration tolerance, provide them with better defenses against impulsivity and depression, and tone down their exploitativeness with others.[25]

---

has some awareness of his predatory intentions in his dealings with others. It might be better to suggest that the narcissist only permits *that kind* of experience with others, even though he may often be entirely unaware of the extent of his parasitic wishes.

But the point that Kernberg is making with this marvelous metaphor, about how value is placed on others in direct relation to their capacity to gratify whatever instinctual longing may be paramount *at the moment* in the life of the narcissist, and, the ease with which the narcissist "disposes" of people when the object is no longer necessary to meet any pressing instinctual needs, is descriptively very accurate.

[25]Kohut's school of Self psychology conceptualizes narcissistic disturbance very differently, and the approach to treatment is also very different. To offer a very brief comparison (that does not do his approach justice): Kohut viewed narcissism and self-experience as operating according to an entirely separate line of development from that of object-libidinal strivings; whereas, in the traditional analytic model, narcissistic development grows directly from the matrix and vicissitudes of object-libidinal investments. In this way, Kohut raised the concept of narcissism to that of a psychic structure equivalent

to, and as highly organized as, the "traditional" structures—the id, the ego, and the superego. The Freudian approach uses a "conflict model" of development, whereas Kohut had a view more in line with a self-actualization model, in which progressive development is virtually automatic as long as certain conditions are met: in this case, parenting that supports the early expansive grandiosity of the child, that mirrors the child's self-investments, and that smoothly supplies, externally, the internal psychic functions that the child, through immaturity, has not yet developed. Kohut's model is one of arrested development, whereas the Freudian model is geared to the concept of fixations influenced by ensuing pathological defenses and fantasy-organized distortions of object relations.

Using a developmental arrest model, the concept of recapitulating fixated object relations loses its centrality as the linchpin of the treatment. It does not matter whether the patient's object relations are shallow or rich, nor is it critical that the patient's approach to the treatment is basically manipulative. As an alternative to the classical model, Self psychology has developed a reparative model of empathic relatedness, emphasizing the therapist's ability to permit the patient to experience his narcissism in precisely the ways that his parents could not (Kohut's *self-object, mirroring*, and *idealizing* transferences). The assumption is that an intersubjective sharing of the patient's and analyst's experience will emerge, restoring an equivalent empathic relatedness to that which should have existed in the patient's childhood, which then enables the patient to continue with the development that was arrested in the past.

The Freudian model has not accepted the idea that pathological narcissism in an adult mirrors the stage of narcissism in which the patient was arrested as a child, arguing instead that disruptions in normal development result in disturbed structural operations, disturbed object relations, disturbed identification processes, and deformations of narcissistic functioning in adults which *do not* parallel the quality of childhood narcissism. "Classical" analysts view these patients as having a characterological organization that is too disordered for them to be able to make effective use of analytic treatment, which, they all agree, has clear limitations in this area: it was never assumed to be capable of dealing with every kind of psychopathology. Self psychologists see narcissistic patients as eminently treatable since, given the right conditions in the treatment (i.e., an empathic therapist who can permit the patient's self–object, mirroring, and idealizing transferences), the normal progression of narcissistic development will be restarted.

11

Interpretation

The Concept of Interpretation

Interpretation has been previously touched upon, sometimes in some depth, under other subject headings. Indeed, a number of key issues could not have been properly conceptualized without having confronted the critical and often central role played in them by interpretation. To cite just a few examples: it was necessary to look at interpretation in discussing what is considered curative in analysis; in considering the problem of "wild analysis"; in reviewing the tools that classical analysis uses, compared with the tools used by other, nonclassical and anticlassical, analytic approaches; in examining the working-through process; in identifying numerous subtle components of the analytic object relationship; in contemplating the role of the integrative and synthetic functions of the ego in psychoanalysis; in studying the nature, development, and management of the transference neurosis; in thinking about the management of analytic regressions; and in surveying the differences in working with neurotic patients versus patients who are character-disordered. There are still a number of significant points about interpretation to be made, however, despite its having been approached from so many different vantage points in previous chapters.

In the popular mythology about psychoanalysis, the *New Yorker* cartoon version, the reverent patient listens breathlessly as the analyst brilliantly pieces together the jigsaw puzzle of his history, his symptoms, his conflicts, his defenses, and, most especially, the current state of his unconscious. Much like a mendicant at the feet of a guru, or a child in the power of a benevolent (but omniscient and omnipotent) parent, the patient gratefully accepts the analyst's interpretations, which then revolutionize the patient's life. The analyst makes his interpretation, the patient sees "The Truth" in it, and the patient is freed from his conflicts and symptoms, his cured self like a phoenix rising from the ashes.

This caricature of what is like to be in a psychoanalysis is very widespread. Many therapists betray their version of this fantasy when they conceive of interpretations as a kind of magic bullet, a special communication about deep unconscious motives that the therapist bestows on the ignorant, but willing, patient. In this sketch it should be noted that the analyst is interpreting the patient's *unconscious* (about which, by definition, the patient can know nothing by himself) rather than interpreting material that has entered *preconsciousness* (about which the patient at least knows *something*, albeit not everything, or as much as he will ultimately need to know). Interpretation of the unconscious involves patient participation only by acquiescence. The patient, having to take the analyst's word about the truth of the interpretation because by definition he cannot know about his own unconscious directly, can only agree or disagree. What is wrong with this lampoon, and what makes it unlike the real experience of a psychoanalysis, is that it is not a collaborative endeavor to understand the patient (with both participants actively engaged in trying to make sense out of the patient's experiences, conflicts, and inner life).[1]

In actuality, the interpretive process is a hesitating, partial, limited, tentative testing-out of both parties' speculations about what might be going on with the patient and unconsciously influencing him. It involves a great deal of back-and-forth hypothesizing based on little, and at times almost inconspicuous, clues picked up sometimes by the patient and sometimes by the analyst. These hypotheses are subjected to considerable further scrutiny. The jigsaw puzzle only gradually emerges to both patient and analyst after laborious examination of the "pieces," which move slowly and in a disorganized fashion from unconsciousness into preconsciousness and then finally (when the interpretations have some validity) into consciousness. Even then, the knowledge alone, the so-called Aha! experience of an insight, is insufficient to make a difference in the patient's functioning. At best, the patient now knows something that he did not know before. But that, unfortunately, is not the same thing as knowing how to put this new knowledge into practice. This has been discussed in detail in Chapter 7, the section devoted to the relationship between insight and working through.

This leads us to another myth about interpretation, namely, that interpretation is directed at symptoms, conflicts, and defenses. In Chapters 8, 9, and 10 we have discussed at length the "classical" position in which interpretation is directed at symptoms, conflicts and defenses specifically as they become expressed in resistances and as they emerge in the transference (or, more precisely, in the transference neurosis), and not as they make their appearance in any other way. When we do comment on the appearance of symptoms, conflicts, and defenses in other contexts, we often regard those interventions as either clarifications or as preparatory comments that will set the stage for a later interpretation.

Preparatory Comments and Clarifications

In one respect, the distinction that something is a *preparatory comment* or a *clarification* rather than being an *interpretation* needs further elucidation. This distinction is not

---

[1]Another thing that is regularly caricatured is the notion that all the patient and the analyst talk about is the past when, in fact, analysis concerns itself with interpretations of unconscious conflict as it is manifested in the present (transference).

being directed at the content of what the analyst has to say about underlying issues for the patient but, rather, at the context in which the communication is made. Setting aside for the moment the question of when and in what circumstances it is given, how should we define an interpretation? In the broadest sense, an interpretation may be anything the analyst says that gives the patient more knowledge about himself. Putting the communication of the analyst into a context of how, when, and in what circumstances it is given is what makes the communication psychoanalytic or psychotherapeutic, and not what defines it as an interpretation. Defined in this way, clarifications and preparatory comments become an intrinsic part of the interpretive process, which ultimately achieves its highest focus in the examination of resistance and the transference neurosis. In this way we can avoid a false distinction in which clarifications, preparatory comments, and everything else that sets the stage for genetic transference interpretations are treated as if they are not part of the interpretive process, as if they are unnecessary, and as if they make no valuable contributions to the final form in which interpretations are made.

Grounding the Interpretation for the Patient

What else can be said about interpretation? Unlike the cartoon figure that opened this chapter, the analytic situation is not one where the analyst knows exactly what is going on with the patient. The analyst does not have a complex, complete picture of the patient's unconscious and the patient's dynamics, the patient's object relations and conflicts. The analyst does not know it all in advance, as it were, simply waiting for the right time to tell the patient about what he (the analyst) has known virtually from the beginning. The analyst listens to the patient for a very long time, slowly building up a fragmentary and partial understanding of the patient's inner life, and in a parallel process the patient is doing the same thing: analyst and patient, together – in response to the patient's verbal productions, the analyst's interpretations, and the material that arises as a result of the analyst's interpretations – learn more about what is meaningful for the patient as the analysis proceeds. The patient associates, resists, makes transference demands, intensifies them, and so on, and the analyst interprets; the analyst's interpretation is based on what the patient has said and done at that very moment, in combination with what the analyst knows about the patient from everything that has passed through the analysis up until that point. Even when the analyst is drawing on material from the history of the analysis, as it were, the interpretation is always grounded in the medium of what was both contained and expressed in the patient's thoughts and feelings, words and behavior. Naturally, only a little can be known at any given time; unlike the popular stereotype, the patient is not an "open book" to the analyst. What actually happens in this slow process of discovery is that the analyst begins to recognize that some of the patient's thoughts, feelings, associations, and behavior can be clustered together; that is, that they have a common underlying unconscious or preconscious thread. The analyst attempts to show the patient how these things, which the patient experiences and presents as if they were unrelated, actually seem to be tied together; how they are connected through some common elements, for example, a wish, a fear, a conflict, a defensive purpose, a way of organizing memory, or the interplay of past and present.

Multiple Levels of Meaning

Communications to the patient are about a combination of observable events and the underlying processes that are not consciously recognized, and a repercussion of this is that the communication itself is not entirely regulated by secondary-process organization. In consequence, what is on the surface of the interpretation is not the only thing that makes an impact; because it is an event that extends beyond the secondary process, the interpretation's impact also derives from its potential to stimulate linkages between different levels of mental functioning. Simultaneous with the conscious and cognitive significance of what the analyst has had to say, this factor in the process of interpretation adds the possibility of reawakening the flow of primary-process connections in the patient's mind, which then brings more material into preconsciousness and into the associative matrix. (It should be noted that this is not the equivalent of recall, and this should not be confused with a description of how, in general terms, recall takes place: this is a description of conditions that may make recall *possible*.) Obviously, for a very long time, what is recalled, presented, and interpreted is fragmentary and incomplete, so that it is only quite late in the analysis that all the pieces come together in the kind of fully articulated, genetic (i.e., the reciprocal relationship between the past and the present) and dynamic (i.e., the origin of ego and superego constituents and id derivatives) transference interpretation that provides the whole picture.[2]

This accessibility to multiple levels of the mind is one of the meanings of what a number of analysts (beginning with Hartmann) have referred to as the "multiple appeal" of interpretation. It not only uses things that the patient knows about himself to help him see some of the things he that does *not* know about himself, it also uses the known material to help bring into a new level of awareness yet additional things that he does not know about himself. The various planes of mental functioning that interpretation taps into is not limited only to an examination of the reciprocal relationship between the past and present, as we provide when we make genetic interpretations; no matter what the subject matter of the interpretation, and no matter at what level of functioning it is directed, it also simultaneously taps into relationships between conflicts and defenses, wishes and fears, object relations,

---

[2]The idea of getting the whole picture is, of course, a metaphor. No interpretation or reconstruction can examine every element of a conflict and every attribute of the unconscious. One is not left at the end of an analysis with no conflicts and no unconscious: this will be discussed in more detail in the chapter on termination (Chapter 13).

identifications, tensions between the psychic structures, fantasy organization, and so on.

A patient began to speak of his dislike for lying on the couch instead of being in a "face-to-face kind of therapy." He expressed his concern that, not being able to see the analyst, he could not tell whether the analyst was really paying any attention to him. Perhaps the analyst was taking notes instead of listening to him, or reading a book. Perhaps the analyst was daydreaming, looking out the window, or even asleep. How would he ever know? He said that he did not like the feeling that this brought up in him, the feeling that he was out of control. He went on to say more, about how he was feeling a lot of anxiety, and feeling that he was getting more and more out of control; he hated losing control of himself, which he speculated was caused by his lying on the couch instead of being able to sit up in a chair, facing the analyst.

The analyst made the observation that his complaint sounded like he was more afraid of not being able to control the analyst than of losing control of himself. The analyst's comment prompted an immediate conscious recognition of what the patient had previously only been preconsciously aware of and, next, a thought about his father, who was a manipulative and untrustworthy man, a liar and perhaps even a bit of a psychopath. The thought about his father, that he was a liar and unable to be trusted, brought up a series of memories concerning disappointments and betrayals with him. These, in turn, stimulated memories of his great admiration for his father in early childhood, how much he adored him and wanted to be like him, how much he loved his father and wanted to be loved back by him.

The patient then commented on the choice of words he used: that he wanted to be loved *back* by his father. He thought that it would have been grammatically more proper to have said that he wanted to be loved *in return*. Initially this led to some ideas about how his father was untrustworthy, and he used the figure of speech that he never felt able to *turn his back* on his father, without worrying about what would happen. He continued for some time in this vein and then commented that, while speaking, a calypso song was running through his head: the words were "Back-to-back, belly-to-belly, I don't give a damn, I don't give a helly," and he became intensely anxious as he repeated them out loud. He cast about for a few moments, trying to ascertain what he was feeling anxious about, without much luck, and in the process his anxiety subsided. He thought about a trip to Jamaica he had taken the previous month, recalling the pleasure of the warmth, swimming in the sea, the contagiously exhilarating music, and eating fresh tropical fruit.

The patient had taken a midwinter vacation, which was outside the regularly scheduled vacation time that he and the analyst had agreed upon. The patient now remembered how indignant he had felt when, after telling the analyst that he had made plans to take that vacation, the analyst had suggested that he had finalized all the arrangements to take time off without even mentioning his plan to take a vacation (rather than having talked with the analyst about the wish to go on vacation), in order to prevent the analyst from being able to interfere with his desires. The patient remembered that conversation, now, with all the anger and emotional vividness it had for him at the time, reiterating, as he had done then, his feeling that the analyst resented any good time he might have, and his conviction that the analyst had a vested interest in trying to limit the patient's fun "in the name of what was good for [him]." The patient then remarked that his wish to control the analyst was not so unreasonable after all; if the analyst was going to oppose the patient's needs, and look after his own (unspecified) needs instead, the patient had every right to protect himself. The patient said that he felt especially bitter about this "because of the kind of father that I had, who had a narcissistic, self-indulgent streak a mile wide," and the patient thought that it was particularly ironic that he should end up with an analyst who had that problem, too.

An incident from childhood entered the patient's mind, from when he was about 5 years old. He and his mother were playing at dancing together: she was holding him straddled on her hip as she swept around the room with him, laughing, and spinning in circles, in time to the music. He was very excited. Father came in and, seeing this, said to him, "No, no, that's not the way to do it. That's the way a baby would do it. Let me show you how to dance like a grown-up," and pulled him out of his mother's arms. Father now swept up mother and danced around the room with her for what seemed like forever, as the patient peevishly watched. Finally, being unable to restrain himself, the patient began to yell, "My turn now! My turn now!", and began to shove his way in between them. Father pushed him aside, telling him to "hold his water" until the song was over. The patient wanted to resume the dancing game with his mother when his turn came, but his father insisted that he should learn how to dance "for real," and proceeded to give him a "dancing lesson" on the spot. Father took the lead, placing the patient in the female partner's position, and made as if to teach him the steps of the dance. The patient quickly became extremely frustrated and began to cry. Father, "misinterpreting" the reason why his son was crying, said to him, "Okay, okay, if you can't remember the steps, watch me," and began to dance once again with the patient's mother, to "illustrate." The patient remarked at this point in the telling, rather archly, "I wish *he* would have taken a vacation."

One can see from this example how much was liberated (and at how many different levels) in response to the analyst's interpretation of the patient's wish to control the analyst rather than himself: initially, we may recall, the patient only expressed the fear of losing control of himself in the presence of the analyst. It would seem, from his original disturbance and from his associative response to the analyst's comment, that his fear of losing control reflects concerns about managing incestuous wishes toward his mother, and concerns about managing both aggressive and homosexual wishes toward his competitive father. In the transference he seems to fear that the analyst, by sleeping, through inattention, or by having daydreams, will "take a vacation" from him as his mother did (when she accepted his father without protest as her dancing partner instead of the patient). A different aspect of the transference suggests the wish that the analyst *should* "take a vacation" from the patient, the way he wished, at the end of telling his story, that his father would. Along similar lines, this "dancing" story clearly explains why the patient, wishing to have a pleasurable experience, maneuvered the therapeutic situation so that the analyst (in the transferential role of his father) would not have an opportunity to frustrate him.

Interpretation and Compromise Formations

Without attempting to illustrate everything about this fragment of a session, one can readily see that the interpretation touched on, and helped bring to the surface, many levels of the patient's conflicts, object relations, drives and defenses, and multiple transference meanings. One also can see how the analyst interpreted something that the patient already knew about, or had the potential to readily know about, as the point of leverage for getting to material that the patient had no way of consciously knowing about (for example, the oedipal nature of his "belly-to-belly, don't give a damn, don't give a helly" dance with his mother; his "back-to-back, belly-to-belly"/"hold your water," homosexual attachment to his father; his oedipal rage and aggressiveness toward his father; and so on). In his interpretation the analyst used the words and imagery of the patient to make his interpretation, rather than similar words and images that could have made the same point to the patient. The analyst could, for example, have said that the patient wanted to take charge of the analyst, or that the patient wanted to have power over the analyst, or that the patient wanted to exercise dominance over the analyst, or that the patient wanted to be able to manage, oversee, regulate, command, subdue, or corner the analyst. However, the patient kept repeating the idea of "control," and so that is what the analyst used in his interpretation.

Using the patient's words and ideas in an interpretation is important for a number of reasons. Most importantly, they have the power of recognizability to the patient. The patient has used them first; thus, when the analyst also uses them and places them in a slightly different framework (the interpretive reorganization), the link between the two contexts is identifiable through the language and imagery that they have in common. This makes the new idea, that is, what the interpretation is about, more easily recognized by the patient and thus more acceptable to the patient. Using words and images different from the ones first used by the patient may be conceptually acceptable to the patient on a purely intellectual level, but it lends an interpretation a foreign or alien quality which makes the content of the interpretation much harder to recognize and to admit into consciousness. Beyond the question of recognizability, however, there is also the consideration that the patient has not chosen his words and imagery at random. They are *compromise formations* that have preconscious importance and are not simply secondary-process modes of story telling in which the choice of words and images is arbitrary and subordinate to the "story." As compromise formations, the patient's words and images also carry with them vestiges of the mental forces that led to the formation of the compromise.

Using the same words and images as the patient, because they are part of the patient's compromise formation, has an interpretive potential that equally accurate, but different, words and images do not. The importance of this in the interpretation process cannot be overemphasized: the use of the patient's choice of words and images has the power to promote a rearrangement of his thoughts and feelings in the compromise formation, and such a reorganization of the thoughts and feelings of the patient is what leads to recall and to insight.

Timing and Depth of Interpretations

This vignette also showed another guiding principle of interpretation, that is, careful attention to the timing and the depth of the interpretation: this is what is meant by *analytic tact*. Because interpretations are based not only on events of the moment in an analysis, but also on everything that has previously occurred as well, the analyst may have been in a position to have known that the patient was alluding to oedipal matters when the patient expressed his suspicions about what the analyst might be doing behind his back. If the analyst had said, *"You are worried about what I am doing behind your back, what I might be depriving you of, and about what pleasures I might be having that you wish to have, in the same way that as a little boy you worried about what went on between your mother and father, behind your back, when you went to sleep,"* he would have been correct. The greatest likelihood, however, is that such an interpretation, in spite of being correct, would have fallen on deaf ears. Interpretations are always given in drips and drabs, as it were, slowly but surely leading to deeper insights and to the liberation of more deeply defended contents. The patient integrates a greater awareness about himself only gradually, and this process is very different from the way one intellectually learns things. Deep interpretations (even those that do not make the patient more guarded) may have a profound emotional resonance for the patient but still be of no real value. Profound emotional resonance is important in interpretation, but the patient has to be able to do more with the information than just resonate.

Both thoughts and feelings are defended against when they are associated with conflict, and the process of unraveling the patient's material also has to take into account the fact that most of the patient's defenses are unconscious, too. Our approach to resistance gives us a good idea of how interpretation is doled out over time, so that the patient can integrate the experience in a new way. At the sign of a resistance, say in a situation where a patient who usually has many associations to dreams reports a dream and then falls silent, the analyst does not initially communicate his understanding of the underlying meaning of the dream or of the motive of the resistance to the patient. The first step is taken just to alert the patient to the fact that a resistance is taking place. One would not suggest the nature of the underlying wishes that are being warded off by the patient's silence, nor would one even suggest that the patient's silence is a way of defending against the emergence of conflictual material: one first observes to the patient that he is in resistance. Naturally, this is not done in an intellectual way or in a way that implies, conceptually, that the patient is resisting: if the object is to identify that a resistive process is underway, one might simply say to the patient, "It is very unlike you to have absolutely no responses to a dream," which then, in a nonchallenging way, alerts the patient to the fact that something unusual has happened and gives him a chance to become curious about his behavior. In gradual steps the patient actively learns that he is being defensive, having been unconscious of his defensiveness (in his lack of associations to the dream) before this was pointed out to him. The patient might at first demur but will usually be able to recognize that what the analyst has said is true, and that his silence is unlike his usual response to dreams. When he wonders why he might be behaving defensively, he will begin an associative process anew, now about his resistance instead of his dream (but still, unconsciously, related to his dream since the resistance is in response to the dream). In this way the examination of the patient's resistance leads to an examination of his defenses. And the examination of conscious defenses leads to the examination of unconscious defenses, as material moves upward into preconsciousness in the process. As defenses are examined in this way, the conflicts that they are associated with begin to become more apparent. Again, conflicts, like defenses, move upward into consciousness as the patient verbalizes more of what is going on. As conflicts become more conscious, the underlying wishes about which the patient is in conflict finally have a chance to surface into consciousness. Through this sequence of analyzing resistance before defense, defense before conflict, and conflict before impulse, the patient has an opportunity to integrate the material rather than just learn about it.

This model, which is so clear in relation to the analysis of resistance, is the same model that is used with all interpretation. This slow and careful interpretive work is necessary because even where the meaning of a patient's production is apparent to the analyst, in fact even where the meaning is so obviously clear that it seems impossible that the patient does not see it, it may not be at all apparent to the patient. Susan Isaacs relates a charming story about how the meaning of something can be completely obvious to the listener but totally obscure to the speaker: ". . . a boy of five years of age, one day at a meal, addressing no one in particular, said in a very subdued voice, 'I don't like dreams: they are horrid things'; and then, after a pause, 'and another thing—I don't have any.' " She goes on to say, "that every hearer, save the most obtuse, appreciates perceptually that in his denial the boy actually makes a positive statement, namely, that his dreams are so horrid that he wishes he did not have any, and cannot bear to remember them. The ordinary hearer does not set out his awareness of this in conceptual terms, as analysts have learnt to do, using it as a means of generalizing the mechanism of denial; but everybody perceives the immediate concrete meaning."[3] Her point was to demonstrate that the analysts

---

[3] S. S. Isaacs, "Criteria for Interpretation," *International Journal of Psycho-Analysis*, vol. 20 (1939), p. 153.

interpret the underlying meaning of a patient's statement on the basis of reasonable assumptions, but her story also fits our purposes perfectly.

It sometimes seems rather remarkable that patients will do and say things that seem to have such obvious meanings, and nevertheless appear to be quite oblivious to the import of what they have said and done. Often the double meaning in a pun, or what is said in a slip of the tongue, is so apparent that it is difficult to believe the patient when he claims not to have heard or to have understood the meaning of what he has said. Denial or reversal may sometimes be so transparent that it seems impossible that the patient believes it himself. It takes considerable experience to appreciate how unconscious (descriptively unconscious, even though not dynamically unconscious) these preconscious eruptions are for patients, because they often seem so glaringly and unmistakably apparent to the observer. It is always necessary to take fully into account the patient's unawareness of what he has just said or done, otherwise the interpretation becomes a confrontation, which may be embarrassing for the patient and which might make him reactively defensive. The patient is quite serious in not understanding his own productions – not because he is stupid but because he is motivated not to see or to understand what he has just said or done.

Accuracy of Interpretations

A related problem, on the other end of the continuum, is that of making an interpretation that is too speculative, too based on inferences that may be taken in too many ways. While keeping ourselves open to the alternate meanings of things, we need to be careful not to indulge in flights of fancy in our interpretive efforts. Isaacs's point was that our interpretation (to ourselves and to the patient) must be based on reasonable assumptions. It is reasonable to say that the little boy found his dreams so horrid that he wished he didn't have any, based on what he said. It is true that this is not what he said; he said that he did not have any dreams, but the meaning fairly jumps out at us in spite of his having said that he does not have any dreams. It would not be reasonable to have interpreted what he said to mean that he was expressing a reaction-formation against anal pleasure, and that the dreams he claimed he didn't have really stood for stools that he was claiming he did not have (as a measure, in reversal, of his anal erotic excitement when moving his bowels). It is certainly possible that an anal reaction-formation might be expressed exactly in this way, but we would have no way of knowing that, based on what we know about this little boy. If we had known, from previous work with him, that this was a major conflict for him, and if we had a lot of past experience with statements of his that, upon analysis, had turned out to have this underlying meaning, we might then be justified in making that interpretation of his statement. Or if he went on to say that he thought dreams were horrid because they were dirty, messy things; that mucking around with them only got people into trouble; and that dreams were a royal pain in the ass, then we might have a case for suggesting that he was talking about his stools using the metaphor of dreams. Interpretations need to be well grounded in what we know about the patient's transformational processes – that is, in what we know about the patient's preferred methods of disguise and defense. They should be well established by what we know about the patient's dynamics, and in what we know about the patient's conflicts. They should follow logically from the information we have on hand, and they need to be rooted in the patient's personal reality.[4]

Affects and Interpretations

The extent of a patient's emotionality, or of warded-off affectivity, is not insignificant for the work of interpretation. Patients have a particular receptivity to interpretation when their associations are richly based in affect. Emotionally shallow presentations are not uncommon and they are not impossible to understand or to interpret, but emotional expressivity is very helpful in bringing material to the surface of consciousness. Even in the case of warded-off emotions, we still have a special entry to unconscious processes. Affect gives the analyst an exceptional approach to the underlying meaning of things. This is because emotions are complex amalgamations of impulse derivatives fused with ego operations. Emotions give us access to paths of mental functioning that are leading both in the direction of the ego and in the direction of the id, simultaneously.

Interpretation, like emotions, are at their most powerful in states of immediacy. When interpretations are too far removed from a current conflict for the patient, the interpretation has hardly any effect. On the other hand, interpretations that are given during an affect storm are equally ineffective. The objective is to try to reach a balance, in which the patient's emotionality works for the interpretation and not against it: the object is to make interpretations that are emotionally alive for the patient, while cautiously titrating interpretation when the patient is too infused with affect.[5]

The importance of the emotional climate in which interpretation occurs is clear; the simultaneous access to both the ego and the id, the hallmark of the examination of emotions, is crucial in interpretation. But, the role of emotions is not the only important variable in what makes interpretation the mainstay of analytic intervention. The role of speech and language in relation to affect, and the special functions they serve in the autonomous, integrative, and synthetic functions of the ego, is

---

[4]At this point we are making no distinctions between the preparatory interpretation of contents, the preparatory interpretation of mechanisms, and genetically organized transference interpretations.

[5]This is not the same thing as what Fred Pine means when he speaks of "striking when the iron is cold." He is referring to working with particularly disturbed patients whose affects are frequently so intense that feeling states become massively disorganizing, for whom the immediacy of interpretation is disruptive, and who need an adequate distance from their emotions before an interpretation can be internalized without having decompensating effects.

another, perhaps even more critical, factor in interpretation. Loewenstein (1956) once described verbalization in psychoanalysis in a vivid kind of architectural metaphor: ". . . language performs the function of a kind of scaffolding that permits conscious thought to be built inside . . . , a kind of scaffolding which the patient's thoughts can gradually fill" (p. 465).

The Roles of Verbalization and Verbal Symbolization

As the patient says aloud the things that are going though his mind, he also hears himself speaking; the special importance that we attribute to the patient speaking out loud, so that he can actually hear himself, is based on strong clinical findings which suggest that inner experience captures a greater sense of vividness, and acquires a greater sense of reality, when it is spoken aloud, and when he patient hears himself, than when it is only being thought of by the patient, or silently felt. Things that the patient previously only thought to himself seem to be very different, qualitatively and quantitatively, after they have been said aloud; they do not just have a different impact on the patient, they become as if they were actually something else.

Every time a patient, behaving protectively, thinks or feels something to himself and decides not to say it out loud, we see a clear example of this. Only when he finally speaks what he has been thinking and feeling, and hears these things spoken of by himself, does he feel that they have become completely real: and at such times, it then may feel, *only on account of finally having been said aloud,* both real and – as such – really dangerous. In regard to how *emotions* can be felt to be made more dangerous through verbal expression: patients sometimes feel that if they say out loud what they are feeling, they will be swept up and swept away by their feelings, carried over the edge by them, as it were, in a way that would not happen if they just would keep their feelings quietly to themselves.

Let us consider another danger, one that some patients fear will be liberated by the verbalization of *thought.* When a patient does not tell the analyst about a conscious thought and is hiding his thought specifically because he believes that the analyst will disapprove of it, he is, in this way, asserting that there is a greater reality to that which is spoken aloud than there is to that which has only been thought. That which is not said is *as if it were not thought,* even though the patient *has* thought it and *knows* that he has thought it. By restricting himself to silent thinking, the patient hopes he is going to be able to avoid certain facets of his superego; however, those very superego aspects that he expects to be able to avoid by silent thinking are believed to be inescapable, if the thought is spoken to the analyst. *That is the point, after all, of not saying what he knows he is thinking.* The patient experiences the analyst, once his unacceptable thought has been said out loud, as if the analyst were a more powerful, external superego than is the patient's internalized superego. The unacceptable thought, after being spoken, has become more real and more powerful, and the external superego's response (in the fantasied form of the analyst, who the patient now has to protect himself against) is inescapable.

To suggest just a few other examples; often an angry or accusatory thought or aggressive feeling toward a love object is not said out loud, because saying it feels like a greater defilement and violation of the love object than does merely thinking it. Also, we see many instances when patients keep silent because they feel that something that they say out loud cannot be undone as easily as something that they have only thought.

The resistance against putting feelings and thoughts into words can be very complex. An alternative problem to what has been said thus far is the case where patients feel that if something has not been said, it can be held onto and preserved; it is not uncommon for patients to safeguard certain conscious and unconscious gratifications that would be interrupted if their thoughts and feelings were to be "shared" with the analyst. Patients sometimes have extremely satisfying fantasies; these are dreams and wishes that the patient feels will remain intact only if they are afforded the opportunity for silent gratification. Speaking about them in the analysis destroys them, it breaks the spell, and causes the patient to have to analyze them – thus, lose them – in place of being able to experience them.

The power of speech in psychoanalysis (and the specifically verbal aspects of interpretation) is readily observable when we see how internal realities take on the character of external realities once they have been spoken about in the analysis; thus the reorganization of inner experience, so that it becomes more "real" through being spoken, is one aspect of the importance of verbalization. Another consideration is that when patients are consciously aware of thoughts and feelings that they have not spoken about, they are maintaining a sense of isolation, reticence, and secrecy that serves to exclude the analyst. Once inner thoughts and feelings have been communicated, however, they are transformed into a social reality of which the analyst is an intrinsic part. The patient's thoughts and feelings, when spoken, take on the quality of an external object that now exists between the patient and the analyst. The words of the patient can, and actually must, become a substitute for solitary psychological action; the psychological form of action referred to here, the action that requires a verbal substitute, is in having solitary thoughts and feelings that are being kept isolated from the analysis and cloistered by the patient.[6] Patients who keep what they are thinking to themselves are not particularly expressing an obstruction between unconsciousness and preconsciousness, or a limitation between preconsciousness and consciousness, as one might think: they are expressing

---

[6]This is one of the senses of what Nunberg (1931) meant when he suggested that speech is a substitute for action; and in this context we might wish to think of talking in psychoanalysis as a form of trial action.

a barrier between conscious thoughts and emotions and their verbalization that, when it is not in the service of specifically behavioral acting out, is still usually designed to permit sustained psychological action rather than reflective analytic insight.

We are well aware of the relationship between verbalization by the patient, acting out, and the analyst's verbal interpretations. When a patient acts out, he is gratifying inner needs that are not being brought into the analysis. It is not until he gives up the commitment to action and begins to verbally express himself, in the analysis, that there is any possibility for him to understand the underlying meaning of what is going on psychologically. (This has been discussed in considerable detail in Chapter 10.) Insight is not possible, motivations cannot become known, without the patient's verbalizations. Correspondingly, the analyst's verbalizations offer the patient more than just an explanation of why he might be functioning in a particular way. The analyst's interpretations offer the patient insight into new aspects of his subjective psychic reality, a reality which the patient has always treated as if it were mainly external, objective, and unchangeable. The patient's communications – when he talks to the analyst instead of acting out – carry with them, in addition to the contents of the patient's thoughts, a wide array of emotions which find some partial discharge in the very act of speaking, and which find some partial discharge in response to the patient having chosen to speak the thoughts and feelings out loud. Verbalizations that lack adequate symbolization, for example, verbalizations that have idiosyncratic meanings (as in word salad, or as one finds in a thought disorder, or in clang associations), verbalizations that are designed mainly to discharge affects (where, for example, the patient curses at the analyst or attempts to humiliate him with what he is saying), and verbalizations in which the purpose of communication is essentially absent (as one frequently finds in narcissistic transferences, where the patient speaks *at* the analyst but not *to* him), do not have the same potential for the development of insight. In the slow building up of insight which is not, as has been pointed out, a notably conceptual or intellectual undertaking, it may well be that the duality that occurs in verbalization – thoughts combined with emotional discharge processes – is a necessary a factor in the communication of the patient. Where acting out is concerned, inhibition of action is possible before insight is achieved (that is, the patient can decide not to do whatever he was doing without having any insight into why he was doing it, or why he stopped), but verbalizations with these dual characteristics are required before insight, rather than inhibition, can be accepted by the patient as a substitution for action.

Another way of looking at the emotional discharge process that occurs as a result of having spoken is to say that speech in analysis tends to bind affects in the patient. Verbalization is a mode, one of our primary modes, of symbolization. Verbal symbolization transforms primitive, previously inchoate affecto-sensory-motor experiences into manageable thoughts and feelings, and into social realities as these internal events are communicatively expressed between people.[7] The symbolized transformations of primitive affective states via the use of language affects more than just the patient's thinking processes, it renovates the patient's experiencing processes. Verbalization has an equivalently transforming effect on the analytic process, in the following sense: much of the neutralized energy that the ego uses in the development of insight derives directly from the binding of the patient's affects by words.

Both the patient's speaking in the analytic process and the analyst's speaking in the analytic process are in a kind of intermediary position between action and emotional expression. It is not only the speech of the patient that has this characteristic, even though the patient's use of verbalization has different effects on his ego than do the verbalizations of the analyst. The dynamic changes that occur in an analysis as a result of interpretation may, in large part, be dependent on the unique position of verbalization between action and emotional expression, reaching to many levels of mental operation at the same time.[8] The important benefits of verbalization notwithstanding, there is always a resistance to verbalization, even in patients who are not "acter-outers." This resistance to verbalization is a last-gasp effort on the part of the ego, when all else fails, to keep unconscious material from entering consciousness. Thus we have yet another reason why verbalization is an essential step in the acquisition of analytic insight, and why it cannot be replaced by reparative actions or corrective emotional experiences on the part of the analyst.

The act of verbalization in analysis is important even when the patient's material is at a preverbal level. A better way to put this is that when the patient's conflicts are at a preverbal level, one of the primary aims of the treatment is to enable the patient to put the relevant inner experience into words, so that it can be dealt with by the more advanced areas of the patient's ego. Because the patient's conflict, and even his current way of experiencing that conflict, is connected with mental processes that were organized before the acquisition of language, verbally symbolizing preverbal experience is not just a matter of finding the right words but, rather, of finding how to use words as a means of representing the experience. Verbalization of material

---

[7]In this regard, Loewenstein suggests that speech can subserve certain functions of the superego as it binds social conventions between people. The basic idea is rather straightforward: verbalization of thoughts and emotions leads to socialization between people.

[8]Here we are distinguishing between a mechanism and contents. In our previous discussion of the analyst's need to use the patient's chosen language, we observed the way in which the patient's choice of words and imagery were organized as a compromise formation. We regularly assume that the mind can go in many directions at once and that many more contents of the patient's mind can be reached by staying, interpretively, within the language of the patient's compromise formation. In the present case we are observing a mechanism, rather than a content, that is relevant to interpretation. Here we are observing the way verbalization is a "compromise mechanism," as it were, somewhere between the expression of emotions and action and, as a result of that, also able to go in many mental "directions" at once. An additional meaning of the distinction between contents and mechanisms, perhaps the most common one, is in the difference between the interpretation, respectively, of a fantasy and of a defense.

that has achieved an adequate degree of symbolization (since conflicts encountered after the acquisition of language can coexist, side by side, with preverbal conflicts) becomes very helpful in bringing preverbal experience to consciousness, as well as in reorganizing the preverbal material into verbal form after it has surfaced.

In certain ways, the verbal interchange between the patient and the analyst, particularly when the material is preverbal and the patient is relating more closely to the analyst's affect (or to the analyst's unconscious) than to his words, is reminiscent of some of the auditory features of the earliest mother–child interactions. The baby lies in his mother's arms *(the patient lies on the couch)*, able to see only indistinctly in earliest infancy *(the patient faces away from the analyst and from other non-internal stimuli)*, the mother croons to him, talks baby-talk, sings, sighs, and laughs with delight *(the analyst's sounds, like "umm" or "uh-huh," which are not uncommon, as well as the analyst's comments, questions, and interpretations, provide an aural experience for the patient and are experienced by the patient more in that sensuous way than they are for the specific words and ideas that the analyst is using)*, the patient senses from his mother's body language, her laugh, her tone of voice, how she is feeling and how she feels toward him *(the patient reads the analyst's explicit emotions and unconscious communications, picking up both conscious and unconscious attitudes and affects of the analyst)*. This feature of the analytic experience serves as a prod (a nudge, as it were), to sensational, affective, and motoric memory in the patient, bringing preverbal conflict material into preconsciousness where it can be transformed from affecto-sensory-motor events, and from thing presentations,[9] into word presentations and ideas, which are formally assigned word-cathexes by the patient's ego, which now, because it is an adult ego, *does* have the capacity to symbolize that which it was too immature to symbolize in the distant past of infancy.

Reconstruction

We have discussed, in this chapter and elsewhere in the book, the questions of the timing, depth, and sequence of interpretations; what we have not yet discussed in

---

[9]Freud used the concept of "thing presentations" to stand for presentations (frequently, but not always, linked to objects) of an essentially visual nature, and used the concept of "word presentations" to stand for presentations of essentially aural nature. This was an important distinction for Freud because of how he understood the dynamics of the movement of mental contents from unconsciousness to preconsciousness, on their way into consciousness; in the system PCS, thing presentations are tied to word presentations, whereas in the system UCS only thing presentations are possible. Actually, thing presentations (which Freud sometimes also called "object presentations") are not exclusively visual: their character is actually visual, acoustic, and tactile. They are commonly described as visual, that is, their visual character is emphasized over the tactile and acoustic features, not because the other features are nonexistent or irrelevant but because in the connection of thing presentations to word presentations the *sound image* of the word presentation gets linked to the *visual association* of the thing presentation. (Word presentations, depending on the individual's level of development, include sound images, motor images, reading images, and writing images.) These PCS dynamics transform mental representations that were exclusively perceptual, motoric, and sensational into mental representations that are also conceptual: from experience-bound mental representations into mental representations that stand for the experience.

any detail is the role of interpretations in the process of reconstruction. Freud made a distinction between interpretive work that has to do with isolated areas of mental functioning and isolated parts of the patient's associations (e.g., a slip of the tongue, a dream, a specific resistance, a defense, a pun, a joke, or an affect), and the reconstructive work involved in elaborating a genetic transference interpretation (that is, in identifying the important events of the patient's past, which, as they make their appearance in the transference, demonstrate that they are still exerting powerful influences on the patient in the present): the latter he called constructions, or reconstructions. A reconstruction is not exactly the same as an interpretation: a reconstruction brings together how the actual circumstances of the patient's childhood were blended with childhood fantasy. The interpretation is in how that historical situation has come to still be an active determinant in the current mental life of the patient.

Kris, in his 1956 paper "The Recovery of Childhood Memories in Psychoanalysis," argues that the attempt to reconstruct exactly what happened in childhood is hopeless. The whole question of the difference between historical truth and narrative truth has been interesting to many analysts; there is general although not universal agreement that historical truth, knowing "what really happened," is useful but not absolutely essential in the conduct of a successful analysis: there is virtually universal agreement that narrative truth, what is *subjectively* real to the patient, must always and in every case be treated with the utmost seriousness in the conduct of an analysis. Narrative truth, the patient's subjective memory of what happened, is generated through the fusion of childhood history and childhood fantasy. Kris felt that reconstructive work in an analysis could not, and should not, work toward the goal of trying to define the objectified or objectifiable truth of what actually happened during childhood. He felt that the purpose of reconstructive work

> is more limited and yet much vaster. The material of actual occurrences, of things as they happen, is constantly subjected to the selective scrutiny of memory under the guise of the inner constellation. What we here call selection is itself a complex process. Not only were the events loaded with meaning when they occurred: each later stage of the conflict pattern may endow part of these events or of their elaboration with added meaning. But these processes are repeated throughout many years of childhood and adolescence and finally integrated into the structure of the personality. They are molded, as it were, into patterns, and it is with these patterns rather than with the events that the analyst deals. [p. 77]

In the end, Freud's ideas about reconstruction were not so different from the conclusions drawn by Kris, although he arrived at them from a slightly different vantage point. In his 1937 paper, on "Constructions in Analysis," he described how hard, usually impossible, it was to achieve the "ideal" of providing a perfectly full and reliable construction: a construction that would prompt the patient to remember, with full accuracy, all of what happened to him as a child and, thereby, eradicate infantile amnesia entirely. The recapturing of infantile memory is difficult for many reasons, not the least of which are the effects of infantile amnesia, the fact that a memory may be preverbal in nature, the fact that memories have been altered by fantasy, and the possibility that very early memories may be stored differently in the brain (and consequently, the mind) than are later memories, inasmuch as the child is not even finished with his full neurological development until he is almost into toddlerhood. Freud was not pessimistic about an analysis that did not capture all of the relevant early memories: he wrote, "Quite often we do not succeed in bringing the patient to recollect what has been repressed. Instead of that, if the analysis is carried out correctly, we produce in him an assured conviction of the truth of the construction which achieves the same therapeutic result as a recaptured memory."[10] Freud was not speaking here of the power of suggestion as it is usually thought of in relation to hypnosis, for example, or where persuasion is attempted. Freud was referring to a conviction of the truth that is based on the patient's experience of the analyst's interpretations and constructions as being eminently reasonable, as based on everything that had been learned in the analysis until then, as rooted in the realities that patient has perceived in the analysis, as being both emotionally and intellectually accurate; these interpretations and constructions being made to the patient at a time when the patient was ready to see the truth in them.

---

[10]S. Freud, "Constructions in Analysis." *Standard Edition* vol. 23 (1937), pp. 265–266.

12

Countertransference and the Analytic Instrument

Evolving Concepts of Countertransference

Countertransference must easily be one of the most variably defined concepts in all of psychoanalysis. Since it was first conceptualized by Freud as a resistance of the analyst and an obstacle to the treatment, it has undergone many transformations of meaning; it is now thought, by some, to be a positive analytic development and an essential analytic tool, without which psychoanalysis would not be possible, thus rendering unrecognizable the original concept of countertransference.

Criticism of Freud's Early Inattention to Countertransference

It has been suggested more than once that the history of the concept of countertransference should properly have begun with a critique by Freud of Joseph Breuer's treatment of Bertha Pappenheim (Anna O.), and particularly with a critique by Freud of how Breuer ended her treatment in response to Anna O.'s hysterical pregnancy fantasy. The critique that is leveled at Freud (for not doing this) starts with the suggestion that Breuer's technical behavior with Anna O. was grossly inappropriate;[1] it goes on to suggest that the strength of Breuer's "overinvolvement" with Anna O. was based on his own transferences to her;[2] and finally, it concludes

---

[1]Behavior that today might be considered quite unorthodox but which was not so obviously improper or so clearly inappropriate in the early 1880s; behavior such as feeding her when she would not eat, holding her hand, visiting her at her home in the country, conducting therapy sessions in her bedroom, and so on. We must remember the context in which Anna O.'s treatment took place: transference was a totally unknown concept and doctors traditionally (as they still do today, if you can find one who makes house calls) treated bedridden patients in their homes. What seems so striking to us today, with the advantage of hindsight, was quite unexceptional and altogether unremarkable (in fact, it was considered entirely appropriate) back then.

[2]One might be tempted to say, "Well, Anna O. was a neurological patient; that's how neurological patients were treated in those days," except that Breuer did seem to have been altogether overinvolved

(the "incriminating" criticism of Freud) that Freud wrote nothing about Breuer's countertransference abandonment of Anna O. because Freud could not face the subject of Breuer's transference to her, squarely and honestly, himself.[3]

Considering that this was the case on which the discovery of psychoanalysis was founded, it seems rather peculiar to single out countertransference as something that Freud should have been focused on – particularly when he had not yet even conceptualized the concept of *transference*. The objection seems rather off the mark, even if in retrospect Breuer's countertransference seems quite obvious to us. Even if we supposed, for the sake of the argument, that he *did* know about transference (and remember that in fact, he did not), he certainly could not have been expected to zero in on such a specialized issue as countertransference – in the very earliest "moments" of psychoanalysis – when he was trying to develop a rational understanding, *for the very first time,* of such basics as psychic conflict, repression, defenses, the dynamics of hysteria, and the unconscious. And if we hypothesize that Freud *did* have such thoughts and judgments about Breuer's conclusion of the case, which seems possible but rather unlikely, they could only have been of a passing and probably latent nature if Freud did not appreciate the implications of transference; concern that Breuer handled the situation badly, even given a compassionate reaction to Anna O.'s situation, would understandably have been secondary to the pressing importance of formulating a general theory of mental functioning and a dependent theory of abnormal psychology.

Freud's Discovery of Countertransference as an Aspect of the Treatment

Freud's first approach to the problem of countertransference was in his 1910 paper, "Future Prospects for Psycho-Analytic Therapy." He wrote: "We have become aware of the 'counter-transference,' which arises in (the analyst) as a result of the patient's influence on his unconscious feelings, and we are almost inclined to insist that he shall recognize this counter-transference in himself and overcome it." He went on: "We have noticed that no psychoanalyst goes further than his own complexes and resistances permit; and we consequently require that he shall begin his activity with a self-analysis and continually carry it deeper while he is making his own observations on his patients. Anyone who fails to produce results in a

---

with her. Many of the things he did were not exceptional in and of themselves, and taken quite apart from one another; but Anna O. may well have received more personal attention from Breuer than any other patient in neurological history has ever received from her doctor. Breuer's wife, too, was troubled by the depth of his involvement with Anna O. and expressed her awareness and discomfort at this.

[3]Having been unaware of the very concept of transference itself and, consequently, ignorant of any of its dynamics (in fact, so much so that he did not even understand the meaning of Anna O.'s transferences to Breuer), it seems hardly likely that Freud would have had any understanding of Breuer's transferences to Anna O. It took many years before Freud began to write about patients' transference to their analysts, and he can hardly be expected, at that time, to have been sensitive to transference in analysts to their patients.

self-analysis of this kind may at once give up any idea of being able to treat patients by analysis" (*Standard Edition* 11:144–145).

Ambiguities in Freud's Description of Countertransference

This statement, which seems at first so clear, actually has some significant ambiguity in it. Is Freud suggesting that all analysts, because they are human and less than perfect, will regularly have inappropriate unconscious reactions toward their patients (the same way that they would toward anyone else), and that these unconscious feelings will prevent them from understanding certain things about their patients (create blind spots, one might say, in the analyst)? Or is Freud concerned here with a more limited class of reactions in the analyst: reactions that form in the matrix of the analyst's personality but which are nevertheless somewhat special and unique to each patient because they are specifically prompted by the different nature of each patient's transference relation to the analyst?

One can never be certain about something like this, but it does not seem likely that what Freud had in mind was the broad scope of the analyst's reactions to the patient (which would encompass the analyst's unconscious neurotic responses toward the patient in the same way that the analyst might have unconscious neurotic responses toward anyone). If this were his concern, would he not have warned us about the dangers of the analyst's *neuroses,* or, more specifically, about the dangers of the analyst's *transferences* to the patient? Freud often changed the meaning of the terms that he used, but he always chose them with great care, and we must assume that he used the term *counter-transference* in preference to other descriptive terms for a good reason.[4] If Freud's concern was that a broad understanding of the patient might be blocked by something in the inner life of the analyst, would he not have warned us about the dangers of the analyst's *unconscious conflicts?* It would seem that Freud was commenting, specifically, on the effect that the patient's transferences may have on the analyst.

It is not unreasonable to assume that Freud was generally interested in the effects of any and all unconscious feeling states in the analyst, including those to the patient's transferences, but this seems not to be the essence of his concern in his warning about countertransference. Hinging on those thoughts of his – about the unconscious reactive states that develop in the analyst in direct response to the patient's transference – Freud appears to have been mainly concerned about how the analyst might put into practice (in the analysis), *behaviorally and without his conscious knowledge,* those unconsciously motivated responses to the patient's transferences.

---

[4]Freud was careful in his thinking and did choose his language with a high degree of intentionality; however, it is also true that Freud did not always say exactly what he meant. One could, on that basis, object to the assertion that if he meant something in a certain way, he would have said it in that way. Taken to an extreme, this objection could throw into doubt even the most explicit and absolute of his statements.

Freud seems to be more concerned with the analyst's potential to gratify the patient's transference instead of analyzing it, than with the reactions in unconsciousness themselves, because if we attend to Freud's description of countertransference as a *resistance* of the analyst's, we know that resistances are events that are *enacted* in an analysis and are not inner states of being (despite the fact that inner states of being are what they grow out of).[5] However, we may feel even more assured, if not entirely confident, that Freud was concerned with the analyst's *actions* in the analysis, rather than essentially with the state of his inner life, by Freud's (1914) next reference to countertransference. Freud refers to the analyst needing to battle "in his own mind against the forces which seek to drag him down from the analytic level," (*Standard Edition* 12:170) and he gives that caution immediately following a detailed description of the destructive effect on the treatment that he believes would occur if an analyst were to respond in kind to a patient's transferential love. Although the issue of disruptive mental forces that may exist in the analyst is the starting point for Freud's caution, the emphasis in the "battle" that Freud recommends is on the fact that mental forces can "drag the analyst down from the analytic level," that is, that they can cause him to *act* unanalytically; his emphasis was not mainly on the fact that there are such forces with that potential. Obviously there is an interconnection between unconscious neurotic mental forces that are triggered by the patient's transferential expectations, and the eventual taking of an inappropriate therapeutic action. It would be impossible to consider countertransferential actions without also including the particular kind of conflict in the analyst that has led to them. But Freud was not especially alerting us, in that context, about the analyst's inner feelings toward the patient (which certainly do have to be considered as a starting point) when he spoke of those forces in the analyst's mind; he was articulating a warning against the analyst permitting those unconscious mental forces to allow him to rationalize "returning the patient's love" in the analysis – in other words, gratifying the transference through psychological or behavioral action.

Countertransference phenomena were distinguished by Freud (above) from the analyst's "complexes and resistances"; *complexes* are a matter of concern because they do undoubtedly interfere with the analyst's ability to appropriately understand the patient, but countertransference as a *resistance* concerned Freud particularly because it

---

[5]One might object to the kind of exegesis necessary in ferreting out Freud's meaning, and one might think: If he meant action, why didn't he specify action? It is certainly a good question. One possible reply might draw our attention to the fact that Freud preferred (not only then, but throughout his entire life) not to write specifically about questions of technique. He discussed technique, explicitly, as little as possible and usually only indirectly (except, for example, in the five "technique papers," and in a very few others, which make up only a tiny fraction of his writings).

This is not a fully satisfying answer, but it might throw some light on why he did not focus his comments more clearly on the analyst's conduct of the treatment. Parenthetically, Freud resisted writing about technique because he did not want to "lock in" a model for analytic work. Freud believed that there were many possible styles in which one could work, assuming, of course, that certain minimum criteria for the work were met (e.g., abstinence and neutrality on the part of the analyst, and the use of free association).

analyst's disposal but, rather, as a destructive activity that needs first to be made conscious, and then, no longer enacted.[8] Countertransference was viewed as something the analyst inevitably got into but was supposed to get out of, so that the analyst could go back to analyzing rather than acting out the transferential conflict along with the patient.

Whether or not he was referring to all of the therapist's reactions to the patient's transference, or mainly to enactments based on those reactions, the spirit of Freud's thoughts on the matter are in direct opposition to some current views that consider countertransference a positive analytic event.[9] Today there seems to be a general collapsing together of the concept of *countertransference* with the concept of *the analytic instrument:* perhaps it was the very ambiguity of Freud's charge that was responsible. But even if that is not a factor, both of these concepts are so interrelated and interpenetrating that the conflation of them comes as no surprise. Ferenczi was one of the first of Freud's circle to challenge the idea that countertransference is, by definition, destructive to the treatment, and he supported his challenge by using this method of blurring the distinctions between the concepts of countertransference and the analytic instrument.

Ferenczi's Reorganization of Freud's Concept of Transference–Countertransference Interactions

Ferenczi believed that free-floating attention also included attention to the analyst's own unconscious processes, and that empathy for the patient came from this source. He challenged Freud's suggestion that countertransference must be mastered, because he believed that the effort involved in doing so would interfere with the analyst's attention to his own unconscious processes and, consequently, block analytic empathy. Ferenczi included analytic empathy in the concept of countertransference; he even suggested a new term, *objective countertransference,* by which he meant the realistic reaction of the analyst to the real personality of the patient.[10] For Ferenczi, the interactions that took place between analyst and patient were not as overwhelmingly dominated by transference distortion as they were for Freud.

---

[8]Freud frequently prefigured many notions that were dependent on a fuller working out of a later concept, of which this is an excellent example; for instance, his early thoughts about defense, in 1895, needed the structural theory, with its concept of the ego as a complex psychic agency, which he did not provide until 1923, to do full justice to the concept.

[9]This does not make those current views automatically wrong (one would not wish to treat any concept of Freud's as if it were holy writ, and therefore not subject to question, modification, and change), but it is useful to be clear about the restricted negative denotations and connotations in the original development and use of this concept, and to the negative status it had, for years, within the profession. Only very recently have analysts suggested anything other than an entirely negative meaning to the concept of countertransference.

[10]It is a bit difficult to distinguish between the personality of the patient and the *real* personality of the patient, unless, by this, Ferenczi meant to suggest that the neurotic constituents of the patient's personality were, somehow, less *real.*

leads to destructive mutual enactments, behaviorally, in the analysis, between the analyst and the patient.

Freud's comments were very preliminary, and this is only one of a number of possible interpretations of his first communication on countertransference;[6] however, it is now generally agreed that the greatest danger that the analyst can present to an analysis is when unconsciously determined neurotic reactions to the patient result in gratification, rather than frustration, of the patient's transference expectations.[7] In Chapter 8, we have discussed in some detail how psychoanalytic treatment depends on a fully developed transference neurosis, and why any behavior that interferes with the full potential of the transference neurosis is destructive to the process. And we have described the theoretical basis underlying the assumption that the transference neurosis is developed, and it matures as a primary tool of the treatment, as a result of the analyst frustrating the patient's transference demands, fears, wishes, expectations, and so on. Unconscious, neurotic gratification of the transference by the analyst, which is what Freud seemed to be addressing in his articulation of the concept of countertransference, puts an obstacle in the way of the treatment by disrupting the development of the transference neurosis. Even though, at that time, he had not yet worked out all of his ideas about the power of the transference neurosis, Freud does seem to have intended countertransference to be understood as a difficulty in the path of the therapy—not a useful tool at the

---

[6]Analysts who prefer the alternative interpretation of the above quote (1910), that is, that Freud *was* referring to the analyst's feelings about the patient and that he was not especially placing particular emphasis on the therapist's actions, frequently trace the lineage of their argument to the following quote from Freud's 1912 paper, "Recommendations to Physicians Practicing Psychoanalysis": ". . . the analyst must turn his own unconscious like a receptive organ towards the transmitting unconscious of the patient. He must adjust himself to the patient as a telephone receiver is adjusted to the transmitting microphone. Just as the receiver converts back into sound waves the electric oscillations in the telephone line which were set up by sound waves, so the doctor's unconscious is able, from the derivatives of the unconscious which are communicated to him, to reconstruct that unconscious, which has determined the patient's free associations. . . . But if the doctor is to be in a position to use his unconscious in this way as an instrument in the analysis . . . he may not tolerate any resistances in himself which hold back from his consciousness what has been perceived by his unconscious" (*Standard Edition* 12:115–116).

Although it is quite true that Freud was concerned here with difficulties that might arise as a result of the analyst's state of mind, the argument for this definition of countertransference would have been more compelling if he had then identified the problem as one of countertransference; after all, the term had been introduced two years earlier, and this would have been a likely place to use it if that is the way he wanted to have it conceptualized. It seems that Freud was making a distinction here between countertransference and the analyst's unconscious participation in the work; rather than describing the analyst's unconscious receptivity and resistiveness as an example of countertransference, he seemed to prefer a different concept, that is, the concept of "the analytic instrument." The distinction between these concepts will be discussed in considerable detail later in this chapter.

[7]Obviously, a psychotic or a grossly unethical analyst has the potential to present greater dangers to an analysis than an analyst who unconsciously gratifies transference expectations. We are speaking here only about dangers to the analytic situation that might arise as the course of a normal, average treatment circumstance, and we are excluding from our consideration any conditions that would not occur as a regular feature of the analytic situation.

Ferenczi thought that every analytic interaction also included, in rather large measure, the experienced effects of the analyst's "real" behavior (that is, as it is unrelated to the patient's transferentially overdetermined perceptions), and most importantly, he thought that patients could clearly distinguish this; that is, that powerful "real" perceptions of the analyst (immune from distortion because they are part of "reality") exist side by side, virtually on a par, with powerful fantasies about the analyst. Thus Ferenczi began to focus on the "real" ways that the analyst's "real" reactions had an effect on the treatment. This led Ferenczi to the position that although the analyst had to carefully control and "correct" his feelings toward patients when necessary, it was also useful in certain circumstances to reveal both his mistakes and his feelings to his patients. Given the culture of psychoanalysis at the time, where the analyst as a "blank screen" or as a "mirror" were the prevailing metaphors, one can imagine the stir this caused!

Not inhibited by the reaction of the establishment, and not intimidated by the role of an iconoclast, Ferenczi carried his theories even further away from the Freudian mainstream. Ferenczi thought that analysts are often made uncomfortable by the feelings and attitudes that their patients' transferences induce in them, and that every patient can accurately perceive the unconscious negative experience of the analyst (directed toward the patient), which then causes the patient to pull back from the analyst.[11] Thus, as a remedy, Ferenczi suggested that it was legitimate to offer his patient "proof" that, whatever else may be true about his unconscious, he really did also care about his patient. The range of what was permissible as proof went from thoughtful accurate interpretation, through telling the patient about his (Ferenczi's) feelings toward him, to hugging and even actually kissing his female patients.

Continuing Specification and Redefinition
of the Concept by Other Analysts

A. Stern

At the same time other analysts, too, began to enlarge on the concept of counter-transference and on the concept of the analytic instrument, sometimes merging them, without, however, moving out of the mainstream of psychoanalysis, as Ferenczi did. Without attempting to present an entire or systematic history of these concepts in psychoanalysis, we can touch on some of the more important ideas. It

---

[11]This was a revolutionary idea for the time, and not within mainstream thinking, but it has certainly become part of mainstream thinking today in relation to work with primitive, psychotic, and certain character-disordered patients, who do have a greater talent than does the neurotic for "reading" the unconscious of the analyst. When applied to neurotic patients this is consistent, of course, with Ferenczi's view that the analytic relationship is not so dominated by fantasy and transference as Freud believed it to be.

was not until the mid-1920s that Stern published the first essay devoted entirely to the concept of countertransference.[12] He discussed the bearing that the analyst's transferences to the patient have on the analyst's ability to process the patient's transferences to him, and suggested a number of factors that could create interferences in the analyst's mode of working with his patient's transferences (for example, the effects of variably intense stresses in the analyst's life).

Helene Deutsch

Helene Deutsch addressed the question, What more than just the analyst's transferences to the patient might his countertransference consist of? and ended up with an early model of intuition and empathy. She wrote about the way that the analyst internally sifts the associations of the patient and the patient's descriptions of his experience, so that it all slowly becomes part of his own psyche, too: he is still able to distinguish, however, while he is permitting this to happen, which part of it originally came from the patient. In this process the analyst identifies emotionally with the infantile character of the patient's ego. And in addition, as the patient transfers his infantile object relations into the medium of the analysis, the analyst also identifies with the significant objects of the patient's past. This set of double identifications by the analyst, quite different from the analyst's conscious experience of the patient, is what Deutsch termed "the complementary attitude," and it was this that she felt to be the basis for the analyst's empathy and intuition.

Wilhelm Reich, Robert Fliess, and Otto Kernberg

Wilhelm Reich, on the other hand, made a clear distinction between empathy and countertransference. Reich believed that it was not possible to understand the patient through examining countertransference, and he recommended instead a reliance on empathy (with which he equated the term *intuitive comprehension*). Some time later, Robert Fliess addressed these issues in a somewhat different way. He introduced the idea that the analyst engages in *trial identifications* with the patient. Fliess differentiated trial identification from Reich's concept of empathy in the following way: empathy, according to Fliess, was a description of a relatively passive emotional state that underwent change only slowly and in very small ways, whereas trial identification was a very active, highly changeable and extremely variable process (not an affect), which the analyst engaged in consciously, preconsciously, and unconsciously. In trial identification the analyst examines his own states of mind, his emotions, his ideation, his fantasies – everything that is aroused in him as a result of his contact with the patient – in order to get a better sense of what the patient might be experiencing. Fliess's assumption was that the analyst, in

---

[12]A. Stern, "On the Countertransference in Psychoanalysis," *Psychoanalytic Review,* vol. 2 (1924), pp. 166–174.

listening to the patient, has access (on many levels of consciousness and unconsciousness) to similar experiences within himself that are analogous to the patient's experiences, and that he trades on this active identificatory capacity to get a more sensitive picture of the patient's inner life and experience. Almost a quarter of a century later, Kernberg took up the topic of the analyst's *capacity for concern,* which he viewed as being broader than prior concepts of empathy that only stressed the analyst's ability to "feel along with" the patient. Kernberg thought that the analyst's capacity for concern was a broader phenomenon than empathy because it trades on an overall regard and consideration for the patient's best interests and includes an identification capacity in the analyst that permits him to recognize, in both the transference and the countertransference, the patient's aggressive and self-aggressive impulses (impulses that are destructive to himself and to the therapy), and to neutralize them – first in the countertransference, and then in the transference. Kernberg elaborated the interactive nature of the capacity for concern in many papers on treatment of narcissistic and borderline patients. At about roughly the same time, Kohut began to write about empathy from a Self psychological point of view. Exactly what Kohut meant by empathy is still a matter of some controversy. However, it appears that he was referring to an identification process in the analyst that involved recognition as well as some kind of accepting mirroring, similar to that which occurs in good parenting, of his patients' needs to experience a wide range of narcissistic satisfactions.

Before leaving the work of Fliess behind us, we should also note that his model also includes the assumption that the analyst (whose ego has not been impaired by transferential regression in the analytic process), unlike the patient (who is not always in the best position to recognize transferentially distorted representations of the analyst), has the ability to differentiate realistically between these identificatory states of mind and the objective reality of what the patient is presenting to him, and that he can move with volition and ease between them. With the concept of trial identification, Fliess is discussing *the analytic instrument* rather than *countertransference* in the sense that Freud seems to have meant it; in discussing countertransference in the more traditional sense, Fliess joined with the prevailing negative view of it and suggested that it occurs when the analyst is having some immature reaction in response to something that has happened in the treatment, and he substitutes the patient for one of his own infantile objects.

Edward Glover

Glover's contributions further emphasized the role that the patient plays in inducing countertransference reactions to his transferences.[13] More importantly, however,

---

[13]This is what is commonly described today as *induced countertransference;* it seems rather a redundant label, although it is presumably meant to differentiate this concept of countertransference from a different countertransference concept that would include all the analyst's reactions (and especially, his transfer-

Glover introduced another new concept to the countertransference literature: *counterresistance*. Glover related the psychosexual stage of the patient's transferences to the analyst, to the (not necessarily complementary) psychosexual stage of the analyst's reciprocal countertransference reaction, which is how he understands the analyst's countertransference to be able to acquire its own subjectivity. For Glover, countertransference was related to preoedipal levels of the analyst's own development, whereas counterresistance was more mature, and related to the analyst's development at least at the oedipal level, and higher.

James Strachey

Strachey also introduced a new term into the countertransference literature: *mutative interpretation*.[14] Strachey was trying to clarify how interpretation worked best, while also discouraging the use of what he viewed as ineffective or, at least, less effective, interventions; for example, advice, suggestion, questions, abreaction, and reassurance. His point was that there was a special value to interpretations that are made strictly within the transference neurosis, as opposed to interpretations of an extra-transferential and nonimmediate nature. Strachey was emphasizing the importance, in the interpretive process, of the intensity of the patient's instinctual and emotional investments in the analyst (as a transference figure). He suggested that there was a special emotional force-field of transference–countertransference connections that exists at special times between the patient and the analyst (mainly at times of transferential regression in the patient). His underscoring of the emotional force-field in the analysis stressed the necessity of making interpretations precisely when the analyst becomes the immediate target of the patient's instinctual wishes; Strachey felt that only in the hothouse of the transference (which is the heart of the patient's neurosis) could the cognitive nature of information acquired through interpretation be transformed into insight – hence, the term *mutative* interpretation. In the process of working out this theory of technique, Strachey observed that considerable unconscious reactivity exists in the analyst when he becomes the target of the primitive and immediate instinctual wishes of the patient; it was in this context that he discussed the potential for countertransference responses in the analyst, and in this context that he described the transference–countertransference matrix in which mutative interpretations are made. His reasoning was as follows: the mutative interpretation is critical for the analyst as well as for the patient because the intensity of the emotional force-field of the patient's transference (and the associated instinc-

---

ences to the patient that are unrelated to the patient's transferences to him). One other, less redundant, use of the concept suggests that induced countertransference may be thought of as the kind of countertransference that would be induced in every analyst, no matter what his conflicts, by certain kinds of patients; for example, the particularly primitive countertransference responses to the especially primitive transferences that are seen in certain borderline patients, which it is assumed all analysts would have.

[14]Kohut's use of this term, with his own particular definition, seems to be the sense in which it is most often used at present.

tual demands) brings the analyst closer to his own unconscious, and this affects how he makes interpretations. As a result, Strachey suggested, mutative interpretations grow out of an intense interaction process and always involve a high degree of mutuality between the patient's unconscious processes and the analyst's unconscious processes.[15]

Revolutionary Shifts in the Concept of Countertransference

D. W. Winnicott

Even though, in the work of all these theorists, there had not been clear distinctions made (nor were any called for) between countertransference and the analytic instrument, attitudes toward the analytic instrument generally ranged from neutral to positive, whereas attitudes toward countertransference ranged from moderately negative to condemnatory (except, perhaps, in the case of Ferenczi). However, Winnicott's paper, "Hate in the Countertransference" (1949), served as a beacon for a change of attitude about countertransference. Winnicott introduced the modern notion of countertransference as something that could be unambivalently positive.[16] Rather than continuing with the standard view that analysts should not have strong feelings toward their patients, Winnicott argued an opposite stance: the analyst is a human being who is entitled to both realistic and unrealistic emotions, no matter how strong, as long as he can be relatively aware of the difference; and, he *should* make them *all* part of the treatment. His paper described working with psychotic and antisocial patients who were, and are, frequently hateful and provoking to the analyst. Winnicott was making the point that there are objective realities about such patient's personalities that the analyst will have strong reality-based responses to, different from the kind of neurotic countertransference that is also possible, and that the analyst has to be able to use them *both* in his interpretive work with the patient. He believed that with certain kinds of primitive and highly provocative patients, the patient needs to acquire a realistically appropriate, genu-

---

[15]Parenthetically, Strachey also suggested that mutative interpretation constituted only a part–perhaps even a small part–of the overall treatment. However, it was his view that it was *only* the mutative interpretation that had the power to deeply affect the patient; that is, the mutative interpretation is (as Strachey put it) "the ultimate operative factor" in the acquisition of insight and in the bringing about of structural change.

[16]It is true that Ferenczi might, technically, qualify for this distinction even though he was generally discredited because of his conduct with patients (which most analysts, rightly or wrongly, considered seductive at best and outright unethical at worst); thus, certain of his views, despite being earlier than Winnicott's work on the positive value of countertransference, never came to have much influence among the general body of psychoanalysts. More recently, however, Ferenczi's work has begun to take on more popularity and has come to be treated with considerably more respect, in a parallel process with (or perhaps because of) the development of Self psychology.

inely hateful, reaction from the analyst in response to his enacted aggression before he can seek, or accept, a loving relationship with the analyst. Winnicott's model was based on the fact that a mother hates her baby (even if awareness of it is warded off) in response to the infant's narcissistic misuse of her and his narcissistic lack of appreciation of her, and that this is an objective aspect of the mother–child dyad which the child can pick up (even if the mother is incognizant of it). This reaction on the mother's part facilitates the maturation that permits the baby to be less narcissistic and more loving in his relations with her, and in that sense it serves an essential purpose in the development of love. Winnicott suggested that patients who are "hateful" in reality often seek the objective hate in the analyst as an evolutionary step in reaching the objective love of the analyst; that the patient needs the analyst's hate in order to tolerate his own; and that the analyst short-circuits this process if he cannot tolerate the objective hate that arises in him in response to such a patient.

Paula Heimann

Winnicott was quickly joined by Paula Heimann, a Kleinian, who challenged Freud's views quite directly. Heimann first suggested that the concept of countertransference should include all of the analyst's reactions to his patient, all of his feelings without exception, and not just his emotional reactions in response to the patient's transference. In addition, she thought that the analyst's attempt to be relatively detached and that his attempts not to be in countertransference was harmful to analytic treatment, not helpful. In her view, all countertransference was a creation of the patient despite the fact that it was occurring in the analyst: therefore, a careful examination of the analyst's countertransference was, as she put it, "an instrument of research into the patient's unconscious." For Heimann, no analyst could adequately interpret a patient's mental condition without carefully examining his own countertransference.[17] Where Winnicott viewed the countertransference as a facet of the real relationship between the patient and the analyst, Heimann understood it to be a way of understanding the inner life of the patient.[18]

Margaret Little

Margaret Little also made a significant contribution in the attempt to remove the purely negative stigma from countertransference and to reconceptualize countertransference as a potentially positive, absolutely necessary, and entirely intrinsic part of analytic work. Little believed that a joining of forces between the id of the

---

[17]Heimann was not suggesting, however, as Ferenczi did, that it would be useful to intentionally share her inner experiences with the patient in making interpretations. The inner experience of the analyst, she thought, was for his educational purposes, and not for illustrative purposes with the patient.

[18]Undoubtedly, the difference between the kinds of patients they were working with and writing about made a big difference in their respective positions: Winnicott had developed his ideas working with psychotics and psychopaths, and Heimann meant her conclusions about countertransference to be applicable to *all* patients.

patient and the id of the analyst is what powers the patient's move to health. However, both the patient and the analyst will not be able to capitalize on this meshing of id interests unless the analyst is capable of a special, complex, multilayered identification with the patient. One part of the identification is conscious: it is with the patient's wish to get better (this would ally the analyst with the patient's ego). The other part of the identification is both conscious and unconscious: this part is with the patient's resistance against getting better (this would ally the analyst with patient's id and also with the patient's superego). As we can see, looked at from Little's perspective, both the transference and the countertransference, in fact, the entire patient–analyst relationship, is a mixture of normal and pathological aspects of the characters of both participants. Thus the analyst's countertransference has as much potential for helping the patient get well as it does for interfering with the treatment, and vice versa. It may be good for the treatment, bad for the treatment, or neither; it may be good for the treatment at some points and bad for the treatment at other points; moreover, countertransference will never be the same from patient to patient in exactly the same way that transference is always different from patient to patient. On the positive side, the analyst has as much investment *in the patient getting well* in order to serve his own aggressive and libidinal purposes as he does in having the patient get well to serve the goals of his and the patient's ego. On the negative side, the analyst has as much investment *in the patient remaining ill* in order to serve his own aggressive and libidinal purposes as does the patient for *his* own reasons.

Little viewed the analytic situation not in the way Freud did, where the analyst is a mirror of the patient's inner life, but rather more like what one would see in a hall of mirrors, in which both parties are holding multiple mirrors up to each other and generating images that eventually blend together and repeat themselves into infinity. In her view, the analyst is much more open to the patient as a result of the interpenetrability of their psyches, and she can be seen as a descendent of Ferenczi (who intentionally and quite calculatingly opened himself up to patients), and an ancestor of those current analysts who view the analytic process as, phenomenologically and dynamically, entirely "intersubjective." However, Little's view about self-disclosure, based on her understanding of the interpenetrability of the analyst's and the patient's psyches, should not be mistaken for Ferenczi's approach to this practice. She, too, felt that it was important for the analyst to acknowledge having made a mistake, but she did not agree with the more "confessional" aspects of Ferenczi's approach. Little believed that self-disclosure in moderation, under special circumstances, may be useful, but when self-disclosure is not absolutely necessary it will constitute an undue burden on the patient.

Annie Reich Responds to the Newly Broadened Definitions of Countertransference

At the same time and, one may assume, very much in response to Little, Annie Reich asserted an even more conservative view than the traditional one (which viewed countertransference as that part of the analyst's neurosis that responded to the patient's transference expectations). Reich thought that countertransference was representative of the analyst's *permanent* neurotic problems; therefore, countertransference does not reflect the problems of the patient but those of the analyst, and thus – as inevitable as it is, and as much as it brings a certain degree of spontaneity to the inner life of the analyst at work – countertransference can only be counterproductive to the treatment and it must remain as much in the background of the analysis as possible. Reich's view of countertransference suggests that it is that part of the analyst's neurotic conflicts that makes it difficult or impossible to do analysis; it is not the equivalent of the analyst's neurosis but, rather, it is the interface between the analyst's neurosis and the analytic tasks with which it is incompatible. Reich's position is directly opposite to the views of those analysts who suggest that there is a "constructive" use of countertransference. She rejects entirely concepts of "useful" countertransference, such as those that have been already discussed above, or, for example, Searles's notions of *therapeutic symbiosis* and *oedipal love in the countertransference,* Towers's notion of *dual analysis,* or Spotnitz's approach (based on Ferenczi) to working with schizophrenics. Reich emphatically argued that there is no way countertransference is, and no way it can become, a tool of the analytic work.

Additional Kleinian Views of Countertransference: Heinrich Racker and Leon Grinberg

Heinrich Racker and Leon Grinberg, Kleinians like Paula Heimann whom we discussed above, have described numerous, highly complex, transference–countertransference paradigms and patterns. Countertransference concepts like *complementary identification, concordant identification* (Racker), and *projective counteridentification* (Grinberg) are notions of theirs that emphasize the patient's use of splitting and projective identification and the correlated internalizations and ejections by the analyst of the patient's fantasies and defense operations. They both, in only slightly different ways, clearly viewed countertransferences as introjective, projective, and counterprojective reactions that match, and act in tandem with, the splitting and projective identification mechanisms of the patient, and in their models we can see that they have closely linked the unconscious processes of the analyst with those of the patient. One of the great strengths of Racker's work, whether or not one is comfortable with Kleinian dynamic formulations, is that he describes in exquisite and wonderfully illuminating clinical detail many different kinds of transference––countertransference matrices. Racker also focused considerable attention on countertransference problems in the training analysis of analytic candidates, not a usual avenue of approach to this topic at the time he wrote, although it is more common today in certain approaches.

Countertransference with the "More Disturbed" Patient

Peter Giovacchini and Joyce McDougall

The kinds of patients who are now treated in analysis, or in somewhat modified analyses, has broadened to include more seriously disturbed kinds of people; a number of writers (in addition to the previously mentioned Winnicott, Searles, Spotnitz, Kernberg, and Kohut) have begun to consider the problem of countertransference in working with the more profoundly disordered patient, and among them analysts like Joyce McDougall and Peter Giovacchini (to mention only two) have made very interesting contributions. Giovacchini, who has had extensive experience in applying psychoanalytic treatment approaches to psychotic disturbances, has discussed the way in which such disturbed patients trigger intensely distressed states of mind in their therapists. He suggests that the analyst may evolve many rigid defenses in such extremely uncomfortable treatment situations, one of which may be a fixed conviction that a patient (who actually might be able to be treated in psychoanalysis) is analytically untreatable. McDougall has focused on the special value that countertransference has for the analyst when he is treating psychotic patients whose central conflictual traumas occurred at a time in their lives prior to the acquisition of symbolizing capacities. She points to two problems in particular for analysts who are working with patients who have been traumatically disorganized so early in life. The inability of the patient to experience conflict in symbolic modes, which has already been mentioned, and the correspondingly primitive nature of such patient's defensive operations – in particular, the extensive use of splitting – are out of sync, as it were, with the defensive modes most comfortable for the analyst. Unlike the case with a neurotic patient, who presents ideas, affects, conflicts, and fantasies in a symbolic form that the analyst can comfortably relate to in an equally symbolic way, these psychotic patients may trigger in the analyst chaotic, fragmented, identificatory responses more in line with affecto-sensory-motor reactions than with traditionally organized thoughts and fantasies. In this case, McDougall argues, because of the deficits in the patient's processing and communicative skills, the only access the analyst may have to the nature of the inner experiences of the patient is through the close examination of countertransference responses of this nature. Compounding the problems of symbolization, the tendency of psychotic patients to use extensive splitting defenses makes the transference relation of the psychotic patient to the analyst very different from that of the neurotic. Neurotic patients displace and project conflicted object relations and object relationships onto the analyst in a coherent and intelligible fashion, even when their transferences are highly symbolized and defensively transformed; psychotic patients, with split and split-off self-representations, treat the analyst as if he were a split-off part of the patient, instead of as a transferentially significant past object. This often makes the analyst miss the patient's transferences: instead the analyst is likely to view these peculiar transferences as if they were a form of tension-releasing activities for the patient. The analyst often has a difficult time decoding the more complex meaning of the patient's transference experience: McDougall uses the example of a mother with a crying baby, trying to understand the nature of her child's distress, as an analogy to how the analyst must use and rely on his inner experiences to make sense out of the patient's poorly organized world. She has also described the need to be able to freely use countertransference in work with certain character-disordered patients whose difficulties in symbolization cause them to present in an altogether different way. These patients seem "too normal"; their transference relations to the analyst remain hidden, and only the analyst's internal responsiveness gives clues to the patient's interior world.

Other Modern Views of Countertransference in the Freudian Model

Charles Brenner

While some modern theorists, like Martin Silverman, for example, see countertransference as always indicating that something is amiss in how the analyst is able to use his analyzing capacities, others, like Brenner, for example, hesitate to even acknowledge the validity of how these concepts are generally thought about. Brenner (1985) writes: "My thesis is this. Countertransference is ubiquitous and inescapable, just as is transference. There is, truly, no need for a separate term. Countertransference is the transference of the analyst in an analytic situation" (p. 156). By viewing countertransference as a set of compromise formations, in which derivatives of drive gratification, defense, and superego functioning are always present, Brenner suggests that the process intrinsically has neither positive nor negative qualities. He suggests that, if anything, this compromise formation is what makes analyzing possible: "The assertion of some colleagues (here he is referring to Heimann) that countertransference is what makes psychoanalysis possible has in it a kernal [sic] of truth, though not what they mean when they say it. Countertransference is not a synonym for intuition or empathy, which is their idea. It is a set of compromise formations which expresses the conflicting and cooperating psychic tendencies at work in the mind of an analyst in his professional capacity. And, just as some circumstances, in particular some patients, make analysis less enjoyable and less easy to do well, other circumstances, in particular other patients, make analysis more enjoyable and easier to do well for a particular analyst" (p. 156).

Jacob Arlow

Arlow also differentiates countertransference from empathy, but on a very different basis (a basis very reminiscent of, although somewhat different from, the one that Fliess suggested). Arlow believes that both countertransference and empathy are based on identifications with the patient, but that the vicissitudes of the identification are very different in each case. He describes the identification in both instances as being with the patient's unconscious fantasies and wishes, which is what gives the analyst his understanding of the patient. However, for Arlow, in empathy the identification is broken off after a period of time, that is, the identification is only temporary; whereas in countertransference, Arlow suggests, the analyst becomes fixated at the point of the identification. In countertransference identifications the analyst's conflicts, identical to the patient's conflicts, have come into play, thus altering his freedom to move in and out of the identification. Arlow emphasizes the importance of these distinctions, between the transient identifications of empathy and the tenacious and resolute identifications of countertransference.[19] Clearly, for Arlow, countertransference always indicates a disruption in the "analytic stance" of the analyst. We can see certain similarities in Sandler's point of view, despite the emphasis that he places on object relations in countertransference. Not exactly like an identification, Sandler discusses the *intrapsychic role-responsiveness* implicated in countertransference, highlighting as does Arlow the idea that countertransference is interactional and not something that the patient imposes on the analyst. In Sandler's view of countertransference, both the patient and the analyst are attempting to impose an intrapsychic object relationship on each other.

Theodore Jacobs

Other analysts have found themselves particularly interested in the subtleties of transference–countertransference interactions, for example Abend, Blum, DeWald, and most notably, Theodore Jacobs. Jacobs has taken a very close look at the difference between grossly enacted and subtly enacted countertransference engagements, describing many of the less obvious ways countertransference can emerge in analytic treatment. He describes how particular countertransferences, the ones he characterizes as being "noisy," "boisterous," and "dramatic," generally inform us about the ways the countertransference is working in direct opposition to the treatment; whereas the subtler countertransferences, enactments that are so deeply embedded in the nuances of the analytic relationship that they are usually concealed by aspects of the work that we take for granted, have a particular promise for our understanding of equally subtle and frequently warded-off aspects of the patient's experience.

Categorizing the Differing Views of Countertransference

When we consider all of these many, quite thoughtful, analysts' ways of conceptualizing countertransference, and setting aside special issues for the moment (like, for example, the question of self-revelation), most of their positions can be categorized under three general groupings, each of which seems to differ in important ways from the way Freud appears to have set up the problem:

Group 1: Countertransference is indistinguishable from the inner life of the analyst at work, and no special distinction should (or must) be made between the emotional responses of the analyst that *are* predicated on the patient's transference

---

[19]In reference to this point, but in a different context, Arlow made the pithy observation that "one man's empathy is another man's countertransference."

relations to him, and those that *are not*. There is acknowledgement of the difference in how the psychological condition was originally prompted in the analyst. However, the argument would be that every response of the analyst must, in some way, eventually be related to the patient once the analyst and the patient are in a relationship–this is an intrinsic part of what is involved in being in an analytic interaction with another human being. Thus there is an artificiality to singling out for special attention only the analyst's reactions to the patient's transference. In addition, making fine discriminations between the concepts of the analytic instrument, empathy, trial identification, and so on, and countertransference, are thought to be both useful and not useful ways of thinking about the issue: useful because they all speak to different aspects of the countertransference, not useful because they are all indices of countertransference. The analyst's entire personality is involved in his relationship to the patient, consciously, preconsciously, and unconsciously; countertransference is virtually an ego function of the analyst that has both positive and negative aspects, and it can equally help and hinder the analytic process.

Group 2: The concept of countertransference should be limited to the analyst's reactions to the patient's transference. Countertransference may still be either helpful or harmful, depending on the manner and extent to which both healthy and unhealthy parts of the analyst's personality are brought into play with the countertransference reaction. Countertransference is still, in this model, not considered identifiably separate from "the analytic instrument" of the analyst, that is, the aspects of the analyst's personality that organize empathy, sensitivity, insight, and so on. Thus this model, too, continues the notion that countertransference can be "constructive."

Group 3: Countertransference is a response in the analyst to the patient's transference relations to him, and this response is destructive to the treatment. It *should* be defined as harmful to the process. This model would differentiate between neurotic reactions that the analyst may independently bring to the analytic situation and that can hinder the work in one way, and the neurotic reactions of the analyst that are directly prompted by the patient's transferences and that hinder the work in a different way. This model makes a distinction, also, between countertransference as a destructive event, on the one hand, which grows out of the chronicity of the analyst's neurosis, and on the other hand, empathy, trial identification, the analytic instrument, and so on; that is to say, the healthiest and most autonomous part of the analyst's personality, the part that helps him in sensitively understanding the psychic experience of the patient. In this model, the analyst may enact the condition of being in countertransference in a variety of ways. To suggest only a few: by having a blocked understanding of the patient; by misidentifying with the patient or by counteridentifying with him; through counterresistance or through projective counteridentification; by gratifying the patient's transference demands; by frustrating the patient's reality needs; by merging the representation of the patient with representations of significant past objects in the analyst's life; by using the patient for the satisfaction of the analyst's instinctual or narcissistic needs or as an extension of him in satisfying action tendencies; or, to give a final example, by becoming emotionally anesthetized in response to the primitivity, demandingness, disorganization, and destructive force of the inner lives of certain profoundly disturbed patients. In this model there is no possibility of the "constructive" use of countertransference. However, this model suggests that once the analyst has freed himself from actively being in countertransference, he can use his having been in the experience – now more autonomously: partly because it is behind him but mainly because he got out of it as a result of *self*-analysis, which has moved the material of the countertransference into his consciousness and into the orbit of the analyst's ego – to gain insight about aspects of the patient's transference and unconscious life that were previously hidden to him.[20] Thus the analyst either makes good use or makes bad use, depending on his personal resources, of *having been in* a countertransference, but he never can make constructive use of *being in* a countertransference.

This last model seems to come closest to what Freud had in mind; however, for comparative purposes, let us outline how Freud's original view differed. If our understanding of him was correct, Freud would have made a distinction between all of the reactions of the analyst that occur internally – that is, as purely psychological events – and the analyst's behaviors with the patient.[21] Also, Freud would have made a distinction between inappropriate behaviors of the analyst that gratify (and satisfy) the patient's transference expectations, and equally inappropriate behaviors on the part of the analyst that do not.

An Argument for Separating the Concept of Countertransference from the General Internal Condition of the Analyst at Work

Does it make sense to abandon this particular notion of countertransference in favor of one, or all, of the models of countertransference that are outlined above? On the

---

[20]Often, analysts engage in countertransferences even though they may have an emotional and nonideational recognition of the patient's inner states and needs. This is a kind of "recognition" that may precede the analyst's intellectual recognition of the nature of the transference and of the patient's internal pressures. It is frequently this particular quality of preconscious awareness that makes it possible for the analyst to merge the patient's conflicts with his own, thus setting a condition for a countertransference response to have taken place. Getting out of a countertransference through self-analysis attaches the conceptual and conscious structure to the original recognition, a key variable that permits the analyst to rework the experience over again, this time analytically, with the patient.

[21]This distinction would be similar to the one, for example, that we make between object relations (as purely internal psychological phenomena within the person) and object relationships (as externalized interpersonal events that occur between the self and others). The similarity would extend even further. We have previously discussed the highly interactive nature of object relations, fantasy, and object relationships. Here, too, we see a clear interactive determinant: the nature of what happens in the psyche of the analyst informs how he behaves in the relationship with the patient; and, conversely, the involvement with the patient that takes place in the analysis contributes to the inner experience of the analyst. Thus the ever-shifting balance between the analyst's inner life and his interpersonal interactions with the patient always exert mutual influences and are always mutually reinforcing.

one hand, it is very clear even from this short survey (which, admittedly, is very selective and incomplete) that our knowledge of how analysis functions, and how the analyst functions within it, has been greatly advanced by contributions of each of the models. On the other hand, there may be some particular usefulness in organizing our thinking along the lines of Freud's model (not because he suggested it and we want to preserve it because it was his, but because it may be advantageous to us on both clinical and theoretical grounds). Is there something to be lost by condensing the concept of countertransference with the broad range of internal experiences of the analyst, which for the rest of this discussion we will call (for the sake of simplicity) the analytic instrument? Is there something to be lost by not differentiating the analyst's motivations from his behavior? And, finally, is there something to be lost by not distinguishing between inappropriate behavior that gratifies transference and inappropriate behavior that does not?

The Nature of the Analytic Instrument

Countertransference is not a value-free concept. It has had negative connotations since it was first conceptualized, and one could argue that despite efforts to view it as neutral or even as something positive, it still retains a negative valence in the unconscious. To make the point more clear, let us draw an analogy to the situation of an "enlightened" parent who determines to toilet train his child in a nontraumatic manner. The parent recognizes that the child needs ample time to learn excretory control, understands that the child's motivations do not originally include disgust toward bowel and urinary products (and thus the child will not have the support of this affect in the early stages of toilet training), intellectually appreciates that his own disgust and his associated aggressive tendencies are not based on any compelling reality requirements (thus he is determined not to let them influence his reactions to his child when the child has "accidents" during the process), and dedicates himself to helping the child to become toilet trained in a way that uses support without physical and emotional coercion. Despite all of his conscious intentions, it seems impossible to imagine that on an unconscious primary process level, this parent could remain "value-free" during his child's toilet training. He may well be com-mitted to certain attitudes consciously, but if, for example, he were a psychoanalyst, we would consider the assumption that he could act exclusively on his conscious attitudes to be extremely naive. In fact, if he were an analyst and he ignored the fact that such an activity can only be undertaken with considerable ambivalence, we would be tempted to argue that the problem is not a lack of sophistication but, rather, a form of denial (quite possibly based on unresolved toilet-training conflicts of his own).

It may well be that analysts who try to approach countertransference as if they did not have unconsciously anchored negative attitudes that have been determined by this concept's history in psychoanalysis, attitudes which are immune to conscious secondary-process reasoning, are not fully taking into account how their conscious ideas are infiltrated with unconsciously conflicting negative superego attitudes. This presents a problem when the concept of countertransference is linked to, or made indistinguishable from, the concept of the analytic instrument; our thinking about the affectively rich internal environment of the analyst that permits understanding, empathy, insight, sensitivity, and intuition becomes contaminated with unconscious feelings of shame and guilt.

The analytic instrument is benefited not only by the unconflicted parts of the analyst's psyche but by the conflicted parts as well. A male analyst working with a female patient who has conflicts about penetration, for example, is negatively influenced by reaction formations against homosexual wishes and against feminine and bisexual identifications that arise in response to the anxieties and fantasies stimulated by his patient; however, he is positively influenced in his appreciation of her situation by the identificatory possibilities inherent in his own conflicts about penetration. His own fantasies about the pleasure of penetration; deeply retained, infantile beliefs about the possibility of incorporatively owning objects and their parts; fears of body damage; conflicts about passivity and activity; positive and negative, active and passive oedipal attachments and fears; superego conflicts about sexuality and aggression: all permit him to intuitively appreciate his female patient's penetration conflicts. Self-reflective awareness of his own psychological condition permits him to decrease the power of his anti-identificatory reaction formations, as he engages in further self-analytic work on his conflicts, and it increases his conscious and preconscious awareness of his patient's internal experiences and conflicts.

The use of reaction formation in his initial, pre–self-analytic opposition to engaging in (trial-) identification with his female patient also includes associated affects of both shame and guilt.[22] These affects serve to reinforce the power of the analyst's reaction formations, which in this case operate as means of maintaining narcissistic balance.[23] If the analyst conceptually views these complex responses as a form of countertransference, making no distinction between countertransference and his emotional aliveness and responsivity to the patient (he may not consciously know it) but unconsciously he adds an additional burden of shame and guilt to that which has already been imposed, defensively. Additional shame and guilt[24] promotes a greater reaction from the superego, and from wishful self-images in the ego,

---

[22]We are aware of the close connection that exists between reaction formation and superego functioning.

[23]We are also aware of the threat that feminine identifications pose to narcissistic balance in men, namely, castration anxiety and all of its ramifications, and of the threat to narcissistic balance that exists when one is in opposition to superego demands and expectations.

[24]Not from his identification with the patient but, now, from his "analytic superego." Also, we want to remember that, in primary-process terms, all shames are equal and all guilts are equal; thus the distinction of where the shame and guilt is coming from is lost.

to inhibit deeply felt (i.e., penetrated) identifications with his female patient. This, then, would make it harder for him to freely use his analytic "instrument" in this patient's service.

It is not necessary, as we have seen, to assume that only unconflicted resonations in the analyst lead him to relate adequately to the psychic life of his patients. Looked at this way, we are under no obligation, theoretically, to separate out the analyst's "healthy" responses and his "unhealthy" responses in positing the suggestion that everything that occurs in the analyst's inner life either is, or has the potential to become, part of the analytic instrument.[25] On the other hand, we can see some of the difficulties (described above) that may be associated with suggesting that both the analyst's neurotic and nonneurotic internal responses are, or may be, counter-transferential. Even if the analyst has an unresolved neurotic response, a neurotic response that has not yet been successfully submitted to self-analysis, we still may not wish to describe this as countertransference or as counter to the analytic instrument.

All analysts have blind spots; this is why Freud explicitly suggested that the analyst's continued self-analysis is a part of every patient's analysis. (In this, at least, there is no disagreement in the literature.) It is certainly true that blind spots in the analyst work against the treatment;[26] however, blind spots are part of the human condition; in his 1937 paper "Analysis Terminable and Interminable," Freud described the impossibility of finally "analyzing away" all the internal conflicts of which a person is capable, no matter how far any analysis goes.[27] To describe a preexisting neurotic conflict as countertransference seems both descriptively and dynamically incorrect, because the neurosis preceded the patient. And if we do so, we fall prey to the same problems associated with describing any of the analyst's internal reactions *to the patient* as countertransferential; our unconscious negative values about countertransference become attached to our neurotic conflicts (about which we already have intensely negative values) even though our neurotic conflicts have nothing to do with the patient,[28] making us more guilty and ashamed of our innate conflicts. Operating like the effect of "wild analysis," this use of the concept of countertransference causes our neurotic difficulties to become more impacted. That is, the inaccurately targeted but nevertheless powerfully affecting augmenta-

---

[25]This is not the equivalent of suggesting that conflict that detrimentally affects the treatment is also part of the analytic instrument. We can readily separate out the difference between using one's own conflicts as a method of trial identification with a patient, and having one's own conflicts work against empathic relatedness. The former is part of the analytic instrument, and the latter is either countertrans-ference (if it gratifies transference) or bad therapy (if it does not).

[26]Conflicts that create "blind spots" should not automatically be equated with conflicts that enhance the analyst's understanding of his patient, based simply on the argument that conflicts are involved in both events.

[27]Martin Silverman, whom I cited earlier in this chapter, pursues this theme in his paper "The Myth of the Perfectly Analyzed Analyst" (see bibliography).

[28]They do exist independently from the patient, as our personal problems, even if in the course of the analysis they become attached to the patient.

tion of shame and guilt inevitably has the net result of making our neurotic conflicts harder to analyze than if we had just viewed them as neurotic instead of, either by intention or by default, defining them as part of the countertransference. Defining the analyst's neurotic conflicts as part of the countertransference becomes a superego posture, whether or not we consciously intend it to, and this works against our best interests and, in analysis, it works against the best interests of the patient. We need not shy away from describing conflicts that impair the therapy as destructive; however, let us consider the following question. If we acknowledge the role that even neurotic conflict plays in enhancing the analyst's sensitivities; and if we no longer view only the unconflicted parts of the analyst's personality as the heart of the analytic instrument; and especially when we are not referring to any destructive behavior of the analyst: what possible advantage is served by describing the mental operations that enhance the analyst's capacity to better understand his patient as a form of *countertransference?*

Separating the concept of countertransference from the concept of the analytic instrument, along the lines of differentiating what the analyst *does* from the state of his *inner life,* seems to have some value if it leads to more effective insight in the working analyst and more effective insight into the patient. This brings us, once again, to our earlier question: assuming that we are only referring to things the analyst does that detrimentally affect the treatment, is there a meaningful difference when what he does wrong *is* transferentially gratifying and when it *is not?*

Let us approach the question by positing a hypothetical analytic situation in which we compare the effects of a consistent neurotic behavior of the analyst on two different patients; in one case it will interface with the patient's transference, and in the other it will not. First, let us have a portrait of each patient, and then a description of the analyst's neurotic problem:

Ms. X. comes to analysis to solve long-standing difficulties in her love relationships. She has had a history of becoming romantically involved with older, married, or otherwise unavailable men. We learn, as the analysis progresses, that she had for many years (in fact, until the onset of adolescence) a grossly overstimulating oedipal relationship with her father, which we understand is being repeated in her current sexual object choices.

Ms. Y. comes to analysis to solve an acute, seemingly reactive, depression. She had not progressed as well as she should have in an educational endeavor, and after she was asked to leave the program, 3 years previously, she became deeply depressed and has not been able to come out of it since. We learn, in the analysis, that Ms. Y.'s mother suffered a psychotic postpartum melancholia and could not tolerate sustained contact with Ms. Y. for the first year or so. We also learn that Ms. Y. came to experience her mother as if she were a dead object and turned away from her reactively as well as defensively. We understand her school behavior to be based on a reenactment of this, and assume Ms. Y.'s apparently reactive (but unconsciously chronic) depression, which consciously started when she was asked to leave school, to have its origins in the earlier rejection of her by her mother.

Dr. Z., like Ms. X., had an oedipally overstimulating childhood, except that his incestuous attachment was passive and negative (i.e., a homosexual attachment to his father in which he [Dr. Z.] took the feminine position). In compensation, Dr. Z.'s defensive resolution was the development of a kind of Don Juanism that has become directed toward all women indiscriminately. We would find it surprising if he did not have difficulty in keeping this way of relating to women out of his work. Therefore, we will posit that (whatever else he may be constructively capable of), at one point or another this difficulty, no mere surface deficiency, will make its appearance in both Ms. X.'s and Ms. Y.'s analyses.

In Ms. X.'s analysis, Dr. Z. is directly satisfying a transference wish, as well as playing into a transference fear, when his seductiveness becomes introduced into the treatment. Let us give Dr. Z. the benefit of the doubt and assume that his behavior is symbolic and not overtly sexual. Ms. X. will, of course, be extremely ambivalent about Dr. Z.'s behavior; on the one hand, she will find it objectionable (she has already had too much sexual overstimulation from her father, and look where it got her), and on the other hand, she will find it irresistible (if she could resist it, she would not be in an analysis to learn to give up incestuous love objects). On balance, because this issue has not yet been analytically resolved by Ms. X., we may predict that she will lean toward being seduced by Dr. Z. rather than rejecting his overtures. At this point, Ms. X. and Dr. Z. have begun to symbolically replay one of the most destructive events of her childhood: a chronic incestuous relationship that prevented her from finding happiness with any man who is not a pathological substitute for her father (Dr. Z. is very much like these other men—no more available in reality than are any of the other unavailable men in Ms. X.'s life). The analysis of Ms. X.'s oedipal difficulties has come to an end, even if they both consciously imagine that they are continuing to meet for that purpose. Because her pathological transference needs are being satisfied by Dr. Z.'s behavior, Ms. X. will have considerably less ego available to recognize the inappropriateness of Dr. Z.'s conduct, and one can also expect that superego functions will also be weakened; and, whereas she came to analysis to break this pattern, she is now locked once again into the pattern, this time by her analyst: Ms. X. is not merely in the situation she was in before—her situation has become immeasurably worse. In a "worst case" scenario, Ms. X.'s transference neurosis has been transformed into a mutually enacted transference psychosis, the two clinical neuroses have become interlocking (a condition that one would expect to remain unchanged in the absence of further analysis for both parties), and no further analysis is possible for Ms. X.

In the second analysis, that of Ms. Y., Dr. Z.'s seductive behavior has much less power because his conduct is not so interlocked with Ms. Y.'s conflicts. It does, on one level, satisfy one aspect of her transference: a hope that she might be able to have in the analysis the opposite of the mother she actually did have during her first year; that is, her wish, in the transference, for an involved mother (in the analyst) who would have adequate libidinal supplies consistently available for her. However, sexual overstimulation is not the same thing as providing appropriate libidinal supplies, and one would not suggest that inappropriately overwhelming sexual overstimulation is the "good mother" opposite of the kind of "bad" mothering that characterized Ms. Y.'s infancy. Dr. Z.'s behavior barely gratifies her transferential wish, and she is much more free than was Ms. X. to continue to unsuccessfully strive for transferential satisfaction in the analysis (leading to continued deepening of the transference neurosis).

On Dr. Z.'s side, the neurotic wish is less satisfied, too, because Ms. Y. (unlike Ms. X.) has frustrated him. This might lead to two possible outcomes: either Dr. Z. may intensify his efforts to seduce Ms. Y., or he may reduce them. In either case, Ms. Y. is in a better position to cope with his behavior than was Ms. X. Unlike the situation with Ms. X., whose ego autonomy was interfered with when her conflictual involvement with Dr. Z. deepened, Ms. Y. will not have had a great deal of ego energy bound up by Dr. Z.'s attempts at seduction, nor will she suffer the same fate in her superego functioning. Therefore, if Dr. Z. intensifies his seductive behavior, it is quite likely that Ms. Y. will call it to his attention in no uncertain terms. If that does not work, then she will be free to leave a treatment (perhaps not easily, but at least it is possible for her) that has clearly deteriorated.

If Ms. Y. calls this to Dr. Z.'s attention (as patients often do when the analyst is having a problem) and Dr. Z. is not so disturbed that his only option is to escalate, Dr. Z. may be able to use her signal to help himself. Granting that Dr. Z. has a pressing investment in gratifying his transference wish on Ms. Y., his inappropriate need would become even more pressing and even less resolvable if they had achieved a meshed neurotic relationship, like the one he had achieved with Ms. X., because such a relationship with his patient would further impair *his* ego and superego functioning. Unless he were very profoundly disturbed, perhaps more than neurotically disturbed, Ms. Y.'s rejection of his behavior would act as a prod to resolution[29] rather than perseverance. He would be prompted by her reaction[29] to engage in the self-analysis that is necessary in every analysis. However, even if he *were* disturbed enough to press on, Ms. Y. is *not* a co-participant at the same level, and thus, she is likely to have the freedom to break off the relationship under those conditions. Clearly an ineffective terminated analysis is a healthier resolution than a perverted one that is perpetuated forever.

One might raise the objection that Dr. Z. is, in fact, gratifying a transference wish of Ms. Y.'s in his seductive behavior; that is, that he is as bad an analyst, under those analogous circumstances, as her mother was during Ms. Y.'s first year. For this to be true, first of all, we would have had to have stipulated in our original description of

---

[29]Of course, this is not the only thing that ever prompts an analyst into self-analysis. Many analysts are of the opinion that there is much greater ego autonomy and considerably more neutralized superego functioning available to the analyst at work than at other times. They suggest that it is this – the enhanced autonomous capacity of the ego and the greater maturity of superego operations that are possible when the analyst is in his professional capacity (whether or not he happens to be in a session) – that prompts the analyst to become uncomfortably aware that something is amiss even when the patient has not called him on it.

the case that Ms. Y. had some wish—perhaps a masochistic wish, perhaps some aspect of a traumatic neurosis, perhaps a need to make a passive experience active—that would have made her *want* to repeat her first-year experience with her mother in the analysis: we must remember that simply being like a significant past object is not the same as gratifying a transference wish.

However, if one were to suggest that this behavior may not have satisfied a transference *wish* but that it did satisfy an *expectation* in the transference, we would have to take the objection more seriously. It is impossible to imagine someone with Ms. Y.'s history *not* expecting that she would find her mother in the analysis. The expectation that she might find the worst aspects of her mother would, if anything, probably make Ms. Y. especially vigilant, perhaps neurotically vigilant, but not about intrusive sexuality. She would be on guard against any evidence of schizoid or depressed functioning in Dr. Z., but would probably be able to generalize his behavior as inappropriate even though it was in the sexual realm. Without our having postulated the *wish* to revive that relationship, the expectation is a feared, rather than a desired, event, and the patient is fixated at that level in an entirely different way than when the event is in satisfaction of something. Not only would Ms. Y. have ego and superego resources available to resist such behavior, she might be even less tolerant of it because it did not capture the way her mother really was inadequate; she would have the reality-testing ability available to recognize that the analyst is not supposed, in reality, to be very much like one's transference objects, especially if they are realistically deficient or malevolent. And if one were to find that the analyst really has those flaws, or other equivalently destructive flaws, the transference would make continuing the relationship even less acceptable rather than more compelling. In either case, Ms. Y. would be able to free herself from Dr. Z.'s neurosis (or if that was not possible, because he could not change, from Dr. Z., himself) in a way that Ms. X. would never have found possible.

We can see from these comparisons that although neurotic conflict in the analyst always leads to difficulties in the treatment, when it gratifies transference wishes instead of frustrating them, it does infinitely more damage. Even though we were making a comparison, one can say, colloquially, that there is no comparison between, on one hand, the damage to the structure of the analysis that neurotic gratification of the transference can do and, on the other, the lack of damage to the structure of the analysis when the analyst has neurotic conflict that the patient does not transferentially join. In the latter case, unless the analyst is very grossly disturbed, analysis is always still possible. In fact, this is the situation that every analyst is in, since no analyst is without neurotic conflict.

Neurotic conflict in the analyst inevitably enters every treatment without every treatment suffering disastrous effects. This is the natural condition of every analysis. In fact, the reason why we can still work as analysts even though we all have neurotic conflicts[30] is because neurotic conflict need not, inevitably, have a destruc-

---

[30]We may not all be clinically neurotic, but no one is without neurotic conflict.

tive effect on the treatment. It may impede it, but it certainly does not make it impossible. If it did, no one would ever be analyzed. It does not seem particularly useful to categorize all neurotic conflict of the analyst that makes its appearance in a treatment in the same class with those situations where we find neurotic conflicts of analysts that actively have a destructive effect on the treatment. And in addition, it may not be in our best interests to lump together all the situations where the analyst's neurotic conflict harms the treatment, because in some of those cases patients will not have their resources impaired by the analyst, and in other cases patients will suffer serious impairment of their resources. In the former case, patients (whose transferences are not being gratified) have the freedom to do something constructive about the damaged analytic situation, and in the latter case, patients (who are locked into the situation because of their gratified transference) have not.

We need a way, as analysts, to investigate our inner processes, the analytic process, and the interface between them, in a value-free and conflict-free way, to the extent that either is possible. It is useful to be able to think about our inner processes, even conflicted ones, without unnecessarily having the participation of intruding and disruptive unconscious attributions of guilt and shame: it is difficult enough to be fully honest with ourselves as it is, because we are investigating our own conflicts and our own unconscious, without adding additional and superfluous burdens. For this reason we may find it desirable to go back to Freud's original use of the two concepts – of countertransference, and of the analytic instrument – as differentiated from one another.[31] And, similarly, we may find it desirable to return to the concept of countertransference where it refers only to those behavioral enactments of the analyst that (because they are unconsciously prompted by neurotic conflict) specifically damage the analysis by interfering with the transference neurosis (i.e., *behaviors* that unintentionally gratify the patient's transference instead of frustrating it).[32]

Differentiating Counter-Therapeutic Behavior from Countertransference

If we make these distinctions, neurotic behavior can simply be described as neurotic behavior, which we then examine to see how it works for or against the treatment,

---

[31]The heightened ego autonomy and heightened superego maturity of the analyst during analytic hours may well provide him with special preconscious signals when something of a countertransferential nature is occurring, specifically because the countertransferential conduct, being neurotic rather than characterological in nature, will be ego-dystonic in a way that other inappropriate behaviors may not be.

[32]We make a clear distinction here between intentionally gratifying transference and unintentionally gratifying it. There are many circumstances in which one chooses to gratify transference. For example, one would not stop being predominantly silent just because one's patient had a verbally inactive but very pleasing parent, with whom he wanted to emotionally reconnect, in the silence. Or one would be supportive with a patient whom one felt would decompensate if left unsupported, even if part of the problem was that he had parents who were too "supportive," in many unnecessary ways, and that was partly what put him in that fragile position to begin with.

without necessarily (and with automaticity) also calling it countertransference. Behavior that is countertherapeutic can be described that way and still not have the additionally guilt-inducing label of countertransference – which label, now adding further burdens to the weight of our knowing that we have been less than we had hoped to be in that situation, makes it even harder for us to resolve. And, most importantly, we can investigate the deepest levels of our emotional resonances to patients, the very thing that makes us analysts instead of educators, without having to devote our energies to coping with inappropriately applied unconscious guilt and shame. Guilt and shame that consciously arises in the process of self-examination and self-analysis is different, and easier to come to constructive terms with, than multiple guilts and shames that we are unaware of and which exhaust our needed resources through our having to defensively generate fantasies that they do not even exist.

A model organized along these lines would go something like this:

Imagine that people's personalities are like a harp,[33] with dozens of strings, some of which stand for conflicts and some of which do not; a harp where one string can be plucked independently, where many strings can be sounded at the same time, and where the sounding of any single string will cause certain other unplucked strings to sympathetically resonate in a series of harmonic overtones on that harp, and also on any adjacent harps that might pick up the vibrations that are in the air. Let us also assume that all strings, across all the octaves, that sound the pitch of C stand for conflicts, different Cs standing each for their own particular kind of conflict.

If it happens that the middle C of the analyst's harp rings out, indiscriminately, with every patient who walks through his door, we can assume that the analyst has a chronic neurotic conflict that is infiltrating all of his work; a conflict that is entirely independent of the conflicts of the particular patient who caused him to sound that pitch, despite the fact that this conflict may subsequently become meshed with the patient's conflicts as the analysis proceeds. If some patients cause him to sound middle C with great volume, if they really run up the decibel level, we can assume that these are the patients whose conflicts resonate with, and may even encourage, the analyst's conflicts.

Now we must make some choices in our model. Our first set of choices would center on what the net effect of the analyst's neurosis is with each different patient. Does the behavior that emerges from the analyst's chronic conflict prevent him from understanding a particular patient? If so, we would suggest that his neurosis is crippling the capacities of his analyzing instrument with that patient. Or, does it help him to understand a particular patient? If so, we would suggest that his neurosis has become subordinated, for the time he can use it in that way, to his analyzing instrument. If the first situation is, in effect, the one where his work is impaired by his conflicts, we would need to ask two further questions. Is the nature of his

---

[33]As long as we have metaphorized the analyst's capacities to function analytically as an "instrument," we might as well stay with it.

impairment limited to his finding it difficult to develop an internal empathic model of his patient? If so, we would still only wish to describe this as an interference in his analytic capacity as a result of his conflicts. Or is the nature of his impairment such that it leads to taking destructive actions with the patient? If this is the case, we would need to ask yet a further question. Does the action he takes in the treatment interfere with the transference neurosis by inappropriately gratifying the transference? If it does, we would call this countertransference; and if it interferes with the treatment, *but not in that particular way,* we would only identify it as bad therapy because of the striking differences in how such things affect patients when their transferences are not implicated.

Actually, the way these things usually happen is very different because most analysts, while having neurotic conflicts of many sorts, usually are not often so clinically disturbed that they have to act their conflicts out with every patient who comes along.[34] The more common situation is that the harp of the analyst is either silent or softly sounding lots of pitches when the patient enters the consulting room. However, there are certain situations in which the analyst notices that something is awry in his understanding of, or in his reaction to, or in his behavior with, a particular patient. Also, he notices this with many patients. But, what seems to be happening is that one patient causes the C *above* middle C to sound, whereas a different patient causes the C *below* middle C to sound. Each patient, then, triggers *different* conflicted responses in the analyst. We can say that, dynamically, one aspect of the analyzing instrument has recognized that something is amiss in the analyst's reaction, and this causes him to become consciously aware that something is wrong (even if he is not immediately able to identify what it is). The analyst is greatly helped in understanding his reactions, and what they mean for the patient, by the fact that different strings on the harp were involved. It is as if he says to himself: "With all the different C strings I have on my harp, how the did patient manage to pluck this particular one, instead of any other?" Whether the analyst's appreciation of the patient was interfered with (in which case we are speaking of the analytic instrument), or whether he was unconsciously gratifying a patient's transference demand (in which case we are speaking of countertransference), the analyst is prompted by his recognition to begin the self-analysis that will complete his rough early understanding that something was going wrong. In the former case, he will enhance his ability to analyze when his analysis of his reactions is successful, and in the latter case, successful analysis of the situation will enable him to stop his countertransferential acting out.

---

[34]This is, after all, one of the purposes of each analyst's own training analysis: not that he should not have conflicts, but that he should not be in such poor control of them that they spill out everywhere. Also, unless we have specific evidence to the contrary, we should assume that analysts can effectively do analytic work even if they have conflicts; it seems an unnecessarily pernicious and cynical attitude – a derivative of the superego's most unneutralized aggression – to start with the assumption that, because analysts are known to have conflicts, that the analyst's motives should always be suspect, and that he is most likely to behave in an unhealthy way, unless he has "proved" otherwise.

The analyst can also make good use of knowing which particular C string on his harp resonated with the patient's conflicts. This is the way that an analyst who has stopped being in countertransference can put his having previously been in counter-transference to some good use, instead of just writing it all off as something unfortunate that he hopes not to repeat. As many of the authors whose work was described above have pointed out, sometimes examining the countertransference[35] is an important way one can know certain things about the patient. At other times it may be the *only* way we can know certain things about the patient. And frequently it is the key that tells us which hidden transferences exist in an analysis. It has the special capacity to make obscure transference postures visible because countertrans-ference is the complementary partner to the patient's transference (another good reason for wanting to define it in a way that keeps it related to the analyst's behavioral reactions to the patient's *transference*). This can all be made even more clear through the use of two actual clinical situations, one of countertransference and one illustrating the use of neurotic conflict constructively in the analytic instrument.

The Contribution of a Neurotic Conflict in Countertransference

A female patient with an explicit erotic transference filled sessions with graphic descriptions of her sexual fantasies and conduct. As the transference deepened, the patient's fantasies became focused on the analyst. When this happened, he found himself uncomfortably stimulated, and he began to feel extremely guilty. He was excited, he wished it would stop, and he wished it would continue: all at once. Being unable to stop having erotic reactions and further eroticized wishes in response to this patient's frank sexual fantasies about him, he began to become furious with himself; and, he was beginning to feel quite angry with the patient, too, for making him aroused during sessions (which she had openly admitted wanting to do).

He was aware of the inappropriateness of his reactions but, nevertheless, was unable to listen to his patient as dispassionately as he wanted to (and as impartially as he felt he needed to be able to), in order to be of any help to her. He determined, quite consciously, that he would not act out either his sexual feelings with this patient or his angry feelings. He also believed that he should not act aggressively toward himself in this situation. He recognized, intellectually, that there was some sort of therapeutic impasse expressed by his sexual response, and he thought that by being actively aware that a problem existed he was, at least, on the way to resolving it. His idea was that as long as he felt out of control—and he did feel badly out of control—it would be best for him to take no actions in the treatment. He recognized that this was exactly the kind of situation in which analysts sometimes take inappropriate action, because they feel too uncomfortable to permit the situation to remain in that condition. His rationale for choosing not to take any therapeutic action (i.e., no interpretations, no limit setting, no questions, no clarifications, no

---

[35]Only possible, however, after the fact—not while one is still in it.

reconstructions) until he felt more in control was his concern that any action he might take would not be an informed action; that is, it would not be based on a neutral decision about what was therapeutically best for the patient.

On the other hand, he was quite suspicious of the idea that he should do nothing, and change nothing, in the treatment until he felt in more control of his responses. This was because he did not entirely trust his own motives: he believed, intellectually, that he had arrived at this as a rational decision; however, because without successful analytic intervention he had no expectation that the situation would spontaneously change, he was worried that he was lying to himself, and that he had arrived at that decision only in order to satisfy a neurotic wish to obtain more sexual satisfaction from the situation. His fear was that this was not really rational but just a rationalization, so that she would be able to keep talking dirty to him, and so that he could keep responding with excitement. These fears notwithstanding, he still felt that it made most sense to take no action until he felt he had a better handle on the situation. And so for a number of weeks the patient recounted her sexual fantasies about him, with intentional provocativeness, uninterrupted and uninterpreted, while he hoped that through simultaneous self-analysis his conflicts would become resolved enough for him to become active once again in the analysis. He felt that this was possible because he had some confidence in the process of self-analysis, and also because he thought that he knew something about the transference paradigm this patient was enacting.

The patient in this illustration is actually Ms. X., from our earlier hypothetical example of Ms. X., Ms. Y., and Dr. Z. You will recall that she had a grossly overstimulating, sexualized relationship with her father until she reached adolescence. Beginning with her earliest memories right until the present, Ms. X. could recall having sexual fantasies, with explicit content about her father. The contents of those sexual fantasies matched the contents of her sexual fantasies about her analyst, and it was apparent that this erotic transference was paternal in nature. She had, from the viewpoint of an oedipal child, an ideal relationship with her father until adolescence; he spent a great deal of time with her, and they regularly played together in ways that were always eroticized and very exciting, even if not explicitly sexual. Ms. X. identified her entry into puberty as the factor that disrupted her libidinized relationship with her father, and recalled longing, desperately, for time to be reversed, throughout adolescence. Sexuality became permitted between them only if it took aggressive forms. The nature of their interactions was that of barely concealed sexual encounters, but concealed enough, through aggression, to make them possible. For example, Ms. X. and her father would have ferocious fights, which would end up with her closeting herself in their finished basement. The fight would continue through closed doors, and the most customary form in which their battles ended was with her father shouting "Fuck you, goddammit," down the stairs, and with Ms. X. screaming back, with equal volume and feeling, "You wish you could!"

The analyst thought that the transference was quite clear, including both the sexuality and the aggressiveness of her relationship with her father: Ms. X. was shouting "You wish you could," with every explicit sexual fantasy she leveled at the analyst, and the analyst was supposed to be responding with frustrated, angry sexuality, just as her father did at the top of the basement stairs. With this knowledge of the transference, the analyst retreated into therapeutic inaction, hoping for continued self-examination to bring about some resolution of his sexual excitement and anger. The neurotic contribution of the analyst, which he conveniently forgot, was his tendency to withdraw from contact when stressed. Things continued this way for some time until one session when Ms. X. added something new to her fantasy; she was describing how much the analyst would enjoy what she was doing to him in the fantasy when she remarked that she would like to be able to see his excitement better. His face was not sufficiently visible to her, so in that fantasy she chose to imagine him without his beard and moustache. The session came to a close with nothing any closer to resolution.

For the rest of that day, the analyst had an aria from Saint-Saëns' opera *Samson et Delila* running through his head. This is an analyst who frequently had music running through his head, and so at first nothing about this seemed remarkable to him. However, at some point, he became aware that this was not typical of the kind of music he usually imagined, and this led him to wonder why *that* opera, on *that* day. As he began to think about the story told in the opera, of Delila emasculating Samson by cutting off his hair, he had a sudden flash of memory – of Ms. X. saying that she would like to have him clean-shaven in her fantasy. He then had the thought, with great amusement (that clearly betrayed as much anxiety as it did insight), "And what happens if you cut off an analyst's beard?"

With that thought, the analyst recognized that underlying Ms. X.'s erotic transference was another destructive transference, in which she emasculated her father as a punishment for sexually abandoning her. Just as in the story of their fights, where Ms. X.'s father was made impotent ("You wish you could!"), the analyst had been made therapeutically impotent by his discomfort with his sexual responsiveness and his anger. He was unable to analyze, emasculated as a professional, truly "an analyst without a beard." In response to this insight his reactive responses subsided, and he was able once again to behave like an analyst instead of her fantasied father. Rather than continuing to shy away from her fantasies, the analyst explored them more deeply, eventually enabling Ms. X. to explore and recognize the angry, destructive, punishing rage underneath her seductiveness and the appearance of sexuality in her fantasies about the analyst.

The Contribution of a Neurotic Conflict to the Effectiveness of the Analytic Instrument

This example is based on the actual treatment of Mr. Y., whose early childhood was represented in the hypothetical example of Ms. X., Ms. Y., and

Dr. Z.[36] Much of Mr. Y.'s treatment had been taken up with his growing understanding of his mother's behavior as a pathological condition, rather than as a personal rejection of him. He had spent much of his childhood trying to figure out what he could conceivably have done that was so wrong that it would have made his mother turn away from him; and much of his early relation to the analyst was a careful, guarded approach designed to make sure that he did not displease the analyst in any way. He seemed a very nice man, with essentially a forgiving nature, until the analyst's view of him was changed by a fantasy he (the analyst) had.

Mr. Y.'s treatment hour was at 9:15 P.M., on a cold wintry night. The streets were deserted, and the analyst was alone in the suite of offices he shared with professional colleagues. By coincidence the 2 hours before Mr. Y.'s session were canceled that evening and the analyst, having been more tired that day than usual, took advantage of the break and dozed off in his chair (having set the alarm to awaken him at 8:45 P.M.). At about 8:30 P.M. the analyst was startled out of sleep by something – perhaps a noise, perhaps a dream – he could not be sure.

With a feeling of considerable unease, the analyst checked the other offices: the suite had been burglarized about 2 months previously, and the analyst feared one of those horrible situations where the burglar finds someone home and shoots him when he is discovered. The offices were empty, and the analyst had no way of knowing what startled him. Growing out of his own castration anxieties, which either stemmed from something that he had dreamt but forgot, or from his fantasy of being shot by a burglar, he began to fantasize about being able to catch the burglar unawares, disarming him, and shooting the burglar himself. In the midst of these narcissistically restitutive fantasies, the analyst began to have a concern about Mr. Y., who was due to appear for his session in about 10 minutes.

The analyst imagined Mr. Y. kicking open his office door and shooting him in the chest with both barrels of a sawed-off shotgun. This fantasy caused the analyst to have the same sweaty palms, palpitations, and shortness of breath that he had experienced earlier when he imagined that a burglar might actually be hidden in the office suite somewhere. He said to himself that this was a ridiculous fantasy, totally unbelievable; Mr. Y. was not the kind of a person who would do something like that! Nevertheless, none of his anxiety symptoms were relieved by these thoughts. He then recalled a story he had heard, earlier that week, about an analyst whose former patient came to the office with a gun and forced the analyst to take him to his bank and withdraw all his money, which the patient then took. He thought to himself that it was fortunate that other analyst was not hurt in the incident, and

---

[36]In that example, the circumstances of Mr. Y.'s childhood were accurate, but Mr. Y. was represented by a female patient, Ms. Y. That being only a hypothetical example, arranged specifically to make an abstract point more clear, permitted the reversal of gender without doing violence to the concept or to the patient. This being a report of an actual treatment makes it necessary to now assign the proper gender to the patient.

then had the thought that the other analyst probably did not expect his patient to behave that way either. This did not make him feel reassured, and his anxiety symptoms began to escalate almost to the point of an attack of panic.

Seeming as if it were just a figure of speech, the analyst said to himself, "Good grief, what did I ever do to deserve this?" Remarkably, the anxiety began to melt away, and the analyst was left with that thought: What did I do to deserve this? Almost instantly, the analyst realized that this really did have something to do with the relationship between Mr. Y. and himself. Underneath Mr. Y.'s friendly and cooperative facade, the "good boy" presentation designed to never make the analyst angry enough at him to abandon him the way his mother did, was a towering rage. The transference had changed without the analyst having consciously become aware of it. The patient, having made considerable gains in analyzing his neurotic guilt, and considerable progress in realistically examining his mother's possible motives, was now free to express his fury (which refused to accept excuses about his mother being ill) at having had the kind of childhood he had with her. This wish to punish his mother, warded off and denied all of his life, was liberated by the work of the analysis and had very subtly entered the transference. The analyst apparently had some unconscious and emotional recognition of this, which is what permitted his castration anxieties to express themselves in the fantasy about Mr. Y. with the shotgun. The fantasy represented, quite graphically, the work of the analyst's comprehension changing from an unconscious awareness to a preconscious aware- ness. With fully conscious recognition of the meaning of the fantasy, the analyst's intellectual, cognitive, ideational awareness of the subtle changes in the transference became possible, and the analyst no longer feared Mr. Y.'s arrival. Mr. Y.'s analysis continued to progress nicely as this aspect of his inner life became subject to the analytic work.

At no time did the analyst enact anything related to the neurotic part of the fantasy with the patient. This fantasy, a blend of the analyst's neurotic castration anxieties and his unconscious recognition of a change in the transference, the subsequent preconscious reorganization of it into the analyst's question, and the conscious insight it led the analyst to about the change in Mr. Y.'s transference relationship to him, exemplifies a concept of the analytic instrument that is free of the complications of unconscious shame and guilt that would be present if this were thought of as countertransference. We can think about this analytic event without the slightest hint of recrimination or any other suggestion that the analyst did anything wrong.

13

Termination

M ost of the issues that are relevant to the early, middle, and late phases of analysis have already been covered as integral parts of the preceding chapters, and further elaboration of them at this time would be, in the main, redundant. The question of termination, however, has been addressed only in a very indirect way in our discussion of the various notions of cure in psychoanalysis, and that creates a necessity to discuss it now.

In "Analysis Terminable and Interminable" Freud (1937) is attempting to sum up what can be expected to be achieved by psychoanalysis in the following way: "Our aim will not be to rub off every peculiarity of human character for the sake of a schematic 'normality', nor yet to demand that the person who had been 'thoroughly analysed' shall feel no passions and develop no internal conflicts. The business of the analysis is to secure the best possible psychological conditions for the functions of the ego; with that it has discharged its task" (*Standard Edition* 23:250). This is somewhat different, because it approaches the question from a different angle, but not unrelated to, his famous prescription that the "normal" individual should be able to freely work, play and love.[1] These goals, although evident, do not help us to determine exactly what criteria we depend on when we are considering whether or not a patient has had "enough" analysis to work, play, and love, free from the incursions of neurotic misery and conflict. What are the "best conditions for the ego?"

---

[1] One way to think about the difference is that the first statement is the statement of an analyst, about how he determines when a patient seems to be ready for termination; that is to say, it is technical in nature. The second statement refers to goals that are more commonsensical, and it expresses the goals in language that could be used by both the patient and the analyst. In what follows in this chapter, the discussion will be mainly from the perspective of the analyst, but it will also, when appropriate, consider the patient's perspective on things as well. It makes sense to distinguish between the perspective of the analyst and the perspective of the patient. Consider: in follow-up studies of successfully terminated analyses, patients frequently had difficulty remembering what had been talked about and often did not know exactly what it was they had learned, or exactly how it was that changes came about; nevertheless, the analysis was successful. Being able to talk in technical terms about goals and processes of an ongoing treatment, or about what was or was not accomplished in a previous treatment, may be necessary for the analyst, but it is certainly not necessary for the patient.

Expectations and Indications

Our primary expectation is that as a result of the analysis, we will have seen significant structural growth in the patient. We will not accept simply the amelioration of symptoms, or even the complete disappearance of the particular symptoms that the patient originally presented with; we usually define the best possible outcome of an analysis as a significant change in the structure of the personality itself, with enhanced superego maturity and autonomy and a clear enhancement of the ego's integrative, synthetic, and other executive functions. Taking a closer look at these structural considerations, we would want to feel secure, at the point of termination, that such changes in the patient are not a transference cure but have come about as a result of a shift in the patient's drives and drive derivatives – away from infantile goals and infantile objects because there has been a marked redirection of them toward genital primacy. We do not require a total abandonment of all infantile aims and objects, but we do expect to see a high degree of sublimation and neutralization associated with prephallic drive derivatives and object attachments. We expect that this will have been achieved as a result of a change in the balance between conflicts and defenses involving major shifts in both ego and superego functioning.

Rather than attempting to suggest a schematic diagram or a shopping list of specific functions within the ego and superego, which we will expect to have become more mature and autonomous, let us suggest instead a description of ideal conditions that would have general applicability for any terminating patient. To begin with, we can say that in the ego we would expect to see greater conscious mastery over problems that had previously been unconscious and preconscious. This would naturally be contingent on a decreased dependence on unconscious defenses, on fewer fractional solutions to conflicts, and on an increased conscious awareness of, and control over, the conflicts that will remain still unresolved at the point of termination. This last is a very important point, because it permits the analyst to consider an analysis ready to be terminated even when he can still point to some continuing conflicts in the patient. To elaborate further on our earlier proposition, in which we said that we would not insist on a full resolution of the patient's conflicts, or on full amelioration of the symptoms that constituted the presenting problem when the patient first entered analysis: we would expect only that there will have been a significant improvement accompanied by some evidence that the patient is capable of tolerating the conflicts or symptoms that have remained unresolved. Concerning the patient's past and current conflicts, we would expect to see a reasonable amount of awareness regarding the infantile sources of these conflicts, as well as substantial insight about the derivative methods in which the conflicts were, and are, expressed. This is such a high degree of self-knowledge and insight that we would not expect to find it in someone who has not been analyzed (although there must be some unanalyzed persons for whom this is true), but it does not seem too much to expect in an analytic patient at the point of termination.

Concerning the patient's superego functioning, we would expect to see some modification of the original infantile superego attitudes that the patient will have brought to the analysis: some examples of this would include a significant decrease in primitive aggressive demands that previously may have led to tyrannical harshness in the regulation of impulses; a decrease in authoritarian moral precepts; a decrease in "talion" morality; a relaxation of unreasonable enforcement functions of the superego that is balanced by a strengthening of the superego's directive functions; solidification in the internalization of the superego that would be demonstrated by a reduction of superego projections, and by an increase in the patient's capacity to make conscious determinations and judgments about his moral attitudes and values; and, last, we would expect the patient to be able to have the capacity for adequately aim-inhibited identifications that are able to be based on a wider range of objects than just his original infantile objects and barely disguised substitutes for them. In addition to the modification of superego attitudes, we would also expect to see adequate methods of regulating self-esteem that do not resort to making use of infantile grandiosity or to a defensive blurring of the distinctions between self-critical superego capacities, self-critical ego capacities, and wishful self-images. And, finally, in managing all the narcissistic regulatory processes we would expect to see a reasonably close cooperation between the ego and the superego; most particularly, we would want to see them securely united in the control of both guilt and shame.

The establishment of mature object relations would go hand in hand with the accomplishments thus far described, and we would expect to see evidence of this in the patient at the point of termination. However, it may be in the area of identification that we find the most crucial expectation of all; that is, our expectation that the patient will have adequately internalized the analytic function established in the analysis. The patient ending an analysis may be free of the conflicts that originally brought him to treatment, but that does not suggest that he will be free of all conflict at the end of his treatment. We know that no analysis can fully rid one of all neurotic conflict, that both the unconscious and the primary process remain as vibrant mental operations, and we can recall Freud's description of the normal (even analyzed) personality as having the same components as does the personality of the psychotic, differing only in degree. The purpose of the analysis was to remove active neurotic misery, and no one expects the patient to be totally conflict-free at the point of termination any more than anyone (except the most naively wishful among us) seriously expects to be unrecognizably changed by an analysis. Also, new situations that the patient will subsequently be exposed to, after the termination is accomplished, will always have the potential to revive conflicts that seemed previously to have been settled in the analysis, and to create new conflicts where previously one may not have existed. When we say that the analytic process should be able to outlive the procedure, and that this is based on an aim-inhibited identification with the analyst's analytic functioning, we mean that one of the results of the analysis should be the patient's capacity to both recognize and explore old and new conflicts as they assert themselves in his life. This analytic identification is frequently underemphasized in favor of an examination of what needs to be apparent in the patient's object relations and what needs to be apparent about the patient's psychic structure if one is to consider termination. However, it may well be that this is the single most important termination criterion of all.

Certainly, all the things about psychic structure and object relations that have been discussed above should ideally be true (for the average expectable patient in the average expectable analysis) at the time of termination. But no matter how much structuralization had taken place, and no matter how mature the patient's object relations have become, the analysis cannot be considered complete until the patient has the capacity for independent self-analysis. If we turn this statement on its head, so to speak, we find ourselves with a very interesting question: no matter what the nature of the patient's psychic structure or the degree of maturity in the patient's object relations – even if clear signs of pathology still exist, as they do at the end of every analysis – why should it be necessary to continue an analysis if the patient has sufficiently internalized the analytic function? The patient's attainment of the analytic function rests on the accomplishments described above, and is not indepen- dent of them; and so there is no contradiction if we were to suggest that in assessing whether a patient is ready to think about termination, the measure best used is an evaluation of the stability of, and the level of aim-inhibition in, the analytic identification.

The Process of Termination

By the time termination becomes an issue, the transference relation to the analyst will no longer be mainly characterized by pathological qualities (since the transfer- ence has been worked through enough to get the patient to that point in the treatment), and remaining transference distortions and wishes will become even more muted as the termination process progresses. But once the process of termi- nation begins, one also may see an exacerbation and reinstinctualization of the previously resolved neurotic transferences with the analyst. This serves a variety of important functions for the patient, some in support of the termination process and others designed to thwart it.

The patient is in the position of having to renounce an important and deeply meaningful object and object relationship when the analysis comes to an end. Whether it is the analyst or the patient who has initially brought up the question of termination, the analyst's acceptance of the end of the relationship is experienced by the patient, on one level, as a repudiation, and it prompts feeling of anger, sadness, grief, and rejection. Both mourning and grief become central issues in the termination process, as the patient responds to the reality loss of the analyst and the analytic relationship (which may have been, for some patients, the most stable reality relationship of their lives), as the patient responds to what he has perceived as the analyst's rejection, and as the patient is reminded in the transference of earlier experiences of loss, loss of love, and separation from significant others. The more intense the transference throughout the analysis, the more we can expect to see sadness, depression, grief, anger, loss, and a sense of helplessness in the face of it, in working through the termination.

In part, the disappointment and mourning also include a response to the abandonment of the patient's last wishful transference hopes and aspirations that have survived the analysis until that point, but that now also have to be abandoned with renunciation of the analysis itself. When the termination has the meaning, unconsciously, of all of the worst frustrations of the transference, one can see a reactive development of intense negative transference, a reactive persistence of fantasied transference gratifications (the ultimate transference gratifications, whatever that might be for each different patient), or both. Some analysts, notably Greenson, have suggested that no analysis can occur without negative transferences (despite the fact that they are often warded off) that are as strong and as meaningful as are the most powerful of the positive transferences that emerge in the course of the analysis; and that, especially where they have been warded-off, no termination process can be complete without the activation and resolution of intensely negative transference configurations. Indeed, Dewald has suggested that negative transference reactions in the termination phase may exceed the severity of any of the negative transferences that have ever appeared in the analysis previously. This may have, in part, to do with the frustrations attendant on giving up the idea that, by having been a "good patient," the patient will at some future time get the analyst's love in reality. The termination destroys the patient's hope that this is a possibility, and thus removes the inhibition that the patient has maintained throughout the analysis against directing aggression toward the analyst. In the best of circumstances, both mourning processes and the final renunciation of vestigial, reactive, and remaining transference attachments are worked through in the termination phase of the analysis.

The frustration of deeply hidden transference wishes, the loss of secondary gains, and the reactivation of painful affects (carried over from past experiences of separation and loss) may cause the patient to reject termination by developing a recrudescence of neurotic symptoms and defenses in the analysis. Some patients may develop entirely new symptoms, urging the analyst to "start over again" with them; some may seek to achieve the satisfaction of remaining transference needs with others outside the analysis, perhaps even by beginning another analysis; some may reactively depreciate the analysis and feel that they have not received any benefit from it, as a means of attempting to avoid the mobilization of sadness and loss, and the experience of grief and other painfully related affects and conflicts (as if to say that if they did not get anything out of it, they are not losing much); and some may develop the fantasy, or heighten an investment in a preexisting fantasy, that contact with the analyst will be possible after the treatment has ended, as a means of avoiding the final renunciation of the analyst even though they have agreed to end the treatment. These are by no means signs that the treatment is not ready to come to an end, and repeated postponements of the termination may also be the method by which the patient puts off working them through, in a "last gasp" attempt to preserve the relationship.

The process of termination begins when the analyst and patient begin to seriously consider ending the treatment, no matter who brings it up first. The process does not begin, however, with transferential threats to end the treatment or with countertransferential destruction of the analyst's therapeutic ambition, even if the treatment should end in that way. The termination phase is above all a working-through process; we are not discussing a situational outcome. The working through of termination differs for every patient. Patients with particularly intense transferences may need more time to work through the termination than do patients whose transferences were comparatively mild; there does seem to be a correlative relationship between the intensity of the transference and the degree of emergent conflict in the working-through process of termination. Thus some patients (like, for example, Dr. A., the patient who will be discussed in the next chapter) will need a comparatively short time for termination, ranging from only a number of weeks to a few months, whereas other patients may need as much as a year or more to come to terms with the termination. Certainly, no matter what the patient's innate transference intensity, patients who have suffered real losses and separations in early childhood will be more susceptible to intense and protracted periods of working through in the termination phase than will patients whose history is not so concretely repeated in the process.[2] In settling upon a date for the termination the patient and the analyst may disagree, largely because the patient is not aware, in the way that the analyst is, of the necessity to allow sufficient time to adequately work such issues through. This can particularly be a problem where the patient wants to end the treatment fast, as a way of avoiding the conflicts, and to avoid the painful reminiscences and affects that would be stimulated by a more prolonged parting. The analyst, knowing the patient's transference condition, and having some sense of how difficult the process may be for the patient in a way that the patient cannot, frustrates the patient's wish to "get it over" as soon as possible. It is not uncommon in such circumstances for the patient to misinterpret the analyst's wish to prolong the process, as (very satisfying evidence of) the analyst's "inability" to give up the patient. Such reactions prolong the process because the patient's wishful fantasy is substituted for having to accept and come to terms with the realistic loss that looms in the future, and with the familiar and repetitive sense

---

[2]We want to keep in mind here that nothing is ever true of every case, and exceptions are not only possible, they are more usually the rule.

of loss that was triggered the moment ending the treatment became a realistic possibility; the substitution of the fantasy is expressly designed to interfere with the production of grief and with stimulation of other emotional reactions related to loss, separation, and mourning.[3]

The termination process also carries, in addition to conflicts centered on separation anxieties (and castration anxieties), an intensified recapitulation of the patient's early childhood conflicts about emancipation, independence, autonomy, success, accomplishment, mastery, triumph, victory, self-fulfillment, self-assurance, self-reliance, self-sufficiency, and so on. Reminiscent of how he might have done so as a young child, the terminating patient oscillates and vacillates between progression and regression, advancement and retreat, as he attempts to achieve his conflicted emancipation from the analysis.

Finally,[4] at least for this portion of the chapter, we should consider the question of slowly tapering off the analysis versus maintaining the analytic frame intact until the very end. When working with patients who have not achieved a very intense and regressed transference neurosis, particularly where this is the case because of limitations in the patient's ego autonomy, one could argue that it may be advisable to slowly taper off the treatment as way of graduating the experience of loss. Graduated appreciation of loss would certainly make the process less anxiety-provoking and stressful, and might afford such patients a better ability to resolve the intensely frustrating experiences in the transference that are part of every termination process. Whether or not one agrees with this approach to patients whose ego autonomy may be compromised, it seems clear that when working with the "average" analysand, maintaining the analytic frame right up through the very last moments of the treatment permits transference to remain at its highest pitch, continuing to mobilize conflict and anxiety within the analysis, which affords the analyst the optimal opportunity to interpretively help the patient to resolve the issues that become triggered in the termination process.

A patient may decide to terminate his analysis in consultation with his analyst, and he may be the one to bring it up first; or it may be the analyst. Patients also terminate their analyses without the agreement of their analysts, and for a variety of reasons; sometimes this is an obvious form of acting out of the transference; at other times it may occur in response to intolerable frustrations in the analysis; sometimes we see it as an attempt to manipulate the analyst or the analytic frame for other reasons; sometimes it is a simple matter of the patient needing to relocate; sometimes it reflects a sign of health – for example, if the patient discovers that the analyst

---

[3]This is an excellent example of what was mentioned in an earlier footnote, that is, the differences between how analysts and patients conceive of, and need think about, termination issues.

[4]The above has not been an attempt to address every conceivable consideration that could possibly be related to the indications for termination or to the process of terminating; our purpose has been to identify the main issues, to suggest some of the complexities involved, and to offer a paradigm for how these matters might be usefully considered.

is not performing properly;[5] and at other times it may reflect a major decompensation. Occasionally, by changing the frame (a reduction of sessions per week, face-to-face meetings, planned transference gratifications, and so on) the analyst is able to wait out the storm, hoping, of course, that a return to regular analytic work will be possible. Analysts frequently find themselves scrambling, one might say, to find an interpretive method of helping the patient to stay in treatment, and often find themselves having to abandon "pure" interpretation for education and suggestion. Too often, when the patient simply leaves the treatment and will not discuss it, there is not much the analyst can do about it. These are familiar and frustrating situations, for the analyst no less than for the patient. Sometimes, when nothing works, the best one can do is to find a way of indicating to the patient that such decisions are never irrevocable.

The Analyst's Reasoned Choice to End a Treatment

Let us close this chapter by shifting our discussion, however, to the least common form of termination, that is, when the analyst decides to terminate an analysis against the patient's wishes. Sometimes an analysis is stalemated, and discontinuing the treatment is the best solution for both parties. Stalemates occur for many reasons; occasionally an analysis seems to be going nowhere and neither the analyst nor the patient has a clue as to what the problem may be. It is customary in such situations to have the patient seen in consultation by a colleague who might be able to figure out, because of his distance from the situation, what the analyst and patient could not. As a result of the consultation, termination is always a realistic possibility.

Sometimes patients have needs that the analyst is simply not prepared to meet. For example, a patient might insist on being treated free or else he will quit, as part of undergoing a severe (but hopefully temporary) regression in the transference. The analyst may feel this to be too burdensome (not everyone would be comfortable in working that way), even if he agrees that such a gratification, if only temporary, would be in the best interests of the patient. When he *does* wish to meet the needs of those kinds of patients, of course he attempts to work through the reality constraints or psychological constraints that have been making it difficult for him to respond in the way he thinks is best. However, when he does not, it makes sense to refer the patient to someone who will not be conflicted about the kinds of demands that are made by such patients (many analysts specialize in creatively working with extremely disturbed patients).

Quite commonly, a patient and an analyst will find themselves in an unresolv-

---

[5]Analysts do sometimes grow too old, or they are made incompetent by an illness, without always being aware of it. Virtually every analytic institute has its own story about the senior training analyst who should not have been working, but was; and the candidate who, when he confronted the analyst (or the institute) with it, was treated as if his perception of the problem was a form of negative transference.

able transference–countertransference bind in which movement in the analysis has either become severely limited or has become nonexistent. Less commonly, but frequent enough nevertheless, and related to this, the analyst encounters a particular type of patient with whom he does not work well; long experience sometimes suggests to an analyst that there is a kind of patient that he is unable to get enough distance on, whose conflicts interface too closely with his own, and he learns to avoid them. If he mistakenly begins to work with such a patient, and something happens in the treatment that makes him realize that the patient's progress will suffer because of his (the analyst's) limitations, he may wish to discontinue the analysis and make a better referral for the patient.

Sometimes the problem is that the patient does not have the psychic resources to be in an analysis, and the analyst had not recognized early enough that the patient needed a supportive or expressive approach to treatment. Depending on many possible circumstances, the analyst may convert the treatment into a psychotherapy, or if there are reasons why the patient should not continue the work specifically with him, he may then refer the patient elsewhere. At other times the problem is with the patient's motivations for treatment; we have already discussed the way certain patients with narcissistic transferences wish to use the analysis for the gratification of narcissistic strivings rather than for the resolution of neurotic conflict. Analysts frequently lose therapeutic ambition when they are "extractively" used, and when in addition to that, the patient seems not to be making (or to be wanting to make) any therapeutic progress, and, in frustration (certainly, an understandable frustration) they sometimes prefer to discontinue working with the patient.

At the end of a very good analysis, where the patient has made much progress, he may still not feel ready to discontinue the treatment, as we have discussed above, and he may first react as if the analyst were pushing him out the door against his will. In this situation, the patient eventually comes to recognize the appropriateness of the analyst's intention to discontinue the analysis, and despite his conflicted feelings, he joins with the analyst and no longer believes that the analyst is discontinuing the treatment unilaterally and against his will. Other patients have difficulty accepting the limitations of what psychoanalysis can ultimately offer, and they too have to come to terms with these residual conflicts before they can feel that termination has been agreed on mutually. There are situations, however, in which the treatment is going badly and it seems irreversible, and both the analyst and the patient are consciously aware of the difficulties, and yet the patient will still refuse to collaborate with the termination. These are usually situations in which a psychotic transference has emerged, and in which the analyst believes that continuing the treatment will be actively harmful to the patient. If the analyst believes that it is best to end the treatment in these very difficult situations, he is always forced to do it whether the patient agrees or not (usually, the analyst is only spared the need to end the treatment himself by patients who preempt him in retaliatory abandonments). One always hesitates in making such a decision because of the possibility of countertransferential and neurotic contributions to it, and it should be made only after long examination, when the analyst feels certain of his conclusion about the harm continued treatment would bring to the patient, and, probably, in formal or informal supervisory consultation. And when it finally does become necessary, it must be handled with a maximum of gentleness and tact. Ms. D., whose treatment is presented at the end of Chapter 16, exemplifies this kind of situation. However, because it is relatively rare that a therapy ever must reach that point, and it is not an event common to the experience of most analysts, I will end this chapter with a short description of another such case.

A Sample Case of Forced Termination

Mr. W. was a third-year medical student, enrolled in a joint M.D.-Ph.D. program, when he presented for analysis. He was quite a brilliant young man who, despite the depth of his pathology, had made a number of excellent adjustments to a very pathological environment. Both of Mr. W.'s parents were psychotic: his father had been permanently placed in a state mental institution since Mr. W. had been a 4-year-old child, and his mother remained at home quietly hallucinating. Mr. W., an only child, had been subject to massive depressions since early childhood, and throughout his childhood he had terrible fears that because insanity was "hereditary" in his family, it was only a matter of time until he was next. Naturally, his extreme depressions, during which he might take to his bed for a month at a time, did nothing to reassure him on that score.

No one's conflicts are so simple that they can be reduced to a single childhood circumstance, but I would like to isolate one kind of continuous event of Mr. W.'s life in particular that had more than just a little significance to his later, disturbed behavior, the behavior that caused his analysis to have to be prematurely terminated by me. Mr. W.'s depressions, which occurred two or three times a year for as long as he could remember, were not always so severe that he would be bedridden; most lasted only a week or two and did not interfere with going to school or playing ball, or any other childhood activities. However, periodically, about once every other year, starting at about puberty, Mr. W. would have depressions of the worst type. At these times, not only did he take to his bed, but his mother would lie down in the bed with him to comfort him (frequently spending days and nights there with him). Needless to say, she brought him all his food in bed. She also would walk him to the bathroom, hold his penis for him when he needed to urinate, and wipe his behind for him when he made bowel movements. This behavior continued from early adolescence until Mr. W. was 22 years old.

When Mr. W. was not depressed, he functioned superbly. He was an excellent student, a better-than-average athlete, popular with the neighborhood kids, and, as he grew older, dated with regularity. A detailed description of how Mr. W. developed these strengths is beyond the scope of this example, but in addition to good genes (despite his fantasies), some of it can be attributed to the fact that Mr. W.

spent considerable time (living off-and-on) with his maternal grandmother, who apparently was extremely nurturing and supportive with him (this capacity seemed to be unrelated to any deficiencies that she might have had in raising her own daughter). Mr. W. was 24 years old at the time he presented for treatment, was happily married (another example of how well he functioned when not acutely depressed), and he had a 3-month-old baby at home. He came to analysis with unfocused complaints, mainly expressing his curiosity about why he was subject to depression (this curiosity superficially masking his terror of becoming psychotic).

In the course of the analytic work it quickly became apparent to me that there was some serious question about the depths of depression that Mr. W. reached, even when they were at their worst. A careful examination of those experiences indicated that Mr. W. was depressed, no doubt, but that he was perfectly able to care for himself, and especially to care for his excretory functions, without his mother's help. In addition, a long pattern of passive-demanding behavior with others began to become increasingly more apparent as the analysis progressed, and it was a monumental exacerbation of this dynamic that led to my having to discontinue his treatment after 3 years of analysis.

About a year after Mr. W. began his analysis, he began to approach many of his faculty, asking them to give him a topic for his doctoral dissertation. At first they patiently explained that Mr. W. would have to find his own topic, and then come back to see whether any of them was interested enough in it to want to sponsor the work, or, as an alternative, that Mr. W. could work as a research assistant on one of their projects, and get a dissertation out of it. Mr. W. refused to accept those replies, and began to plague his teachers with the same request so repeatedly that they lost patience with him. Mr. W. became very depressed and agitated about this, and in the analysis we identified this behavior and his responses as related to his wish to reproduce, with his teachers, the gratifying experiences he had with his mother in the depths of his depressions. The stand-off between Mr. W. and his teachers got so bad that they refused to meet with him any longer, and the only thing that defused the situation was Mr. W. going off to internship at the end of that year. The internship occupied enough of his time so that the dissertation, and the demand for a research topic, was put on a back burner for a while.

The following year, Mr. W. began a residency in medicine and reactivated his interest in forcing his teachers to give him a research topic for his dissertation. This quickly entered into the analysis in the form of having his requests now directed at me: "After all," he said, "you've got a Ph.D. You've been through the process of finding a research topic for yourself, so you know what it's all about, and you can find one for me!" No amount of analysis was to any avail in reducing his unreasonableness or his demandingness in the treatment, and no amount of rejection at the laboratory was able to, either. Mr. W. was asked to take a "leave of absence" from school, a clear warning that if he kept this up he was going to be asked to leave for good. He continued to torment many of his faculty members, threatening me in the analysis with: "If you don't give me a topic, I'm going to eventually get kicked out of school. If I lose the chance to get a Ph.D., it'll be your fault." Again, Mr. W. was refractory to interpretation where this was concerned. We had gone over the ways in which this was a repetition of the event with his mother; how disappointing it was not to get what he was used to; the shift from passive "insanity" to active "insanity"; how he minimized his capacities, even to himself, in order to maintain the wish for reality gratifications equal to the ones he got with his mother; the identifications inherent in this with both of his parents; and especially, how destructive it would be for him if I gave him a suggestion for a topic. We spoke at length about the destructiveness of what he was demanding of me, and of his insistence that he should receive it in reality. We spent time clarifying the point that it would be a barely veiled replay of what happened between him and his mother. And I emphasized as best as I could that I could not, in good faith, give him what he wanted, because to do so would only perpetuate his problem, rather than helping him to give it up; however, nothing helped.

Mr. W., – actually, now Dr. W. – began to spend all of his time in the analysis doing nothing but trying to get me to give him a dissertation topic. He began to bring in stories of how he was having difficulties in his residency training that were directly attributable to his frustration with me, but he told them with a great deal of bravado and provocative insouciance.

Dr. W. next had an incident at home, which he told me about, in which his wife and child were asleep and he was leaving the house. He smelled gas and realized that the pilot light on the stove had gone out. Nevertheless, he left the house without either waking his wife or fixing the stove. He had the thought that if they died, it would serve me right. Not long after that, Dr. W. got into real difficulties on the wards, which again he directly attributed to my not giving him a dissertation topic. Finally, a patient under his care died under circumstances that his director thought Dr. W. could have prevented, and he was asked to leave the program. Again, Dr. W. linked this to my refusal to give him a dissertation topic and my insistence on "analyzing." He managed to get into another residency program, but things began to go sour there, too. And at that time I decided that his analysis should be discontinued. We spoke about how the treatment had become an irritant to him, and a source of provocation rather than a help. I suggested that he would not have to be so destructive to others, or to himself, if I were not in his life and he did not have to force me into compliance with his wishes. If he was not in treatment, there would be no pressure to get me to give him anything, and he could stop behaving in such destructive ways as a method of leverage against me.

Dr. W. was, for the most part, refractory to these explanations, and insisted that I continue his treatment or make a referral to somebody else. I gave him the name of a colleague whom I held in great respect, harboring the fantasy that she could do with him what I could not. To the best of my knowledge, he never contacted her.

III

DEVELOPMENT OF THE THERAPEUTIC PROCESS

14

The Case of Dr. A.

This case report describes the psychoanalysis of a woman with an obsessive-compulsive neurosis who entered treatment suffering from a reactive depression precipitated by a broken love affair. The acuteness of her feelings was reactive, but her depression itself had roots leading back to early childhood.

This report is divided informally into a first section in which I present an overview of the patient and of the treatment, and a second section in which detailed descriptions of our patient–therapist interactions are provided. Naturally, you will find some degree of overlap between the two sections despite differences in format and concentration.

The first section, using the initial period of consultation as a fulcrum, provides the patient's history, dynamics, conflicts, and other aspects concerning her mental functioning. It also indicates the course of treatment, from beginning to end, and focuses on the specific points in her analysis at which structural growth was facilitated. In general, the first section of this case presentation is very much the way a clinical case report would appear in a professional journal, and although it is informative, it has the same flaw that clinical reports in the literature invariably have; that is, the reader often understands the points the author is trying to make but does not have a sufficient sense of what actually happened in the analysis, what the analyst said and what the patient said, and what the regular quality of sessions was like. Although this problem is understandable, given the constraints journals place on the length of articles they can accept for publication, the worst possible thing that could happen in a case presentation of this type would be for the reader to walk away with the feeling that he or she did not have a concrete sense of how I work. Thus the second part of this report, using the patient's first and most important dream as its fulcrum, I have used to present clinical material in considerable detail.

My hope is that despite the other side of the problem, which is having a lengthy report to read, you will get a convincing sense of what this patient was like as a person, and that you will have a satisfying sense of the mechanics involved in how this analysis was actually conducted.

Dr. A., a 37-year-old white female, in good physical health but suffering from depression, was referred by a former student of mine. She was treated, successfully, in psychoanalysis at the rate of five sessions per week for a period of 6 years.

Dr. A., a Catholic theologian on the faculty of a university, had dated a fellow faculty member four or five times and had grown rather fond of him. They had kissed and engaged in some mutual fondling, and at the time that Dr. A. expected the relationship to proceed further, both physically and emotionally, this man told her that he was engaged to be married and liked her too much to go any further in their relationship (it having been entered into by him under false pretenses). He hoped they could still be good friends. Dr. A. was infuriated, humiliated, and subsequently became deeply depressed. She had liked him very much, had had no conscious awareness of signs that she actually could have used that might have prepared her for this, had no awareness of how the nature of this relationship reenacted intense and central childhood conflicts, and was left both hurt and confused by the wish to keep on seeing him and the simultaneous wish never to see him again. She determined not to see him again, even as a friend, because of her humiliation in having been rejected and especially because of her humiliation in continuing to want him. She felt that her best protection was to break off all contact, but this was impossible because their paths crossed frequently at the university, and every time she saw him there he would try to engage her in friendly relations. In times between these occasions Dr. A. would be enraged with him; she was aware of being (as she put it) "naturally enraged at him" and also of consciously attempting to reinforce her rage as a means of countering her wishes to be romantically reattached to him.

After a number of months of unsuccessfully attempting to diminish her longing for him in this way, she began to become infuriated with herself because of her inability to abandon her attachment to him. She then became very depressed both by her feeling of frustration in not being able to have him in the way she wanted and by her loss of self-esteem in not being able to control her wishes. She discussed her situation on a number of occasions with her closest female friend, a professor of psychology, who recommended that she enter psychoanalysis and gave her my name.

Her friend gave her good support and sensitive counseling and explained to her in detail the limitations in what even the very best of friends could do, and why she thought Dr. A. should undertake an analysis (including a description of how and why it worked). It was under these circumstances that Dr. A. called me to ask if I had the time available to begin work with a new patient five times a week. I indicated that I would be able to see her and suggested that we treat our initial sessions as a consultation period in which we could explore her situation to see whether analysis was the treatment of choice for her and, if so, whether it looked as if we could work well together (the fit between analyst and analysand was one of the topics her friend had discussed with her). An appointment was then scheduled.

Dr. A. appeared for her first session exactly on time, as she did throughout her analysis unless conditions that were genuinely out of her control interfered. She was well groomed, although unnaturally so. The fact that she wore no make up was unremarkable, but her hairstyle, and most particularly the clothes she wore, looked as if they were from the 1950s instead of the 1970s. In addition, the colors she chose were dark and dull and the fabric patterns were either entirely muted or solids. She certainly did not look inappropriate but there was nonetheless a strikingly mousy, sedate, drab quality to her appearance that she looked like she worked (albeit unconsciously) to achieve.

We spent the greater portion of the first two sessions with her telling me, in greater detail than I have presented here, the material described above. Dr. A. was extraordinarily intelligent and articulate, more so than the average bright and verbal patient: but as intellectually spectacular as she was, she was proportionally muted in her affect. She described her feelings of humiliation, rage, and frustration in such exquisite detail that one could clearly appreciate how intensely unhappy she was, but the description was absolutely flat affectively; she was like a good therapist sensitively describing the unhappiness of a patient in a case presentation.

In the next half-dozen or so sessions Dr. A. related the following version of her history. She was the oldest of three children (no other pregnancies). She had a sister 3 years younger than herself who was a nun, working toward a doctorate in church history, and who had been assigned to the Vatican for the past few years. Dr. A.'s youngest sister, 5 years her junior, was a college graduate with an education major. She had two daughters, ages 2 and 5 (same age relationship as Dr. A. and the middle sister), was happily married, and never worked after receiving her B.A. This woman appears to be closely identified with her mother, who graduated from a normal school, married Dr. A.'s father, and then never held employment outside the home; whereas the middle sister and Dr. A. seem more identified with Dr. A.'s father, who was initially an academic research scientist and eventually founded a world-famous scientific business. His doctorate was in engineering; Dr. A. was a mathematics major in college, and then went on to obtain a master's degree in a branch of mathematics essential to engineering, before pursuing her doctorate in philosophy (theology). Dr. A. never really understood her shift in interest from mathematics to theology, except to say that her family was intensely religious and deeply involved in the church.

Some time later she mentioned that mathematics was both too exciting and paradoxically too boring to want to spend the rest of her life with it; however, it was not until well into her analysis when our focus was centered on her attachments to her father and her identification with him, the pacifying effects (on sexual excitement) of Catholic doctrine and practice, and her characteristic use of suppression, inhibition, and aggression as a defense against libido, that she fully appreciated how she ended up as a theologian.

Dr. A. described her father as an irascible man of violent temper who seemed to exist in a continuous state of angry tension, punctuated by furious outbursts and tantrums. His explosions of temper were always extreme and without regard to the importance or triviality of their precipitating factors. He was a tyrant, a martinet, a dictator who terrified everyone. Everything had to be his way and only his way or he would fly into a rage, and he needed to control the actions and even thoughts of everyone around him. He was hypertensive and there was always the hint, expressed by Dr. A.'s mother, that if anyone argued with him (let alone actively opposed his wishes) he could have a stroke or a heart attack. This suggestion was never medically verified as far as Dr. A. was aware, but the hint was not subtle, never denied by her father, and used as the guiding force behind the demand that he never be opposed in gesture or in thought.

Dr. A. opposed him in thought but perpetually felt guilty because it placed his life in danger. She tried her best to have only thoughts that pleased him (the thought of actually *doing something* to displease him was inconceivable), and she was perpetually guilty and angry with herself for being unable to control thoughts she had that she knew would upset him. One cannot fail to note the parallel to her guilt and anger about thoughts and wishes she could not control in her presenting problem.

Two incidents were described in these early sessions, one from childhood and one from her adult life, that will illustrate the picture she drew of her father. At 6 years of age Dr. A. stated at the breakfast table that she would like her mother to buy a new brand of vitamin, as the brand she had been using tended to uncomfortably repeat on her throughout the morning. She described her father as having begun to "huff and puff" by the middle of her sentence. By the time she finished her request "he had turned absolutely crimson with rage" and began to pound the table with his fist. He screamed, in a way that seemed totally out of control, that he had purchased the best vitamins available and that she had no right to question his decisions; he was acting in her best interests, with only her welfare at heart; she was ungrateful, and despicable; she would take those vitamins, appreciate what her parents did for her, *and like it* – or else! Of course for Dr. A. the implication was clearly that the "or else" was not only that she would be punished, but also that he would continue to be so angry that he would die and it would be all her fault.

Her mother's behavior in this, and in similar situations, was to be completely noninterfering except for afterwards, in private, when she would remind Dr. A. not to get her father too upset because of his high blood pressure.

The second incident occurred during her early twenties and also had to do with a dinner-table scene. Throughout her adult life, in fact up until the middle of her analysis, Dr. A. spent every weekend (with only a few, very rare exceptions) at her parents' home. One Friday evening during the traditional fish dinner, Dr. A.'s mother served her two filets of sole on the same plate. They were not overly large and together added up to about the amount she would ordinarily eat, and Dr. A. got up from the table to return one to the oven to stay warm while she ate the other. She sat back down and her father leaped up, grabbed her plate from in front of her, ran into the kitchen and threw open the oven door, dumped the filet back on to her plate, and ran back to the table upon which he slammed down her plate in its place. Dr. A. sat in stunned silence. "How dare you refuse this food your mother prepared for you!" he bellowed. "Do you know how much work she went to just to prepare this for you? Don't you have any awareness of how expensive this fish is? God gives you food while, all the time, other people in the world are dying of starvation: and you have the nerve, the unmitigated gall, to throw it away? How dare you?

How dare you?" Trying to pacify him, Dr. A. began to explain that she only wanted to keep it warm. Her frenzied, apoplectic father shrieked at her that she had no right to accuse her parents ("i.e., him; i.e., God;" she now acidly commented) of providing inappropriately served meals, that no one in possession of his senses needed to keep food warm that was already hot, that she was disrespectful and disobedient, that such behavior would not be tolerated in his house, that she would eat her food as it was served *and* (once again) *like it,* and that she had better mend her ways and begin to appreciate her parents – after all, some people have none – for all that they do for her. Dr. A. ate her fish.

Dr. A.'s choice of examples was significant on a number of accounts. To begin with, these memories were served up to me the way she received her vitamins and her fish. The fact is that her father was an extremely complex man who had many other facets to his personality, and he was also capable of warm, tender, loving, friendly, and affectionate relations. And if you, as the reader, have developed the impression that Dr. A.'s father was an absolute monster, then you share not only Dr. A.'s conscious view of him when she entered treatment but also the view that she insisted that I share with her, too, even long after there was ample evidence to the contrary.

It turned out that up until the middle of the oedipal complex, when both father and daughter seemed to be becoming progressively more overstimulated and disorganized, Dr. A. and her father had a close and loving relationship quite unmarred by the aggressions described above. As will be described in more detail below, it appears that both father and daughter retreated from their incestuous involvement (psychologically, not physically) via a retreat to anal aggression in which the phallic and then genital relationship was played out in sadomasochistic terms. Dr. A.'s memory and perceptions of her father were dominated by the need to inhibit oedipal love through anger and seemingly ego-dystonic masochistic submission; however, this process by its very nature acted simultaneously as both a defense against incestuous wishes and a transformed gratification of them. When material arose in her associations that suggested that her descriptions of her father were uneven and perhaps even inaccurate, and I would then comment on this, Dr. A. would fly into a prolonged rage, accusing me of accusing her of being a liar; describing me as attempting to (as she put it) force interpretations down her throat (a very overdetermined accusation very much in accordance with Dr. A.'s fears and wishes); questioning my integrity, my intelligence, and my honesty; and attempting to engage me in a variety of other ploys designed to make me feel guilty, humiliated, and afraid to speak my mind again.

Her rage at me for pointing out that clues from her preconscious productions suggested that there was another version of her father hidden behind the one she was consciously aware of, and her intensified rage at me for pointing out (some time later) that these were not merely memories and perceptions but a set of memories and perceptions that she was committed to, and committed to preserving, reflected both an intensification of her attempts to keep her incestuous attachments suppressed and an acting out by her of the sadomasochistic oedipal relationship in the transference. Thus, for both defensive as well as transferential motives, Dr. A. served up these images of her father the way he served up her vitamins and fish, from the onset of the very first hours to the middle of her analysis.

Here, too, we once again can see a reflection of the material in Dr. A.'s presenting sessions, in which she described native rage and a kind of conjured-up rage, in connection with an intense romantic setting as well as acting as a defense against unwanted thoughts and feelings. It is also worth noting that the first real break-through of affect (active vibrant rage) occurred in the conditions just described; that is, when evoked by a more regressed transferential condition associated with the deepening quality of the transference neurosis. Up until this point Dr. A. was able to inhibit the external display of affect although she reported, quite believably, feeling her feelings deeply. But, we get ahead of ourselves.

Another significant feature of Dr. A. having chosen these two examples, by way of giving me her history, is the conspicuous absence of her two sisters. One would imagine, listening to these stories, that Dr. A. was an only child. Such was the intensity of Dr. A.'s involvement with her parents, particularly her father; that she experienced the world as if there were no one else in it except for her and them. It was not until the end phase of her analysis, when Dr. A.'s oedipal attachments were in the final process of stage-specific renunciation, that her sisters entered her thoughts, and consequently her analysis, with any frequency and in a continuously meaningful fashion.

From material presented in the middle of her analysis, Dr. A. discovered (with a sense of surprise equal to an explorer's on discovering a new land never before even conceived of in human history, and with a great deal of discomfort, too) that she and her father had an especially close and intense relationship until she was about 6 years old. So very special was this relationship, and with so great an intensity was it, that Dr. A. (at a slightly later date) put it this way: "We formed a closed unit between us. Of course my mother was important to me, but she was more like a necessary servant (I am embarrassed now to say), whereas my father was my very life itself. He made the world come alive. We were so very, very involved with one another that everyone else existed only in the abstract. I know the theories about sibling rivalry, but in my case I don't think they applied. I got so much from my father that I barely noticed when X. and Y. [she names her sisters] were born. If my mother withdrew from me at those times, I wasn't aware of it. Probably because my father did not. I think the petty jealousies I felt toward X. were of so little consequence to me because I was more involved with my father when she was born than I was with my mother, even though I was only a little over 3. The same seems true of my lack of rivalry with Y. I was just 5 when she was born. You know, I don't think my sisters were quite real to me until my father changed and rejected me when I was 6. Isn't that peculiar? [Pause] After things became so different between us, when my father seemed so angry with me and I was so preoccupied with attempting to find out what he wanted and how to be that way, even then I think my sisters still weren't entirely real. I was so caught up by that conflict between us that I do believe that my sisters still existed for me only on the peripheries. To some extent, mother, too. [*Very lengthy pause*] Dr. Lasky, did it ever occur to you that the nature of my relationship with my father never really changed, even if it looked on the surface as if it went from good to bad? [*Another lengthy pause*] Can it really be true that I still am just as enmeshed with him now?" Dr. A. quickly, but only temporarily, left the final question, which, although it did surface, she was unready to contend with at that time; and at that point she began the serious analytic investigation of the sadomasochistic transformation of the oedipal love she and her father shared. It was a relationship so compelling and engrossing that they two were, for all practical purposes, the only two people in the world.

Before understanding this transformation, Dr. A. first had to recall the suppressed memories of her early relationship with her father. And despite the conspicuous absence of material about her sisters in the early stages of treatment, interestingly enough, the way we first began to see the emergence of these memories was in connection with one of her few references to a sibling. This event, which ushered in "the return of the repressed," occurred 2 years prior to the statement just described, in the twenty-sixth month of Dr. A.'s analysis. But before moving back from the fifth year of Dr. A.'s analysis to its third year, let us go back even further for some additional background. Dr. A., as you will recall, initially insisted on presenting her father as a fuming, fire-breathing dragon, belching noxious fumes in every direction, with no redeeming qualities whatsoever, and she forcefully resisted any exploration of her presentation. Direct interventions pointing out any inconsistencies in her description of him or calling her attention to preconscious evidence to the contrary were rejected in anger. However, midway into the second year of her treatment Dr. A. did become responsive to some expression of my interest in examining her experience of her father if I were to raise the issue in a somewhat indirect way. Naturally, before she could remember other more pleasant aspects of their relationship she had to first question her current perceptions, memories, attitudes, and beliefs; and her readiness to begin this process became apparent (even though it was, at first, a limited readiness) in interchanges such as the one that follows. I had been preparing (with smaller comments) for some time to make the lengthy interpretation described below.

Dr. A. had been describing a typically horrendous story, in which she was home for a weekend visit and had spent all day housecleaning in her parents' home. "Finished at last," she thought to herself, when her father began to complain, in his typically critical and overly angry fashion, that the bathrooms looked terrible. Dr. A. was not able to understand what it was he found at fault, but her mother took her aside and suggested to her that in order to keep him from becoming too upset (which could affect his blood pressure) perhaps Dr. A. might want to go over the bathrooms (all three of them) once again. Dr. A. sighed in frustration and resignation, and in order to keep the peace, got down to work.

At that time in her treatment both the analization of her relationship with her mother and the role it played in the sadomasochistic compromise formations of her oedipal conflict (which will be discussed in greater detail below) were too far from Dr. A.'s consciousness to be investigated in that context. Instead, because it was more immediately germane and because it offered her a chance to examine her ideas about her father without specifically singling him out for attention, I offered the following comments: "This story supports all you have said for many months now about your parents, and how impossibly selfish, brutalizing, and self-centered they are. Everything you have told me about your childhood is entirely in character with this extremely abusive conduct. In fact, this is even rather mild compared to the kinds of abuse, and the continuing stream of abuse, you suffered throughout childhood. But, you know, there is something that puzzles me. It is usually true that severely abused children, particularly when there has been a profound a lack of love, comfort, and support as you have described, turn out rather badly. I mean, given your childhood, one might have expected you to have grown up to be psychotic, or at the very least, a mean, hateful, supremely destructive person. One might expect lots of other kinds of problems, too, like reduced intelligence, learning difficulties, an inability to develop close friendships or to offer love to another person, and other stuff like that. But none of that is true of you. You are extremely bright; you've racked up an impressive array of degrees; you have close relationships in which you are very open, warm, and giving; you are extremely ethical and have moral attitudes that are based on kindness to others as well as doing what's right; and your intrinsic belief in the rightness of loving others is not based only on the teachings of the church but also on a deep inner conviction that love between people is possible. What puzzles me is where you developed these ideas, how you were able to become so accomplished, and how you turned out to be, at heart, a basically decent human being. In other words, I don't understand why you did not develop into the monster the events of your childhood seem to call for. Are you sure there wasn't someone else in your childhood you haven't told me about? Someone who treated you right, who loved you and loved you properly, and gave you what a person needs in order to grow up with decent values and a capacity to care for others?"

Dr. A.'s response to this was much better than to earlier, more partial attempts on my part that more directly challenged (although they were by no means confrontational) her determinedly rigid presentation of her father. Also, putting it into the intellectual arena (without transforming it into something intellectualized), an arena where she was able to function in a more conflict-free fashion, was quite helpful. Given the fact that she could not identify anyone else in her childhood who could account for this, Dr. A., too, found herself puzzled. Now, however, she found the puzzle intriguing rather than threatening. Not immediately, but within a short time, she, in her typically tenacious fashion, grabbed on to the puzzle like a bulldog with a bone (with all the aggressiveness implied in that simile). Over a number of months, during which this comment and other, shorter comments like it were offered, Dr. A. finally came to the conclusion that she must have some defect in her memory. She asked if I thought this was true.

Given Dr. A.'s propensity for power struggles, about which I had learned a great deal by this time, I chose, instead of confirming this, to remind her (based on a number of other considerations about the number 6, too) that she had never spoken about a memory earlier than age 6. With the further passage of time Dr. A. decided that the defect in her memory had two characteristics: first, that since the age of 6 she must be blocking out all positive experiences with her parents, and second, that she must be actively blocked from remembering anything earlier than the age of 6. Before my comment it had just never registered on her that her memory began at age 6. Following my comment she thought that memories of being 6 years old ought in fact to be considered very early memories, and perhaps earlier memories were just lost to childhood, in general, for all people. Being too smart for that, she soon gave up this idea and concluded that she had a conspicuously motivated absence of memory.

Ultimately we reached a point where she decided that 6 years of age must have been some sort of turning point in her life, and that the positive experiences that would account for the healthy aspects of her personality must have taken place during the period she was actively blocking out. We are now nearing the twenty-sixth month of Dr. A.'s analysis when, as I mentioned earlier, a reference to her sister led to retrieval of the facts of her life before age 6. In the session immediately preceding the one we are leading up to, Dr. A. expressed her readiness, preconsciously, to retrieve some of the lost period of her childhood, saying: "I wonder how long one must *play* [my emphasis] with ideas before they become translated into memories, insights, and change." In the next session she was speaking of a weekend at home with her parents during which her sister came to dinner (another dinner scene) with her husband and children. Dr. A. was describing, in her characteristically martyred presentation of herself, how her parents, sister, and brother-in-law and nieces were romping and playing in the living room after dinner while she was in the kitchen washing the dishes and scrubbing the pots and pans. Mother was embroidering; Y. and her husband were playing Scrabble and listening to Beethoven's Sixth Symphony (Yes, it really was the Sixth. The fates were with us this time!); periodically, Y.'s husband would leap up from his chair when the music was particularly stirring and would make believe he was vigorously conducting it, to great hilarity all around; and father was bouncing his little granddaughters up and down in time to the music, one on each knee.

"Quite a happy little family scene," I said, "it sounds really very nice." "Sure," she replied, "as long as you don't take into account my slaving away over the sink, and having housecleaned all day, and my having spent more time than my mother on cooking and serving supper. You don't see them expecting all that from Y., do you?" "Yes," I said, "that's true. But if we don't take all that into account, it really does sound lovely." "What's your point?" Dr. A. asked, somewhat more warily than belligerently. "Just that it's a nice picture of your family. Particularly your father, bouncing your nieces on his knees in time to the music. I didn't know he had it in him." "Why that's not true at all," she said in a huff, "I happen to have a very nice family, and my father and I played that way lots of times when I was their age." "Really?" I said. Dr. A. gasped in surprise and burst into tears, "Yes. Yes, we did. I never remembered before, but we did. We played together all the time." This session ushered in a period of concentrated effort to remember and integrate her happy memories of childhood with her father, which brought us eventually to the session early in the fifth year of her analysis (described above) in which she first consciously identified the sadomasochistic transformation of their relationship, and after which the oedipal nature of their love began to become explicitly revealed. But, more of this below.

Let us return once again to those introductory hours to see how they presaged the conflicts Dr. A. would explore regarding her relationship with her mother. She did not say a great deal about her mother, describing her most graphically only as a by-product, as it were, of an accounting of the antagonism between her father and herself. Dr. A., referring directly to her mother, described how mother would absent herself psychologically when father and daughter were battling, sometimes even leaving the room to absent herself entirely. The usual case, however, involved mother being present but fading quite actively into the background when father would begin to rant and rave. It was Dr. A.'s understanding that her mother behaved in that way because she fostered the hope that by not interfering she would cause, or help, the situation to de-escalate that much sooner. Any active role her mother played involved reminding Dr. A. not to upset father, or suggesting that Dr. A. agree with him or do what he wanted. It was Dr. A.'s impression that her mother always agreed with father: she may have had reservations about her husband's style of delivery, but these reservations had to do with his health rather than with his right to be dictatorial or abusive. Mother was experienced by Dr. A. as if she were a facet of father instead of a separate person with distinct characteristics of her own. Dr. A. was aware of the many objective ways in which mother and father were unalike, but her emotional perception of them, consciously, indicated a distinct lack of differentiation. She could intellectually acknowledge many differences between them, but nonetheless thought about them rather monolithically, as if there were only a father and his shadow with which to interact. And in doing this, Dr. A.'s mother was both present and made to disappear simultaneously. This reflected a partial truth about Dr. A.'s mother, who did generally defer to her husband, and who did, all too often, subtly encourage the sadomasochistic scenes between Dr. A. and her father through her behavior during and after their imbroglios; it also reflected, however, Dr. A.'s unconscious wish that her mother not come between her and her father; it also reflected how the intensity of Dr. A.'s oedipal involvement with her father overshadowed and even blocked from memory the libidinally gratifying relationship she had (as was later confirmed) with her mother in infancy, in childhood, and as an adult; and, it reflected too, in her seeing her mother as the sadistic colleague of her husband, an aspect of the ascendancy of aggressively anal-erotic factors in her relationship with her mother which, itself, played a significant role in shaping her oedipal relationship with her father.

Dr. A. described herself as usually getting along well with her mother, and although she tended to treat her mother dismissively in those initial sessions, she did comment on how obsessively clean her mother was, and how that was one of her finest characteristics. One got the impression that her mother was very much a lady, genteel, reserved, rather immaculate in her personal habits and in how she kept her home. Yet Dr. A., unintentionally I think, conveyed a sense that there was some pathological urgency to her mother's gentility and orderliness, and then this sense of impression of mine (for it was nothing more than that at first) was verified by considerable material about her mother and about Dr. A.'s toilet training as her analysis progressed. Dr. A.'s mother seemed to be an upper-middle-class version of the housewife whose furniture is always shielded by fitted clear plastic covers, and on further examination of the bathroom-cleaning scene (which we went over many times between the session in which it was introduced until the end of her analysis, in much the same way that dreams may be returned to again and again) Dr. A. eventually concluded that despite outward appearances, the reason why her father could not make himself clear about what was wrong with how she cleaned the bathrooms was because it was never really his complaint to begin with; Dr. A. thought that her father was really acting as her mother's agent (probably, although she was never certain, unconsciously), even though it looked on the surface as if Dr. A.'s mother suggested a recleaning of the bathroom only to pacify father. She also thought (although, again, never with any sense of final certainty) that in such circumstances, her mother's communication of her needs to her husband was as unconscious as was his knowledge that he was acting out her wishes for her.

Dr. A. also mentioned that she and her sisters were supposed to have been toilet trained at very early ages, with no particular difficulties. Her mother told her this, and although she considered her mother to be trustworthy and reliable she nonetheless viewed this claim with some suspicion. Her disbelief was based on recollections of what she described as major battles between her mother and both of her sisters over toilet training. Dr. A. initially remembered nothing about her own toilet training, but her memory of her sisters' toilet training was particularly vivid. She first referred to this in one of those early sessions rather offhandedly and in a different context: "I don't know if it is true that opposites attract one another, but in the case of my parents that does seem to be true. As volatile and 'Hitlerish' as my father can be, my mother is just the opposite. She is very quiet and gentle. The only time I ever remember my mother having anything in common with my father was when she was toilet training X. and Y. I used to be frightened of her then because she used to become so angry when they had accidents. But that's the only time she was scary to me, and that passed as soon as they were both out of that stage. Other than that she was, and is, the sweetest and most considerate person imaginable. It is as relaxing to be around her as it's agitating to be around my father. I guess she calms him down, and that's one of the things that attracted him to her. Goodness knows, he needs some calming down!"

Late in her analysis Dr. A. retrieved many active memories of her own toilet training, replete with recollections of struggles of intense and considerable magnitude in which she and her mother were almost constantly at odds with one another. Dr. A. also came to the realization that many of the struggles she remembered as having been between her mother and her sisters were really about her mother and herself. She also concluded that the fear she experienced when watching the struggles between her mother and her sisters were really about her mother and herself. She also concluded that the fear she experienced when watching the struggles between her mother and her sisters was compounded by fears of her mother that were active but carried with her only internally and unconsciously, and which were then especially triggered by those scenes.

What emerged during this period of analysis, when early childhood memories had finally become accessible to her, was a picture of an extremely good mother–daughter relationship that turned unbearably sour at the time of toilet training. Dr. A. had active memories of extremely satisfying experiences with her mother in relatively early infancy. Such memories included images of being held, sung to, played with, fed well, being dressed in her pajamas (with the feet attached and a real flap in the back, although at that early age it was just for show), and being dressed in snowsuits. Parenthetically, we may note that the memory of the pajamas with the flap in the seat reflects the unfortunate analization in her retrospective memory of some of Dr. A.'s happiest and most conflict-free years. Dr. A.'s memories were, as might be expected, confused and incomplete. They were remembered more as snatches of experience than as complete and coherent memories. They carried with them, in the telling, both an intensity and an internal consistency that convincingly gave the impression of a very happy and secure childhood prior to toilet training. Apparently, for whatever reasons, Dr. A.'s mother seemed able to suspend her anal reaction formations when her children were truly infants, but when it came time for them to be toilet trained her anal conflicts, which seem to have been quite severe, asserted themselves with a vengeance.

One may wonder, in the light of her subsequent behavior, what gave Dr. A.'s mother the ability to be what appears to be very truly supportive and unconflicted in nurturing before her children were to be toilet trained, and one may also wonder how she seemed able to genuinely maintain her mothering equilibrium with her younger children when she was, at the very same time, so out of control with the older siblings at the toilet-training stage. In other words, Dr. A.'s mother could be more than adequately nurturing with her infant while simultaneously being overpowering and destructive with a slightly older child, and the key to the change in her capacities seem to be related to her expectations and demands around toilet training. One may wonder how she simultaneously kept these separated with two children of different ages and one may wonder why, with such anal conflicts, they did not also contaminate her initial capacities for good mothering with any of her children. Unfortunately, we do not have these answers and all we may do is wonder, but there seems to be no question that she was initially sufficiently supportive and adequately nourishing emotionally for each of her three children. Dr. A. valiantly struggled (always a struggle, of course) with an attempt to understand why and how her mother went through such a sudden and startling transformation: how could she be so selfless and giving before toilet training, and then turn so demanding and rejecting during toilet training, and then seem to disappear into the woodwork from then on?

Naturally, Dr. A.'s attempt to analyze her mother was frustrating because it was, as an objective task, impossible. In the process, however, she acquired a great deal of information about herself and her own childhood. A critical thing she learned was about the many hidden ways in which her mother and her father were alike. This recognition, that the anal power struggles she suffered with her mother were essentially no different from, or at the very least inextricably interwoven with, the constant power struggles she had been having, incessantly, with her father since she had been 6 years old, affected Dr. A. profoundly. To summarize a very complicated sequence, Dr. A. first recognized that struggles with mother and struggles with father were in essence the same and then linked this up with another recognition previously noted in this presentation, that is, that in the current struggles with her father (the struggles that her mother seemed to have no part of) the truth was that both her father and her mother were actually acting in concert with one another. He may have initially been the primary focus because he became the highly visible enactor of both their wishes (and perhaps even sometimes only of hers), but Dr. A. finally became aware of this and came to realize that the struggle with her father also couched within it an ongoing struggle with her mother as well.

As a consequence of these realizations Dr. A. was brought to an appreciation of two points of the utmost significance. First, she was able to speculate that the quality of her relationship with her mother in the anal stage actually served as a template for maintaining an oedipal attachment, in its final form, to her father. Dr. A., it should be remembered, was analyzing this material with her mother during the same general time in which she became aware of her happy oedipal love for her father, and in which she also began to recognize how and why it deteriorated into an endless and perpetually pathological attachment. She thought that when she was 6 and their relationship changed, her father chose an anally-tinged sadomasochistic compromise formation (my words, of course, not hers) because his dynamics were similar to the dynamics of her mother, and that she, Dr. A., entered into that mode of compromise with him because it directly paralleled her immediately previous sequence of experiences with her mother. She said once, pensively, "You know, when you do something once, it's easier to do it again the next time. My life with my mother went from good to bad, and the bad was as bad as the good was good. And the kind of bad it was, even if it didn't last forever, was a life-and-death struggle—or so it seems to me now. My life with my father went from good to bad, and with him too the bad was as bad as the good was good. And the kind of bad it is now, which has lasted forever, is a life and death struggle. I wonder if I would be in such constant conflict over everything with my father if I didn't do it first with my mother. [*She laughs.*] I just had the thought that my toilet training was a rehearsal for the rest of my life."

The second item of significance, and one which was of the utmost importance, that thrust itself into Dr. A.'s awareness was that her continuing pathological oedipal relationship with her father, and its amazing tenacity, was also reflective of a deep and continuing attachment to her mother. She now fully appreciated the condensation that she had maintained between her parents, based in part on features of reality and in part on her inner needs. When she began to be able to see that the overt aggression in her relationship with her father was a reversed form (and a reliable measure) of the depth of their oedipal love, she was then also able to see that in this condensation between her parents there was the representation of her preoedipal aggression with her mother, and not only that, but also of her earlier happy love for her mother and their prior, almost idyllic, relationship. It was when she began to see how she and her father were too threatened by the closeness of their relationship and so, in order not to give each other up, transformed it into a disguised–consequently less threatening–anally organized sadomasochistic relationship of equal intensity and involvement, that all these insights and their working through became possible. This work was accomplished in the end phase of Dr. A.'s analysis, and what I have summarized here in one long paragraph represents, in actuality, about 2 years of work. Dr. A.'s ultimate recognition was that, even up until the present, her involvement with both her parents (and not just her father) was so deep and compelling that it was finally clear why there never was room for anyone else in her life; that is, why no one ever came along to take their place the way it happens for other people who grow up, marry, and establish families of their own.

This comment leads us back once again for a final look at the series of Dr. A.'s initial consultation sessions, to acquire the last piece of critical information about Dr. A.'s circumstances that led her to treatment: information that, in light of everything said thus far, will make perfect sense. Dr. A. was once again reviewing that recent disappointment in her love life, and after having discussed this from a number of vantage points in the preceding sessions, suddenly revealed that her frustration was especially compounded by the fact that although she was 37 years old she was still a virgin. Holding back information was a very characteristic pattern of behavior throughout much of her analysis. It was particularly painful to her that he rejected her when she cared so much for him that she had decided finally, for the first time in her life, to have sexual intercourse. If she had had the expectable sexual experience of a woman of 37, perhaps she would not have been so devastated, she said. But she felt so very intensely, profoundly hurt because she cared so much; so much, in fact, that it was enough to want to take a step that she had feared and avoided up until she met him. Much later in her analysis she became aware of signals he gave off that should have clued her in to his unavailability, and subsequently she came to the conclusion that if she were really ready for sex at that time she would have picked a man who would have been happy to accommodate her physically and emotionally. But lacking that insight at the time we are speaking of, she then also feared that her anger and her pain at his incomprehensible and mortifying rejection might make it impossible for her to ever again feel ready to have a sexual relationship with anyone (also, in and of itself, a hidden wish). It felt to her, she said, that she had lost both her first and last chance. By the end of that session Dr. A. indicated that she had major sexual problems, problems that went beyond just the fact that she was still a virgin, problems that she could not yet tell me about (of course), problems that she thought for years she should have been in therapy because of, and which she would like to try to resolve in this analysis. We were agreed by this time, without particularly formal declaration, that we would undertake to work together, and the period of consultation shifted into the beginning of the work of analysis.

The preceding material, using Dr. A.'s initial period of consultation as a fulcrum, has been an overview of Dr. A.'s presenting problems, her history, the nature of her basic conflicts, a description of some of her key dynamics, and a summary of the course of her treatment with reference to the order in which various issues in the working-through process were addressed. The following section of this exposition will present, in greater detail, what analytic sessions with Dr. A. were like; how the transference issues emerged and were explored; how we worked with fantasies, dreams, and other primary-process material; some further remarks on Dr. A.'s defenses, identifications, object relations, and psychic structuralization; and, finally, the particulars under which Dr. A.'s analysis was successfully concluded.

Dr. A. spent the first few months of sessions going over her anger at herself for wanting her "almost boyfriend," her anger at him for deceiving her, her feelings of longing for him and her sense of loneliness whenever he would come to mind. She never referred to her virginity or to the more profound sexual problems she had alluded to earlier, and which she had claimed at that time were probably the most important reasons for her needing to be in analysis. She described this man in high detail: his appearance, his attitudes, his conduct, and so forth. She gave, in fact, an overabundance of detail. It was an overabundance of detail because her descriptions were extremely lengthy and included a degree of thoroughness that was most extraordinary, yet for all her protracted discussion of him, none of what she originally began to say ever led her to any associative material. Her inner feelings and particularly her interactions with him were described as if they were a reading of a picaresque, epic novel. Although much reference was made to her feelings, and it was apparent that she was in true distress, her manner of delivery was essentially narrative in form. Her descriptions of how she thought about him, and her feelings in the process of thinking about him, were also detailed to excess.

She might, for example, spend an entire session describing how she was dusting her furniture while reviewing in her mind what he had said to her when he told her that he wanted to discontinue the romantic aspect of their relationship. I learned about all her furniture: what each piece looked like; which one she was dusting when she had each thought about him; the kinds of materials she used for dusting and for polishing; which pieces of furniture required only dusting, and which also needed to be polished; where in the room they were sitting when he told her; which was his favorite chair, and which was hers; where she stood up and walked to in the room when he gave her the bad news (to the window); what the view is, and was that day, from that particular window; her sense of shock, and the chair she walked to and sat down in while attempting to compose herself before making a reply to him; the problems she had had in trying to find exactly the right place in the room for that chair, and the questions she had about whether it would look better in some other room entirely or, on the other hand, whether she should just get rid of it and replace it with another one; the words she thought of using as well as the reply she actually made; the look on his face; how at one point the tea kettle began to whistle, and her feeling of relief at having an excuse to leave the room in order to attend to it; her thinking, once she was in the kitchen, about whether she should just turn it off and return immediately to the living room, or whether she should bring back a cup of tea only for herself, or whether she should bring back tea for both of them; and if she was going to bring back tea for both of them, should she ask him what kind of tea he would like; the fact that he liked herbal teas whereas she did not; what kinds of teas she liked; what kinds of teas she had in the house; what kinds of teas were readily available in local stores, and where one might have to go in order to find the others; the various methods she had devised for storing tea in an airtight fashion to keep it from going stale; the relative merits of tea bags versus loose tea bought in bulk; her thoughts about purchasing a new kind of electric tea kettle that had just come out on the market; the eruption of her tears as she imagined passing the herbal teas in the supermarket; how she wiped away her tears before returning to the living room so as to hide how upset she was; her brand of tissues; why she liked them best; and so on.

There is no question but that listening to Dr. A.'s monologues was informative in a variety of important ways, and there was clearly a great deal of symbolic significance in her exquisitely detailed "digressions." However, such intensely obsessional delving into detail also made listening to her difficult at times (this was an inevitable and unavoidable countertransference trap). The aspect of the process that was difficult was made even harder by the fact that Dr. A. had a relatively monotonal manner of speaking, even when the content of what she was saying was highly charged: a subdued and muted quality of presentation that did not seem to be attributable entirely to her depression. During the early months of her analysis Dr. A. also spoke frequently about her father, the conflicts between them, and every other conceivable detail concerning her "weekend visits home." Her extraordinary attention to detail of even the most insignificant kind (to the extent that anything in analysis can ever be insignificant) was equally true of this material. Her sessions illustrated, in addition to her extreme obsessionalism, a characteristic use of intentional and quite actively boring repetition and attention to detail (notwithstanding the fact that her intentions were unconscious) to serve multiple purposes.

One set of purposes centered around issues related to her father and sexuality:

(1) it reflected an attempt to keep her own excitement in check, to keep herself muted; (2) it was designed, through attempting to bore me, to keep any excitement I was capable of feeling equally muted; (3) it had the purpose of trying at the very same time to elicit excitement from me: angry, restless, frustrated feelings I was intended to have in response to being bored by her, which would in symbolic fashion place me in a similar affective posture to the one she experienced in the emotional climate with her father; (4) both this veiled seduction and the repetitive aspects of her presentation were separately, and together, highly transformed masturbatory equivalents, the aggressive components of which will become particularly clear in a later discussion of the specific nature of Dr. A.'s masturbatory fantasies; (5) it was a means of expressing both erotized and nonerotized aggression.

A second set of purposes centered around the maternal transference: (1) it was a means of repeating, with the roles reversed, the anal power struggles she experienced with her mother in which one powerful and dominating figure could keep the other, weaker, one immobilized and restrained for long periods; and (2) by initially emphasizing that specifically sexual problems were her most long-standing and important reason for requiring treatment and then never again explicitly or implicitly returning to the topic, she was able to maintain a sense of narcissistic integrity: this was accomplished by making a presentation permitting her to seem as if she were entirely forthcoming and totally cooperative, saying everything that came to mind faithfully and without censorship, while actually withholding that which, by her very definition, was of most importance.

Dr. A.'s first recognition of some of these purposes, centering on both her defensive maneuvering and the paternal transference, was achieved late in the first year of her analysis following a number of sessions in which she began to comment, with increasing frequency, on the inconsequentiality of many of the details she related, on the repetitiveness of what she had to say, on her emotional flatness (except for the several times she became excessively angry with me when I questioned her perceptions about her father), on the fact that her subdued nature seemed somewhat contrived in the sense that it could not be adequately accounted for by depression alone, and also on the lack of intensity in our relationship. Her general but reliable knowledge of psychoanalysis had led her to expect that the transference relationship in analysis would always be particularly strong, emotional, and stormy, and yet ours seemed so mild and pallid to her. She speculated that perhaps this was so because she was simply a boring patient. She began to express the fear that she was not just simply a boring patient, but that she was a very boring patient indeed, and that, compared with my other patients, who were unquestionably more animated and interesting, working with her must really be a trial for me. She became anxious that I might secretly be harboring a wish (her projected version of her own many secret wishes) to discontinue her analysis, if I actually were as bored with her as she supposed I must be.

She went on to speak of the many happy hours I could be having, and that I might resent not having with her, if I had an interesting patient to work with instead of one who, in her words, was boring me to death. It was this particular idea, *that she was boring me to death,* that gave direction to the subsequent sessions despite the many alternative associative paths she could have chosen to follow (such as the issue of rivalry with my other patients). It was as a result of using the expression "boring [me] *to death"* that material began to coalesce into a number of insights concerning the hidden aggression in her manner of relating to me, and in how she presented herself. Finally, she came to the insight (in a way that greatly upset her) that behind the fear of boring me to death was the active wish to do so. Dr. A. then returned to the idea she had expressed, about ten sessions previously, that I might resent not having happy and pleasurable sessions with her.

After making some inquiries for the purpose of clarification, I pointed out the difference between not having happy and pleasurable sessions *because of her,* which is what she thought she meant to be saying, and what she actually did say, which was that I might resent not having happy and pleasurable sessions *with her.* In great embarrassment she became aware of the wish that we should have pleasurable hours together, and with even greater embarrassment she revealed (as much to herself as to me) that it would be nice if I looked forward to her sessions as much as she did. Feeling extremely guilty and uncomfortable, as if she had done something terribly wrong, Dr. A. returned to her earlier idea about wishing to bore me to death: partly as a defense that substituted a challenging intellectual puzzle for an extremely disquieting emotional condition, and partly as a genuine attempt to understand this seeming contradiction.

Eventually, and of course inevitably, Dr. A. recognized that we did, in fact, have a very intense relationship. It was a relationship in which she wanted love, attentiveness, interest, concern, and involvement, but which existed under a surface of disinterest and unrelatedness. This was also a camouflaged need being given expression, to make the relationship implicitly hateful even if the quality of hatefulness never became overtly revealed. With a shock of recognition Dr. A. saw, for the very first time in her analysis, a replay of the most essential part of her current relationship with her father in the treatment setting with me: the hateful part of their relationship in which she wished him as punished and humiliated as she was by him.

It was not until much later in her analysis that Dr. A. understood that the love, attentiveness, interest, concern, and involvement she wanted from me stood for what she wanted from her father, wanted from her mother, had (in original and transformed fashion) from him, and had had prior to toilet-training from her mother. But what she did understand at that time was that she, through her angers both at me and her boringness, had been creating in her mind a relationship of antagonism between us that directly paralleled the overwhelming antagonism and discomfort she currently experienced with her father.

A more detailed reflection about the problem of countertransference is useful at this time. Although there were many reasons why Dr. A. chose to begin reflecting on her repetitiveness and boringness, some of which would suggest both good therapeutic technique on my part and strong autonomous ego functions on Dr. A.'s part, there is no doubt in my mind that some part of the explanation must be that when Dr. A. was at the heights of obsessional detail and repetitiveness I was often bored, and that Dr. A. must have picked that up in some way I had not intended (or was even aware of).

Bored was certainly not the only thing I was, but I *was* often bored and there simply is no way of getting around that fact. And it seems to me that it is not possible that this could have been lost on Dr. A., who was a sensitive and highly alert person. Her fears that I found her boring were not only fears and wishes but were also preconscious perceptions, correctly identifying an aspect of my emotional reaction to her. I have the impression that her unconscious recognition of this existed long before she began to address the issue, and that the gratifications inherent in having successfully seduced me into establishing an oedipal relationship with her (hidden deeply within the healthier aspects of our analytic relationship) served to reinforce, if not prolong, this trend in the nature of her emotional, cognitive, and behavioral conduct in her sessions.

I think the trigger that started Dr. A. working analytically on this issue, in the context of the healthier and more executive ego-functioning of both of us (which was also in continuous operation on other levels), was the shift in her from unconscious to preconscious recognition of the gratifying but also destructive elements of this aspect of my emotional state, and also some preconscious aware-ness of her pleasure in it. Initially, she broached the subject through some accurate, and some self-attacking and not entirely accurate, observations of herself, and then opened the topic for true analysis with the expression of her fantasies and fears.

Dr. A. succeeded in recognizing some of the aggressive components, including the importance of inhibition, that characterized her relationship with her father as this was being emotionally replayed with me in her analysis. But, as has been mentioned, she did not yet appreciate the defensive roles that inhibition played, and that transformations of libido into aggression played, in her relationship with her father himself. And she also did not yet appreciate the ways they reflected a relation to her mother as well as to her father. Nevertheless, her first profound recognition of a major transference relationship with me was a turning point in her analysis, and there was a marked shift (following the reintroduction of an old dream) in the content and style of her presentations. Mainly, Dr. A. began to focus on the sexual problems she had previously been withholding. This realignment of her approach signaled the beginning of a libidinally tinged paternal transference, still predomi-nantly colored by aggression but no longer entirely bereft of the libidinal aspects of her ambivalence. In addition, it also demonstrated a partial relaxation of the anal power struggle being enacted in her maternal transference relation to me.

Dr. A. began to tell me about her sexual difficulties by informing me that except for the man whose rejection drove her to treatment, she had had a relationship with only one other man in her entire life. What that meant was that there was only one other man in her whole life she had ever dated, held hands with, or kissed. That relationship too, which she began to describe, was remarkably oedipal, and also clearly replayed the anal-erotic relation attached to both of her parents. It significantly demonstrated her addiction to her father as the only true love object: the relationship was so obviously oedipal (but not to her, of course) by virtue of its having been so triangular in nature.

The man in question was the husband of her best friend: the husband of the psychologist on the faculty of her university in whom she had confided her troubles and who had recommended to her that she enter treatment. Part of her relationship with this man was a secret, and part of it was with her friend's blessings. Nearing the end of Dr. A.'s analysis we explored some unconscious homosexual wishes she had regarding her friend (reflecting underlying wishes for an oral, not genital, reconnection to her mother) based on other aspects of the triangularity of the relationship (in which the man they both shared were substitutes for each other), but at this stage of her treatment the primary focus was on heterosexuality and on telling me of the secrets she had been keeping back.

The entire subject was opened up, as was previously mentioned, by the reintroduction of the first dream Dr. A. presented in analysis; a dream she had one profitable idea about on its first report and one which she returned to repeatedly as is not surprising given the nature of her dynamics. However, her repeated forays into examining this dream did not grow only from her obsessive nature but also from its innate importance: it was the first dream, it was the dream she always returned to (and she had many others, so it was not as if she had to return to this one for lack of any other opportunity), and it was a dream in which all the central features of her neurotic conflicts were reflected (although we know that in theory this is true of any dream, it was through this dream more than through any other that we were able, at various times during her treatment, to learn about and address ourselves to her wishes, anxieties, guilts, and conflicts). The dream was as follows:

I was a little girl and my mother had baked a chocolate cake with an icing of fudge. The cake was going to be a birthday present to me from my father. The cake was on a counter in the kitchen and was going to be served at dinner that evening. I knew that it was my birthday cake. It was no secret. I mean that it was not intended as a surprise. My mother was elsewhere in the house and I don't know whether my father was home or not. I decided to eat some now, even though I was supposed to wait until dinner. I began by scraping some of the icing off with my finger and tasting it. It tasted luscious and my mouth began to water profusely. I quickly scooped off some more and put it in my mouth, and that made me want even more. In my home one does not stick one's finger into things, and if they saw that I had done that, my parents would have considered me crude and been angry with me. I cut a thin slice out of the cake to hide what I had done, and even though I needed to eat it to hide what I had done I was also looking forward to eating it with tremendous excitement. I ate that slice of cake and savored every bite. The taste was so exquisite. Then the scene changed. I was still in the kitchen but my parents were there and about three-quarters of the cake was gone. I had a terrible stomachache: awful cramps. Apparently, I had gotten carried away and eaten all that cake. I had a memory of eating slice after slice in a rapture of pleasure, but that was only a memory in the dream. I didn't actually dream the part in which that happened. In the new scene I had a terrible feeling of being too full and I had those awful pains in my stomach, and my parents were there and very angry with me. I think they had already told me how I ruined my father's present for me, and all my mother's work. But when the scene changed they were just standing there angrily staring at me. I had to get to the bathroom desperately, but I don't think it was to relieve my bowels. Then I woke up.

Dr. A.'s initial interpretation of this dream, when it was first reported, was that it represented both her insatiable hunger for the man who rejected her and the punishment she was suffering for having indulged her appetite to begin with. When the dream came to mind this time, immediately following the exploration of her "boringness" and her first recognition of the intensity of her transference, the part she focused on was "the open secret" of the birthday cake. She remembered the dream somewhat differently, saying that it was a paradox that the chocolate cake was definitely a secret birthday treat from her father but openly displayed in the kitchen for all to see. She then had two particularly vivid memories: of seeing herself eating the cake, and of the end of the dream in which her parents were staring at her angrily after having observed what she had done. She said that she had felt a deep sense of shame. After a lengthening pause I asked her why she had become silent. She said that she was flooded with the same sense of shame and that it was an intense feeling accompanied by visual imagery that didn't have words attached to it, which was why she wasn't speaking. All she had was this vision, "that we looked at together just now," and the terrible sense of shame it engendered. I commented that looking and seeing seemed to be emphasized in her recollection of her dream, central to her sense of having done something wrong, and central to the intense shame she was now feeling: seeing something that was supposed to be a secret (the cake); being shown something she did not know whether she should or should not be seeing (the cake being left out by her parents for anyone to see); seeing herself doing something wrong (in the dream memory of eating the cake); being seen doing something wrong (her parents angrily staring at her); the active looking at something bad (her) that her parents were doing—as a separate issue from the one where she is the focus by being observed; her seeing the dream's visual components in the retelling and the flooding of shame in her silence; and finally, me looking on (as we looked at these memories and her feelings together) to add its own ingredient to her shame. All issues of looking, seeing, and being seen, inextricably tied into her profound sense of shame. I further remarked that the essence of the dream in her prior telling of it seemed to emphasize the eating of the cake as something she did wrong, whereas now it seemed as if her sense of shame had shifted and even intensified around issues that had to do with looking, seeing, and being seen.

There now followed another silence, lengthier than the previous pause, but one in which I did not get the impression that further comments from me would be of use. After some time, Dr. A. indicated that she was silent this time not because she had no words but because she was aware of something, an association specifically related to looking that was directly relevant to what we had been speaking of and to her sense of shame, that was also partly a dark secret, and which she was trying to work up the courage to speak about. And thus the material referred to earlier as having been immediately freed to emerge by the first successful analysis of a transference resistance (but by no means of the transference itself) began, from out of this dream context, to be brought into the analysis.

Dr. A.'s secret involved two elements, one of which she had been withholding from me and the other of which she had been hiding from her friend. She began by telling me that one of her secrets, of which she was particularly ashamed, was her interest in looking at pornography: not reading pornographic stories but looking at the pictures in pornography magazines and going to pornographic movies. Dr. A. was raised in a home where no explicit mention of sex was ever made except to point out its sinfulness. In fact, even what was being pointed out as sinful was always inexplicit and unclear. An amusing anecdote (which once again illustrates the anal and phallic condensation in Dr. A.'s conflicts) gives one a sense of this quite clearly: Dr. A. was told once, but at the time with great emphasis, that when she was in the bath she should not touch herself. She spent many years wondering how one could get clean if one never touched oneself while bathing. She knew that this was not a topic she could pursue because the ominous manner in which the instruction was delivered made it clear that the subject, including even talking any more about it, was seriously taboo. She resolved the dilemma, saying that she never had even the slightest idea that masturbation was being referred to, by deciding that her mother must have meant that when soaping and rinsing her body she should always use a washcloth rather than her bare hands. She had sexual interests and fantasies throughout her childhood about which she had felt quite guilty, and which will be described in the discussion of her masturbation fantasies later in this case report. These fantasies were carried forward into adulthood (which was when she actively began to masturbate) essentially unchanged from the forms they took in childhood.

Dr. A. had no traditionally romantic fantasies throughout her childhood or adolescence that she was aware of, and never had any interest in dating in high school or in college. She was spared provocation by the fact that she attended a parochial all-girls' high school and college. The nuns referred to love and sex strictly in vague admonitions about the sins of getting boys excited, a concept that Dr. A. said was not relevant to her because she had no interest in boys and which she didn't understand anyhow, and in repeated reminders that love and "the rest" were to be engaged in only within "the holy sacrament of marriage in which Catholic babies were made to house Catholic souls."

When Dr. A. left home for the first time it was to attend graduate school, studying the subject of her father's profession, and reflecting one highly personified aspect of her strong identification with him. She lived in a dormitory for girls, most of whom were enrolled in the undergraduate division of this coed secular university. Her roommate was an undergraduate sophomore who was sexually active and who frequently spent her weekends elsewhere. On one of those weekends when her roommate was away, Dr. A. discovered a pornographic magazine hidden behind some books. She was first shocked and offended, then fascinated, and eventually reached a stage where she actively looked forward to her roommate's absences so that she could look at the magazine again and again, despite her intense feelings of guilt and shame (but mostly guilt) at doing so. After a few months the magazine suddenly was missing, and she never again discovered any others (and you can be certain that she made thorough searches) for the rest of the year that they roomed together. She was intensely disappointed and would have liked to get some pornographic magazines of her own, but she was afraid that her roommate might discover them as she did hers.

Dr. A. decided that she would room alone for the second year of graduate school, not as a sign of growing independence or in order to have the sexual privacy of the usual sort desired by young adults, but in order to have a place of her own in which she could accumulate a collection of pornographic magazines safe from discovery. The decision to do this was a major one for her, obviously fraught with conflict, but one she was determined to do, and did. This ushered in the period of actively acknowledged masturbation in her life, which would begin with a viewing of her magazines and was completed to orgasm through sexual fantasies only partially related to what she saw in the magazine pictures.

She did not, at the time of relating this material, indicate the nature of her fantasies and how they differed from what she saw in the magazines, but these fantasies were described later in her analysis (also in the context of returning to that dream). At this time, however, Dr. A. simply mentioned in passing that there was a difference between what initially excited her and what finally brought her to orgasm, as part of the story of how over a number of years she accumulated an extensive collection of pornographic magazines.

Amazing as it seems, Dr. A. would regularly drive to adult book stores in many locations outside the area where she lived and worked to buy her magazines. She described herself as going through a transformation directly from a sexual innocent with anaesthetized impulses to a sexually obsessed onanistic nymphomaniac, being entirely unaware at the time of the connections of all of this to her infantile sexual preoccupations and to the hidden but continuingly unrenounced sexual nature of the relationship with her father.

For years Dr. A. bought these magazines and would masturbate frequently, yet she still never dated nor did she have any interest in becoming involved with men. Her sexual interests were centered on her inner world of objects, rather than on the object world itself. The years passed, Dr. A. changed graduate programs, received her doctorate in the new program, began teaching at the religiously supervised university where she was employed when she entered treatment and where she met, and became very close to, the psychologist who referred her to me. Their friendship deepened, this female friend serving as a representative of her parents prior to the conflicts with her mother in the anal period and with her father in the phallic stage, and eventually they began to speak about Dr. A.'s lack of involvement with men.

A most bizarre arrangement emerged from these discussions, which was most unusual in that Dr. A.'s friend was usually sensible, levelheaded, and constructive in her judgments and in the advice she offered to Dr. A. In talking about the lack of romance in Dr. A.'s life, Dr. A. revealed that she had strong sexual interests and that she was involved with "magazine masturbation." She also told her friend that she was very interested in going to see pornographic movies, but of course this was impossible since she had no one to go with and could never have the courage to go to one by herself. Her friend said that her husband was very interested in pornography but that she was not. He had brought home some magazines that turned him on incredibly but that did nothing for her. Recently he had been "pestering" her to attend a pornographic film with him, which she had been resisting. Very uncharacteristically for her, and obviously in relation to some conflicts of her own, Dr. A.'s friend suggested that since both her husband and Dr. A. were very interested in seeing these films, they could go together: it would be a perfect arrangement – Dr. A. would have an escort, and her husband would be going with someone who he could see these movies with and who would be "safe" because she would not involve him in any sexual entanglements outside their marriage. And so Dr. A. and her friend's husband began to go to porno films together about once every other week. Afterwards they would go to a diner for a light supper, or coffee and cake, and then he would drop her off at her apartment on his way back home. Dr. A. and her friend continued to talk about the need for Dr. A. to find a romance in her life, a real romance with a real live man, and scrupulously (and rather conspicuously, I think) avoided discussing her going to the porno flicks with her friend's husband.

As Dr. A. and her friend's husband got more comfortable together they began to discuss, in their post-movie time together, which parts of the movies turned them on. Dr. A. found the fellatio scenes most exciting, especially when the man ejaculated and the semen could be seen in the woman's mouth or when he withdrew his penis at the point of ejaculation and the semen was directed onto the woman's face. She also found exciting scenes in which a woman would masturbate a man to ejaculation and then lick up the semen. She also found it very exciting, she told me, but not him, the fact that in all these pornographic movies women were obviously merely sexual objects for men – receptacles and tools to be used for their sexual gratifications without the pretense of emotional involvements.

She interrupted her narrative at this time for two brief departures. First, she said she didn't tell *that* part to him, and felt very uncomfortable admitting *that* part to me. In fact, *that* admission was even more uncomfortable than the explicit descriptions of the sexual activity, and her associated excitement, because she was a strong supporter of the women's movement and was quite active in it. In principle she understood and supported women's resentment of men's treatment of them as mere sexual objects, and thus she was terribly embarrassed about the fact that this attitude on a man's part was a special kind of excitement for her. She then wondered whether I was the sort of man who viewed women as whole people or only as sexual objects, and this was the very first emergence of a clearly libidinally tinged transference in the analysis.

She paused, and then introduced the second departure from her story in the form of a memory about the chocolate cake dream. She said that the idea of the dream had just "popped" into her mind, and she was remembering the profuse salivation and the rapturous pleasure she experienced, both in contemplating tasting the cake and while eating it. She connected this to what she had been saying about fellatio and seeing the semen in the women's mouth, but then dismissed the connection impatiently, saying that it was "just too pat" and that "symbolism and connections of this sort could be made about just about anything."

I did not pursue this for two obvious reasons: first of all, she rejected the idea rather forcefully, and any further attempt at focusing on it on my part would have made her defensive reaction more extreme and also would have probably played into the other, hidden, transference demand that I enter into a sadomasochistic anal-erotic power struggle; and second, she did, after all, make the connection, so why continue to press the issue any further at that time? Naturally, this also was definitely not the time to point out that fellatio stood for reparative oral satisfactions from her mother (who baked the cake), and that oral excitations regarding the cake stood for fellatio (an oralization of genital contact) with her father (since the cake was to be *his* present even though it was her mother who baked it). All of this material was analyzed, however, and quite fully so, at the proper times later in her analysis.

After dismissing this association, Dr. A. continued her story. Not surprisingly, discussions between Dr. A. and her friend's husband went from talking about what excited them in the movies to discussing the fact that they were highly excited in the presence of each other during the watching of the movies together, and finally to the immediate sexual excitement that they were feeling both as they were talking, each to the other, about their sexual responses to and also during the movies.

This information emerged over a number of analytic hours, and Dr. A. referred again to the cake dream reference of a few weeks earlier, mentioning how obvious the relation was to her of all this material to the emphasis in the dream on looking at forbidden things and then the sense of shame that ensued. To which I added, in a subsequent session, the remark that another aspect of the dream that made her ashamed was being seen doing something forbidden or bad.

She picked up on that immediately and said that telling this man about her sexual excitement both at the movies and with him afterwards was a form of exhibition-ism, a way of actively being looked at or passively being seen while being very bad; but, she said, it was both paradoxical and puzzling to her that she felt some shame in the process but much less than she ever would have expected to feel. What she was feeling in ascending order of intensity was shame, guilt, anxiety, and sexual excitement—but mainly sexual excitement. She then said that telling me about all this, in analysis, was a similar form of exhibitionism.

Pausing for a moment, she then said that she was very surprised that she could tell me about all of this without being bombarded by shame and guilt. Did that mean she was feeling sexually excited now, or sexually attracted to me? she asked rhetorically. No, she decided, that couldn't be true because she was not aware of any such feelings, and besides which, I looked too much like her father to be an object of sexual interest for her. And with these negations she both demonstrated the intensification of the erotic transference developing in the analysis and specifically introduced for the first time an element of information about the underlying erotic nature of her relationship with her father (which, up until then, was expressed only in terms of overt hostilities).

Returning to her only other experience with a man, Dr. A. described how it came to pass that quite expectedly one thing led to another, and that she and her friend's husband ended up at Dr. A.'s apartment one night after the movies instead of going to the diner for coffee and talk. They began to kiss and to pet: Dr. A.'s first kiss ever, the first time anyone ever touched her, and the first time she ever touched a man. Dr. A. and her friend's husband were kissing and mutually masturbating one another when he suddenly drew back from her and said, "I'm going to come soon. Do you want to watch?" Dr. A. stopped her kissing and her manipulations immediately and said, "No!" He was surprised and very disappointed, and when he wanted to continue she refused. She would not explain herself, adding to his confusion and frustration. They argued, he left, and they never went to the movies together again. Dr. A. continued to meet socially with her friend and her friend's husband, and neither of them acted as if they had had a falling out. But they never went out together again, and that never was acknowledged as a topic of conversation between the three of them; in fact, throughout all of this and afterwards as well, Dr. A. and her friend (once the arrangement was suggested) never discussed either Dr. A.'s excursions with her friend's husband or the fact that they had abruptly stopped.

During one of the hours in which this was being reviewed (Dr. A. still expressed her obsessionalism through overly repeated returns to material, even if much of the overtly aggressive element in this was reduced), Dr. A. returned once again to the cake dream and noted that there was a parallel between the conspicuous avoidance of this topic in her relationship with her friend and an aspect of that dream. Did her friend know what happened between her husband and Dr. A., or did she not? Was that (one) sexual encounter unknown to Dr. A.'s friend and therefore truly a secret, or was it an open secret in the sense that she knew about it but never acknowledged it between them? Did her friend know about all the verbal foreplay between her husband and Dr. A.? Her friend knew that something sexual was happening, inasmuch as she was the one who suggested that Dr. A. go to porno flicks with her husband, but it was presented at the time as if Dr. A. and her husband would be like children engaged in parallel play rather than in mutual play. Could she really have meant that, or have believed that that was possible?

This reminded Dr. A. of the ambiguous nature of the birthday cake that was a secret, or supposed to be a secret, or wasn't supposed to be a secret but yet somehow was supposed to be a surprise, or wasn't supposed to be either a secret or a surprise but just a special treat.

Dr. A. could not explain to that man why she abruptly stopped when he asked if she wanted to watch him ejaculate because she herself didn't know. She was not consciously aware of anything other than the feeling that she didn't want to, and wouldn't, continue. The question of what he was feeling, or for that matter what she was feeling, was nonexistent outside of her wish to stop what was happening. This seeming blankness to everything but a stubborn refusal to continue when he asked her not to stop was what she emphasized in the telling of this incident in the analysis. She fluctuated between a very fleeting and mild curiosity about why she had said no: after all, he was, she said, being thoughtful rather than selfish, considering the fact that he knew that she was tremendously excited by seeing ejaculations in the movies, and, on the other hand, an adamantly angry feeling (predominating in most of her reaction) that she was not going to continue if she didn't want to, and nobody was going to make her.

When I pointed out to her the fluctuations in her attitudes about examining what had happened, she treated me as if I were him and was asking her for something sexual. She took the position that I was telling her what to think about, and that if she was more involved in expressing her feeling that no one could force her to do what she decided she didn't want to do, then that was her right, and where did I get off telling her what to think or how to think about it?

For a number of sessions Dr. A. either angrily, or in softly intellectualized and highly rational-seeming statements, condemned me for abandoning an analytic posture. I had told her, she reminded me, that she was to say everything that came to mind without censorship or regard to its apparent relevance or rationality, and here I was now, telling her *not to talk about what was on her mind* and recommending— no, insisting—that she *talk about what was not on her mind!*

I reminded her that curiosity about what had happened and her angry reactions were both on her mind at the time I made my comment, and that what seemed to happen, once I said what I did, was that she determined that one thing, the curiosity part, was not going to enter her mind again. She grudgingly acknowledged this but reiterated that no one could make her think about anything she didn't want to. I asked her if there was any reason why she might not want to think about her original curiosity, and focus so exclusively on the rest, and we were off and running again, with her accusing me of trying to trap her into talking about something she didn't want to.

A number of sessions then passed with Dr. A. maintaining an angry, stubborn silence. In the midst of one she said, "Have I made my point?" "Yes," I replied. After another few moments of silence I commented that although I still thought it worth her while to follow up all her reactions, I understood that such a remark was experienced by her as a provocation because it was something that I seemed, to her, to want for me: to serve some purpose of mine, instead of something I commented on in order to help her. "True," she said, "and that's why I am not going to discuss it and you aren't going to be able to make me."

My comment, she amplified, caused her to stop what she was doing–purely free associating–and instead forced her to have to protect herself from being pressured into doing what she thought I wanted her to do. I asked her if she would be willing to discuss with me what she thought my motives might be if I wanted her to investigate this for me rather than for her, and she said she'd give it some thought. Another session passed in silence.

In the following session Dr. A. began speaking immediately, saying that she had been trying to figure out why I was so insistent that she examine her curiosity when it suddenly occurred to her that I had never insisted on any such thing–all I had done was to point out that there were alternations in her reactions, one of which was that curiosity. Somehow, she realized, she had translated that into my having made a condemnation of her; at the point when I observed that her curiosity was fleeting and mild in comparison to her other reactions. Then she ended up feeling that I was demanding that she drop everything else and relate to what she thought I believed was an inappropriateness in her. She was insulted and hurt at what she saw as a harsh criticism I made of her and by my demand that she comply with my wishes, when in reality, she now said, I had done nothing of the sort. Thus, she said, the question was not one of figuring out what ulterior motives I might have had, but of trying to understand why she felt so hurt and criticized by me, and why she saw me as so selfishly demanding.

Dr. A. soon came to the realization that she was feeling with me exactly what she felt with her father, but, she said triumphantly, with one important difference: this time, finally, she did not have to give in. And she went on to describe, at length, the extraordinary sense of satisfaction she was feeling as she imagined that I was becoming increasingly more frustrated by her. As she repeated the description of her pleasure in imagining her leading me on with "tantalizing associations" and then frustrating me "to the point of bursting," I commented on the similarity of this behavior with me and her behavior with her friend's husband. "Exactly," she exclaimed, "exactly!" "Did you know at the time it was happening that this was behind your refusal to continue, or to discuss it with him?" I asked. "No, no, of course not," she replied. "Then I didn't know anything about why I was doing that. I just had to stop. It didn't feel like something I was doing, it just felt like something that had to happen."

She then paused, seeming uncomfortable rather than withholding, and as the pause continued to lengthen I said, "Did you think of something you didn't want to say?" "Yes," she said, "something I feel very ashamed of. That what I did with [*she names her friend's husband*] and what I did with you were both sexual. And there's something even worse. Somehow it's connected to my father." "Why do you say that?" I asked. She laughed, and chided me good-naturedly, "Don't worry. You don't have to be so cautious–I'm not going to bite your head off, or accuse you of asking leading questions, or of attempting to direct my train of thought. I think I'm over my craziness now. If what I was doing with [*she names her friend's husband*] and you are connected, and what I was doing with you is connected to my feelings about my father, then obviously what I was doing with [*she names her friend's husband*] must somehow be connected with my father. What connection there is to my father is beyond me, I can tell you that, because, given our relationship – you know that this is true, Dr. Lasky – I would be the last person in the world to be suffering from an oedipal complex."

Dr. A.'s behavior with her friend's husband, and her transferential conduct with me in the analysis, were highly overdetermined and, of course, served a multiplicity of functions. Some of the things most clearly revealed by this included her identification with her mother and the remarkably anal-demanding and anal-inhibiting aspects of her mother's character; her identification with her father and his rages, and his bullying and domineering characteristics; and her identifications with the controlling and manipulating aspects in the functioning of both of her parents. This also revealed the anal-aggressive transformations characterizing her object relations and illustrated the intrusion of pregenital influences into her libidinal interests and, consequently, how some of this was exhibited in her interpersonal relationships. Most glaringly, this showed the extensive degree of oedipal organization influencing her functioning. And through this vignette one may see that as treatment progressed there was an intensification of regressive features in the transference neurosis in which the anally dominated struggle with her mother was clearly enacted, and in which the sexual attachment to me became intensified and more dramatically colored by anal-erotic transformations (as had been, and at the time this was happening, still was the actual case with her father).

As the segment of analysis just described was drawing to a close, Dr. A. began to be concerned about her lack of publications and the implications of that, since her faculty position at the university was in a tenure track. Dr. A. had no publications to her credit, and she was naturally troubled about this, being acutely aware of the "publish or perish" realities of academic employment. Using the insights gained from the above material, in combination with later insights (previously described) about the transformation of her happy early experiences with her mother into an anal power struggle of seemingly life-and-death proportions, Dr. A. recognized that her lack of publications was a statement and not just a fact.

This problem occupied a considerable amount of time in Dr. A.'s analysis, continuously being woven in and out of the material revealed about her sexual life and her relations with her family, and was also included within the regressed transference interactions occurring with me. The gains accrued by Dr. A. via the working through of much of this material permitted her to write and to have published enough so that she was able to acquire tenure, although she managed to do so with absolutely no time to spare. The true measure of her having solved this inhibition in her work productivity was demonstrated not so much by the fact that she managed to publish enough to get tenure (since in this situation she was still influenced by strong outside pressures) but by the fact that after receiving tenure she continued to be able to write freely and to publish.

Equivalent gains were made in her teaching and in her relationships with her students. As Dr. A. gained meaningful insights about her identifications with her mother, and then her father, she changed from being an authoritarian, distant ideologue in the classroom and she became more friendly and relaxed, while still maintaining her authoritative competence in the teaching of material about which she had strong views. Her relationships with individual students also underwent changes in which she no longer played the primary role of a disciplinarian with them and was able to meet and talk with them in a more collegial fashion. She found herself able to act, with some of them, as a counselor and confidante, and could converse with them about many topics and not just those that had relevance to the course they were taking with her.

Also, and of great significance, Dr. A. began to make friends among a number of her faculty colleagues, expanding her social life beyond a single, intense relationship she had had with her psychologist friend. And in this process, Dr. A. finally began dating.

In the context of Dr. A.'s interest in dating, another significant transference regression occurred, and it is in that context that Dr. A.'s masturbatory fantasies were revealed and then integrated into an important insight about the oedipal nature of her relationship with her father: the insight that fully prepared her for the return of her memories of her happy love relationship with her father, which occurred in the third year of her analysis.

Dr. A.'s social life had expanded greatly and she reported dating various men who she would see once or twice and with whom she shared, at most, a good-night kiss. As the frequency of her dating increased, particularly as she would see a man more than just once or twice, Dr. A. began to become rather conspicuously secretive about this. She would drop hints, saying that she was seeing someone more frequently or that she had met a particularly interesting man but that she preferred not to go into any details.

After this happened about a half-dozen times (over a period of about 4 months) I mentioned to her that I thought she was trying to get me both interested and frustrated by what she was doing, and recounted to her how often this pattern of telling and then not telling had happened. Dr. A. immediately brought into the open the transference regression that had been quietly but increasingly building, by charging me with having an impatience to hear what she was not yet ready to talk about. I described this as seeming more like something she wanted me to be feeling than a true description of something I was doing. Dr. A. begged to differ. And furthermore, she told me, if anything ever did happen between her and a man, I was the last person she would tell.

There then followed a series of sessions in which Dr. A. would repeat that if she decided "to go all the way" she would definitely not tell me. I asked her if this was still because she felt I was too intrusive (another accusation added to that of my impatience to hear what she was not ready to say) and she said, "No, not at all. I don't want to tell you what I don't want to tell you, and you can't make me." "Sounds more than just a little familiar," I said. "This has nothing to do with my mother and her toilet training or my fighting with my father," she shot back. "So what does it have to do with?" I asked. "Up yours!" she exclaimed, and started to cry. Within a few minutes the session ended.

At the start of her next session she began to examine what had been happening: a not uncharacteristic pattern for her, in building to peaks of transference regression with quick, abrupt, and relieving shifts back to her more autonomous and observant attitudes; a sequence which had undeniably masturbatory and orgasmic qualities, as well as reflecting the strength of her ego.

In that following session Dr. A. began by saying that she just couldn't figure out what was going on between us. She recognized that she was acting something out with me, of that she was sure, but what it was seemed unclear because she was certain that she was not, as she said, having an anal power struggle with me like the ones she had had with her mother, and she was certain that she was not just repeating the typical kinds of fighting she did with her father. "So what's left?" she asked. "Up yours?" I replied, reminding her of her final comment to me.

She did not see what was significant about that: it was just an expression of anger. True, I told her, but it was not the kind of language she typically used with me. Not entirely untypical, she demurred, reminding me that she sometimes said "Oh, shit!" Throughout the preceding months I had been developing the notion that Dr. A. had something she needed to talk about but couldn't. I began, increasingly, hearing the statement "If something did happen I wouldn't tell you" as really meaning "There is something happening, *not* having to do with *what I do* with men, but *stimulated by* what is going on between me and men, that I have to tell you about, but it makes me too ashamed." Dr. A. seemed genuinely curious despite her continued demurrals, and so I told her this idea of mine and asked her if it made any sense to her in the context of "up yours" and "oh shit," and, happily, struck gold.

"Oh, shit!" said Dr. A. in true distress (and totally unaware of the humor in her reply), "I certainly do know what this is about, and I certainly don't want to talk about it. How can I have been so stupid? [*Pause*] Now, how do I talk about it?"

Dr. A. had, in all her dating thus far, maintained her virginity. She kissed, and engaged in mutual masturbation (to orgasm for both parties), but went no further. However, the increase in her sexual activities kept her in a highly stimulated state of arousal much of the time, and consequently she had begun to masturbate much more frequently than was usual for her, at times even twice daily. "Up yours" and "oh, shit" were directly related to her masturbation fantasies, which were her last and most closely guarded (conscious) secret.

Dr. A. would begin to browse through her magazines, building up feelings of high arousal without active masturbatory manipulation. This would always be in preparation for physical masturbation itself. You already know what excited her in these preparatory activities from previously presented material. However, while actively engaging in genital masturbation she discarded her magazines for other images of an entirely different nature. Dr. A.'s masturbatory fantasies, the ones that ultimately brought her to orgasm, were enema fantasies. Certainly not fantasies one could have been in a position to actively predict but fantasies that are not surprising, however, given what we know about her. She had a variety of enema fantasies, but the one she came back to most frequently was one where she was a novice in a convent being punished for something, something that was never clearly defined, that she had done wrong. *She is naked and tied face-down, hand and foot, with her legs spread, and her body curved over a large barrel. Surrounding her and grimly looking on is a circle of cassocked monks. A priest enters, with a furious look on his face, holding a giant enema. Dr. A. says, as in the confessional, "Forgive me, Father, for I have sinned."* (Only much later in her analysis, in the fifth year, when Dr. A. was finally working through the anal sado-masochistic transformation of her sustained oedipal relationship with her father, did she come to fully recognize which "Father" she was involved with in this favorite masturbation fantasy.) *The priest looks her in the eye, long and sustained, but does not speak. He walks behind her and inserts into her rectum the enormously long and thick nozzle of the enema. He drains a copious amount of water into her. Her bowel is enormously and painfully distended, and compressed terribly by her posture, being draped forward face-down on the barrel as she is. She experiences awful cramps. The priest removes the nozzle and Dr. A. is required to retain her bowel contents while reciting the rosary in penance. The group of monks silently looks on with Dr. A. experiencing acute humiliation. She must recite the rosary slowly in genuine repentance, terrified that her cramps will overpower her attempts, her exquisite efforts, to hold the water in.* And with this imagery Dr. A. would achieve orgasm, during which the image disappears and she focuses intensely on her physical sensations.

A similar masturbatory fantasy revealed to Dr. A. both the fact and the nature of her childhood masturbation. As a child she would, on occasion, be invited to other children's homes for dinner. At night, in bed, when she was a little girl, she would imagine that at one of those dinner visits she would do something (unspecified) wrong at the dinner table and that her friend's father (each friend's father, changing with each occasion) would then take her down to the basement to give her an enema as punishment. She would think about this, with no further specific images, feeling very excited without identifying her excitement as sexual, until she fell asleep.

It was in the recounting of this as a current masturbatory fantasy, replete with highly detailed images of being given the enema, that Dr. A. suddenly remembered the setting of her fantasy as having had its origin in her childhood presleep experiences. And in the late phase of her analysis, it was through reviewing this fantasy, with a father in the central role, that she made the proper connection to the "Father" in her favorite masturbation fantasy, and finally began to understand the central role her father played in her sexual life.

Dr. A.'s understanding of the fantasies, as she revealed them at this time, however, was essentially a view of them as a reflection of the hateful anal transformation of the early happy relationship with her mother, arrived at through a variety of associative material clearly directing her there; and she was, of course, quite right since one in that level of understanding does not in any way preclude the other; because her understanding of the corollary issues with her father was not yet advanced enough in the analysis to properly place this material into that context as well; and because the reality of how her fixations centered on her mother was significant in its own right despite the high degree of condensation of parental representations held by Dr. A. (in fact, the inability to simultaneously see and work with both parental representations was itself significant in undoing the highly condensed representations she had maintained until she started her analysis).

Dr. A. arrived at the idea that these fantasies had to be purely anal representatives having to do with her mother because, despite the fact that they were used sexually, the idea of any such things in reality was actively repugnant to her. She would never think of having "enema-play" with any man; she never used an enema for any sexual purposes; she abhorred the idea of pain; she had absolutely no wish for humiliation in her sexual relationships; in short, these ideas were for the end-stage purposes of masturbation only, and any possibility of acting any portion of them out in reality was not simply unwelcome but anathema to her. Therefore, she reasoned, although the sexual purpose was undeniably present it was "unfortunately totally inscrutable," and thus she would be able to address the other issues (which were "not only apparent but transparent") more profitably.

At a later point in her treatment Dr. A. was able to appreciate that wonderful pun on the word "transparent" (trans-*parent*) both in terms of the relation it had to overdetermined investments in looking and being seen, and in terms of its condensation of both parents. But at this time, in order to de-genitalize this material, to place it as purely as possible into the anal-sadistic realm of her conflicts with her mother, Dr. A. hearkened back to the way her masturbatory fantasies had emerged in the analysis, that is, by remembering the statements that preceded them—"Up yours," in its anal connection to, "Oh, shit"—and by remembering and emphasizing the quality of anal struggle in the relationship between us as exemplified by her feelings that I was demanding things from her that she was not going to be forced into giving, and as exemplified by her statement to me that if anything did happen between her and a man, I would be the last person she would tell.

In this context some of Dr. A.'s most vivid memories of her own toilet training emerged to augment much of our earlier work and her previously less vivid recollections, clearly illustrating the prophetic nature of her prior negation, that is, her claim that our "conflict" was not reflective of anal power struggles with her mother.

The retrieval of some (very few) of her even earlier memories of her relationship with her mother, prior to toilet training, and her sense of that stage as having been a happy one (which was strongly reinforced in both our minds through inferences based on those memories, and by other memories, sparse and vague but nevertheless present, and recounted at other times) was prompted by her once again remembering her "chocolate cake" dream and her integration of it into the material with which we were then working. She focused on the chocolate cake itself in the dream and began by relating her view of it as having an anal nature by remarking on the fact that it was chocolate "which stands for shit," and by rather pointedly observing that chocolate was not her favorite flavor. She always preferred vanilla, and when all the kids in the neighborhood got ice cream they always got chocolate and she always got teased for being the only one to choose vanilla. Even as an adult she had joked that the proof that something must be radically wrong with her was that unlike the rest of the world she was not a chocolate addict. And so, she concluded, the fact that her mother made the cake even though it was supposed to be her father's present, and that her mother chose to make a chocolate cake rather than vanilla, her real favorite, was a demonstration of how her "mother turned everything shitty with her hang-ups about toilet training."

This next led her to a new and important direction, that is, to think about the fact that something good must have been happening between her and her mother, "otherwise there would be nothing to turn into shit." Her next associations were to the extraordinary oral pleasure she remembered while eating the cake in the dream, and from these thoughts Dr. A. recovered hazy but undeniably happy memories of being held and sung to by her mother when she was just a little baby, and some other early memories of a rather vague but nonetheless idyllic nature.

Such memories and material as these were short-lived and fleeting, and never occupied a sustained arena of focus for Dr. A., in part as a reflection of how brief was the period of her life in which she actually did have happily unconflicted relationships with her parents, and in part as a reflection of how little influence this era of her life played in her conscious memories and her conscious experience of herself. But this turn of events in her analysis, in which the anally sadistic transformation of a satisfactory earlier state of affairs became an ongoing part of Dr. A.'s memories, documented for her that there were previously hidden experiences of a positive and unambivalent relationship with her mother. And this answered for her the question, to some extent, that I had raised so much earlier in her analysis about why she didn't develop into an unreachable psychotic monster if she came from such an unrelievedly horrible home environment with no redeeming features.

The other important influence on the analysis that occurred as a result of this "discovery" and its integration into Dr. A.'s view of herself, her past, and the puzzles she still felt were left unsolved about her development was that she began, for the first time and quite seriously, to ask: if there was a whole period of her life that she didn't know about in which she had had a happy and satisfying relationship with her mother, was it possible that there was also an unremembered earlier relationship with her father that was equally positive and pleasurable? This question ushered in the period of Dr. A.'s analysis in which those paternally linked memories were retrieved, which opened the analysis to what actually did happen with her father: that is, it exposed their early oedipal love and the nonerotic love that preceded it, which eventually led to the brutal (but still erotic) transformation of their relationship ever after.

This "discovery" about her relationship with her mother and this major new question it raised for Dr. A. also had two other major effects, one in the analysis itself and one in her social life. In her analysis there was a permanently marked reduction of maternally organized anal-withholding and anal-sadistic transference demands, leaving the transference more clearly colored by considerations of a more specifically anal-erotic quality. And in her social relations, Dr. A. finally went "all the way."

Just the asking of the question, the new question about her father, did not start an automatic flow of germane memories, of course, but the process was unequivocally set in motion. Dr. A. spent a considerable amount of time working on this question, retrieving memories, and confirming the period of seemingly conflict-free love with her father, one example of which was reported earlier (in the first section of this presentation) in her description of having little or no sibling rivalry because of the specialness and intensity of her relationship with her father.

The reconstruction of this period of her life occupied almost 2 years of Dr. A.'s time in analysis, and from no conscious knowledge of her satisfactory love with her father she came eventually (as you will also recall from that earlier vignette) to an intuition that she was still deeply involved in some sort of obscured and camouflaged love affair with him. But what she still had not yet been able to confront in her memories was the specifically and oedipally erotic character of their relationship and then the sadomasochistic anally-defined transformation it underwent.

This material, the erotic component of her love affair with her father, emerged not from an uninhibited flow of associative and connective memories but quite naturally, in the course of a resistance embedded in another transference regression, which will be described presently. After Dr. A.'s insight, that she was still deeply enmeshed in her relationship with her father (despite the fact that the nature of her enmeshment with him was recognized but unclearly understood), some of the strength of her immediate ties to him became loosened. This began a working-through process that permitted her to begin to have more normalized sexual relations with stage-appropriate men. An important regressive element in her sexual functioning played a key part in how the transference regression intensified, or at least in her conscious experience of it, but there is no question that from this point on Dr. A. began to achieve genital primacy in her sexual functioning and had made an irreversible step into the world of nonincestuous object choices.

At first, when Dr. A. began to have sexual intercourse she described her initial experience, and her reactions to it afterwards, quite vividly. While certainly not being promiscuous, Dr. A., over a period of time, had relations with several men, which she spoke about freely in analysis. Then Dr. A. began to become secretive about her relationships, particularly regarding physical activity.

When I asked whether she was aware that there seemed to be a change in how she was behaving with me she first protested ignorance, saying, "I'm not aware of anything different. I come in, lie down, talk. You listen. What's different?" I did not reply, and the session continued, focusing on related but other issues concerning her social and professional life. A short time later she brought it up again: "I don't know what you were referring to before. It just came into my mind again but I don't know what you are pointing out to me." "You don't even have a guess about what I mean?" I asked. "Nothing," she said. "I have no idea." And within a few minutes the session came to an end.

About midway into her next session she raised the question again. I was in some conflict about how to proceed. On the one hand, if I took her statement of total ignorance entirely seriously, I would not want to prematurely present to her any information about her resistance that would address either the underlying conflicts or the defenses associated with them too soon, since the net effect ("wild analysis") would cause her to become increasingly defensive. On the other hand, she did keep returning to the question, asking me to clarify what I had meant, which could be understood as a preconscious recognition of the problem that would indicate some readiness to be further informed. In addition, there was also the question of Dr. A.'s propensity toward power struggles, and I was concerned about the potential of this interaction turning into a scuffle over whether or not I was going to explain what I meant.

Given all these considerations, I opted to repeat that I had noticed a change in our sessions, and I added that the change was not radical but readily observable nonetheless. What surprised me, I then told her, was not so much that she hadn't noticed anything different, but that she couldn't even offer a guess as to what it might be or what might be going on. I said that it was certainly reasonable that she might not know about it, and that there was certainly nothing wrong with asking me to clarify what I had in mind, but that I found it striking, nevertheless, that she couldn't even fantasize about what I had been drawing her attention to. I reminded her that there had been many past occasions in which I said something that she did not immediately understand, and that she usually had some guesses about what I meant. She would usually explore them and reject the ones that didn't make sense, or in the process figured out what I meant, or when that was impossible, I would then say more about it. Usually, however, she was able to follow my meaning within a reasonably short time when she began to try to imagine what it was I was commenting about.

Somewhat sarcastically she said, "So this is supposed to be a guessing game?" "No," I said, "not a guessing game. But it's not unfair to say that in some ways it is a fantasizing and imagining game. And on that level it's a game you usually are rather adept at. Doesn't it strike you as unusual that in this case you can't even have a single idea about what I mean, even if it immediately proves not to be true?"

She admitted that I seemed to have a good point there, and added the fact that her recent sarcasm seemed unwarranted too. "Now," she laughed, "I really am in a quandary. I still don't have any idea what you are talking about but it's obvious that demanding that you explain yourself is inappropriate." The subject changed, and the session came to an end.

In Dr. A.'s next session she said that she wished she had had a dream the previous night in the hope that it might explain something about this; but, no such luck. I asked her if any of her other dreams came to mind and she immediately thought of the "chocolate cake" dream. "What do you remember about it?" I asked her, and she replied that eating the cake and having her mouth fill with saliva in anticipation was very vivid in her memory. Also, she remembered, very vividly, both the memory in the dream of watching herself do something bad (eating the cake) and the memory of how angrily her parents were looking at her.

Her next association was to her "enema in the monastery" masturbation fantasy, particularly how all the monks silently watched her punishment and how sternly the priest looked at her before administering the enema. "Aha, Dr. Watson," she suddenly said, "the clues are beginning to unravel." She went on: "I have been hiding what I have been doing with [*she names her current boyfriend*] from you. I didn't realize that I was hiding anything from you, but I can see now that I was. You are the angry, stern person looking at something bad that I'm doing, and I keep what I do with [her boyfriend] secret to protect myself from being punished by you. I know that's silly, but I feel that way even if it probably isn't true. I guess I suspected that this was what you were talking about, but because I did not feel free to talk about it I pushed down and interiorized [the word she characteristically used interchange- ably for suppression or identification] my recognition so that I somehow didn't know what you meant, even though I think I did."

I asked which "clue" made what was going on between us obvious to her now, in a way that it wasn't before. "Eating the cake," she replied, "with my mouth full of saliva in anticipation, and the swallowing of the copious water; eating the cake with such a delicious taste in my mouth and such delicious feelings. I knew it was bad but I never realized, until today, that this was bad because it was sexual."

After some further remarks (delaying tactics as well as observation of her ego functioning) about how clever and subtle the mind is, she drew the following conclusion: "First," she said, "I represent a sexual function and sexual feelings and sensations in a totally nonsexual image, and then, despite all the times I have returned to that image in analysis, I managed to keep its sexual meaning completely hidden from myself – isn't that just amazing?" Dr. A. finally got down to brass tacks and told me what was going on, what she had been keeping secret.

Dr. A.'s current boyfriend was willing to have intercourse but mainly preferred fellatio. Dr. A. had experimented with fellatio before, but only infrequently and as a part of foreplay, and never to the point of her partner's orgasm. In this relationship, however, Dr. A. performed fellatio so frequently that its novelty effect wore off enough for her to become involved in what she was doing beyond its uniqueness as a new experience, and she found that she loved it. She liked the taste of his penis and how it filled up her mouth. She liked the copious flow of saliva produced in performing fellatio, and she liked the taste of his semen and the experience of swallowing it when her boyfriend came. His intense excitement and his orgasm in her mouth were frequently so exciting to her that she, too, had an orgasm herself, simultaneously with him, in the process. (Cunnilingus was a practice both he and she were indifferent to.)

Dr. A. had been vague and somewhat withholding in this transference regression for three reasons. First, she was embarrassed by her behavior and felt guilty about it, such practices having had (for so much of her life) the connotation of sinfulness and evil perversity. Second, she felt especially reluctant to speak because she could not think about it without becoming actively excited, and she did not want to be sexually aroused while actually in the consulting room with me. And finally – and this she derived directly from her associations to the dream and the masturbation fantasy – she imagined telling me all about this very graphically, and in such a way so that I would have an almost visual image of her doing these things.

It would be, through her telling of it, as if I were "sitting there watching a porno film unfold" before my very eyes. And naturally, I, too, would become excited. Thus, to "protect" me from losing my analytic neutrality, Dr. A. would have to keep down both of our sexual excitements. She would be able to have a "safe analytic haven" only if she were not compelled to control the emergence of inappropriate and unacceptable feelings on her part or mine. It was necessary then, in transferential terms, to keep the analysis free of anything that would contaminate our relationship and change it. "Things were going so well between us"; she was making so much progress in reconstructing her past; everything was going so perfectly; "it would be such a shame to break us up," she said, "if all that sexual stuff were to get between us."

One can see how much more influenced by phallic and oedipal considerations her withholding was in this instance than had been the case in the much more anally sadistic organization of the withholding she had engaged in with me previously in the transference. The dream and masturbation fantasy led her to a quick statement of this radical shift in the transference. I call it radical not so much because it was particularly unexpected; it had, after all, a "gestation period," which in retrospect could be traced, and which in terms of its form was not unlike other transference regressions. But I call it radical nonetheless because it was remarkably abrupt in comparison to the way previous transference regressions intensified.

We went through a long period of good relations in which Dr. A. made much progress and was feeling very close to, grateful to, and comfortable with me, and then, all of a sudden, because of what seemed to be an outside influence (the relationship with that man), the very fabric of our connection to each other felt endangered to her. The abruptness and intensity of this shift directly parallels the shift from a relatively uninhibited relationship with her father to a highly conflicted oedipal one. The specifically erotic components of her relationship with her father, and how they were transformed into sadomasochistic derivatives, was made more explicit by what next emerged that Dr. A. also felt at first the need to suppress.

Although Dr. A. had long ago abandoned her attachment to her pornographic magazines and was masturbating only infrequently, she had added to her repertoire of masturbatory fantasies a new fantasy, a fantasy that made her extremely anxious when she revealed it. She and her boyfriend had recently seen the film *Deep Throat* and they had been practicing to see if she could develop Linda Lovelace's capabilities.

Dr. A. was surprised to find that the gagging sensation she experienced was not entirely unpleasant to her.

I asked if it brought anything to mind, and she replied that it *reminded her* of what it would be like if a little girl were to try to take a grown man's penis in her mouth. This seemed, at the time, to lead nowhere and Dr. A. moved on to other ideas that seemed to her to be more productive. But this was subsequently used in the new masturbation fantasy, and it is by no means insignificant that her fantasy used an image that derived at least in part directly from a kind of reality contact with me.

One important thing it illustrates, in addition to making the specific current nature of the transference more explicit to us, is how Dr. A.'s openness (which existed side by side with her bouts of secretiveness) was also an acting-out of the transference under the guise of analysis. She did, in fact, in a form of pornographic display, describe her actual behavior and her fantasies in remarkably graphic detail — a degree of detail equal to her earlier penchant for obsessive detail, but now serving quite a different purpose. When Dr. A. finally was able to bring the fantasy into analysis, in the context of examining her reluctance to do so, it became clear that her reluctance this time was not based only on the fear that one or both of us would become sexually aroused but also on a "sickening awareness" that it was somehow connected to me as a direct object of her sexual interest.

In her fantasy she is *a little girl, about 6 years old, sitting on a grown-up man's lap. The man is faceless; she does not know who he is, and she never speculates as to who he might be. No words ever pass between them. He is dressed in a business suit, with a vest and a tie, and she is in a party dress, with white lacy socks and patent leather shoes. He is gently rubbing her back and she slides off his lap so that she is standing in profile between his legs. His hand drops down to include her buttocks in his rubbing, and then moves down to her bare legs. His hand slides up the back of her legs and he insinuates it into her underpants and fondles her. She sees that he has an erection and is extremely curious about it. She places her hand on it to feel it, and when he makes no objection she opens his pants and takes out his penis. She puts both her hands around his penis and he shows her, with his free hand, how to move her hands up and down. She sees a drop of lubricating fluid well up out of the tip of his penis and drip onto her hand. Without any thought, automatically, as if it were the most natural thing in the world, she leans forward and licks it off her hand. He senses her excitement and gently pushes her head down toward his penis, which she tries to take into her mouth. As he gets more excited he becomes slightly rougher with her, jamming his penis into her mouth and pushing her head up and down, until he finally ejaculates. She is gagging and swallowing,* and with that image the masturbatory fantasy brings her to orgasm.

After exposing her usual fears about the possible emergence of sexual arousal threatening to interfere with our relationship, that fantasy was reluctantly but finally presented. It was in the context of discussing those concerns that Dr. A. expressed her first awareness of how she used the actual reporting of sexual material for exhibitionistic purposes in relation to me, but this was not fully confirmed for her until some time later when, transferentially, she recognized me as an object of her active sexual wishes.

Her first glimpse of this was through worrying about the possibility that even the rigorous training undergone by psychoanalysts would be insufficient to protect us from me also getting aroused along with her by what she had to say: not a new concern. At the cost of intense embarrassment, she said, she could talk about such things and actually be aroused in my presence if, and only if, there was some guarantee that I would remain erotically uninvolved; but how would it be possible for anyone, no matter how much training they have received, to be unmoved by all this explicit sexuality? I commented, "There really is quite a lot of very explicit sexual description in what you have to tell me, isn't there?" "Well, of course," she replied, "it's only natural that sex is a main topic of my sessions. After all, I began analysis to solve sexual problems, so why shouldn't I speak about it in many of my sessions?"

"You sound like you heard my comment as a criticism," I said, which led us to the fact that Dr. A. had been slowly becoming aware of the pleasure she was taking in describing herself, how this did include an attempt to get me aroused, and how guilty she felt about that. Her defensiveness, and her awareness of it as soon as I pointed it out to her, quickly brought into consciousness the partially hidden wish expressed in her fear, so that she was then able to consciously experience them both simultaneously; and this was part of what eventually led to Dr. A.'s speculation, "with a sickening awareness of the truth," that I must be an object of her sexual interests.

How did she arrive at that? I asked when she reported this, and she replied that she had the evidence (just arrived at) of knowing that she was sexualizing her relationship with me in analysis, and had another two reasons for this belief. First of all, the first time she ever thought of a little girl sucking on a grown man's penis was in a session with me when "you asked me what the gagging during deep-throat *reminded me* of," which clearly suggested to her some connection to me in the contents of her subsequent masturbation fantasy. Second, and with considerable discomfort, Dr. A. revealed that as she began to discuss the fantasy and her concerns about it, over a number of sessions, she developed a growing awareness (which she tried to push out of her consciousness) that the man in the fantasy bore a faint resemblance to me both in build and in manner of dress. She then added a third reason – her comment that no words passed between the man and the girl, and that reminded her of my silence in analysis.

There then followed a number of sessions in which she obsessively went over the fantasy: whether it really could be me in the fantasy; how it absolutely had to be me in the fantasy; how it absolutely couldn't be me in the fantasy; and why (if it was me in the fantasy) didn't she in reality feel actively attracted to me sexually, or in love with me as happens with so many women in analysis? These sessions, and many sessions that followed, finally brought to the surface a replication of the quality of the intense and compelling sexuality of her relationship with her father. What it did not bring to the surface was conscious memories of having had such an intensely sexual relationship with him (those memories having yet to wait for activation). Those memories became available only at the time that an examination of the sadomasochistic transformation of their relationship was undertaken.

The examination of that transformation began when Dr. A. once again brought up my having asked her what "gagging during deep-throat" *reminded her of;* I told her that I had never said that. I pointed out to her that I had only asked if it brought anything *to mind,* and then specified that it was she who had substituted the notion that it *reminded her of something* and who had been referring to it as a kind of reminiscence ever since.

She first rejected this angrily, saying that that was not the way she remembered it, claiming that I was trying to force an unwholesome idea on her, and she eventually escalated the disagreement to the point where she was threatening to terminate analysis over it.

I then recalled to Dr. A. the session in which she was talking about her sisters and the question of sibling rivalry (which had occurred not too long ago) and in which she mentioned the sudden, horrible, and inexplicable downhill turn in her relationship with her father. I suggested that there was a parallel there for what had happened between us now and said that examining it further could serve to make both hateful transformations more comprehensible.

Dr. A. rejected this too, quite angrily, saying that any parallels between sexual feelings toward me and sexual feelings for her father was an impossibility and that if I was suggesting that she gave her father a blow-job when she was 6 years old I was absolutely out of my mind.

I replied that I was not suggesting any such thing, but that there was some evidence that she did remember something sexual from her childhood, even if what happened may not have been so explicitly sexual, or if the memory itself is not entirely conscious. I reiterated, trying to be as nonprovoking as possible, that I derived my impression strictly from her immediate and unconscious translation of what I said in which the concept of a reminiscence was so highly emphasized by her.

I went on to say that the age of 6 was apparently significant: in the masturbation fantasy she was 6, she dated the horrible change in her relationship with her father as occurring when she was 6, and that we were just on the verge of entering her sixth year of analysis. I added the information that the massive deterioration of our relationship seemed to be more a reaction to the emergence of actively sexual and romantic fantasies about me (which were being alluded to with greater frequency) than a reaction to any intellectual connections that might be made about her past; in other words, that her resistance to my showing her some evidence that her masturbation fantasy had elements of reminiscence in it was at least, in part, a smoke screen to undo something that had directly happened between us that was unbearably anxiety-provoking.

I backed away from direct investigation of reminiscences at this point because I had some concern about Dr. A.'s actually acting out her threat to leave (another countertransference trap I fell into). It seemed a small concession to make (I rationalized to myself), and it was made directly on the heels of a series of statements that kept the material attached where it belonged so as to be ready for use at a later date (which was true but nevertheless still more rationalization).

In any event, it didn't help (which is the fated outcome with countertransferences, even when the analyst's intervention is consciously well intended). Dr. A. continued to be angry, challenging, accusatory, and belligerent. I was no longer making interpretations but was, rather, like a turtle with its head pulled into its shell, waiting to weather out the storm (now very deep into the countertransference, although I had no idea of it at the time). Dr. A. continued to hammer away at me, constantly interspersing threats to terminate treatment with her criticisms of me.

During the time I became so passive externally (while Dr. A. was subsequently bombarding me with threats and accusations), I was internally quite active. I began to feel very anxious about the seemingly unstoppable quality of Dr. A.'s transference regression, and eventually I began to frantically search for an answer to the question of how to stop the regression and keep her from terminating prematurely. In other words, clearly in a transference–countertransference matrix, I was repeating Dr. A.'s experience with her father: something sexual happened between them, he became hateful and accusatory, she frantically searched for a way to please him, and the transformed relationship was then maintained forever.

It was this last quality, the way the relationship stabilized on that level, that finally permitted me to begin to address my dilemma in the countertransference as well as the transference–countertransference dilemma we both were in as long as this were to continue. As the result of a dream I had, I recognized what I was feeling and why, and with a great sense of relief I also recognized that Dr. A. was committed to remaining in treatment so as to perpetuate her ability to flay me with accusations and threats: our relationship was in no more danger of ending than was her relationship with her father, no matter how realistic his threats, accusations, and rejections seemed on the surface. Thus, with a restored sense of confidence, I capitalized on my prior state of countertransference with a full description of what was going on between us. Instead of telling her what I was feeling, however, I showed her how her behavior was specifically intended to make me feel those things.

I began by telling her that although she had been threatening to quit for weeks, I thought that she had no such intentions. Not that she was being consciously dishonest, but if she really stood back from the process for a moment she would see that these were actually very powerful fantasies rather than actual statements of intent. But the problem was not just her, I went on, but me, too: we were both missing the point about this and taking it at surface value.

I then described her behavior with me and showed her how this was exactly how, in many other contexts, her father behaved with her. I indicated how I thought I was supposed to be experiencing this and how I thought I was expected to react, and showed her how, in those other contexts, this was exactly the way she had actually felt with her father.

I then went back to my earlier point about her threats to quit, saying that given the intensity of her feelings and the fact that this was going on for some time, it honestly seemed to me that if she was really serious about leaving she would already have done so. My impression was that this state of conflict between us was intended (in fact, unconsciously predetermined) to be perpetuated indefinitely, and then showed her how this, too, was a direct parallel to her extremely intense and prolonged relationship with her father.

Finally, I reviewed for her the direct parallels between the abrupt and hateful contamination of her ideal relationship with her father when she was 6 and the abrupt and hateful contamination now of our previously excellent relationship, concluding that I must have been very much on target in pointing out to her (a few months ago) the importance of her having introduced the possibility of sexual reminiscences.

I reasoned that if it was true that sexual issues were both the most potentially and the most realistically destructive influences on what had been our previously excellent relationship, and if everything else paralleled her relationship with her father so perfectly, then it was not unreasonable to assume that sexual considerations were involved in the transformation of the relationship with her father. And given the fact that her fantasy of a little girl (of exactly the age she was when the relationship with her father went bad) with a grown man was described in terms of a reminiscence (whether or not that was her conscious intention), I could not see how we had any choice but to assume that sexual issues with her father were somehow involved in the transformation of their relationship.

Within a reasonably short time Dr. A. was in agreement with me, and her behavior changed. She began to search for evidence that she had had some overtly sexual experience with her father, but without success (not, however, for lack of trying, because her attempts seemed to be quite genuine and not a disguised form of anal compliance). I suggested (in an inappropriately supportive fashion, because I was still partly under the influence of the countertransference that had been mainly, but apparently not yet entirely, resolved) that her initial objections were both right and wrong. Perhaps it was a mistake to look for an explicitly sexual act of the sort that might take place between two adults. It was not unreasonable to assume that she was right, I told her, in protesting that it was crazy to imagine that as a 6-year-old she would have given her father a blow-job, given the reality of what both he and she were like. But maybe she was being too literal. Perhaps she would find the answer by looking for what a child and an adult might do together that could have sexual undertones without their relationship being explicitly sexual, in the way that two extremely close adults might be with each other.

This was helpful only in that it gave Dr. A. a different avenue of approach, because it turned out that there was, in fact, something very explicitly sexual that had occurred between Dr. A. and her father. But the reason why it was helpful at getting to this, despite the countertransferential motive behind this supportive intervention, was because it provided Dr. A. with a direction in which to take her thoughts that was less closely guarded. Just prior to our vacation break, Dr. A. unearthed the critical memory.

After having closely examined her physical and emotional contact with her father in many situations while their relationship was still good, Dr. A. began to speak about a way of playing with her father which finally seemed to account for the deterioration in their relationship.

On Sunday mornings Dr. A.'s mother went to early Mass, visited with her sister briefly, did some light shopping, and came home. Dr. A. would climb into bed with her father, and they would romp, cuddle, and play. This was their regular routine, which never varied, and it was a review of this Sunday morning play-time (that ended when she was 6) that finally solved the mystery. *Dr. A. and her father would do lots of wrestling, tickling, and poking when they played. One morning Dr. A. was astride her father, while he lay on his back, and they were tickling and wrestling in such a way that they were moving their bodies in exactly the way bodies would be moving if two adults were having sexual intercourse in that position.* Dr. A. recalled something she never remembered before, even though she had thought about those Sunday mornings previously. It happened when she began to wonder why, and exactly when, those play-times with her father ended. *She remembered sitting astride him on that morning, and without actually realizing what she was feeling or what she was doing, feeling (through both their pajamas) that he had an erection. His erection was flat against his belly and she was sitting on it, with her vagina straddling it. She remembered, almost as if it were a dream, that their tickling and horsing around stopped and she gradually entered an almost trancelike reverie in which she gazed into his eyes and rocked herself gently on his penis.*

In retrospect it is clear how sexually stimulating it was, but at the time it was not a fully conscious sexual event for her. She said that it felt like a combination of things, but the closest image she could use to describe it was to say that she felt like how a 3- or 4-year-old might feel being rocked on a warm, comfy, adult's lap with her eyes closed while she sucked her thumb and held her ear, and while the adult softly scratched her back: a warm, dreamy feeling that was both languorous and sensual, exciting but soothing and relaxing at the same time.

She said that there is a kind of gentle, dreamy masturbation she sometimes engages in that is sexually stimulating but also a satisfaction in itself, so that the act of masturbating is for its own sake and not to build up the tension for an orgasm: "sexual, but on some level not sexual. Sort of like a sexual substitute for a baby being rocked to sleep." And that was the situation she felt was the best adult analogue for the sexual, but not consciously and explicitly sexual, sensations and state of mind she had been experiencing then with her father. The major difference being her adult awareness that she is, in fact, masturbating: an awareness she felt was only a "subliminal" experience for her as a child in bed with her father. The parallel between sucking her thumb and sucking a penis was not lost on her.

Dr. A. thought that this experience must have continued uninterrupted for perhaps 30 seconds or a minute, because the memory included the idea of a long time doing this and not just a fleeting sensation. But she could not be absolutely certain of that because of the timeless sense of the reverie experience as she now remembered it (which was one of the reasons why the memory itself had a dreamlike quality). The haziest part of the memory was how it ended. The best she could make out was, that after what must have been a short but not insignificant time her father, who had remained absolutely still with his eyes half closed, and who seemed in a reverie of his own, seemed to be startled into an awareness of what was happening. She remarked that they seemed at first to exchange guilty glances, but then seemed *"unable to look each other in the eye. Just the opposite of how we were dreamily looking into each other's eyes, before."* He roughly pushed her away and told her to go to her room. It was the last time they ever played together, and from that time on their relationship turned sour and deteriorated. From that time on she was a bad girl, and he was the outraged and morally incorruptible adult.

In Dr. A.'s reconstruction of all of this, she eventually decided that her father must have been having sexual feelings for her and must have been aware of her sexual feelings for some time, but that his feelings and his awareness were kept unconscious until that incident, during which they both did something so overt that he could no longer make believe to himself that he did not know what was going on. However, he was too guilty to face his own feelings so he blamed it all on her, as if she were the bad one and he was the good one who had been victimized somehow.

Next, he kept himself safe from ever being forced to face his own involvement by hiding from himself, once again, even after this happened, the true nature of this oedipal seduction by generalizing the issue. In this way no remnant of the underlying sexual involvement would become visible: it was simply a matter of a child needing correction, guidance, direction, punishment, limits, and external control, in life itself.

He collapsed together both of their sexual feelings and then acted as if they were hers alone, and then he acted as if they were not sexual feelings but bowel contents and as if she was a bad little girl who was refusing to be toilet trained. His anger at her, the impossibility of her ever pleasing him, and why he always seemed so agitated by her, now became understood in an entirely different light.

During this work, the last few weeks of Dr. A.'s fifth year of analysis drew to a close, and we took our summer break.

During the vacation Dr. A. met a new man who quickly took the place of the fellatio-oriented man with whom she had been involved for quite some time. He was also a college professor, but at a midwestern school. He was in New York, teaching a summer session at Dr. A.'s school on a visiting professorship, and it was love at first sight. Dr. A. came back to analysis ecstatic. Everything about him was right: his looks; his gentleness and warmth; his political, social, religious, and philosophical orientations; his shared interests with her; his sexual tastes (which were primarily genital); his economic status; his sensitivity; his generous nature; in short, everything. The only problem was that he lived in Indiana and she lived in

New York. The way they solved this, as the year progressed, was for him to fly to New York to be with her every other weekend, and for every long break from school (holiday recesses, intersession, and so on).

During the 3½ months between Labor Day and Christmas, Dr. A.'s analysis was essentially occupied with two things: her new man, and a further exploration of her relationship with her father. In particular, the focus was on why, after the transformation of the relationship, it was perpetuated for the rest of her life with such intensity.

Once again her "chocolate cake" dream surfaced and shed light on this question, as well as the question of why Dr. A. experienced so much visual excitement. Attached to the Sunday play ritual was another ritual that now came under scrutiny. During the Sunday light shopping Dr. A.'s mother always stopped off at the bakery "for their most famous product, a black-out cake." This was a super-heavy, super-rich chocolate cake with a chocolate fudge icing very similar to the cake in Dr. A.'s dream. The minute mother came home, everyone (including her younger sisters when they were old enough) would swarm into the kitchen and with great pleasure devour massive chunks of the cake with enormous glasses of milk.

This ritual, a cause for considerable excitement (despite the fact that chocolate was not her favorite flavor), did not stop when her ritual play sessions with her father did, and it became embossed on her psyche as their substitute. Dr. A. was able to recognize immediately why so much guilt was attached to eating the cake in her dream.

She next had her attention captured by the fact that the cake ritual was never abandoned. Even to this very day, when Dr. A. is home for the weekend (and, she believed, even when her parents were by themselves for the weekend), Sunday morning is "cake morning." I mentioned that she, too, had an internal version of this in the fact that the dream kept resurfacing in her analysis: she began with the dream, it came to mind more often than any other dream she ever reported, it surfaced quite regularly (not exactly every Sunday morning, but with a regularity not dissimilar to that), and it was still on her mind now. "So," she said, "it never ends."

She began to work with the idea that "it never ends," and at one point I drew her attention to the fact that she had begun calling the playtimes with her father "play sessions." This allusion to "sessions" led her to an examination of the "play-ritual" elements of our relationship, and to the miserable transformation of our relationship some half-year earlier, with the same conclusion: "So, it never ends."

Through a more thorough examination of the hidden pleasures in torturing me, Dr. A. came to see how much of the pleasure was actually erotic despite the heavy blanket of camouflage under which it rested. And shortly thereafter, Dr. A. was able to conclude that her father's behavior was not just a defense against his sexual feelings but also a way of secretly gratifying them. Thus, finally, Dr. A. came to know why she was so involved with her father and could never give him up:

"Because he could never give me up. How can a girl leave her father until he gives her up first?"

It was at this time also that the linkage between these events and the intensity of Dr. A.'s visual excitement became clarified. Her visual libidinization, as she discovered, started in the dreamy gazing-into-each-other's-eyes that was described in the sexual encounter between Dr. A. and her father. It went through the following sequence of transformations: (1) Father and daughter looked deeply into each other's eyes as they stimulated each other and themselves (with each other) sexually. (2) Father and daughter abruptly (and traumatically, for Dr. A.) broke eye contact—a clear and unequivocal part of, and response to, the intensity of their excitement. (3) They revived the experience, in transformed fashion, by then sharing guilty (i.e., sexual) glances. (4) They once again broke eye contact, this time as a statement of their excited behavior *in reverse*. (5) Almost immediately afterward (actually within about 30 minutes of the incident), mother came home and the exciting chocolate cake was served. (6) The intense excitement of the "chocolate-cake morning" became condensed with the sexual excitement that Dr. A. had just previously been feeling with her father, and could not fully inhibit. Her sexual excitement was not yet reorganized as "visual," but it was then, as the first step, associated with this new experience. It became "allowable" if it were expressed in this highly transformed context (not, however, entirely without conflict, as we came to see). (7) An important part of the cake ritual, and much of the excitement associated with it, was in *looking* at the cake before it was served and in measuring each piece *(visually)* with great care as they were handed around the table. Thus, (8) looking and seeing become highly sexualized.

Looking, seeing, and being seen became Dr. A.'s main outlet for the expression of these incestuous wishes. In this way it was possible for Dr. A. to "see my cake and eat it, too" (which is how she amusingly put it) even though the transformation was not sufficient to entirely prevent conflicts.

During this period Dr. A. was visiting with her parents less frequently than ever, much to their dismay. Her father disapproved of her new relationship because, as he put it, "a daughter's involvement with a man, even if it is a husband, is not supposed to be cause for disrupting the solidity of a family's relationship. If a relationship with a man puts a daughter in an either-or relationship with regard to the rest of her family, perhaps he is the wrong man." Dr. A.'s father could not have been more helpful to her analysis if he were reading from a prepared and prearranged script, and his competitive reactions made things even more clear for her.

On Christmas Day, Dr. A.'s man presented her with an engagement ring, and on New Year's Day she accepted.

The arrangements they made were that they would be married in June when the teaching year ended. They would spend the last half of June through August in Europe, honeymooning. Dr. A. would make arrangements to take a one-year unpaid leave of absence from the college (she was not yet eligible for sabbatical leave), and would give up her apartment and return with her husband to Indiana. During that year she would devote most of her time to completing a book she was two-thirds finished with and would perhaps do some teaching on a visiting or adjunct basis. Since they were both tenured, she would look for a new tenured position in his area and he would look for a new tenured position in the New York area, and eventually one or the other would permanently relocate.

Following the New Year, and as these arrangements were being worked out, Dr. A. was very happy and excited. This was marred only by her father's lack of enthusiasm and his pessimism about whether one or the other of them could find a tenured teaching position elsewhere within a year's time. Dr. A. told him that his attitude was throwing a pall over the proceedings and said that it was like raining on her parade when all he could relate to were the possible problems that might exist. He blew up and furiously chastised her for being disrespectful. She sat quietly through all he had to say, and then with her heart beating wildly she said, "I did not mean to be disrespectful to you, and I intend none now, but what I said is true. And you ought to know you are hurting me." Father "looked fit to bust a gut," she told me. Mother looked at her and nervously whispered, "Blood pressure, blood pressure!" Dr. A. stalked out of the room in a rage. Dr. A.'s father lived, and Dr. A. remained quite furious with both parents for about 2 weeks.

Dr. A. next raised the question (in a concrete sense) of ending her analysis, indicating that she thought that she had changed considerably over the past 5½ years. She now explicitly set the date for the summer: a good choice, because it left enough time for termination issues to arise and to be addressed.

The question of children soon came up as Dr. A. began the mourning-work of termination, and she entered a rapidly formed and deep depression. She had never given much thought to the idea of having children before, but now she bitterly regretted the fact that she was just turning 44, and she felt that this placed her over the age of childbearing capacity. After medical confirmation of this, Dr. A. began to fume at her father, her rage dominating everything in her sessions, blaming him for keeping her attached to him during her "prime childbearing years."

I pointed out to her that although she had ample justification for most of her feelings there was, nonetheless, a quality to her feelings that seemed too intense even for this situation (and there was no question that this was an absolute tragedy in reality). Where we eventually got, from two images Dr. A. had (of a lioness continuing to shake her prey by the throat long after it was already dead, and of a "bulldog with a bone"), was to an understanding of how she was prolonging her relationship with her father. This was a "last-gasp attempt" on her part, she thought, to hold onto her father using the very same angry, blaming, accusatory tactics they had shared for years.

This next led us to consider her remaining concrete identifications with him, as evidenced by that tactic, which she felt as both ego-dystonic (most of the time, when she was not directly acting out the identification) and also still, to some extent, ego-syntonic. What she learned here was that the experience of actively being enraged with him was only the "next to the last gasp" attempt to hold on to her old oedipal attachment to her father, and that the "very last gasp" attempt was her identification with him on this level. This was a very powerful period of mental reorganization for Dr. A., in which her identifications underwent a renovation similar to that of her object relations.

As Dr. A. began to relegate those identifications (with both parents) more to the peripheries of her mental functioning, and identifications with those aspects of her parents' functioning that did provide her with a healthy and loving environment came to the fore, Dr. A. once again became very depressed about not being able to have children (but this time without the rage). She reviewed some of the very best of her childhood memories of being with her parents, and felt terrible about the fact that she would not be able to have those experiences with a child of her own. And what was worse was that she could not give a child a better experience than the one she had undergone.

She spoke very movingly about her belief that every mother and father has an opportunity to almost magically undo the worst experiences of their own childhood by doing better with children of their own. And now she suffered a double loss: no children (the reality), and the loss of the fantasy that through having children and raising them well, one can achieve narcissistic restitution (my words, not hers) for injuries of the past.

Dr. A.'s depression continued to increase beyond this point until it began to take on some exaggerated characteristics. In particular, the quality of her depression included a kind of mourning process over the children she could not have, as if they were once alive and had actually died. Through an investigation of this, Dr. A. came to realize that the exaggerated part of her depression was related to the actual loss of the active attachment to her father, and to her abandonment of both of her parents as anal-erotic and oedipal love objects. She felt that "no matter how long ago I physically moved out of the house, for the first time I am finally (fully emotionally) leaving home."

There was still, even after these insights and their working through, a sense of loss that felt as if it was connected to something real. After going over the fact a number of times, that it wasn't as if she would never see her parents again after she was married (after all, they would be able to visit each other at will), Dr. A. realized that it was me she was now talking about, who she would never see again, and began to review our relationship and what it had done for her (and meant to her).

On the last Friday in June, the one immediately preceding the weekend on which she was married, Dr. A. had her last session.

15

The Case of Ms. B

D
r. A. was diagnostically neurotic, a classic patient as it were, and she was eminently suited for classical analytic treatment. To put it simply, her treatment did not require the use of any major parameters or modifications. Psychoanalysis is usually thought of as best serving neurotic patients, but it is regularly used with more profoundly disturbed patients also, frequently with considerable success, by employing a variety of modifications in the classical technique. Although these modifications were designed specifically to accommodate the structural deficiencies in ego and superego organization of some patients who fall into the category of the character disorders, even the most useful of these modifications has not proved sufficient for the analytic treatment of all character-disordered patients. It sometimes seems apparent even at the time of the initial consultation that a patient may seem remarkably well suited for a generally psychoanalytic treatment, despite some serious characterological disturbances. On the other hand, it often seems obvious to the analyst that a patient would probably not be helped by an essentially analytic treatment, given the ego organization the patient seems to have. Notwithstanding the usual reliability of these early judgments, they are proven wrong frequently enough, as the treatment progresses, for the analyst to be careful not to set any precedents in the earliest phase of the work that might make a switch in treatment modality difficult or impossible. In some cases, one only appreciates that there has been a mismatch between the patient and the treatment modality (and hopefully, but not always, learns why) when a psychoanalysis proves to be ineffective. Ideally, in such cases, a therapeutic contract remains intact and the analyst can shift to a psychotherapy without treatment having to be abandoned; in other cases it may prove more useful for the patient to be referred elsewhere. Of course there will be instances in which the mismatch only becomes clear as a result of the patient having irrevocably terminated the treatment, and in such circumstances nothing can be salvaged by the analyst.

In this chapter, and in the following chapter, we will look at the treatment of three patients who were diagnostically categorized as suffering from character disorders. This chapter will consider the case of Ms. B., who, despite the depth of her pathology, had a character structure that made her amenable to a psychoanalytic treatment. Her analysis had a number of modifications, but none were so extreme as to have turned the treatment, basically, into a psychotherapy. We will take a clinical (rather than theoretical) look at how her psychic organization differed from what one finds in the neuroses; a look at a major and quite striking modification in the approach to her treatment that became necessary as a result; and a look at what it was in her particular resources that permitted the psychoanalytic process to take hold.[1] Ms. B. will be familiar to the reader because an abbreviated vignette about her was presented in Chapter 3 as part of our discussion of overdetermination and genetic theory. However, we will now have an opportunity to go into her history and her treatment in much greater detail. In presenting the case of Dr. A. the main intention was to give the reader some concrete sense of how an analysis is conducted. It is unnecessary to repeat this with Ms. B. and with the two cases to be discussed in the next chapter. Now our primary goal is to examine the interplay between disordered character structure and the modifications in technique it necessitates.

Ms. B. was 32 years old when she began her analysis. She had been married for 5 years, with no children and no pregnancies, by choice. She began treatment after having discontinued, and in her mind as the result of, a *ménage à cinq* that involved in addition to Ms. B. and her husband, a man and two women who had been previously living together in their own *ménage à trois*. Despite their superficially genuine claims that they wanted such a relationship, this created intense tension between Ms. B. and her husband, which culminated in furious arguments that led, eventually, to a series of actual fistfights between them.

Fights between Ms. B. and her husband originally were precipitated by some jealousy over a relationship with someone else in the "extended marriage" (which is how they referred to it). However, by the time she came for treatment the *ménage* was over and it seemed to her that anything, even highly unpredictable and improbable things, could now start an argument that led to physical violence between them. Ms. B. and her husband, as well as the other members of their

---

[1]Psychoanalysis is not the treatment of choice for everyone who needs some form of psychotherapeutic intervention; sometimes considerations of time, or finances, make analysis impossible: sometimes patients wish to undergo a particular form of treatment other than psychoanalysis (and whether or not one feels that analysis might actually be best for them, one still must respect their wishes in the matter): and, of course, sometimes the quality of the patient's ego suggests that the regressive or frustrating features of the analytic process will be essentially disorganizing, that in the end the treatment will be counterproductive, and that the patient will be harmed rather than helped – mainly by having been put into a circumstance for which he or she is unequipped, and thus one that is more stressful than he or she can effectively tolerate. The next chapter will describe two patients who fall into this last category. They had, in each instance, a failed analysis. We will not undertake this to demonstrate how and why they were "bad" patients but, rather, to show how this kind of patient and the psychoanalytic treatment approach were inappropriate for each other. These were not "unsatisfactory" patients: they simply were treated in a fashion unsuitable for their needs; psychoanalysis was not an "impotent" treatment: it is extremely effective with a different kind of patient. We will focus in on the problems in their treatments, attempting in the process to specify what, precisely, made the patient and the treatment a bad match for each other and suggesting, with the advantages of hindsight, what therapeutic alternatives to analysis might have been more useful at various points in each of the cases.

ménage, were manifestly influenced not only by the time in which they lived (this all took place in the late 1960s and early 1970s when many people were experimenting with group marriage, extended family structures, and communal living) but also by the science fiction writers Heinlein and Rimmer (who posited the notion that not only was it possible to have such relationships in a manner that was free of conflict, but that such extended marriages were the only means by which genuine and intimate relationships were possible once one freed oneself of bourgeois conflict: you can see how easily writing science fiction came to them). As one might imagine, all five found the idea easier to live with than the reality, and considerable tension between all of them soon began to surface. They thought of themselves as psychologically minded people who believed in talking things out, despite the obvious action tendencies we see expressed by their "marital arrangement." They found, however, that they could not speak to each other as freely as they wished: anger and jealousy frequently interfered with both their ability to speak to each other and the wish to do so. They felt that they should not give in to "politically incorrect emotions" that they did not value and so they hired a sensitivity trainer to meet with them "to help [them] to express [their] inner feelings better." This was also a time when T-groups, encounter groups, and other sensitivity-training group processes were greatly in vogue.

The sensitivity trainer did help to bring out their inner feelings, but he did not encourage them to keep the expression of their feelings within verbal limits. One of the exercises involved wrestling with the person with whom one was angry, and this in particular seemed to open up the floodgates of real physical violence between Mr. and Ms. B. Their fights became so frightening and so distasteful to the other members of their *ménage* that they eventually decided to go their own way. Mr. and Ms. B. were now left alone with each other: arguments escalating into fights became even more frequent, Ms. B. became more sick over them, felt more out of control and in danger of carrying things too far, and she entered analysis.

Her eruptions of rage and ultimately her inability to, as she put it, "contain [herself] when so furious" made her physically ill for days before a fight and for days afterward. Her "stomach would be tied in knots" when she argued with her husband. She would experience a continuous urge to vomit, as tension between the couple mounted. Finally they would reach the point of physically fighting with each other and, whether she lost or won, she would then spend a number of days afterward in bed in a state of physical exhaustion and depression. At the time she began treatment Ms. B. was concerned about the depression and exhaustion following such fights, but what she was mainly focused on was her rage and her inability to regulate it: as pressures between them mounted she would become so angry that she felt very much out of control and, most recently, when she fought with her husband she felt that she had no restraint and she was afraid of the possibility that she might kill him. She had harbored the faint hope that these fistfights were just a passing phase and that they would diminish over time. Instead, each time they argued the conflict became more likely to escalate into physical violence, and each time they hit each other they were fighting for longer periods, hitting harder, adding kicks and punches to what began as slaps, and generally doing more damage. Ms. B. sought analysis when it became apparent to her that, despite being consciously distressed by this problem she was nevertheless unable to do anything about it and that she was becoming progressively more enraged and violent with every ensuing fight.

Ms. B. was born with severe rectal and anal deformities, and in her first years of life had a number of major surgical procedures. The first was when she was only hours old, to create an excretory channel, without which she could not have lived. Others followed regularly and unrelentingly, in infancy and childhood, in an effort to provide her with an excretory system that was, mechanically and cosmetically, as close to normal as was possible. Her parents lived in an agricultural area of the South, and Ms. B. was their third and last child. Their baby needed specialists in this kind of surgery and would continue to need specialists in the extensive physical therapy that would be required, and their own geographical area did not have any. Wanting to give their baby every resource to lead as close to as normal a life as might be possible, they moved to a city in a different area of the country where the necessary facilities existed but where, much to their distress, they had no family and no easy access to any family.

Her father, who had never worked anywhere but on his father's farm, managed to find work as a linotype setter, and her mother was a housewife who had never been otherwise employed. Ms. B.'s parents were married very young: father was 18 and mother was 17, and they had their first baby within a year of the wedding. Ms. B. had two brothers, one 5 years her senior and the other her senior by 7 years, and her mother had not had any other pregnancies that Ms. B. knew about. Fortunately for Ms. B. they were in their mid-twenties when she was born, because it is hard to imagine parents who are still teenagers themselves being able to care for her in the way that she needed and, additionally, to do this in the almost total absence of familial support. They each came from large families, mainly farm workers and laborers, and they enjoyed a close relationship with their own family, and with each other's. Both Ms. B.'s brothers had unremarkable childhoods, inasmuch as anyone can be said to have had an unremarkable childhood with such a sick child in the family.[2] Both were in school by the time she came into the home, but they were also very involved with her. Never having to participate in what was painful for her, and treating her "like a favorite toy," they were very available to her at times

---

[2]Obviously their childhoods were deeply marked by the illness of their sister, by the special focus of attention placed on her in the family, and by what they witnessed as she was cared for. However, neither brother was reported to have evidenced any particular pathology that could be directly traced to this, despite our expectation that there must have been some whether or not it was identified as such. Fortunately they both had successfully passed through important developmental stages before their sister was born, giving them resources that likely would not have been available to them if they had been younger when their sister came upon the scene.

of stress.[3] Both completed college, married early, went to graduate school as married students, had young children of their own, and entered the professions; they remained close to each other, to Ms. B., and to their own parents, a rich testimony to the excellent and nurturing atmosphere of their childhood.

After I had achieved some analytic distance it became quite clear that Ms. B. had excellent parents, although this was by no means apparent to either of us at first. In the early stages of her analysis Ms. B. presented her family in a way that put them in a rather unfavorable light, in a similar way to that which we saw with Dr. A., in the sense that many of her stories were about the horrible things that her parents had done to her (told from the emotional perspective of the little child to which it had all been happening).[4] As a baby she was in pain and discomfort most of the time. She was in pain because of the physical difficulties that made both feeding as well as excreting rather excruciating experiences for her (you will recall from our earlier discussion that when she was fed, not only did peristalsis actively cause pain but also that the pain blocked the acquisition of pleasure and of relief from hunger and psychic tension). She was in pain because of the many required surgeries, occurring time and time again throughout her infancy and childhood. And every day, many times each day, her parents performed necessary – but painful and humiliating – ministrations concerning her excretory functioning. Some of Ms. B.'s experience of her parents as "horrible people who mainly brought [her] grief, mortification, and pain" was simple stimulus-response learning. It had to do with the direct environmental effect of having been subject to those experiences for so long and with such regularity, at a time in her life before she had the conceptual maturity to rationally and objectively understand either what was happening to her or what may have been motivating her parents. She learned to associate her parents mainly with the pain and with her subjective experience, which was one of being tortured, an association which the many positive interactions with her parents were not sufficient to counterbalance. Whatever positive representations she was able to develop of her parents – and they did exist to some extent – were always contaminated by aggression as a result and thus were always highly equivocal by comparison with their negative counterparts.

Another part of Ms. B.'s experience of her parents, in fact the main part of it, did not have to do so directly with what actually happened to her in life but, rather, with

---

[3]One is not in a position to know how much of what sounded like genuine loving kindness toward her was truly conflict-free, and how much may have been due to reaction formation.

[4]This kind of inaccuracy at the onset of their analyses were not unique to Dr. A. and Ms. B.: all patients express distortions, it would seem quite unintentionally but nevertheless in a highly motivated fashion despite being unconscious, at the beginning of treatment. Even at the end of a successful treatment one can never be sure of the objectivity of memory; however, at the outset of a treatment one can always be quite certain that the effects of fantasy on memory are most profound, and this will always play a significant role in how patients recall and present their childhoods and the significant figures of their past.

the fantasies she developed in association with her experiences. For example, because she experienced pain when her mother cleaned and changed her she learned to associate this with mother, but then she also developed fantasies during that experience: fantasies about *why* her mother was causing her such pain. One might say that at that time her fantasy life was developing an infantile theory of motivation, in which her parents' actions could come to have psychological as well as sensational and experiential meanings. She was not in a position to be realistic about her actual situation, including her mother's motivations, but she was in a position to generate fantasies about what was happening and about why her mother, and often her father, would be doing such painful things to her. Being only a baby, and later only a small child, she did not have sophisticated reality-testing skills against which to measure her fantasies. Through both spontaneous memory as well as during further analytic investigation, we found that many of her infantile fantasies were about her mother being "a witch who loved to see small children suffer," clearly suggesting that from a very early age Ms. B. imagined that her mother was hurting her intentionally. That is, that her mother did not *have* to do it to her; she could have chosen not to if she wanted but instead *did* choose to do it, and she chose to do it because she was sadistic and because it gave her personal pleasure to do so. Ms. B. had many other fantasies about this: she imagined that she had something her mother wanted and that her mother would stop at nothing, even to the extent of destroying her baby's body, to get it; she imagined that she was a bad girl who was being punished, and wondered what she did that was so wrong as to deserve such brutal reproof; she imagined that her parents were killing her, sometimes her mother and sometimes her father (although her fantasies about her father were quickly subjected to suppression), in retaliation for having been forced to give up their own parents when they had to move to the city to take care of her; she imagined that her mother was mentally disturbed, "an out-of-control monster who would get too carried away with a punishment, even if it were deserved," and who might "batter her child to death over a triviality." Such fantasies came to greatly overshadow the realities in which they originated, and it was the elaborations of these early fantasies throughout childhood and later into adulthood that came to be presented as the original "data" of her history when she first presented it in her analysis.[5]

Many of the contents of Ms. B.'s fantasies reflected the frustrations and pain associated with early feeding experiences, others were condensed with phallic-narcissistic concerns, but most of them acquired their special character from her toilet experiences. In some respects Ms. B. underwent both a precocious and

---

[5]Fantasies such as these were developed in the context of what she suffered, but they were not developed simply because she was suffering a special situation that other children normally do not: everyone develops fantasies about the events of their childhood, no matter what the nature of their experiences. The specific contents of Ms. B.'s fantasies were shaped by her experiences, without a doubt, but it would be a mistake to assume that her recollection of the "actual" events of her childhood would have been essentially accurate if she had not been so traumatized.

protracted anal stage, having its beginning virtually at birth and extending well into, and beyond, the phallic stage. Anal factors (anal in the psychological sense, as well as in the physical) became immediately prominent because of the special circumstances that focused uncommonly early attention on her anus and on her bowel products and, most especially, on her having to passively accept what was painfully being done to her. For many years, in fact not until after her final operations in midlatency, Ms. B. had little or no voluntary sphincter control. Even as an adult she had residual difficulties that could not be further rectified: it took about 30 minutes after a bowel movement before her anal sphincter fully closed, and thus Ms. B. had to undergo a tense half hour after every bowel movement before she could confidently feel that no bowel contents might inadvertently leak out (this was a realistic concern as well as an overdetermined fantasy). As an infant, just the necessary manipulation of her raw, open wounds as she was cleaned and changed was enough to have forced anal preoccupations to the foreground, but her problems did not end after the surgical procedures were no longer necessary. Even after the surgical creation of her anus, and after she did begin to acquire some control over her anal sphincter, further painful manipulations were required because of her bowel functioning (functioning that was initially tied simply to her physical condition and which then, naturally, became psychologically elaborated). Throughout early childhood Ms. B. suffered from alternating bouts of diarrhea and constipation, and constipation presented a particular problem. Her diarrhea could usually be controlled by medication, and sometimes her constipation was helped by laxatives, but most frequently her parents had to rely on enemas and, on many occasions, her constipation was so severe, and her feces became so impacted, that her parents had to digitally clear her rectum prior to administering an enema.

These were horrible experiences, and Ms. B. had many partial and fragmentary memories of occasions on which they were necessary. Her brothers never actively took part in helping to excavate her feces or in giving her enemas, and she never remembered her father having done either (although she was told that he regularly did, and also that her brothers were frequently present even if they did not actively participate).[6] What she did remember, or thought she remembered, in these fragmentary and shifting reminiscences of being constipated was the sense of being painfully full, packed, laden, brimming; feeling as if her body should have long ago burst because of it; and of feeling absolutely and unmanageably frantic because she had no way to relieve this pressure.[7] And conversely, of saying to herself that it had to end soon, that at some point her feces would have to come out or she would just

---

[6]Ms. B.'s memories and fantasies focused primarily on her mother. One purpose of being unable to recall her father's active participation was to be able to unambivalently preserve him (at least, consciously) as a "savior" to whom she could turn for protection from her mother, whom she just as unambivalently (again, consciously) saw exclusively as a persecutor.

[7]This is a paradigm of what may be the most basic and profound anxiety, derived directly from instinctual pressure; that is, mounting, uncontrollable excitation leading to a destructive inundation and overwhelming of the psyche.

explode, sometimes imagining the explosion as a relief and at other times imagining it as a rending and damaging of her body. She remembered with particular poignancy, even if the details were indistinct, the terror, rage, and sense of violation she felt at being held down when impacted feces had to be removed. She fractionally and incompletely recalled episodes of explosive diarrhea; of struggling to hold in her feces; her shame and her disgust at soiling herself; and the cramping pains in her stomach that attacked her in waves (and which created both pain and an appalling sense of foreboding) as she anticipated the inevitable "accident."

At the beginning of her analysis her memories were mainly impressionistic and fragmented in detail and sequence, and she had only a single coherent and fully formed memory of any kind about "toilet-training" experiences. This memory, which had particular vividness for her, was of an incident in which her mother digitally extracted her feces and then administered an enema. In addition to her mother's participation it included, in a symbolic form, her father and both of her brothers. In the memory Ms. B. was a child of about 3 or 4 and she was in the bathroom with her mother who was somehow holding her, face down, on the floor (perhaps with her foot in the small of Ms. B.'s back). Ms. B. was shrieking in rage and frustration, flinging her body about wildly, as her mother was spreading her buttocks with one hand and was using the tube of an enema, with her other hand, to dig feces out of Ms. B.'s rectum.[8] Ms. B. recalled seeing neighbors watching this through the open bathroom window, and experienced intense mortification at their being able to see what her mother was doing to her. We learned, however, from extensive analysis of this memory that it was not a depiction of an actual single incident but of an accumulation of incidents, and the presence of her father and her brothers in the memory required decoding their representation as neighbors (having been symbolized there in much the same way that a dream makes use of disguises). At no point in her analysis, from beginning to end, and even after she was aware of the distortions in this "memory," was Ms. B. able to think about this without passionate rage and humiliation.

One can readily see from what has been presented thus far how some of the influences from Ms. B.'s childhood were represented in her current life at the time she presented herself for analysis. The psychic bonding between her rage and her altered physical sensations, including nausea and vomiting, "knots" in her stomach, cramps, other sensations of illness, is apparent. Her inability to moderate mounting uncontrollable rage, to the point where she felt it would kill her (and even then it *still* would not stop), was connected to her chronic, malignant constipation. The episodes of mounting uncontrollable rage, finally spilling over into actual violence, is obviously connected to innumerable episodes of explosive diarrhea, as well as to the domestic "violence" of her actual toilet experiences (in which she felt that she was literally fighting for her life). Clearly, the escalation from "wrestling exercises" into full-scale physical assaults occurred in response to the unconsciously provoked

---

[8]It later became clear that this was actually her mother's finger, encased in a rubber sanitary covering.

memories of being held down and invaded during the removal of feces and the administration of enemas. And not least, her fights with her husband and the fear that she might actually kill him appears to be reflecting an identification with her fantasied mother, the insane, impulse-ridden sadist who attacked her child's body without regard for the consequences, indicative of a basically sadomasochistic formulation of love founded on her subjective experience of the mother–infant bond.

Most of Ms. B.'s identifications and object relations were highly instinctualized, given her special circumstances, making sublimated psychic alliances with her parents and brothers next to impossible.[9] One sees this reflected in the extreme infantile libidinization and aggressivization of her actual relationship with her husband. One also sees this heightened instinctualization in her participation in an "extended marriage" whose members, both male and female, stood for her father and for her brothers (and their unconsciously remembered participation in the sexual and aggressive dramas of the toilet).

In addition, one also gets some sense of how certain unneutralized and unsublimated childhood events affected her ego: first and foremost, Ms. B. often took action in the place of having conscious memories. And, unlike the case where one has a more highly structured ego in which affect storms can degenerate into moods that are expended through multiple channels of discharge, Ms. B. was overwhelmed by her affects: for her, strong affects, particularly when they were reminiscent of her childhood conflicts, had a profoundly disorganizing effect and they were discharged most effectively, again, essentially through action. Given these particular difficulties, one might wonder how she came to be considered a candidate for a psychoanalytic treatment, in which these factors would be expected to present major difficulties; however, Ms. B. had other resources that seemed to be (and proved to be) a powerful counterbalance to her deficits. The childhood events thus far described have been artificially excerpted or singled out, as it were, in order to make some pathological aspects of her adult functioning comprehensible. Let us now look at some other important variables of her history that account for the strengths she did have as an adult (and she had many), including those qualities of ego strength and superego maturity that made her amenable to psychoanalysis.

Although Ms. B. may have been unable to use mature reality testing in her

---

[9]The fact that her relation to all of her family members was highly instinctualized in no way suggests that they gave her any *inappropriate* cause for this. Her degree of acutely heightened instinctualization (even when the conscious representations of it were suppressed) was a result of a chronic traumatic life circumstance; her handicap and its subsequent ramifications were just too traumatic and created too much psychic havoc for noninstinctualized identifications and object relations to have been readily established by her. In addition, the degree of her instinctualized identifications and object relations is in no way indicative that her mother's, her father's, and her brothers' relations to her were equivalently instinctualized; this is a crucial consideration in explaining how they could have served as such healthy, reliable, and trustworthy resources for her development despite the intensity of instinctualization directed from her toward them.

infantile theory of parental motivation, she did not have a severe, or even a general, impairment of reality testing in other areas. As an adult the residue of her childhood conflicts was to be found not so much in limitations of reality testing but, rather, mainly in the areas of impaired judgment and impaired impulse control, and to some extent in her difficulties with symbolization that sometimes led her to actions, as we have seen, that were inconsistent with her best interests. To some extent reality testing plays a role in all those other things and thus some faulty reality testing was always involved, but in Ms. B.'s case we are speaking of a matter of degree: there is considerable difference between, on the one hand, the impairment of reality testing that leads one to believe that it is possible for a group marriage to take place without jealousy and, on the other hand, the impairment of a schizophrenic's reality testing when he is hallucinating voices, totally misperceiving the source of the "stimulus" and being totally unable (at that time) to distinguish between a thought and an event.

Ms. B. was a good student despite everything, making friends easily at school and in the neighborhood, and had many happy memories of her childhood – in addition to the bad ones. She went to college, completed graduate work in Far Eastern Area Studies, and was working as a simultaneous translator when she met her husband. Her frequent sadomasochistic object choices caused her to have had a number of frustrating and unsatisfactory relationships and played a role in how she chose her husband. With her previous lovers she had always had the option of breaking off the affair when the sadomasochistic character of the relationship began to get out of control and began to be expressed physically instead of only psychologically. She chose her husband because he was the first man to whom she was attracted who did not seem have this side to his nature: this was an expression of her ambivalence about the kinds of relationships she had been drawn to previously, of her conscious recognition that something in her choice of men was suspect, and it was a conscious wish to find a better alternative to the kind of relationships she had been having in the past; all evidence of considerable ego autonomy standing in opposition to the instinctualized parts of her ego. On the unconscious, pathological, side of her ambivalence she was aware (without realizing it consciously) that his gentleness was superficial, a reaction formation against the very kind of sadism that she found most attractive: naturally this served as a powerful unconscious attraction. As time passed, their marriage began to take on a sadomasochistic coloration, as one would expect, but in this case – because marriage is much harder to leave than a "relationship" – Ms. B. did not have the same freedom to leave, and so the relationship became progressively more disturbed even though it was not what the healthy part of her wanted, until it reached the point of crisis that brought her to analysis.

One might argue that she chose not to leave precisely because the marriage satisfied her need for a sadomasochistic relationship, but one might also argue that because the relationship was harder to leave, Ms. B. got drawn in deeper and deeper against her conscious and healthy wishes, in conformity with her unconscious and pathological needs as they were given greater expression and more scope for satisfaction. By the time her analysis was concluded it was clear that, her sadomasochistic needs notwithstanding, Ms. B. had been primarily making an attempt to break free of her pathology. *"It was like,"* she said, *"someone with a weight problem who was trying to diet. If she didn't have the problem, she wouldn't be trying to diet. No one disputes that she has the problem. But the point is that she's trying to diet! So she and her husband get invited to dinner and she vows that she's going to eat reasonably: and then the appetizers come out, and the soup, and the wine, and the main course, and the desserts, and the coffee, and the after-dinner drinks, and what do you expect? Of course she loses it. It's just too much, to have it all in front of her, and to see everyone else being able to eat when she feels so deprived. Everything, all her self-restraint, all her good intentions, all the work she did on her diet up until then, it all goes out the window! She eats, knowing she shouldn't, knowing she'll be sorry, and hating herself for it. All those people who think 'What a pig. Doesn't she have any self-control? She's not even trying!' don't have the vaguest idea what it's about; they don't have a clue. It's not about what made her fat to begin with, at least it's not about that just then: it's about desperately trying to do something about it, and getting into a situation that is just too much for her. My father had an expression: 'The road to Hell is paved with good intentions.' He was a good man, very kind to me, but he didn't know the first thing about the importance of a good intention."*[10]

Both her healthy conscious wishes and her unconscious pathological needs were met in the marriage. Along with the underlying psychopathology that dictated much of her marital choice we see considerable ego strength in her recognition that something was amiss in how she chose men and in her attempt, however unsuccessful, to form a relationship (at least consciously) with her husband on other than a sadomasochistic basis. One could choose to emphasize her psychopathology in this, but the fact that she was in considerable conflict about it, and that she was attempting to do what she could to remedy it, reflects considerable assets that one would not wish to ignore simply because they stand side by side with an area of unresolved difficulty. A common mistake in assessing the ego strengths of characterologically disturbed patients is to suppose that only the disturbed alterations of

---

[10]Ms. B. added the comment about her father because this was at a time in the transference when she was experiencing me as someone who could not accept her healthy wishes and as being gratified only by "therapeutic evidence" of her illness. Despite the reference to her father this was actually a maternal transference dynamic, hidden in the cloak of a paternal image. She had been working very hard to identify her motives in choosing her husband and was experiencing me as questioning her honesty in that process. She saw me as hostile to any view of her but an unhealthy one. Her accusations, motivated by the transference, included the idea that I wanted her to be sick, that I resisted her getting well, and that I felt deprived by any sign of health in her because it would mean that she would leave and then I would lose income. Parenthetically, the fact that she could be having such a strong transferential reaction to me and, in another realm, be working so effectively, illustrates some of the autonomous features of her ego that helped the analysis along.

the ego are significant, and this can lead to an underestimation of the patient's potentials.

Many characterologically disturbed patients, like Ms. B., have a kind of florid pathology that permeates much of their functioning without, however, ravaging other equally established and equally important constructive assets. It is this peculiar combination of organization and disorganization that sometimes makes these people good candidates for psychoanalysis, despite many of their deficits. We are familiar with the way most characterologically disturbed patients tend to flood, even saturate, the treatment with transference from the outset. However, despite this inclination, many patients who are on the healthier end of the character-disorder spectrum seem also to be able, simultaneously, to retain some residual access to the "as if" quality of transference experiences.[11] This permits healthier, but nevertheless characterologically disordered, patients to experience many of the more powerfully affecting phenomena in their treatments, such as major transference regressions, as a psychological events, rather than as actual repetitions of the past (which is frequently all that is possible for patients who are unable to achieve any distance from the transference and whose transferences are essentially narcissistic, delusional, or psychotic). What was it about Ms. B.'s background that gave her these resources, despite the chronically traumatic nature of her childhood?

Let us begin to answer this by noting that the traumatic nature of many of her childhood experiences should not be equated, in and of itself, with a pure measure of how traumatized Ms. B. actually ended up being as an adult. There is not a one-to-one, direct correspondence between reality events and their representation in the psyche; nor is there a pure "stimulus-response learning theory–like" mechanism between what happens, especially the actual events, in one's childhood and how one is affected by it (particularly after fantasy has influenced it) in later years. Given her anatomical difficulties and the chronic pain and discomfort (and rage and humiliation) associated with excretory activity, and associated with being anally ministered to by her parents, there is no doubt that Ms. B. had a childhood situation that was extremely traumatizing and which had the potential to be extremely traumatic.[12] If one were to consider *only* the actual traumatizing factors (pain, repeated surgeries, removal of impacted feces, and so on), and *no* other issues (like, for example, the degree of ego strength present in her, or the amount of external support available to her in going through these experiences) one would expect considerably more disruption in Ms. B.'s ego than actually seemed to be the case. Serious trauma in childhood inevitably affects development, not only in the stage in which it occurs but also in subsequent stages. In addition to dynamic evidence in adulthood of having been exposed to trauma during childhood, one might also have

---

[11]This particular dynamic and, in fact, the differences in how neurotic versus character-disordered patients approach the treatment process has been discussed in some detail in Chapter 8 (Transference).

[12]I am making a distinction here between a situation that is traumatizing and the subsequent degree of traumatization that actually occurs.

expected clear clinical signs of a serious traumatic neurosis. Ms. B. certainly showed signs of her past, as one would expect, but signs of a *traumatic neurosis* were essentially absent, and most certainly did not function as a primary organizing force in Ms. B.'s mental life.[13] Again we must ask, Why not?

Before looking at the specific factors that helped Ms. B. to negotiate her traumatic childhood situation without being psychologically devastated by it, we might look at the following preliminary question: how, concretely, did evidence of trauma from Ms. B.'s earlier developmental stages (the "analized" oral stage, and the anal stage, proper) show up in the phallic stage, and then, how did it make its appearance in the analysis?

In her maturation the development of reaction formations, as well as other means of suppressive anal-stage solutions and compromises, were insufficient: they existed, to some measure, but they were inadequate. Because of that she was unable to enter the phallic stage with the same repertoire of defenses and skills that other children usually have; that is, the defenses and skills needed to abandon the anal stage and to reorganize mental events along primarily phallic lines. Ms. B. reported at various times in the analysis early childhood memories of imagining that she must have once had a penis; however, instead of the typical rather stereotypic fantasy that her mother deprived her of a penis, as a punishment for masturbating, Ms. B. thought of castration (and penis envy) in an essentially analized context. The continuing experience of her mother's persisting involvements in her toilet activities (in the phallic stage) was a powerful organizer in her fantasy life, and she also heightened and augmented this aspect of her phallic-stage experience by unconsciously attaching to it memories of her mother's past ministrations during the anal stage; this reinforced the conviction that her mother was a "punishing anal destroyer" who did, literally, remove her child's offending body parts. She based her phallic-stage penis-envy/castration fantasy on a superstructure of events that had, actually, some support in reality even if they were subject to considerable distortion. This inner manipulation is, of course, radically different from the conventional situation in which the idea is essentially rooted in fantasy. Ms. B.'s fantasy was concretized by a realistic role that her mother played in her life: needing to be helped with her bowel movements by her mother occurred repeatedly despite any change taking place in Ms. B.'s psychosexual stages (and partially blurring the distinctions between them). This fantasy (now altered as well as reinforced by experiences that, in reality, played right into it) was then further used, in a kind of "compounding" process, as a "reality" confirmation of Ms. B.'s phallic-stage castration fantasy. As an example of how this analization of phallic and genital functioning was expressed

---

[13]Ms. B.'s situation, this kind of *chronically* traumatizing circumstance, is often described as a "strain" trauma. The concept of "stress" trauma is, on the other hand, usually reserved for single acutely traumatic situations with discrete beginnings and endings like, for example, being in an automobile accident or having one's tonsils removed. If Ms. B. had only undergone a single major surgery, we would have described that as a stress trauma, whereas the long sequence of interlocking traumata we describe as a strain trauma.

in the present: Ms. B. regularly amalgamated the experience of genital masturbation with the back-and-forth repetitiveness of trying to squeeze out constipated feces, and also, very concretely and consciously (as expressed in her associations),[14] with the pleasurable relief that she felt when she was finally able to void her bowel. She had condensed her phallic masturbatory experiences with anal tension-and-discharge experiences in such a way as to always give masturbation, and in fact, all genital excitement, an analized quality. Masturbation was always a very lengthy event for her (frequently lasting as long as 2 or more hours) before orgasm, and usually only a partial feeling of relief could be achieved. She also reported always experiencing a feeling of subtle pain and tension, in both the genital and the anal regions, during masturbation. These disagreeable feelings always existed concomitantly with her feelings of intense excitement and, eventually, relief. What was true of masturbation, in this regard at least, was also true of her experience of sexual intercourse.

Ms. B.'s analization of phallic material, particularly the oedipal conflict, was readily discernible in the transference neurosis. As had been mentioned earlier, her father was preserved as an idealized figure, split off in her mind—despite his participation in caring for her bodily needs—from the mother of painful anal caretaking, in order to keep him available as a love object about whom she could feel, at least consciously, relatively unambivalent. From the opening of the analysis until midway into the second year the analyst was the *good father* in her transference, to whom she could bring her problems, who would listen patiently, and who would never force her to any "premature conclusions" about anything. She described her husband and the various members of their prior *ménage* as "bad mothers who made me feel too full of feelings and who gave me no room in which to let them (the feelings) go. Even if this (analysis) is not always pleasant for me, at least you don't overstimulate me and you let me get on at my own pace." Her husband was the *bad mother,* many of her feelings and most of her conflicts (when conscious) were experienced as the *bad mother,* the people at work who hassled her were the *bad mother,* economic pressures were the *bad mother;* everything that pained her not only pained her but felt as if it were a torture, a torture forced on her by pitiless fate (the

---

[14]Associative processions of this nature began from initial comments, like "the orgasm finally comes out," "when I can finally make an orgasm come," "my rocking back and forth during it," "holding the excitement in and then letting it out," "making a big orgasm" (or "a little one"), "letting the excitement out slowly" (or "in a rush"), "feeling the pressure of the excitement build up in me until it is painful," and so on. Some of these comments are obvious condensations between anal and phallic sensations, to her as well as to us, and they led her very quickly to some of the ways in which anal experiences and phallic masturbatory experiences were amalgamated. Other condensations and amalgamations were not so immediately obvious, for example, the compound meaning to be found in her description of rocking herself back and forth during masturbation. However, her associative material to masturbatory rocking eventually led her to memories of sitting on the toilet rocking herself back and forth with cramps, squeezing to evacuate her bowels, and feeling the alternating internal movement of the fecal column that she could not express.

ultimate *bad mother*). I and the analysis, on the other hand, were "the oasis in the desert, the place of relief," as if the bad feelings she felt had not arisen in direct response to talking to me and as an essential part of the analysis. Of course this view of her analytic experience duplicated more than just the split she made between her parents. It reflected, on a different level, how out of control she felt about what had happened to her and how helpless she felt about what she was forced to experience as a child. And it indicated, in addition, how much she attributed internal experience as a child to an outside cause (instead of recognizing it as having arisen within herself).

During this time I had made a number of interpretations that were (even more than I anticipated) extremely anxiety-provoking, and on occasion I had even made some "against-the-grain" interpretations that Ms. B. strongly rejected. By splitting off her distressing experiences, and by fragmenting her view of me (so that I was never experienced as the agent of anything painful), Ms. B. experienced me as providing the kind of almost perfect "holding environment" that some "object relations" analysts describe attempting, intentionally, to furnish. Her conscious associations always identified me as her father in the transference, and whatever characteristics our relationship had that duplicated the good *mothering* she received was unacknowledged by her (and recognized only in an unconscious way by her).

Partway into the second year of her treatment Ms. B. began to think about what a good husband I would make: never hitting her, never getting angry at her, and never giving her cause for complaint. As soon as these ideas emerged Ms. B. began to have a number of psychosomatic symptoms, mainly expressed in the analytic hours themselves and only occasionally represented elsewhere. They primarily took the form of stomach pains, gaseousness and borborygmi, feelings of being "bloated" and of nausea, and they reflected the condensation between her sexual feelings and the anal contamination always associated with them. Slowly, as the erotic nature of the transference intensified, Ms. B. began to get attacks of diarrhea during the hour, which frequently caused her to have to bolt out of the consulting room in midsession to use the bathroom. Some time later she was able to say that she felt somewhat stimulated and not just in pain when she was on the toilet voiding her bowels, and she found that very peculiar and baffling. This was the event that opened up exploration in her analysis of how her sexuality was intertwined with anal preoccupations, but the specifically oedipal component of it had to wait until much later. One also could see the way sexual function was influenced by anal fixation outside the analysis, in her actual sexual conduct, where, during this time frame in her analysis, her preferred form of intercourse was anal rather than vaginal.

Now that we have looked at how some of Ms. B's earlier conflict was expressed in later developmental events, let us go back to the question of what gave her the ability not to have developed a major traumatic neurosis under these conditions. Although overwhelming mental and physical events are real things and not figments of one's imagination (despite their susceptibility to fantasy elaboration), the way one processes these events frequently becomes as important as, or even more important than, the "real" nature of the event itself.[15]

Despite all the terrifying and infuriating aspects involved in the necessary manipulation of her body, Ms. B. was being *taken care of* and not just being assaulted and harmed. Neither of her parents seemed to use the caretaking activity mainly to express or to achieve secondary aggressive gains. They basically took no pleasure from the pain that they caused, and they hated the unfortunate aspects of what they had to do, in part because of their psychological health and in part because they

---

[15]If one is tempted to suggest that there are some events that are so momentous that no manner of processing them could matter, we can recall our earlier description of how infants learn to organize and make sense out of their perceptions, using the ego of their mother as a means of mastering not only what is happening but also its impact, to assert that this is not the case. Every "real" event is susceptible to the influence of how it is processed.

For example, in the earliest stages of life being hungry and unfed, being physically tense and unable to discharge the tension in order to relax, or needing to be held and comforted without any way of bringing it about, is the equivalent of any trauma of cardinal importance for an older person. Without any sense of cause and effect, without any sense of how time passes, or a concept of the future, with no control over memory (which can often serve substitutive functions until the need is met in reality), without cognitive organization (which could permit the use of fantasy to facilitate a surrogate aim until the need is met in reality, and which would permit some purposive action in order to bring about a change in the infant's reality), a baby is as helplessly at the mercy of its painful experiences (both mental and physical) as is any adult who is menaced by a disaster, facing severe bodily damage, or confronting the loss of a dearly loved person. In fact, if we really pay sufficient attention to what we know about the skills that adults have to defeat the impact of reality when necessary, and then compare that with the lack of skills infants have for that very same (and often imperative) purpose, it becomes clear that the subjective experience of infants can at times be more traumatic than any comparable reality experience could be for older children, adolescents, and adults. Indeed, Henry Krystal forcefully argues that no trauma of adulthood is as potentially destructive as are the traumas of infancy that one rather tends to ignore and to minimize.

Infants have a counterbalance to the effects of trauma that adults do not have at their disposal: sleep, the way only an infant can. But maturity, the very thing that the infant lacks, provides multiple internal means of helping after the impact of trauma (ranging from countercathexis and denial to – at worst, and if necessary – psychotic withdrawal). Lacking maturity, the only mechanism that the infant brings on his own to the experience (that is, one that is not borrowed temporarily from his mother) is the unpleasure principle – negative hallucination, stimulus barrier, call it what you will – and this quickly breaks down as a safety device in unpleasant situations of any significant duration and certainly deteriorates greatly in any situations of real traumatic impact. And yet infants regularly and repeatedly go through terrible psychic experiences, such as being left without the assurance that anyone will ever come back again. Or being in pain from illness, injury, or hunger: a pain that is unstoppable and unmanageable on the infant's own, with no mental approximation of aspirin or even of the bottle, and also (in earliest life) with no firm idea that there is anyone that the baby can definitely count on to bring any relief. Infants manage to survive these ordeals without serious and enduring traumatic damage when they are properly supported by their parents (usually their mother) in the process. Probably some deficiency of memory protects infants from retaining these traumas, but even if that is the case, it is a protection of a lesser sort than the mother's ability to intervene in the experience, to ameliorate the event, or at the very least (when she can not change the traumatic situation itself), to make sense out of it for her baby.

identified and empathized with their daughter. Their ability to keep doing what was necessary for Ms. B.'s welfare, no matter how unpleasant it became, was an act of love not aggression. We know that there are circumstances where parents may not always do everything necessary for a child in trouble, mainly when the situation becomes intensely unpleasant and particularly when this is compounded by a child who is extremely uncooperative (as children in these situations often are). Even serious developmental defects may remain unaddressed when the painfulness of the situation, for the parent or for the child, becomes unbearable. It is by no means certain that everyone could satisfactorily meet the demands of raising a child in Ms. B.'s situation. For Ms. B.'s parents there must certainly have been times when their deprivation, frustration, and anger – especially when Ms. B. was being particularly difficult and resentful (as, from her perspective, she had every right to be) – came to play a part in their caretaking activities. There surely must have been times when either consciously or, more likely, unconsciously, there were some active retaliatory satisfactions in the pain that they caused. And surely what they had to do must have also interfaced (in a passive sense) with unconscious aggressive trends in their personalities. These factors notwithstanding, their relation to their child was *dominated* by love: their passing, partial, or deeply unconscious aggressive gratifications in no way canceled out the essentially loving, supportive, and nurturing (physical and mental) environment that they offered their child. This rich environment could not prevent the impact of Ms. B.'s condition on the general structure of her psyche, but it served to protect her from the development of a severe traumatic neurosis. The key to how traumatizing an event will become depends in large measure on the reality, but in much larger measure on whether the child is helped to negotiate it by the supportive interventions of healthy parents.

Even if we view adversity as an unfortunate event that is to be avoided whenever possible, when it is unavoidable it can be a good, if hard, teacher. So much so that we can say that when supportive parents are on the scene to help the child through the experience, even adversity, painful experiences, disappointments and frustrations – unpleasant, traumatic, and potentially disorganizing as they may be – can play a role in the advancement of psychic structuralization. The extreme dependency of a child on the external provision of its parents' psychic capabilities makes a clear statement of the child's vulnerability, but this is not the only characteristic of the situation that demands our attention. The use of the parents' ego functions is a complicated activity that involves a combining of ego identifications with defensively motivated, regressive identificatory mergers. When young children experience themselves as merged with the fantasied invulnerability of their parents, to defend against narcissistic dangers, the fantasy provides them with "protections" that are not even available to adults (who are more constrained to operate within the limits of reality). With this sort of magic the child is no longer subject to the disorganization an adult might have to experience when confronted with real helplessness in a threatening situation with no one's resources to fall back on but his own. At its worst, this can develop into a permanent turning away from reality; but as an interim measure it provides the child with a kind of temporary relief from the overwhelming situation that then makes other approaches to it more possible.

Actually, this grandiose merger fantasy – that one is one's omnipotent, impervious parent – is a fiction that has a small measure of support from reality. Children in these circumstances can, to some real extent, use some of their parents' ego strengths as if they were their own. Subjectively this seems to lend credence to the fantasy, to support it, to blow it out of proportion, to make it greater than it is, and to perpetuate it. No matter that from our point of view, rather than the child's, this involves the use of a grandiose and narcissistically restitutive fantasy which relies mainly on a rather primitive type of merger-based identification. It is not totally devoid of any kind of reality, however, because it is, in fact, accompanied by an actual merger of some part of the child's ego with his parents' egos. That is to say that there is a very constructive (and very real) ego identification taking place in this activity – not just primitive mergers alone – in which some of the features of the parents' egos do become incorporated into the child's ego.

The ego of a child is limited by immaturity but it still benefits from this operation. We can think of this as happening in much the same way that an appropriate response from a parent to a crying baby helps the baby to make sense out of its experiences. The same potential for growth also exists for the child in traumatic adversity. In an environment with adequately supportive parents, the process operating for the child in trauma is the same as the one that causes the ego of the baby to begin to model itself on the capable ego functioning of the parent, thus furthering structuralization despite the miserable circumstances that prompted it.

It may seem somewhat paradoxical to suggest that for Ms. B. the trauma itself also served as a stimulus to ego development, but the paradox is only superficial, insofar as her environment also included other, extremely supportive features along with the traumatic situation. Even though her trauma absorbed considerable psychic resources and produced considerable "psychic scar tissue" it also stimulated adaptive struggles: adaptive struggles that met with considerable success precisely because her adaptive strengths were enhanced by her parents' support throughout it all. Ms. B. did not end up with a traumatic neurosis, despite the extensive strain trauma of her childhood, because of the adequacy of her parents and their ability to support her through it all. If they had not been able, themselves, to cope as well with the situation, or if they had not been so appropriately supportive with Ms. B., we would expect to have precisely the kind of character-disordered patient that we will encounter in Mr. C. and in Ms. D., in the next chapter (and who, interestingly enough, did not have anywhere near the extremity of actual realistic trauma throughout their childhoods). The role of external support in traumatic situations cannot be overemphasized, and in many cases, as we can see with Ms. B., it makes all the difference in the world.

Having addressed the question of how she came to have the resources to be analyzable, let us return once more to Ms. B.'s analysis, to see how the extent of her difficulties did show up in it, the situation in which she appeared to be least analyzable, and the modifications that were necessary in response. You will recall that until midway into the second year of the analysis, Ms. B.'s transference was paternal. She slowly shifted to a maternal transference, so that by early into the third year it was there with a vengeance.[16] Where I had previously been experienced as if I were her idealized father, who never moved the analysis along too fast, now Ms. B. began to experience me as intrusive and as trying to get her to deal with the material that she was thinking about "too quickly." From having been patient and understanding with her, she now always had the feeling about me: "What's the big rush?" She began to wonder whether I disliked her. "Perhaps," she wondered, I was "annoyed with her for some reason." Did I appreciate how hard she was working at "getting things out" in analysis?

As this maternal transference regressed and became increasingly more intense, Ms. B.'s characterological difficulties became more pronounced in the analysis. The nature of her character organization did not pose any particular obstacles in the early part of the analysis; she showed a slight tendency to invest herself in the relationship a bit more passionately than do most neurotic patients early in the treatment, but she was not even remotely like some more profoundly disturbed patients who become so focused on the analyst, right from the beginning, that it is as if what had originally brought them to the treatment no longer exists for them, and – all of a sudden – they have no concerns beyond what the analyst means to them (which then becomes their sole preoccupation: whether the analyst can really be trusted; whether the analyst is really the right analyst for them; whether the analyst has his own problems that will get in the way of the therapy; whether the analyst will be sufficiently "validating"; whether the analyst's orientation is "legitimate"; whether the analyst is going to hurt them, or is sufficiently sensitive, or is too old or too young, or demonstrates his deficiencies with everything he says; and so on). However, under the regressive pulls of this more profound transferential pressure, Ms. B.'s strengths, which were most apparent in the early part of the analysis, began to become enfeebled by conflict.

Her treatment took a rather dramatic turn one day, when in a deep regression, she could no longer continue to verbalize her conflicts and began to put them into action. As Ms. B. began to reexperience the worst parts of her infantile relationship with her mother with more vividness and immediacy in the work, the analysis had been becoming gradually more difficult for her, and she was finding it increasingly difficult to continue to talk in sessions. We were able to discuss, albeit much too superficially, how much the analysis was beginning to feel like a demand, but without any relief for her. One day she came in and could not talk at all. She lay down on the couch as usual and remained silent for quite some time. I remarked on

---

[16]It is interesting to note, if somewhat facile to suggest it as a determinant, that she shifted into an anal-aggressive transference in her analysis in the about the same period of time that it takes a child to reach that stage in normal development.

how much more difficult it seemed for her to talk these days, and she made no reply. After some further period of time I asked if there was anything that I could do to help her to say what was on her mind, and again she could not respond. A few minutes before the end of the session I made a joking comment about how my describing her situation as one where "it was a bit more difficult for her to talk these days" was quite an understatement (hoping to capitalize on her sense of humor, which had always been quite excellent and a source of particular strength), but again I did not meet with any success in helping her to say anything. Ms B. did not talk to me for the next 10 months.

Five days a week, like clockwork, Ms. B. would come into the office, lie down on the couch, and remain silent for the rest of the hour. She was never late in coming to sessions, never late in payment, and never able to speak. Her posture suggested that she was quite uncomfortable; however, this was not expressed in any grossly physical way. The signals of her discomfort were subtle, having more to do with the appearance of tension than with gestural behavior. During the first week of this I attempted a number of different approaches to examining this behavior, in every instance trying to do so without also being demanding in the process (of course, given her state of mind, this was not possible). I had the impression that her silence did not particularly have the character of being withholding, despite her growing anger at me in the transference. She seemed psychologically unable, rather than unwilling, to talk. In any event, none of my efforts met with any success.

At the start of the next week, when Ms. B. resumed her silence, I had the impression that this was going to be difficult to work through because I had seen a pattern slowly but inexorably developing: an increasing tendency for Ms. B. to lose symbolizing skills as the transference became more difficult for her to tolerate. Without suggesting that I knew everything I needed to about her and the situation, I appreciated some of her limitations as well as many of the strengths she had available to her; and I had some confidence, based on the strength of the work in the analysis up until that time, that she would, after a period of enactment, be able to adequately symbolize and communicate her experiences to me. Despite this, however, I would not have guessed that the period of enactment would be 10 months long!

Given my expectation that some enactment was inevitable, I engaged in the first of two particular modifications in her treatment that I want to highlight in this case report. Ms. B. was silent for about 10 or 12 minutes when I again asked whether there was anything useful I could do to help her to talk about what was going on. As had become habitual by now, Ms. B. did not reply. I waited about 15 more minutes, and then I said, "*Although I would like to help you to find a way to talk about what is going on, I recognize that if I keep asking you what is happening, or what I can do to help, that you will only experience me as putting pressure on you. After all, by now, if you could tell me what is going on, you would have done so when I asked; and if you could tell me what I could do to help, you would have. I think I understand that you are not choosing not to talk, as if you could but you didn't feel like it, and that you are not on the couch with nothing going through your mind to talk about. You look full of tension to me as you lie there, as if you are ready to burst. If anything, I imagine that you are filled with feelings and emotions and thoughts that you can't say and can't find a way to get out. If anything, rather than being empty, I imagine you are too filled up with what you are feeling; filled ready to practically explode, and not able to do anything about it. I want to help you, but I don't want to harass you, and I can appreciate that my continuing to ask you if there's something I can do to help you talk could also feel like badgering to you. If you cannot talk, next time you come in here, or anytime you come in here, I will wait a reasonable amount of time and then ask you if there's anything I can do to help. If you don't reply, I will not pursue it again for the rest of the session. After all, we can't pull it out of you. I will wait, and I'll be there for whenever you can talk again. I know that you're cooperating in every way that you can, otherwise you wouldn't come in here the way you do, day after day; you'd quit instead. I'm telling you why I will behave this way so that you'll know that when I don't ask you a second time, after the first time, it's because I know you can't.*[17] Ms. B. did not verbally reply to this, any more than she had verbally responded to anything else I had said in the previous six sessions, however I either saw, or fantasied that I saw, a fleeting relaxation in her posture.

And that is the way that sessions went for the next 10 months. I would open the door to the waiting room; say, "Hello. Please come in"; Ms. B. would lie silently on the couch; after about 10 or 12 minutes I would make my comment; Ms. B. would remain silent; at the end of the session I would say, "We have to stop now"; and that was it for 10 months. Waiting 10 months for her to talk, not realizing that it would take that long but committing myself to waiting for as long as it took, even longer if necessary, for her to be able to make a shift in her internal situation, was the other parameter I introduced into Ms. B.'s treatment that I wanted to highlight in this discussion.

Ms. B. was clearly enacting, in this silence, multiple problems associated with her early excretory difficulties.[18] In one sense, perhaps the most important, she was repeating both the experience of being helpless at the mercy of a cruel fate that she had no control over, and the suffering itself that she underwent when she had deeply impacted feces that she could not move in the chronic constipations of infancy and early childhood. There were a number of additional, associated conflicts and memories, quite important in themselves, represented in her behavior. For example: in childhood, Ms. B. mainly employed the very limited control that she did acquire over her bowel functions for the purpose of warfare with "bad objects," rather than for self-mastery. She had learned, by midlatency, how to actively withhold bowel products (which became one of the nonbiological sources of some

---

[17]This is, as well as I can tell, an exact quote. The situation was so unusual that, later that evening, when writing the day's notes, I recorded my words as exactly as I could remember them. Not terrific English, I must admit, but I think the point got across.

[18]The discussion that follows is not an attempt to exhaustively describe all of the possible meanings of Ms. B.'s behavior; in fact, it will not even come close to a full accounting of everything that was important in this. It is an attempt to identify and to focus in only on the particular meanings that were major determinants of her behavior and the major determinants of the choices that I made in the treatment.

of the worst impacted constipations of Ms. B.'s later childhood years). She also learned by then how to eject them, in retaliatory opposition to the enforced passivity in infancy and in early childhood that she underwent during enemas and when impacted feces were manually dug out of her anus. If her mother forced her to do battle over her body and its productions (which is how she experienced it), then Ms. B. would, to the extent that she could, "fight fire with fire," and turn her passive experience active to the extent that she was able. Her silence clearly had this quality, too, although that was not what I chose to emphasize in what I said to her (since I thought that her current behavior was more influenced by the earlier experience of passive constipation than by the later one of active, defensive, and aggressive constipation).

Related to the question of passivity-activity, but also different, there was clearly a provocativeness to what she was doing with her silence; in it there was an appeal for me to force her to talk, to make her be a Good Analytic Patient, to require her compliance with the "fundament"(al) rule. At the same time, the other side of her ambivalence about this was that she needed to be permitted to learn how to use the toilet/analysis at her own pace, as a personal act of mastery instead of rebellion, in a way that way took into account her limitations physically/psychologically.

And still along those general lines, but again with a somewhat different cast to it, there was her need to put me into a passive constrained predicament similar to the way she had been psychologically bound and physically constrained as a child. This last point has a particular complexity to it because it was not only an attempt to make me suffer what she had suffered, and still suffered, it was also an attempt to make psychic contact with me in the only way left to her (since the symbolic, verbal pathway of communication had been slowly under attack and had now become no longer available). Ms. B. needed me to feel what she had been feeling, to go through what she had been going through, to suffer along with her, as a form of communion, not communication. Her regression into behavioral reenactment painfully fractured the most mature part of our relationship, the aspect of it in which things could be talked about, and in which her experience could be represented in that symbolic way. It is perhaps in this sense that the concept of projective identification as a mode of restitution in analysis (which frequently obscures more that it clarifies because of how inexactly it is used, and because of how differently it is used depending on who is using it) may have its clearest and most accurate meaning: Ms. B. needed me to identify with her and to become fixated at the level of that identification, putting us both into the same emotional condition of pressured misery, in order to feel that contact between us was still possible. If I were not also the child along with her, if I were not also her as well as being me, bursting with fecal pressure and being unable to do anything about it, strangulated by the experience, immobilized, paralyzed by it; if I only understood her situation but did not experience it too, then I was the mother with the enema, with the prying, digging tubes and fingers. Ms. B. had been, gradually, over time, losing contact with me in this transferential regression, and this reminded her of how she lost contact with the mother who fed her and who loved her so adequately when she was in the presence of the other mother, the mother who ministered to her anal needs. The enactment began because she lost symbolizing functions, but maintaining the enactment was a highly overdetermined action. Despite the content of what she felt she needed to induce in me, in this primitive restitutive fashion, Ms. B. was attempting to recreate the original, untainted mother–infant experience of psychic (rather than physical) interpenetrability. The painful, immobilized version of the mother–child bond that she was attempting to create was still better than being out of contact entirely (which is exactly what, on the healthiest side of her personality, being in that transference and unable to talk to me felt like: it was not just an inability to communicate as effectively as she wished to, but an inability to make contact itself). It is characteristic of all patients, and not just character-disordered patients, that symptoms, transference, and acting out – even if the form they take in neurotics is not so extreme – has multiple and often contradictory meanings.

My decision to introduce these two parameters into the treatment was, as is always the case with parameters, a combination of choice and necessity. Let us consider the necessity first. When a patient begins to act in such a way as to make further analysis impossible, at least according to the customary ways in which it is conducted, one has no choice but to alter the treatment in some way. Ms. B. had remained silent for six sessions at the time I introduced the parameter of my statement of intention, and one might ask, Why then? Why not wait longer before taking action? You will recall that she had been gradually showing impairment of autonomous ego functioning over some time. I was not measuring the difficulty in the analysis from the day she fell silent, but instead saw this as the culmination of a developing trend. I had been partially aware, but clearly not aware enough, of the faltering of Ms. B.'s symbolizing capacities as the transference was growing progressively more intense. One wonders, if I had paid sufficient attention to it at the time, whether there might have been some possible way of interpreting this in the treatment so that the treatment would have not reached the point that it did, but that is only an interesting speculation inasmuch as that is not, in fact, what happened. In retrospect, my lack of full recognition of the developing complication appears to have been due to two faulty assumptions: first, that this was a normal deterioration that would remain within manageable limits, very little different from the reinstinctualizations one sees in neurotic patients; and second, a faulty assumption based on the remarkable ego strengths (given her history) that she showed when she was not deeply regressed, that is, that they would still be available to her as she became more deeply regressed. I did not attend, as much as it was later clear to me that I should have, to the available signals that she was getting into trouble in the analysis, and her prolonged silence finally crystallized in my consciousness what I had only been preconsciously aware of until that time. However, once I was aware of this as a relatively long-standing difficulty that had slowly been building over time, it became clear that there was no point in waiting to see if this was going to be only transitory. I had no way of predicting that it would be a 10-month wait, but given my thinking after I had reorganized my thoughts about the recent history of the treatment, I also did not think that it would resolve itself soon. My thought was that if it were not therapeutically addressed in some way, that is, if I merely matched her silence with silence of my own, or if I simply insisted – whether it felt possible or not – that she talk, the outcome would only be a deeper and more unproductive regression. It took me the six sessions to recognize the preliminaries to her current silence and to fully appreciate the importance of it. However, as soon as that became clear to me, it seemed that waiting any longer would quickly bring us to a point of further diminishing returns.

If that reply is satisfactory, one could still ask why I made that statement of intent to her and then let her remain silent for such an extended time instead of transforming the treatment into a supportive or expressive psychotherapy. After all, Freud pointed out as long ago as 1914 (in "Remembering, Repeating, and Working Through") that "allowing repetitions during analytic treatment . . . constitutes a conjuring into existence of a piece of real life, and can therefore not always be harmless and indifferent in its effect"; and Fenichel suggested that in analysis we have three techniques for managing acting out, namely, interpretation, prohibition, and strengthening of the ego; and my choice of technique did not obviously fall into any of those categories.

Interpretation and prohibition did not appear to be useful possibilities at the time, and to understand whether any other choices seemed possible we need to review some of the things we know about the relationship between trauma and acting out. We know that traumatic events in childhood tend to be repeated in a variety of ways later on, very frequently in episodes of acting out during adulthood (and the tendency of the adult to act out the childhood trauma, if it is extreme and pervasive enough, will constitute, then, a classical traumatic neurosis), so an acting-out episode in analysis – even if not established within a traumatic neurosis as part of her general symptomatic organization – is not unusual or to be unexpected with a patient having Ms. B.'s background. Also, we know that the quality of acting-out episodes in adults frequently tends to be extreme and recurrent when the traumatic conditions in childhood involved forcible passivity, and that acting out episodes in adulthood seem to be especially problematic when this occurred to the child in particularly humiliating conditions. Additionally, this seems to be compounded further when the child's situation alternated between being (or experiencing herself as being) forcibly switched from a highly valued active position into a devalued passive position. We would expect, then, that whatever kind of acting out Ms. B. was going to be engaged in, it would not be mild, short-lived, or innocuous. Considered in this way, Ms. B.'s acting out was extremely restrained, and although it posed serious problems it took on a less troubling quality than there was potential for, particularly when taking into account the fact that it was kept well within the transference rather than erupting into all areas of her life.[19]

---

[19]However, this last point was not something that I knew for sure; it was only an educated guess until after the acting out episode had come to an end and we were then able to talk about it in detail.

Ms. B.'s acting out was severe, even if it was not as serious as it could have been, and she was not amenable to interpretation at that point. That was not an educated guess, it was a fact arrived at by my lack of interpretive success when, during the first 6 weeks of silence, I was attempting to deal with the situation. Greenacre (1975) makes a point about severe episodes of acting out that seems to capture certain aspects of Ms. B.'s situation quite well, but not others: "During the period of acting out, the analysand generally loses all communication with the judging self-critical part of the ego and the therapeutic alliance is consequently diminished to the vanishing point. Interpretation therefore cannot be given at such times" (p. 701). It was not my impression that Ms. B.'s ability to sustain analytic work had vanished, although she certainly seemed to be unable to use any self-critical faculties that might have leveraged her into speaking, but then Greenacre's comment was made in reference to patients with much more disorganizing kinds of acting out.

Ms. B.'s choice of the acting-out symptom, not speaking, is also comprehensible in a variety of ways. We have focused thus far on the particular events of her childhood that might have prompted her not to speak (e.g., a replay of constipation); however, there are some strictly developmental issues that also contributed to her choice of silence in her analytic hours. These developmental considerations illustrate the overdetermined nature of her use of speech, in this case nonspeech, and they become particularly important because they militate against our having to consider Ms. B.'s acting out to be, necessarily and only, an unresolvable impasse in the analysis. That is because they indicate other possibilities besides only ego impairment as a result of a current regression that could have led to silence as her choice of an acting-out symptom. Let us start with a general consideration that many analysts have suggested; that is, that the repetitions involved in acting out establish a condition in the transference that makes it unmanageably burdened by conflicts from the second year of life, in which the relationship of speech to action is crucial. We can see the direct applicability here to Ms. B., whose conflicts were not literally from the second year of life, but who had the conflicts that children ordinarily, in normal circumstances, would be exposed to in the second year of life, in other words, the anal stage. More specifically, however, we want to zero in on the *disturbances of speech* that are possible if too much conflict exists in the second year of life—and in this case, we can take the time frame literally. In the second year of life a number of developmental accomplishments are mastered at the same time, and in relation to one another. For example, the mastery of speech takes place at exactly the same time that the special motility of walking is being accomplished, and at the very same time that *sphincter control* is in the process of being established. All three things happen together and exercise mutual influences on each other. Many psychoanalytic students of development have reported on the ways that speech and mouth movements become combined with, or become influenced by, the organization of bladder and bowel control (particularly the expulsive sphincter movements that are involved), which has led them to suggest that speech is always and clearly marked by the imprints derived from these retentive and ejective bodily constituents. A disturbance in speech during analysis is considerably less disconcerting from a patient with Ms. B.'s history, for whom one would almost have to predict such a disturbance given her history, than if one were to find it in a patient whose disturbance was linked to conflicts at a developmental period for which it would not be appropriate; for example, a disturbance of speech linked to the phallic stage or to latency and the organization of the superego. This does not reduce Ms. B.'s silence to an insignificant event, but it places it in an important perspective. Her behavior in the analysis does not have the same ring of extreme abnormality that it necessarily would have, were one not attending to how such massive anal difficulties, naturally, will inevitably have an effect on the autonomy of speech and language in the presence of conflict, later in life. This seems to have been as much a developmentally overdetermined event as it was a sign of regression of the symbolizing function under transferential stress, and in that sense the behavior is not as prognostically grave in a patient who shows in other areas of the analysis, as did Ms. B., very good to excellent ego and superego organization.

With all the above considerations of both content and function in mind, it seemed that neither prohibition of her behavior nor interpretation of it was possible at that time (in Ms. B.'s sixth session of silence). But it did not seem that this state of affairs was entirely irreversible, and it also seemed that abandoning the treatment or converting it into a supportive psychotherapy so quickly was premature. If the treatment were causing her actual harm, perhaps then there would have been a reason to take a decisive action. Although no obvious technical avenue of approach had occurred to me, simply a lack of clear direction did not seem sufficient justification to ignore all of the proficiencies that Ms. B. had previously demonstrated in the analysis. Was there ample enough evidence that this change had to be viewed as conclusive and final? If anything, there was evidence of more than 2 years of Ms. B.'s having demonstrated adequate insight, satisfactory verbal capacities (at least until that point), clear introspective capacity, and considerable self-reflectiveness in the analysis. On the other hand, one would not wish to take action[20] without some rationale for it, even if one's justifications are forced to be speculative and based on one's "best guess."[21] During the time separating her fifth and sixth sessions of silence, I consolidated some of the ideas that had been percolating in me (during the previous week): ideas about what this all meant, why it was happening just then and in that particular form (these were the ideas that I

---

[20]And we must make no mistake about it: my statement to her was an action, and my intention to do nothing but wait until she could once again begin to speak was also an action. Even the analyst sitting silently, in the more normal analytic situation, letting the patient free-associate in an unhindered way, is taking an action.

[21]The assumption that some therapists make, that "I can do it as long as there is no reason not to," is a dangerous therapeutic posture. We are much better off taking the position that "I can only do it if there is a reason for me to do so. The reason why I am doing this is. . . ." Unfortunately, the clarity of our reasons is not always as plain as we would like it to be, that is the nature of working with obscure mental forces and contents, but the principle of acting *for a reason,* rather than acting because one cannot think of a reason why one shouldn't, is quite important.

have just outlined above), and about what stance might be appropriate for me to take with Ms. B. under these circumstances.

The rationale for my parametric approach, then, was as follows: I thought that by permitting her to do what she clearly needed to do (even if it meant that she did not fit the typical analytic model of a standard patient and the analysis did not fit the model of a standard analysis), nothing major was to be lost, in that the analysis was stymied anyhow for the moment. But, as I have stated, that did not seem to me to necessarily be a permanent condition. If I permitted Ms. B. to be silent for as long as necessary, and in that situation to experience a fantasy of merger based on my forced identification with her,[22] then the sense of reconnectedness that Ms. B. would be able to achieve through these sustained periods of projective identification (as I have defined its operation above) would have a temporary healing effect; a salutary effect that would in no way be equal to what interpretation might offer in more ideal circumstances, but nevertheless a salutary effect that, after sufficient time, would then permit the analysis to progress once again along more standard lines. At least, this is what I hoped (perhaps as much out of desperation as out of conviction). And the passage of time, I thought, would in itself provide Ms. B. with a "cooling-off" period, a time in which she could feel reconstituted by the lack of overt stress, which I assumed would be supportive (in this period of crisis) to her otherwise good ego and superego functioning.

This approach would be considered a variant of the third technique that Fenichel suggested (although not at all an obvious one); that is, supporting the patient's ego at times of acting out. Taking this analytic stance[23] seems now, with hindsight, to have been correct (even though I certainly could have been wrong, and even though I did not imagine that it would take quite so much time). The decision seems to have been appropriate because once Ms. B. began talking again, her treatment was able to continue without any repetitions of this kind; it was a treatment with a number of other, but more minor, impediments, however, and most significantly, it ended as a successfully completed analysis that did not require the use of any other equivalently major parameters. The nature of her conflicts was such that it was a complicated and protracted analysis, but it was an analysis from that point on that was very little different, at least where technique was concerned, from that of a profoundly neurotic patient.

The manner in which the impasse of silence came to an end is very interesting because it involved an enacted but symbolic depiction of soiling in the office. For some time, exactly how much time it is impossible for me to say, I had been aware of considerably less tension in the room (whether the reduction was in her tension,

---

[22]Mainly, but only partly, illusory, because it was realistically impossible for me to be comfortable under such circumstances, and that is what she would be able to pick up and "feed off."

[23]I want to emphasize that various temporary alterations of the analytic stance, what we call modification of technique, are frequently what character-disordered patients require of their analysts, if the analysis is to remain intact in the long run.

or in mine, or in both of ours, is also impossible to say) despite the fact that Ms. B. was just as silent as ever. It is difficult to say over what period of time this took place because, once again, I recognized it only preconsciously during the hours. My conscious recognition of it as a process occurred in retrospect, after the impasse was bridged. I also find it difficult to identify whose tension was lifted, and in what order, although I am sure it must have been reciprocal, because in working with patients whose conflicts are preverbal the analyst's resonating responses and identifications are frequently, in fact almost always, matched at first in the level of primitivity. As a consequence, the intellectual organization of one's responses is minimal despite one's best attempts to translate them into the symbolic terms with which one is more comfortable, and which come more easily into the analyst's consciousness. In any event, at around that time, I opened the door to my waiting room one day to invite Ms. B. in, and found her on her hands and knees cleaning up the mess from an ashtray she had spilled. With great embarrassment and profuse apologies, she explained that she was feeling a bit unsteady and had bumped into the table while sitting down, overturning the ashtray in the process. After she settled herself on the couch I inquired as to whether she was still feeling unsteady, and Ms. B. began to describe having been feeling unwell for a few days, as if talking to me were the most natural thing in the world and we had not just been through 10 months of silence in the analysis.

After about a dozen sessions of "filling me in," in actuality solidifying her reestablished resources by avoiding conflictual material, Ms. B. was able to mention the silence and we began to talk about it quite productively. She described herself, during the silence of those hours, as having been in a kind of limbo, thinking very little but feeling intense emotional pressures that she could not define. During the next year, interspersed with other matters of more immediate importance to her, we were able to closely examine her experience of the silence and, even more importantly in some ways, what had been happening between us that had led up to her needing to stop speaking. Near the end of her analysis, some 4 years later, she said: "You know, it's really quite amazing that you managed to use just the language of my constipations and diarrheas when you first talked to me about my state of mind, that time when I stopped talking. It was really a lucky break that you came up with those specific images. Your unconscious was really on the right track, even if I didn't understand all of what you were saying to me at the time. I guess you didn't, either."

I was, of course, setting her up for the conceptual interpretation that I had hoped to be able to make with effect when the impasse was broken, and was depending on her unconscious recognition of its correctness at that time. I just did not realize that it would, literally, be years before that was possible. The rest of her analysis was sufficiently unremarkable, despite her having still had some considerable problems, that there would be no value in describing it in detail. In the 4 remaining years of her analysis, Ms. B. divorced her husband (but not until after they got into a fight in which her nose was broken) and decided that when her analysis was over, she would go to law school (a childhood wish that she had abandoned in favor of simultaneous translation, which she eventually had come to consider "a grind"). She was unmarried when the analysis came to an end, but she was in a relationship with a man that was quite serious, and which seemed free of the sadomasochistic character of her previous relationships. I did not hear from her again until 4 years later, when she sent me an office announcement celebrating her having joined a prominent Wall Street law firm. Six months later, I received a birth announcement; Ms. B. had a son (I had no way of knowing whether this was a childbirth or an adoption, not an unreasonable thing to wonder about, given her age at the time). From a note she included, I learned that she had married the man that she was involved with at the end of her analysis, that they now owned both an apartment in the city and a house in the country, that they had two cats and a dog, and that she was very happy.

The purpose of this case report, and the reason why it has been presented in truncated fashion, was to focus in on the particular difficulties that can be encountered in the analytic treatment of severely character-disordered patients who, in the long run, still remain amenable to analytic treatment. With what has come to be known as "the widening scope of analysis," we find ourselves constantly pushed to find creative solutions to treatment problems of patients who would have been considered unanalyzable not very long ago. In considering how to treat neurotic patients, we are confronted with the nature of the right interpretation and how it may best be delivered for the patient to make good use of it; with such difficult patients we are confronted, in addition to the question of whether our interpretation is correct, even more with the question of what makes an interpretation possible when weak or distorted ego functioning and highly pathological object relations are prominent features of the patient's character.

16

The Cases of Mr. C. and Ms. D.

This chapter will examine the treatment of two patients affected by a special form of sexual acting out between parent and child that interferes with the capacity for analytic treatment, even many years into adulthood; specifically, an oedipal relationship that leads up to, but stops just short of, explicit and consummated sexual relations. This creates a character disturbance rather than a neurosis, despite the central pathology being oedipal and phallic in nature; however, in each of these cases considerable disruption of the preoedipal environment also contributed greatly to the patients' character structure and subsequent unanalyzability.

The insistent libidinization of the relationship on the part of the parents creates an environment which is, for the child, traumatically intense (without the sheltering parental supports that existed for Ms. B.) and utterly absorbing; it chronically contaminates the conditions of the child's existence, interfering in a variety of ways with the happiness and welfare of the child and impeding the child's capacities for progressive development. The cost to the child goes beyond a fixation in object choice and extends to a constant hindrance in appropriate stage-specific attempts to develop ego autonomy and superego structuralization. Conflict resolution can be close to impossible in such circumstances, leading to inevitable disruptions in the child's struggle for psychic equilibrium which are reflected in the adult's inability to find the analytic process of therapeutic value.

As a shorthand term I will use the designation *oedipal winner;* the designation will refer to an individual who, throughout childhood, was grossly overstimulated by the parent of the opposite sex in a setting where the same-sex parent competed inadequately or not at all. Children who score an oedipal "victory" focus on the readiness of their parents to permit them to become the object of adult sexual interests and genital wishes. In the child's mind there is a genuine possibility of a gratifying, but highly traumatic, incestuous encounter. The possibility that this may become a reality presents a multitude of threats to the child's immature psychic organization, and goes on to have serious repercussions in adolescence when the physical reality and its possibilities become crystallized.

The relationship of innate drive endowment to aspects of ego strengths within the oedipal configuration, and the interplay between preoedipal mental functioning and oedipal stage-specific dynamics, has been extensively described in the first part of this book, in the section covering development and the nature of conflict formation. Much of that will be kept in the background here and not particularly singled out, although it will necessarily be touched upon in discussing these two patients' narcissism, the development of their psychic structure, and their object relations. Acknowledging the full importance of those components, and granting the influence of some other significant constituents in mental functioning that will not be addressed at length here, the major focus will be on the serious disturbance in personality and character structure in individuals who can generally be classed as oedipal winners and who seem to need an approach that is somewhat different from psychoanalysis (even with considerable modifications).

We should be cautious however in our use of the term *oedipal winner*. The concept of an oedipal winner should be distinguished from those terms that describe diagnostic categories. In a parallel precaution, the theoretical sections of this chapter should not be equated with a fully developed clinical theory, as there is no question but that the conflicts of the oedipal complex become expressed and/or resolved in a variety of ways.

The theoretical and clinical formulations developed in this chapter also occur in individuals who are not oedipal winners. However, in those cases these dynamics are not only less intense, but they frequently play a different role in the general development of mental functioning. In the oedipal winner, the conflicts to be described are primary mental organizers. Such conflicts tend to predominate, act as mental *dis*organizers, and thus have a disproportionately large influence in the ultimate development of symptoms, character, and later accessibility to the analytic undertaking. One of the differentiating characteristics between oedipal winners and other individuals who make use of similar or related dynamics may have to do with the use of global and archaic defenses in combinations with a particular primitivity of object relations. This concept will be clearly detailed as the chapter progresses. There may be no reason, or need, to describe oedipal winners as if they are in a class by themselves; nevertheless, a study of these dynamics can aid in understanding their inner life, their plight in reality, and their difficulties with psychoanalysis.

Depending on the depth of family pathology there are some interesting characteristics (especially in profoundly disturbed environments) that oedipal winners sometimes hold in common. The more profound the disorder of the childhood environment, the more similar these individuals seem, until, at worst, they come to approximate the two patients, Mr. C. and Ms. D., described in this chapter, whose lives and analyses were simply a shambles. Thus it seems that the specific dynamics and structural propositions advanced here gain in explanatory power as pathological conditions and compromise formations intensify, and therefore the term oedipal winner becomes more apropos as the trauma becomes more central in mental organization. This still leaves ample room for the variants many analysts see as less saturated dynamic and structural possibilities evolve in response to less contaminating and paralyzing circumstances of childhood. The generalized description of the oedipal winner and the attending dynamics refers, then, to the worst possible outcome barring development of a psychosis, and the reader who extrapolates backwards will see the relevance of these dynamics in less disturbed individuals.

If it is true that oedipal winners have a particular hardship throughout life in the regulation of drive fusions and the neutralization and sublimation of conflictually bound resources, it comes as no surprise that when they wish to begin an analysis they frequently have difficulties in establishing a flexible interchange between regressive elements (and resistive inclinations) in the transference neurosis, and the autonomously organized aspects of the working alliance. As a consequence, they may fail, or usually fail, to complete a successful analysis, or may do so only with the greatest possible modifications and only after protracted treatment.

I have chosen to present a male patient and a female patient here, to demonstrate similarities and contrasts which follow generally accepted notions in current psychoanalytic thinking that differentiate certain aspects of development according to sex. These cases were chosen to illustrate how analytic treatment and some patients do not mix, and so I picked patients who showed severe oedipal winner characteristics; that is, they were the most extreme examples available to me. It is well to remember that most cases are not so flagrant, and that these cases were selected for heuristic considerations. In both cases the analyses were unsuccessful and uncompleted, and although this is not an uncommon occurrence with such patients, it is by no means a preordained fate. Most certainly it is not the universal experience of all analysts working with oedipal winners. It is necessary to keep in the forefront of one's mind that these dynamics are only a part of these patient's overall mental functioning, chosen and highlighted specifically to illustrate how they made analysis impossible (and not intended to describe the general nature of these patients' entire mental economies). Also, it is necessary to be aware that even the most extreme cases can fall into a wide variety of diagnostic categories. Finally, the clinical material is provided to illustrate a hitch in the process: no attempt is made here to fully delineate the entire course of these two unsuccessful analyses, and the focus, clinically, is on problems in treatment as they reflect problems in mental organization, and not on the general conduct of the rest of the analysis. There is also a loss in the phenomenological aspects of these patients, as there was with Ms. B., which is inevitable in a truncated report; many aspects of these patients are lost or minimized, and suffer in the microscopic view of them necessitated by limiting our goals for this chapter. In any event, we can now proceed to our patients.

Before doing so, however, it would be useful, as a necessary background, to consider some conceptual issues affecting the development of narcissism, object relations, and psychic structure in the male oedipal winner. Children who are free from inordinate oedipal trauma are able to structure the superego at the end of the phallic stage by replacing considerable quantities of object-libidinal striving with sublimated and neutralized identifications. The formation of parental introjects enables the child to shift away from, and significantly decrease, the sexual longings, fears, and hatreds of the oedipal complex. The child may then enter latency replacing these intense preoccupations with ample capacities for nonsexual affection, positive regard, and the wish to identify in an aim-inhibited fashion.

For all oedipal winners, but particularly for the male, this capacity is significantly diminished. The constant readiness of the male oedipal winner's mother to provide libidinal gratification (in concert with the meaningful absence of a competing father, or at least, with a competing paternal psychic representation) does not prompt the child to relinquish object-instinctual ties. In fact, if anything, it leaves the way open for continual development of ever more heightened sexual interests in his mother. The freedom to sublimate, neutralize, and fuse those drives that usually becomes more available to a child (in a healthy environment) as the impulses characterizing the oedipal complex undergo repression (and other transformations), remains mostly unavailable to the male oedipal winner. This creates significant defects in the capacity of the ego to develop and maintain its functions at a constructive level of secondary autonomy, which then leads to equivalently major defects in the super-ego.

In normal circumstances the paternal representation has the strength necessary (whether based mostly or entirely on fantasy) for a boy to experience an intense castration anxiety.[1] A powerful and inescapable paternal imago is a helpful tool for the management of oedipal aspirations. Lacking an appropriate object in reality because his father does not compete, the male oedipal winner turns to grandiose and omnipotent preoedipal parental imagoes. These identifications combine archaic representations of the grand and powerful mother of the oral stage with some demanding and punishing aspects of the mother of the anal stage, which develops in the psyche of the little boy a phallic maternal object representation. This complicated, layered mental representation is then merged further with an idealized representation of phallic paternal strength (despite its obvious ambiguity, being based essentially in fantasy), which is "fueled" essentially by derivatives of the child's own projected aggression.

The male oedipal winner must rely on exaggerated powerful representations in the superego to balance and combat his instinctual wishes and inclinations. Because the father has not presented himself as sufficiently threatening in reality, nor has he supported a complementary fantasy, the boy turns to memory traces of his earliest experiences with his mother (where grandiose-narcissistic self-representations were merged with grandiose-omnipotent maternal representations) to provide the needed

---

[1] This fantasy may be strongly reinforced by the revival of the father's own oedipal conflicts, as he becomes a significant player in his son's oedipal drama. The father's unconscious wishes to defeat and kill his own infantile competitors may be communicated to his son who can then use the unspoken, but clearly hostile, intent in the unconscious of his father to confirm his worst suspicions. Normally, in response to his own and his father's combined fantasies, the boy is able to repress his sexual wishes, to substitute affection in his relations with his mother, and identification and admiration in his relations with his father.

external, reality-supported if not determined, resources necessary for the creation of internalized restraints.

As this pathological identification (although identification is not exactly the right concept, in the sense of how we usually use it) enters into a further merger with the actual aspects of whatever paternal representation exists, expressly for the purpose of controlling instinctual impulses, it gains its power and its efficacy not from its paternal components but, rather, from the underlying archaic self–maternal object representation. The male oedipal winner magnifies the paternal object representation to threatening proportions based, paradoxically, on the characteristics of his mother rather than his father. In some cases, where there *is* a remnant of oedipal competitiveness in the father's character (but still not enough to present a sufficiently threatening challenge to the son), this remnant is magnified and enlarged upon in an attempt to fix the restraint on a reality confirmation (to reinforce the idea that is not just a fantasy) so as to support the notion that the father is a real threat to the son's phallic assertions. When the little boy further enhances the paternal identification (representation) by adding to it the power of his own projected aggression, he is attempting to develop an inner representation of a powerful father who is frightening enough to enforce (and to, at first, potentiate) selective uses of repression, suppression, neutralization, and inhibition. The problem here for the male oedipal winner is that because he identifies with a memory trace of infantile and regressive experience he is unable to establish a durable *stage-specific* set of identification-based mechanisms for the control of his impulses, or an appropriate set of *stage-coordinated* aspirations in the ego ideal.

The ego ideal of the male oedipal winner contains, among a variety of pathological aspirations and identifications, an unconscious identification based on the passive-feminine position of his mother. This identification is modified by the mother's sexually aggressive stance in reality, and also by the retention in the boy's superego of her grandiose infantile representation. The male oedipal winner's need for power, assertiveness, and phallic-narcissistic integrity in the ego ideal leads him to rely almost exclusively on the omnipotence of the infantile representation of his mother (which predates stage-specific devaluations). In consciousness, and to a much greater extent in unconsciousness, the grandiose feminine representation is masculinized by being transformed into a caricature of a powerful phallic father; other possibilities might also include homosexual resolutions that are limited and/or avoided to preserve genital (phallic-narcissistic) integrity.

Even into adulthood the ego ideal of the male oedipal winner may contain another category of pathological aspirations and identifications, consisting of a set of "heroic" paternal representations of the kind most often associated with the champions (Superman, The Hulk, et al.) of the latency stage. The powerful superhero imago serves as a caricature of the powerful and awe-inspiring hero (and threat) the father should have been; and in other, more transformed derivatives, serves a variety of other purposes for the male oedipal winner as he moves from the phallic stage into latency. We can enumerate some of these purposes as follows: (1) it strengthens the influence of aggressive projections and identifications put to use by the superego; (2) it influences the development of aspirations and controls that can be based on reaction formations against sexual-aggressive pleasures; (3) it channels a quantity of unbound aggression into socially acceptable modes of expression; and, certainly of tremendous importance, (4) it helps to further masculinize an essentially feminine identification.

Another major element in the male oedipal winner's ego ideal uses the father's passivity as a competitor, in effect his "silence" in the oedipal triangle, to create an image for the boy of a strong, silent, uncommunicative, inscrutable, powerful man whose impulses are tamed and completely under control (which stands side by side with the boy's use of these things as he identifies, now in the ego, with his father's passivity). When this cartoon of noncommunicative inscrutability is an ego-syntonic posture, we see in the male oedipal winner an attempt to have the ego ideal take over from his inadequate ego, which has failed in the task of setting limits on the expression of dangerous impulses. It is not surprising, then, that, also in analytic treatment, this particular aspect of the ego ideal (because of its ego syntonicity) is used to justify, legitimize, and even to ensure a treatment milieu replete with guarding, withholdingness, a refusal to be intimate, and prolonged and highly motivated bouts of silence. The ambivalence about being able to expose material from the unconscious that is seen in most patients appears to be almost entirely absent in the male oedipal winner. If one takes all of the aspects of the ego ideal that have just been mentioned, and adds to that the extraordinarily high levels of anxiety male oedipal winners constantly undergo as incestuous wishes threaten to become a reality, and if we also add the inordinately severe demands on the ego (motivated by the superego without regard to reality considerations of appropriateness, as is usually the case with the superego) which uncompromisingly insists on repression, suppression, and inhibitions, we can readily understand how disruptive and harmful will be their effects on the ego's capacity to act as a successful psychic regulator. In its application to treatment we can see how this places the male oedipal winner in a very unfavorable position regarding the free exploration of his mental conflicts.

In addition to a number of narcissistic mortifications inherent in such rigid and overly severe demands of the superego, the male oedipal winner also has to cope with further ramifications of the fact that a large percentage of his major identifications are feminine even though they take the form of phallic-male caricatures. Included in the underlying, generally feminine set of identifications is an additional identification on a different level with his mother's sexual impulse-ridden acting out. The male oedipal winner must devote considerable amounts of effort, using energy that might have been directed to relatively autonomous pursuits, toward keeping this impulsively disordered identification under control. In the service of this goal, the male oedipal winner may hypercathect oral-satisfying or anal-demanding representations of his mother. Such retreats to orality and to anality are adaptive, although quite regressive, in that they are designed to keep the sexually active maternal identification suppressed (in terms of action as well as in consciousness) and, in turn, to keep his own sexual impulsivity under control.

The male oedipal winner's identifications are based on maternal representations in greater proportion than paternal representations, and therefore may be considered to be essentially female identifications. If so, they carry a strong strain of passivity and latent homosexuality, which may be acted out in treatment. He often presents himself to the analyst in a passive/negative oedipal stance, and may try to cajole or to challenge the analyst to assert himself (or herself) over him (the patient). He acts out the suppressed wish for a powerful assertive father by trying to get the analyst to engage in a variety of symbolic shows of strength (which may also include symbolic rape and castration, both as a punishment and a preventative). Although much of his stubborn silences and his wish to defeat the treatment may stem from the oedipal winner's need to keep his impulses in check, he is also motivated by the wish to get the analyst to forcibly break past his defenses and invade him internally (as the analyst grows frustrated with the patient's silences, stubbornness, and resistance to insight). In some circumstances the patient even tries to get the analyst to make an explicit attack upon him (as the analyst grows irritated with the patient's passive-aggressive provocativeness). These transference demands present themselves simultaneously, and alternatively, with the more obvious maternal transference (erotic imago), where the analyst is seen as annihilatingly threatening because of the capacity to be overstimulating.

Let us now look at how this was played out in the unsuccessful analysis of Mr. C., who entered treatment suffering from premature ejaculation and *globus hystericus*.[2] Other symptoms included depression and an aversion to washing.

Mr. C.'s father was a career Navy man who spent most of his time at sea. Mr. C.'s mother was extremely seductive, and she grossly overstimulated him throughout his childhood and adolescence. She frequently would undress in front of him. In adolescence, Mr. C. tried to set limits on his impulses (and, apparently, on hers, as well) by asking his mother to undress only in the privacy of her bedroom. She grudgingly agreed but made no real attempt to frustrate her exhibitionistic needs: whether she was partially dressed or totally undressed, she always kept her bedroom door completely open. As a measure of his own ambivalence, Mr. C. often managed to be walking by at such times.

Mr. C.'s mother constantly gave him detailed accounts of her sexual life, including her extramarital affairs, which seemed to be short-lived but frequent. She was not only overstimulating her son with all this information but also signaling her availability. It was in this context that Mr. C. developed a complicated, obsessive, masturbation fantasy which excited him intensely, but puzzled him, because its contents were not explicitly erotic. When the symbolic presentation gave way to

---

[2]This symptom existed as a *lump* in Mr. C.'s throat that caused him to be unable to comfortably swallow food, eventually becoming severe enough to prevent him from eating almost entirely.

the true meaning of his imagery, in analysis, the masturbation fantasy became anathema to him:

Mr. C. is a swashbuckling pirate chieftain roaming the world searching for booty. A Spanish galleon [Mr. C. was of Hispanic descent] laden with gold from the New World is crossing the hot and humid Caribbean on its way to Europe, escorted by a 74-gun man o'war. "Captain C." attacks the convoy and sinks the escort, despite the fact that he is badly outgunned. His pirate crew boards the treasure ship and kills all aboard with the one exception: the warship's or treasure-ship's "First Officer" [his not being sure which kind of ship may reflect his multiple identifications in projected form]. Captain C. and his crew set the "First Mate" [now, to us, making his identity even clearer] adrift in a tiny rowboat [deprived of "oars," of course], and spitefully laugh in his face. Captain C. sails off with the other man's property and, looking off into a blazing sunset, wonders to himself what will kill the marooned sailor first; hunger, thirst, exposure, or the sharks.

Mr. C. was involved with weight lifting and body building beginning in midlatency and continuing until late adolescence. Each day Mr. C.'s mother would give him "post-workout rubdowns." While admiring his bulging muscles she would massage his entire body, telling him how excited the neighborhood girls would be if they could see and feel his muscles. It remained unclear whether Mr. C. was dressed or undressed during these "rubdown sessions," but it is not unreasonable to assume that some counterparts to his mother's behaviors are represented here. At one point in treatment he mentioned casually, almost as if in passing, that during these "sessions"[3] he was always intensely excited and that he had, on occasion, erections which he and his mother ignored.[4]

In late adolescence Mr. C. had a fistfight with his father, and Mr. C. beat the daylights out of him. Beginning then, when reality and Mr. C.'s masturbation fantasy began to resemble each other too closely, augmented by the surfacing into consciousness of a fellatio fantasy of "swallowing [his] father whole," Mr. C. stopped lifting weights, developed the first of a series of attacks of *globus hystericus,* became quite slovenly, had a brief but powerful period of anxiety attacks which ultimately resolved into numbing and deadening depression, and hastily fled into a precipitous marriage. He eloped with a girl whom he knew for only 2 months, within a week or a bit more after the fight with his father. Not long afterward the marriage dissolved, and shortly thereafter he presented for treatment. At that time Mr. C. was eating at a bare minimum because of the *globus hystericus,* bathing and washing rather infrequently, was feeling only mildly depressed ("on the few occasions when I feel anything at all"), and was in clear distress. Mr. C. claimed to have absolutely no feelings most of the time, "as if I were already dead and buried."

The reality of having bested his father, compounded by the encouraging seduc-

---

[3]He described them, repeatedly, as "sessions," suggesting both the overexciting and homosexual character of analysis for him.

[4]It should come as so surprise that he never chose to attend to what we might see as an obvious parallel between rubdown "session" and analytic "sessions."

tiveness of his mother, forced Mr. C. to inaugurate massive inhibitions designed to stand in opposition to his oedipal wishes. These heightened interests, emerging in a pathogenic environment, required extremely powerful defensive strategies. In such a situation the need to decrease oedipal strivings is not merely urgent, it becomes paramount; Mr. C.'s parents, by both commission and omission, were hardly of use to him in achieving the structuralizing sublimations, neutralizations, and drive fusion that are generally available to the ordinary child in a more "normal" environment.[5] Mr. C.'s parents were unable to provide the necessary auxiliary ego and superego capacities (and here we might particularly note the striking difference between Mr. C.'s parents' deficits in this regard, and Ms. B.'s parents' assets) that are available to a child in a healthier family when instinctual strivings threaten to overcome the infantile ego's limitations in the ability to set and follow limits. Mr. C.'s solution was to globally encompass all impulses with the potential for danger by inhibiting virtually all spontaneous thinking and feeling; hence he felt "dead."[6] Aided and abetted by the liberal use of repression, suppression, and inhibition, such a massive commitment to not having any dangerous thoughts and feelings protects both self and object from the destructive possibilities inherent in the real, or fantasied, consummation of such illicit love.

Despite the similarity of aim in many of his defensive configurations one could sense, underneath his rigidly nonaffective presentation of himself, a genuine quality of pathos. In addition to its obvious role in limiting unacceptable impulses, Mr. C.'s depression reflected his misery as he attempted to renounce his pathological attachment to his mother.

Mr. C.'s precipitous rush into marriage appears to have been an attempt to extricate himself from the destructive home environment. His wife was particularly unattractive, and a conspicuously deformed victim of a serious childhood illness. One may assume that the choice of "a woman who was thoroughly repulsive to me" was an attempt to keep his sexual impulses at a minimum. On the rare occasions that "my sexual needs overcame my revulsion," either coitus was interrupted or intromission was unsuccessful because of premature ejaculation. This resulted from the generally high level of his anxiety when Mr. C. was unable to distinguish his wife and her mental representations from the mental representations of his mother.

We can also identify some of the more important aims of his *globus hystericus* symptom: (1) It caused Mr. C. to lose weight rapidly. In reality, and in his mental representation of himself, it decreased his physical size and diminished his dangerous physical potentials. (2) If he and his mother treated his muscular body as a

---

[5]Normal environments have conflict but they are not *saturated* with conflict: in addition, normal environments offer the possibility of an adaptive resolution of emergent conflicts.

[6]Without fine discriminations this is tantamount to attempting to oppose and defy every impulse except those that have undergone drastic transformations, and which then may only occur in a form that appears as a most unrecognizable derivative.

phallic equivalent, then this weight loss was a way of going from erection to flaccidity. (3) If his powerful body was a significant contributor to the literal defeat of his father in the fistfight, then reversion to "puniness," as he put it, might help to restore the proper hierarchical order of the family. And finally (4), if he reverted to "puniness" he also reproduced a stage of his life when he was not physiologically mature enough to take part in an act of genital sexuality.

In a set of dynamics with a different organization, and ignoring for the moment the previously mentioned "fellatio fantasy" (which clearly was implicated in the feeling of a lump in his throat, and in his inability to swallow without gagging), the inability to swallow helped him to avoid the powerful regressive temptation to displace genital conflict onto conspicuous, debilitating, passive orality. Thus, in a compromise formation of dubious value, he attempted to block the possibility of instinctual gratifications on a variety of levels, with most of his efforts directed toward the ideal of achieving an objectless, angry anality.

Considering this last point, an interesting aspect of his default in personal hygiene was that it quite naturally caused him to be unattractive and repellent (matching his stance toward his wife, and intended to keep her sexual and affec-tionate feelings low, so that a decrease of sexual excitement and opportunity would be a mutually desirable goal). The more important aspect of his refusal to keep clean was its role in setting the stage for a retreat to an anal passive-aggressive state where sadism was meant to overpower libido: the intention was to replace conscious and unconscious sexual wishes with unconscious aggression.

Mr. C.'s treatment followed the pattern of the conflicts that dominated his life. He expressed considerable affect whenever inhibition was decreased, and his at-tempts to institute this defense usually involved a furious enmity toward the analyst, which served conflicting purposes: his enmity was intended to reduce his current involvement with the analyst and with the analysis; however, it also expressed, at the same time, the disdain and contempt in which he held his father. On rare occasions he became consciously angry with the analyst and accused the analyst of a wide variety of personal and professional deficiencies that, transferen-tially, were aimed at his father (who failed to best him in the oedipal struggle), at his mother (who failed to master her sexual impulses), and at both parents simulta-neously (who were unable, or unwilling, to protect him from his own impulses). Mr. C.'s most characteristic pattern in treatment was expressed by flat affect, halting and shallow verbalizations, body rigidity, an unconscious but quite deliberate and intentional refusal to associate freely, and a motivated lack of both introspection and insight. If Mr. C. had a family coat-of-arms, the motto would surely be "Hear no evil; see no evil; speak no evil." Throughout the course of treatment there were infrequent but consistent statements to the analyst that the analysis did not seem to be helping (which, in addition to a realistic perception and assessment, was also a symbolic transferential defeat of his father by rendering the treatment impotent), accompanied at such times by reassurances to the analyst that he would never leave the analysis until he had achieved a complete success (which was hypocritical and a reflection, really, of his continuing attachment to his mother combined with the wish to make a passive surrender to his father).

After approximately 475 sessions of extremely nonconfrontational analysis, Mr. C. began to experience a more generalized lessening of defensive rigidity. Until then the analysis seemed to be progressing, although with a plodding slowness that was not recognized, at that point, as a harbinger of the insurmountable difficulties to follow. He was able at that point to remember, in an emotionally charged context, many sexual and sexualized childhood experiences with his mother, and it was in this stage of his treatment that most of his history (which has already been presented here) became a matter of record. These memories were accompanied by overtly sexual dreams and associations, which increased regularly in both content and frequency. Shortly thereafter Mr. C. became quite anxious. From few or no feelings he was now overwhelmed by too many feelings. Not unexpectedly, he intensified his customary global defenses (mainly repression and severe inhibition). When these psychological gestures proved inadequate in regulating his mounting anxiety, he attempted to regulate it behaviorally by missing sessions. His absences eventually became frequent enough to be a matter of real concern and were not responsive to interpretation. They were also unresponsive to increasingly greater parameters and, eventually, modifications in the analysis, such as fewer interpretations of unconscious defenses; fewer interpretations of preconscious wishes; substitution of intellectual formulations instead of eliciting memories; planned transference gratifications; and eventually, even a reduction in the number of sessions per week, to decrease the pressure he was under. Eventually Mr. C. caused the majority of his disturbing conscious memories and fantasies to be suppressed, but there was still no real easing of the tension for him, no real easing of the negative transference eruptions, and no real easing of the downward spiral in his ability to internally control his anxiety (a perfect replica of the childhood situation, in which his sexual wishes as well as terrible anxiety were unmanageable and out of his voluntary control). For example, absences continued to increase, which demonstrates how little he was helped, once his anxiety was too greatly mobilized, by the analyst's interventions and by the attempt of the analyst to slow down the rate of regression and reinstinctualization. As conscious anxiety was replaced with unconscious anxiety that continued to mount, Mr. C. precipitously terminated the analysis.[7]

The termination of his analysis was not something that just seemed to happen as his anxiety mounted, it was connected to a trauma in the treatment itself. Termination followed an sharp awareness about one of the unconscious meanings of his

---

[7]This suggests some additional hypotheses about his motivation as well as about his eventual use of the treatment. Mr. C. fled from Mother to Analysis, just as he fled from Mother to Marriage; not *to Analysis* but *from Mother*. If he did not enter treatment but, instead, as a way of concretely seeking shelter from an unmanageable situation, was an analytic treatment, that by necessity would revive his relationship to her, doomed from the start? Is it also possible that analysis and marriage were unconscious equivalents and, if so, does his entry into analysis reflect some attempt at enactment of an unconscious homosexual resolution of both active and passive oedipal relations to both parents?

repetitive masturbation fantasy. He could not tolerate an insight that occurred to him, which first connected that fantasy to the "rubdown sessions" with his mother and then to the fight with his father. Treatment itself became a noxious stimulus that needed inhibition, as suppressed and repressed wishes and ideas emerged into consciousness and preconsciousness and, more importantly, threatened to keep continuing to emerge. Defeat of the analysis became the equivalent of his defeat of his father, but–again, more importantly–defeat of the treatment became the equivalent of defeat (and therefore mastery) of his forbidden oedipal desires. Such extreme responses to considerable anxiety are by no means the special preserve of the oedipal winner or the only resolution possible for oedipal winners, but Mr. C. felt he had no choice at that time but to discontinue a treatment he could not cope with or otherwise defeat.

Let us turn now, before discussing further the pitfalls of analysis for such patients, to the female oedipal winner and look at some considerations in the development of her narcissism, object relations, and psychic structure to see how they played a role in an equivalently disastrous analysis. One frequently encounters the suggestion that a relationship exists between some forms of antisocial acting out in children and various superego lacunae in their parents. Whereas it is true that acting out in all oedipal winners, male and female, is not limited to the realm of antisocial activity, much of it can be contrary to socially expected norms. In particular, this is the case with female oedipal winners, when it takes the form of promiscuity (also promiscuity supplemented by other sexual misbehavior). Why is this the case with females more than with males, and why does it take the form of promiscuous acting out? Rather than merely engaging in wholesale internalization within their own superegos, of the lacunae in the superegos of both their parents, female oedipal winners appear to develop partial identifications with the impulse disorders of their fathers which are then represented, as a narcissistic restitution, in the ego ideal.[8]

The unique life circumstances of the female oedipal winner (discussed in greater detail below) promote the formation of gaps in the ego ideal and, in addition, leave them vulnerable to the establishment of a "negative" ego ideal. In normal family constellations, females begin the development of a healthy ego ideal with positive and nurturing maternal identifications strengthened by reaction formations against anal pleasures. The mothers of female oedipal winners seem to lack a commitment to safeguarding their daughters' best interests that goes deeper than mere culpability in the unfolding oedipal seduction with the father. The mothers of female oedipal winners have not only abdicated the responsibility of being consistent providers of internal and external protection but also may have been unavailable, throughout the female oedipal winner's childhood, for the task of providing reasonably continuous libidinal gratifications. Thus they would appear to be, in a variety of ways,

---

[8]This would be impossible for the male oedipal winner. Such a cross-gender identification in the ego ideal of the male would represent castration, rather than narcissistic balance, as it does for the female.

genuinely inadequate objects on which to base a set of positive and constructive identifications.

Disappointing mothers (and mothering experiences), and the severe frustrations that accompany disappointment, may lead the female oedipal winner to shift object representations in the ego ideal; in place of the more normally expected positive maternal identifications, the female oedipal winner seems to substitute a set of transient identifications based on her father's sexually aggressive posture. Excepting the timing, we can see the obvious parallel to the equivalent mechanism of the male. These pathological, initially transient, paternal identifications become stabilized and more permanent as they become strengthened and reinforced by a special preconscious and unconscious libidinal gratification: the gratification inherent in being the object of their father's frequently symbolic, but nevertheless intense, sexual desires. This mode of influencing the contents of the ego ideal is designed to provide the female oedipal winner with a sense of narcissistic intactness as the child is subjected to narcissistic injuries which are the consequences of at least two major factors: (1) her mother's gross inadequacies, dating from earliest infancy, stage-specifically reflected in the abandonment of her daughter, who is being overwhelmed in the oedipal seduction; and (2) overwhelming levels of continuously mounting excitement caused by the incestuous attentions showered upon her by her father.[9] The blending of self-representations with representations of the assertive phallic father, and in particular with his destructive intrusiveness, is designed to support the need for narcissistic intactness, but beyond this, it is also an attempt to concretize a grandiose fantasy of omnipotent phallic power, which the female oedipal winner carries as an "internal selfobject possession." That is, the identification is treated in two ways: as if omnipotent phallic power is an intrinsic part of the self; and as if omnipotent phallic power is a possession of the self which could be concretely used as a tool in the warfare with anxiety.

Under the impact of such traumatic overexcitation and, paradoxically, in response to the gratifications of both the sexual attentions and development of such constructs in the ego ideal, the little girl's ego is motivated to blur the distinction between self and object. Thus another major problem for the female oedipal winner, in both childhood and as an adult, is that she experiences herself as the equivalent of her ego ideal. This process helps the little girl avoid having to experience her vulnerability, which, because of disappointment and the internal mechanisms just described, is so frightening to the child. Even as an adult, the female oedipal winner will go to almost any lengths to avoid the feeling of vulnerability (which seems to be experienced only in terms of being at the mercy of an unmerciful someone else).

---

[9]Despite current attention to the potential for narcissistic injury in the processes of differentiation, separation, and individuation, and notwithstanding all the obvious ramifications of castration anxiety and other body-damage fears, the most basic threat to the mental apparatus would seem to be mounting, unavoidable, uncontrollable overexcitation.

She expects that the wishes, needs, hopes, desires, and expectations (and any other drive-related activity) of anyone else she is with will inevitably result in damage to her, in that despite her attempts at invulnerability she is susceptible to considerable disorganization in the presence of impulses and the demand for their gratification. This paradigm may also help our understanding of what appears to be a common problem for the female oedipal winner. Although she may be aware that her environment is permeated with sexual feelings and may also be quite consciously aware that these feelings are dangerously out of control, she never seems to be able to determine whose sexual feelings are being expressed. When with a sexual partner, or a potential sexual partner, even the slightest sexual signalling by her partner becomes elevated to the intense and insistent demands made upon her during childhood. Having exaggerated her apperception all out of proportion she cannot figure out whether she is having such strong feelings or if it is her partner who is threatening her with powerful and destructive sexuality. We can see that in the attempt to preserve narcissistic integrity the female oedipal winner develops impediments that are slightly different, but equal in seriousness, to those of the male in defensive, narcissistic, object relational, identificatory and structural development.

Compounding her difficulties is the further complication that there is, after all, some important internalization of the "superego lacunae" of her father. Superficially, one might assume a moderately reasonable degree of intactness of superego functioning in the fathers, as the explanation of why they seem to limit their acting out to symbolic and only partial seductions rather than overt and consummated exploitations. It might be more correct, however, to view their functioning as a reflection of severely pathological ego and superego disruption, even though one can point to evidence that suggests a capacity for some control of their impulses. What we see as we examine the histories of female oedipal winners is that their fathers' capacities for the control of their impulses was minimal, at best, and often bordered on no control at all. Such marginal accomplishments ought not to be thought of as evidence of structural maturity and autonomy.

The little girl does not identify with the minimal level of control the father is able to exercise, but internalizes instead the impulsive configurations of her father's ego and superego. In this way she is deprived of many of the most beneficial attributes of superego functioning: (1) protective sexual and aggressive taboos; (2) the safety and protective structuralization commonly afforded by the achievement of conventional behavioral and other social demands (usually present in the form of parental introjects); and (3) the opportunity for narcissistic expansion when compliance with demands of the superego are achieved. She is also deprived of significant portions of many important ego functions: (1) areas of reality testing; (2) the capacity to keep defenses adaptive; (3) neutralizations, sublimations, and the ability to achieve and use drive fusion (i.e., much of the capacity for deinstinctualization); and, among still others, (4) the effective use of signal anxiety.

In consequence, with the possible exception of the single life-preserving narcissistic fantasy of her phallic power, the inner world of the little girl is not nurturant and trustworthy but depriving, empty, frustrating, hostile, overstimulating, and a genuine source of danger. We see in this a reflection of her outer environment, which has been for the most part uncaring, exploitive, and destructive.

In the female oedipal winner, direct identification with the superego lacunae of her parents (and here we can definitely include the superego lacunae of the mother, in the sense that she was in covert collusion with the father) and indirect identifications (which place omnipotent and grandiose narcissistic fictions in the ego ideal) together combine to foster an eventual compulsion to victimize others in precisely the way she has been victimized.[10] The aim of this complex operation is to acquire control over passively being excited and actively being overexcited, over passive and destructive (in the sense of being empty) maternal identifications, and over the trauma of having been a captive victim of her father's sexual pathology.

Let us now look at the analysis of Ms. D. (like Mr. C.'s, also unsuccessful) to see how this was played out in actuality and the effect that it had on the usefulness of analysis for her. Ms. D. entered analysis after a previously unsuccessful therapy. She entered both therapies because of conflicts at home and depression. Ms. D. spent much of her time in her first treatment crying miserably, which seems to have been more complicated than one would assume from first appearances. In response to her seductive appeal, her obvious unhappiness, and his own neuroses, her previous therapist ended up with her frequently in his arms as he patted her and soothed her into quiet relaxation, in his mind, much as a good mother would with a distressed infant, but less superficially, with many more meanings for them both. She was aware of her pleasure at this, but also of its inappropriateness, and she terminated that treatment feeling (rightly so) that the therapist could not maintain the proper distance to help her solve her problems. Her therapist was the casualty of his sexual feelings toward Ms. D. and appeared, to both of them, to be out of control despite his rationalizations, which he understood on another level to be rather hypocritical. Being out of control was precisely what he was intended to be feeling in the context of Ms. D.'s hidden transference demands. Although this behavior is not excusable

---

[10]In cases of this kind of child sexual abuse, and worse, one often sees the victim described as an "incest survivor." First of all, one must question this tendency to lump together overstimulation, even extreme overstimulation of the sort being described here, with actual instances of incest. Second, this designation, "survivor," seems to be a romantic exaggeration closely tied into the therapist's feelings about what has happened to the child who is now his or her patient. Even taking into consideration the analyst's commitment to a neutral stance, the analyst is nevertheless an agent of reality, and cannot afford to dramatize the patient's situation (in his or her own mind) because of the effect that will have on how the analysis is subsequently conducted. In fact the child was not physically damaged in a potentially life-threatening way nor in any other way literally threatened with an actual loss of life, for which the "survivor" designation would be applicable. Rather, these children experience a particular kind of victimization which is terribly unfortunate, not simply because no child should be treated in that way, but especially because of how tremendously destructive it becomes in the child's psychic life. Despite the emotional damage it can, and inevitably will, bring about (and which is not meant to be minimized in this discussion), the seduction, no matter how reprehensible, is not life-threatening in and of itself, and the victimization of the patient, not the patient's "survivorship," is what needs analyzing.

on the grounds that countertransference reactions play a part in every treatment, it would also be unfair to suggest that this therapist's problem was a completely alien intrusion into that particular therapy. If it is true that Ms. D. was motivated, in large part, by a wish to receive transference gratifications rather than transference resolutions in therapy, we can hypothesize that her therapist's inappropriate behavior was enormously rewarding for her. If so, why did she terminate? Perhaps her rational reasons were an indication of sovereign ego functioning, but the decision may also have been a vehicle for diminishing the accompanying overexcitement, which must have been of overwhelming proportions even if it was self-engineered at first. In that case, the situation was *intolerable* and not merely undesirable.

Ms. D.'s mother was mentioned infrequently in the treatment and seemed to be almost nonexistent. Apparently she lived in constant fear of her husband, a physically large and psychologically dominating man. She never opposed him and never protected Ms. D. when a variety of conflicts and fights broke out between father and daughter. Time and time again Ms. D. would turn to her mother for interventions or support of some kind, and her mother would tell her, "This is between you and your father. Leave me out of it!"

Ms. D.'s father was sometimes violent, always seductive, and sometimes quite overpowering with his daughter. He would sit her on his knee and tell her stories of his romantic and sexual exploits, frequently in quite explicit detail, from the days before he was married. He made it a practice to walk around the house in only a pair of loose, boxer-type undershorts. Ms. D. remembered having her eyes constantly drawn to the open fly or the loose leg of the shorts, where she could see his genitals. She was fascinated by them and although she often thought to herself that she should not have been looking, she did so anyhow and eagerly awaited every opportunity.

As Ms. D. grew older and began dating, she went through a peculiar and disturbing ritual with her father. He would sit up waiting for her to come home after a date; on her return she would have to sit on his knee, again with him only in his underpants, while he questioned her about what happened on her date. In the dimly lit room his grip on her wrist would painfully tighten as he demanded the details of every kiss and of every caress. He would eventually explode in a rage at her and push her from him, calling her a tramp and a slut. He often threatened to beat her during those episodes.[11] Ms. D. remembered these numerous incidents with a mixture of fear and excitement.

The fact is that she did permit boys and, later, men, greater liberties more quickly than was usual. She was marginally aware of her father's pathological need for these

---

[11]The fact that this was not merely angry excitement was confirmed when Ms. D. recalled that he would breathe heavily and get red in the face, "with the veins throbbing on his forehead," well before the time when he actually "exploded." She remembered that as he would insist on more and more details he would get progressively more agitated (excited), until he "exploded." Further confirmation came when she was describing this in analysis and suddenly remembered that he looked just the way her boyfriend did prior to, and during, his orgasm.

reports. Her frank promiscuity was a sign of her gross overstimulation, which was complicated by her wish to meet her father's constantly pressing demands. His vicarious enjoyment of her sexual exploits was paramount in their relationship; he insistently communicated hidden messages that required her to act out with other men that which he was barely able to keep himself from acting out with her. We can see in this situation another root of her chronic confusion as a child, as to just whose sexual impulses were expressed and being acted upon.

In a final but important note regarding her father: he used to threaten her constantly with beatings. On the occasions when he had his pants on, he would remove his belt and brandish it menacingly. Ms. D.'s constant fantasy, even in the midst of subjective feelings of terror, was that his underpants would fall down and then she could again see his genitals.[12]

Ms. D. began her analysis by making the same attempt to seduce the analyst that she had made with her previous therapist. She needed to create in the treatment the same environment of unclear but insistent excitement as that which existed at home for her during childhood. When I did not respond sexually, Ms. D. became very anxious. This frightened her, and she intensified her efforts to have me respond to her with sexual interest and excitement.

I continued to remain unresponsive to what began as subtle sexual invitations; after some frustration, they became quite explicit. Later, she began to become "bad" in the hope of being "punished" by me. If she could not provoke me in a sexual way, then she would try to engage me in the other, apparently aggressive, mode. At first she treated only herself badly. When I responded in each instance in a concerned but uncritical manner, she switched the attack from herself to me. In verbal form she attacked with accusations, and in behavioral form she escalated the assault, trying harder and harder to get me provoked into anger by actively behaving badly toward me (this included not flushing toilets in the patients' bathroom, paying me late, burning a hole in the covering of a waiting room chair with a lit cigarette, misbehaving in the lobby of my building, and other, similar provocations).

Ms. D. had intellectual insight as to what she was doing, and why, but it proved not to be of any real help to her: she even said at one point, "I know what is happening and how crazy it is. But I can't believe that you care about me if you won't even get angry. I can't get a *rise*[13] out of you. I know that I am trying to get you to act with me like my father did, but I need to get you to respond to me somehow and I don't care whether it is crazy or not." Clearly, she meant that there was something quite basic that was missing in my response to her plight, and she was not referring only to my refusal to respond to her sexual invitations. When we

---

[12]It is not uncommon for young children to mistake the sexual act for an aggressive one, and this misconception is often carried forward consciously or unconsciously into adulthood. It is clear that for Ms. D., sexuality and aggression were interchangeable and, at the very least, merged in her mind.

[13]This pun, in which the amalgamation of sexuality and aggression is so very clear, was not noticed by her at first but she came back to it somewhat later that week. She was able to make intellectual sense out of it then, but it still did not help in decreasing the pressure to act.

consider some of the preoedipal dynamics in this stance of Ms. D., we may wonder if she is not also expressing a feeling of deadness within herself and within her mother (based on the lack of empathic responsiveness she reported in her mother). This would seem to be a conflict equal in importance to the phallic and oedipal difficulties of Ms. D., and probably set the stage for Ms. D.'s readiness and willingness to respond to her father (even when she was made anxious and fearful by him) in her later development. It certainly made her predicament in the analysis particularly painful: any lack of mirroring response, even if it was withheld so as not to repeat the experience with her father, was the equivalent of having an emotionally dead mother. Suffice it to say, then, that her desperation in the search for a response may have been so intense because the lack of a response suggested to Ms. D. that there was no basis whatsoever for relating; aggression and sexuality may have been all that she knew, but it was at least proof that she had an impact and that she was in a room with another live human being.

One warm summer day nearing Ms. D.'s 600th session, she came in wearing a light, one-piece shift. She told me that she had nothing on underneath, that she was minus all the usual undergarments, and spent the rest of the session giving me all the details.

The next day she came in minus the shift, as well!

By coming into the room, stripping off her shift, and lying down completely naked on the couch (all in a split second), Ms. D. intended me to be sexually excited, nonplussed, extremely uncomfortable, and furious (also, all in a split second). I insisted in as bland a way as possible (as if one could be bland under such circumstances) that she get dressed, and we began to speak of the incident. Ms. D. got all the "mileage" she could out of my informing her that such behavior was unacceptable. She chose not to see that as a helpful limit that I was setting for her (since she seemed unable to set it for herself), and focused instead on the obvious fact that this same limit would also make the situation more comfortable for me. She insisted that I was personally furious with her. This made her extremely anxious, but she was more than willing to put up with the anxiety because of its exciting repetitive symbolic qualities and because, on a very conscious level, it also made her feel reassured that at least I cared for her.

Just as in the many incidents with her father, where exhibitionism was a commonplace mode of relating, Ms. D. never expressed any shame, humiliation, or embarrassment (except in the form of projections). Ms. D. began threatening me with a repetition of her getting undressed each time she wanted to "regulate" my reactions to her. Again, she had considerable intellectual awareness about why she was doing this, but it did not help to reduce the compulsion to repeat it. She was completely clear on why such behavior in her analysis was harmful to her and thus prohibited, but this understanding was only superficially intellectual. Not unexpectedly, she needed to challenge my proscription against any further undressing in the consulting room. I tried to show her the destructive circularity of the situation she was creating, where she could gain gratification only on the most symbolic and unhealthy of levels, but to no avail. Her expectation was that she could master the traumas of her childhood by recreating them in the present, while forcing me to "participate." Permitting her to undress in my presence could serve no objectively useful purpose, although it would give her a passingly subjective feeling of power, closeness, and satisfaction. The expense, in terms of increased damage to the ego and its autonomous functioning, was much too high to justify even passive acceptance of this enaction in the analysis. I tried to make it clear, despite her insistence on misconstruing it in terms of her desires, that I felt that I had no choice but to prohibit her disrobing, acknowledging that it would make me more comfortable, but emphasizing the necessity of this interdiction because of what the cost would be for her, in reality, if I did not.

After about 6 weeks (thirty continuous sessions) of incessant threats to repeat her performance, Ms. D. once again took off her dress in the office. At that time I discontinued her treatment.

By way of some brief closing discussion, it is typical of the male oedipal winner that, at worst, all situations are charged with oedipal undertones, which can be managed only by implementing the strictest possible controls. The inability to use repression and suppression, reaction formation, drive substitution, isolation, reversal, and so on more effectively and with greater selectivity, and the poverty of the person's defensive resources in general, leads to unfocused prohibitions based on nearly global inhibitions. When augmented by immense pathology in both the contents and the functions of the superego, the outlook appears rather grim. Male oedipal winners experience life as being saturated, contaminated, and polluted by instinctual dangers which must be prevented from reaching fruition at all costs. There is no neutral territory and there are no neutral people. They have a fixed conviction based on the interplay between unconscious fantasy and traumatic reality which is compounded by the inability to distinguish between thoughts and action. Thus they are involuntarily immobilized by the dangers that they fear, and they immobilize themselves even further in the attempt to cope.

Female oedipal winners are disorganized by situations reminiscent of those parts of their childhoods in which they were the passive (captive) victims of their parents' sexual pathologies. The pathological compromise formation of the female oedipal winner is to try to make the passive experience an active one. She attempts to avoid the danger to her tenuous psychic equilibrium in a manner similar to that employed in the "classic" traumatic neurosis. In a traumatic neurosis the aim of the repetition is multifold and includes, among other goals, an attempt to prepare the ego for an experience (rather than having it meet the experience unprepared to cope), and to have the traumatic event reoccur with a magically transformed outcome. The aim of the female oedipal winner is directed somewhat differently; her goal is to create a magical transformation of the *source,* in addition to the outcome, of the trauma. The female oedipal winner, by creating an explicit sexual atmosphere wherever she goes can, in this way, "take charge" of the sexual atmosphere wherever she finds herself. She cherishes the notion that she can regulate her own, and everyone else's, impulses, and she hopes in this way to successfully master her chronic state of overexcitement.

The degree and extent of trauma inflicted in a home where sexual feelings and actions are unable to be channeled constructively pervades the entire quality of the oedipal winner's childhood. The problem rests on more than just a few bad childhood experiences, or some compelling fantasies mostly unjustified in reality, but on scarring, pervasive, stressful saturation, which inevitably leads to crippling psychological sequelae.

Bibliographic Essay[1]

For excellent overviews of *development* one can look at **Jacobson,** *The Self and the Object World,* and at **Blos,** *On Adolescence: An Introduction.* **Spitz's** work, *The First Year of Life,* not only outlines infant development in the first year, it also shows how empirical infant research is applied to the psychoanalytic theory of development. Other interesting work on what the condition of the baby is, just after birth, includes **Hamburg,** *A developmental approach to human aggressiveness;* **Hendrick,** *Instinct and the ego during infancy;* and **Kaywin,** *An epigenetic approach to the psychoanalytic theory of instincts and drives.*

Concerning the concept of *drives,* and how instincts operate, one can see **Alpert, Neubauer, and Weill,** *Unusual variations in drive endowment;* **Arlow and Brenner's** landmark book, *Psychoanalytic Concepts and the Structural Theory;* **Beres,** *Clinical notes on aggression in children;* **Brenner,** *The psychoanalytic concept of aggression;* **Hartmann,** *Comments on the psychoanalytic theory of instinctual drives;* **Jones,** *Psychoanalysis and the instincts;* **B. Rank,** *Aggression;* and **Max Schur's** undervalued masterpiece, *The Id and the Regulatory Principles of Mental Functioning.*

For coverage of the *criticisms of instinct theory,* and to see how they have been answered, one can see **Apfelbaum,** *Ego psychology, psychic energy, and the hazards of quantitative explanation in psychoanalytic theory,* **E. Bibring,** *The development and problems in the theory of instincts;* **Brenner,** *Problems in the psychoanalytic theory of aggression;* **Modell,** *The concept of psychic energy;* and **Slap,** *Freud's view on pleasure and aggression.* One can examine the question of the *transformations in aggression,* which has been singled out here because it is more problematic a concept than is libido, in much of the above work and, most especially, in the work of **Bak,** *Aggression and symptom formation;* and **A. Freud,** *Aggression in relation to emotional development.*

The concept of *metapsychology,* and critiques of the concept, can be found in much of the above work on drive and instinctual endowment. Some particularly interesting and useful readings on this topic include **Hartmann,** *Comments on the psychoanalytic theory of the ego;* **Rapaport and Gill's** classic, *The points of view and*

---

[1]The materials contained here are for the reader who wishes to examine some of the concepts in this book more closely, and who wishes to look at some of the sources used for the various chapters. This is not, however, a complete list of every contribution to the literature that was used in the writing of this book. Full references for every book or article described in this essay can be found in the Bibliography.

assumptions of metapsychology; and **Sandler and Nagera,** *Aspects of the metapsychology of fantasy.* The question of ***structure formation*** is nicely addressed by **Alexander,** *Relation of structural and instinctual conflict;* by **Hartmann, Kris, and Loewenstein,** *Comments on the formation of psychic structure;* and by **Schur,** *Phylogenesis and ontogenesis of affect- and structure-formation and the phenomenon of the repetition compulsion.*

Schur's article covers not only structure formation, but includes in addition a good discussion of both ***the regulatory principles of mental functioning*** and ***intra- and intersystemic conflict.*** Other good and interesting work on regulatory principles is found in **Hartmann,** *Notes on the reality principle.* Additional important work on intra- and intersystemic conflict can be found in two articles by **Lustman,** *Psychic energy and the mechanisms of defense,* and *The economic point of view and defense.* We see the interaction of such concepts as structure, regulatory principles, and conflict in the work of **Rapaport,** *On the psychoanalytic theory of affects,* and in **Schur,** *The ego and the id in anxiety.*

In looking at ***the oral stage*** one can consider a number of different points of view about development—for example, the work of **M. Balint,** *Primary Love and Psychoanalytic Technique,* or the work of **Klein.** Klein has postulated the very early development of certain psychic structures and defenses, as one sees quite clearly in her book (with **Riviere**), *Love, Hate, and Reparation,* or in her articles *Early stages of the Oedipus conflict; The importance of symbol formation in the development of the ego; The early development of conscience in the child;* and *The Oedipus complex in the light of early anxieties.* An interesting Freudian review of Klein's work is provided by **Glover,** in *Examination of the Klein system of child psychology.* Other, more traditional, views of the oral stage are found in the work of **Hoffer,** *Development of the body ego;* **Rubinfine,** *Maternal stimulation, psychic structure, and early object relations: With special reference to aggression and denial;* and, of course, **Spitz's** *The First Year of Life.* An interesting addition to this may be found in **Spitz and Wolff,** *Anaclitic depression: An inquiry into the genesis of psychiatric conditions in early childhood.*

Other important work on ***the early mother–child relationship,*** particularly with reference to ***object relations*** and ***identifications,*** is found in the many books of **Bettelheim** (*Love is Not Enough, The Empty Fortress,* and *The Uses of Enchantment*). One would also like to look at **Boyer,** *On maternal overstimulation and ego defects;* **Brenner,** *Archaic aspects of ego functioning;* **Bychowski,** *The preschizophrenic ego;* **Gould,** *Child Studies Through Fantasy: A Cognitive-Affective Approach;* **Heimann,** *Certain functions of introjection and projection in early infancy;* **Hendrick,** *Early development of the ego;* **Hoffer,** *Mutual influences in the development of ego and id;* **Maenchen,** *Notes on early ego disturbances;* two very excellent articles by **Annie Reich,** *Early identifications as archaic elements of the superego,* and *Pathologic forms of self-esteem regulation;* and at **Spitz's** article, *Some early prototypes of ego defenses.*

Interesting work on ***conflict-free spheres of the ego*** has been done by **Apfelbaum,** *On ego psychology;* by **Hoffer,** *Mouth, hand, and ego integration;* by **Lampl-de Groot,** *The preoedipal phase in the development of the male child;* and, of course, by **Winnicott** (particularly his *Collected Papers,* and *The Maturational Process and the Facilitating Environment*).

Some work on the earliest (that is, oral) stage of *infantile sexuality* that is very interesting, but which one could not recognize from their titles, is found in two articles by **Frank,** *The development of Freud's concept of primal repression,* and *The unrememberable and the unforgettable: Passive primal repression.* One would also like, in that context, to look at **Jones's** *Love and morality.*

Some of the earliest, and best, work on *anality,* and the narcissistic trauma (and other ramifications) of *toilet training* was done by **Abraham,** in *Selected Papers on Psychoanalysis.* Other important contributions include the work of **Brenner,** *Archaic aspects of ego functioning;* **Bychowski,** *Patters of anger;* **Jones,** *Anal-erotic character traits;* **Lampl-de Groot,** *The preoedipal phase in the development of the child;* **Mahler's** article, *Notes on the development of basic moods;* and **Rubinfine,** *Maternal stimulation, psychic structure, and early object relations: With special reference to aggression and denial.*

Concerning the question of *overdetermination* and *genetic conflicts of the anal stage,* one would wish to see **Heimann,** *Certain functions of introjection and projection in early infancy;* **Niederland,** *Early auditory experiences, beating fantasies, and the primal scene;* **Solnit,** *Some adaptive functions of aggressive behavior;* and **Steingart,** *On self, character, and the development of a psychic apparatus.*

Margaret Mahler's works on *separation, differentiation, and individuation* have become classics in the field: (with **Bergman, Feuer,** and **Pine**) *On Human Symbiosis and the Vicissitudes of Individuation,* and *The Psychological Birth of the Human Infant.* Her article *Sadness and grief in infancy and early childhood: Loss and restoration of the symbiotic love object* is a fascinating counterpoint to the work of **Klein,** and to the work of **Joffee** and **Sandler** (*Notes on pain, depression, and individuation*).

In a sense, one can say that the history of the psychoanalytic literature is based on a consideration of *the phallic stage* and its influences. Almost all of the articles thus far recommended, with only a few rare exceptions, are highly informative about development in the phallic stage. There are some articles and books of unique interest, however, which are worth singling out for particular attention, for example **Helene Deutsch's** two-volume set, *The Psychology of Women.* **Deutsch's** work is a classic, despite coming in for much criticism in recent years, and it sets out *feminine development* as it was understood by psychoanalysts for generations. Other work of interest is **Bak's** *The phallic woman: The ubiquitous fantasy in perversions;* and **Greenacre's** *Respiratory incorporation and the phallic phase.* The impact of *fantasy* on the events of the phallic stage have been discussed by **Frankl,** in *Some observations on the development of integration in childhood;* **Kennedy,** in *Cover memories in formation;* and **Lampl-de Groot,** in *On masturbation and its influence on general development.* The phallic-level *oedipus complex in girls* has been discussed in an interesting fashion by **Horney,** in *On the genesis of the castration complex in women;* and, from a different slant by **Keiser,** in *A manifest oedipus complex in an adolescent girl.* A particularly interesting article covering the borderground between the anal and phallic stages is **Sperling's,** *An imaginary companion, representing a pre-stage of the superego.*

Without a doubt, however, some of the most interesting work in *feminine psychology* has challenged our traditional notions about *gender identity and stage specificity;* for example, **Applegarth,** *Some observations on work inhibitions in women;* **Barnett,** *Vaginal awareness in the infancy and childhood of girls;* **Bernstein,** *The female superego: A different perspective;* **Chassequet-Smirgel,** *Feminine guilt and the Oedipus complex;* **Fast,** *Developments in gender identity: Gender differentiation in girls;* **Fliegel,** *Women's development in analytic theory: Six decades of controversy;* **Horney,** *The flight from womanhood;* **Jacobson,** *Ways of female superego formation and the female castration complex;* **Kubie,** *The drive to become both sexes;* **Mayer,** *'Everybody must be just like me': Observations on female castration anxiety;* **Parens, Pollack, Stern,** and **Kramer,** *On the girl's entry into the Oedipus complex;* and **Stoller's** critical works, *Sex and Gender: On the Development of Masculinity and Femininity; Primary femininity;* and *A contribution to the study of gender identity.*

Superego organization has been closely studied by **Beres,** *Vicissitudes of superego functions and superego precursors in childhood;* **Hartmann** and **Loewenstein,** *Notes on the superego;* **Jacobson,** *The effect of disappointment on ego and superego development;* **Jones,** *The genesis and structure of the superego;* **Kernberg,** *Structural derivatives of object relations;* **Sandler,** *On the concept of the superego;* **Schafer,** *On the loving and beloved superego in Freud's structural theory;* and **Spitz's** *On the genesis of superego components.*

The ego ideal has come in for special attention in the work of **Bibring,** *Some considerations regarding the ego-ideal in the psychoanalytic process;* **Hendrick,** *Narcissism and the pre-puberty ego-ideal;* **Kahn,** *Ego ideal, excitement, and the threat of annihilation;* **Kaplan** and **Whitman,** *The negative ego ideal;* **Lampl-de Groot,** *Ego-ideal and superego;* **Murray,** *Narcissism and the ego ideal;* **Novey,** *The role of the superego and ego ideal in character development;* and, **Sandler, Holder,** and **Meers,** *The ego ideal and the ideal self.* Specific issues of *conscience* have been discussed by **Maenchen,** *A case of superego disintegration;* **Malquist,** *Conscience development;* **Nass,** *The superego and moral development in the theories of Freud and Piaget;* and in the work of **Rosenfeld,** *Notes on the psychoanalysis of the superego conflict in a schizophrenic girl,* and *Psychotic States.* **Identification** issues as they are **related to superego development** have been discussed by **Greenson** in his famous paper *The struggle against identification;* and by **Tyson,** in *A developmental line of gender identity, gender role, and the choice of love object. Latency* has come in for particular attention in the work of **Bornstein,** *On latency,* and *Masturbation in the latency period;* and of **Sarnoff,** *Latency;* and one finds an excellent review of the subject by **Fries,** *Review of the literature on the latency period.*

Adolescence is covered extremely well by **Blos's,** *On Adolescence,* and by **Jacobson's** *The Self and the Object World.* **Jacobson's** *Adolescent moods and the remodeling of psychic structures in adolescence* is an excellent addition, and **Blos** has a series of other works on adolescence that are particularly illuminating (*The Adolescent Personality; Prolonged adolescence: The formulation of a syndrome and its therapeutic implications; The initial stage of adolescence; The second individuation process of adolescence; The function of the ego ideal in late adolescence;* and *Character formation in adolescence*). Volume 27 (1972) of *The Psychoanalytic Study of the Child* has an entire section devoted to adolescent development, with articles of particular interest by **Lustman** (*Yale's year of confrontation: A view from the master's house);* **Settlage,** (*Cultural values and the superego in late adolescence);* **Solnit**

(Youth and the campus: The search for social conscience); and, **Schowalter** and **Lord** *(On the writings of adolescents in a general hospital ward).* Among the earliest psychoanalytic writings on adolescence, **Aichorn's** 1925 work, *Wayward Youth,* is considered a classic. Other important work on delinquency in adolescence was contributed by **Redl,** *The psychology of gang formation and the treatment of juvenile delinquents,* as well as by **Eissler's** book of readings, *Searchlights on Delinquency.* **Bernfeld's** *Types of adolescence;* **Gitelson's** *Direct psychotherapy in adolescence;* and **Hoffer's** *Diaries of adolescent schizophrenics* were other important early contributions to our understanding of adolescent processes, normal and abnormal. **Beres** and **Obers's** paper, *The effects of extreme deprivation in infancy on psychic structure in adolescence,* provides a good view of the interrelationship of adolescence and the preceding psychosexual stages. And of course no discussion of the work on adolescence would be adequate without mentioning **Anna Freud's** 1958 paper, *Adolescence.*

More recently, **Ritvo's** *Late adolescence: Developmental and clinical considerations,* and **Marjorie Sprince's** *An adolescent boy's battle against recovery: The analysis of an adolescent whose ongoing preoedipal tie to the mother aroused massive treatment resistance and a terror of health,* provide an interesting counterpoint and addition to the earlier work of **Beres** and **Obers. Furman's** *A contribution to assessing the role of infantile separation-individual in adolescent development,* and **Laufer's** *Ego-ideal and pseudo ego-ideal in adolescence* carry this theme yet further, and a final recommendation on readings in adolescence is **Novick's** *Termination of treatment in adolescence.*

The nature of the psychoanalytic situation itself has been discussed from many different theoretical points of view, including differing ideas about what the patient brings to the process and what is brought to the process by the analyst. We can see great agreement and divergence in the work of **Arlow,** *Conflict, regression, and symptom formation;* **E. Balint,** *On being empty of oneself;* **Brenner,** *Depression, anxiety, and affect therapy,* and also *Archaic aspects of ego functioning;* **Chasseguet-Smirgel,** *Illness of ideality,* and also *On the therapeutic alliance and "pervert" patients;* **R. Fliess,** *The metapsychology of the analyst;* **Kohut's** many works, which would include *The Analysis of the Self, The two analyses of Mr. Z, The Restoration of the Self, Thoughts on narcissism and narcissistic rage, The psychoanalytic treatment of narcissistic personality disorders,* and *Forms and transformations of narcissism;* **Langs,** *The Listening Process,* and *The therapeutic relationship and deviations in technique* (to mention only a few of his numerous works); **Levin,** *The self: a contribution to its place in theory and technique;* **Loewald's** classic, *On the therapeutic action of psychoanalysis;* **McDougall's** *The psychosoma and the psychoanalytic process,* and her *Plea for a Measure of Abnormality* (to mention only a few of her numerous works, as well); **Modell,** *The conceptualization of the therapeutic action of psychoanalysis;* **Stolorow** and **Lachman,** *Psychoanalysis of Developmental Arrests;* **Stone's** seminal contributions, *The widening scope of indications for psychoanalysis,* and *The Psychoanalytic Situation;* and, finally, **Volkan,** *Primitive Internalized Object Relations.*

The general questions of **insight** and its acquisition, **working through, symptom amelioration, structural change,** and **the ego's synthetic and integrative functions** have been examined by **Brickman,** *Pre-oedipal development of the superego;* **Clark,** *The question* *of prognosis in narcissistic neuroses and psychoses;* **Dickes,** *Severe regressive disruptions of the therapeutic alliance;* **Lax,** *Libidinal objects and self constancy enhanced by the analytic process;* **Niederland,** *The role of the ego in the recovery of early memories;* and **Searles,** *Transitional phenomena and therapeutic symbiosis.*

The nature of **the analytic contract** as well as the nature of **the analytic object relationship** has been discussed in a variety of ways by **Bibring,** in *Some considerations regarding the ego-ideal in the psychoanalytic process;* **Blum,** *The forbidden quest and the analytic ideal: The superego and insight;* **Dorpat,** *Internalization of the parent–analyst relationship in patients with narcissistic disorders;* **Easser,** *Empathic inhibition and psychoanalytic technique;* **Ferreira,** *Empathy and the bridge function of the ego;* **Gitelson,** *The emotional position of the analyst in the psycho-analytic situation;* **Grunes,** *The therapeutic object relationship;* **Loewald,** *On the therapeutic action of psychoanalysis;* **Modell,** *The "holding environment" and the therapeutic action of psychoanalysis;* and by **Strachey,** *The nature of the therapeutic action of psychoanalysis.* The nature of **analytic identifications** has been interestingly investigated by **Filho,** in *Vicissitudes of identification as observed in character pathology;* by **Greenson,** *The struggle against identification;* and by **Meissner,** *The earliest internalizations.*

Basic concepts of transference, particularly regarding whether they are to be considered displacement phenomena or projection phenomena, have been considered by **Bak,** *Being in love and object choice;* in two papers by **Gill** with the same title, *The analysis of the transference* (one in 1979 and the other in 1982); by **Kernberg,** *An ego psychology–object relations approach to the transference;* by **Loewald,** *The transference neurosis: The concept and the phenomenon;* and by **Zetzel,** *Current concepts of transference.* **The relationship of transference to the repetition compulsion** has been discussed by **Berliner** in two interesting papers, *The role of object relations in moral masochism* and *On some psychodynamics of masochism;* by **Bernstein,** also in relation to masochism, *The role of narcissism in moral masochism;* by **Blum,** *Superego formation, adolescent transformation, and the adult neurosis;* by **Bychowski,** *Some aspects of masochistic involvement;* by **Gedo,** *Forms of idealization in the analytic transference;* by **Greenacre,** *Problems of overidealization of the analyst and the analysis;* by **Hanley,** *Narcissism, defense, and the positive transference;* by **Peto,** *The fragmentizing function of the ego in the transference neurosis;* and by **Sterba** in his well-known paper *The dynamics of the dissolution of the transference neurosis.* The relation of the ego's autonomous functions to **ubiquitous transference phenomena** has been discussed by **Buxbaum,** *Transference and group formation in children and adolescents;* **Dorpat,** *An object relations perspective on masochism;* and **Fleming,** *Early object deprivation and transference phenomena: The working alliance.* **Pathological transference manifestations** have been discussed both by **Beland,** *Alterations of the ego due to defensive processes and the limitations of psychoanalytic treatment;* and by **Kernberg,** *Transference regression and psychoanalytic technique with infantile patients.* Other considerations of pathological transference states have been considered by **Blum,** *Object inconstancy and paranoid conspiracy;* **Kron,** *Psychoanalytic complications of a narcissistic transference;* **Little,** *Transference in borderline patients;* and by **Rothstein,** *The implications of early psychopathology for the analyzability of narcissistic character disorders.* Specific discussion of the nature of **the transference neurosis** as an artifact of the psychoanalytic process has been provided by **Gedo,** *Notes on the psychoanalytic management of archaic transferences;* **Greenacre,** *Certain technical problems in the transference relationship;* and **Nacht,** *The curative factors in psychoanalysis.* **Special problems in the transference** have been described by **Blum,** *The concept of erotized transference;* and by **Searles,** *The functions of the patient's realistic perceptions of the analyst in delusional transferences.* And the most severe transference problems have been discussed by **Atkins,** *Comments on severe and psychotic regressions in analysis;* by **Little,** *On delusional transference (transference psychosis);* by **Reider,** *Transference psychosis;* and by **Wallerstein,** *Reconstruction and mastery in the transference psychosis.*

Discussion of what has been termed *the "ground rules" of psychoanalysis* is not easily broken down into subcategories, since most of the "rules" are not considered separately in the literature; the material tends to be addressed somewhat as a "conceptual mass" (with different "conceptual masses" posited for the differing theoretical stances). Some of the literature that is of particular interest includes **Arlow,** *Silence and the theory of technique;* **Bach,** *Self constancy and alternate states of consciousness;* **Bouvet,** *Technical variation and the concept of distance;* **Boyer,** *Psychoanalytic technique and the treatment of certain characterological and schizophrenic disorders;* **Brenner,** *Psychoanalytic Technique and Psychic Conflict;* **Eichler,** *Notes upon the emotionality of a schizophrenic patient and its relation to problems of technique;* two papers by **Eissler,** *The effect of the structure of the ego on psychoanalytic technique* (one of the most influential papers in the technique literature), and *Notes upon the emotionality of a schizophrenic patient and its relations to problems of technique;* **Fenichel,** *Concerning the theory of psychoanalytic technique;* **Glover,** *Lectures on technique in psychoanalysis;* two papers by **Kernberg,** *Factors in the psychoanalytic treatment of narcissistic personalities,* and *Further contributions to the treatment of narcissistic personalities;* **A. Kris,** *Determinants of free association in narcissistic phenomena;* **Nacht,** *Variations in technique;* **Nunberg's** paper, *Problems of therapy,* and his book, *Practice and Theory of Psychoanalysis;* three important papers by **Peto,** *The fragmentizing function of the ego in the analytic session,* and two papers of the same name, *Dedifferentiations and fragmentizations during analysis* (one appearing in the *International Journal of Psycho-Analysis* and the other in the *Journal of the American Psychoanalytic Association*); **Rangell,** *Structural problems in intrapsychic conflict;* **Schafer,** *Wild analysis;* **Silverman,** *The voice of conscience and the sounds of the analytic hour;* **Stein,** *The unobjectionable part of the transference;* and, finally, **Waldhorn's** paper, *Assessment of analyzability; Technical and theoretical observations.*

The concept of resistance, both as a psychoanalytic notion and as a psychotherapeutic notion, has had an interesting discussion by **Adler,** *Psychotherapy of the narcissistic personality disorder patient: Two contrasting approaches;* and one can capture some of the history of this concept in **W. Reich's** *Character Analysis;* and in **Schafer's** well-known paper, *The idea of resistance.* **Ego resistances** have been interestingly demonstrated and discussed by **Easser** and **Lesser** in two articles, *Hysterical personality; A re-evaluation,* and *Transference resistance in hysterical character neurosis: Technical considerations;* and by **Marmor,** who also has an interest in hysteria, *Orality in the hysterical personality.* **Lichtenstein's** article, *The malignant no;* and **Morse's** *The afterpleasure of suicide* are interesting in their discussion of *id resistance.* **Superego resistance** is considered by **Loewald** in *Freud's conception of the negative therapeutic reaction, with comments on instinct theory;* **Malcolm,** *Technical problems in the analysis of a pseudo-compliant patient;* **Modell,** *On having a right to a life: An aspect of the superego's development;* **Novey,** *The role of the superego and ego ideal in character formation;* **Riviere,** *A contribution to the analysis of the negative therapeutic reaction;* and **Valenstein,** *On attachment to painful feelings and the negative therapeutic reaction.* Both **acting out** and **resistance to regression** are considered by **Atkins,** *Acting out and psychosomatic illness as reflected regressive trends;* **Bird,** *A specific peculiarity of acting out;* **Boesky,** *Acting out: A reconsideration of the concept;* **J. Frank,** *Treatment approach to acting out character disorders;* in two important papers by **Greenacre,** *General problems of acting out,* and *Acting out in the transference relationship;* by **Naiman,** *The role of the superego in certain forms of acting out;* **Novotny,** *Self-cutting;* in a comprehensive review article by **Olinick,** *The negative therapeutic reaction;* by **Sperling,** *A contribution to the treatment of character disorders with acting out behavior;* and in a symposium reported in the 1968 issue of the *International Journal of Psycho-Analysis* (in which there are important contributions by **Deutsch, Garabino, Greenacre, Grinberg, Lebovici, Moore, Mitscherlich-Nelson, Rangell, Rowart, Schwartz,** and **Vanggard**). **The role of both character and character pathology in resistance** is discussed by **Altman,** *A case of narcissistic personality disorder: The problem of treatment;* **Angel,** *Unanalyzability and narcissistic transference;* two excellent papers by **Baudry,** *Character, character-type, and character organization,* and *The evolution of the concept of character in Freud's writings;* **Gitelson,** *The problem of character neurosis;* two **Kernberg** papers, *Object relations theory and character analysis,* and *Contrasting viewpoints regarding the nature and treatment of narcissistic personalities;* **Kinston,** *A theoretical and technical approach to narcissistic disturbances;* **Lebovici** and **Kitakine,** *The contribution of the theory and technique of child analysis to the understanding of character neuroses;* **Liebert,** *The concept of character: A historical review;* and **Parkin,** *On masochistic enthrallment: A contribution to the study of moral masochism.*

The chapter on **interpretation** has in it a number of interesting and important references, to which may be added: **Arlow,** *The genesis of interpretation;* **Blum,** *The position and value of extratransference interpretation;* **James,** *Preverbal communication;* **E. Kris,** *Ego psychology and interpretation in psychoanalytic theory;* **Racker,** *The study of some early conflicts through their return in the patient's relationship with the interpretation;* and **Valenstein,** *Pre-oedipal reconstructions in psychoanalysis.*

The literature on **countertransference,** and on what I have singled out as *"the analytic instrument"* is not discrete, nor is there a discrete literature on the condition of the analyst under abnormal conditions (with only a few notable exceptions, such as when the analyst has been ill or pregnant). Thus the following suggestions, which supplement the references already provided in Chapter 12, are intended to provide a broad coverage of the topic (without attempting to provide an entire review of the literature): **Abend,** *Serious illness in the analyst: Countertransference considerations;* **Arlow,** *Some technical problems of countertransference;* **Beres** and **Arlow,** *Fantasy and identification in empathy;* two papers by **Blum,** *Countertransference and the theory of technique: Discussion,* and *Countertransference: Concepts and controversies;* **Brenner,** *Coun-*

tertransference as a compromise formation; **Buan**, *Countertransference and the vicissitudes in an analyst's development;* a paper by **Deutsch** with the exotic title *Occult processes occurring during psychoanalysis;* **Dewald**, *Serious illness in the analyst: Transference, countertransference, and reality responses;* **Ferenczi**, *Further Contributions to the Theory and Technique of Psychoanalysis;* **R. Fliess**, *Countertransference and counteridentification;* four contributions by **Giovacchini**, *The treatment of characterological disorders, Technical difficulties in treating some characterological disorders, Countertransference with primitive mental states,* his book *Treatment of Primitive Mental States;* and a contribution by **Giovacchini** with **Boyer**, *Psychoanalysis of Character Disorders;* two excellent **Greenson** articles, *Empathy and its vicissitudes* and *The "real" relationship between the patient and the psychoanalyst;* two contributions by **Grinberg,** *Projective counteridentification and countertransference* and *On a specific aspect of countertransference due to the patient's projective identification;* three articles by **Heimann,** *Countertransference, On countertransference,* and *Further observations on the analyst's cognitive process;* two very excellent articles by **Jacobs**, *Countertransference enactments* and *The analyst's and the patient's object world: Notes on an aspect of countertransference;* **Kern,** *Countertransference and spontaneous screens: An analyst studies his own visual images;* **Kernberg,** *Notes on countertransference;* two important papers by **Little,** *Countertransference and the patient's response to it* and *"R"– The analyst's total response to the patient's needs;* **McDougall**, *Primitive communication and the use of countertransference;* **McLaughlin,** *Transference, psychic reality, and countertransference;* an article with a somewhat different slant by **Oremland** and his co-workers, *Some specific transference, countertransference, and supervisory problems in the treatment of the narcissistic personality;* two articles by **Racker**, *The meanings and uses of countertransference* and *A contribution to the problem of countertransference,* and **Racker's** landmark book on the topic, *Transference and Countertransference;* three particularly valuable articles by **Annie Reich**, *On countertransference, Further remarks on countertransference,* and *Empathy and countertransference;* **Sandler,** *Countertransference and role-responsiveness;* **Savage**, *Countertransference in the therapy of schizophrenics;* **Schafer,** *Generative empathy in the treatment situation;* four contributions by **Searles** with his own distinctive view of things, *The patient as therapist to his analyst, Oedipal love in the countertransference, Countertransference as a path to understanding and helping the patient* and *The schizophrenic's vulnerability to the therapist's unconscious processes;* **Silverman,** *Countertransference and the myth of the perfectly analyzed analyst;* **Slakter,** *Countertransference: A Comprehensive Review of Those Reactions of the Therapist to the Patient that May Help or Hinder the Treatment;* a paper by **Spotnitz**, who also has a uniquely different view of things, *The toxoid response;* **Stern**, *On the countertransference in psychoanalysis;* **Tower**, *Countertransference;* two **Winnicott** papers, *Countertransference* and the famous *Hate in the countertransference;* and finally a paper by **Wolf**, *Countertransference in disorders of the self.*

The literature on **termination** is quite extensive. Some of the more interesting contributions include: **Aarons**, *On analytic goals and criteria for termination;* **Bond, Franco,** and **Kramer-Richards**, *Dream Portrait: Nineteen Sequential Dreams as Indicators of Pretermination;* **Bridger**, *Criteria for termination of an analysis;* **Buxbaum,** *Technique of terminating analysis;* **Ekstein**, *Working through and termination of analysis;* **Fenichel**, *From* *the terminal phase of analysis* (in his *Collected Papers*); **Ferenczi,** *The problem of termination of psychoanalysis* (in his *Final Contributions to Psycho-Analysis*); **Firestein,** *Termination of psychoanalysis of adults: A review of the literature;* **Glover,** *Termination* (in his *Technique of Psychoanalysis*); **Horn,** *Toward a paradigm of the terminal phase;* **Jones,** *The criteria of success in treatment* (in his *Papers on Psycho-Analysis*); **Kubie,** *Unsolved problems in the resolution of the transference;* **Laforgue,** *Resistance at the conclusion of psychoanalytic treatment;* **Lehr-man,** *On termination of analysis;* **Limentani,** *Some positive aspects of the negative therapeutic reaction;* **Lipton,** *The last hour;* **Lorand,** *Termination* (in his *Technique of Psychoanalytic Therapy*); **McDougall,** *The anti-analysand in analysis;* **Miller,** *On the return of symptoms in the terminal phase of psychoanalysis;* **Milner,** *Note on the ending of an analysis;* and **Nacht,** *Criteria and technique for the termination of an analysis.* Finally, there was an excellent panel on the topic of termination which was published in the *Journal of the American Psychoanalytic Association* (1969, Vol. 17, pp. 222–237) and reported on by **Firestein.**

References

Aaron, R. (1974). The analyst's emotional life during work: panel report. *Journal of the American Psychoanalytic Association* 22:160–169.

Aarons, Z. (1965). On analytic goals and criteria for termination. *Bulletin of the Philadelphia Association for Psychoanalysis* 15:97–109.

Abend, S. (1982). Serious illness in the analyst: countertransference considerations. *Journal of the American Psychoanalytic Association* 30:365–380.

Abrams, L., and Shengold, L. (1974). The meaning of "nothing." *Psychoanalytic Quarterly* 43:115–119.

Adler, A. (1917a). *The Neurotic Constitution.* New York: International Universities Press.

———— (1917b). *A Study of Inferiority and Its Psychical Compensation.* New York: International Universities Press.

Adler, G. (1986). Psychotherapy of the narcissistic personality disorder patient: two contrasting approaches. *American Journal of Psychiatry* 143:430–436.

Aichorn, A. (1925). *Wayward Youth.* New York: Viking.

Alexander, F. (1933). Relation of structural and instinctual conflicts. *Psychoanalytic Quarterly* 2:181–207.

Alpert, A., Neubauer, P. B., and Weil, A. P. (1956). Unusual variations in drive endowment. *Psychoanalytic Study of the Child* 11:125–163. New York: International Universities Press.

Altman, L. (1975). A case of narcissistic personality disorder: the problem of treatment. *International Journal of Psycho-Analysis* 56:187–195.

Angel, K. (1971). Unanalyzability and narcissistic transference. *Psychoanalytic Quarterly* 41:264–276.

Anthony, E. J. (1961). A study of screen sensations. *Psychoanalytic Study of the Child* 16:211–245. New York: International Universities Press.

Apfelbaum, B. (1965). Ego psychology, psychic energy, and the hazards of quantitative explanation in psychoanalytic theory. *International Journal of Psycho-Analysis* 46:168–182.

———— (1966). On ego psychology. *International Journal of Psycho-Analysis* 47:451–475.

Applegarth, A. (1976). Some observations on work inhibitions in women. *Journal of the American Psychoanalytic Association* 24 (Suppl.):251–268.

Arlow, J. (1961a). Silence and the theory of technique. *Journal of the American Psychoanalytic Association* 9:44–55.

―――― (1961b) Ego psychology and mythology. *Journal of the American Psychoanalytic Association* 9:371–393.

―――― (1963). Conflict, regression, and symptom formation. *International Journal of Psycho-Analysis* 44:12–22.

―――― (1979). The genesis of interpretation. *Journal of the American Psychoanalytic Association* 27 (Suppl.):193–206.

―――― (1985). Some technical problems of countertransference. *Psychoanalytic Quarterly* 54:164–174.

Arlow, J., and Brenner, C. (1964). *Psychoanalytic Concepts and the Structural Theory.* New York: International Universities Press.

Asch, S. S. (1966). Depression: three clinical variations. *Psychoanalytic Study of the Child* 21:150–171. New York: International Universities Press.

Atkins, N. (1967). Comments on severe and psychotic regressions in analysis. *Journal of the American Psychoanalytic Association* 15:584–605.

―――― (1968). Acting out and psychosomatic illness as reflected regressive trends. *International Journal of Psycho-Analysis* 49:221–223.

Bach, S. (1985). *Narcissistic States and the Therapeutic Process.* Northvale, NJ: Jason Aronson.

―――― (1986). Self constancy and alternate states of consciousness. In *Self and Object Constancy: Clinical and Theoretical Perspectives,* ed. R. Lax, S. Bach, and J. A. Burland, pp. 135–152. New York: Guilford.

Bak, R. (1951). Fetishism. *Journal of the American Psychoanalytic Association* 1:285–298.

―――― (1966). Regression of ego-orientation and libido in schizophrenia. *Psychoanalytic Study of the Child* 11:64–71. New York: International Universities Press.

―――― (1973). Being in love and object loss. *International Journal of Psycho-Analysis* 54:1–8.

Bak, R. C. (1943). Dissolution of ego, mannerism, and delusions of grandeur. *Journal of Nervous and Mental Disease* 98:457–468.

―――― (1968). The phallic woman: the ubiquitous fantasy in perversions. *Psychoanalytic Study of the Child* 23:15–36. New York: International Universities Press.

Balint, E. (1963). On being empty of oneself. *International Journal of Psycho-Analysis* 44:470–479.

Balint, M. (1952). *Primary Love and Psychoanalytic Technique.* London: Hogarth.

Barnett, M. (1966). Vaginal awareness in the infancy and childhood of girls. *Journal of the American Psychoanalytic Association* 14:129–141.

Baudry, F. (1983). The evolution of the concept of character in Freud's writings. *Journal of the American Psychoanalytic Association* 31:3–31.

―――― (1989). Character, character type, and character organization. *Journal of the American Psychoanalytic Association* 37:655–686.

Beland, H. (1988). Alterations of the ego due to defensive processes and the limitations of psychoanalytic treatment. *International Journal of Psycho-Analysis* 72:189–200.

Beres, D. (1952). Clinical notes on aggression in children. *Psychoanalytic Study of the Child* 7:241–263. New York: International Universities Press.

———— (1956). Ego deviation and the concept of schizophrenia. *Psychoanalytic Study of the Child* 11:164–235. New York: International Universities Press.

———— (1958). Vicissitudes of superego functions and superego precursors in childhood. *Psychoanalytic Study of the Child* 13:324–351. New York: International Universities Press.

Beres, D., and Arlow, J. (1974). Fantasy and identification in empathy. *Psychoanalytic Quarterly* 43:26–50.

Beres, D., and Obers, S. J. (1950). The effects of extreme deprivation in infancy on psychic structure in adolescence: a study in ego development. *Psychoanalytic Study of the Child* 5:212–235. New York: International Universities Press.

Berkowitz, D. (1974). Family contributions to narcissistic disturbances in adolescents. *International Review of Psycho-Analysis* 1:353–362.

Berliner, B. (1947). On some psychodynamics of masochism. *Psychoanalytic Quarterly* 16:459–471.

———— (1958). The role of object relations in moral masochism. *Psychoanalytic Quarterly* 27:38–56.

Bernfeld, S. (1938). Types of adolescence. *Psychoanalytic Quarterly* 7:243–253.

Bernstein, D. (1983). The female superego: a different perspective. *International Journal of Psycho-Analysis* 64:187–201.

Bernstein, I. (1957). The role of narcissism in moral masochism. *Psychoanalytic Quarterly* 26:358–377.

Bettelheim, B. (1967). *The Empty Fortress.* New York: Free Press.

———— (1977). *The Uses of Enchantment.* New York: Knopf.

Bibring, E. (1941). The development and problems of the theory of instincts. *International Journal of Psycho-Analysis* 22:102–131.

———— (1953). The mechanism of depression. In *Affective Disorders,* ed. P. Greenacre, pp. 13–48. New York: International Universities Press.

Bibring, G. L. (1964). Some considerations regarding the ego-ideal in the psychoanalytic process. *Journal of the American Psychoanalytic Association* 12:517–521.

Bird, B. (1957). A specific peculiarity of acting out. *Journal of the American Psychoanalytic Association* 5:630–647.

Blanck, G., and Blanck, R. (1974). *Ego Psychology.* New York: Columbia University Press.

Blank, H. (1954). Depression, hypomania, and depersonalization. *Psychoanalytic Quarterly* 23:20–37.

Blatt, S. (1974). Levels of object representation in anaclitic and introjective depression. *Psychoanalytic Study of the Child* 29:107–157. New Haven, CT: Yale University Press.

Blos, P. (1941). *The Adolescent Personality.* New York: Appleton-Century-Crofts.

———— (1954). Prolonged adolescence: the formulation of a syndrome and its therapeutic implications. *American Journal of Orthopsychiatry* 24:733–742.

———— (1962). *On Adolescence.* New York: Free Press.

———— (1965). The initial stage of male adolescence. *Psychoanalytic Study of the Child* 20:145–164. New York: International Universities Press.

———— (1967). The second individuation process of adolescence. *Psychoanalytic Study of the Child* 22:162–186. New York: International Universities Press.

———— (1968). Character formation in adolescence. *Psychoanalytic Study of the Child* 23:245–263. New York: International Universities Press.

———— (1972). The function of the ego ideal in late adolescence. *Psychoanalytic Study of the Child* 27:93–97. New Haven, CT: Yale University Press.

Blum, G. S., and Miller, D. R. (1952). Exploring the psychoanalytic theory of the "oral character." *Journal of Personality* 20:287–304.

Blum, H. (1973). The concept of erotized transference. *Journal of the American Psychoanalytic Association* 21:61–76.

———— (1976). Masochism, the ego ideal, and the psychology of women. *Journal of the American Psychoanalytic Association* 24:157–191.

————, ed. (1977). *Female Psychology: Contemporary Psychoanalytic Views.* New York: International Universities Press.

———— (1978). An unusual perversion. *Journal of the American Psychoanalytic Association* 26:789–792.

———— (1981). The forbidden quest and the analytic ideal: the superego and insight. *Psychoanalytic Quarterly* 50:535–556.

———— (1982). The position and value of extratransference interpretation. *Journal of the American Psychoanalytic Association* 31:587–618.

———— (1985a). Superego formation, adolescent transformation, and the adult neurosis. *Journal of the American Psychoanalytic Association* 33:887–909.

———— (1985b). Countertransference and the theory of technique: discussion. *Journal of the American Psychoanalytic Association* 34:309–328.

———— (1986a). Object inconstancy and paranoid conspiracy. In *Self and Object Constancy: Clinical and Theoretical Perspectives,* ed. R. Lax, S. Bach, and J. A. Burland, pp. 253–270. New York: Guilford.

———— (1986b). Countertransference: concepts and controversies. In *Psychoanalysis: The Science of Mental Conflicts: Essays in Honor of Charles Brenner,* ed. A. Richards and M. Willick, pp. 229–244. New York: Analytic Press.

Boesky, D. (1982). Acting out: a reconsideration of the concept. *International Journal of Psycho-Analysis* 63:39–55.

Bond, A., Franco, D., and Kramer Richards, A. (1992). *Dream Portrait: A Study of Nineteen Sequential Dreams as Indicators of Pretermination.* Madison, CT.: International Universities Press.

Bornstein, B. (1951). On latency. *Psychoanalytic Study of the Child* 6:279–285. New York: International Universities Press.

_____ (1953). Masturbation in the latency period. *Psychoanalytic Study of the Child* 8:65–78. New York: International Universities Press.

Bouvet, M. (1958). Technical variation and the concept of distance. *International Journal of Psycho-Analysis* 39:211–221.

Boyer, L. (1956). On maternal overstimulation and ego defects. *Psychoanalytic Study of the Child* 11:236–256. New York: International Universities Press.

_____ (1971). Psychoanalytic technique in the treatment of certain characterological and schizophrenic disorders. *International Journal of Psycho-Analysis* 52:67–85.

Brenman, E. (1985). Cruelty and narrowmindedness. *International Journal of Psycho-Analysis* 66:273–281.

Brenner, C. (1959). The masochistic character: genesis and treatment. *Journal of the American Psychoanalytic Association* 7:197–226.

_____ (1968). Archaic aspects of ego functioning. *International Journal of Psycho-Analysis* 49:426–429.

_____ (1970). Problems in the psychoanalytic theory of aggression. *Psychoanalytic Quarterly* 39:666–667.

_____ (1971). The psychoanalytic concept of aggression. *International Journal of Psycho-Analysis* 52:137–144.

_____ (1974). Depression, anxiety, and affect therapy. *International Journal of Psycho-Analysis* 55:25–32.

_____ (1976). *Psychoanalytic Technique and Psychic Conflict.* New York: International Universities Press.

_____ (1982). The concept of the superego: a reformulation. *Psychoanalytic Quarterly* 51:501–525.

_____ (1985). Countertransference as compromise formation. *Psychoanalytic Quarterly* 54:155–163.

Brickman, A. (1983). Pre-oedipal development of the superego. *International Journal of Psycho-Analysis* 64:83–92.

Bridger, H. (1950). Criteria for termination of an analysis. *International Journal of Psycho-Analysis* 31:202–203.

Bruch, H. (1973). *Eating Disorders: Obesity, Anorexia, and the Person Within.* New York: Basic Books.

Buan, O. (1977). Countertransference and the vicissitudes in an analyst's development. *Psychoanalytic Review* 64:539–550.

Burland, J. A. (1986). The vicissitudes of maternal deprivation. In *Self and Object Constancy: Clinical and Theoretical Perspectives.* ed. R. Lax, S. Bach, and J. A. Burland, pp. 291–303. New York: Guilford.

Buxbaum, E. (1945). Transference and group formation in children and adolescents. *Psychoanalytic Study of the Child* 1:351–365. New York: International Universities Press.

_____ (1950). Technique of terminating analysis. *International Journal of Psycho-Analysis* 31:184–190.

Bychowski, G. (1947). The preschizophrenic ego. *Psychoanalytic Quarterly* 16:225–233.

––––––– (1959). Some aspects of masochistic involvement. *Journal of the American Psychoanalytic Association* 7:248–273.

––––––– (1966). Patterns of anger. *Psychoanalytic Study of the Child* 21:172–192. New York: International Universities Press.

Chasseguet-Smirgel, J. (1970). Feminine guilt and the Oedipus complex. In *Feminine Sexuality,* pp. 94–134. Ann Arbor: University of Michigan Press.

––––––– (1984). On the therapeutic alliance and "pervert" patients. In *Creativity and Perversion,* pp. 109–119. New York: Norton.

––––––– (1985). *The Ego Ideal: A Psychoanalytic Essay on the Malady of the Ideal.* New York: Norton.

Clark, L. (1933). The question of prognosis in narcissistic neuroses and psychoses. *International Journal of Psycho-Analysis* 14:71–86.

Clerk, G. (1972). An ego psychological approach to the problem of oral aggression. *International Journal of Psycho-Analysis* 53:77–82.

Cooper, A. (1989). The narcissistic-masochistic character. In *Essential Papers on Character Neurosis and Treatment,* ed. R. Lax, pp. 288–309. New York: Guilford.

Deutsch, H. (1926). Occult processes occurring during psychoanalysis. In *Psychoanalysis and the Occult,* ed. G. Devereux, pp. 418–433. New York: International Universities Press.

––––––– (1942). Some forms of emotional disturbance and their relationship to schizophrenia ("as if"). *Psychoanalytic Quarterly* 11:301–321.

––––––– (1944). *The Psychology of Women.* Vols. 1 & 2. New York: Grune & Stratton.

––––––– (1955). The imposter: ego psychology of a type of psychopath. *Psychoanalytic Quarterly* 24:483–505.

Dewald, P. (1982). Serious illness in the analyst: transference, countertransference, and reality responses. *Journal of the American Psychoanalytic Association* 30:347–364.

Dickes, R. (1967). Severe regressive disruptions of the therapeutic alliance. *Journal of the American Psychoanalytic Association* 15:508–533.

Dorpat, T. (1974). Internalization of the patient-analyst relationship in patients with narcissistic disorders. *International Journal of Psycho-Analysis* 55:183–188.

––––––– (1982). An object-relations perspective on masochism. In *Essential Papers on Character Neurosis and Treatment,* ed. R. Lax, pp. 267–287. New York: International Universities Press, 1989.

Druck, A. (1989). *Four Therapeutic Approaches to the Borderline Patient: Principles and Techniques of the Basic Dynamic Stances.* Northvale, NJ: Jason Aronson.

Easser, R. (1974). Empathic inhibition and psychoanalytic technique. *Psychoanalytic Quarterly* 43:557–580.

Easser, R., and Lesser, S. (1965). Hysterical personality: a re-evaluation. *Psychoanalytic Quarterly* 34:390–405.

––––––– (1966). Transference resistance in hysterical character neurosis: technical considerations. In *Essential Papers on Character Neurosis and Treatment,* ed.

R. Lax, pp. 249–260. New York: International Universities Press.

Eichler, M. (1976). The psychoanalytic treatment of an hysterical character with special emphasis on problems of aggression. *International Journal of Psycho-Analysis* 57:37–47.

Eidelberg, L. (1959). Humiliation in masochism. *Journal of the American Psychoanalytic Association* 7:274–283.

Eisenbud, R. J. (1967). Masochism revisited. *Psychoanalytic Review* 54:561–582.

Eissler, K. R., ed. (1949). *Searchlights on Delinquency.* New York: International Universities Press.

_____ (1953a). The effect of the structure of the ego on psychoanalytic technique. *Journal of the American Psychoanalytic Association* 1:104–143.

_____ (1953b). Notes upon the emotionality of a schizophrenic patient and its relation to problems of technique. *Psychoanalytic Study of the Child* 3:199–251. New York: International Universities Press.

_____ (1966). A note on trauma, dream, anxiety and schizophrenia. *Psychoanalytic Study of the Child* 21:17–50. New York: International Universities Press.

Ekstein, R. (1965). Working through and termination of analysis. *Journal of the American Psychoanalytic Association* 13:57–78.

Elkisch, P. (1957). The psychological significance of the mirror. *Journal of the American Psychoanalytic Association* 5:235–244.

Erikson, E. H. (1956). The problem of ego identity. *Journal of the American Psychoanalytic Association* 4:56–121.

Fairbairn, R. (1952). *An Object Relations Theory of Personality.* London: Hogarth.

Fast, I. (1979). Developments in gender identity: gender differentiation in girls. *International Journal of Psycho-Analysis* 60:443–453.

Federn, P. (1926). Some variations in ego feeling. *International Journal of Psycho-Analysis* 7:434–444.

_____ (1952a). *Ego Psychology and the Psychoses.* New York: Basic Books.

_____ (1952b). On the distinction between healthy and pathological narcissism. In *Ego Psychology and the Psychoses,* pp. 323–364. New York: Basic Books.

Fenichel, O. (1955). *Psychoanalytic Theory of Neurosis.* London: Hogarth.

_____ (1981). *Collected Papers.* New York: Norton.

Ferenczi, S. (1919). On the technique of psycho-analysis. In *Further Contributions to the Theory and Technique of Psychoanalysis,* pp. 177–189. London: Hogarth.

_____ (1920). The further development of an active therapy in psychoanalysis. In *Further Contributions to the Theory and Technique of Psychoanalysis,* pp. 198–217. London: Hogarth.

_____ (1950). *Further Contributions to the Theory and Technique of Psychoanalysis.* London: Hogarth.

_____ (1952). *Contributions to Psychoanalysis.* London: Hogarth.

_____ (1955). *Final Contributions to Psycho-Analysis.* New York: Basic Books.

Ferreira, A. F. (1961). Empathy and the bridge function of the ego. *Journal of the American Psychoanalytic Association* 9:91–105.

Filho, G. (1986). Vicissitudes of identification as observed in character pathology. *International Journal of Psycho-Analysis* 67:193-199.

Firestein, S. K. (1975). Termination of psychoanalysis of adults: a review of the literature. *Journal of the American Psychoanalytic Association* 24:873-893.

Fischer, N. (1981). Masochism: current concepts: panel report. *Journal of the American Psychoanalytic Association* 29:673-678.

Fleming, J. (1972). Early object deprivation and transference phenomena: the working alliance. *Psychoanalytic Quarterly* 41:23-39.

Fliegel, Z. O. (1986). Women's development in analytic theory: six decades of controversy. In *Psychoanalysis and Women: Contemporary Reappraisals,* ed. J. Alpert, pp. 3-31. New York: Analytic Press.

Fliess, R. (1942). The metapsychology of the analyst. *Psychoanalytic Quarterly* 11:211-227.

_____ (1953). Countertransference and counteridentification. *Journal of the American Psychoanalytic Association* 1:268-284.

Frank, A. (1969). The unrememberable and the unforgettable: passive primal repression. *Psychoanalytic Study of the Child* 24:48-77. New York: International Universities Press.

Frank, A., and Muslin, H. (1967). The development of Freud's concept of primal repression. *Psychoanalytic Study of the Child* 22:55-76. New York: International Universities Press.

Frank, J. (1959). Treatment approach to acting out character disorders. *Journal of Hillside Hospital* 8:42-53.

Frankl, L. (1961). Some observations on the development and disturbances of integration in childhood. *Psychoanalytic Study of the Child* 16:19-61. New York: International Universities Press.

Freedman, A. (1978). An unusual perversion. *Journal of the American Psychoanalytic Association* 26:749-778.

Freeman, T. (1964). Some aspects of pathological masochism. *Journal of the American Psychoanalytic Association* 12:540-561.

Freud, A. (1946a). *The Ego and the Mechanisms of Defence.* London: Tavistock.

_____ (1946b). Aggression in relation to emotional development: normal and pathological. In *Writings of Anna Freud,* vol. 4, pp. 489-497. New York: International Universities Press.

_____ (1958). Adolescence. *Psychoanalytic Study of the Child* 13:255-278. New York: International Universities Press.

_____ (1965). Normality and pathology in childhood: assessment of psychopathology. In *Writings of Anna Freud,* vol. 6, pp. 148-212. New York: International Universities Press.

Freud, S. The complete sum of Freud's psychoanalytic writings, from the first paper in which he displayed the discovery of psychoanalysis (1893) to his final work (1939) published posthumously, has been collected and translated into English (in twenty-three volumes) under the general editorship of James Strachey in collaboration with Anna Freud (Freud's daughter, and the only one of Freud's children to pursue this field professionally) and assisted by Alix Strachey and Alan Tyson. A twenty-fourth volume, an index, was compiled by Angela Richards after Strachey's death. This set known as the *Standard Edition* is published by The Hogarth Press and The Institute of Psycho-Analysis in London.

Fries, M. E. (1958). Review of the literature on the latency period. *Journal of Hillside Hospital* 7:3–16.

Fromm, E. (1941). *Escape From Freedom.* New York: International Universities Press.

Furman, E. (1973). A contribution to assessing the role of infantile separation-individuation in adolescent development. *Psychoanalytic Study of the Child* 28:193–207. New Haven, CT: Yale University Press.

Gedo, J. (1975). Forms of idealization in the analytic transference. *Journal of the American Psychoanalytic Association* 23:485–505.

_____ (1977). Notes on the psychoanalytic management of archaic transferences. *Journal of the American Psychoanalytic Association* 25:787–803.

Gero, G. (1962). Sadism, masochism and aggression: their role in symptom formation. *Psychoanalytic Quarterly* 31:32–42.

Gill, M. (1959). The present state of psychoanalytic theory. *Journal of Abnormal Social Psychology* 58:1–8.

_____ (1979). The analysis of the transference. *Journal of the American Psychoanalytic Association* 27 (Suppl.):263–288.

_____ (1982). *The Analysis of Transference.* New York: International Universities Press.

Gillespie, W. H. (1958). Neurotic ego distortions. *International Journal of Psycho-Analysis* 39:258–259.

Giovacchini, P. (1972a). The treatment of characterological disorders. In *Tactics and Techniques of Psychoanalytic Therapy,* pp. 236–253. New York: Science House.

_____ (1972b). Technical difficulties in treating some characterological disorders: countertransference problems. *International Journal of Psychoanalytic Psychotherapy* 1:112–128.

_____ (1979a). *Treatment of Primitive Mental States.* New York: Jason Aronson.

_____ (1979b). Countertransference with primitive mental states. In *Countertransference,* ed. L. Epstein and A. Feiner, pp. 235–266. New York: Jason Aronson.

_____ (1986). Psychic integration and object constancy. In *Self and Object Constancy: Clinical and Theoretical Perspectives,* ed. R. Lax, S. Bach, and J. A. Burland, pp. 208–232. New York: Guilford.

Giovacchini, P., and Boyer, L. (1975). *Psychoanalysis of Character Disorders.* New York: Jason Aronson.

Gitelson, M. (1942). Direct psychotherapy in adolescence. *American Journal of Orthopsychiatry* 12:1–23.

_____ (1952). The emotional position of the analyst in the psycho-analytic situation. *International Journal of Psycho-Analysis* 33:1–10.

_____ (1958). On ego distortion. *International Journal of Psycho-Analysis* 39:243–257.

_____ (1963). On the problem of character neurosis. *Journal of Hillside Hospital* 12:3–17.

Glover, E. (1927). Lectures on technique in psychoanalysis. *International Journal of Psycho-Analysis* 8:311–338.

_____ (1945). Examination of the Klein system of child psychology. *Psychoanalytic Study of the Child* 1:75–118. New York: International Universities Press.

_____ (1955). *Technique of Psychoanalysis.* New York: International Universities Press.

_____ (1956a). *Collected Essays.* London: Hogarth.

_____ (1956b). *On the Early Development of the Mind.* New York: International Universities Press.

_____ (1958). Ego disturbances. *International Journal of Psycho-Analysis* 39:260–264.

Goldberg, A. (1974). On the prognosis and treatment of narcissism. *Journal of the American Psychoanalytic Association* 22:243–254.

_____ ed. (1980). *Advances in Self Psychology.* New York: International Universities Press.

Gould, R. (1973). *Child Studies Through Fantasy: A Cognitive-Affective Approach.* New York: Quadrangle.

Greenacre, P. (1950). General problems of acting out. *Psychoanalytic Quarterly* 19:455–467.

_____ (1951). Respiratory incorporation and the phallic phase. *Psychoanalytic Study of the Child* 6:180–205. New York: International Universities Press.

_____ (1952). *Trauma, Growth, and Personality.* New York: International Universities Press.

_____ (1968a). Perversions: genetic and dynamic background. *Psychoanalytic Study of the Child* 23:47–62. New York: International Universities Press.

_____ (1968b). Acting out: symposium. *International Journal of Psycho-Analysis* 49:171–230.

_____ (1971). *Emotional Growth.* Vols. 1 & 2. New York, International Universities Press.

_____ (1975). Acting out in the transference. In *Emotional Growth,* vol. 2, p. 701. New York: International Universities Press, 1963.

Greenson, R. (1954). The struggle against identification. *Journal of the American Psychoanalytic Association* 2:200–217.

_____ (1960). Empathy and its vicissitudes. *International Journal of Psycho-Analysis* 41:418–424.

_____ (1971). The "real" relationship between the patient and the psychoanalyst. In *The Unconscious Today,* ed. M. Kanzer, pp. 213–232. New York: International Universities Press.

Grinberg, L. (1957). Projective counteridentification and countertransference. In *Countertransference,* ed. L. Epstein and A. Feiner, pp. 168–192. New York: Jason Aronson.

_____ (1962). On a specific aspect of countertransference due to the patient's projective identification. *International Journal of Psycho-Analysis* 43:436–440.

Grolnick, S. (1986). The relationship of Winnicott's developmental concept of the transitional object to self and object constancy. In *Self and Object Constancy: Clinical and Theoretical Perspectives.* ed. R. Lax, S. Bach, and J. A. Burland, pp. 107–134. New York: Guilford.

Grossman, W. (1991). Pain, aggression, fantasy, and concepts of sadomasochism. *Psychoanalytic Quarterly* 60:22–52.

Grunberger, B. (1979). *Narcissism: Psychoanalytic Essays.* New York: International Universities Press.

Grunes, M. (1984). The therapeutic object relationship. *Psychoanalytic Review* 71:123–143.

Hamburg, D. (1973). An evolutionary and developmental approach to human aggressiveness. *Psychoanalytic Quarterly* 42:185–196.

Hanley, C. (1982). Narcissism, defense, and the positive transference. *International Journal of Psycho-Analysis* 63:427–444.

Hartmann, H. (1948). Comments on the psychoanalytic theory of instinctual drives. In *Essays in Ego Psychology,* pp. 69–89. New York: International Universities Press.

_____ (1951). Technical implications of ego psychology. In *Essays in Ego Psychology,* pp. 142–154. New York: International Universities Press.

_____ (1952). The mutual influences in the development of ego and id. In *Essays in Ego Psychology,* pp. 155–181. New York: International Universities Press.

_____ (1955). Notes on the theory of sublimation. In *Essays in Ego Psychology,* pp. 215–240. New York: International Universities Press.

_____ (1956). Notes on the reality principle. *Psychoanalytic Study of the Child* 11:31–53. New York: International Universities Press.

_____ (1958a). Comments on the psychoanalytic theory of the ego. *Psychoanalytic Study of the Child* 5:74–96. New York: International Universities Press.

_____ (1958b). *Ego Psychology and the Problem of Adaptation.* New York: International Universities Press.

_____ (1964). *Essays in Ego Psychology.* New York: International Universities Press.

Hartmann, H., Kris, E., and Loewenstein, R. (1946). Comments on the formation of psychic structure. *Psychoanalytic Study of the Child* 2:1–38.

Hartmann, H., and Loewenstein, R. (1964). Notes on the superego. In *Papers on Psychoanalytic Psychology,* pp. 144–181. New York: International Universities Press.

Havighurst, R. (1948). *Developmental Tasks and Education.* Chicago: University of Chicago Press.

Heimann, P. (1950). On counter-transference. *International Journal of Psycho-Analysis* 31:81–84.

_____ (1952). Certain functions of introjection and projection in early infancy: part I - mental structure, part II - early object relations. In *Developments in Psychoanalysis,* ed. M. Klein, P. Heimann, S. Isaacs, and J. Riviere, pp. 122–168. London: Hogarth.

_____ (1960). Counter-transference. *British Journal of Medical Psychology* 33:9–15.

_____ (1977). Further observations on the analyst's cognitive process. *Journal of the American Psychoanalytic Association* 25:313–333.

Hendrick, I. (1942). Instinct and the ego during infancy. *Psychoanalytic Quarterly* 11:35–58.

_____ (1951). Early development of the ego. *Psychoanalytic Quarterly* 20:44–61.

_____ (1964). Narcissism and the prepuberty ego-ideal. *Journal of the American Psychoanalytic Association* 12:522–528.

Hoffer, W. (1946). Diaries of adolescent schizophrenics (hebephrenics). *Psychoanalytic Study of the Child* 2:293–312. New York: International Universities Press.

_____ (1949). Mouth, hand, and ego integration. *Psychoanalytic Study of the Child* 3,4:49–56. New York: International Universities Press.

_____ (1950). Development of the body ego. *Psychoanalytic Study of the Child* 5:18–24. New York: International Universities Press.

_____ (1952). Mutual influences in the development of ego and id. *Psychoanalytic Study of the Child* 7:31–41. New York: International Universities Press.

Holt, R. (1965). Ego autonomy re-evaluated. *International Journal of Psycho-Analysis* 46:151–167.

Horn, H. T. (1971). Toward a paradigm of the terminal phase. *Journal of the American Psychoanalytic Association* 19:332–348.

Horney, K. (1924). On the genesis of the castration complex in women. *International Journal of Psycho-Analysis* 5:50–65.

_____ (1926). The flight from womanhood. *International Journal of Psycho-Analysis* 7:324–339.

_____ (1937). *The Neurotic Personality of Our Time.* London: Hogarth.

_____ (1940). *New Ways in Psychoanalysis.* New York: International Universities Press.

_____ (1945). *Our Inner Conflicts.* New York: International Universities Press.

_____ (1950). *Neurosis and Human Growth.* New York: International Universities Press.

Isaacs, S. (1939). Criteria for interpretation. *International Journal of Psycho-Analysis* 20:148–160.

Jacobs, T. (1983). The analyst's and the patient's object world: notes on an aspect of countertransference. *Journal of the American Psychoanalytic Association* 31:619–642.

_____ (1986). Countertransference enactments. *Journal of the American Psychoanalytic Association* 34:289–307.

Jacobson, E. (1937). Ways of female superego formation and the female castration conflict. *Psychoanalytic Quarterly* 45:525–537, 1976.

_____ (1946). The effect of disappointment on ego and superego development. *Psychoanalytic Review* 33:129–147.

_____ (1954). The self and the object world: vicissitudes of their infantile cathexes and their influence on ideational and affective development. *Psychoanalytic Study of the Child* 9:75–127. New York: International Universities Press.

_____ (1957). On normal and pathological moods: their nature and functions. *Psychoanalytic Study of the Child* 12:73–113. New York: International Universities Press.

_____ (1959). The "exceptions": an elaboration of Freud's character studies. *Psychoanalytic Study of the Child* 14:135–154. New York: International Universities Press.

_____ (1961). Adolescent moods and the remodeling of psychic structures in adolescence. *Psychoanalytic Study of the Child* 16:164–183. New York: International Universities Press.

_____ (1964). *The Self and the Object World.* New York: International Universities Press.

_____ (1971). *Depression.* New York: International Universities Press.

James, M. (1972). Preverbal communication. In *Tactics and Techniques in Psychoanalytic Therapy,* ed. P. Giovacchini, pp. 436–454. New York: Science House.

Jessner, L., and Abse, C. (1960). Regressive forces in anorexia nervosa. *British Journal of Medical Psychology* 33:301–312.

Joffee, W. G., and Sandler, J. (1965). Notes on pain, depression, and individuation. *Psychoanalytic Study of the Child* 20:392–424. New York: International Universities Press.

Johnston, Mc. (1963–1964). Features of orality in an hysterical character. *Psychoanalytic Review* 50:663–681.

Jones, E. (1918). Anal-erotic character traits. In *Papers on Psychoanalysis,* pp. 413–437. Boston: Beacon.

_____ (1926). The genesis and structure of the superego. In *Papers on Psychoanalysis,* pp. 145–152. Boston: Beacon.

_____ (1929a). Fear, guilt and hate. In *Papers on Psychoanalysis,* pp. 304–319. Boston: Beacon.

_____ (1929b). The psychopathology of anxiety. In *Papers on Psychoanalysis,* pp. 294–303. Boston: Beacon.

_____ (1930). Jealousy. In *Papers on Psychoanalysis,* pp. 325–340. Boston: Beacon.

_____ (1935). Psychoanalysis and the instincts. In *Papers on Psychoanalysis,* pp. 153–169. Boston: Beacon.

_____ (1937). Love and morality. In *Papers on Psychoanalysis,* pp. 196–200. Boston: Beacon.

_____, ed. (1949). Karl Abraham: *Selected Papers on Psychoanalysis.* London: Hogarth.

_____ (1961). *Papers on Psychoanalysis.* Boston: Beacon.

Joseph, B. (1959). An aspect of the repetition compulsion. *International Journal of Psycho-Analysis* 40:213–222.

Jung, C. G. (1941). *Symbols of Transformation.* New York: Pantheon.

Kaplan, S. M., and Whitman, R. M. (1965). The negative ego-ideal. *International Journal of Psycho-Analysis* 46:183–187.

Kafka, E. (1971). On the development of the mental self, the bodily self, and

self-consciousness. *Psychoanalytic Study of the Child* 26:217–240. New Haven, CT: Yale University Press.

Kafka, J. (1976). The analysis of phallic narcissism. *International Review of Psycho-Analysis* 3:277–282.

Kaywin, L. (1960). An epigenetic approach to the psychoanalytic theory of instincts and affects. *Journal of the American Psychoanalytic Association* 8:613–658.

Keiser, S. A. (1953). A manifest oedipus complex in an adolescent girl. *Psychoanalytic Study of the Child* 8:99–107. New York: International Universities Press.

Kennedy, H. E. (1950). Cover memories in formation. *Psychoanalytic Study of the Child* 5:275–284. New York: International Universities Press.

Kern, J. (1978). Countertransference and spontaneous screens: an analyst studies his own visual images. *Journal of the American Psychoanalytic Association* 26:21–47.

Kernberg, O. (1965). Notes on countertransference. *Journal of the American Psychoanalytic Association* 13:38–56.

⸻ (1966). Structural derivatives of object-relationships. *International Journal of Psycho-Analysis* 47:236–253.

⸻ (1967). Borderline personality organization. *Journal of the American Psychoanalytic Association* 15:641–685.

⸻ (1970a). Factors in the psychoanalytic treatment of narcissistic personalities. *Journal of the American Psychoanalytic Association* 18:51–85.

⸻ (1970b). A psychoanalytic classification of character pathology. *Journal of the American Psychoanalytic Association* 18:800–822.

⸻ (1974a). Further contributions to the treatment of narcissistic personalities. *International Journal of Psycho-Analysis* 55:215–240.

⸻ (1974b). Contrasting viewpoints regarding the nature and treatment of narcissistic personalities. *Journal of the American Psychoanalytic Association* 22:255–267.

⸻ (1975). *Borderline Conditions and Pathological Narcissism.* New York: Jason Aronson.

⸻ (1976). *Object Relations Theory and Clinical Psychoanalysis.* New York: Jason Aronson.

⸻ (1983). Object relations theory and character analysis. *Journal of the American Psychoanalytic Association* 31:241–271.

⸻ (1987). An ego psychology-object relations theory approach to the transference. *Psychoanalytic Quarterly* 56:197–221.

⸻ (1991). Transference regression and psychoanalytic technique with infantile patients. *International Journal of Psycho-Analysis* 72:189–200.

Kestemberg, E. (1964). Problems regarding the termination of analysis in character neuroses. *International Journal of Psycho-Analysis* 45:350–357.

Kestenberg, J. S. (1969). Problems of technique of child analysis in relation to various developmental stages: prelatency. *Psychoanalytic Study of the Child* 24:358–383. New York: International Universities Press.

Khan, M. (1963). Ego ideal, excitement, and the threat of annihilation. *Journal of Hillside Hospital* 12:195–217.

_____ (1979). *Alienations in Perversion.* London: Hogarth.

Khantzian, S., and Mack, W. (1983). Self preservation and the care of the self. *Psychoanalytic Study of the Child* 38:209–232. New Haven, CT: Yale University Press.

Kinston, W. (1980). A theoretical and technical approach to narcissistic disturbance. *International Journal of Psycho-Analysis* 61:383–394.

Klein, M. (1927). Criminal tendencies in normal children. In *Contributions to Psychoanalysis: 1921–1945,* ed. E. Jones, pp. 185–201. London: Hogarth.

_____ (1928). Early stages of the oedipus conflict. In *Contributions to Psychoanalysis: 1921–1945,* ed. E. Jones, pp. 202–214. London: Hogarth.

_____ (1929). Infantile anxiety situations reflected in a work of art and in the creative impulse. In *Contributions to Psychoanalysis: 1921–1945,* ed. E. Jones, pp. 227–235. London: Hogarth.

_____ (1930). The importance of symbol formation in the development of the ego. In *Contributions to Psychoanalysis: 1921–1945,* ed. E. Jones, pp. 236–250. London: Hogarth.

_____ (1931a). A contribution to the theory of intellectual inhibition. In *Contributions to Psychoanalysis: 1921–1945,* ed. E. Jones, pp. 254–256. London: Hogarth.

_____ (1931b). The early development of conscience in the child. In *Contributions to Psychoanalysis: 1921–1945,* ed. E. Jones, pp. 267–277. London: Hogarth.

_____ (1932). *The Psychoanalysis of Children.* London: Hogarth.

_____ (1934). On criminality. In *Contributions to Psychoanalysis: 1921–1945,* ed. E. Jones, pp. 278–281. London: Hogarth.

_____ (1935). A contribution to the psychogenesis of manic-depressive states. *International Journal of Psycho-Analysis* 16:282–310.

_____ (1940). Mourning and its relation to manic-depressive states. *International Journal of Psycho-Analysis* 21:311–338.

_____ (1945). The oedipus complex in the light of early anxieties. In *Contributions to Psychoanalysis: 1921–1945,* ed. E. Jones, pp. 339–390. London: Hogarth.

_____ (1973). *Contributions to Psychoanalysis: 1921–1945,* ed. E. Jones. London: Hogarth.

Klein, M., Heimann, P., Isaacs, S., and Riviere, J. (1952). *Developments in Psychoanalysis.* London: Hogarth.

Klein, M., Heimann, P., and Money-Kyrle, R. (1955). *New Directions in Psychoanalysis.* London: Tavistock.

Klein, M., and Riviere, J. (1964). *Love, Hate and Reparation.* New York: Norton.

Kohut, H. (1962). Thoughts on narcissism and narcissistic rage. *Psychoanalytic Study of the Child* 27:360–400. New York: International Universities Press.

_____ (1966). Forms and transformations of narcissism. *Journal of the American Psychoanalytic Association* 14:243–272.

_____ (1968). The psychoanalytical treatment of narcissistic personality disorders. *Psychoanalytic Study of the Child* 23:86–113. New York: International Universities Press.

_____ (1971). *The Analysis of the Self.* New York: International Universities Press.

_____ (1977). *The Restoration of the Self.* New York: International Universities Press.

_____ (1979). The two analyses of Mr. Z. *International Journal of Psycho-Analysis* 60:3–27.

Kramer, P. (1955). On discovering one's identity. *Psychoanalytic Study of the Child* 10:47–74. New York: International Universities Press.

Kris, A. (1983). Determinants of free association in narcissistic phenomena. *Psychoanalytic Study of the Child* 38:439–458. New Haven, CT: Yale University Press.

Kris, E. (1938). Ego development and the comic. *International Journal of Psycho-Analysis* 19:77–90.

_____ (1947). The nature of psychoanalytic propositions and their validation. In *Selected Papers of Ernst Kris,* pp. 3–23. New Haven, CT: Yale University Press.

_____ (1950a). Ego psychology and interpretation in psychoanalytic theory. *Psychoanalytic Quarterly* 5:15–30.

_____ (1950b). Notes on the development and on some urgent problems of psychoanalytic child psychology. *Psychoanalytic Study of the Child* 5:24–46. New York: International Universities Press.

_____ (1950c). On preconscious mental processes. *Psychoanalytic Quarterly* 19:540–560.

_____ (1952). *Psychoanalytic Explorations in Art.* New York: International Universities Press.

_____ (1956). The recovery of childhood memories in psychoanalysis. *Psychoanalytic Study of the Child* 11:54–88. New Haven, CT: Yale University Press.

Kron, R. (1971). Psychoanalytic complications of a narcissistic transference. *Journal of the American Psychoanalytic Association* 19:636–653.

Krystal, H. (1977). Aspects of affect theory. *Bulletin of the Menninger Clinic* 41:1–26.

_____ (1978a). Trauma and affects. *Psychoanalytic Study of the Child* 36:81–116. New Haven, CT: Yale University Press.

_____ (1978b). Self representation and the capacity for self care. *Annual of Psychoanalysis* 2:93–113.

_____ (1982). Alexithymia and the effectiveness of psychoanalytic treatment. *Journal of Psychoanalytic Psychotherapy* 9:353–78.

Kubie, L. (1968). Unsolved problems in the resolution of the transference. *Psychoanalytic Quarterly* 37:331–352.

_____ (1974). The drive to become both sexes. *Psychoanalytic Quarterly* 43:349–426.

LaFarge, L. (1989). Emptiness as a defense in severe regressive states. *Journal of the American Psychoanalytic Association* 37:965–996.

Laforgue, R. (1934). Resistance at the conclusion of psychoanalytic treatment. *International Journal of Psycho-Analysis* 15:419–434.

Lampl-de Groot, J. (1946). The preoedipal phase in the development of the male child. *Psychoanalytic Study of the Child* 2:75–83. New York: International Universities Press.

_____ (1950). On masturbation and its influence on general development. *Psychoanalytic Study of the Child* 5:153–174. New York: International Universities Press.

_____ (1962). Ego-ideal and superego. *Psychoanalytic Study of the Child* 17:94–106. New York: International Universities Press.

_____ (1964). Some remarks on genesis, structuralization, and functioning of the mind. *Psychoanalytic Study of the Child* 19:48–57. New York: International Universities Press.

_____ (1965). Superego, ego-ideal and masochistic fantasies. In *The Development of the Mind*, pp. 351–363. New York: International Universities Press.

Landauer, K. (1939). Some remarks on the formation of the anal-erotic character. *International Journal of Psycho-Analysis* 20:418–425.

Langs, R. (1975). The therapeutic relationship and deviations in technique. *International Journal of Psychoanalytic Psychotherapy* 4:106–141.

_____ (1978). *The Listening Process.* New York: Jason Aronson.

Lasky, J. (1985). Midlife change. In *From Research to Clinical Practice,* ed. R. Keisner and G. Stricker, pp. 327–350. New York: Plenum.

Lasky, R. (1977). The study of object relations theory as a ritual killing of the father. Presented August 1977, Sixth International Forum of Psychoanalysis, Berlin Psychoanalytic Institute. Summarized in *Colloquium* 1:6–9.

_____ (1978a). The impact of object-relations theory on psychoanalysis: theory and technique. In *Changing Perspectives in the Psychotherapies,* ed. H. Greyson and C. Loew, pp. 35–53. New York: Spectrum.

_____ (1978b). The psychoanalytic treatment of a case of multiple personality. *Psychoanalytic Review* 65:355–380.

_____ (1979a). Archaic, immature and infantile personality characteristics. In *Integrating Ego Psychology and Object Relations Theory: Psychoanalytic Perspectives on Psychopathology,* ed. L. Saretsky, G. Goldman, and D. Milman, pp. 47–64. Dubuque, IA: Kendall/Hunt.

_____ (1979b). Thoughts on Kernberg and Kohut: treatment of the narcissistic character disorder. *Colloquium* 2:2–6.

_____ (1981). Comments on multiple personality: letter. *International Journal of Psycho-Analysis* 62:489–490.

_____ (1982). *Evaluating Criminal Responsibility in Multiple Personality and the Related Dissociative Disorders: A Psychoanalytic Perspective.* Springfield, IL: Charles C Thomas.

_____ (1984). Dynamics and problems in the treatment of the "oedipal winner." *Psychoanalytic Review* 71:351–374.

_____ (1985). Primitive object relations and impaired structuralization in the "abusive" patient. *Psychotherapy Patient* 1:95–109.

_____ (1989). Some determinants of the male analyst's capacity to identify with female patients. *International Journal of Psycho-Analysis* 70:405–418.

_____ (1990a). Catastrophic illness in the analyst and the analyst's emotional reactions to it. *International Journal of Psycho-Analysis* 71:455–473.

_____ (1990b). Keeping the analysis intact when the analyst has suffered a catastrophic illness. In *Illness and the Analyst,* ed. H. Schwartz and A. Silver, pp. 177–198. New York: International Universities Press.

_____ (1990c). The influence of neurotic conflict on the analyst's choice of theory and technique. *Psychoanalytic Reflections* 1:110–134.

_____ (1992). Some superego conflicts in the analyst who has suffered a catastrophic illness. *International Journal of Psycho-Analysis* 73:127–136.

Laufer, M. (1964). Ego-ideal and pseudo ego-ideal in adolescence. *Psychoanalytic Study of the Child* 19:196–221. New York: International Universities Press.

Lax, R. (1977). The role of internalization in the development of certain aspects of female masochism: ego psychological considerations. *International Journal of Psycho-Analysis* 58:289–300.

_____ (1980). The rotten core: a defect in the formation of the self during the rapprochement subphase. In *Self and Object Constancy: Clinical and Theoretical Perspectives,* ed. R. Lax, S. Bach, and J. A. Burland, pp. 439–456. New York: Guilford.

_____ (1986). Libidinal object and self constancy enhanced by the analytic process. In *Self and Object Constancy: Clinical and Theoretical Perspectives,* ed. R. Lax, S. Bach, and J. A. Burland, pp. 271–290. New York: Guilford.

_____ ed. (1989). *Essential Papers on Character Neurosis and Treatment.* New York: New York University Press.

_____ (1990). An imaginary brother: his role in the formation of a girl's self image and ego ideal. *Psychoanalytic Study of the Child* 45:257–272. New Haven, CT: Yale University Press.

_____ (1992). A variation on Freud's theme in "A Child Is Being Beaten": mother's role; some implications for superego development in women. *Journal of the American Psychoanalytic Association* 40:455–474.

Lax, R., Bach, S., and Burland, J. A., eds. (1986). *Self and Object Constancy: Clinical and Theoretical Perspectives.* New York: Guilford.

Lebovici, A., and Kiatkine, L. (1964). The contribution of the theory and technique of child analysis to the understanding of character neuroses. *International Journal of Psycho-Analysis* 45:344–349.

Lehrman, P. (1950). On termination of analysis. *Psychoanalytic Quarterly* 19:291–292.

Lerner, H. (1977). Parental mislabeling of female genitals as a determinant of penis envy and learning inhibitions in women. In *Female Psychology: Contemporary Psychoanalytic Views,* ed. H. Blum, pp. 269–283. New York: International Universities Press.

Levin, D. (1969). The self: a contribution to its place in theory and technique. *International Journal of Psycho-Analysis* 50:41–51.

Lewin, B. (1950). *Psychoanalysis of Elation.* New York: Norton.

_____ (1961). Reflections on depression. *Psychoanalytic Study of the Child* 16:321–331.

Lewis, H. B. (1971). *Shame and Guilt in Neurosis.* New York: International Universities Press.

Lichtenstein, H. (1964). The role of narcissism in the emergence and maintenance of a primary identity. *International Journal of Psycho-Analysis* 45:49–56.

_____ (1976). The malignant no. In *The Unconscious Today,* ed. M. Kanzer, pp. 147–176. New York: International Universities Press.

_____ (1977). *The Dilemma of Human Identity.* New York: Jason Aronson.

Liebert, R. (1989). The concept of character: a historical review. In *Essential Papers on Character Neurosis and Treatment,* ed. R. Lax, pp. 46–64. New York: International Universities Press.

Limentani, A. (1981). Some positive aspects of the negative therapeutic reaction. *International Journal of Psycho-Analysis* 62:379–390.

Lipton, S. (1961). The last hour. *Journal of the American Psychoanalytic Association* 9:325–330.

Little, M. (1951). Countertransference and the patient's response to it. *International Journal of Psycho-Analysis* 32:32–40.

_____ (1957). "R" – The analyst's total response to his patient's needs. *International Journal of Psycho-Analysis* 38:240–254.

_____ (1958). On delusional transference (transference psychosis). *International Journal of Psycho-Analysis* 39:134–138.

_____ (1966). Transference in borderline patients. *International Journal of Psycho-Analysis* 47:476–485.

Loewald, H. (1960). On the therapeutic action of psychoanalysis. *International Journal of Psycho-Analysis* 41:16–33.

_____ (1971). The transference neurosis: the concept and the phenomenon. *Journal of the American Psychoanalytic Association* 19:54–66.

_____ (1980a). *Papers on Psychoanalysis.* New Haven, CT: Yale University Press.

_____ (1980b). On internalization. In *Papers on Psychoanalysis,* pp. 69–86. New Haven, CT: Yale University Press.

_____ (1980c). Some considerations on repetition and repetition compulsion. In *Papers on Psychoanalysis,* pp. 87–101. New Haven, CT: Yale University Press.

_____ (1980d). Instinct theory, object relation, and psychic structure. In *Papers on Psychoanalysis,* pp. 207–218. New Haven, CT: Yale University Press.

_____ (1980e). On the therapeutic action of psychoanalysis. In *Papers on Psychoanalysis,* pp. 221–256. New Haven, CT: Yale University Press.

_____ (1980f). Internalization, separation, mourning, and the superego. In *Papers on Psychoanalysis,* pp. 267–276. New Haven, CT: Yale University Press.

_____ (1980g). Freud's conception of the negative therapeutic reaction, with comments on instinct theory. In *Papers on Psychoanalysis,* pp. 315–325. New Haven, CT: Yale University Press.

_____ (1980h). Comments on some instinctual manifestations of superego formation. In *Papers on Psychoanalysis* pp. 326–341. New Haven, CT: Yale University Press.

_____ (1986). Transference-countertransference. *Journal of the American Psychoanalytic Association* 34:275–287.

Loewenstein, R. M. (1956). Some remarks on the role of speech in psycho-analytic technique. *International Journal of Psycho-Analysis* 37:460–468.

_____ (1957). A contribution to the psychoanalytic theory of masochism. *Journal of the American Psychoanalytic Association* 5:197–234.

Loewenstein, R. M., Newman, L. M., Schur, M., and Solnit, A. J., eds. (1966). *Psychoanalysis: A General Psychology.* New York: International Universities Press.

Lorand, S. (1946). *Technique of Psychoanalytic Therapy.* New York: International Universities Press.

Lustman, S. (1957). Psychic energy and the mechanisms of defense. *Psychoanalytic Study of the Child* 12:19–57. New York: International Universities Press.

_____ (1962). Defense, symptoms, and character. *Psychoanalytic Study of the Child* 17:19–62. New York: International Universities Press.

_____ (1968). The economic point of view and defense. *Psychoanalytic Study of the Child* 23: 1968. New York: International Universities Press.

_____ (1972). Yale's year of confrontation: a view from the master's house. *Psychoanalytic Study of the Child* 27:57–73. New Haven, CT: Yale University Press.

Maenchen, A. A. (1946). A case of superego disintegration. *Psychoanalytic Study of the Child* 2:257–262. New York: International Universities Press.

_____ (1953). Notes on early ego disturbances. *Psychoanalytic Study of the Child* 8:262–270. New York: International Universities Press.

Mahler, M. (1961). On sadness and grief in infancy and childhood: loss and restoration of the symbiotic love object. *Psychoanalytic Study of the Child* 16:332–351. New York: International Universities Press.

_____ (1966). Notes on the development of basic moods. In *Psychoanalysis: A General Psychology,* ed. R. Loewenstein, L. Newman, and M. Schur, pp. 152–168. New York: International Universities Press.

_____ (1968). *On Human Symbiosis and the Vicissitudes of Individuation.* New York: International Universities Press.

_____ (1972). On the first three sub-phases of the separation-individuation process. *International Journal of Psycho-Analysis* 53:333–338.

Mahler, M., Pine, F., and Bergman, A. (1975). *The Psychological Birth of the Human Infant.* New York: Basic Books.

Malcolm, R. (1981). Technical problems in the analysis of a pseudo-compliant patient. *International Journal of Psycho-Analysis* 62:477–484.

Malmquist, C. P. (1968). Conscience development. *Psychoanalytic Study of the Child* 23:301–331. New York: International Universities Press.

Marmor, J. (1953). Orality in the hysterical personality. *Journal of the American Psychoanalytic Association* 1:656–671.

Masterson, J. (1981). *The Narcissistic and Borderline Disorders: An Integrated Developmental Approach.* New York: Brunner/Mazel.

Mayer, E. (1985). 'Everybody must be just like me': observations on female castration anxiety. *International Journal of Psycho-Analysis* 66:331–348.

McDevitt, J., and Mahler, M. (1986). Object constancy, individuality, and internalization. In *Self and Object Constancy: Clinical and Theoretical Perspectives,* ed. R. Lax, S. Bach, and J. A. Burland, pp. 11–28. New York: Guilford.

McDougall, J. (1974). The psychosoma and the psychoanalytic process. *International Review of Psycho-Analysis* 1:437–59.

———— (1979). Primitive communication and the use of countertransference. In *Countertransference,* ed. L. Epstein and A. Feiner, pp. 267–303. New York: Jason Aronson.

———— (1980). *Plea for a Measure of Abnormality.* New York: International Universities Press.

———— (1989). The anti-analysand in analysis. In *Essential Papers on Character Neurosis and Treatment,* ed. R. Lax, pp. 363–384. New York: Guilford.

McLaughlin, J. (1981). Transference, psychic reality, and countertransference. *Psychoanalytic Quarterly* 50:639–664.

Meissner, W. W. (1986). The earliest internalizations. In *Self and Object Constancy: Clinical and Theoretical Perspectives,* ed. R. Lax, S. Bach, and J. A. Burland, pp. 29–72. New York: Guilford.

Mendelson, M. (1960). *Psychoanalytic Concepts of Depression.* Springfield, IL: Charles C Thomas.

Menninger, K. (1934). Polysurgery and polysurgical addiction. *Psychoanalytic Quarterly* 3:173–199.

Meyer, J., and Weinroth, B. (1957). Observations on psychological aspects of anorexia nervosa. *Psychosomatic Medicine* 19:389–398.

Meyers, H. (1988). A consideration of treatment techniques in relation to the functions of masochism. In *Self and Object Constancy: Clinical and Theoretical Perspectives,* ed. R. Lax, S. Bach, and J. A. Burland, pp. 331–345. New York: Guilford.

Miller, I. (1965). On the return of symptoms in the terminal phase of psychoanalysis. *International Journal of Psycho-Analysis* 46:487–501.

Milner, M. (1950). Notes on the ending of an analysis. *International Journal of Psycho-Analysis* 31:191–193.

Milrod, D. (1972). Self-pity, self-comforting and the superego. *Psychoanalytic Study of the Child* 27:505–528. New Haven, CT: Yale University Press.

Modell, A. (1963). The concept of psychic energy: scientific proceedings. *Journal of the American Psychoanalytic Association* 11:605–618.

———— (1965). On having a right to a life: an aspect of the superego's development. *International Journal of Psycho-Analysis* 46:323–331.

———— (1975). A narcissistic defense against affects and the illusion of self-sufficiency. *International Journal of Psycho-Analysis* 56:275–282.

———— (1976). The "holding environment" and the therapeutic action of psychoanalysis. *Journal of the American Psychoanalytic Association* 24:285–307.

———— (1978). The conceptualization of the therapeutic action of psychoanalysis. *Bulletin of the Menninger Clinic* 42:493–504.

Morse, S. (1973). The after-pleasure of suicide. *British Journal of Medical Psychology* 46:227–238.

Munro, L. (1955). Steps in ego integration observed in a play analysis. *New Directions in Psychoanalysis,* ed. M. Klein, P. Heimann, and R. Money-Kyrle, pp. 109–139. London: Tavistock.

Murray, J. M. (1964). Narcissism and the ego ideal. *Journal of the American Psychoanalytic Association* 12:477–511.

Nacht, S. (1958a). Causes and mechanisms of ego distortion. *International Journal of Psycho-Analysis* 39:271–273.

———— (1958b). Variations in technique. *International Journal of Psycho-Analysis* 39:235–237.

———— (1962). The curative factors in psychoanalysis. *International Journal of Psycho-Analysis* 43:206–212.

———— (1965). Criteria and technique of the termination of analysis. *International Journal of Psycho-Analysis* 46:107–116.

Nagera, H. (1976a). Obsessional characters and obsessional neurosis. In *Essential Papers on Character Neurosis and Treatment,* ed. R. Lax, pp. 261–263. New York: Guilford.

———— (1976b). Comparing obsessional and hysterical personalities. In *Essential Papers on Character Neurosis and Treatment,* ed. R. Lax, pp. 264–266. New York: Guilford.

Naiman, J. (1966). The role of the superego in certain forms of acting out. *International Journal of Psycho-Analysis* 47:286–292.

Nass, M. L. (1966). The superego and moral development in the theories of Freud and Piaget. *Psychoanalytic Study of the Child* 21:51–68. New York: International Universities Press.

Neugarten, B., ed. (1968). *Middle Age and Aging.* Chicago: University of Chicago Press.

Niederland, W. G. (1958). Early auditory experiences, beating fantasies, and the primal scene. *Psychoanalytic Study of the Child* 13:471–504. New York: International Universities Press.

———— (1965). The role of the ego in the recovery of early memories. *Psychoanalytic Quarterly* 34:564–571.

Novey, S. (1955). The role of the superego and ego-ideal in character formation. *International Journal of Psycho-Analysis* 36:254–259.

Novick, J. (1976). Termination of treatment in adolescence. *Psychoanalytic Study of the Child* 31:389–414.

Novotny, P. (1972). Self-cutting. *Bulletin of the Menninger Clinic* 36:505–514.

Nunberg, H. (1928). Problems of therapy. In *Essential Papers on Character Neurosis and Treatment,* ed. R. Lax, pp. 145–159. New York: International Universities Press.

———— (1931). The synthetic function of the ego. *International Journal of Psycho-Analysis* 12:123–140.

Olinick, S. (1964). The negative therapeutic reaction. *International Journal of Psycho-Analysis* 45:540–548.

Oremland, P. (1971). Some specific transference, countertransference, and supervisory problems in the treatment of the narcissistic personality. *International Journal of Psycho-Analysis* 52:267–275.

Orens, M. (1955). Setting a termination date: an impetus to analysis. *Journal of the American Psychoanalytic Association* 3:651–665.

Ornstein, P. (1974). Discussion of Kernberg. *International Journal of Psycho-Analysis* 55:241–247.

Ostow, M. (1974). *Sexual Deviation: Psychoanalytic Insights.* New York: Quadrangle.

Panken, S. (1973). *The Joy of Suffering.* New York: Jason Aronson.

Pao, P.-N. (1971). Elation, hypomania and mania. *Journal of the American Psychoanalytic Association* 19:787–798.

Parens, H., Pollack, L., Stern, J., and Kramer, S. (1976). On the girl's entry into the Oedipus complex. *Journal of the American Psychoanalytic Association* 24 (Suppl.):79–107.

Parkin, A. (1980). On masochistic enthrallment: a contribution to the study of moral masochism. *International Journal of Psycho-Analysis* 61:307–314.

Peto, A. (1961). The fragmentizing function of the ego in the transference neurosis. *International Journal of Psycho-Analysis* 42:238–245.

_____ (1964). The fragmentizing function of the ego in the analytic session. *International Journal of Psycho-Analysis* 44:334–338.

_____ (1967a). On affect control. *Psychoanalytic Study of the Child* 12:36–51. New York: International Universities Press.

_____ (1967b). Dedifferentiations and fragmentizations during analysis. *Journal of the American Psychoanalytic Association* 15:534–550.

Piaget, J. (1954). *The Construction of Reality in the Child.* New York: Basic Books.

Pulver, S. (1970). Narcissism: the term and the conflict. *Journal of the American Psychoanalytic Association* 18:319–341.

Racker, H. (1953). A contribution to the problem of countertransference. *International Journal of Psycho-Analysis* 34:313–324.

_____ (1957a). Contribution to the problem of psychopathological stratification. *International Journal of Psycho-Analysis* 38:223–240.

_____ (1957b). The meanings and uses of countertransference. *Psychoanalytic Quarterly* 26:303–357.

_____ (1960). Study of some early conflicts through their return in the patient's relationship with the interpretation. *International Journal of Psycho-Analysis* 41:47–58.

_____ (1968). *Transference and Countertransference.* New York: International Universities Press.

Rado, S. (1956). *Psychoanalysis of Behavior.* New York: International Universities Press.

Ramazy, I., and Wallerstein, R. S. (1958). Pain, fear and anxiety. *Psychoanalytic Study of the Child* 13:147–189. New York: International Universities Press.

Rangell, L. (1963). Structural problems in intrapsychic conflict. *Psychoanalytic Study of the Child* 18:103–138. New York: International Universities Press.

Rank, B. (1949). Aggression. *Psychoanalytic Study of the Child* 3,4:43–48. New York: International Universities Press.

Rank, O. (1945). *Will Therapy and Truth and Reality*. New York: International Universities Press.

Rapaport, D. (1951). The autonomy of the ego. In *Collected Papers*, ed. M. Gill, pp. 357–367. New York: Basic Books.

———— (1953). On the psychoanalytic theory of affects. In *Collected Papers*, ed. M. Gill, pp. 476–512. New York: Basic Books.

———— (1954). Clinical implications of ego psychology. In *Collected Papers*, ed. M. Gill, pp. 586–593. New York: Basic Books.

———— (1957a). A theoretical analysis of the superego concept. In *Collected Papers*, ed. M. Gill, pp. 685–709. New York: Basic Books.

———— (1957b). The theory of ego autonomy: a generalization. In *Collected Papers*, ed. M. Gill, pp. 722–744. New York: Basic Books.

———— (1958). The theory of ego autonomy: a generalization. *Bulletin of the Menninger Clinic* 22:13–55.

———— (1967). *Collected Papers*, ed. M. Gill. New York: Basic Books.

Rapaport, D., and Gill, M. (1959). The points of view and assumptions of metapsychology. In *Collected Papers*, ed. M. Gill, pp. 795–811. New York: Basic Books.

Redl, F. (1945). The psychology of gang formation and the treatment of juvenile delinquency. *Psychoanalytic Study of the Child* 1:367–377. New York: International Universities Press.

Reich, A. (1940). A contribution to the psychoanalysis of extreme submissiveness in women. *Psychoanalytic Quarterly* 9:470–480.

———— (1951). On counter-transference. *International Journal of Psycho-Analysis* 32:25–31.

———— (1953). Narcissistic object choice in women. *Journal of the American Psychoanalytic Association* 1:22–40.

———— (1954). Early identifications as archaic elements in the superego. *Journal of the American Psychoanalytic Association* 2:218–238.

———— (1960a). Pathologic forms of self-esteem regulation. *Psychoanalytic Study of the Child* 15:215–232. New York: International Universities Press.

———— (1960b). Further remarks on counter-transference. In *Psychoanalytic Contributions*, pp. 271–287. New York: International Universities Press.

———— (1966). Empathy and countertransference. In *Psychoanalytic Contributions*, pp. 344–360. New York: International Universities Press.

———— (1973). *Psychoanalytic Contributions*. New York: International Universities Press.

Reich, W. (1945). *Character Analysis*. New York: Orgone Institute.

———— (1949). On the technique of character-analysis. In *Character Analysis*, 3rd ed., pp. 39–113. New York: Noonday.

Reider, N. (1957). Transference psychosis. *Journal of Hillside Hospital* 6:131–149.

Reik, T. (1941). *Masochism in Modern Man*. New York: International Universities Press.

Renik, O. (1990). Comments on the clinical analysis of anxiety and depressive affect. *Psychoanalytic Quarterly* 59:226–248.

Rinsley, D. (1984). A comparison of borderline and narcissistic character disorders. *Bulletin of the Menninger Clinic* 48:1–9.

_____ (1986). Object constancy, object permanency, and personality disorders. In *Object and Self Constancy: Clinical and Theoretical Perspectives,* ed. R. Lax, S. Bach, and J. A. Burland, pp. 193–207. New York: Guilford.

Ritvo, S. (1971). Late adolescence: developmental and clinical considerations. *Psychoanalytic Study of the Child* 26:241–263. New Haven, CT: Yale University Press.

Riviere, J. (1936a). On the genesis of psychical conflict in early infancy. *International Journal of Psycho-Analysis* 55:397–404.

_____ (1936b). A contribution to the analysis of the negative therapeutic reaction. *International Journal of Psycho-Analysis* 17:304–320.

Rochlin, G. (1953). Loss and restitution. *Psychoanalytic Study of the Child* 8:288–309. New York: International Universities Press.

_____ (1965). *Griefs and Discontents.* Boston: Little, Brown.

_____ (1973). *Man's Aggression.* Boston: Gambit.

Roiphe, H. (1978). An unusual perversion. *Journal of the American Psychoanalytic Association* 26:779–784.

Roiphe, H., and Galenson, E. (1986). Maternal depression, separation, and a failure in the development of object constancy. In *Self and Object Constancy: Clinical and Theoretical Perspectives,* ed. R. Lax, S. Bach, and J. A. Burland, pp. 304–323. New York: Guilford.

Rosenfeld, H. (1952). Notes on the psychoanalysis of the superego conflict in an acute schizophrenic patient. *International Journal of Psycho-Analysis* 33:111–131.

_____ (1965). *Psychotic States.* London: Tavistock.

Rothstein, A. (1982). The implications of early psychopathology for the analyzability of narcissistic personality disorders. *International Journal of Psycho-Analysis* 63:177–188.

_____ (1984). The fear of humiliation. *Journal of the American Psychoanalytic Association* 32:99–116.

Rubinfine, D. (1962). Maternal stimulation, psychic structure, and early object relations: with special reference to aggression and denial. *Psychoanalytic Study of the Child* 17:265–282. New York: International Universities Press.

_____ (1968). Notes on a theory of depression. *Psychoanalytic Quarterly* 37:400–417. New York: International Universities Press.

Rycroft, C. (1960). The analysis of a paranoid personality. *International Journal of Psycho-Analysis* 41:59–69.

Sandler, J. (1960). On the concept of the superego. *Psychoanalytic Study of the Child* 15:128–162. New York: International Universities Press.

_____ (1976). Countertransference and role-responsiveness. *International Review of Psycho-Analysis* 3:43–47.

_____ (1986). Comments on the self and its objects. In *Self and Object Constancy: Clinical and Theoretical Perspectives,* ed. R. Lax, S. Bach, and J. A. Burland, pp. 97–106. New York: Guilford.

Sandler, J., Holder, A., and Meers, D. (1963). The ego ideal and the ideal self.*Psychoanalytic Study of the Child* 18:139–158. New York: International Universities Press.

Sandler, J., and Nagera, H. (1963). Aspects of the metapsychology of fantasy. *Psychoanalytic Study of the Child* 18:159–194. New York: International Universities Press.

Sarlin, C. (1962). Depersonalization and derealization. *Journal of the American Psychoanalytic Association* 10:784–804.

Sarnoff, C. (1976). *Latency*. New York: Jason Aronson.

Saul, L., and Warner, B. (1967). Identity and a point of technique. *Psychoanalytic Quarterly* 36:532–545.

Savage, C. (1987). Countertransference in the therapy of schizophrenics. In *Countertransference*, ed. E. Slakter, pp. 115–130. Northvale, NJ: Jason Aronson.

Schafer, R. (1959). Generative empathy in the treatment situation. *Psychoanalytic Quarterly* 28:342–373.

_____ (1960). The loving and beloved superego in Freud's structural theory. *Psychoanalytic Study of the Child* 15:163–188. New York: International Universities Press.

_____ (1973). The idea of resistance. *International Journal of Psycho-Analysis* 54:259–285.

_____ (1975). Psychoanalysis without psychodynamics. *International Journal of Psycho-Analysis* 56:41–55.

_____ (1976). *A New Language for Psychoanalysis*. New Haven, CT: Yale University Press.

_____ (1985). Wild analysis. *Journal of the American Psychoanalytic Association* 33:275–299.

Scharpe, E. F. (1950). *Collected Papers*. London: Hogarth.

Schowalter, J. E., and Lord, R. D. (1972). On the writings of adolescents in a general hospital ward. *Psychoanalytic Study of the Child* 27:181–202. New Haven, CT: Yale University Press.

Schur, M. (1958). The ego and the id in anxiety. *Psychoanalytic Study of the Child* 13:199–220. New York: International Universities Press.

_____ (1960). Phylogenesis and ontogenesis of affect- and structure- formation and the phenomenon of repetition compulsion. *International Journal of Psycho-Analysis* 41:275–287.

_____ (1966). *The Id and the Regulatory Principles of Mental Functioning*. New York: International Universities Press.

Searles, H. (1958). The schizophrenic's vulnerability to the therapist's unconscious processes. *Journal of Nervous and Mental Disease* 127:247–262.

_____ (1960). *The Nonhuman Environment in Normal Development and in Schizophrenia*. New York: International Universities Press.

_____ (1965). *Collected Papers on Schizophrenia and Related Subjects*. London: Hogarth.

_____ (1972). The functions of the patient's realistic perceptions of the analyst in delusional transference. *British Journal of Medical Psychology* 45:1–18.

_____ (1975). The patient as therapist to his analyst. In *Tactics and Techniques in Psychoanalytic Therapy*, vol. 2, ed. P. Giovacchini, pp. 95–151. New York: Jason Aronson.

_____ (1976). Transitional phenomena and therapeutic symbiosis. *International Journal of Psychoanalytic Psychotherapy* 5:145–204.

_____ (1987). Countertransference as a path to understanding and helping the patient. In *Countertransference*, ed. E. Slakter, pp. 131–164. Northvale, NJ: Jason Aronson.

Segel, N. (1981). Narcissism and adaptation to indignity. *International Journal of Psycho-Analysis* 62:465–476.

Seigman, A. (1954). Emotionality–a hysterical character defense. *Psychoanalytic Quarterly* 23:339–354.

Settlage, C. F. (1972). Cultural values and the superego in late adolescence. *Psychoanalytic Study of the Child* 27:74–92. New Haven, CT: Yale University Press.

Shengold, L. (1989). *Soul Murders: The Effects of Childhood Abuse and Deprivation.* New Haven, CT: Yale University Press.

_____ (1991). A variety of narcissistic pathology stemming from parental weakness. *Psychoanalytic Quarterly* 60:86–92.

Silverman, M. (1982). The voice of conscience and the sounds of the analytic hour. *Psychoanalytic Quarterly* 51:196–217.

_____ (1985). Countertransference and the myth of the perfectly analyzed analyst. *Psychoanalytic Quarterly* 54:175–199.

Slakter, E., ed. (1987). *Countertransference: A Comprehensive Review of Those Reactions of the Therapist to the Patient that may Help or Hinder the Treatment.* Northvale, NJ: Jason Aronson.

Slap, J. (1967). Freud's view on pleasure and aggression. *Journal of the American Psychoanalytic Association* 15:370–375.

Smith, J. A. (1970). On the structural view of affect. *Journal of the American Psychoanalytic Association* 18:539–561.

Solnit, A. (1966). Some adaptive functions of aggressive behavior. In *Psychoanalysis: A General Psychology*, ed. R. Loewenstein, L. Newman, M. Schur, and A. Solnit, pp. 169–189. New York: International Universities Press.

_____ (1972). Youth and the campus: the search for social conscience. *Psychoanalytic Study of the Child* 27:98–105. New Haven, CT: Yale University Press.

Sperling, M. (1974). A contribution to the treatment of character disorders with acting out behavior. *Annual of Psychoanalysis* 2:249–267.

Sperling, O. E. (1954). An imaginary companion, representing a prestage of the superego. *Psychoanalytic Study of the Child* 9:252–258. New York: International Universities Press.

Spiegel, L. (1959). The self, the sense of self and perception. *Psychoanalytic Study of the Child* 14:81–109.

_____ (1966). Affects in relation to self and object. *Psychoanalytic Study of the Child* 21:69–92. New York: International Universities Press.

Spitz, R. (1958). On the genesis of superego components. *Psychoanalytic Study of the Child* 13:375–404. New York: International Universities Press.

_____ (1959). *A Genetic Field Theory of Ego Formation.* New York: International Universities Press.

_____ (1961). Some early prototypes of ego defenses. *Journal of the American Psychoanalytic Association* 9:626–651.

_____ (1965). *The First Year of Life.* New York: International Universities Press.

Spitz, R., and Wolf, K. M. (1946). Anaclitic depression: an inquiry into the genesis of psychiatric conditions in early childhood. *Psychoanalytic Study of the Child* 2:313–342. New York: International Universities Press.

Spotnitz, H. (1983). The toxoid response. In *Active Psychotherapy,* ed. H. Greenwald, pp. 49–62. New York: Jason Aronson.

Sprince, M. (1971). An adolescent boy's battle against recovery: the analysis of an adolescent whose ongoing preoedipal tie to the mother aroused massive treatment resistance and a terror of health. *Psychoanalytic Study of the Child* 26:453–484. New Haven, CT: Yale University Press.

Stein, M. H. (1956). The problem of masochism in the theory and technique of psychoanalysis: panel report. *Journal of the American Psychoanalytic Association* 4:526–538.

_____ (1981). The unobjectionable part of the transference. *Journal of the American Psychoanalytic Association* 29:869–891.

Steingart, I. (1969). On self, character, and the development of a psychic apparatus. *Psychoanalytic Study of the Child* 24:271–303. New York: International Universities Press.

Sterba, R. (1934). The fate of the ego in analytic theory. *International Journal of Psycho-Analysis* 15:117–126.

_____ (1940). The dynamics of the dissolution of the transference resistance. *Psychoanalytic Quarterly* 9:363–379.

Stern, A. (1924). On the countertransference in psychoanalysis. *Psychoanalytic Review* 2:166–174.

Stoller, R. (1968a). The sense of femaleness. *Psychoanalytic Quarterly* 37:42–55.

_____ (1968b). *Sex and Gender: On the Development of Masculinity and Femininity.* New York: Science House.

_____ (1975). *Perversion: The Erotic Form of Hatred.* New York: Delta.

_____ (1976). Primary femininity. *Journal of the American Psychoanalytic Association* 24:59–78.

_____ (1979). A contribution to the study of gender identity. *International Journal of Psycho-Analysis* 60:220–226.

Stolorow, R. (1975). Towards a functional definition of narcissism. *International Journal of Psycho-Analysis* 56:179–185.

Stolorow, R., and Lachman, F. (1980). *Psychoanalysis of Developmental Arrests.* New York: International Universities Press.

Stone, L. (1954). The widening scope of indications for psychoanalysis. *Journal of the American Psychoanalytic Association* 2:567–594.

_____ (1962). *The Psychoanalytic Situation*. New York: International Universities Press.

Strachey, J. (1934). The nature of the therapeutic action of psychoanalysis. *International Journal of Psycho-Analysis* 15:37–68.

Sugarman, A. (1979). The infantile personality: orality in the hysteric revisited. *International Journal of Psycho-Analysis* 60:501–513.

Sullivan, H. S. (1947). *Conceptions of Modern Psychiatry*. Washington, DC: Georgetown University Press.

Ticho, E. (1977). Varieties of oedipal distortions in severe character pathologies. *Journal of the American Psychoanalytic Association* 25:201–218.

Tolpin, M. (1971). On the beginnings of a cohesive self. *Psychoanalytic Study of the Child* 26:316–352. New Haven, CT: Yale University Press.

Tower, L. (1956). Countertransference. *Journal of the American Psychoanalytic Association* 4:224–255.

Tyson, P. (1982). A developmental line of gender identity, gender role, and choice of love object. *Journal of the American Psychoanalytic Association* 30:61–86.

_____ (1985). Perspectives on the superego: panel report. *Journal of the American Psychoanalytic Association* 33:217–231.

_____ (1986). Countertransference evolution in theory and practice. *Journal of the American Psychoanalytic Association* 34:251–273.

Valenstein, A. (1973). On attachment to painful feelings and the negative therapeutic reaction. *Psychoanalytic Study of the Child* 28:365–392. New Haven, CT: Yale University Press.

_____ (1989). Pre-oedipal reconstructions in psychoanalysis. *International Journal of Psycho-Analysis* 70:433–460.

Volkan, V. (1976a). *Primitive Internalized Object Relations*. New York: International Universities Press.

_____ (1976b). Introjection of and identification with the therapist, and alterations of the patient's psychic structure. In *Primitive Internalized Object Relations*, pp. 87–118. New York: International Universities Press.

Waelder, R. (1936). The principle of multiple function. *Psychoanalytic Quarterly* 5:45–62.

Waldhorn, H. (1960). Assessment of analyzability: technical and theoretical observations. *Psychoanalytic Quarterly* 29:478–506.

Wallerstein, R. (1967). Reconstruction and mastery in the transference psychosis. *Journal of the American Psychoanalytic Association* 15:551–583.

White, R. W. (1963). *Ego and Reality in Psychoanalytic Theory: A Proposal Regarding Independent Ego Energies*. New York: International Universities Press.

Winnicott, D. W. (1949). Hate in the countertransference. *International Journal of Psycho-Analysis* 30:69–74.

_____ (1958). *Collected Papers*. London: Tavistock.

_____ (1960). Countertransference. *British Journal of Medical Psychology* 33:17–21.

_____ (1965). *The Maturational Processes and the Facilitating Environment.* New York: International Universities Press.

_____ (1968). *Playing and Reality.* London: Tavistock.

_____ (1972). *Therapeutic Consultations with Children.* London: Hogarth.

Wolf, E. (1979). Countertransference in disorders of the self. In *Countertransference,* ed. L. Epstein and A. Feiner, pp. 445–464. New York: Jason Aronson.

Zetzel, E. (1949). Anxiety and the capacity to bear it. *International Journal of Psycho-Analysis* 30:1–12.

_____ (1956a). An approach to the relation between concept and content in psychoanalytic theory: with special reference to the work of Melanie Klein and her followers. *Psychoanalytic Study of the Child* 11:99–121. New York: International Universities Press.

_____ (1956b). Current concepts of transference. *International Journal of Psycho-Analysis* 37:369–376.

_____ (1965a). Depression and the incapacity to bear it. In *Drives, Affects, Behavior,* vol. 2, ed. M. Schur, pp. 243–274. New York: International Universities Press.

_____ (1965b). The depressive position. In *Affective Disorders,* ed. P. Greenacre, pp. 184–216. New York: International Universities Press.

_____ (1970). *Capacity for Emotional Growth.* New York: International Universities Press.

Index